Democratic Resilience

Politics in the United States has become increasingly polarized in recent decades. Both political elites and everyday citizens are divided into rival and mutually antagonistic partisan camps, with each camp questioning the political legitimacy and democratic commitments of the other side. Does this polarization pose threats to democracy itself? What can make some democratic institutions resilient in the face of such challenges? *Democratic Resilience* brings together a distinguished group of specialists to examine how polarization affects the performance of institutional checks and balances as well as the political behavior of voters, civil society actors, and political elites. The volume bridges the conventional divide between institutional and behavioral approaches to the study of American politics and incorporates historical and comparative insights to explain the nature of contemporary challenges to democracy. It also breaks new ground to identify the institutional and societal sources of democratic resilience.

Robert C. Lieberman is Krieger-Eisenhower Professor of Political Science at Johns Hopkins University. He is a scholar of American political development, race and politics, public policy, and democracy and the author of several prize-winning books, including *Four Threats: The Recurring Crises of American Democracy* (2020), coauthored with Suzanne Mettler.

Suzanne Mettler is the John L. Senior Professor of American Institutions in the Government Department at Cornell University. Her research and teaching interests include American political development, inequality, public policy, political behavior, and democracy. She is the author of six books, including *Four Threats: The Recurring Crises of American Democracy* (2020), coauthored with Robert C. Lieberman.

Kenneth M. Roberts is the Richard J. Schwartz Professor of Government at Cornell University. His research explores democratic representation and its defects, including the study of parties, populism, and social movements from a comparative perspective. He is the author of *Changing Course in Latin America: Party Systems in the Neoliberal Era*.

Democratic Resilience

Can the United States Withstand Rising Polarization?

Edited by

ROBERT C. LIEBERMAN
Johns Hopkins University

SUZANNE METTLER
Cornell University

KENNETH M. ROBERTS
Cornell University

CAMBRIDGE
UNIVERSITY PRESS

University Printing House, Cambridge CB2 8BS, United Kingdom

One Liberty Plaza, 20th Floor, New York, NY 10006, USA

477 Williamstown Road, Port Melbourne, VIC 3207, Australia

314–321, 3rd Floor, Plot 3, Splendor Forum, Jasola District Centre, New Delhi – 110025, India

103 Penang Road, #05–06/07, Visioncrest Commercial, Singapore 238467

Cambridge University Press is part of the University of Cambridge.

It furthers the University's mission by disseminating knowledge in the pursuit of education, learning, and research at the highest international levels of excellence.

www.cambridge.org
Information on this title: www.cambridge.org/9781108834100
DOI: 10.1017/9781108999601

© Cambridge University Press 2022

This publication is in copyright. Subject to statutory exception and to the provisions of relevant collective licensing agreements, no reproduction of any part may take place without the written permission of Cambridge University Press.

First published 2022

A catalogue record for this publication is available from the British Library.

Library of Congress Cataloging-in-Publication Data
NAMES: Lieberman, Robert C., 1964– editor. | Mettler, Suzanne, editor. | Roberts, Kenneth M., 1958– editor.
TITLE: Democratic resilience : can the United States withstand rising polarization? / Edited by Robert C. Lieberman, Johns Hopkins University, Suzanne Mettler, Cornell University, New York, Kenneth M. Roberts, Cornell University, New York.
DESCRIPTION: Cambridge, United Kingdom ; New York, NY : Cambridge University Press, 2022. | Includes index.
IDENTIFIERS: LCCN 2021017219 (print) | LCCN 2021017220 (ebook) | ISBN 9781108834100 (hardback) | ISBN 9781108999601 (ebook)
SUBJECTS: LCSH: Democracy – United States – History. | Polarization (Social sciences) – United States. | Political culture – United States – History. | United States – Politics and government. | BISAC: POLITICAL SCIENCE / American Government / General
CLASSIFICATION: LCC JK1726 .D457 2022 (print) | LCC JK1726 (ebook) | DDC 306.20973–dc23
LC record available at https://lccn.loc.gov/2021017219
LC ebook record available at https://lccn.loc.gov/2021017220

ISBN 978-1-108-83410-0 Hardback
ISBN 978-1-108-99564-1 Paperback

Cambridge University Press has no responsibility for the persistence or accuracy of URLs for external or third-party internet websites referred to in this publication and does not guarantee that any content on such websites is, or will remain, accurate or appropriate.

For Rick Valelly, our brilliant colleague and dear friend

Contents

List of Figures page ix
List of Tables xi
List of Contributors xii
Acknowledgments xviii

PART I WHY MIGHT POLARIZATION HARM DEMOCRACY? THEORY AND COMPARISON

1 How Democracies Endure: The Challenges of Polarization and Sources of Resilience
  Robert C. Lieberman, Suzanne Mettler, and Kenneth M. Roberts — 3

2 Polarization and the Durability of Madisonian Checks and Balances: A Developmental Analysis
  Paul Pierson and Eric Schickler — 35

3 Pernicious Polarization and Democratic Resilience: Analyzing the United States in Comparative Perspective
  Jennifer McCoy and Murat Somer — 61

PART II POLITICAL INSTITUTIONS IN POLARIZED TIMES

4 Crosscutting Cleavages, Political Institutions, and Democratic Resilience in the United States
  Frances E. Lee — 95

5 Unilateralism Unleashed? Polarization and the Politics of Executive Action
  Douglas L. Kriner — 118

6 Court-Packing and Democratic Erosion
  Thomas M. Keck 141

PART III SOCIAL POLARIZATION AND PARTISANSHIP

7 The Social Roots, Risks, and Rewards of Mass Polarization
  Lilliana Mason and Nathan P. Kalmoe 171

8 The Great White Hope: Threat and Racial Resilience in Trump's America
  Christopher Sebastian Parker and Matt A. Barreto 195

9 The Religious Sort: The Causes and Consequences of the Religiosity Gap in America
  Michele F. Margolis 226

10 Weaponized Group Identities and the Health of Democracy: Why the National Rifle Association Is Good *at* Democracy but Bad *for* It
  Matthew J. Lacombe 246

PART IV VICIOUS CIRCLES? THE RELATIONSHIP BETWEEN POLARIZED BEHAVIOR AND INSTITUTIONS

11 Polarization, the Administrative State, and Executive-Centered Partisanship
  Desmond King and Sidney M. Milkis 267

12 Laboratories of What? American Federalism and the Politics of Democratic Subversion
  Philip Rocco 297

13 Conservative Extra-Party Coalitions and Statehouse Democracy
  Alexander Hertel-Fernandez 320

PART V CAN POLITICAL ACTION SAVE DEMOCRACY IN POLARIZED TIMES?

14 Elections, Polarization, and Democratic Resilience
  David A. Bateman 343

15 Citizen Organizing and Partisan Polarization from the Tea Party to the Anti-Trump Resistance
  Theda Skocpol, Caroline Tervo, and Kirsten Walters 369

Index 401

Figures

3.1	The path from polarization to democratic erosion	*page* 67
4.1	Women in Congress by party	100
4.2	Evangelicals in Congress by party	101
4.3	Nonwhites in Congress by party	103
4.4	Educational attainment in Congress by party	104
4.5	Median net worth of Members of Congress by party	105
5.1	Partisan polarization over time	128
5.2	Total number of executive orders, memoranda, and proclamations, 1977–2018	129
5.3	Significant executive actions, 1977–2018	130
5.4	Executive actions on front page of *New York Times*, 1977–2018	132
7.1	Partisan moral disengagement (CCES 2017)	181
7.2	Correlates of moral disengagement (CCES 2017)	183
7.3	Partisan violence (CCES 2017)	185
7.4	(a–e) Distributions of election confidence and radical partisanship	186
8.1	Estimated change in Trump thermometer rating among whites moving each variable from minimum to maximum value	211
8.2	Estimated point change in oppose Trump (FT) among POC moving each variable from minimum to maximum value	212
8.3	Estimated point change in strongly oppose Trump among POC moving each variable from minimum to maximum value	213
8.4	Estimated probability of strongly opposing Trump by race	214
8.5	Combined impact of perceived racism on anti-Trump attitudes among POC	214

8.6	Predicted probability of political participation 2016 by race	216
8.7	Threat and political engagement, by race	217
9.1	Attachment to Christian and secular identities	234
11.1	Highest and lowest percent changes in employment within the federal bureaucracy under Trump (2016–2020)	278
11.2	On-board personnel (federal civilian employees), 2016–2019	279
12.1	Electoral democracy index scores for US and older federal democracies, 1958 and 2018	300
12.2	Subnational election evenness in US and older federal democracies, 1958 and 2018	300
15.1	Local Tea Parties/resistance group and partisan turnover in the 2010 and 2018 congressional midterm elections	393

Tables

8.1	Predictors of support for Donald Trump by race in ANES 2016	page 219
8.2	Among POC: Predictors of support for Donald Trump (2016 CMPS)	221
8.3	Predictors of political participation (0–10) in 2016 by race in ANES	223
8.4	Predictors of total participation count (0–13) among whites in CMPS	224
8.5	Predictors of total participation count (0–13) among POC in CMPS	225
11.1	Trump Administration Executive Actions: 2017–2019	280
12.1	Significant features of subnational democracy	308

Contributors

Matt A. Barreto is a professor of political science and Chicano/a studies at the University of California, Los Angeles.

David A. Bateman is an associate professor in the Government Department at Cornell University. His research focuses on democratic institutions, American political development, and ideological change. He is the author of *Disenfranchising Democracy: Constructing a Mass Electorate in the United States, United Kingdom, and France*, and coauthor of *Southern Nation: Congress and White Supremacy After Reconstruction*.

Alexander Hertel-Fernandez is an associate professor of public affairs at Columbia University, where he studies American political economy, with a focus on the politics of business, labor, wealthy donors, and policy. His most recent book, *State Capture* (Oxford University Press, 2019), examines how networks of conservative activists, donors, and businesses built organizations to successfully reshape public policy across the states and why progressives failed in similar efforts. His previous book, *Politics at Work* (Oxford University Press, 2018), examines how employers are increasingly recruiting their workers into politics to change elections and policy. His research has appeared in leading academic research journals and media outlets.

Nathan P. Kalmoe is an associate professor of political communication in Louisiana State University's Manship School of Mass Communication and the Department of Political Science. He is the author of *With Ballots and Bullets: Partisanship and Violence in the American Civil*

War (Cambridge University Press) and coauthor of *Neither Liberal nor Conservative: Ideological Innocence in the American Public* (University of Chicago Press).

Thomas M. Keck holds the Michael O. Sawyer Chair of Constitutional Law & Politics at Syracuse University's Maxwell School. He is the author of *The Most Activist Supreme Court in History* and *Judicial Politics in Polarized Times*.

Desmond King is the Andrew W. Mellon Professor of American Government at the University of Oxford and is a Fellow of the American Academy of Arts and Sciences, the British Academy, and the Royal Irish Academy. His publications include *Separate and Unequal: African Americans and the US Federal Government* (Oxford University Press, 2007), *Making Americans: Immigration, Race and the Origins of the Diverse Democracy* (Harvard University Press, 2000); with Rogers M. Smith, *Still a House Divided: Race and Politics in Obama's America* (Princeton University Press, 2013); and with Stephen Skowronek and John Dearborn, *Phantoms of the Beleaguered Republic: The Deep State and the Unitary Executive* (Oxford University Press, 2021).

Douglas L. Kriner is the Clinton Rossiter Professor in American Institutions in the Department of Government at Cornell University. He is the author of five books, including most recently *The Myth of the Imperial President: How Public Opinion Checks the Unilateral Executive* (University of Chicago Press 2020; with Dino Christenson) and *Investigating the President: Congressional Checks on Presidential Power* (Princeton University Press 2016; with Eric Schickler). His research has also appeared in the *American Political Science Review*, *American Journal of Political Science*, *Journal of Politics*, *JAMA Network Open*, and *Science Advances*, among other outlets.

Matthew J. Lacombe is assistant professor of political science at Barnard College, Columbia University. He is the author of *Firepower: How the NRA Turned Gun Owners into a Political Force* and the coauthor of *Billionaires and Stealth Politics*.

Frances E. Lee is professor of politics and public affairs at Princeton University. Her most recent book is *The Limits of Party: Congress and Lawmaking in a Polarized Era* (2020), coauthored with James M. Curry. She is also author of *Insecure Majorities: Congress and the Perpetual*

Campaign (2016) and *Beyond Ideology: Politics, Principles, and Partisanship in the U.S. Senate* (2009).

Robert C. Lieberman is Krieger-Eisenhower Professor of Political Science at Johns Hopkins University. He is a scholar of American political development, race and politics, public policy, and democracy and the author of several prize-winning books. His most recent book is *Four Threats: The Recurring Crises of American Democracy*, coauthored with Suzanne Mettler. He previously served as provost of Johns Hopkins and as dean of the School of International and Public Affairs at Columbia University.

Michele F. Margolis is an associate professor of political science at the University of Pennsylvania. She holds a PhD from the Massachusetts Institute of Technology, a master's degree from the London School of Economics, and a bachelor's degree from the University of California, Berkeley. Michele is the author of *From Politics to the Pews* (2018), which won the Distinguished Book Award from the Society for the Scientific Study of Religion.

Lilliana Mason is the author of *Uncivil Agreement: How Politics Became Our Identity*. She is also an associate research professor at the SNF Agora Institute and the Department of Political Science at Johns Hopkins University.

Jennifer McCoy, Professor of Political Science at Georgia State University, is a specialist in comparative and international politics, political polarization and democratic erosion, and Latin American politics. Author or editor of six books, most recently she coedited with Murat Somer the volume *Polarizing Polities: A Global Threat to Democracy* (Annals of the American Academy of Political and Social Science, 2019).

Suzanne Mettler is the John L. Senior Professor of American Institutions in the Government Department at Cornell University. Her research and teaching interests include American political development, inequality, public policy, political behavior, and democracy. She is the author of six books, including, most recently, *Four Threats: The Recurring Crises of American Democracy* (St. Martin's Press, 2020), coauthored with Robert C. Lieberman. She is a member of the American Academy of Arts and Sciences, the recipient of Guggenheim and Radcliffe Fellowships, and serves on the boards of the Scholars Strategy Network and the American Academy of Political and Social Sciences.

Sidney M. Milkis is the White Burket Miller Professor of Politics and a Faculty Fellow of the Miller Center at the University of Virginia. His books include: *The President and the Parties: The Transformation of the American Party System Since the New Deal* (1993); *Political Parties and Constitutional Government: Remaking American Democracy* (1999); *Presidential Greatness* (2000), coauthored with Marc Landy; *The American Presidency: Origins and Development, 1776–2018* (2019), 8th edition, coauthored with Michael Nelson; *Theodore Roosevelt, the Progressive Party, and the Transformation of American Democracy* (2009); and *Rivalry and Reform: Presidents, Social Movements and the Transformation of American Politics*, coauthored with Daniel Tichenor (2019). He is currently completing a study on political parties and populism.

Christopher Sebastian Parker is professor of political science at the University of Washington. A graduate of UCLA and the University of Chicago, Parker also served in the United States Navy. He is the author of *Change They Can't Believe In: The Tea Party and Reactionary Politics in America* (Princeton University Press, 2013), and *Fighting for Democracy: Black Veterans and the Struggle Against White Supremacy in the Postwar South* (Princeton University Press, 2009). Parker is currently at work on *The Great White Hope: Donald Trump, Race, and the Crisis of American Democracy* (University of Chicago Press, forthcoming). He resides in Seattle with his dog, Brooklyn.

Paul Pierson is the John Gross Professor of Political Science at the University of California, Berkeley. He is the director of Berkeley's Center for the Study of American Democracy and former codirector of the Successful Societies Program of the Canadian Institute for Advanced Social Research. He is the author or coauthor of six books on American and comparative politics, a recipient of a Guggenheim Fellowship, and a member of the American Academy of Arts and Sciences.

Kenneth M. Roberts is the Richard J. Schwartz Professor of Government and Binenkorb Director of Latin American Studies at Cornell University. His research focuses on the comparative study of democratic representation, including party systems, populism, and social movements. He is the author, most recently, of *Changing Course in Latin America: Party Systems in the Neoliberal Era* (Cambridge University Press). He has been a Fulbright scholar in Spain and Chile, and a recipient of grants from the National Science Foundation, the US Department of Education, and the Mellon and MacArthur Foundations.

Philip Rocco is an associate professor of political science at Marquette University. He is the coauthor of *Obamacare Wars: Federalism, State Politics, and the Affordable Care Act* (University Press of Kansas, 2016) and the coeditor of *American Political Development and the Trump Presidency* (University of Pennsylvania Press, 2020). His research has been published in, among other venues, *Publius: The Journal of Federalism*, *Public Administration Review*, *Health Affairs*, and the *Journal of Health Politics, Policy, and Law*.

Eric Schickler is Jeffrey & Ashley McDermott Professor of Political Science and codirector of the Institute of Governmental Studies at the University of California, Berkeley. He is the author of six books, including *Investigating the President: Congressional Checks on Presidential Power* (2016, with Douglas Kriner) and *Racial Realignment: The Transformation of American Liberalism, 1932–1965*, winner of the Woodrow Wilson Prize for the best book on government, politics, or international affairs published in 2016. Schickler was elected to the American Academy of Arts and Sciences in 2017.

Theda Skocpol is the Victor S. Thomas Professor of Government and Sociology at Harvard University. She has done work on comparative revolutions, the US welfare state in comparative perspective, civic associations in America, and the politics of health care reform. Her current work focuses on the evolution of the Republican Party and on recent citizen movements on the right and left in US politics.

Murat Somer is a professor of political science and international relations at Koç University, Istanbul. His writings on polarization, autocratization and democratization, religious and secular politics, and ethnic conflict have appeared in books, book volumes, and journals such as *Comparative Political Studies*, *Democratization*, and the *ANNALS of the American Academy of Political and Social Sciences*.

Caroline Tervo is a research coordinator in the Harvard Government Department. She is the coeditor (with Theda Skocpol) of *Upending American Politics: Polarizing Parties, Ideological Elites, and Citizen Activists from the Tea Party to the Anti-Trump Resistance* (Oxford University Press, 2020). Her research focuses on citizen grassroots organizing and on state and local political party building.

Kirsten Walters is a PhD student in government at Harvard University and a James M. and Catherine D. Stone Scholar in inequality and wealth concentration. She studies the influence of economic and mass membership interest groups in subnational electoral politics and the implications of this influence for economic inequality and disparities in political representation.

Acknowledgments

This book began as a project of the American Democracy Collaborative, formed in early 2017 by the three of us along with Tom Pepinsky and Rick Valelly (Jamila Michener has subsequently joined the group). Our aim in organizing it was to bring together scholars of American and comparative politics to better understand the crisis of democracy that was engulfing the United States and for which political scientists who primarily study the United States seemed to have a limited analytical vocabulary. Our premise was that in order to understand contemporary political developments in the United States, we need to think more broadly than has been the norm, learning from scholars who study democracy in other countries, those who think about American politics historically, and a wide array of experts on specific American political institutions and aspects of behavior.

The collaborative has convened a number of extraordinarily stimulating and generative meetings and public activities. We initially focused our work on uncovering and explaining the roots of the crisis of American democracy that was exposed and exacerbated, although not caused, by Donald Trump's election as president in 2016. But as we, along with many others, made progress on that issue we discovered that few, if any, scholars were turning the question around and trying to understand not "how democracies die" (to borrow a phrase from Steven Levitsky and Daniel Ziblatt) but how they endure: how they carry on in the face of the core challenges that threaten them, including extreme political polarization, racial and ethnic conflict, rising economic inequality, and concentrated executive power. What, we wondered, makes democracies resilient?

Acknowledgments xix

To explore that question, the ADC convened a conference on Democratic Resilience at Cornell University in November 2019. Our goal was to bring together scholars who crossed numerous disciplinary divides – American vs. comparative politics, political institutions vs. mass behavior, contemporary vs. historical – to help develop what we believe is the first systematic account of "democratic resilience." Almost all of the chapters in this volume were originally presented as papers at that meeting, and all benefited from the lively discussions that ensued. In addition to the authors, we are grateful to Tom Pepinsky and Rick Valelly for their contributions to organizing the conference and to the other participants, who provided helpful commentary and stimulating company: Richard Bensel, Val Bunce, Nick Casey (who wrote about the conference in the *New York Times*), Sergio García-Rios, Hahrie Han, Adam Levine, Steven Levitsky (who also kicked off the conference with a keynote address), Jamila Michener, Sid Tarrow, and Nic van de Walle. Jane Mansbridge read the entire manuscript and offered tremendously helpful feedback, as did an anonymous reviewer. The Hewlett Foundation provided generous funding for the conference and volume and we are grateful to Daniel Stid for his wise counsel and consistent support of this and other ADC projects. Thanks are also due to the College of Arts and Sciences at Cornell University, as well as the Einaudi Center for International Studies and the Center for the Study of Inequality, both at Cornell, and their directors, Rachel Beatty Riedl and Kim Weeden, respectively, for financial support.

Our editor at Cambridge University Press, Sara Doskow, championed the book from the beginning; she joined us in Ithaca and has expertly guided us through planning and execution along with her colleague, Cameron Daddis. At Cornell, Jerrica Brown, Laurie Dorsey, and Dinnie Sloman provided exemplary logistical and administrative support; Clara Elpi's striking design for the conference program captured the essence of our topic in graphic form; and Claire Leavitt prepared the index with care. Rob also thanks the graduate students in his Fall 2020 seminar on Democratic Resilience at Johns Hopkins for their penetrating insights on these and related topics, along with their good humor.

Rick Valelly has spent his career thinking deeply about American democracy, about what has made it sometimes grow more robust and resilient, what has at other times endangered it and provoked backsliding, and the crucial role of political parties in each of these dynamics. We have learned so much not only from his distinguished scholarship but also – luckily for us – from years of probing conversations, always laced with laughter. Neither the American Democracy Collaborative nor this volume would have come into being without his indelible influence. We dedicate this volume to him, our cherished friend.

PART I

WHY MIGHT POLARIZATION HARM DEMOCRACY?

Theory and Comparison

I

How Democracies Endure

The Challenges of Polarization and Sources of Resilience

Robert C. Lieberman, Suzanne Mettler, and Kenneth M. Roberts

Politics in the United States has become more polarized in recent decades as both political elites and everyday citizens have been divided into mutually antagonistic partisan camps. Increasingly, these rival camps question the political legitimacy and democratic commitments of the other side. Such polarization or "teamsmanship" can have a number of important political consequences: it can drive actors further apart, intensify political conflict, impede negotiation and compromise, and block the construction of bipartisan legislative and policymaking coalitions.[1] Since polarization makes it difficult, if not impossible, to find common political ground, it can prevent democratic institutions from making important policy choices and responding to the critical issues of the day. Polarization, in short, can easily lead to democratic gridlock, paralysis, the decay of rights, and, in the extreme, violent conflict, as the Trump administration's waning weeks so vividly demonstrated.[2]

---

[1] Frances E. Lee, *Insecure Majorities: Congress and the Perpetual Campaign* (Chicago: University of Chicago Press, 2016), chap. 3; Thomas E. Mann and Norman J. Ornstein, *It's Even Worse Than It Looks: How the American Constitutional System Collided with the Politics of Extremism* (New York: Basic Books, 2012); Barbara Sinclair, *Party Wars: Polarization and the Politics of National Policymaking* (Norman: University of Oklahoma Press, 2006).

[2] Sarah Binder, "Polarized We Govern?" in *Governing in a Polarized Age: Elections, Parties, and Political Representation in America*, ed. Alan S. Gerber and Eric Schickler (Cambridge: Cambridge University Press, 2017), 223–42; Nolan McCarty, "The Policy Effects of Political Polarization," in *The Transformation of American Politics: Activist Government and the Rise of Conservatism*, ed. Paul Pierson and Theda Skocpol (Princeton: Princeton University Press, 2007), 193–222.

Beyond these widely recognized paralyzing effects, however, lies a deeper and more troubling set of questions regarding the political consequences of polarization. Is polarization a threat to democracy itself? That is, does polarization make democratic institutions susceptible to forms of political manipulation that "stack the deck," "tilt the playing field," or otherwise confer advantages on some partisan actors over their rivals? Does it foster antidemocratic political behavior among rival elites who seek to concentrate power, neutralize or circumvent institutional checks and balances, and delegitimize or incapacitate political opponents? Does polarization undermine national cohesion by making common citizens less tolerant of others who belong to different social groups or espouse different political beliefs and values? Indeed, does it induce citizens to support political leaders who openly challenge democratic norms and procedures in their pursuit of public office and the control it provides over resources and the levers of public policy?

Democratic institutions in the United States were explicitly designed to provide for political stability and guard against unwarranted concentrations of power by fragmenting authority across different branches and levels of government and by providing multiple points of entry for diverse actors who seek to participate in the public sphere. Is it possible, however, for political polarization to negate the multiple veto points erected by the separation of powers and federalism, two primary vehicles of institutional fragmentation embedded in the constitutional order? The Constitution does not prevent a party that dominates multiple institutions from using its power to control judicial nominations, neutralize legislative oversight, and establish electoral rules and procedures that increasingly tilt the political system in its favor. Moreover, many ordinary American citizens may be drawn into polarization, as partisan affiliation increasingly reflects and reinforces cleavages of race, ethnicity, religiosity, place (e.g., urban versus rural), and economic status; as a result, mass polarization may reinforce and exacerbate the divisions spurred by political elites.

Each of these challenges confronts one or more of the key attributes of a functioning democracy – free and fair elections, the idea of legitimate opposition, inclusive participation, the protection of civil rights and liberties, and the rule of law – and cumulatively they risk rendering American democracy precarious and uncertain.

Although the dynamics of polarization have been widely studied, scholars have made less progress toward understanding either how it affects the health of democracy or the extent to which democratic political systems might prove resilient to it. In this volume, we ask our contributors to consider both questions, investigating whether polarization leads to democratic erosion and also what resources democratic systems may have to resist or overcome the negative effects of polarization. Can democracy maintain itself when it is exposed to the kind of intensified polarization that the United States, along with other democracies, has experienced in recent decades? To the extent that it can, we would describe that system as *resilient*.

Our contributors – experts on a wide array of political institutions and processes – tackle these questions from a range of different analytical perspectives, bridging the conventional divide between institutional and behavioral approaches to the study of American politics. They break new ground in assessing polarization's implications for democratic governance and, more fundamentally, the resilience of democratic institutions in the United States. We seek to understand the conditions under which polarization does and does not become a threat to democracy itself and the conditions under which democratic institutions and processes prove resilient in the face of threats to their guiding principles and common practices. At a time of rising concern about "democratic backsliding" and the strengthening of authoritarian currents around the world, we explore whether the United States is also prone to such tendencies and we analyze what features of American society and US democratic institutions make them more or less resilient in the face of such pressures.

Clearly, Donald Trump's presidential campaign and his polarizing administration lent a new sense of urgency to the questions our contributors address in this volume. To buttress his appeal as an antiestablishment political figure, Trump brazenly fanned the flames of tribalism, defied constitutional requirements, and flouted democratic norms. Nevertheless, the trends that endanger American democracy are not the product of a single presidency; rather, they have been on the rise for decades and they threaten to persist well beyond the Trump administration.[3] And while not all observers are equally alarmed about the prospects for the American democratic regime, it is clear that the Trump era has exposed a critical question with which political scientists have not yet fully grappled: how resilient will American political

---

[3] Robert C. Lieberman, Suzanne Mettler, Thomas B. Pepinsky, Kenneth M. Roberts, and Richard Valelly, "The Trump Presidency and American Democracy," *Perspectives on Politics* 17, no. 2 (June 2019): 470–79; Mann and Ornstein, *It's Even Worse Than It Looks*; Suzanne Mettler and Robert C. Lieberman, *Four Threats: The Recurring Crises of American Democracy* (New York: St. Martin's, 2020); Sam Rosenfeld, *The Polarizers: Postwar Architects of Our Partisan Era* (Chicago: University of Chicago Press, 2018).

institutions and civil society prove to be in the face of the dramatic transformations of recent decades?[4]

To answer this question, we begin by explaining our approach to the two critical concepts that are the analytical cornerstones of this volume: democratic resilience and polarization. These concepts have both institutional and behavioral properties and they are intrinsically multidimensional in character.

DEMOCRACY AND DEMOCRATIC RESILIENCE

We define democracy as a system of government in which citizens are able to hold those in power accountable, primarily through regular competitive elections, and in which representatives engage in collective and cooperative decision-making.[5] Some theorists of democracy, notably the economist Joseph Schumpeter, define democracy in strictly procedural terms as a political system in which citizens choose their rulers through competitive elections.[6] But others argue that holding elections is not sufficient to classify a regime as a democracy. Many nations, for example, hold elections that confer power but simultaneously violate other important conditions for effective democratic accountability, such as free and fair elections, universal voting rights, and the protection of civil rights and liberties that are necessary for effective debate and contestation. Steven Levitsky and Lucan Way categorize these regimes as "competitive authoritarianism," a hybrid form of governance in which some of the forms of democracy are preserved but other conditions create a substantially uneven playing field that unfairly advantages incumbents against challengers. In these systems, elections do not provide accountability.[7]

---

[4] See, for example, Raúl L. Madrid and Kurt Weyland, "Why US Democracy Will Survive Trump," in *When Democracy Trumps Populism: European and Latin American Lessons for the United States*, ed. Kurt Weyland and Raúl L. Madrid (Cambridge: Cambridge University Press, 2019), 154–86.

[5] Philippe C. Schmitter and Terry Lynn Karl, "What Democracy Is ... and Is Not," *Journal of Democracy* 2, no. 3 (Summer 1991), 76–80; see also Robert A. Dahl, *Democracy and Its Critics* (New Haven: Yale University Press, 1991).

[6] Joseph A. Schumpeter, *Capitalism, Socialism, and Democracy* (New York: Harper & Brothers, 1942), 269; see also Adam Przeworski, "Minimalist Conception of Democracy: A Defense," in *Democracy's Value*, ed. Ian Shapiro and Casiano Hacker-Cordón (Cambridge: Cambridge University Press, 1999), 23–55.

[7] Steven Levitsky and Lucan A. Way, "The Rise of Competitive Authoritarianism," *Journal of Democracy* 13, no. 2 (April 2002), 52–53.

American history, not to mention global experience, reinforces the obvious point that democracies, once established, do not automatically remain strong and robust or even endure. Democracies come and go, and although a democratic regime's longevity makes democracy more likely to persist, even long-established democracies can deteriorate toward autocracy.[8] But democracy's end does not necessarily come suddenly, with tanks in the street and a sudden seizure of power as in the classic coup d'état; more often, especially in recent decades, democracies erode, through apparently legitimate democratic processes.[9] Democratic erosion might appear as the measurable decline of key democratic attributes: free and fair elections, the recognition of a legitimate opposition, the rule of law, institutional checks and balances, and the integrity of rights, all of which are susceptible to decay over time if they are not tended and protected. In the United States, in fact, each of these attributes has suffered harm in recent decades, as evident in the country's declining scores on numerous comparative democracy indices in the decades since the enactment of the Voting Rights Act.[10] Like sand dunes that become more vulnerable to storms as they gradually erode, democracies can grow increasingly susceptible to more sudden destructive forces through erosion.

We thus define "democratic resilience" broadly as a system's capacity to withstand a major shock such as the onset of extreme polarization and to continue to perform the basic functions of democratic governance – electoral accountability, representation, effective restraints on excessive or concentrated power, and collective decision-making. Democratic resilience has both institutional and behavioral components. Institutionally, effective democracies are able to preserve what Guillermo O'Donnell calls "horizontal accountability" – a system of checks and balances in which

---

[8] Adam Przeworski, Michael Alvarez, José Antonio Cheibub, and Fernando Limongi, "What Makes Democracies Endure?" *Journal of Democracy* 7, no. 1 (January 1996): 39–55.

[9] Nancy Bermeo, "On Democratic Backsliding," *Journal of Democracy* 27, no. 1 (January 2016): 5–19; Larry Diamond, *Ill Winds: Saving Democracy From Russian Rage, Chinese Ambition, and American Complacency* (New York: Penguin, 2019); Steven Levitsky and Daniel Ziblatt, *How Democracies Die* (New York: Crown, 2018).

[10] See, for example, the indices compiled by the Varieties of Democracy Project (www.v-dem.net/en/), Freedom House (https://freedomhouse.org/countries/freedom-world/scores), the Economist Intelligence Unit (www.eiu.com/topic/democracy-index), and Bright Line Watch (http://brightlinewatch.org). See also Levitsky and Ziblatt, *How Democracies Die*; Mettler and Lieberman, *Four Threats*; Robert Mickey, *Paths out of Dixie: The Democratization of Authoritarian Enclaves in America's Deep South, 1944–1972* (Princeton: Princeton University Press, 2015).

different government institutions are able to challenge and restrain each other and thereby prevent excessive concentrations and abuses of power.[11] In the United States, horizontal accountability arises principally from institutional arrangements such as federalism, bicameralism, and the separation of powers, which tend to fragment power and induce office holders in one branch of government to resist domination by the other branches, as James Madison foresaw in *Federalist* no. 51 ("ambition must be made to counteract ambition").

Social scientists generally regard political institutions, by their very nature, as sources of stability. Whether we understand institutions as formal organizations, networks of rules, recurring patterns of behavior, or widely shared cultural understandings, institutions across the social sciences are generally interpreted as promoting order, even in changing social or political circumstances.[12] This is especially the case with the United States Constitution, which is commonly seen as imparting particular stability to American politics by establishing enduring structural features such as the separation of powers, the bicameral legislature, and federalism. But the stability of constitutional arrangements does not foreclose the possibility, even the likelihood, of profound change; political development – a "durable shift in governing authority," in Karen Orren and Stephen Skowronek's often-cited definition – is an equally persistent feature of the American regime.[13] As Paul Pierson and Eric Schickler show in their contribution to this volume, checks and balances are not self-executing; the Madisonian view of institutions-as-clockwork does not account for the threat that polarization can pose to the system of checks and balances and its ability to ensure horizontal accountability.

---

[11] Guillermo O'Donnell, "Delegative Democracy," *Journal of Democracy* 5, no. 1 (January 1994): 61.

[12] See Orfeo Fioretos, Tulia G. Falleti, and Adam Sheingate, "Historical Institutionalism in Political Science," in *The Oxford Handbook of Historical Institutionalism*, ed. Orfeo Fioretos, Tulia G. Falleti, and Adam Sheingate (Oxford: Oxford University Press, 2016), 3–28; Samuel P. Huntington, *Political Order in Changing Societies* (New Haven: Yale University Press, 1968); Robert C. Lieberman, "Ideas, Institutions, and Political Order: Explaining Political Change," *American Political Science Review*, 96, no. 4 (December 2002): 697–712.

[13] Karen Orren and Stephen Skowronek, *The Search for American Political Development* (Cambridge: Cambridge University Press, 2004), 123. See also Stephen Skowronek and Karen Orren, "Pathways to the Present: Political Development in America," in *The Oxford Handbook of American Political Development*, ed. Richard M. Valelly, Suzanne Mettler, and Robert C. Lieberman (Oxford: Oxford University Press, 2016), 27–47.

In the first impeachment of Donald Trump, for example, rather than hold the president to account for his evident abuse of presidential power and obstruction of Congress – or even, indeed, conduct a thorough trial and hear from witnesses who might have shed light on the charges – the Senate's Republican majority protected the president. It is instructive to compare the Trump impeachment episode with the near-impeachment of Richard Nixon almost a half-century earlier, at a moment of considerably lower polarization in American politics. In addition to unanimous Democratic support, each of the three articles of impeachment against Nixon approved by the House Judiciary Committee received Republican votes. Nixon's eventual resignation was precipitated by the collapse of Republican support for his acquittal in the Senate in the face of overwhelming evidence, much of which had been uncovered by a series of investigations conducted by federal government institutions acting independently (notably Congress and the Department of Justice). By contrast, in the polarized contemporary Congress, not a single Republican voted in support of articles of impeachment in the House, either in the Judiciary committee or on the floor, and in the Senate trial, only one Republican, Mitt Romney, voted for conviction on one of the two articles.[14] Trump's unprecedented second impeachment, in the wake of the January 6, 2021, insurrection at the United States Capitol, came a bit closer to a bipartisan reckoning with presidential misconduct; ten Republicans in the House voted to impeach and seven Republican Senators supported conviction, still ten votes short of the two-thirds majority needed for a guilty verdict. The inability of a highly polarized system to rein in evident executive wrongdoing raises serious questions about the system's ability to preserve democratic accountability in the face of extreme polarization.

On the institutional dimension, then, democratic resilience entails the maintenance of the checks and balances and restraints on concentrated power that the constitutional system promises but does not always ensure. Some of the observable manifestations of institutional resilience might include the avoidance of deck stacking in electoral rules, the preservation of incentives for public officials to cooperate across party lines and seek policy compromise, or restraint in the use of constitutional hardball tactics that can send democratic regimes into a cascade toward authoritarianism. Likewise, institutional resilience requires that institutions

---

[14] Romney and one other Republican senator, Susan Collins, also voted to call witnesses in the Senate impeachment trial. But aside from these anomalies, the impeachment and trial of Donald Trump proceeded entirely along party lines.

designed to perform "watchdog" functions for the regime itself – including the courts, the Justice Department (including the FBI), and executive branch inspectors general – maintain a significant measure of professional independence from overt partisan manipulation; this is necessary in order to preserve the rule of law and protect against officials who are tempted to abuse their authority to pursue their own personal or political gain. Our contributors differ on the extent to which they see American institutions as resilient in the face of contemporary polarization. Frances Lee and Douglas Kriner, for example, argue that polarization has not fundamentally eroded at least some important checks and balances. Paul Pierson and Eric Schickler, Desmond King and Sidney Milkis, Thomas Keck, and Alexander Hertel-Fernandez, on the other hand, see more threats in contemporary circumstances.

Democratic accountability runs not only horizontally, among officials empowered by governing institutions, but also "vertically," through mechanisms that enable citizens to hold their representatives accountable.[15] The ability of citizens to replace those in power stands as the ultimate tool of representation and check against abuses of power. We expect office holders to hold each other to account, but when they fail to do so the electorate gets the final say. As the capacity erodes to hold those in power accountable, democracy risks further decay. Effective vertical accountability requires electoral practices that maintain a level playing field for voters and protect free and fair elections. Practices such as gerrymandering and various means of voter suppression risk distorting electoral accountability by giving those in power a built-in advantage in their quest to defeat challengers and retain power. Vertical accountability, moreover, also requires action; the government's perceived failure to address social problems effectively – which is often a product of the very checks and balances that enable horizontal accountability – can produce frustration, cynicism, and anger toward government, which themselves contribute to the erosion of democracy.[16]

On the behavioral side, moreover, polarization among the electorate can affect the possibility of electoral accountability. To the extent that partisan attachments among voters reinforce rather than cut across social divisions such as race, ethnicity, gender, and religiosity, electoral polarization can further buttress the "teamsmanship" that impedes

---

[15] O'Donnell, "Delegative Democracy," 61.
[16] Suzanne Mettler, *The Government-Citizen Disconnect* (New York: Russell Sage Foundation, 2018).

institutional accountability. Such teamsmanship is especially dangerous when it induces voters to tolerate or even reward violations of democratic norms by officials of their own party because they so loathe the other "team." For democracy to be resilient, it is essential that voters be willing and able to recognize and electorally sanction antidemocratic behavior, whatever its source. Where polarized teamsmanship impedes such recognition or electoral sanctioning, vertical accountability is seriously impaired, and politicians can transgress democratic norms with impunity.

In the 2016 and 2020 elections, for example, despite widespread anxiety about Trump's suitability for the presidency, Republicans eventually fell in line behind him; 88 percent of Republican voters chose him in 2016 and 94 percent in 2020. Despite his overall unpopularity, Trump has successfully mobilized and energized his electoral base around an extreme and dangerous set of antiestablishment impulses and extreme positions on immigration, race, and America's role in the world.[17] His persistent high levels of approval from his core constituencies – Republicans and older, wealthier, white, male, rural, and Christian voters – even through the trials of impeachment, a global pandemic, and a precipitous plunge into a deep recession have underscored the challenges of vertical accountability in the face of polarization. Voters did hand Trump and the Republican party a rebuke in the 2018 midterm, electing a Democratic majority in the House of Representatives, and ultimately ousted him and elected an evenly split Senate in 2020. Still, events that would likely have dramatically diminished another president's support – impeachment, a mismanaged pandemic, and the rapid onset of a recession – seem to have had little impact on Trump's public approval. And although he lost in 2020, he outperformed his own previous vote total and percentage and gained ground among a number of constituencies, including African Americans, Latinos, and women. Moreover, the president's conspiratorial and dishonest fury over the conduct of the 2020 election, amplified by the right-wing media echo chamber, not only impelled many of his followers to parrot his grievances but also incited some of them to mount what can only be described as an insurrection at the US Capitol on January 6, 2021, at the very hour that Congress was meeting to ratify Joe Biden's Electoral College victory.

---

[17] Desmond King and Rogers M. Smith, "White Protectionism in America," *Perspectives on Politics* 19, no. 2 (June 2021): 460–78.

Behavioral resilience might mean the rejection or marginalization of extreme views; the ability of political leaders to mobilize voters and compete for power on the basis of broad and inclusive (rather than divisive and polarizing) appeals; the emergence or persistence of cross-cutting rather than reinforcing cleavages among the electorate; and the maintenance of a sense of legitimacy for the democratic system as a whole. Politics will function better to protect democracy when leaders attempt to unite broad and diverse coalitions, as that process in itself requires participants to recognize the need to compromise, diffusing the tendency for politics to be perceived as mortal combat. In addition, it can make political losses less threatening to the social identity of particular groups, thus making partisanship less likely to inculcate polarized perceptions of one another as "us versus them."

POLARIZATION: A MULTIDIMENSIONAL APPROACH

Polarization is hardly a new phenomenon in American politics. The United States, after all, fought a civil war over slavery in the 1860s, and the extension – or denial – of citizenship rights to African Americans remained deeply divisive issues thereafter. In contrast to European democracies, however, the United States never developed a strong, labor-based socialist party in the twentieth century and levels of class and ideological polarization in the American two-party system were markedly lower than in most other industrialized societies in the post–World War II era.[18] This postwar political landscape, which was dominated by two large, ideologically eclectic, and socially heterogeneous "catch-all" parties, weighed heavily on scholarly thinking about how American democracy "works." Given the presence of liberal northern Republicans and conservative southern Democrats, the two parties overlapped ideologically and created a centripetal dynamic of political competition. They competed for support around the median voter, as Anthony Downs theorized, and they adopted moderate programmatic positions that eased the construction of bipartisan legislative and policymaking coalitions.[19] The most contentious and polarizing issues – particularly

---

[18] Seymour Martin Lipset and Stein Rokkan, "Cleavage Structures, Party Systems, and Voter Alignments: An Introduction," in *Party Systems and Voter Alignments: Cross-National Perspectives*, ed. Seymour Martin Lipset and Stein Rokkan (New York: Free Press, 1967), 1–64; Seymour Martin Lipset and Gary Marks, *It Didn't Happen Here: Why Socialism Failed in the United States* (New York: W. W. Norton, 2000).

[19] Anthony Downs, *An Economic Theory of Democracy* (New York: Harper & Row, 1957).

desegregation and civil rights – had begun to realign the parties at the state and local levels during the New Deal era, but these issues did not structure interparty competition at the national level until the passage of the Civil Rights Act in 1964, as they cut across the partisan divide.[20] Civil rights, in other words, divided both parties internally (the Democrats, in particular, along regional lines), rather than aligning one party against the other on opposing sides of the political cleavage.

The transformation of this postwar order into the polarized political landscape of the early twenty-first century was a prolonged, complex, and multifaceted process, one that involved both institutional and behavioral components. Since that story has been told very capably elsewhere, we will not repeat it here, other than to say that the process was heavily conditioned by the civil rights revolution, crystalized by the Civil Rights Act of 1964, and the conservative backlash against it.[21] This backlash was subsequently reinforced by other cleavages in the "culture wars," and by the patterns of social mobilization and countermobilization they elicited among movements and activist networks on both sides of the divide. Social and political mobilization around cultural issues brought new grassroots activists with strong policy and ideological commitments into the parties, helping to push them further apart. The Supreme Court's decision on abortion in *Roe v. Wade* had a significant effect on the decision of evangelical Christians to abandon their earlier reticence and enter politics. The fight over the Equal Rights Amendment, too, energized conservatives, enabling Phyllis Schlafly and her followers to reinvigorate the waning anti-communist movement with support for "family values."[22] Similarly, rising immigration has invigorated the right, divided the left, and become a key flashpoint in ideological and partisan battles. It

---

[20] Eric Schickler, *Racial Realignment: The Transformation of American Liberalism, 1932–1965* (Princeton: Princeton University Press, 2016).

[21] Doug McAdam and Karina Kloos, *Deeply Divided: Racial Politics and Social Movements in Postwar America* (Oxford: Oxford University Press, 2014); Mickey, *Paths out of Dixie*; Schickler, *Racial Realignment*; Nolan McCarty, Keith T. Poole, and Howard Rosenthal, *Polarized America: The Dance of Ideology and Unequal Riches*, 2nd ed. (Cambridge: MIT Press, 2016); Lilliana Mason, *Uncivil Agreement: How Politics Became Our Identity* (Chicago: University of Chicago Press, 2018); Angie Maxwell and Todd Shields, *The Long Southern Strategy: How Chasing White Voters in the South Changed American Politics* (Oxford: Oxford University Press, 2019).

[22] Jane J. Mansbridge, *Why We Lost the ERA* (Chicago: University of Chicago Press, 1986); Donald T. Critchlow, *Phyllis Schlafly and Grassroots Conservatism: A Woman's Crusade* (Princeton: Princeton University Press, 2008); Marjorie J. Spruill, *Divided We Stand: The Battle over Women's Rights and Family Values That Polarized American Politics* (New York: Bloomsbury, 2017); Alice Kessler-Harris, "Engendering Democracy in an

has joined other sources of division, including religion, LGBTQ rights, and gun control, in gradually realigning the conservative South from the Democratic to the Republican camp. Partisan realignment thus produced a more consistently liberal Democratic Party and a more deeply conservative Republican Party, sharpening the programmatic distinctions between the two parties on a wide range of social and cultural issues.

Realignment, however, was not simply a matter of ideological sorting and polarization. It also transformed and differentiated the social bases of the two major parties, with each party becoming more closely identified with specific social and cultural groups. Whites, evangelicals, and small-town and rural America gravitated toward the Republican camp, which became increasingly homogenous in its social composition and possessed fewer crosscutting ties to diverse social groups. On the other hand, racial and ethnic minorities, secular and non-evangelical voters, and urban America moved toward the Democrats. This "sorting" of different social groups into rival partisan camps was parallel to the sorting of liberal and conservative voters into parties with distinct ideological or programmatic brands. As Lilliana Mason demonstrates, however, these dual sorting processes were analytically distinct and not reducible to each other, even if they were mutually reinforcing.[23] Similarly, Frances Lee identifies the important phenomenon of partisan teamsmanship among lawmakers, a polarizing dynamic that is rooted in organizational self-interest and is not dependent on either ideological or social differentiation. The need for cohesive teamsmanship within parties has, she points out, grown far greater since 1980, when the Democrats lost their hegemonic control of Congress – and especially since the Gingrich era in the 1990s – and it became possible for either party to win or lose the majority.[24]

These distinctions are indicative of the multidimensional character of polarization processes and the diverse mechanisms that can drive them. Therefore, to assess the implications of polarization for democracy, it is important to look beyond the ideological plane to these social and organizational dimensions and the complex – and often synergistic – interactions

---

Age of Anxiety," in *Who Gets What? The New Politics of Insecurity*, ed. Frances Rosenbluth and Margaret Weir (Cambridge: Cambridge University Press, 2021).

[23] Mason, *Uncivil Agreement*.

[24] Frances E. Lee, *Beyond Ideology: Politics, Principles, and Partisanship in the U.S. Senate* (Chicago: University of Chicago Press, 2009). See also Mann and Ornstein, *It's Even Worse Than It Looks*; Julian E. Zelizer, *Burning Down the House: Newt Gingrich, the Fall of a Speaker, and the Rise of the New Republican Party* (New York: Penguin Press, 2020).

among them. The following sections analyze these three dimensions of polarization and their mutually reinforcing properties, which help to explain polarization's inertial tendencies and the challenges they pose to democratic resilience.

Ideology and Issue-Based Polarization

Political parties routinely seek to develop reputations or "brands" to differentiate themselves from opponents and cultivate a loyal core of followers in the electorate. Voters, in turn, rely on such brands as heuristics or shortcuts to reduce the information costs of voting decisions.[25] Although party brands can be based on "valence" reputations for competence, clean government, or other values that are broadly shared in the electorate, the adoption of policy or programmatic positions on issues that divide the electorate is standard fare for the construction of party brands that appeal to the interests or values of loyal core constituencies.[26] Spatial models of party competition assume that parties differentiate themselves on such "positional" issues, and research in both American and comparative politics suggests that this differentiation is healthy for democratic representation. A special committee of the American Political Science Association famously recommended that the United States needed parties that were more programmatically differentiated to offer "a proper range of choice" to voters in the more consensual postwar period.[27] Likewise, comparativists have argued that a lack of programmatic differentiation may cause some societal interests to be excluded from effective representation, enhancing the appeal of populist outsiders who challenge established parties[28]

There is no clear benchmark, however, for determining when "healthy" programmatic differentiation gives way to dysfunctional or

---

[25] John H. Aldrich, *Why Parties? A Second Look* (Chicago: University of Chicago Press, 2011), 47–48.
[26] Donald E. Stokes, "Spatial Models of Party Competition," *American Political Science Review* 57, no. 2 (June 1963): 368–77.
[27] American Political Science Association, "A Report of the Committee on Political Parties: Toward a More Responsible Two-Party System," *American Political Science Review* 44, no. 3 (September 1950, Part 2): 15.
[28] Sheri Berman and Maria Snegovaya, "Populism and the Decline of Social Democracy," *Journal of Democracy* 30, no. 3 (July 2019): 5–19; Noam Lupu, *Party Brands in Crisis: Partisanship, Brand Dilution, and the Breakdown of Political Parties in Latin America* (Cambridge: Cambridge University Press, 2017); Kenneth M. Roberts, *Changing Course in Latin America: Party Systems in the Neoliberal Era* (Cambridge: Cambridge University Press, 2014).

even threatening forms of ideological polarization. In general, ideological polarization is a function of three basic factors: (1) the gap or distance between the policy positions adopted by major parties on key issues under dispute; (2) the internal cohesion or consistency of each party around their modal position; and (3) the mapping or "bundling" of multiple issues onto the same axis of programmatic contestation (such as the conventional left-right or liberal-conservative axis). So conceived, polarization is magnified when parties move toward opposite ideological "poles" on an axis of issue competition, when their positions are not watered down by more centrist internal factions, and when the parties bundle social, cultural, and economic issues onto the same competitive axis.

A large body of literature attests to the reality of issue-based polarization in late-twentieth- and early-twenty-first-century US politics.[29] The Republican and Democratic parties moved further apart in their policy positions, the Democrats became more internally cohesive in their programmatic stands with the gradual exodus of southern conservatives, and both parties mapped a wide range of social, cultural, and economic issues onto an underlying liberal-conservative axis of competition. As Nolan McCarty, Keith Poole, and Howard Rosenthal report, interest-group rankings of members of Congress indicate that "moderates are vanishing," the two parties "have pulled apart," and individual issue areas no longer have a "distinctive existence," since they are increasingly bundled onto a "single, liberal-conservative dimension."[30] Although the two parties occasionally manage to work together, as in their joint development of a stimulus package in response to the COVID-19 pandemic and its economic effects, the ideological overlap between them disappeared after 2005, as every Democratic member of Congress had a voting record "ideal point" to the left of every Republican.[31]

Although the process of ideological polarization reflects changes in both major party organizations, it has not been a symmetrical process. As Matt Grossmann and David Hopkins note, congressional Democrats have moved modestly left since the 1970s while Republicans have moved much more dramatically to the right. Moreover, Democrats remain more ideologically heterogenous.[32] Given the Democratic Party's centrist

---

[29] Geoffrey C. Layman, Thomas M. Carsey, and Julianna M. Horowitz, "Party Polarization in American Politics," *Annual Review of Political Science* 9 (2006): 83–110; McCarty, Poole, and Rosenthal, *Polarized America*.
[30] McCarty, Poole, and Rosenthal, *Polarized America*, 4–5.   [31] Ibid., 33–34.
[32] Matt Grossmann and David A. Hopkins, *Asymmetric Politics: Ideological Republicans and Group Interest Democrats* (Oxford: Oxford University Press, 2016), 11.

positioning on economic issues under Bill Clinton – whose presidency introduced NAFTA, welfare reform, and financial deregulation, reflecting a general pro-market policy orientation – polarization on economic issues was largely attributable to the Republicans' shift toward market-fundamentalist positions on the far right pole. In that sense, the competitive dynamic on economic issues was arguably one of unilateral radicalization rather than bilateral polarization, at least until the rise after 2016 of Bernie Sanders, whose politicization of economic inequalities pulled the Democratic Party further to the left. On a wide range of other social and cultural issues, however – including abortion rights, LGBTQ rights, gun control, and eventually immigration – the two parties gradually moved in opposite directions, staking out sharply polarized positions that mapped onto the liberal-conservative axis. Ideological identities were especially prominent on the conservative side of the divide under the Republican Party, which bundled multiple issues into a form of conservative orthodoxy that gave it, according to Grossmann and Hopkins, "the most consistently conservative positions of any political party in the world."[33] Indeed, the GOP's current positions on gun rights, climate change, taxes, and deregulation are striking for the lack of parallels among any other mainstream conservative parties elsewhere in the world today, including throughout Europe and Latin America.

Although this partisan polarization has induced voters to sort into one party or the other depending on their policy or ideological preferences, it is important to recognize that many voters do not have consistent or well-defined ideological worldviews. Consequently, scholars have debated whether the mass public itself has polarized on the issues or whether polarization is largely a function of party elites' efforts to differentiate their brands, discredit their rivals, and turn out the vote.[34] Even where moderate or ill-defined policy positions predominate in the general

---

[33] Grossmann and Hopkins, *Asymmetric Politics,* 108. Data from the comparative Manifesto Project, which analyzes political parties worldwide based on their election platforms, similarly locate the Republican Party well to the right of most mainstream European conservative parties and closer to explicitly xenophobic nationalist parties such as the Austrian Freedom Party and Alternative for Germany. Sahil Chinoy, "What Happened to America's Political Center of Gravity?" *New York Times,* June 26, 2019, www.nytimes.com/interactive/2019/06/26/opinion/sunday/republican-platform-far-right.html.

[34] Alan I. Abramowitz, *The Disappearing Center: Engaged Citizens, Polarization, and American Democracy* (New Haven: Yale University Press, 2011); Christopher H. Achen and Larry M. Bartels, *Democracy for Realists: Why Elections Do Not Produce Responsive Government* (Princeton: Princeton University Press, 2016); Morris P. Fiorina, Samuel J. Abrams, and Jeremy C. Pope, *Culture War? The Myth of a Polarized America* (New York: Pearson Longman, 2005).

electorate, however, non-elite societal actors can play a central role in the process of partisan and ideological polarization. A wide range of interest groups, activist networks, and social movements have contributed to the realignment of the Republication and Democratic parties and the definition of their respective policy platforms, as each party came to be seen as the primary representative of particular societal interests in the democratic arena.[35]

On the left, labor unions' traditional ties to the Democratic Party were supplemented after the 1960s by new ties to the movements for civil rights, women's rights, LGBTQ rights, environmental protection, and eventually immigrants' rights. On the right, the Republican Party – traditionally associated with pro-market business interests – became a staunch ally of the antiabortion and evangelical Christian movements by the 1980s as well as guns rights activist networks and, increasingly, white ethno-nationalist currents. The anti-Obama Tea Party movement stitched together these diverse currents on the right flank of the Republican Party after 2009, combining grassroots mobilization with elite financial and organizational support from free market think tanks and advocacy networks, such as the Koch brothers–aligned Americans for Prosperity and Freedom Works.[36] As Theda Skocpol, Caroline Tervo, and Kirsten Walters show in this volume, Tea Party groups at the local level tilted the Republican Party further to the right, embracing more extreme candidates, policy positions, and tactics. Notably, the anti-Trump resistance groups have not pulled the Democratic Party in analogous ways, but rather have been willing to embrace moderate and incrementalist approaches as they face practical challenges in efforts to achieve and retain national power. With that exception, most of these forms of civic activism, beyond their impact on the policy agendas and the ideological polarization of the two major parties, were also instrumental in shaping a second key dimension of polarization, that of social sorting, as explained in the following.

---

[35] Daniel Schlozman, *When Movements Anchor Parties: Electoral Alignments in American History* (Princeton: Princeton University Press, 2015).
[36] Rachel M. Blum, *How the Tea Party Captured the GOP: Insurgent Factions in American Politics* (Chicago: University of Chicago Press, 2020); Christopher S. Parker and Matt A. Barreto, *Change They Can't Believe In: The Tea Party and Reactionary Politics in America* (Princeton: Princeton University Press, 2013); Theda Skocpol and Alexander Hertel-Fernandez, "The Koch Network and Republican Party Extremism," *Perspectives on Politics* 14, no. 3 (September 2016): 681–99; Theda Skocpol and Vanessa Williamson, *The Tea Party and the Remaking of Republican Conservatism* (Oxford: Oxford University Press, 2013).

Group Identities, Social Sorting, and Partisan Polarization

Although many voters do not have consistent and well-defined policy preferences, neither do they approach each election with a blank state or *tabula rasa*. Beyond – and typically complementing – their programmatic identities, political parties develop brands for representing the interests and values of particular social groups in the democratic arena. Analogous to ideological branding, citizens' identification with social groups bound to a specific party can provide a convenient heuristic to simplify vote choices; as Alan Zuckerman, Josip Dasović, and Jennifer Fitzgerald pithily state, "Partisanship is a socially derived choice."[37] Voters, in short, may learn through family or social ties that a given party stands for "people like me" and internalize partisan loyalty as a natural extension of their social group identity. This extension is clearly facilitated where a party establishes political ties to social group organizations or activist networks and embraces their policy preferences, but it cannot be reduced to such programmatic considerations; voters with strong social identities but hazy or diverse policy preferences may still vote on the basis of their primary group identity.

In her careful work on social sorting and social polarization in contemporary US politics, Lilliana Mason persuasively demonstrates the extent to which "the American electorate has become deeply socially divided along partisan lines," undermining "the cross-cutting social ties that once allowed for partisan compromise."[38] In a competitive environment, she argues, strong in-group identities can be a source of political conflict with out-groups even in the absence of significant differences in group-based policy preferences. Where social group identities *are* aligned with parties and policy preferences, as in the United States, those social identities clearly magnify polarization on the party dimension and may have an even stronger effect in shaping citizens' attitudes.

The problem, then, is not only that the Republican and Democratic parties have moved further apart in their programmatic stands, but also that they represent very different sectors of the American electorate, divided on lines of race and ethnicity, gender, religion, and place. Such patterns of social sorting can produce a cultural divide and forms of mutual intolerance or antagonism that magnify policy or issue-based

---

[37] Alan S. Zuckerman, Josip Dasović, and Jennifer Fitzgerald, *Partisan Families: The Social Logic of Bounded Partisanship in Germany and Britain* (Cambridge: Cambridge University Press, 2007), 1.

[38] Mason, *Uncivil Agreement*, 3, 6.

differences. Indeed, social sorting is central to the forms of "negative partisanship" that have been identified in the American electorate, whereby voters have stronger adverse reactions to the "other side" than they do positive affect toward their own preferred party. As Alan Abramowitz and Steven Webster state, "Americans largely align *against* one party instead of affiliating with the other"; this negative partisanship is deeply rooted in the racial divide between the two parties and rising levels of racial resentment among white Republicans.[39] Negative partisanship is also fueled by highly partisan media outlets and the sorting of voters into separate and insular networks of political information and communication.

Partisan Competition, Teamsmanship, and Polarization

If social sorting is capable of exerting an independent effect on political polarization above and beyond its association with deep ideological or policy divides, so also can the dynamics of partisan competition contribute toward polarization. As Frances Lee argues, "there is far more party conflict in the Congress than one would expect based on the ideological content of the congressional agenda or the policy differences between liberals and conservatives." Party competition for "elected office and chamber control" helps to explain this surfeit of conflict; competition creates shared interests among partisans as well as shared risks, and it ensures that the personal and professional interests of individual members of congress "are bound up with the fate of their parties." Competition between rival partisan "teams," therefore, tends to "institutionalize, exploit, and deepen" policy-based differences, or even "create conflict where it would not have otherwise existed" by encouraging forms of "reflexive partisanship."[40] In short, partisans in Congress reflexively try to discredit their opponents, highlight issues that differentiate the rival camps, and oppose any initiatives introduced by the other side, even when they do not invoke core ideological principles.

This teamsmanship or competitive polarization is caused in significant part by the dynamic that arises when the two parties approach electoral parity and a competitive equilibrium. Under such conditions, institutional

---

[39] Alan I. Abramowitz and Steven W. Webster, "Negative Partisanship: Why Americans Dislike Parties but Behave Like Rabid Partisans," *Advances in Political Psychology* 39 (2018, Supplement 1): 119, 124–27.

[40] Lee, *Beyond Ideology*, 3–4.

control of the executive and legislative branches is at stake in every election cycle, and congressional majorities become highly insecure. As insecurity intensifies interparty competition, it also transforms parties' strategic behavior; simply put, "competition for institutional control focuses members of Congress on the quest for partisan political advantage."[41] Not surprisingly, then, political polarization in the United States in recent decades was driven by the erosion of the majoritarian status of the Democratic Party's New Deal coalition, and by the rise of a new competitive equilibrium. Since 1980, the two major parties have become more equally balanced in their electoral appeal and in the size of their congressional blocs; the two parties have alternated in the presidency, divided government has become the norm, and the majority party in both houses of Congress has changed hands multiple times (seven times in the Senate, and four times in the House). Razor-thin electoral margins have allowed the last two Republican presidents – George W. Bush and Donald Trump – to win the Electoral College despite losing the popular vote.

On multiple fronts, then, political polarization has raised the stakes of partisan competition and intensified the battle to win elections, control institutions, and dictate the terms of public policy formation. The two major US parties have grown further apart on the issues, sorted distinct social groups into rival partisan camps, and become locked in a competitive equilibrium whereby electoral outcomes, institutional leverage, and policy orientations are highly uncertain and tenuous.

Because these multiple dimensions of polarization are increasingly aligned and mutually reinforcing, they impede the construction of bipartisan legislative and policymaking coalitions, producing either gridlock and paralysis or narrow partisan-based policy initiatives that are bitterly opposed by the rival camp. The central question we pose in this volume, however, is whether these multiple forms of polarization also create novel political temptations to manipulate different institutional sites for partisan advantage in ways that undermine democratic norms and practices. Such forms of manipulation – for example, efforts to stack the courts, circumvent or "weaponize" oversight institutions, or tilt the electoral playing field – can be induced by polarization, but they also exacerbate it, since they are intrinsically threatening to the other party and its social constituencies. Indeed, they are central to the dynamics of the inertial or self-reinforcing "pernicious polarization" that Jennifer McCoy and

---

[41] Lee, *Insecure Majorities*, 2.

Murat Somer examine in this volume. Is polarization, then, a threat to democracy itself? And if it is, what institutional mechanisms and forms of societal resistance are available to counteract these threats, temper polarization, and buttress democracy as a system of governance? In short, what makes democracy resilient?

BRIDGING INSTITUTIONAL, BEHAVIORAL, AND HISTORICAL ANALYSIS

The central questions of this volume are whether contemporary polarization presents a serious threat to US democracy itself, and whether the nation has the institutional and political capacity to resist or recuperate from the harm it may experience. It is well known that polarization has transformed numerous aspects of government and politics, for example, by altering standard operating procedures in Congress, deterring policy enactment, and prompting voters to align their policy preferences with one party or the other. Might it also endanger the United States' character as a democratic regime?

Both polarization and democratic resilience, as we have seen, engage multiple dimensions of American politics. Polarization presents a challenge to American politics at the system level, as mass and elite actors affect one another, and numerous institutions and political processes come into play and interact. Resilience, too, involves both mass and elite actors and the institutions and political practices that connect them and foster (or undermine) democratic accountability. Understanding polarization's impact on democracy and evaluating democratic resilience, therefore, require a system-level response that brings together diverse analytical threads. Yet scholars of American politics typically study the political system through what Paul Pierson calls a "pizza-pie approach," concentrating on a particular part of the political system and specializing deeply in it.[42] This has led to the accumulation of sophisticated literatures on each part of the system, and yet it leaves us ill-prepared to analyze developments that transcend particular components; in fact, we may even fail to recognize their emergence, much less understand them.

As we have argued elsewhere, both history and comparison are essential to meeting the system-level challenge of understanding the dynamics

---

[42] Paul Pierson, "The Costs of Marginalization: Qualitative Methods in the Study of American Politics," *Comparative Political Studies* 40, no. 2 (February 2007): 147.

of democracy and democratic resilience in the United States.[43] Throughout its history, American democracy has weathered numerous shocks that have threatened the integrity of democracy – from the nearly ruinous polarization of the 1790s and the conflict over slavery to the violent rollback of voting rights for African Americans after Reconstruction and the presidential excesses of the twentieth century such as the mass incarceration of Japanese Americans during World War II and the misadventures of Watergate. In each case, certain features of the democratic regime have proven resilient, while others have sustained serious damage. Frequently, these two dynamics have coincided; the resolution of democratic crises in American history has often entailed a compromise of democratic values that reaffirmed or perpetuated racial hierarchy and exclusion.[44] Historical inquiry can be useful as a way to examine these patterns of resilience and backsliding in American democracy and probe their causes. A historical approach can help identify the processes of change that drive resilience and might (or might not) be at work in the contemporary crisis of American democracy.[45] Polarization in particular, as Pierson and Schickler have argued, has been an ever-changing and dynamic force in American politics that has become increasingly self-reinforcing in recent decades, heightening the challenge of resilience.[46]

The problem of democratic resilience is also a global one, and comparison can also illuminate it. Events around the world suggest that the challenges to democracy in the United States are not unique. Previously democratic regimes are under threat or have turned in an authoritarian direction around the world in countries such as Russia, Hungary, Poland, Turkey, Venezuela, and the Philippines. Viewing the United States in a comparative context provides more data with which to develop and test theories of democratic resilience. Although the prospect of democratic backsliding or breakdown has long seemed outside the realm of

---

[43] Lieberman et al., "Trump Presidency." See also Kimberly J. Morgan, "Comparative Politics and American Political Development," in *The Oxford Handbook of American Political Development*, ed. Richard M. Valelly, Suzanne Mettler, and Robert C. Lieberman (Oxford: Oxford University Press, 2016), 166–84.
[44] Mettler and Lieberman, *Four Threats*.
[45] Theda Skocpol, "Analyzing American Political Development as It Happens," in *The Oxford Handbook of American Political Development*, ed. Richard M. Valelly, Suzanne Mettler, and Robert C. Lieberman (Oxford: Oxford University Press, 2016), 48–68.
[46] Paul Pierson and Eric Schickler, "Madison's Constitution Under Stress: A Developmental Analysis of Political Polarization," *Annual Review of Political Science* 23 (2020): 37–58.

reasonable speculation in the United States, comparative scholars have made substantial progress toward understanding and explaining why democracies emerge, how they fail, and under what conditions they might survive.[47] Comparative studies have shown that several conditions pose especially grave threats to democracy: conflict over the boundaries of membership in the political community, particularly on the basis of race, ethnicity, national origin, or other "formative rifts" that predate democratization; high and rising economic inequality; the decay of democratic norms and institutional restraints; and high levels of political polarization.[48]

Guided by this analytical framework, we have gathered first-rate scholars of American politics, both students of institutions and of political behavior. Our aim has been to bring them into dialogue with one another, by asking them to think about how each other's research findings might have a bearing on their own area of study. We have also encouraged them to think about how time matters in their analysis, as circumstances unfold and change dynamically. The authors in this volume probe the historical currents and developmental processes that have helped produce current conditions, asking how the American experience might compare to that of other countries where democracy has been under threat. The resulting analyses take us far in understanding the dangers to US democracy posed by polarization and the capacity of the political system to prove resilient.

The next two chapters – the first by Paul Pierson and Eric Schickler and the second by Jennifer McCoy and Murat Somer – address the

---

[47] Some works have explicitly treated American democracy as congenitally compromised, fragile, and subject to reversal, but these have been the exception. See W. E. Burghardt Du Bois, *Black Reconstruction: An Essay toward the Part Which Black Folk Played in the Attempt to Reconstruct Democracy in America, 1860–1880* (New York: Harcourt, Brace, 1935); Ira Katznelson, *Desolation and Enlightenment: Political Enlightenment After Total War, Totalitarianism, and the Holocaust* (New York: Columbia University Press, 2003); Desmond King, Robert C. Lieberman, Gretchen Ritter, and Laurence Whitehead, eds., *Democratization in America: A Comparative-Historical Analysis* (Baltimore: Johns Hopkins University Press, 2009); Mickey, *Paths out of Dixie*; Richard M. Valelly, *The Two Reconstructions: The Struggle for Black Enfranchisement* (Chicago: University of Chicago Press, 2004).

[48] Jennifer McCoy and Murat Somer, "Toward a Theory of Pernicious Polarization and How It Harms Democracies: Comparative Evidence and Possible Remedies," *Annals of the American Academy of Political and Social Science* 681 (January 2019): 234–71; Dankwart Rustow, "Transitions to Democracy: Toward a Dynamic Model," *Comparative Politics* 2, no. 3 (April 1970): 337–63; see also Bermeo, "On Democratic Backsliding"; Levitsky and Ziblatt, *How Democracies Die*; Przeworski et al., "What Makes Democracies Endure?"

question of polarization's consequences for resilience from this broad historical and comparative perspective. American political institutions, including the structures of separation of powers and federalism, have long been regarded as fragmenting political power by facilitating widespread access to the political system and at the same time impeding efforts by one side or the other to stage a takeover. Nevertheless, the escalation of polarization threatens to overwhelm these institutions. Polarization is not static; rather, it can take on a life of its own and eventually generate different effects than earlier on, as it intensifies and metastasizes. Pierson and Schickler demonstrate this in their developmental analysis of polarization, in which they show that the United States' "meso-institutions" – including interest groups, state parties, and news media – have ceased to operate as countervailing mechanisms that constrain polarization, and have either weakened or turned into engines of polarization. As a result, partisan public officials increasingly run roughshod over checks and balances, seek to delegitimize and incapacitate the political opposition, and aim to rig the system to cement their dominance.

Growing social polarization that emanates from ordinary Americans, moreover, may also increasingly affect how these institutions operate. It may undermine national unity and constrain political elites from working across the aisle, effectively exacerbating harmful consequences. Put differently, mass and elite polarization may feed each other, leading to a spiraling of both. McCoy and Somer view the United States today as subject to "pernicious polarization," a process that transforms the incentives of political actors in ways that can lead to the demise of democratic resilience. Surveying polarization in countries around the world, they observe that it can be most corrosive to democracy when it revolves around unresolved "formative rifts," debates over who is considered a citizen that may date back to the nation's origins, as is the case in the United States. Such developments raise the question of whether the political system can withstand these mounting challenges and permit democracy to survive.

National Institutions

To investigate whether the dispersion and fragmentation of power underlying the US constitutional system remain sufficient to weather the onslaught of threats the nation is confronting presently, we then shift to a focus on institutions themselves. In three chapters, specialists examine the extent to which polarization hinders or obstructs the capacity of national institutions, along with the arrangements of separation of powers, to protect democracy.

Rising polarization in Congress and its impact on the policy process has received considerable attention from scholars, but notwithstanding these problems, Congress may still remain the most resilient of the national institutions to democratic erosion. Frances Lee observes that the political parties in Congress, reflecting their membership across the nation, have grown more socially sorted, more differentiated along lines of race, gender, and religion. Yet while she agrees with Pierson and Schickler that cross-cutting cleavages no longer play the role in ensuring democratic stability that they did in the past, Lee argues that US institutions themselves retain consensus-promoting abilities, enabling them to thwart and restrain such social divides. The separation of powers, strong bicameralism, and federalism still promote power-sharing between the parties and therefore safeguard democratic stability. Some chapters (such as Pierson and Schickler's and McCoy and Somer's) point out that growing dysfunction in Congress impedes the policymaking process, but while acknowledging these concerns, Lee maintains that the institution continues to force bipartisan compromise and negotiation.

Some scholars suspect that ascendant polarization and its accompanying legislative gridlock and failure of responsiveness are leading to the greater assertion of unilateral power by presidents, as they seek alternate means of delivering to the public. Certainly the rise of presidential power is nothing new; presidents of both parties, at least since Franklin D. Roosevelt (and with precedents dating back to George Washington) have exerted it in efforts to respond to the public's demands. Examining trends since the mid-1970s, however, Douglas Kriner finds only slim evidence that contemporary polarization has exacerbated presidential power grabs in the form of executive orders, memoranda, and proclamations. He then investigates the Trump presidency and finds it to be neither imperial nor exceptional in these respects, largely because Republican leaders in Congress themselves have pushed back on several of Trump's key policy initiatives. Yet when it comes to oversight – a critical factor for democratic resilience – Kriner explains that the Trump administration has engaged in almost total obstruction of Congress, in ways that might have the "most dangerous and long-lasting consequences for the balance of power between the branches." Such developments, if they pass judicial muster, threaten to decimate the capacity of Congress to check the power of presidents and the administrative state, especially when executive malfeasance and obstruction are aided by the president's own party in Congress. Taken together, these assessments offer a fair amount of confidence in Congress's ability to restrain presidential unilateralism in policy-making, but Kriner raises grave concerns about the effectiveness of legislative checks on executive misconduct in a context of acute partisan polarization. Such polarization threatens to neutralize congressional oversight or render it strictly partisan in character, posing a risk to democratic resilience.

By contrast, Thomas Keck's chapter on the courts indicates that democratic erosion is already long underway in that domain. It is often assumed that courts can act as guardrails of democracy by restraining the partisan excesses of the "political" branches of government. In the face of worries about the Supreme Court's "countermajoritarian" tendencies in the postwar era, for example, Robert Dahl famously argued that the Court tends to be constrained by the political system and, given the political method of judicial selection, eventually catches up with political majorities.[49] But as Keck explains, courts can also be effective agents of democratic erosion. The long history of court-packing in the American past offers instances of efforts at facilitating both outcomes. In the contemporary era, since the 1970s, Republicans in particular have taken action to stack the judiciary, including the Supreme Court, and conservatives now stand to dominate it for years to come, regardless of the outcome of elections. This dominance threatens democracy given that the courts in recent years have often proven willing to block efforts at democratic renewal and to permit unfair procedures to persist.

Social Polarization and Partisanship

As polarization has grown, many ordinary Americans themselves have been drawn into it. Four chapters explore how social polarization and partisan affiliation have come to be mutually reinforcing and what this trend means for democratic resilience.

Lilliana Mason and Nathan Kalmoe introduce the concept of "social sorting," showing how social identities have increasingly aligned with

---

[49] Alexander M. Bickel, *The Least Dangerous Branch: The Supreme Court at the Bar of Politics* (Indianapolis: Bobbs-Merrill, 1962); Robert A. Dahl, "Decision-Making in a Democracy: The Supreme Court as a National Policy-Maker," *Journal of Public Law* 6, no. 2 (Fall 1957): 279–95; Richard H. Pildes, "Is the Supreme Court a 'Majoritarian' Institution?" *Supreme Court Review* (2010): 103–58.

political identities. The mid-twentieth-century political parties that featured overlapping social identities have become transformed into a Republican Party made up primarily of white Americans, including those who strongly identify as evangelical Christians and those who are particularly concerned with maintaining their privileged status, while the Democratic Party has grown increasingly diverse in its composition and simultaneously more affirming of inclusive policies. Drawing on psychological theories, Mason and Kalmoe illuminate how such social sorting can lead to intergroup conflict and political intolerance. These developments, in turn, may put the polity at risk by leading to greater emotional hostility, moral disengagement, the possibility of violence, and the rejection of election results that threaten one's own party. Mason and Kalmoe draw on the historical record to demonstrate that such outcomes are not only well within the American experience but in fact have been commonplace, making their reemergence today highly conceivable.

Social sorting can facilitate what Matthew Lacombe calls "identity-based mobilization," the political rallying together of those who share a common identity. While such mobilization is fueled by democratic processes, it can have deleterious consequences for democracy if it fosters the kinds of intolerant and exclusionary political reactions that Mason and Kalmoe discuss. The next three chapters explore how this has occurred in recent decades around race, religion, and gun ownership.

Although many journalists widely attributed support for Trump in the 2016 election to economic anxiety, Christopher Parker and Matt Barreto show that support for him was fueled more heavily by white identity. They examine the role of fears on the part of some whites that they were losing "their country" or "way of life," as they perceived growing racial and ethnic diversity in the US population – and the election of the nation's first black president – as a threat to their status.[50] The capacity of such fears to fuel conservative, and in some instances, authoritarian political movements has a long history in the United States, encompassing the Ku Klux

---

[50] See also Katherine J. Cramer, *The Politics of Resentment: Rural Consciousness in Wisconsin and the Rise of Scott Walker* (Chicago: University of Chicago Press, 2016); Arlie Russell Hochschild, *Strangers in Their Own Land: Anger and Mourning on the American Right* (New York: New Press, 2016); John Sides, Michael Tesler, and Lynn Vavreck, *Identity Crisis: The 2016 Presidential Campaign and the Battle for the Meaning of America* (Princeton: Princeton University Press, 2018). For a more nuanced view of the mutually constitutive roles of economics and identity in the 2016 vote, see Andrew J. Cherlin, "Why Did So Many Urban Working-Class Whites Support President Trump?," *Contexts*, contexts.org/articles/why-did-so-many-urban-working-class-whites-support-president-trump/.

Klan, John Birch Society, and the Tea Party. These movements risk harm to democracy because they stoke intolerance of social difference that can activate and mobilize latent authoritarian currents that are intrinsically threatening to democratic resilience.[51]

Religious sorting plays a crucial role in contemporary politics, as Michele Margolis explains. Today's religious divisions, different from those of the past, cut across denominations, joining together active evangelical Protestants and Catholics in the Republican Party, and a religiously pluralistic coalition among Democrats, with its quickly growing contingent of less religious or unaffiliated Americans joining highly religious African Americans. This partisan cleavage, which has been growing for forty years, has become extremely consequential for American politics as highly mobilized religious conservatives have become a core constituency of the Republican Party. Margolis argues that such mobilization threatens democracy by weakening political accountability, stymying political discourse and dissenting views, and undermining the possibility for compromise and negotiation.

The identity of gun ownership has been actively cultivated in recent decades by the National Rifle Association (NRA), one of the largest mass-based interest groups in the United States. Matthew Lacombe explains that the NRA portrays candidates and legislative proposals as a fundamental threat to gun owners' interests and values, generating fear and mobilizing them politically. The tactics it uses make compromise harder to attain, encourage supporters to delegitimize opponents and think of them as enemies, and spur political leaders to engage in constitutional "hardball." These developments therefore harm democratic accountability and responsiveness.

By these accounts, social sorting can be used by political leaders to generate voter turnout and political participation and to promote a policy agenda. While such mobilization itself fosters democratic values, including civic engagement and representation, the goals and tactics it features can undermine democratic norms and capacity, particularly when it is in the service of a narrow social base or ideological stance.

Related to this point, several chapters point to a fundamental asymmetry between today's Republican and Democratic parties. The Republican Party is more socially homogenous, predominantly white and Christian, and as a result its supporters are more likely to feel that

---

[51] Karen Stenner, *The Authoritarian Dynamic* (Cambridge: Cambridge University Press, 2005).

their identity itself is at stake in elections and the policy process. It has also become more ideologically grounded and homogenous over time, with a well-defined set of issue positions defining conservative orthodoxy. The Democratic Party, by contrast, encompasses greater diversity on multiple dimensions, including race, ethnicity, religion and religiosity. As a coalition of different and often crosscutting interests, it encompasses a broad ideological spectrum ranging from moderate-liberals to left-progressives.[52] This structural asymmetry between the parties fosters a different kind of politics in each; Republicans, who are able to mobilize around targeted policy arenas that offer their constituencies more concentrated costs and benefits, are more likely than Democrats to eschew compromise and negotiation and to treat politics as mortal combat. Democrats, on the other hand, tend to develop a list of policy stands that appeal to specific constituencies but often struggle to connect those policy stances to overarching identities or principles.[53] Finally, as Pierson and Schickler point out, the meso-institutional processes that fuel contemporary polarization are more intense on the right and provide continuing incentives for Republicans, more than Democrats, to pursue polarizing political strategies.

Interplay of Mass and Elite Political Behavior and Institutions

If mass and elite polarization are exacerbating each other, might checks and balances that proved reliable at other earlier points in time grow increasingly unlikely to function reliably? Several chapters investigate this possibility by exploring the interplay between institutions and political behavior amid rising polarization and investigating how they have developed over time.

Desmond King and Sidney Milkis continue our focus on national political institutions by analyzing the contemporary administrative state. They argue that presidents of both parties, from Nixon onward, have sought to deploy state power in order to cater to partisan constituencies. Partisanship no longer entails a battle over the size of government; rather, both parties pursue the enlargement of particular programs and policies. With a polarized Congress often hamstrung in its ability to deliver on

---

[52] Grossmann and Hopkins, *Asymmetric Politics*.
[53] Theodore J. Lowi, *The End of Liberalism: Ideology, Politics, and the Crisis of Public Authority* (New York: W. W. Norton, 1969); James Q. Wilson, *Political Organizations* (New York: Basic Books, 1973); Grossmann and Hopkins, *Asymmetric Politics*.

major party goals, presidents now take the lead in responding to party activists and social movements, many of whom eschew deliberation and compromise. Trump has nurtured executive-centered partisanship, as Obama did before him. These dynamics, which have been intensifying for decades, disrupt the constitutional system.

Another pair of chapters turn to developments at the state level, and in the process interrogate the long-standing assumption that federalism necessarily protects democracy. Historically, the southern states long served as what Robert Mickey terms "authoritarian enclaves," and many other states, too, were slow to extend political, civil, and social rights.[54] At the same time, some have argued that the states present greater and more diverse opportunities for democratic renewal than the sclerotic and increasingly hollow federal government.[55] Phillip Rocco shows that even today, the states remain uneven in the extent to which they protect democracy. Collectively these American subnational units continue to lag well behind those of comparable nations in this protection. Democratic erosion in the states, which is fostered by polarization and party extremism, matters also for national politics since state governments run elections, determine congressional districts, implement many federal policies, and define the scope of many rights. Alexander Hertel-Fernandez explains how conservatives captured control of many state governments in recent decades owing to the efforts of wealthy donors, ideological activists, and private-sector businesses. Working together, these groups have pushed the Republican Party in many states to the right on its policy agenda, which means that the priorities of the average citizen (including most Republicans) lack representation, undermining the quality of democracy. In addition, they have pushed those in power to tilt the playing field, aiding Republicans' electoral prospects for years to come; these changes harm democracy in more fundamental and enduring ways.

As these three chapters illustrate, key aspects of contemporary polarization emanate from long-term organizational and institutional changes. In combination, these have played crucial roles in transforming the political landscape, leading the United States to a political moment of democratic erosion. These studies highlight the value of scholarship that probes the intersection between mass and elite politics, or political behavior and

---

[54] Mickey, *Paths out of Dixie*. See also David Brian Robertson, *Federalism and the Making of America* (New York: Routledge, 2012).
[55] Heather K. Gerken, "A New Progressive Federalism," *Democracy: A Journal of Ideas* 24 (Spring 2012): 37–48.

institutions. The long-term dynamic interplay between them reveals troubling developments for American democracy than would not be visible through a narrower analytical lens.

Whereas this volume's four chapters highlighting national institutions offer a somewhat mixed assessment of democratic resilience, the two analyses of state governments present a more troubling portrayal. As Rocco observes, democratic erosion at the state level matters for national political outcomes given the states' role in running elections and creating congressional districts. How might political change come about? Next we turn to this question.

Possibilities for Democratic Renewal

Does the American polity currently have the capacity to foster countercurrents that can reverse or repair damage to democracy that may have already occurred? One might hope that threats to the political system will provoke a democratic backlash that will set the system right. Several chapters consider how this might occur or is already occurring, and in keeping with the volume's dual approach, our contributors offer a range of approaches that focus on both institutions and mass mobilization.

Some authors argue that in circumstances of polarization in which one party has taken the lead in advancing democratic erosion, the opposition party can choose to safeguard and restore democracy. McCoy and Somer note that the Democratic Party, though it has itself engaged in some polarizing strategies, has also demonstrated the political will and capacity to choose a nonpolarizing leader and to avoid extra-constitutional measures. Mason and Kalmoe observe that the contemporary Democratic Party is highly motivated to press for the advancement of previously marginalized groups, embracing a democratizing agenda.

Another approach to democratic renewal might be through elections, which are widely viewed as the most fundamental feature of democracies. Yet as David Bateman explains, elections are inherently paradoxical. Although they have the potential to strengthen democracy, they are also vulnerable to becoming tools of those who seek to restrict it. Elections serve two functions in a democracy that exist in tension to one another: first, giving voters a meaningful choice, which by definition makes them polarizing, and second, an integrative role, by serving as processes through which those who govern can be regarded as legitimate. In addition, political leaders themselves are in a position to structure elections and set the rules of the game, and when the parties compete intensely with one another, this can encourage electoral manipulation – a frequent occurrence in American history. Today, as Bateman explains, such manipulation emanates almost entirely from hardball efforts by partisans rather than from fraud or malfeasance. In order to make democracy resilient, reformers need to protect the electoral process from political self-entrenchment. Like Keck, Bateman ultimately argues that democracy's defenders must be prepared to take some hardball measures in order to renew democratic institutions, and he offers several possibilities.

Finally, we address the potential of grassroots organizing to restore democracy. As Skocpol, Tervo, and Walters argue in their chapter, the two nationwide waves of such voluntary citizen efforts that commenced after the 2008 and 2016 elections – the Tea Party movement and the resistance groups, respectively – can both be credited with engaging more citizens in collective action and boosting voter turnout, and in those respects are democratizing. Yet the Tea Party also fueled the ethno-cultural and authoritarian tendencies that led to Trump and the subsequent willingness of the GOP to override legal practices in its quest to retain power. Nationally organized progressives, distinct from the grassroots resistance groups, have been willing to embrace maximalist and moralistic positions that lack broad support, which can be problematic for democracy. In sum, though civic engagement is certainly democratic in and of itself, it has the potential to both engender greater democracy and, conversely, to heighten the existential warfare for power that has been on the rise for four decades. As it so often has in American history, this conflict is increasingly manifesting itself in a partisan divide over fundamental questions of democratic participation: should we make it easy or hard (or even impossible) for Americans to exercise their right to vote?[56] The record to date suggests that the Tea Party led to a rightward shift of the Republican Party, exacerbating polarization and undermining possibilities for compromise and negotiation. The resistance groups, by contrast, have facilitated the election of a broad range of Democratic candidates, from moderates to progressives, thus reducing polarization. Similarly, Parker and Barreto observe that people of color have become particularly mobilized in response to Trump's election, with the aim of protecting and renewing democracy. In short, when some groups become

---

[56] Alexander Keyssar, *The Right to Vote: The Contested History of Democracy in the United States* (New York: Basic Books, 2000); Valelly, *The Two Reconstructions*; Mettler and Lieberman, *Four Threats*.

mobilized to roll back democracy, countermobilization by others may occur to protect and expand it.

Taken together, the chapters in this volume identify myriad ways in which polarization can strain democratic institutions and foster political behavior that challenges democratic norms. Yet they also provide evidence of the subtle ways in which institutions can restrain autocratic behavior and foster democratic resilience by providing leverage to countervailing forces and offering channels of access to society actors who seek democratic renewal. Our contributing authors offer no simple formulas to gauge the prospects for American democracy in the years to come. Collectively, however, they shed new light on the dynamic forces that work both for and against it.

2

Polarization and the Durability of Madisonian Checks and Balances

A Developmental Analysis

Paul Pierson and Eric Schickler

Since the 1970s the American political system has undergone a dramatic increase in partisan polarization. By polarization, we mean that the parties are "far apart" from each other. This is largely, but not exclusively, a matter of policy views, although it may include important elements of identity-based tribalism. In a highly polarized environment, parties view one another as competing camps engaged in a battle where the stakes attached to victory or defeat are extremely high.

Scholars have a growing understanding of some of the forces that fostered this high-polarization setting and have begun to advance our understanding of many of its characteristics as well.[1] Yet we are just beginning to wrestle effectively with the profound consequences of

---

We thank the Hewlett Foundation's Madison Initiative for financial support. For comments on earlier drafts, we are grateful to Peter Hall, Alexander Hertel-Fernandez, Daniel Hopkins, Frances Lee, Steve Levitsky, Robert Lieberman, Thomas Mann, Jane Mansbridge, David Mayhew, Suzanne Mettler, and Daniel Stid, as well as participants in the Berkeley meeting on Madisonian Institutions and Polarization, the Conference on Political Institutions and Challenges to Democracy sponsored by the Social Science Research Council, Stanford's Freeman Spogli Institute for International Studies, a meeting of the Canadian Institute for Advanced Research Successful Societies Group, and the Cornell Conference on Democratic Resilience.

[1] Daniel J. Hopkins, *Red Fighting Blue: How Geography and Electoral Rules Polarize American Politics* (Cambridge: Cambridge University Press, 2018); Frances E. Lee, *Insecure Majorities: Congress and the Perpetual Campaign* (Chicago: University of Chicago Press, 2016); Nolan McCarty, *Polarization: What Everyone Needs to Know* (Oxford: Oxford University Press, 2019); Nolan McCarty, Keith T. Poole, and Howard Rosenthal, *Polarized America: The Dance of Ideology and Unequal Riches* (Cambridge: MIT Press, 2006); Eric Schickler, *Racial Realignment: The Transformation of American Liberalism, 1932–1965* (Princeton: Princeton University Press).

modern polarization for our politics. In this chapter, we explore some aspects of how that polarization is influencing executive-legislative relations, a potentially vital domain for democratic resilience. We devote considerable attention, however, to specifying some of the broader elements of this reconfigured polity, because we consider this essential to explaining why executive-legislative relations no longer work the way they once did.

Much of the literature on today's polarized system has been fairly reassuring, suggesting that an extended period of polarization – which now spans at least a quarter-century – reaffirms the flexibility of our Madisonian framework. A number of propositions bolster this position, ranging from the assertion that American politics has often been equally polarized in the past to the claim that partisan tactical battles in a closely divided Congress greatly accentuate the divisions seen in congressional roll-call votes, which are usually interpreted solely as evidence of deep ideological polarization.[2]

In recent work we have raised doubts about this assessment.[3] Adopting a developmental approach to polarization, we investigate how broad institutional configurations, extending beyond formal political institutions, might either dampen or intensify polarization once it emerges. From this perspective, contemporary polarization looks quite distinctive. In past eras, what we term meso-institutions – systems of interest intermediation, state parties operating within a geographically extensive and decentralized federal polity, and the ecology of news media – typically acted as important countervailing mechanisms. By fostering robust factional divisions in the parties, they repeatedly constrained or undermined polarization. The polarization that developed over the past generation, by contrast, has altered this meso-institutional landscape. It has encouraged

---

[2] John H. Aldrich, Mark M. Berger, and David W. Rohde, "The Historical Variability in Conditional Party Government, 1877–1994," in *Party, Process, and Political Change in Congress: New Perspectives on the History of Congress*, ed. David W. Brady and Mathew D. McCubbins (Stanford: Stanford University Press, 2002), 17–35; David W. Brady and Hahrie Han, "Polarization Then and Now: A Historical Perspective," in *Red and Blue: Characteristics and Causes of America's Polarized Politics*, vol. 1, ed. Pietro S. Nivola and David W. Brady (Stanford: Hoover Institution of War, Revolution and Peace; Washington DC: Brookings Institution, 2006), 119–51; Marc J. Hetherington, "Putting Polarization in Perspective," *British Journal of Political Science* 39, no. 2 (April 2009): 413–48; Frances E. Lee, *Beyond Ideology: Politics, Principles, and Partisanship in the U.S. Senate* (Chicago: University of Chicago Press, 2009); Lee, *Insecure Majorities*.

[3] Paul Pierson and Eric Schickler, "Madison's Constitution under Stress," *Annual Review of Political Science* 23 (2020): 37–58.

the rise of new organizations and transformed existing ones, creating new relationships, balances of political power, and incentives. These changes, in turn, have generally discouraged the activation of divisions *within* the parties while intensifying the divisions *between* the parties, their supporting coalitions, and voters.[4] In short, many of the self-correcting mechanisms of the Madisonian polity so often celebrated in the past have either weakened or themselves been transformed into engines of polarization. At the same time, these changes have had large effects on the workings of formal institutions. By undercutting the separation of political incentives necessary to make a separation-of-powers system robust, the rise of intense polarization dividing two increasingly coherent and cohesive political teams introduces new instabilities into the American political system. We argue that these changes in meso-institutions are particularly acute on the right, with important implications for the robustness of American democratic institutions.

THE MADISONIAN SYSTEM: A SHIELD AGAINST EXTREME POLARIZATION?

Briefly connecting our arguments about the intensification of polarization explicitly to the structure of American political institutions can clarify the potential impact on critical dimensions of governance. The standard, Madisonian account of American politics emphasizes the ways in which core political institutions encourage compromise and stability. The Founders were, of course, preoccupied with the question of how to create a stable republic. Understanding that factional divisions are inevitable, Madison famously argued that American political institutions could prevent all-out conflict between competing camps. Critical mechanisms that would tend to attenuate or countervail against polarization, rather than reinforce it, were built directly into the constitutional system. Others, such as the development of what were by comparative standards highly

---

[4] The intraparty divisions that do tend to emerge in the present context are very different from those that were most important in earlier eras. The silver Republicans of the 1890s, progressive Republicans of the 1900s–20s, and Dixiecrats of the 1930s–70s each sought a working alliance with the opposing party on key issues of concern. By contrast, intraparty factions now generally seek to offer a "purer" version of the party's policy agenda than their "establishment" colleagues, as in the case of Bernie Sanders' followers and Freedom Caucus Republicans. The contending sides within each party are not characteristically seeking to work with the other party; instead, they draw upon their own party's core fundraising and media/online constituencies in a fight for control of the party's message and identity.

decentralized and geographically factionalized political parties, were crucial (if unintended) outgrowths of the constitutional framework.

Most obviously, separation of powers, checks and balances, and federalism divide power, making it less likely that any single group will gain control of the entire government. This, in turn, means that governance will routinely require accommodating a range of group interests. The rules structuring elections require the assembly of different kinds of coalitions for different offices, discouraging the emergence of a single coherent and dominant cleavage. The creation of an extended republic with immense geographic diversity reinforced the institutional obstacles to polarization. Madison lays out the logic of this argument in Federalist 10: The scope of the new nation implied a diversity of viewpoints, which would make the emergence of a majority faction unlikely.[5] Creating a majority would require broad appeals to widely shared interests, rather than narrow, parochial appeals to a particular faction. As Dahl and Lindblom argue, social pluralism, when combined with America's fragmented constitutional structure, forces bargaining among diverse groups in order to achieve policy success.[6]

Federalism, from this perspective, interacts with the extended republic in critical ways. It is not just that the national government shares power with fifty separate state governments: The diversity of state circumstances and the relative autonomy of state political institutions together foster the emergence and sustenance of a diversity of interests and groups. This, too, promotes carefully brokered compromises that are mindful of an array of distinctive interests.[7]

These core institutions of American government tend to frustrate efforts of a particular coalition or individual to consolidate power. Crucially, it is not just that the division of authority encourages a search

---

[5] Samuel Kernell, "'The True Principles of Republican Government': Reassessing James Madison's Political Science," in *James Madison and the Theory and Practice of Republican Government*, ed. Samuel Kernell (Stanford: Stanford University Press, 2003), 92–125.

[6] Robert A. Dahl and Charles E. Lindblom, *Politics, Economics, and Welfare* (New York: Harper & Brothers, 1953), 307. See also John G. Gunnell, *Imagining the American Polity: Political Science and the Discourse of Democracy* (University Park: Pennsylvania State University Press, 2004), 224; David B. Truman, *The Governmental Process: Political Interests and Public Opinion* (New York: Alfred A. Knopf, 1951), 514.

[7] William Anderson, *The Nation and the States: Rivals or Partners?* (Minneapolis: University of Minnesota Press, 1955), 135–36; Daniel J. Elazar, *A View from the States* (New York: Thomas Y. Crowell, 1966), 6, 203; David B. Truman, "Federalism and the Party System," in *American Party Politics*, ed. Donald G. Herzberg and Gerald M. Pomper (New York: Holt, Rinehart and Winston, 1966), 24–34.

for broad consensus that can accommodate opposing interests. In addition, the allocation of authority to distinct, geographically organized representatives actively encourages the generation and maintenance of diverse interests. Moreover, under many conditions, we can think of these institutional arrangements as functionally equivalent mechanisms for attenuating polarization. Even if one mechanism weakens in a particular context – such as when unified government reduces Congress's incentive to check the president – there are built-in redundancies that reinforce the overall tendency toward stability and moderation. Finally, these institutional arrangements have a homeostatic quality. Given the diversity of interests, and the independence and diversity of political settings and roles, politicians unwilling to engage in compromise are likely to face increasing resistance.

The American constitution left a powerful mark on American political parties, rendering them unlikely vessels for intensely and durably polarized politics. From the start, American political institutions helped produce parties that were federal in character and decentralized in many of their operations.[8] In the words of V. O. Key, American parties were "confederative," consisting "of a working coalition of state and local parties" that provided pluralistic representation of diverse interests.[9] A critical source of power and independence for state parties has been their control of nominations and, more generally, their role in shaping career paths for ambitious politicians. Truman observes that "the basic political fact of federalism is that it creates separate, self-sustaining centers of power, privilege, and profit ... [and] bases from which individuals may move to places of greater influence and prestige in and out of government."[10] Polsby, echoing an earlier comment from Dwight Eisenhower, argues that "one may be justified in referring to the American two-party system as masking something more like a hundred-party system."[11] A Massachusetts Democrat and an Alabama Democrat might belong to the same formal organization at the national level, but they need not agree on much of anything when it comes

---

[8] Daniel DiSalvo, *Engines of Change: Party Factions in American Politics, 1868–2010* (Oxford: Oxford University Press, 2012).

[9] V. O. Key Jr., *Politics, Parties, and Pressure Groups*, 5th ed. (New York: Thomas Y. Crowell, 1964), 315. See also Leon Epstein, "Party Confederations and Political Nationalization," *Publius* 12, no. 1 (1982): 67–102; E. E. Schattschneider, *Party Government* (New York: Holt, Rinehart and Winston, 1942).

[10] Truman, "Federalism and the Party System," 30.

[11] Nelson W. Polsby, "The American Party System," in *The New Federalist Papers*, ed. Alan Brinkley, Nelson Polsby, and Kathleen Sullivan (Washington: Brookings Institution, 1997), 40.

to policy. Hershey, in her textbook on American parties, concludes that federalism and separation of powers mean that American legislative parties "can rarely achieve the degree of party discipline that is common in parliamentary systems."[12]

This feature of party politics lowered the stakes of political conflict – an effect that comparativists have long stressed is conducive to democratic stability.[13] Even if one party wins power, it is forced to accommodate a diverse array of interests that likely will make its ultimate policies broadly acceptable. Furthermore, the crosscutting cleavages and fluidity of alliances ensure that even if one's side loses today, the outcome could easily change soon.[14] The operations of the constitutional system might be remade on the ground over time by assertive presidents or new ideological formations (e.g., the New Deal), but the core features that gave rise to pluralism and fragmented power remained: separation of powers, checks and balances, territorially grounded representation, and the extended republic.[15] The modern presidency is a much more powerful office than Madison anticipated, yet modern presidents continued to be frustrated by the need to deal with contending power centers in Congress, the Courts, the bureaucracy, and the states.[16] The New Deal remade the role of the national government, yet also had to confront fundamental limitations imposed by separation of powers, federalism, and the Democrats' north-south regional coalition.[17]

In summary, while political parties might bridge the differences across branches, institutions, or localities in a way that the Framers had not anticipated, sustained, intense policy polarization at the national level has been rare. Even in periods of high party voting in Congress, substantial intraparty divisions limited the scope of partisan battles. A fragmented party and interest group system meant that national party lines failed to

---

[12] Marjorie Hershey, *Party Politics in America*, 17th ed. (New York: Routledge, 2017), 26.
[13] Daron Acemoglu and James A. Robinson, *Economic Origins of Dictatorship and Democracy* (Cambridge: Cambridge University Press, 2006).
[14] Earl Latham, "The Group Basis of Politics: Notes for a Theory," *American Political Science Review* 46, no. 2 (June 1952): 376–97.
[15] On "reconstructive" leadership, see Stephen Skowronek, *The Politics Presidents Make: Leadership from John Adams to Bill Clinton*, rev. ed. (Cambridge: Harvard University Press, 1997).
[16] Terry M. Moe, "The Politicized Presidency," in *The New Direction in American Politics*, ed. John E. Chubb and Paul E. Peterson (Washington, DC: Brookings Institution, 1985), 235–71; Richard E. Neustadt, *Presidential Power: The Politics of Leadership* (New York: Wiley, 1960); Skowronek, *The Politics Presidents Make*.
[17] Margaret Weir, "States, Race, and the Decline of New Deal Liberalism," *Studies in American Political Development* 19, no. 2 (October 2005): 157–72.

capture or contain many of the critical disputes animating politics. Because this system created institutional spaces within which these divisions could operate and shape the incentives of important political actors, they countered the force of national party polarization. For all of its acute limitations, the Madisonian system was, for much of American history, a robust obstacle to narrow and durable consolidations of power.

It bears emphasis that comparativists, concerned about the stability of democracy and that of presidential systems in particular, have also noted the impact of these unusual institutional arrangements. Linz argues that presidential systems tend to be less stable due to dueling bases of legitimacy.[18] Viewing the United States as an exception, Linz suggests that our weak and fragmented parties have prevented this kind of all-or-nothing showdown between branches under the control of competing parties. We argue below that this confidence in the moderating influence of American political institutions may no longer be justified. Moreover, the particular perils Linz associates with presidentialism might obscure several different challenges for democracy associated with intensifying polarization within a Madisonian framework. First, however, we briefly describe how the transformation of "meso-institutions" of interest intermediation, state parties, and media has contributed to the reconfiguration of the American polity.

MODERN POLARIZATION AND THE REMAKING OF MESO-INSTITUTIONS

The initial development of modern polarization had profound consequences for the American polity. Standard accounts of its emergence emphasize the sorting of the parties, at both the elite and mass levels, which flowed from realignment of the political parties around issues of race.[19] In this necessarily abbreviated account, we do not challenge that basic depiction, but wish to stress that the initial rise in polarization – against a backdrop of technological change and a vastly expanded role of the federal government – helped to transform what we call meso-institutions: interest groups, state parties, and the media. In earlier eras,

---

[18] While there is now considerable doubt about Linz's assertion that presidential systems are more vulnerable to breakdown, it remains important to explore the distinctive mechanisms through which instability might emerge in such settings. Juan J. Linz, "The Perils of Presidentialism," *Journal of Democracy* 1, no. 1 (Winter 1990): 51–69.

[19] Schickler, *Racial Realignment*; McCarty, Poole, and Rosenthal, *Polarized America*.

these arrangements had been crucial bulwarks of the formal institutions of our Madisonian system, tending to attenuate partisan polarization. Today, they instead encourage further national party polarization.[20]

We briefly recap the analysis we have offered of interest groups, state parties, and media.[21] Traditionally, American political structures encouraged a diffuse and fluid structure of interest intermediation – interest group structures were both unusually fragmented, and only weakly aligned with national parties.[22] Growing polarization (intersecting in important ways with the expanding role of the national government during what Skocpol has called "the long-1960s") led to a proliferation and nationalization of interest group activity (Skocpol 2003). Over time, the new environment produced a second major shift: a growing inclination of powerful groups to align with a party – to try to achieve their policy goals by working with, and in support of, a durable political coalition (Pierson 2014; Krimmel 2017). Rather than being a source of incentives and action that crosscut parties and thus restricted polarization, interest groups became yet another factor reinforcing the divide between them. A powerful self-reinforcing logic was at play. As a party moves closer to an interest group's preferred policy positions (and the other party moves in the opposite direction), the stakes in the outcome of interparty conflict increase. As groups join teams, see increasing benefits of victory by their team, and thus work to ensure those victories while punishing defectors, interest group political behavior can intensify polarization rather than moderating it.

Indeed, the transformed interplay between groups and parties does more than just remove one of the traditional mechanisms that limit polarization. Many of these contemporary groups are national in scope and invested in an ambitious policy agenda. They eagerly push their partisan allies to advance that agenda wherever possible, helping to pull

---

[20] For a more detailed exploration of the causal sequence between changes in polarization and changes in these meso-level institutions, see Pierson and Schickler, "Madison's Constitution under Stress." The transformations we describe have also had important effects on mass politics, helping to fuel the development of tribalism and affective polarization. Due to space constraints we cannot pursue these linkages here, but see the chapters by Margolis (Chapter 9) and Kalmoe and Mason (Chapter 7) on the growth in tribalism at the mass level.
[21] Pierson and Schickler, "Madison's Constitution under Stress."
[22] John Mark Hansen, *Gaining Access: Congress and the Farm Lobby, 1919–1981* (Chicago: University of Chicago Press, 1991); Katherine Krimmel, "The Efficiencies and Pathologies of Special Interest Partisanship," *Studies in American Political Development* 31, no. 2 (October 2017): 149–69.

state parties more tightly into this nationalized system (Hertel-Fernandez 2020).[23] Parties have contracted out mobilizing voters to groups, which may also have considerable influence over fundraising and candidate recruitment. The fixation on winning elections that characterized many traditional party elites encouraged moderation. Party networks, however, increasingly lack the kind of robust organizational infrastructure that might limit extremism. Under conditions of polarization, they may cede power to groups whose strategies of organizational maintenance often rely on extreme appeals and who may be more accepting of electoral risk to achieve potentially extreme ends (Azari 2018).[24]

This dynamic of intensifying partisan polarization and weakening of crosscutting cleavages is equally evident in state parties. For much of its history, America's federal party system tended to act as a countervailing mechanism limiting partisan polarization. Even when the national parties were relatively polarized on a given set of issues – such as the tariff in the late nineteenth century – state and local parties provided a partially independent, geographically rooted power base to represent competing interests that crosscut that division. Perhaps even more important, the geographically decentralized party system provided a mechanism to incorporate new interests that fit uncomfortably with existing national party coalitions. National parties lacked a veto over state party positions. Nor did they have any effective way of preventing the entry of new groups into a state party coalition, even when those positions and groups undermined an existing line of cleavage. This process of geographically rooted factional entry repeatedly drove change in partisan alignments and coalitions.[25]

It is far more difficult for today's state parties to play this countervailing role. They are more tightly integrated into national party networks. Key resources are outside the control of state party leaders. National party organizations have become more active as a source of funds and professional services for local candidates, encouraging greater coordination

---

[23] Jacob M. Grumbach, "From Backwaters to Major Policymakers: Policy Polarization in the States, 1970–2014," *Perspectives on Politics* 16, no. 2 (June 2018): 416–35; Alexander Hertel-Fernandez, *State Capture: How Conservative Activists, Big Businesses, and Wealthy Donors Reshaped the American States – and the Nation* (Oxford: Oxford University Press, 2019).

[24] Jacob S. Hacker and Paul Pierson, "After the 'Master Theory': Downs, Schattschneider, and the Rebirth of Policy-Focused Analysis," *Perspectives on Politics* 12, no. 3 (September 2014): 643–62; Daniel Schlozman and Sam Rosenfeld, "The Hollow Parties," in *Can America Govern Itself?*, ed. Frances E. Lee and Nolan McCarty (Cambridge: Cambridge University Press, 2019), 120–51.

[25] Schickler, *Racial Realignment*.

across states (Lunch 1987, Paddock 2015). Nomination process reforms that empower ordinary voters have also shifted influence within states from professional, locally rooted politicians to policy-oriented activists who often focus on hot-button issues that divide the parties nationally (La Raja & Schaffner 2015).[26] Meanwhile, fundraising has been nationalized. Drawing on Federal Election Commission data, Hopkins finds that the share of itemized campaign contributions that cross state lines increased from 31 percent in 1990 to 68 percent in 2012.[27] The nationalization of politics, including of communication networks, has made it harder for state parties and politicians to tailor their identity to local conditions. As Hopkins notes, "state parties themselves ... especially as voters perceive them, have increasingly come to mirror their national counterparts."[28]

As with the transformed role of interest groups, these changes in state party politics help make polarization self-reinforcing. When it becomes harder for state politicians to distinguish themselves from the national party brand in the eyes of voters, their incentives change. As Hopkins puts it, state politicians "may well come to see their ambitions as tethered more closely to their status in the national party than their ability to cater to the state's median voter."[29] When an issue potentially separates the state's median voter from the position of the national party, politicians' incentives to toe the national party line have grown stronger, as voters prove less attentive to state-level differences and as the relevant audience for their behavior (interest groups, donors, etc.) becomes more nationalized. The result is a more integrated party system. What were once relatively autonomous state and local party organizations that provided a basis for dissident factions to form and challenge national party lines now appear to be "rather small cogs" in a nationally oriented network.[30] Within this

---

[26] Geoffrey C. Layman, Thomas M. Carsey, and Juliana Menasce Horowitz, "Party Polarization in American Politics: Characteristics, Causes, and Consequences," *Annual Review of Political Science* 9 (2006): 83–110; Joel W. Paddock, *State and National Parties and American Democracy* (New York: Peter Lang, 2005).

[27] Daniel J. Hopkins, *The Increasingly United States: How and Why American Political Behavior Nationalized* (Chicago: University of Chicago Press, 2018).

[28] Ibid., 15. See also Devin Caughey, James Dunham, and Christopher Washaw, "The Ideological Nationalization of Partisan Subconstituencies in the American States," *Public Choice* 176, no. 1/2 (July 2018): 133–151.

[29] Hopkins, *Increasingly United States*, 6.

[30] Joel W. Paddock, "Local and State Political Parties," in *The Oxford Handbook of State and Local Government*, ed. Donald P. Haider-Markel (Oxford: Oxford University Press, 2014), 165.

new, more integrated system, state-level politicians find it in their interest to reinforce or even intensify existing national alignments.

Federalism has become, increasingly, yet another arena and instrument of national party competition. State party actors now use their power – particularly under conditions of unified control – to pursue policies that are in line with their national party's agenda, and, at times, to shape the electoral rules of the game in ways that boost the national party's chances (see Hertel-Fernandez, this volume, and Rocco, this volume).[31] A state under the control of the party opposing the president – Texas in the Obama years or California in the Trump years – can serve as an important power base challenging national-level policies, at times uniting with other states of a similar partisan complexion to forge a new front in policy battles. But in doing so, these states reinforce, rather than undermine, the intense national party divide.

Media represents a third "meso-institution" that once helped to limit polarization but now intensifies it. The presence of partisan or ideological news outlets is nothing new in American history. But the party press of the nineteenth century was not nationalized. Although more research is required on this topic, case study evidence suggests that voters in different regions who belonged to the same party did not necessarily receive the same messages about key issues. For example, as the fifty-first Congress debated the tariff and currency in 1890, GOP newspapers were divided regionally and thus provided a crosscutting set of cues for many voters as well as local political elites.[32]

Technological and commercial developments, such as the rise of cable news, talk radio, and social media, have created a much more nationalized media infrastructure, diminishing the role of locally grounded information and issues. These trends have also fueled the growth of an "outrage industry," especially on the political right, that is increasingly geared to partisans.[33] This industry has powerful incentives to intensify polarization in two respects. First, to attract an audience it inflames negative views about political opponents and makes exaggerated claims about the political stakes involved. Second, to capture and hold its audience, it makes it

---

[31] As Rocco (this volume) observes, Republicans have been particularly aggressive in shaping state electoral rules in ways that advantage their party and may undermine democratic norms.

[32] Eric Schickler, *Disjointed Pluralism: Institutional Innovation and the Development of the U.S. Congress* (Princeton: Princeton University Press, 2001).

[33] Jeffrey M. Berry and Sarah Sobieraj, *The Outrage Industry: Political Opinion Media and the New Incivility* (Oxford: Oxford University Press, 2013).

a priority to de-legitimate other sources of information.[34] If a party's voters come to rely on media outlets with incentives to polarize, and increasingly dismiss alternative sources of information, polarization is likely to become more intense and durable.

This is a necessarily truncated description of just some of the ways in which ongoing processes of nationalization and polarization have transformed critical meso-institutions. Even as formal institutional arrangements remain largely unchanged, these transformations – and the effects they in turn help generate, such as increasing tribalism and affective polarization among voters – may fundamentally alter the way discrete elements of the American polity fit together. In many cases, these developments did not just weaken the traditional generators of Madisonian pluralism; they transformed them into generators of intensified polarization. Interest groups and issues do not crosscut; they stack, one on top of the other, along partisan lines. When new issues arise, party politicians, existing groups, and politically aligned (and increasingly national) media, have incentives to push them into existing lines of partisan cleavage.[35] Reflecting the growing forces of nationalization at work in our polity, geography no longer encourages pluralism, as it often did even during what are typically characterized as highly partisan eras. If state party competition focuses on intrastate dynamics, it will tend to be multidimensional, distinctive across states, and a source of moderation and plausible bipartisanship at the national level.[36] However, where media and interest groups are nationalized, the role of geography may reverse. Nationalization puts the focus of state politics on the main national dimension, which means that even modest geographically based partisan inequalities may intensify over time.[37] These conditions create incentives for local parties to elevate polarizing issues when they feel that highlighting the national partisan divide gives them an edge. Rather than serving as a brake, the strong role of territorially grounded representation in the American system may come to act as an engine of polarization.

Meso-institutions – social arrangements that are not formal (constitutional) rules – play a crucial and often underappreciated role in mediating

---

[34] Yochai Benkler, Robert Faris, and Hal Roberts, *Network Propaganda: Manipulation, Disinformation, and Radicalization in American Politics* (Oxford: Oxford University Press, 2018).
[35] Layman, Carsey, and Horowitz, "Party Polarization."
[36] Hopkins, *Increasingly United States*.
[37] David A. Hopkins, *Red Fighting Blue: How Geography and Electoral Rules Polarize American Politics* (Cambridge: Cambridge University Press, 2017).

interactions among American citizens, among political elites, and between elites and ordinary citizens. In earlier periods of polarization, these meso-institutions operated as countervailing mechanisms that (often quickly) dampened the intensity and breadth of partisan warfare. Partisan pushes away from centrist or consensus positions triggered a reaction. Crucially, these reactions did not simply depend – as they do in many traditional (Downsian) models of party competition – on the median voter's political moderation and the responsiveness of officials to that voter. Downs postulated that electoral competition *between* parties would force parties to the middle. Yet many of the mechanisms limiting stark polarization, working mainly through the meso-institutional features described previously, operated primarily *within* parties rather than between them. American parties have been pluralistic and resistant to central direction, reflecting the competing concerns of interest groups, geographically diverse state parties, locally embedded media, and the distinct institutionally derived interests of politicians situated in different positions within our fragmented system of political authority.[38]

If polarization helps transform these intermediary institutions and their associated incentives, however, these self-correcting processes may cease to operate. When interest groups have strongly committed to a party and regard the stakes of party defeat as very high, they may find it prohibitively costly to push back against unwanted initiatives. State parties, operating in an increasingly nationalized system of incentives, may cease to produce the political diversity that would generate intraparty backlash. The same would be true for highly partisan media. In a transformed polity, all of these forces, which might in the past have generated dissent and signaled to voters that a party had moved to the extreme, may falter.

CHECKS AND BALANCES IN AN AGE OF INTENSE POLARIZATION

The changes in meso-level institutions described here have critical implications for the Madisonian system famously described by Neustadt as one of "separated institutions sharing powers." We wish to focus on one particular implication, because it has such important ramifications for democratic stability and other key aspects of governance: the new political configuration changes the incentives of individual members of Congress in

---

[38] Schickler, *Disjointed Pluralism*; Schickler, *Racial Realignment*.

ways that make it considerably less likely that they will act in a manner that provides an effective check on executive power.

This is most obvious when there is unified party control of Congress and the White House. Shared partisanship has always encouraged members of Congress to be more receptive to presidential power claims and less likely to fight back when the president steps beyond prior understandings of the president's role. Recent studies have shown, for example, that investigative oversight of the president by the House of Representatives was systematically lower under unified party control than divided control throughout the twentieth century. The impact of unified government on House oversight was higher in periods of high polarization than when polarization has been more muted, suggesting that when policy alignment between the president and the congressional majority is tighter, the incentives to investigate decline.[39]

Nonetheless, serious oversight was by no means absent in earlier periods of unified government. Indeed, the volume of Senate investigative activism was far less tied to divided versus unified control throughout the twentieth century, even under conditions of high polarization.[40] The structure of meso-level institutions afforded substantial space for the president's co-partisans to take on the White House in earlier eras. In particular, the relative autonomy of state parties meant that members' career paths were far less dependent on pleasing the national party and its constituencies than is currently the case.

Perhaps the clearest example of this dynamic occurred during the New Deal and World War II. When southern Democrats became alarmed that the Roosevelt administration's embrace of organized labor posed a threat to Jim Crow, southern members of Congress led aggressive investigations. Their oversight was designed not just to target particular Roosevelt policies, but to weaken an interest group that was a key pillar of the electoral base for both the president and their northern co-partisans. Noteworthy cases targeting the Roosevelt administration and its allies include Martin Dies' (D-TX) investigation of Un-American Activities, Howard Smith's (D-VA) onslaught against the National Labor Relations Board (and, a few years later, against the Office of Price Administration), and Eugene Cox's (D-GA) investigation of the Federal Communications Commission.[41] For southern Democrats, the benefits of challenging a co-partisan president

---

[39] Douglas L. Kriner and Eric Schickler, *Investigating the President: Congressional Checks on Presidential Power* (Princeton: Princeton University Press, 2016).
[40] Ibid.   [41] Schickler, *Disjointed Pluralism*.

were substantial, while the costs were low. Those who led these investigations faced little risk of electoral repercussions for taking on the Democratic administration. Their own re-election was not contingent on either the national party's standing or on the perception of national party leaders that they were "team players." Roosevelt's failed 1938 purge brought home the critical point: in a decentralized party system, winning reelection depended on appealing to locally rooted constituencies, regardless of whether this pleased either the president or other national party constituencies.

This relative autonomy of state parties was linked to another core aspect of meso-level institutions: the structure of interest group–party relations. The interest group coalition that backed Democrats in the north was fundamentally different from the constellation of interests critical in the south – indeed, in key respects the interest groups backing these party factions were fundamentally at odds.[42] Rather than relying on a nationally based network of activists and donors, Democrats in different regions were dependent on different groups. Some of these interests – such as business – were associated with different parties in different regions. For example, where business groups in much of the north gave mostly to Republicans, many businesses in the south and in New York City (the latter often led by Jewish entrepreneurs who were tied to the Democrats for ethno-cultural reasons) gave heavily to Democrats (Webber 2000). Instead of confronting an interest group universe that was nationally organized and often closely aligned with one party or the other, as is the case today, politicians of the same party often relied upon different types of groups depending on their local political economy and demographics. This again freed individual members to take on the president and his allied groups: the coalition of groups backing a southern Democrat in the 1940s did not view its interests as inextricably tied to the national-level party's success.

A further crucial difference was the absence of a nationalized partisan media. Democrats in Congress could count on very different press coverage for either supporting or challenging national Democratic policies and groups depending on whether they were in the north or the south. Today's national and partisan media supplies a key mechanism for enforcing cross-branch discipline, but the more decentralized press landscape in this earlier period operated very differently.

---

[42] See Ira Katznelson, *Fear Itself: The New Deal and the Origins of Our Time* (New York: Liveright, 2013).

One might object that the New Deal era was an aberration, but other periods show some of the same dynamics, even if less dramatically. The Republican majorities of the 1920s repeatedly wrestled with regionally based party factions of farm and progressive members who dissented from key party positions and were willing to take coordinated actions that undermined the standing of the GOP administration (Bloch Rubin 2017). Most notably, progressive Republicans worked closely with Democrats in the early 1920s on the series of investigations that led to the disclosure of the Teapot Dome scandal and that ultimately forced the resignation of the attorney general. Unified Republican control did not prove a serious obstacle to major investigative oversight that seriously damaged the Republican administration's standing.

Again, the space to criticize or challenge the president of one's own party depended on meso-institutions working in a way that allowed members to see their own fortunes as not too dependent on their national party's standing and success. For progressive Republicans, their nomination to office depended on appealing to voters who did not share the conservatism of national Republican leaders. They worked within a regionally based interest group landscape that was not a simple mirror of national-level Republican groups. They also could rely upon more localized press outlets that shared their skepticism of the national party's positions and approach.

One indicator of the extent to which progressive Republicans saw their interests as partially independent of the national party was their willingness to cooperate with Democrats to scrutinize the "excessive" campaign spending of a handful of Republican Senate candidates. These actions actually resulted in the Republican Senate's failure to seat incoming Republican members William Vare of Pennsylvania and Frank Smith of Illinois in 1927.[43] The crucial point is that progressive Republicans of this era viewed their main constituency as fundamentally rooted in their home states. They believed that wooing those constituents was consistent with (and at times required) taking on their own national party.

Earlier periods of progressive activism within the GOP featured similar dynamics: the Ballinger-Pinchot investigation during the Taft administration – in which dissident Republicans joined with Democrats to attack the administration's handling of public lands – is another example of the recurrent tendency for party factions to capitalize on their relatively

---

[43] George H. Haynes, *The Senate of the United States: Its History and Practice* (Boston: Houghton Mifflin, 1938).

independent electoral constituencies to take on a president of their own party.

Stepping back, these dynamics speak to a central theme in David Mayhew's (2000) incisive account of the durability and flexibility of America's Madisonian system. Repeatedly, members of Congress have engaged in significant actions in the public sphere that challenge or undermine the president. Mayhew's systematic coding suggests that while clusters of opposition to the president may have been somewhat more likely under divided government, they have also been a recurrent feature of unified government. Mayhew argues that these oppositions have played a central role in checking presidential aggrandizement, alerting the public when the system of separated institutions sharing powers is under threat, and providing opportunities for the public to weigh in on major policy questions dividing the branches.

Today, the incentives facing members of Congress are far less conducive to this role. Consider a Republican member of Congress deciding how to respond to President Donald Trump. Regardless of one's home state, the fear is the same: undermining the president carries serious political risks, particularly in a party primary. This fear reflects the changes in meso-level institutions. In place of the relatively autonomous state parties of earlier decades, Republican members are embedded in a national party network of activists and donors who share a commitment to much the same conservative policies, and to the established partisan alliances that support them. Given the sharp divide between the two parties, they are deeply hostile to any actions that would benefit the Democratic opposition. They also confront an interest group universe that is more national in scope and more clearly tied to party. There is no major alternative source of support out there if a member alienates the groups with strong ties to their party. Because today these groups identify their own success much more closely with that of the party, they have a stronger incentive to penalize failures to be a good team player. Perhaps most importantly, the nationalized and partisan media – Fox News, talk radio, and online – mean that a member risks coordinated, concerted criticism for taking on the president.

All of this adds up to a strong incentive for members to stick with a president of their own party. Indeed, the current institutional configuration makes remaining loyal to one's party by far the easiest choice. Denying everything and attacking the other side is a safe strategy, particularly when one can count on partisan media to amplify this message and discount alternative narratives. The net result looks a lot like tribalism, but for those valuing political survival it can be firmly grounded in a cold calculation of personal interest rather than emotion or identity.

This tribalism has different – yet perhaps equally troubling – implications for the resilience of Madisonian separation of powers under divided and unified government. As noted, the primary concern under unified government is that the majority party in Congress will block serious efforts to investigate or roll back presidential excesses. Under divided government, one surely can expect plentiful congressional efforts to investigate and fight back against the president – indeed, intense polarization sharply increases the incentives of the other party to go after the White House. But absent any significant buy-in from the president's party, the risk is that these congressional actions will be far less effective.

We conventionally classify government as divided if the president's party does not control at least one chamber of Congress; but it may make a big difference to Congress's ability to fight back on policy if different parties control the House and Senate.[44] Losing control of a single chamber can create problems for the president's party. In the process they lose considerable agenda control, greatly increasing the prospects for potentially damaging investigations. Yet retaining control of a single chamber limits the capacity of Congress to take robust action.[45] This distinction likely existed in earlier eras, but it is exacerbated when intense polarization leads the president's co-partisans to view defecting from the White House as prohibitively costly.

When it comes to direct policy-making, polarization under divided government makes it harder for Congress to fight back effectively against presidential unilateral actions. President Trump's decision to shift funds to build the border wall is a telling example. The president's declaration of a national emergency was widely understood to be a breach of prior use of emergency declaration powers, and was directly counter to Congress's

---

[44] Indeed, some of the dynamics identified here would also apply to another category: cases where the opposition party controls both the House and Senate but does not have a filibuster-proof super-majority. Given the filibuster, the case that most worried Linz (where a legislature under the complete control of one party faces off against a president of another party) remains a rarity in the United States.

[45] The Trump case suggests that control of a single branch also makes it much harder for the opposing party's chamber to use its legislative tools to force the executive to provide even the most limited cooperation with its investigative efforts. With control of both chambers, the majority party might use the threat to withhold appropriations to force the president to provide documents. But with control of the two chambers divided, it is easier for the executive to resist providing any cooperation.

decision with respect to its core power of the purse. Yet even in the presence of expedited procedures that allowed a simple majority in each chamber to pass a resolution overturning the president's action, Trump's veto power, backed by a clear majority of House and Senate Republicans, proved sufficient to block a reversal. Congressional efforts to fight back on policy are also hampered when control of the two chambers is divided. The need to win Senate Republicans' agreement has undermined House Democrats' efforts to use subsequent spending bills to block further reprogramming of funds. This stands in sharp contrast to the early 1970s, when Nixon threatened congressional control of the purse with his aggressive use of impoundments. Then, a near-unanimous Congress adopted the Congressional Budget and Impoundment Control Act of 1974, which imposed major restrictions on the president's ability to control spending.[46]

Although this warrants more discussion than we can offer here, it is important to emphasize that the character of modern polarization we have described has other worrisome effects on the complex interplay within a system of fragmented political authority. Even if Congress is able to limit or neutralize presidential unilateral actions, continuous interbranch battles under divided control may give rise to policy immobilism and a sense of deep political dysfunction that contributes to long-term democratic erosion. The American political system has generally required the construction of broad, cross-party coalitions to enact major legislative change. Intense polarization sharply diminishes the prospects for such coalitions. It is not just that the parties are further apart, although it is obviously harder to compromise when the two parties want to move in opposite directions. Irrespective of policy goals, the political competition between the parties is increasingly zero-sum, making it difficult or impossible to locate agreements that both sides will see as wins. And the challenge is worsened when affective polarization, egged on by partisan media and extreme groups, bolsters the view that compromise constitutes betrayal. When such coalitions are much harder to construct, policy challenges may fester, heightening frustration with existing institutions. A sense of democratic dysfunction is particularly dangerous in a context of tribalism where an aspiring demagogue can count on party loyalty to

---

[46] The final bill passed the House with just six no votes and it passed the Senate unanimously. It is true that Republicans were less enthusiastic about the impoundment control provisions of the Budget Act, but they agreed to them as part of a broader package of reforms that included congressional mechanisms to limit spending and deficits.

provide a solid base of support for efforts to sweep aside traditional institutional constraints on their actions.

Increasing party loyalty doesn't just make it more difficult for Congress to take action. Solidarity within the president's party makes it much harder to portray investigative efforts as transcending partisan conflict. As a result, investigations may have less impact on public opinion (which in turn makes it easier for co-partisans to stay loyal to the president). Changes in the media environment further weaken the potential impact of Congressional action. The decline of "neutral arbiters" in the press means that the main signals that the public will receive inevitably come from partisan elites on either side. If Republicans can be counted on to stick with a president of their party and if Democrats can be assumed to have strong political incentives to oppose the president, many voters will be tempted to view what happens in congressional hearing rooms as little more than partisan position-taking. Mayhew's concept of members taking significant actions in a "public sphere" presupposes sufficient member independence so that citizens may well change their minds in response to what they see members doing. But if the president's party is unified in dismissing serious investigations as mere partisan witch-hunts, voters may be resistant to updating their views in response. In sufficiently extreme cases, the sheer weight of evidence may move enough voters and elites for investigations to have a meaningful impact. But the hurdle for doing so is arguably much higher than it had been in the past. Even as most Republicans stuck with President Nixon throughout the Watergate scandal, consequential fissures emerged among Republicans. These fissures, in turn, likely reinforced the public's sense that the scandal was not simply "politics as usual."

We have described these incentives in general but the focus here on Republicans is not simply illustrative. These dynamics are especially strong for Republicans due to differences in the meso-institutional environment facing the two parties' members – indeed one of the important analytical advantages of our approach is its utility for exploring and explaining differences between the two party coalitions in contexts where each operates within identical formal institutions. The polarizing role of contemporary federalism that we have noted operates more weakly for Democrats, given the unfavorable geographic distribution of the party's voters. The growing concentration of Democratic voters in urban areas is, within the American electoral framework, politically inefficient (Rodden 2019). As a result, a Democratic victory in Congress requires winning red-leaning districts and states, creating an incentive to moderate and/or tolerate heterogeneity within the party. Republicans, by contrast, receive an electoral bonus from this political geography, facilitating a move to the right and diminishing the need to tolerate intraparty dissent. Speaker Pelosi's delicate balancing act in approaching competing views of impeachment through much of 2019 was a telling example of Democratic leaders' perception that protecting their vulnerable members has to be a top consideration if the party is to retain its majority.

At least as important, the media environment for the two parties is fundamentally different. As Grossmann and Hopkins show, the conservative media ecosystem, which developed partly in response to perceived mainstream media bias, created news outlets that were explicitly tied to conservative organizations and causes.[47] From the outset, conservative media placed considerable emphasis on the task of discrediting alternative sources of information. Grossmann and Hopkins note, "the strategy was self-reinforcing, as right-leaning citizens came to rely more on conservative media and become less trusting of other news sources."[48] The media ecosystem on the right is far more isolated from the informational mainstream than that of the left.[49] Messages from conservative media sources have worked to activate the existing symbolic predispositions of their audience, insulated viewers from countervailing forms of influence, and have increased vulnerability to conspiracy thinking.[50] Recent evidence suggests that Fox News – itself just one part of the conservative media ecosystem – has in fact pushed viewers' opinions further to the right.[51] Fox now finds itself challenged from outlets that are more extreme, such as One America News and Newsmax, reinforcing the message that on the conservative side, there is a strong incentive not to be outbid from the right.

Although empirical research on this topic is less developed, these differences seem likely to exist on the interest group side as well. GOP networks seem to involve fewer, but very powerful groups – especially the Christian right and organized economic elites – with ambitious policy agendas that drive the entire party rightward. The Democratic coalition, by contrast, is made up of a wider range of interests, each of them demanding a say but none of them (especially given the decline of organized labor) large enough to

---

[47] Matt Grossmann and David A. Hopkins, "Placing Media in Conservative Culture" (Paper presented the New Agendas Conference, University of Texas, Austin, 2018).
[48] Ibid., 11.   [49] Benkler, Faris, and Roberts, *Network Propaganda*.
[50] Russell Muirhead and Nancy L. Rosenblum, *A Lot of People Are Saying: The New Conspiracism and the Assault on Democracy* (Princeton: Princeton University Press, 2019).
[51] Gregory J. Martin and Ali Yurukoglu, "Bias in Cable News: Persuasion and Polarization," *American Economic Review* 107, no. 9 (September 2017): 2565–99.

dictate priorities. Furthermore, the shift of political resources to the wealthy and corporations amid rising inequality has different implications for the two parties.[52] For a left-leaning party, growing inequality in economic and political power exerts a moderating influence at least on many economic issues, encouraging the party to resist pulls to the left. For the GOP, however, a growing concentration of economic power, mobilized by organizations like the Koch network and the Chamber of Commerce, has pushed the party to the right (Hertel-Fernandez and Skocpol 2016).[53]

Republicans also face a distinct and formidable challenge: powerful demographic trends that are unfavorable to its existing coalition. In the past, parties facing such trends would have had both strong incentives and considerable capacity to adapt. Indeed, a striking feature of American political history is the impressive ability of parties to shift their positions on issues and incorporate appeals to rising demographic groups, even when doing so required weakening ties to groups in decline.[54] Some Republican moderates have urged the party to act similarly, most famously with the RNC's "autopsy report" after Mitt Romney lost in 2012, but the shifts in the meso-environment we have described have made this kind of adaptation considerably more difficult. As the party and aligned interest groups become more tightly intertwined, organized resistance to efforts to moderate and to incorporate new groups is likely to grow.[55] Groups will often be far less willing than politicians to throw prized policies overboard. The emergence of partisan media, working with a profit model based on stoking identity and outrage, only worsens the problem. Adaptation may be labeled betrayal, and the capacity of partisan media to punish undesired behavior has grown. Rather than reaching out to ascendant groups and incorporating new issues, a party facing demographic threats under current conditions may choose to intensify efforts to mobilize its existing coalition. Even more troubling, it may see advantages in restricting access of these ascendant groups to the public sphere. The associated risk for democratic backsliding is evident.

---

[52] Hacker and Pierson, "After the 'Master Theory'."
[53] As Margolis (this volume) demonstrates, the GOP coalition at the mass level is also more cohesive in important ways: for example, GOP partisans are overwhelmingly religious, where Democrats include large numbers of both believers and nonbelievers.
[54] David Karol, "American Political Parties: Exceptional No More," in *Solutions to Political Polarization in America*, ed. Nathan Persily (Cambridge: Cambridge University Press, 2015), 208–17.
[55] Jacob S. Hacker and Paul Pierson, *Let Them Eat Tweets: How the Right Rules in an Age of Extreme Inequality* (New York: W. W. Norton, 2020).

CONCLUSION: POLARIZATION IN A MADISONIAN FRAMEWORK

Intensifying polarization in the context of the transformed meso-institutional environment that we have described poses a genuine challenge to the robustness of Madisonian separation of powers and checks and balances. This is by no means the first threat to American democratic institutions. Political scientists and historians have long made it clear that these institutions were woefully flawed when it comes to critical dimensions of inclusion and responsiveness for much of American history. Our argument is that the particular threats and problems we face today are distinctive – and that they jeopardize core assumptions about the self-correcting tendencies of a system in which "ambition is made to counteract ambition."

We have emphasized some of the ways in which the current configuration of meso-institutions, formal institutions and party competition can erode the quality of governance, undercutting the capacity to reach a consensus on and address major problems, and diminishing the prospects for effective oversight. In this conclusion we focus, however, on how our developmental perspective allows us to situate the evolution of the American polity within the ongoing comparative discussion of democratic backsliding. We have already noted the efforts of Juan Linz to draw out the ways in which American institutions generated weak parties, which limited the dangers he saw lurking in presidential systems. In the contemporary period of intense polarization, however, American parties look less distinctive. Most important, this new political configuration seems far less effective at generating crosscutting pressures and a multiplicity of fluidly aligned interests. Increasingly, incentives for party loyalty appear to trump incentives associated with the particular institutional location of a political representative within our institutionally complex constitutional order.

Yet the challenge this new configuration creates doesn't simply involve the potential conflict between two branches, each with well-grounded claims to legitimacy, stressed in Linz's account. While this remains a plausible scenario, the rise of stronger incentives for party loyalty also suggests new vulnerabilities in a system that relies heavily on each branch to police the others.

The strengthening pull of party loyalty across the separation of powers system has been on vivid display in the final year of Donald Trump's presidency. Republicans' near-perfect unity in defending President Trump during the impeachment battle in early 2020 begged the question of whether there was any *possible* evidence of wrongdoing that would lead a substantial number of Republicans to emulate the conduct of their fellow-partisans during the Nixon years. While Nixon-era Republicans showed a strong inclination to side with the president, in the end a third of Republicans on House Judiciary backed impeachment, and pivotal senators eventually made it clear to the president that they would vote to convict. It is hard to imagine any "smoking-gun" evidence that would have led more than a very small handful of Republicans to take such action in 2020.

The willingness of elected Republicans to tolerate or openly support President Trump's baseless attack on the legitimacy of the 2020 election was equally revealing. When 126 House Republicans signed an amicus brief adopting the unprecedented position that the electoral votes of four states should be thrown out in order to overturn President Trump's defeat, many speculated on whether these members truly believed their own argument or were simply position-taking to curry favor with Trump. But this misses the essential point. A clear majority of House Republicans – and a considerably higher proportion of those who were not retiring – adopted a position that would have been politically inconceivable a few decades ago: that millions of votes ought to be thrown out in order to secure their candidates' victory. Regardless of whether these members believed their own argument or expected to have any concrete impact on the Court, their willingness to sign the brief was a clear indicator that loyalty to the president outweighed any commitment to long-standing democratic rules of the game.

Our analysis supports the view of Roberts and others that these new circumstances have made the parties, and especially the GOP, vulnerable to what comparativists call "bandwagoning."[56] Bandwagoning is a process in which disparate elites within a coalition face growing incentives to go along with extremist or antidemocratic practices.[57] A developmental perspective suggests that the prospects for bandwagoning are much greater in today's GOP than they might have been a few decades ago. What Roberts calls the "movementization" of the GOP creates new incentives for political elites to stick with their team on matters – including challenges to established norms of restraint and tolerance, the rule of law, and the integrity and autonomy of

---

[56] Kenneth M. Roberts, "Parties, Populism, and Democratic Decay: A Comparative Perspective on Party Polarization in the United States," in *When Democracy Trumps Populism: European and Latin American Lessons for the United States*, ed. Kurt Weyland and Raúl L. Madrid (Cambridge: Cambridge University Press, 2019), 132–53.

[57] Steven Levitsky and Daniel Ziblatt, *How Democracies Die* (New York: Crown, 2018).

core democratic institutions – where previously they might have chosen to dissent.[58] In this chapter, we have focused on Congress, but we should note that while some of the analysis would require modification, many elements would also apply to the courts. Partisan loyalty and fealty to party-aligned groups and causes are increasingly important parts of the process through which judges are selected.

The American system of checks and balances, with its unusual dispersal of political authority, has long generated formidable barriers against democratic backsliding.[59] Yet many of the stabilizing forces that traditionally were linked to these institutions seem much weaker today. In fact, in some cases, these arrangements now introduce new polarizing elements. For instance, the Madisonian system of territorial representation may create a powerful incentive for bandwagoning that is absent in systems lacking that feature. The stacking of cleavages in our polarized system has helped to deepen the territorial divide between the electorates of the two parties. Increasingly, elected officials find themselves facing local electorates dominated by a single party, further undercutting the effectiveness of traditional Downsian mechanisms for limiting extremism.

Most important, the United States is unusual in its heavy reliance on checks and balances to insure democratic stability. In many democracies, electoral arrangements that encourage multiparty systems in which no single party is likely to dominate play a central role. Our two-party system has been grounded in a structural decentralization of political authority. Yet the emergence of hyper-partisanship means that the check on authoritarian developments in the presidency that the Madisonian system relies on most, Congress, may not work. Instead, GOP members of Congress in particular face multiple incentives to bandwagon rather than resist. Among those incentives are the intense preferences of the party's interest groups, the heavily "red" and negatively partisan electoral bases of these politicians, and the likelihood that influential partisan media will exact a very high price for defection. Given these realities, it is perhaps unsurprising when even the most extreme and disquieting

---

[58] Roberts, "Parties, Populism, and Democratic Decay."
[59] These obstacles were not impermeable, of course. The imposition of disfranchisement and Jim Crow following Reconstruction constitute the most glaring instance of backsliding in US history, though it is not alone. On the successful moves to disenfranchise free black citizens in several states during the antebellum years, see, for example, David A. Bateman, *Disenfranchising Democracy: The Construction of the Electorate in the United States, United Kingdom, and France* (Cambridge: Cambridge University Press, 2018).

behavior in a Republican White House fails to shake the solidarity of Republican members of Congress. In short, the developmental perspective we offer raises a disturbing prospect: Under conditions of hyperpolarization, with the associated shifts in meso-institutional arrangements and the growth of tribalism, the Madisonian institutions of the United States may make it more vulnerable to democratic backsliding than many other wealthy democracies would be.

3

Pernicious Polarization and Democratic Resilience

Analyzing the United States in Comparative Perspective

Jennifer McCoy and Murat Somer

This chapter unpacks and critically discusses the idea of democratic resilience vis-à-vis polarization that becomes "pernicious," that is, it divides societies into mutually distrustful Us vs. Them camps. Democratic resilience, we argue, is a polity's ability to produce electoral, programmatic, discursive, and organizational behavior that can jointly contain and reverse pernicious polarization and its democracy-eroding consequences. We apply comparative lessons to assess US resilience and vulnerability to such consequences, focusing on three factors: institutional constraints, formative rifts, and opposition capacities and strategies.

Our analysis views polarization as both a process and a condition. As a process, it changes the incentive structure and even the composition and predisposition of the collective political actors themselves. It becomes an endogenous factor, as opposed to responding to exogenous factors. Consequently, the ability of the same institutions to contain pernicious consequences of polarization will change as the process deepens and becomes entrenched in an equilibrium condition. Our prior research further indicates that pernicious polarization is more likely to become entrenched when it involves formative rifts, that is, unresolved debates over citizenship, national identity, and state roles from the country's founding or refounding, and when it captures mass-based and institutionalized political parties. Finally, agency is critical to the deepening of polarization as the choices and capacities of both polarizing incumbents and opposition actors will determine whether they become locked into a self-propagating logic of dangerous polarization, or whether they are able to contain polarization before it reaches that level, or reverse it once it is reached. Mobilization, institutional accountability, and collective self-reflection capacities all matter here, the latter including such ideational capacities as high-quality universities and other self-reflective institutions.[1]

The first section discusses the political and relational aspects of our concept of pernicious polarization, as well as the role of formative rifts and institutional constraints. In the second section, we turn to the incentives produced by a polarizing logic that induce political actors and citizens to take or endorse actions undermining democratic institutions and the rule of law. The third section draws on comparative country research to lay out the common patterns of incumbent democracy-eroding behavior, that is, the pernicious consequences for democracy of Us vs. Them polarization, as well as our typology[2] of the array of possible opposition strategies that may contain, reverse or deepen pernicious polarization.

The last section discusses the implications of the argument for the case of the United States, as it analyzes the sources of vulnerability and resilience to the common patterns of political-societal polarization contributing to democratic erosion from a comparative perspective. We focus on three key factors in analyzing the United States: the strength of consensus-promoting institutions, polarization around formative rifts at the nation's founding centered on national identity and citizenship, and opposition strategies/capacities of polarization and depolarization.

POLITICAL AND RELATIONAL ASPECTS OF PERNICIOUS POLARIZATION

In recent years, the relationship between polarization and democracy, and in particular between polarization and democratic backsliding, has re-emerged as an important question of comparative politics.[3] Polarizing politics is considered a major factor underlying the proliferation of democratic backsliding, executive takeovers and hybrid regimes in recent

---

[1] Sheri Berman, "Ideational Theorizing in the Social Sciences since "Policy Paradigms, Social Learning, and the State," *Governance* 26, no. 2 (2013): 217–37.

[2] Murat Somer, Jennifer L. McCoy, and Russell E. Luke, "Pernicious Polarization, Autocratization, and Opposition Strategies," *Democratization* 28, no. 5 (2021): 929–48.

[3] Thomas Carothers and Andrew O'Donohue, *Democracies Divided: the Global Challenge of Political Polarization* (Washington: Brookings Institution, 2019); Matthew H. Graham and Milan W. Svolik, "Democracy in America? Partisanship, Polarization, and the Robustness of Support for Democracy in the United States," *American Political Science Review* 114, no. 2 (2020): 392–409; Jennifer McCoy and Murat Somer, eds. "Special Issue on Polarized Polities: A Global Threat to Democracy," *ANNALS of the American Academy of Political and Social Science*, 1, 681 (2019).

decades.[4] A significant challenge is to conceptually and empirically distinguish between polarization that can be part and sometimes conducive of normal, democratic politics, and severe polarization that undermines democracy.[5] We contribute to this question by defining "pernicious polarization" as a democracy-eroding *process* as well as, eventually, an equilibrium *condition* where a society is split into mutually distrustful Us vs. Them camps.

In addition, we contribute to extant research on the relationship between polarization and democracy by offering a political and relational concept of pernicious polarization, and, thus, by treating polarization as an endogenous aspect of democratic erosion and autocratization. While explaining how polarization facilitates the emergence and endurance of authoritarianism, most studies treat polarization as exogenously given.[6] By contrast, we offer an endogenous explanation of polarization and its democracy-eroding effects, in two senses.

First, we argue that *difference*, as in the ideological distance between political parties, is not the same as polarization.[7] Difference may be produced by exogenous factors such as history and socioeconomic dynamics, or cultural or ethnic cleavages. Polarization, on the other hand, arises as a result of political behavior that acts on differences based on an Us vs. Them logic that overrides crosscutting ties in order to pursue political goals, such as mobilizing a constituency or weakening rivals. It becomes pernicious if and when a country's level of democratic resilience is overcome by the self-fulfilling logic of polarization, as an endogenous product of the causal mechanisms that transform political actors and their behavioral incentives. Second, once the resulting polarization begins to erode democracy, we maintain that fissures over the workings and future of democracy – even disagreements over whether democracy is eroding or advancing – are likely to arise as a built-in property of the process. When this happens, polarization and democratic backsliding can reinforce each other. A *political* perspective on

---

[4] Nancy Bermeo, "On Democratic Backsliding," *Journal of Democracy* 27, no. 1 (2016): 5–19; Larry Diamond, *Ill Winds: Saving Democracy from Russian Rage, Chinese Ambition, and American Complacency* (New York: Penguin Press, 2019); Graham and Svolik, "Democracy in America?"

[5] Murat Somer and Jennifer McCoy, "Déjà Vu? Polarization and Endangered Democracies in the 21st Century," *American Behavioral Scientist* 62, no. 1 (2018): 3–15.

[6] Milan W. Svolik, "Polarization versus Democracy," *Journal of Democracy* 30, no. 3 (2019): 20–32.

[7] Jennifer McCoy, Tahmina Rahman, and Murat Somer, "Polarization and the Global Crisis of Democracy: Common Patterns, Dynamics, and Pernicious Consequences for Democratic Polities," *American Behavioral Scientist* 62, no. 1 (2018): 16–42.

polarization argues that political entrepreneurs often activate and reframe societal divisions as a tool to simplify politics and consolidate supporters, weaken opponents, and achieve political goals. Thus, while societal polarization is a major challenge to democracy, it becomes a major threat insofar as it also involves political polarization – when political identities also become social identities, or vice versa. Research on political polarization, for example, highlights the importance of sorting, where voters with particular characteristics line up their interests and support with particular political parties.[8] Parties and their bases diverge from each other even when society does not become more differentiated. While organizational and demographic factors may be important in explaining this sorting, we emphasize the political will and purposes that lead to such changes. We argue that political polarization is often started when political actors use divisive discourse and draw attention to issues in such a way that they line up divisions that had been crosscutting and vaguely experienced into an overarching Us vs. Them (or Our worldview vs. Theirs) wedge. While doing so, they also reinterpret existing divisions and may construct new ones. This type of polarization then becomes the linchpin of politics, regrouping citizens in terms of their party attachments and, over time, social relations, with pernicious consequences for democracy.

A *relational* perspective, in turn, implies that polarization always is an interactive phenomenon. Those political actors who initiate the process and those who respond to it jointly produce enduring polarization, which may otherwise be short-lived. They also jointly determine whether or not it becomes pernicious. In this process, various factors play important causal roles. These include political agency, resources, and creativity; the nature of the cleavages around which a society is polarized; and mobilizational repertoires and capacities of each camp. Also important is the extent to which political actors and institutional players understand the dynamics of polarization and its consequences for democracy, and how a vicious cycle of polarization and democratic erosion can be prevented.

Political polarization is thus both a process and a condition. Its endogenous character indicates that the process of deepening polarization changes the incentives, and at times also the profile of collective actors themselves as they respond to a changing incentive structure. For example, more principled and centrist actors often become marginalized or purged in intraparty politics under deepening polarization, changing the

---

[8] Lilliana Mason, *Uncivil Agreement: How Politics Became Our Identity* (Chicago: University of Chicago Press, 2018).

composition of collective actors and moving them toward more extreme positions. Further, the same actors may become more predisposed to display in-group favoritism as the society becomes more polarized. Such changes also alter the capacity of the existing institutions to contain the negative consequences of polarization, as the institutions themselves become politicized and perceptions of them polarize among the public. As political parties and leaders and social actors employ reciprocal tactics that deepen polarization, the logic of pernicious polarization sets in and becomes entrenched in the political system, and then it proves difficult to reverse.[9]

Formative Rifts and Institutional Arrangements

In our comparative study of eleven polarized cases globally, we found that those countries that polarized around unresolved debates that stem from the nation's founding are the most pernicious and tend to become the most entrenched.[10] These issues include questions of who is considered a citizen with full rights and who legitimately represents them, as well as the myths about the nation's founding and what comprises the nation's core culture and identity. Some examples would be the legacy of unequal citizenship rights that were conferred upon African Americans, Native Americans, and women during the foundation of the United States; the claim that political legitimacy is to be conferred only on those with national liberation war experience in Zimbabwe; and whether language and ethnicity, or religion should be the basis of national identity in Bangladesh.

These rifts tend to have a particularly divisive quality because "they cannot be eliminated without fundamentally reconfiguring these states, and because people often find themselves on one side of these rifts or the other by birth. As a result, formative rifts can have a powerful impact on political attachments when activated."[11] We find that polarizing political actors often seek to activate these rifts to mobilize their constituencies, and build a cohesive and emotionally appealing group identity. Such polarization becomes threatening and induces mutual polarizing reactions in a relational way, leading to democratic erosion. It becomes an enduring

---

[9] Murat Somer and Jennifer McCoy, "Transformations Through Polarizations and Global Threats to Democracy," *The ANNALS of the American Academy of Political and Social Science* 681, no. 1 (2019): 8–22.
[10] McCoy and Somer, "Special Issue on Polarized Polities"; Somer and McCoy, "Transformations Through Polarizations."
[11] Somer and McCoy, "Transformations Through Polarizations," 15.

feature of democratic politics because the competing political identities extend into the society such that even if one political actor is able to dominate over the other and temporarily defuse the polarization episode, the latent polarization residing in the society will facilitate its resurgence unless the political actors take constructive steps toward resolving the historic national debates.

Finally, of the cases we examined in our prior research, polarization was not associated with any particular institutional arrangements, such as presidential vs. parliamentary, or strong or weakly institutionalized party systems.[12] Nevertheless, one institution stands out – majoritarian electoral systems that give disproportionate representation to the largest party tend to raise the stakes of elections, contribute to zero-sum perceptions of politics, and deepen pernicious polarization. Further, the capacity of one political bloc to use existing accountability mechanisms, such as courts, bureaucracy, impeachment, or the military to pressure an opposition or remove an incumbent may deepen pernicious polarization when used extra-constitutionally or when these mechanisms are already politicized by polarization. If they are used constitutionally before pernicious polarization is entrenched, however, such accountability mechanisms may be able to keep the polarization from deepening into a severe state.

POLITICIAN AND CITIZEN INCENTIVES TO ERODE DEMOCRACY IN CONTEXTS OF SEVERE POLARIZATION

In McCoy and Somer (2019),[13] we developed the following summary of the most striking features of pernicious polarization that distinguish it from a healthy pluralism in a democratic society or, for that matter, from a polarization that can contribute to democratic governance by clarifying choices for citizens:

(a) Division of the electorate into two hostile camps, where multiple cleavages have collapsed into one dominant cleavage or boundary line between the two camps.
(b) The political identity of the two camps becomes a social identity in which members feel they belong to a "team" or bloc and

---

[12] Jennifer McCoy and Murat Somer, "Toward a Theory of Pernicious Polarization and How It Harms Democracies: Comparative Evidence and Possible Remedies," *The ANNALS of the American Academy of Political and Social Science* 681, no. 1 (2019): 243–71.
[13] McCoy and Somer, "Special Issue on Polarized Polities."

demonstrate strong loyalty to it. Political demands and interests become formed around those identities.

(c) The two camps are characterized in moral terms of "good" and "evil."
(d) The identities and interests of the two camps are viewed as mutually exclusive and antagonistic, thus negating the possibility of common interests between different groups.
(e) Stereotyping and prejudice builds toward the out-group due to lack of direct communication and/or social interaction.
(f) The center drops out and the polarized camps attempt to label all individuals and groups in society as one or the other.
(h) Institutions, including media, become either bifurcated or dominated by one bloc or the other through discursive changes as well as changes of ownership, management, and staff, weakening the middle ground in public and political discourses.
(i) The antagonistic relationship manifests in spatial, social, and psychological separation of the polarized groups.[14]

The logic of such a situation of pernicious polarization creates a perception of politics as being in a state of emergency, even a state of exception à la Carl Schmitt, and a zero-sum game. It leads both sides to see the other as an existential threat to the nation and way of life if they were to gain (or retain) power. Elections become high-stakes affairs, and control of other levers of power (security and intelligence forces, bureaucracies, ownership or regulation of economic activity, media, civil society organizations) becomes an aim as well. Such polarization provides incentives for political actors and citizens alike to take or endorse actions that undermine the independence of democratic institutions and the rule of law.

Figure 3.1 graphically depicts the path from polarization to democratic erosion. Political actors who employ polarizing electoral and governing

FIGURE 3.1 The path from polarization to democratic erosion

---

[14] McCoy and Somer, "Toward a Theory of Pernicious Polarization," 246–47.

strategies contribute to the Us vs. Them logic of intergroup conflict and resulting negative perceptions of the out-group. Growing perceptions of out-group threat and in-group self-defense then create incentives for violations of democratic norms.

For citizens, the social-psychology of inter-group conflict plays an important role in the logic of polarization. As political, economic, or cultural grievances deepen, citizens become receptive to political entrepreneurs who draw attention to or magnify these grievances for electoral or other mobilizational purposes. Polarizing rhetoric that divides an electorate, identifies enemies, and/or appeals to anger and anxieties are often successful electoral strategies. Populist polarizers, for example, rely on an Us vs. Them rhetoric that demonizes a perceived enemy identified as a nefarious elite (political establishment, economic elites, intellectuals, or foreigners) taking advantage of the common people, while ethnic polarizers identify an ethnic "Other" as the perceived enemy. Social psychologists have long demonstrated that a perceived out-group threat strengthens in-group loyalty and favoritism while increasing out-group stereotyping and hostility. As the divides grow and partisan social identity and sorting deepens, perceptions of politics as a zero-sum game increases. Eventually both camps perceive the policies and projects of the Other as an existential threat to their way of life or the well-being of the nation.

For politicians, either an intra-elite power struggle or mass-based popular demands may motivate a political entrepreneur to utilize a polarizing strategy. In the case of an intra-elite power struggle, the polarizing politician may attempt to mobilize masses to support his/her aims. In the case of mass-based popular demands for or against fundamental change, polarization becomes a transformative or obstructive political strategy, whether on the Left or the Right. The dominant political motive and discursive focus seem to be either active-inclusionary – seeking to include previously marginalized sectors, or reactionary-exclusionary – seeking to exclude threatening outsiders. In these patterns, polarizing politicians challenge the status quo, often with populist undertones.

COMMON PATTERNS OF INCUMBENT-LED DEMOCRATIC EROSION AND OPPOSITION REACTIONS

Gridlock and paralysis, democratic backsliding, or outright democratic collapse are all potential outcomes of pernicious polarization. Whether political actors become locked into a pattern of deepening polarization or strive to contain or reverse it will depend on their discursive and behavioral choices and interactions within the institutional constraints functioning in a given political system.

Comparative case studies have highlighted a common set of tools of democratic erosion from the logic of severe polarization.[15] By themselves, none of these democracy-challenging tools, which arise as undesirable yet perhaps also unavoidable by-products of democratic competition, is destructive of functioning democracies. In combination and coupled with pernicious polarization, however, they cause erosion.

Electoral Engineering. First, the governing party in highly polarized contexts almost always attempts to enhance and entrench their electoral advantage through constitutional or electoral law reform, creating an unlevel playing field by restricting media access or campaign finance, gerrymandering, impeding voter registration of opponents, or intimidating voters on election day. Polarizing populists in particular tend to claim a natural majority as they uniquely represent "the people," and preemptively allege fraud or discredit the electoral process if they risk losing an election.

Discredit the Opposition. Second, a perniciously polarizing leader often uses insults and denigration to discredit his/her political opposition by linking them to domestic or foreign enemies. Examples include Hugo Chávez's charge that Venezuela's opposition were puppets of the "imperial" United States or Victor Orbán's charge that George Soros was carrying out the European Union's bidding to force Hungary to accept burdensome refugees.

Restrict Media, Dissent, and Criticism. Third, a polarized media often transforms to a state-dominated media as state media is expanded and independent media is squeezed out of business by tax harassment or restrictions on newsprint and broadcast licenses, with actors sympathetic to the government buying up the weakened media. Intraparty rivals and opposition challengers alike may be eliminated by trumped up corruption or criminal charges, or blatant disqualification of political parties. Dissidence and protest may be dealt with harshly with repression, arbitrary detention, and absence of due process.

---

[15] Carothers and O'Donohue, *"Democracies Divided"*; Robert R. Kaufman and Stephan Haggard, "Democratic Decline in the United States: What Can We Learn from Middle Income Backsliding?" *Perspectives on Politics* 17, no. 2 (2018): 417–32; McCoy, Rahman, and Somer, "Polarization and the Global Crisis of Democracy"; Somer and McCoy, "Special Issue on Polarized Polities."

Enhance Institutional Control and Politicization. Fourth, public institutions such as security and intelligence agencies, government bureaucracy, oversight bodies, and courts are politicized with the appointment of partisan or personal loyalists. Civil society institutions may become polarized as each camp develops its own interest groups, NGOs, media outlets, universities, and labor and business associations. Commonly, however, a polarizing incumbent will attempt to control rival civil society actors through co-optation or coercion, such as Orbán's pressure campaign to force Central European University to leave the country and the government's assertion of budgetary control over the Hungarian Academy of Sciences.

Weaken Horizontal Accountability. Fifth, polarizing incumbents, no matter the type of government system, concentrate power in their office. In the case of Turkey, Prime Minister Erdoğan passed constitutional reforms in a free and fair referendum that opened the judiciary to partisan packing in 2010.[16] Seven years later and free from judicial oversight, he orchestrated an unfair and partially free constitutional referendum, which replaced the parliamentary system with hyper-presidentialism.[17] Presidents weaken the separation of powers and practice executive overreach, claiming a popular mandate above the legislative branch or ignoring court decisions until they can transform those institutions into loyalist branches unwilling to challenge the executive. On the other hand, oppositions may attempt to use their influence in those very accountability mechanisms (courts, bureaucracies, security and intelligence forces, media) to challenge a polarizing figure. They may do so following constitutional impeachment procedures, but they may also stretch to extra-constitutional court decisions, questionable impeachment and party-closure cases, or military threats and actual coup attempts, as in Thailand against Thaksin and his successors, the Philippines in 2010, Turkey in 2007 and 2008, and Venezuela in 2002.[18]

---

[16] Murat Somer, "Turkey: The Slippery Slope from Reformist to Revolutionary Polarization and Democratic Breakdown," *The ANNALS of the American Academy of Political and Social Science* 681 (2019): 42–61.

[17] Berk Esen and Sebnem Gumuscu, "Building a Competitive Authoritarian Regime: State–Business Relations in the AKP's Turkey," *Journal of Balkan and Near Eastern Studies* 20, no. 4 (November 2017): 1–24.

[18] Aries Arugay and Dan Slater, "Polarization Without Poles: Machiavellian Conflicts and the Philippines' Lost Decade of Democracy, 2000–2010," *The ANNALS of the American Academy of Political and Social Science* 681, no. 1 (2019): 122–36; Jennifer McCoy and Díez Francisco, *International Mediation in Venezuela* (Washington: United States Institute of Peace, 2011); Dan Slater and Aries A Arugay, "Polarizing Figures: Executive

Scapegoat and Blame. Finally, polarizing actors thrive on perceptions of a threatening enemy to blame for the society's ills. While the identity of the enemy may change, there always must be one to motivate supporters to rally around the leader. For instance, polarizing incumbents have scapegoated a revolving range of external and domestic critics in Turkey, immigrants in Italy or Hungary, or domestic or American economic saboteurs in Venezuela.

Two points are crucial to note here to conceptualize democratic resilience. First, polarizing incumbents resort to these democracy-eroding behaviors to differing degrees. Incumbents are not homogenous. An incumbent political party, for example, may include principled actors who exercise forbearance to avoid these behaviors or engage in them with restraint, or simply self-interested actors who do so for strategic reasons. Demonization, discrediting, or bullying tactics are often employed against non-polarizing or bridge-building actors, who may be labeled as too soft, naïve, or treasonous, by their own party. Second, incumbents resort to polarizing politics to pursue various political interests, which can also be pursued, as many political actors do, in non-polarizing ways. Hence, part of a country's democratic resilience can be conceptualized as the ability of incumbents to protect their interests and settle intra-incumbent power struggles without resorting to pernicious polarization and authoritarianism.

Opposition Reactions and Strategies

Confronting a polarizing incumbent, oppositions are faced with difficult ethical and political choices. Ethically, they may abhor the divisiveness of the incumbent's behavior, but feel pressed to reciprocate, pushed by their base to react strongly. Politically, they may fear that such polarizing behavior may succeed in consolidating a winning pro-government majority, but fear that foregoing a reciprocal response may also lead to their own loss. The more the incumbent engages in "creeping authoritarianism," the more the ethical and political urgency escalates. However, the options available to oppositions are all costly with uncertain outcomes. The ability to choose and implement better options for democracy require political will and learning, acumen, and creativity in addition to the other resources previously mentioned. Oppositions across the world may be

Power and Institutional Conflict in Asian Democracies," *American Behavioral Scientist* 62, no. 1 (2018): 92–106; Somer, "Turkey: The Slippery Slope."

involved in a process of learning to cope with the novel and challenging aspects of polarization and democratic backsliding in recent decades.

Hence, we maintain that the concept of democratic resilience should include the ability of opposition actors to produce and implement strategies that prevent or reverse rather than reinforce pernicious polarization. What we refer to as "opposition" here overlaps with the conventional incumbent-opposition distinction but should be interpreted more dynamically. It can potentially include those agents within the incumbent political bloc who aim to reverse pernicious polarization and thereby may either split from the incumbent or cooperate with the opposition from within. It should also involve political parties as well as movements.

The Reciprocate-Avoid Dilemma of Oppositions. Oppositions face two basic choices. First, they can respond to the incumbents with polarizing or non-polarizing politics of their own. Second, they can either pursue a preservative strategy by conducting politics on the existing axes of politics or develop a generative strategy by politicizing new axes/cleavages. We discuss each in the following.

Avoid Polarization: Passive and Active Depolarization

Avoiding polarization may be a normative choice as many people realize its dangers for democracy and coexistence. Alternatively, it may be a strategy to improve political prospects. Hence, avoidance can have two versions. A passive version would simply reject polarization and avoid polarizing politics along the existing axes of politics, as a normative choice or out of weakness. In the interwar era, many European democracies fell to authoritarianism, among other reasons, because indecisive centrist parties failed to counter fascist rivals who exploited left-right polarization and fear of communism. An active version purposefully tries to appeal to centrist voters by proactively highlighting and mobilizing around crosscutting ties downplayed by the incumbent, hence shifting from polarized to pluralist politics. In recent examples of the latter, opposition mayoral candidates in Istanbul and Budapest defeated incumbent candidates by actively seeking depolarization and pursuing moderate voters based on crosscutting identities and interests.

The risk of avoidance is that it may fail to mobilize the opposition's own base enough to defeat the incumbent, and it may be seen as too soft and legitimizing the incumbent's divisive and antidemocratic behavior. If avoidance fails to deliver political gains, the resulting internal rivalries within opposition coalitions, demoralization, or apathy can cause oppositions to fragment and send mixed messages to their supporters, generally strengthening a polarizing incumbent.

As polarization deepens, oppositions become faced with their own existential threat perceptions and growing internal pressures to "act firmly" as well as "reach out to the other side." They face the dilemmas of choosing strategies that can either deepen or diminish pernicious polarization and democratic erosion, hence our argument that the concept of democratic resilience should include the capacity to resolve these dilemmas.

Counter-Polarization: Reciprocal and Transformative Repolarization

Counter-polarization is aimed at returning the previous elites to power by fostering a backlash to a new group that won the past election, or mobilizing the society against an unscrupulous incumbent by presenting the electorate with a Manichean binary choice. Counter-polarization can be both a political strategy and a principled stand against a polarizing incumbent. Under this larger rubric, comparative examples indicate two versions, one reciprocal and one transformative. In the *reciprocal counter-polarization* version, the primary purpose is to restore an old elite displaced from power or stop the rise of an authoritarian polarizer by conducting politics on the same axis politicized by the incumbent. The main means seem to be protests and judicial or military interventions. Since the principle aim is to stop the advances of an incumbent and his/her base, this strategy comes close to what we have called exclusionary-reactionary polarization.[19] For example, the Turkish opposition tried to block the incumbent party's rise through massive anti-Islamist protests in 2007 and a Constitutional Court case to de-register the party for its anti-secularism in 2008.[20] Since the main axis of these opposition mobilizations was the defense of secularism, they were perceived as exclusionary by pro-incumbent pious Turks.

Reciprocal counter-polarization, even to prevent democratic erosion, risks deepening polarization and moving to a pernicious equilibrium. Even if such a politics of counter-polarization manages to unseat the incumbent, it may also end up killing democracy, as in the extreme version of "autocracy under the old elites" in post-Thaksin Thailand or post-Morsi

---

[19] Somer and McCoy, "Toward a Theory of Pernicious Polarization."
[20] Murat Somer, "Moderate Islam and Secularist Opposition in Turkey: Implications for the World, Muslims and Secular Democracy," *Third World Quarterly* 28, no. 7 (2007): 1271–89.

Egypt.[21] It can also produce governance dysfunction where democracy is paralyzed between mutually opposed forces in a context of discredited and politicized institutions of horizontal accountability.

An alternative form of counter-polarization is *transformative repolarization*, which aims to mobilize the society against the incumbent based on new axes of politics such as a platform of large-scale socioeconomic and institutional transformations to achieve democratic reforms. Insofar as the transformative aims of this polarizing politics rest on changes that empower new groups in society, including some supporters of the incumbent, it resembles what we have called in general inclusionary-progressive polarization.[22] Transformative repolarization was perhaps exemplified recently by the US presidential campaigns of Bernie Sanders and Elizabeth Warren in 2020.

VULNERABILITY AND RESILIENCE OF THE UNITED STATES TO THE DEMOCRACY-WEAKENING TENDENCIES OF PERNICIOUS POLARIZATION

Analysts have varied in their assessments of the risks facing US democracy. Expert surveys measure a decline in democratic quality since 2015 (Brightline Watch, Authoritarian Warning, Varieties of Democracy). Comparativists warn about the risks based on examples abroad,[23] primarily focusing on the rise of affective polarization and the erosion of informal norms. Yet another group of comparativist and Americanist political scientists see continued substantial bulwarks protecting the United States from a serious risk of democratic reversion arising from either populism or extreme polarization.[24] These more optimistic views primarily offer institutional defenses, focusing on constitutional rigidity and consensus-promoting

---

[21] Prajak Kongkirati, "From Illiberal Democracy to Military Authoritarianism: Intra-Elite Struggle and Mass-Based Conflict in Deeply Polarized Thailand," *The ANNALS of the American Academy of Political and Social Science* 681, no. 1 (2019): 24–40; Somer and McCoy, "Special Issue on Polarized Polities."

[22] McCoy and Somer, "Toward a Theory of Pernicious Polarization."

[23] Kaufman and Haggard, "Democratic Decline in the United States"; Jennifer McCoy, "Pernicious Polarization's Threat to Democracy: Lessons for the U.S. from Abroad," *Newsletter of the Organized Section in Comparative Politics of the American Political Science Association* 29, no. 1 (2019): 22–30; Somer and McCoy, "Transformations Through Polarizations."

[24] Kurt Weyland and Raúl L. Madrid, eds., *When Democracy Trumps Populism: European and Latin American Lessons for the United States* (Cambridge: Cambridge University Press, 2019); Kurt Weyland, "Populism's Threat to Democracy: Comparative Lessons for the United States," *Perspectives on Politics* 17, no. 2 (January 2020): 1–18.

mechanisms baked into the US political system. In some ways, it is a glass-half-full vs. glass-half-empty debate. But we also contend there are theoretical differences in the factors to be emphasized and the sources of threat. In particular, we argue that the process of polarization changes the incentives of the political actors and alters the conflict management and consensus-promoting capacities of institutions.

We argue that the United States is in a process of pernicious polarization that has involved the country's formative rifts, two mass-based parties, and social identities – all risk factors according to our argument.[25] It has also already caused significant democratic erosion. As highlighted elsewhere in this volume, the United States exhibits symptoms in all six categories of incumbent-led democratic erosion found in our comparative research: electoral engineering to enhance the governing party advantage; discrediting the opposition; restricting the media, criticism, and dissent; politicizing and controlling institutions and bureaucracies; weakening horizontal accountability; and scapegoating and blaming.

In the remainder of this section, we turn to our analysis of three key factors in analyzing the United States: the weakened capacity of consensus-promoting institutions under polarization, polarization around formative rifts at the nation's founding centered on national identity and citizenship, and opposition strategies/capacities of polarization and depolarization.

Institutions as a Source of Resilience and Vulnerability: Why American Institutions Are Not as Resilient as We Think They Are

The most commonly cited sources of resilience for the American democracy are its institutions rooted in a rigid constitution, its strong opposition party, and its vibrant civil society.[26] Lijphart characterized the United States as a medium plural society divided on race and geography.[27] (A plural society is one in which partisan lines reinforce other social cleavages.) To govern with such divisions, he recommended consensus-promoting and supermajority institutions. Frances Lee points out that of Lijphart's list of ten such institutions, the United States has six which serve

---

[25] McCoy and Somer, "Toward a Theory of Pernicious Polarization."
[26] Weyland and Madrid, *When Democracy Trumps Populism*; Weyland, "Populism's Threat to Democracy."
[27] Arend Lijphart, *Democracy in Plural Societies: A Comparative Exploration* (New Haven: Yale University Press, 1977).

to "lower the stakes in any particular election outcome, force broader consensus-building in policymaking, and necessitate bipartisan negotiation in governance, even under contemporary party-polarized conditions."[28] Since Lijphart's writing in the 1970s, however, the reinforcing cleavages in the United States have only deepened, putting more pressure on the consensus-promoting institutions.

The institutional sources of resilience identified by scholars of American politics include both the formal institutions of federalism, separation of powers, bicameralism, and an independent judiciary, and the informal institutions that have bolstered the consensus-promoting ideals of the constitution, such as the filibuster and cloture norm created in 1917, a strong defense of states' rights, a shared Judeo-Christian culture, a strong civil society, dispersed economic power, and an independent media. Beginning in the 1990s, however, changes in information and communication technologies (ICTs) and growing identity-based partisanship and affective partisan polarization[29] weakened the capacity of the American formal and informal institutions to protect against the centrifugal forces unleashed by technological, demographic, and economic change. The creation of the Internet and rise of social media removed the filter provided by an establishment media that interpreted information in a common vein for the public.[30] The resulting fractured information environment produced a society with no consensus even on facts. Affective partisan polarization provoked distrust and dislike of the out-party and impeded compromise.[31]

The diverging narratives based on competing information sources combined with strong affective polarization to weaken the institutional

---

[28] Lee, Ch.4, this volume.
[29] A recent study by Boxell et al. (2020) finds that the United States has experienced the largest increase in affective polarization since 1980 among nine OECD countries studied. Levi Boxell, Matthew Gentzkow, and Jesse Shapiro, "Cross-Country Trends in Affective Polarization," Cambridge, MA: National Bureau of Economic Research, January 2020. https://doi.org/10.3386/w26669.
[30] S. Rosenberg, "Democracy Devouring Itself: The Rise of the Incompetent Citizen and the Appeal of Right Wing Populism," 2019. https://escholarship.org/uc/item/8806z01m#main.
[31] Alan Abramowitz and Jennifer McCoy, "United States: Racial Resentment, Negative Partisanship, and Polarization in Trump's America," *The ANNALS of the American Academy of Political and Social Science* 681, no. 1 (2019): 137–56; Mason *Uncivil Agreement*; Shanto Iyengar and Sean J. Eastwood, "Fear and Loathing Across Party Lines: New Evidence on Group Polarization," *American Journal of Political Science* 59, no. 3 (2015): 690–707; McCoy, Rahman, and Somer, "Polarization and the Global Crisis."

guardrails. As Levitsky and Ziblatt argue, constitutional consensus-promoting mechanisms depend on the informal norms of mutual forbearance and restraint.[32] But when instead political actors use constitutional hardball (pushing their advantage to the legal limit to protect their party's status), those consensus-promoting mechanisms lose their capacity to manage conflict peacefully as well as serve the purpose of checks and balances to hold public officials accountable. Nowhere is this more clear than in the 2019–20 impeachment investigation and trial of President Donald Trump. The very institution of impeachment as an accountability mechanism in Congress's constitutional duty to oversee the executive and judiciary branches became politicized *because* the actors charged with carrying out the impeachment process were not trusted by the other side. Democrats were seen by the president and Republicans as having waged a vendetta against Trump since his election, and thus as being motivated by partisan interests to remove him from power; Republicans were seen by Democrats as enabling and protecting a corrupt leader to protect their own partisan interests of retaining power.

The abandonment of the informal norm of the filibuster and cloture by both parties in a reciprocal tit-for-tat strategy, discussed further in the following, undermined another consensus-promoting mechanism – that of requiring a 60 percent supermajority to move to a vote for the appointment of lifetime federal judges and the Supreme Court. The resulting party-line votes on judicial appointments have politicized that mechanism of democratic accountability and resilience. Accordingly, the judiciary may lose its legitimacy in the eyes of a significant portion of the population. Indeed, while federal courts have blocked some Trump-era administrative policy changes, the Supreme Court in 2019 and 2020 (with the addition of three Trump appointees to the conservative majority) largely upheld his policies and those state policies that have been more exclusionary than inclusionary in voting rights. The institutions that should be a bulwark *against* the pernicious logic of polarization thus became a mechanism *of* deepening polarization.

Perhaps the most threatening legacy of the Trump administration for American democracy is Trump's refusal to accept his electoral defeat to Joe Biden. The sowing of disinformation in the 2020 election cycle came not from outsiders like Russia, but much more insidiously, from the very government itself.[33] The Trump administration's months-long campaign

---

[32] Steven Levitsky and Daniel Ziblatt, *How Democracies Die* (New York: Crown, 2018).
[33] www.nytimes.com/2020/11/23/opinion/trump-republicans-election-2020.html?referringSource=articleShare.

to sow distrust in mail-in balloting prior to the election, and the pursuit of multiple strategies to overturn the election results after, was reiterated by Republican officials even after the electoral college vote confirming Biden's victory in December 2020. Despite the commitment of state-level election officials to protect election integrity, destroying trust in elections incentivizes voters and political leaders alike to engage in the democracy-destroying behavior we described here as a consequence of pernicious polarization.

Not only informal institutions, but the very institutional DNA of the United States political system is turning into a source of polarization that may no longer be able to serve the protective role that Frances Lee foresees, to "thwart and restrain the ambitions of today's more socially sorted and ideologically distinctive political parties."[34] Instead, the constitutional compromises made to forge a new nation from a group of disparate states in the 1700s – a federal system with a weak national government and strong states, the electoral college, and bicameral legislature – have gradually shifted toward a nationalization of power with a strong presidency and a disproportionate scheme of representation in the twenty-first century that is reminiscent of other polarized, backsliding democracies, which we discuss in the following.

The federal nature of the US political system with its strong decentralization should diffuse power and serve as a check on national government power.[35] Nevertheless, as Pierson and Schickler show, the meso-institutions that historically countervailed polarization have now been transformed into engines of polarization[36]: decentralized political parties in which state-level parties controlled their own nominations, with ambition rooted in the states and new cleavages that could crosscut existing divisions, have now become dominated by national political parties and fundraising; interest group/party coalitions that varied across regions have now become nationalized; and local media is nationalized, providing a single national message, even if divided between partisan and ideological bias of the particular news media. Studies by Hertel Fernandez and Rocco further show both a nationalization of state politics and an asymmetrical polarization with the Republican-led states more likely to support antidemocratic measures, including failing to respond to democratic mandates from the public, curbing political participation, using policy to tilt

---

[34] Lee, Ch.4, this volume.
[35] Lee, Ch.4, this volume; Lijphart, "*Patterns of Democracy.*"
[36] Pierson and Schickler, Ch.2, this volume.

the electoral playing field in one's favor, and rejecting progressive policies approved by municipalities.[37] Funded by large donors such as the Koch Brothers and policy advocacy organizations such as ALEC, Republican-controlled legislatures now respond to a common national agenda rather than local constituencies.

Even the bicameral national legislature is weakening as a consensus-building mechanism, and has delegated much of its power to the executive in the last half century.[38] Granted, despite the rise of party polarization in Congress, there has been no meaningful increase in the tendency of legislation to be adopted on narrow party lines or over the opposition of a majority of the minority party.[39] The landmark legislation enacted on party line votes – the 2010 Affordable Care Act and the 2017 tax cuts – are the exception rather than the rule.[40] Yet, with the Republican party blocking most legislation after winning majorities in the House in 2010 and the Senate in 2014, Obama resorted to executive orders to implement policy. Trump then revoked many of those orders when he entered the White House in 2017, but struggled to achieve unity within his own party to pass significant legislation beyond the 2017 tax bill even while he retained unified government in 2017–18. The pernicious outcome of the deep polarization may well be government paralysis and dysfunction, or a careening between ideological extremes as each new governing party strives to undo the advances made by the prior administration, at the cost of bipartisan law-making.[41]

Disproportionate Representation

Our prior comparative research indicated that representative institutions, both formal and informal, are a key factor in determining whether polarization is contained within normal democratic boundaries, or deepens with pernicious consequences for democracy.[42] As we show in McCoy and Somer, the common practice of a polarizing political actor is to seek

---

[37] Hertel-Fernandez, Ch. 12, and Rocco, Ch.13, this volume.
[38] Philip A. Wallach, "How Congress Fell behind the Executive Branch," in *Congress Overwhelmed*, ed. Timothy LaPira, Lee Drutman, and Kevin Kosar (Chicago: University of Chicago Press, 2020), 51–73.
[39] James M. Curry and Frances E. Lee, "Non-Party Government: Bipartisan Lawmaking and Party Power in Congress," *Perspectives on Politics* 17, no. 1 (2019): 47–65.
[40] Lee, Ch.4, this volume.
[41] Ibid.; Somer and McCoy, "Toward a Theory of Pernicious Polarization."
[42] Somer and McCoy, "Special Issue on Polarized Polities."

constitutional or legislative changes to entrench their electoral majority into the future.[43] Granted, given the difficulty of amending the US constitution, we do not see the same resort to constitutional change to engineer electoral rules or extend term limits so prevalent in our other cases. Nevertheless, recent Supreme Court decisions privileging corporate actors in campaign finance, gutting the Voting Rights Act, and upholding partisan gerrymandering and restrictive voter identification laws have helped to enhance Republican electoral advantages at a time when Republicans dominate the state legislatures who make many of these decisions.

The implications of the majoritarian electoral systems are profound: the winner-take-all logic produced by institutional rules in disproportionate systems, combined with the psychological elements of the Us vs. Them discourse employed in severely polarized party systems, provide perverse incentives in favor of de-democratization. As Vegetti argues, the resulting electoral immobilism entrenched with institutional disproportionate rules contributes to the extension of political polarization to the societal level, and makes polarization even more difficult to overcome.[44]

Two counter-majoritarian institutions were designed to protect against tyranny of the majority in the US constitution – the Electoral College and the Senate. Like Australia, Brazil, and Mexico, the upper chamber in the US Congress is designed to give less populous, often rural, states equal sway within that institution. The United States Electoral College – the method of indirect election of president and vice president that began as a compromise between free states and slave-holding states, and as an elitist method to insulate the presidency from "popular passions" – further distorts the equality of the individual vote both by providing smaller states an advantage with the inclusion of two electors per state as in the Senate, and by the practice of winner-take-all electoral votes used by forty-eight of the fifty states.[45] In these minority-empowering institutions,

---

[43] McCoy and Somer, "Toward a Theory of Pernicious Polarization."

[44] Federico Vegetti, "The Political Nature of Ideological Polarization: The Case of Hungary," *The ANNALS of the American Academy of Political and Social Science* 681, no. 1 (2019): 78–96.

[45] Alexander Keyssar, *Why Do We Still Have the Electoral College?* (Cambridge: Harvard University Press, 2020). A single electoral vote in California represents nearly four times the number of voters as an electoral vote in Wyoming. Katy Collin, "The Electoral College Badly Distorts the Vote. And It's Going to Get Worse," *Washington Post*, Nov 17, 2016. In the House of Representatives, a 2018 model by *The Economist* predicted that the Democrats need to win 53.5 percent of all votes cast for the two major parties just to have a 50/50 chance of winning a majority in the House. They found a similar Republican advantage in the Senate: "adding together all the votes from the most recent election of

then, it can be "loser-take-all" when the popular vote-winning party fails to win a majority of the Senate seats or Electoral College votes.[46]

The practice of partisan gerrymandering upheld by the Supreme Court in the 2019 case of *Rucho vs. Common Cause*[47] reduces the competitiveness of representative elections and enhances the partisan advantage of whichever party controls a state legislature in the year following the census every decade.[48] Further, the shift toward binding primaries to choose candidates in both parties over the last several decades rewards the extremes in a polarized context because partisan activists are the ones who vote in primary elections and who exhibit the most affective polarization.[49] As Milkis and King note: "the pursuit of 'participatory democracy' did not empower the Downsian median-voter; rather, the weakening of traditional party organizations enhanced the influence of donors, interest groups and social activists who scorned the pragmatic politics and compromises hitherto credited with forging majority coalitions."[50]

In 2020, following a long period of deepening polarization including along urban-rural lines, all of these institutional factors favored the Republican Party: The chances of an inversion of the Electoral College, where the winner of the popular vote loses the Electoral College, favored the Republican Party 65 percent of the time in close elections.[51] The Republican Party controlled twenty-nine state legislatures compared to the Democratic Party controlling nineteen and two states with split legislatures; thus the Republican Party had an advantage going into the 2021–2 redistricting period. And while the disproportion in the Senate has historically given 30 percent of the population 70 percent of the Senate

---

each senator, Republicans got only 46% of them, and they hold 51 of the seats," www.economist.com/briefing/2018/07/12/americas-electoral-system-gives-the-republicans-advantages-over-democrats.

[46] The concept of "loser-take-all" was suggested by Dan Slater.

[47] www.supremecourt.gov/opinions/18pdf/18-422_9ol1.pdf.

[48] State legislatures normally draw state and Congressional legislative districts; in 2019, only eight states had independent redistricting commissions, https://ballotpedia.org/Independent_redistricting_commissions.

[49] Leonie Huddy, Lilliana Mason, and Lene Aarøe, "Expressive Partisanship: Campaign Involvement, Political Emotion, and Partisan Identity," *American Political Science Review* 109, no. 1 (2015): 1–17; Lilliana Mason, *Uncivil Agreement: How Politics Became Our Identity* (Chicago: The University of Chicago Press, 2018).

[50] Milkis and King, Ch. 11, this volume.

[51] Michael Geruso, Dean Spears, and Ishaana Talesara, "Inversions in US Presidential Elections: 1836–2016," Working Paper, National Bureau of Economic Research, September 2019. https://doi.org/10.3386/w26247.

vote,[52] the increasing geographic sorting of the parties into rural and urban states tilted this advantage, and its accompanying advantage in the Electoral College, toward the Republican Party with its rural base.[53]

We argued previously that as the perception of existential threat from the "Other" camp rises, the incentive to hold onto, or gain power, at all costs is strong. The normal centralizing logic of the Downsian median voter in a two-party system instead shifts toward a centrifugal pressure in a polarized system with disproportionate representation. Though Republicans have consistently been a minority party in the national popular vote since 1992 (winning a popular vote majority for president only in 2004), the incentive to diversify and expand their voter base is changed by the institutional advantages described here. As Ezra Klein notes, "Republicans are trapped in a dangerous place: They represent a shrinking constituency that holds vast political power."[54] Rather than support reforms to ensure more equal representation, the logic of polarization further incentivizes and capacitates the party to lock in their base with polarizing emotional appeals and entrench their majority using legal maneuvers such as gerrymandering and questionable practices of voter suppression to survive in the face of demographic changes predicting a continually shrinking base of their core identity voters.

Polarizing Around Formative Rifts: A Vulnerability

As discussed earlier, we identify formative rifts as unresolved debates over citizenship, national identity, and state roles from the country's founding or refounding.[55] Polarizing around these debates appears to contribute to more entrenched pernicious polarization. In the United States, the basic question of citizenship and who enjoys the rights espoused by the founding fathers has been debated since the establishment of the republic and its differentiated citizenship for African slaves, Native Americans, and women. Subsequent divisive issues centered on birthright citizenship and

---

[52] www.washingtonpost.com/news/politics/wp/2017/11/28/by-2040-two-thirds-of-americans-will-be-represented-by-30-percent-of-the-senate/.

[53] Bill Bishop, *The Big Sort: Why the Clustering of Like-Minded America Is Tearing Us Apart* (Boston: Mariner Books, 2009); Matt Motyl, "Liberals and Conservatives Are (Geographically) Dividing," in *Social Psychology of Political Polarization*, ed. P. Valdesolo and J. Graham (New York: Routledge, 2016).

[54] Ezra Klein, *Why We're Polarized* (New York: Avid Reader Press, 2020). Steven Levitsky made the same point at a keynote speech at Cornell University on Nov. 8, 2019.

[55] Somer and McCoy, "Transformations Through Polarizations."

naturalized citizenship. As Jill Lepore argues, at the heart of these conflicts is the dispute over the origin of truth, whether from God or the laws of nature, and the application of Thomas Jefferson's "these truths" of political equality, natural rights, and sovereignty of the people.[56] The deep polarization over these competing narratives of citizenship rights and roles of faith and reason led to the 1860–5 Civil War, evolving versions of legal and informal discrimination against and segregation of African Americans during the Jim Crow era of 1877–1964, and repolarization in the late twentieth century that turned particularly rancorous during the Obama and Trump administrations.

The identity-based sorting of political parties over the last fifty years is rooted in the formative rifts over race and religion. The movement of white working-class voters from the Democratic camp to the Republican camp has been occurring since 1964, when Lyndon Johnson firmly aligned the Democratic Party with the cause of civil rights for African Americans in the passage of the Civil Rights Act.[57] The Christian Right movement became active politically, marginalizing moderate Republicans, as early as Jimmy Carter's administration in the late 1970s, first in reaction to the Supreme Court's abortion decision in *Roe v. Wade* (1973) and then in reaction to Carter's attempts to revoke tax exemptions for segregated religious schools.[58] The movement of white evangelicals and other religious conservatives to the Republican Party continued in the 1980s when Ronald Reagan and the party came out for the repeal of *Roe v. Wade*. These voter shifts and the Southern Democratic political party realignment in the 1970s and 1980s led to increased party polarization in the 1990s and 2000s as Americans sorted into more ideologically homogeneous political parties, perceived the parties as growing further apart on policies, and their representatives in Congress voted in more lock-step party unity roll-call votes.[59]

By the twenty-first century, the Republican Party had become more homogenous with its core of white, older, and evangelical Christian voters, while the Democratic party became more diverse but concentrated

---

[56] Jill Lepore, *These Truths: a History of the United States* (New York: W.W. Norton, 2019).
[57] Robert Mickey, *Paths out of Dixie: The Democratization of Authoritarian Enclaves in America's Deep South* (Princeton: Princeton University Press, 2015).
[58] Daniel Schlozman, *Achieving Radical Change: Social Movements and the Partisan Promise* (Princeton: Princeton University Press, 2015).
[59] James E. Campbell, *Polarized: Making Sense of a Divided America* (Princeton: Princeton University Press, 2018); "Partisanship and Political Animosity in 2016," Pew Research, 2016.

in racial minorities, non-Christian identifiers, and urban voters.[60] Obama's presidency disappointed those who hoped that the United States had entered a post-racial political era. Instead, scholars argued that racial resentment, ethno-nationalism, and racial prejudice played a major role in predicting voting choice among whites in the next two presidential elections, costing Obama votes in his second election in 2012 and lending votes to Trump in 2016.[61]

Scholars analyzing the 2016 campaign and election of Donald Trump have argued that the prior alignment between racial and religious social identities and partisanship, along with the candidates' activation of ethnic and racial identities, determined the outcome. Sides, Tesler and Vavreck argue not only that racial anxiety rather than economic anxiety explained the 2016 outcome, but also that longer-term trends of increasing partisanship and growing alignment between group identities and partisanship since the Civil Rights Act of 1964 intensified the party divisions and resulting polarization during the Obama presidency.[62] Likewise, Abramowitz and McCoy show how racial resentment in the United States – responding to perceived unfair benefits or redress for historical legacies of discrimination – helps to explain voter realignment after 1964 and to predict the vote for Trump in the 2016 US elections. They argue that Donald Trump's candidacy "reinforced some of the deepest social and cultural divisions within the American electorate – those based on race and religion."[63] Thus, longer-term trends of partisan realignment along racial and religious social identities combined with the Trump and Clinton campaigns' emphasis on gender and racial identities. These emphases renewed the salience of historic unresolved formative rifts from the nation's founding, contributing to the potential for a pernicious polarization.

---

[60] Lee, Ch.4, this volume; Mason, *Uncivil Disagreement*.

[61] Alan I. Abramowitz, "Donald Trump, Partisan Polarization, and the 2016 Presidential Election," *Sabato's Crystal Ball*, 2016; Jonathan Knuckey and Kim Myunghee, "Racial Resentment, Old-Fashioned Racism, and the Vote Choice of Southern and Nonsouthern Whites in the 2012 U.S. Presidential Election," *Social Science Quarterly* 94, no. 4 (2015): 905–22; Stephen Morgan and Lee Jiwon "The White Working Class and Voter Turnout in U.S. Presidential Elections, 2004 to 2016," *Sociological Science* 4, no. 27 (2017): 656–85; Michael Tesler, "Analysis | Views About Race Mattered More in Electing Trump than in Electing Obama," *Washington Post*, 2016.

[62] John Sides, Michael Tesler, and Lynn Vavreck, *Identity Crisis the 2016 Presidential Campaign and the Battle for the Meaning of America* (Princeton: Princeton University Press, 2019).

[63] Abramowitz and McCoy, "United States: Racial Resentment," 137–38.

After four contentious years and the increasing visibility of white nationalist and white supremacist movements during the Trump administration, the Black Lives Matter movement begun earlier in the decade in response to police shootings of unarmed Black persons suddenly took on a visibility in the wake of massive, multiracial protests following the May 2020 murder of George Floyd by a Minneapolis policeman. The formative rift over racial inequities and injustice came to center stage in the country's polarized election campaign.

Opposition Mobilization and Strategy

As we described previously, both political incumbents and oppositions have incentives to polarize to achieve their goals, whether to simply gain and retain power or to achieve more transformative political, social, and economic change. When an opposition chooses to reciprocate polarization, it risks moving toward an equilibrium of pernicious polarization, resulting either in government dysfunction and careening between roughly balanced poles, or killing democracy with an authoritarian backlash (e.g., military coup or extra-constitutional impeachment) to remove the polarizing incumbent. Likewise when an opposition abdicates due to weakness or internal rivalries, they can also kill democracy as a polarizing incumbent enhances his/her own political power.

Nevertheless, we posit three strategies that could potentially contain or reverse pernicious polarization and its harm to democracy: use legal institutional means to constrain incumbent abuses of power; counter-mobilize to proactively depolarize with national unity messages and centrist policy proposals to reach across the divide, particularly in electoral mobilization; and re-polarize around an inclusive, transformative social justice or democracy-reforming program. In other countries, oppositions often turn to the first two of these containment strategies after failing with strategies that deepen pernicious polarization. For example, in Venezuela the opposition first attempted to counter-mobilize against Hugo Chavez in 2002–5 with massive protest marches, a failed coup attempt, a national strike, a recall referendum, and an electoral boycott all aimed at removing Chavez from power. Chavez retained power and strengthened his position, particularly after a legislative boycott in 2005 gave him the means to constitutionally appoint all the members of the public accountability entities with no opposition participation. After a demoralizing and fragmented period, the opposition parties regrouped and by 2010 they had united sufficiently to win a significant number of governorships and representation in the legislature, and by 2015 a unified opposition won two-thirds of the national legislative seats.

In the United States, evidence of movement toward a pernicious equilibrium became clear with the reaction to the 2008 election of the first African American president, Barack Obama. McAdam and Kloos identify the Obama era as a peak of polarization and a lack of cooperation between the two parties to that date, contending that nothing (up to that point) compares "to the acrimony, bitterness, and willful sabotage of policymaking that has characterized Barack Obama's time in office."[64] Counter-mobilization both by citizens and the opposition Republican party in the Congress heightened polarization even when the incumbent president was striving to unify the nation and overcome partisan divides.

At the societal level, Obama's election spurred a counter-mobilization of white, conservative, and evangelical voters in the Tea Party movement. The early Tea Party movement expressed anger and resentment at the distributive injustice of welfare programs for "undeserving" immigrants, minorities, and youth, while favoring entitlement programs like Social Security and Medicare for "hard-working" Americans.[65] For McAdam and Kloos, the harsh response to Obama's administration is rooted in "a racially inflected Tea Party movement that is largely responsible for the deepening divisions and government dysfunction"[66]

Partly responding to pressure from this mass-level organization, the Republican party adopted an obstructionist policy and the Democratic party failed to resist the temptation to engage in a tit-for-tat exchange, locking both into a negative-sum game of constitutional hardball. The pernicious consequences of this polarization resulted in government dysfunction, unilateral policymaking by the Obama administration, and abandonment of longstanding democratic norms, particularly the consensus-promoting mechanism of the filibuster and cloture rules of the US Senate used in appointment processes in the Senate. Even as a Senate minority, Republicans used institutional means to block Obama's nominees, and Democrats responded by eliminating the filibuster for federal judicial appointments and presidential appointments in 2013. This strategy would come back to haunt the Democrats when

---

[64] Doug McAdam, and Karina Kloos, *Deeply Divided: Racial Politics and Social Movements in Post-War America* (Oxford: Oxford University Press, 2016): 253.
[65] Theda Skocpol, and Vanessa Williamson. *The Tea Party and the Remaking of Republican Conservatism* (Oxford: Oxford University Press, 2016).
[66] McAdam and Kloos, *Deeply Divided*, 255.

they became the minority party first in 2015 and continued into the next Republican administration of Donald Trump. Republicans employed a particularly egregious tactic of constitutional hardball when they blocked Obama's Supreme Court nominee during the last year of his presidency. The mutual reciprocity of constitutional hardball continued into the Trump administration as Democrats called the Republican bluff and the latter employed the "nuclear option," removing the filibuster for a second Trump Supreme Court Justice nominee and swinging the balance to a conservative majority. The Republican-led Senate also filled a record number of lower-level judicial nominations in rapid succession with their newfound freedom, provided by the Democrats in 2013, to bypass the sixty-vote rule.

In 2016, the identity-based partisan sorting and accompanying affective polarization of the previous two decades produced a surprising win for Donald Trump, whose campaign rhetoric was starkly polarizing and antiestablishment, dividing the country between "Us" – the "real" Americans who hungered for a return to an idealized past when industrial jobs provided for upward mobility and white males were in charge in the workplace and the family – and "Them" – the immigrants, minorities, and liberal elites who had wrought "American carnage."[67] In an example of using polarizing tactics to sideline critics and potential moderates within a polarizing leader's own camp, Trump's strategy to capture the Republican Party from the outside first used polarizing tactics during the Republican presidential primary to outbid his rivals. After taking office, he continued to use an Us vs. Them logic to discredit his critics within the party. For example, he described Mitt Romney, who voted for his impeachment in 2020, as "too weak to beat the Democrats then so he's joining them now. He's officially a member of the *resistance* [emphasis ours]."[68]

Levels of existential threat were also rising as affective polarization deepened. The Pew Research Center documents a rise in just three years in perceptions of existential threat that supporters of each party viewed as being posed by the other party: in 2014, 27 percent of Democrats viewed Republican policies as threatening to the nation's well-being, and 36 percent of Republicans viewed Democratic policies as such a threat. By 2016, those numbers had risen, and converged, to 41 percent and 45 percent,

---

[67] Trump Inaugural speech. January 21, 2017.
[68] Brakkton Booker, "Trump Blasts Romney Over Impeachment Vote." National Public Radio, February 6, 2020.

respectively.[69] Following the causal chain we posited earlier, these mutual perceptions of existential threat are expected to incentivize voters and politicians alike to contemplate and tolerate abandonment or violation of democratic norms. They create perceptions of a zero-sum game and a state of exception, and change the incentives for political actors and their respective bases.

In this context of hyper-partisanship and existential threat, Trump's victory spawned another grass-roots counter-mobilization, this time on the left and among college-educated women, who marched and ran for political office in massive numbers, as well as among scientists. Citizens poured into the street to protest specific Trump policies early on, judges blocked some of the early attempts to curtail Muslim immigration, and civil servants resisted impetuous decision-making.

The Democratic Party, however, pursued a bifurcated policy: it both engaged in reciprocating polarization tactics, replicating constitutional hardball maneuvers described here under extreme pressure from its base to oppose the Supreme Court nomination of justice Brett Kavanaugh, while also pursuing a depolarizing counter-mobilization strategy – recruiting new moderate candidates for the 2018 midterms and mobilizing electorally. The results of this bifurcated strategy were, not surprisingly, mixed: the Democratic party in opposition was unable to slow or change the course of the tidal wave of Republican appointments of Supreme Court justices and lower-level judges. But its electoral counter-mobilization succeeded in producing a massive Democratic victory to take back the House of Representatives in the 2018 midterm elections. The winning strategy there was flexibility – allowing states and local electorates to nominate candidates appropriate for their districts, whether more moderate to conservative, or more progressive.

The second impetus from the Democratic base – the growing cry to impeach Donald Trump – was resisted by House Speaker Nancy Pelosi for some time for fear of the politicization of that accountability mechanism in the hyperpolarized Congress. It was not until she determined that the president's alleged attempt to pressure the Ukrainian government to intervene in the 2020 elections was so grave that the threat of inaction was greater than the threat of a politicized process further dividing the country that she decided to move forward with an impeachment inquiry. As described here, the result was deepened polarization.

---

[69] Pew Research Center, "Partisanship and Polarization," 2016.

The Democratic Party thus entered the 2020 election year with heightened polarization and a strong desire to defeat the incumbent electorally as its first priority. One strategic dilemma for the party and its voters in nominating a candidate was to decide between two of the strategic choices we outlined: seek to actively depolarize through a centrist, unifying message focused on the safest candidate to oust a threatening incumbent through democratic means; or counter-polarize with a transformative programmatic message calling for radical change that might also address some of the underlying grievances that had opened the door to Trump's style of polarizing populism. Neither of the Democratic offerings employed the exclusionary logic of the Trump administration. Instead, both strategies focused on electoral mobilization and emphasized the need to restore and protect democratic norms.

The Democrats chose, in the end, the depolarizing, centrist strategy of candidate Joe Biden, based on safety and familiarity in a time of heightened threat, over the more transformative but also class-based repolarization strategy of Bernie Sanders. Learning from the costs of a similar division in 2016, the party united more energetically in 2020 to defeat Donald Trump. Nevertheless, while distaste for Trump personally contributed to his defeat, the status quo results down the ballot, eschewing the wave election the Democrats had hoped for, reflected the persistent deep divides in the country.

A second strategic dilemma was whether to mobilize by appealing to identity politics or programmatic policy ideas. As we argued earlier, appealing to identity politics can be more polarizing. The Democrats' mobilization against Trump since his election has been two-pronged. One was linked with the formative rift originating in differential racial and gender rights, in which Democrats targeted what they perceived as the Trump camp's racism and misogyny. The other, however, led by the "progressive" wing of Sanders and Warren focused on socioeconomic injustice and corruption. While African Americans played a big role in both Obama's and Biden's election, the Democratic Party is not anchored in any single racial movement.[70] Add to this the continuing demographic change toward a majority-minority society, and the Democrats are likely to have more flexibility to avoid forming their programs around the identity-based formative rifts than the Republicans, who have

---

[70] Daniel Schlozman, *When Movements Anchor Parties: Electoral Alignments in American History* (Princeton: Princeton University Press, 2015).

increasingly been anchored in the Christian Right movement and white identity politics.

CONCLUSION

We have argued that the United States has been in the process of pernicious polarization since at least the Obama election. However, the United States may not yet have reached a pernicious equilibrium that renders pernicious polarization self-propagating by locking both incumbent and opposition actors into polarizing behavior. We are less sanguine than some scholars that the constitution and democratic institutions will guarantee democratic resilience in the United States. The reason is that once institutions are politicized, or captured by polarized partisan interests to do their bidding, they become an engine of polarization and consequent democratic erosion, rather than serve as a constraint on such behavior. We also highlight the importance of electoral institutions at times of polarization and the need for reform to make them more transparent and less vulnerable to partisan gerrymandering and voter suppression.

As we have argued, the United States exhibits vulnerabilities that we have identified in our comparative work as risk factors for pernicious polarization and harmful consequences to democracy: majoritarian electoral institutions that can be manipulated to award increasingly disproportionate representation to the governing party and engender perceptions of winner-take-all outcomes; polarization around formative rifts rooted in race, gender, and religion; mass-based political parties each with mobilization capacity that can be used for divisive, polarizing mobilization and counter-mobilization; and partisanship linked to social identities that gives rise to affective polarization.

At the same time, sources of resilience that we identified in the introduction are evident, at least to a nascent degree: opposition capacities for counter-mobilization around democracy-enhancing aims, institutional accountability mechanisms that resist politicization, and collective self-reflection capacities that may give rise to internal party renewal and social learning. Grass-roots mobilization and creativity provided resistance to what these groups saw as the most egregious policies of the Trump administration, and recruited new political candidates from underrepresented groups, especially women, to expand representation in elected institutions in the 2018 mid-term and state-level elections. Both political parties mobilized the largest turn-out in American electoral history in the 2020 elections and characterized the election as decisive for the survival of

American democracy and its way of life. In this case, the Democratic party successfully employed an active depolarization strategy to mobilize its traditional base and new voters to defeat the incumbent Republican party's continuation of its polarizing rhetoric.

Institutional accountability mechanisms have functioned to a large degree, in spite of Donald Trump's attempts to politicize them, as judges, intelligence agents, internal watchdogs, and federal and state civil servants provided a bulwark to resist implementing his most divisive and exclusionary policies. In the 2020 elections, state-level election officials maintained election integrity amidst a pandemic and resisted, along with state and federal courts, Trump's attempts to overturn the results.

Finally, the society's capacity for collective self-reflection was evident in the emergence of grass-roots organizations bringing citizens together across the partisan divide in depolarizing efforts after the 2016 elections. In the wake of the massive protests following George Floyd's murder in May 2020, we saw a significant change in attitudes toward racial injustice and attempts by many citizens to educate themselves about the history of American systemic racism and white privilege. This could provide the basis for the generative change needed to address the formative rift of racial injustice in the coming years.

Our account of the US resilience and vulnerability to pernicious polarization has emphasized the importance of agency, particularly of incumbent and opposition leaders and parties. Whether American democracy becomes locked into a self-propagating equilibrium of pernicious polarization depends not only on the societal and institutional capacities of resilience discussed here, but crucially on the mobilizational and self-reflective capacities of the political parties themselves, and on their willingness to choose strategies to overcome rather than deepen polarization and its democracy-threatening consequences.

In the opposition during the Trump administration, the Democratic party showed the political will and deliberative capacity to at least consider multiple strategies in their opposition to a polarizing president and governing party. While the Democratic party has not consistently resisted the temptation to engage in reciprocal polarization in the form of constitutional hardball, neither has it succumbed to extra-constitutional measures or the abuse of institutional oversight mechanisms. The party's internal divisions, on the other hand, may hinder its ability to mobilize public opinion and political leverage to implement the generative policies that could turn polarization's vicious cycle into a virtuous one.

The Republican party, on the other hand, has demonstrated a new source of polarization – the role that an opposition party can play in initiating a process of pernicious polarization, unlike most of our comparative cases focusing on polarizing figures who become incumbents. Beginning with Newt Gingrich's Contract for America in the House of Representatives in 1994, the party has consistently pursued an obstructionist strategy when in the opposition.

The Republican party's refusal to fulfill its oversight role in the face of Trump's breaches of democratic norms throughout his administration, or to stand up to Trump's blatant attempts to destroy confidence in the electoral process when he refused to accept his 2020 defeat, raise serious alarms that one US political party has converted to instrumental rather than principled democrats. The asymmetric polarization led by the Republican party and its apparent willingness to subvert democratic norms to entrench its political advantage using minoritarian institutions, gerrymandering, and voter suppression pose a significant threat to American democratic resilience. Four years of Donald Trump deliberately stoking rage and hate within the electorate, and destroying trust in critical electoral, media, scientific, and government institutions, ensures that societal polarization and mutual distrust will continue for some time. The perpetration of electoral disinformation by Republican insiders and the refusal of elected Republican officials to recognize Biden's victory, even after the electoral college vote on December 14, 2020, are the most serious threat to American democracy in the current era, following patterns of autocratizers worldwide.

The endogenous nature of polarization thus provides both hope and pessimism about American democracy's resilience: our analysis of the crucial role of agency points to the pernicious consequences of political actors choosing divisive polarizing strategies to further their aims, locking a polity into a downward spiral of Us vs. Them mutual distrust and incentivizing the erosion of democratic norms. But it also instills hope that collective learning and the deliberate choice of democratic values that benefit the national over narrow partisan interests might prevail and break the vicious cycle.

PART II

POLITICAL INSTITUTIONS IN POLARIZED TIMES

4

Crosscutting Cleavages, Political Institutions, and Democratic Resilience in the United States

Frances E. Lee

The evidence available suggests that the chances for stable democracy are enhanced to the extent that social strata, groups, and individuals have a number of cross-cutting politically relevant affiliations. Seymour Martin Lipset, 1959[1]

In the most deeply divided societies ... majority rule spells majority dictatorship and civil strife rather than democracy. What such societies need is a democratic regime ... that tries to maximize the size of the ruling majority instead of being satisfied with a bare majority. Arend Lijphart, 2012[2]

Crosscutting cleavages have long moderated party conflict in American politics and thereby contributed to democratic stability. Big-tent parties encompassing different races, ethnicities, religions, regions, classes, and other social identities tend to recruit and nominate moderate political leaders who can knit together disparate interests and avoid aggravating internal party divides. At the same time, crosscutting cleavages also make voters themselves less partisan and ideological, as various social affiliations pull and push them toward different parties.[3] In these ways,

---

For helpful comments on earlier drafts, I am grateful to the editors of this volume, Jim Curry, Jenny Mansbridge, Nicholas van de Walle, and Peter Katzenstein.

[1] Seymour Martin Lipset, "Some Social Requisites of Democracy: Economic Development and Political Legitimacy," *American Political Science Review* 53 (1959): 69–105, 97.

[2] Arend Lijpart, *Patterns of Democracy: Government Forms and Performance in Thirty-Six Countries* (New Haven: Yale University Press, 2012), 32.

[3] A large body of both recent and older scholarship offers evidence on this point. See, as prominent examples: Bernard R. Berelson, Paul F. Lazarsfeld, and William N. McPhee, *Voting: A Study of Opinion Formation in a Presidential Campaign* (Chicago: University of Chicago Press, 1954); Ted Brader, Joshua A. Tucker, and Andrew Therriault, "Cross

a political system characterized by two large, socially diverse, cross-pressured parties both lowers the stakes of politics and promotes moderation and compromise.

By a variety of indicators, however, American political parties in the electorate today increasingly diverge along lines of social identity.[4] In this chapter, I take stock of changes in the social composition of the parties in government. Concurrent with social sorting in the electorate, the parties in Congress have also differentiated along lines of race, gender, and religion. The result is a party system in which one congressional party is overwhelmingly white, male, and increasingly homogeneous in religious affiliation, while the other congressional party is more socially diverse than at any previous point. These deepened partisan social divides contribute to polarization and raise the perceived stakes of politics. With one congressional party less socially diverse than the country as a whole and the other more diverse than the country as a whole, congressional party composition amplifies America's identity-based political divides. Such divisions pose challenges for democracy inasmuch as perceived threats to personal and group identities "evoke deep and powerful emotions" and conflicts over "identities and ways of life cannot readily be settled by negotiation."[5]

Drawing on comparative work on democracy-building in divided societies,[6] I argue that the deeper social divide between the parties

---

Pressure Scores: An Individual-Level Measure of Cumulative Partisan Pressures Arising from Social Group Memberships," *Political Behavior* 36 (2014): 23–51; Paul Felix Lazarsfeld, Bernard Berelson, and Hazel Gaudet, *The People's Choice* (New York: Columbia University Press, 1948); Lilliana Mason, "'I Disrespectfully Agree': The Differential Effects of Partisan Sorting on Social and Issue Polarization," *American Journal of Political Science* 59 (2015): 128–45; Lilliana Mason, "A Cross-Cutting Calm: How Social Sorting Drives Affective Polarization," *Public Opinion Quarterly* 80 (2016): 351–77; Lilliana Mason, *Uncivil Agreement: How Politics Became Our Identity* (Chicago: University of Chicago Press, 2018); G. Bingham Powell, Jr., "Political Cleavage Structure, Cross-Pressure Processes, and Partisanship: An Empirical Test of the Theory," *American Journal of Political Science* 1 (1976): 1–23.

[4] Shanto Iyengar, Gaurav Sood, and Yphtach Lelkes, "Affect, Not Ideology: A Social Identity Perspective on Polarization," *Public Opinion Quarterly* 76 (2012): 405–31; Mason, "A Cross-Cutting Calm"; Mason, *Uncivil Agreement*.

[5] Robert A. Dahl, *Democracy and Its Critics* (New Haven: Yale University Press, 1989), 255.

[6] Donald I. Horowitz, *Ethnic Groups in Conflict* (Berkeley: University of California Press, 1985); Donald I. Horowitz, *A Democratic South Africa? Constitutional Engineering in a Divided Society* (Berkeley: University of California Press, 1991); Arend Lijphart, *Democracy in Plural Societies: A Comparative Exploration* (New Haven: Yale University Press, 1977); Lijphart, *Patterns of Democracy*.

makes the stability of American democracy more dependent upon its complex political institutions. Structural features of US national government – especially, separation of powers, strong bicameralism, and federalism – routinely impose power-sharing requirements on the major parties. These features of the American political system thwart and restrain the ambitions of today's more socially sorted and ideologically distinctive political parties.

Even amidst the pressures of rising party polarization, US governing institutions continue to force bipartisan accommodation, conciliation, and compromise. Despite intense and pervasive partisan conflict, legislation enacted by the polarized Congress rests on the same large, bipartisan majorities characteristic of the less polarized era.[7] Congress retains considerable capacity to check the executive, both in legislation and oversight.[8] Bicameralism[9] and federalism[10] likewise force bipartisan negotiation between and across institutions and levels of government. No doubt, power sharing in a deeply divided polity risks policy immobilism and ineffectiveness.[11] But the system erects high hurdles to partisan action, forces accommodation, and promotes democratic stability – all valuable features for governing a divided polity.

---

[7] James M. Curry and Frances E. Lee, "Non-Party Government: Bipartisan Lawmaking and Party Power in Congress," *Perspectives on Politics* 17 (2019): 47–65; James M. Curry and Frances E. Lee, *The Limits of Party: Congress and Lawmaking in a Polarized Era* (Chicago: University of Chicago Press, 2020).

[8] Douglas L. Kriner and Eric Schickler, *Investigating the President: Congressional Checks on Presidential Power* (Princeton: Princeton University Press, 2016); David R. Mayhew, *Partisan Balance: The Presidency, the Senate, and the House* (Princeton: Princeton University Press, 2010).

[9] Sarah A. Binder, *Stalemate: Causes and Consequences of Legislative Gridlock* (Washington, DC: Brookings Institution Press, 2003).

[10] Jessica Bulman-Pozen and Heather K. Gerken, "Uncooperative Federalism," *Yale Law Journal* 118 (2009): 1256–310; David Brian Robertson, *Federalism and the Making of America* (New York: Routledge, 2011).

[11] Binder, *Stalemate*; Sarah A. Binder, 2014. "Polarized We Govern?" Center for Effective Public Management, Brookings Institution, www.brookings.edu/wp-content/uploads/2016/06/BrookingsCEPM_Polarized_figReplacedTextRevTableRev.pdf; Nolan McCarty, "Polarization and the Changing American Constitutional System," in *Can America Govern Itself?*, eds. Frances E. Lee and Nolan McCarty (Cambridge: Cambridge University Press, 2019), 301–28; Suzanne Mettler, "The Policyscape and the Challenges of Contemporary Politics to Policy Maintenance," *Perspectives on Politics* 14 (2016): 369–90.

SOCIAL SORTING AND THE DECLINE OF CROSSCUTTING CLEAVAGES

Crosscutting cleavages in American politics have markedly declined since the mid-twentieth century when scholars regularly pointed to them as a strength of American democracy. Most notably, religion, region, race, ethnicity, and gender now tend to distinguish the parties from one another. Rather than cutting across the parties, fundamental societal identities and affiliations tend to cumulate in one direction and push voters toward a single party.

Describing these reinforcing and overlapping social identities, Mason terms partisanship in contemporary American politics a "mega identity," such that "a single vote can now indicate a person's partisan preference *as well as* his or her religion, race, ethnicity, gender, neighborhood, and favorite grocery store."[12] Theorizing about the likely effect of cumulating cleavages, Lipset wrote:

> The more reinforced and correlated the sources of cleavage, the less the likelihood for political tolerance. Similarly, on the level of group and individual behavior, the greater the isolation from heterogeneous political stimuli, the more that background factors "pile up" in one direction, the greater the chances that the group or individual will have an extremist perspective.[13]

Recent developments lend new credence to longstanding hypotheses that cumulative, reinforcing social cleavages drive extremism and reduced toleration. The decline of identity-based cross-pressures likely stands at the root of some of the growing partisan gap in voters' policy preferences,[14] though there remains considerable debate about the extent of issue polarization in the mass electorate.[15]

There is less debate about the growth of partisan affective polarization in American politics, meaning the extent to which partisans feel animosity, dislike, and distrust toward their partisan

---

[12] Mason, *Uncivil Agreement*, 14. [13] Lipset, "Some Social Requisites," 97.
[14] Alan I. Abramowitz and Kyle L. Saunders, "Is Polarization a Myth?" *Journal of Politics* 70 (2008): 542–55; Pew Research Center, "Political Polarization in the American Public," June 2014, www.people-press.org/wp-content/uploads/sites/4/2014/06/6-12-2014-Political-Polarization-Release.pdf.
[15] Morris P. Fiorina, Samuel A. Abrams, and Jeremy C. Pope, "Polarization in the American Public: Misconceptions and Misreadings," *Journal of Politics* 70 (2008): 556–60; Morris P. Fiorina, Samuel A. Abrams, and Jeremy C. Pope, *Culture War? The Myth of a Polarized America*, 3rd ed. (Pearson, Longman, 2011).

opponents.[16] Americans clearly harbor more aversion and animus toward the opposing party now than in past decades.[17] Declining cross-pressures among social identities have contributed to this increase in affective polarization.[18] Indeed, the intensity of partisan animosity can even be independent of opinion on policy issues.[19] Put differently, Americans do not even need to disagree on policy issues to dislike or even detest the opposing party on the basis of social identity.

Building on this research on the mass electorate, I review trends here on the extent of social sorting in Congress. As will be evident, several fundamental social identities crosscut the parties less today than in the 1970s and 1980s. The two parties in Congress have grown markedly more distinct in terms of gender, race, and religion. Sorting, however, has not occurred in terms of members' social class background.

Gender

Before 1990, women were gradually increasing their presence in both congressional parties. After 1990, the two parties diverged. As displayed in Figure 4.1, women steadily and sharply increased as a share of the Democratic Party in Congress following the so-called "Year of the Woman" in 1992. By contrast, Republicans in Congress stopped becoming more gender diverse after 2004.

No doubt, the congressional parties' divergence in their share of women has its root in both voter preferences and recruitment processes. Over the period, women increased as a share of the Democratic Party in the

---

[16] Iyengar et al., "Affect, Not Ideology"; Shanto Iyengar and Sean J. Westwood, "Fear and Loathing Across Party Lines: New Evidence on Group Polarization," *American Journal of Political Science* 59 (2015): 690–707.
[17] Shanto Iyengar, Yphtach Lelkes, Matthew Levendusky, Neil Malhotra, and Sean J. Westwood, "The Origins and Consequences of Affective Polarization in the United States," *Annual Review of Political Science* 22 (2019): 129–46.
[18] Mason, "I Disrespectfully Agree"; Mason, *Uncivil Agreement*.
[19] Leonie Huddy, Lilliana Mason, and Lene Aarøe, "Expressive Partisanship: Campaign Involvement, Political Emotion, and Partisan Identity," *American Political Science Review* 109 (2015): 1–17; Iyengar et al., "Affect Not Ideology," 2012; Mason, *Uncivil Agreement*; Lilliana Mason and Julie Wronski, "One Tribe to Bind Them All: How Our Social Group Attachments Strengthen Partisanship," *Political Psychology* 39 (2018): 257–77.

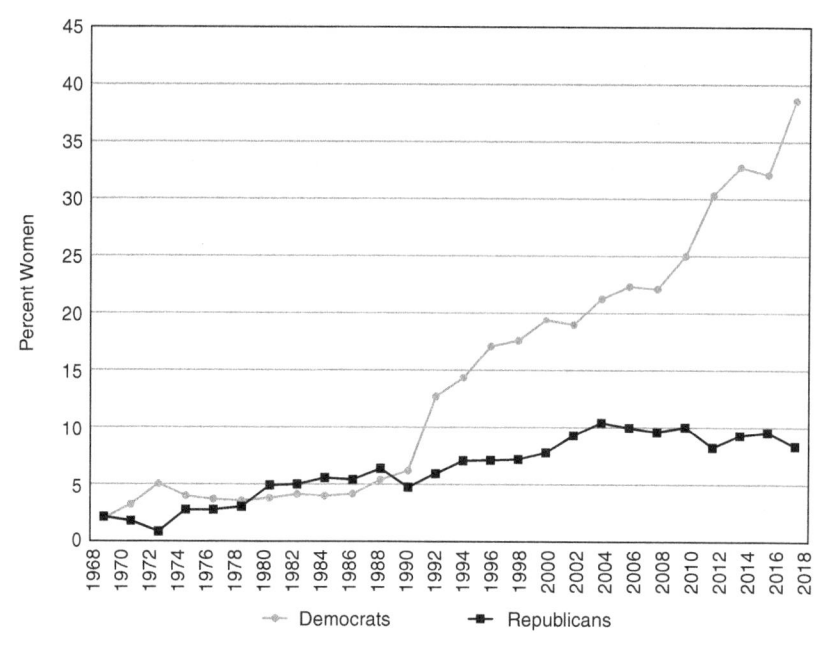

FIGURE 4.1 Women in Congress by party
Source: *Vital Statistics on Congress*; House and Senate data combined

electorate.[20] Comparative work has also shown that women make up a larger share of left- and center-left legislative parties cross-nationally.[21] Thomsen contends that partisan sorting on gender occurred partly due to a relative dearth of conservative women who had won office at lower levels and were available in the pipeline as potential Republican candidates for Congress.[22]

Regardless of the causal mechanisms driving the shift, the resulting contrast is stark: among members of the 116th Congress (2019–20), nearly 40 percent of Democrats are women, as compared to only 8 percent of Republicans. Congress's partisan gender divide reflects the gender gap

---

[20] Pew Research Center, "Wide Gender Gap, Growing Educational Divide in Voters' Party Identification," March 2018, www.people-press.org/2018/03/20/wide-gender-gap-growing-educational-divide-in-voters-party-identification/.

[21] Miki Caul Kittilson, *Challenging Parties, Changing Parliaments: Women and Elected Office in Contemporary Western Europe* (Columbus: Ohio State University Press, 2006).

[22] Danielle M. Thomsen, "Why So Few (Republican) Women? Explaining the Partisan Imbalance of Women in the U.S. Congress," *Legislative Studies Quarterly* 40 (2015): 295–323.

in the electorate. The gender gap in presidential voting first emerged in 1964 and has tended to grow, albeit with fluctuation, over time.[23] But even at its highest point to date – 24 percentage points in the 2016 presidential election[24] – the gender gap in presidential voting pales in comparison with the 32-percentage point gender difference in the composition of the parties in Congress.

Religion

As gauged by the presence of evangelical Christians – the largest religious group in the United States, constituting just over a quarter of the population – the parties in Congress have also sorted out along religious lines. As is evident in Figure 4.2, evangelicals made up roughly the same share

FIGURE 4.2 Evangelicals in Congress by party
Source: Nicole Asmussen Mathew (2018); House and Senate data combined

---

[23] Karen M. Kaufmann, "The Gender Gap," *PS: Political Science & Politics* 39 (2006): 447–53.
[24] Danielle Paquette, "The Unexpected Voters Behind the Widest Gender Gap in Recorded Election History," *Washington Post*, December 9, 2016, www.washingtonpost.com/news/wonk/wp/2016/11/09/men-handed-trump-the-election/.

of both congressional parties in the late 1960s. But since the 1970s, evangelicals have steadily sorted out of the Democratic Party and into the Republican Party.[25] The entry of evangelical Christians as an organized movement in American politics – along with the rise of the culture-war issues of abortion, feminism, and gay rights – helped drive this partisan sorting along religious lines.[26] But the effect also runs the other direction, with voters' partisan affiliations affecting their religious commitments.[27]

No matter the causal roots of the change, the result is a deep partisan-religious divide in Congress. In recent Congresses, evangelicals make up almost 40 percent of Republicans but less than 5 percent of Democrats, a 35-percentage point partisan gap. In voting behavior, by comparison, white evangelical Christians are roughly 20–25 percentage points more likely to support Republicans than other white voters.[28]

Race

As the US population has become more racially diverse since the 1960s, virtually all of that diversity is represented in the Democratic Party in Congress. Put differently, the congressional Democratic Party has grown steadily more racially and ethnically diverse since the late 1970s, such that nearly 40 percent of the party is currently Black (20 percent), Hispanic (13 percent), or Asian (5 percent). Meanwhile, as shown in Figure 4.3, the nation's increasing diversity has bypassed the congressional Republican Party, leaving its racial composition largely unchanged. Nonwhites have never made up more than 5 percent of Republicans in Congress.

As stark as is the racial divide between the parties in Congress, the racial gap in the electorate yawns just as wide. In 2016, for example, 58 percent of white non-Hispanic voters preferred candidate Trump as compared to only 8 percent of Black voters and 36 percent of Hispanics,

---

[25] Nicole Asmussen Mathew, "Evangelizing Congress: The Emergence of Evangelical Republicans and Party Polarization in Congress," *Legislative Studies Quarterly* 43 (2018): 409–55.

[26] Geoffrey Layman, *The Great Divide: Religious and Cultural Conflict in American Party Politics* (New York: Columbia University Press, 2001).

[27] Michele F. Margolis, *From Politics to the Pews: How Partisanship and the Political Environment Shape Religious Identity* (Chicago: University of Chicago Press, 2018).

[28] Jessica Martinez and Gregory A. Smith, "How the Faithful Voted: A Preliminary 2016 Analysis," Pew Research Center, November 9, 2019, www.pewresearch.org/fact-tank/2016/11/09/how-the-faithful-voted-a-preliminary-2016-analysis/.

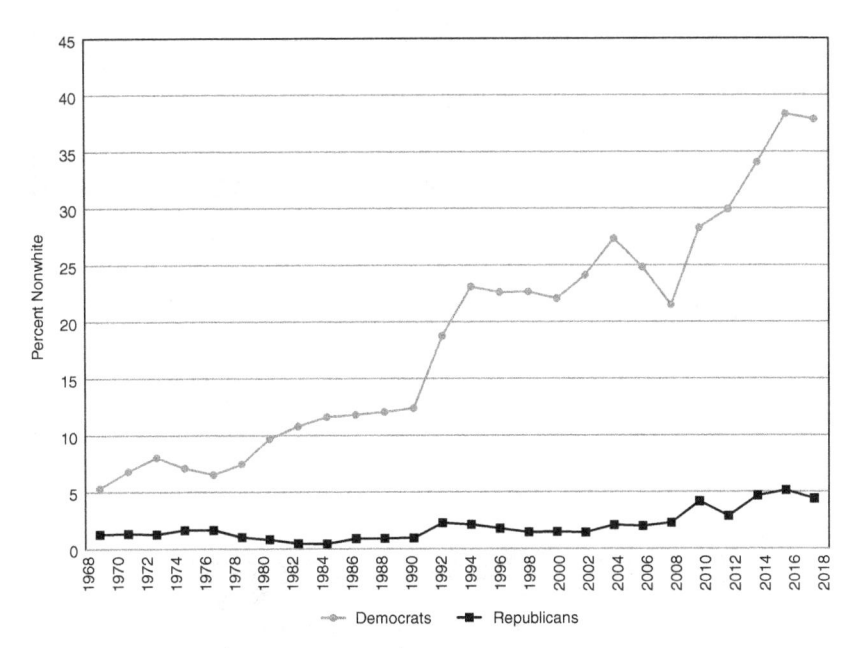

FIGURE 4.3 Nonwhites in Congress by party
Source: *Vital Statistics on Congress*; House and Senate data combined

yielding a racial gap of 50 and 22 percentage points respectively.[29] Without a shift in trendlines, the partisan-racial divide will also increase if racial and ethnic minorities achieve congressional representation proportionate to their share of the electorate. If the Democratic Party continues to absorb the nation's growing racial diversity, the racial gap between the parties in Congress will increase further. Projecting into the future, congresses of future decades may well pit a majority white party against a majority nonwhite party.

Social Class

Interestingly, there has been no trend toward congressional party sorting along the lines of educational background or income. The two parties in Congress do not differ much if at all on this dimension. Both parties

---

[29] Alec Tyson and Shiva Maniam, "Behind Trump's Victory: Divisions by Race, Gender, Education," Pew Research Center, November 9, 2019, www.pewresearch.org/fact-tank/2016/11/09/behind-trumps-victory-divisions-by-race-gender-education/.

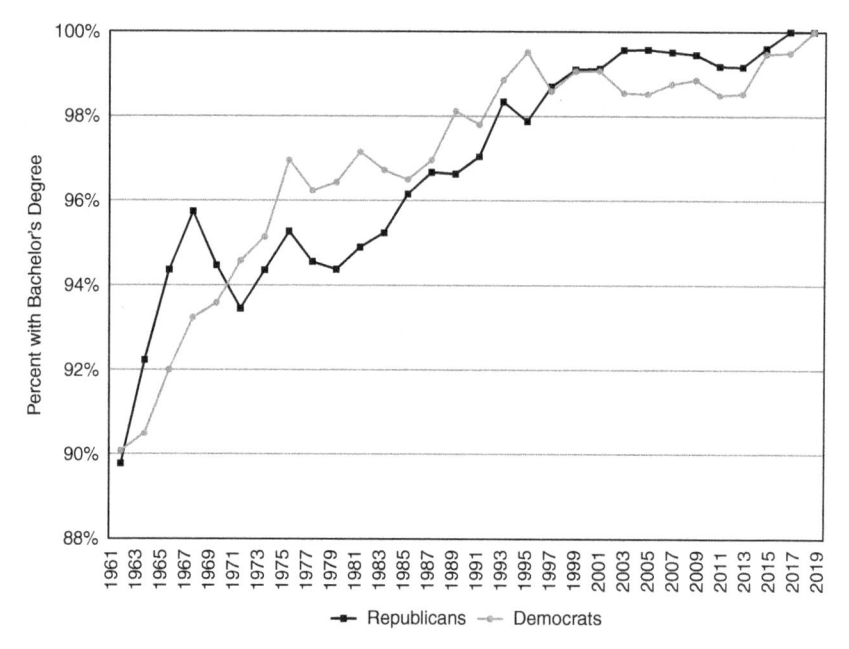

FIGURE 4.4 Educational attainment in Congress by party
Source: Casey Burgat and Charles Hunt (2018); House only

recruit from an elite stratum of society. There just simply is not much social class diversity in Congress.[30] People from working-class backgrounds do not and never have had much representation in Congress in either party. As shown in Figure 4.4, almost all members of the contemporary Congress have college degrees, as compared to 1/3 of American adults. The share of members with college degrees increased in both parties in tandem.

There is also little difference between the parties in Congress in the members' median net worth, as shown in Figure 4.5. Roughly 40 percent of Congress have a net worth in excess of a million dollars, while only about 3 percent of Americans have a net worth that high. Congressional Republicans were somewhat better off than Democrats in the first decade of the twenty-first century, but there is currently no overall difference

---

[30] Nicholas Carnes, *White-Collar Government: The Hidden Role of Class in Economic Policy Making* (Chicago: University of Chicago Press, 2013).

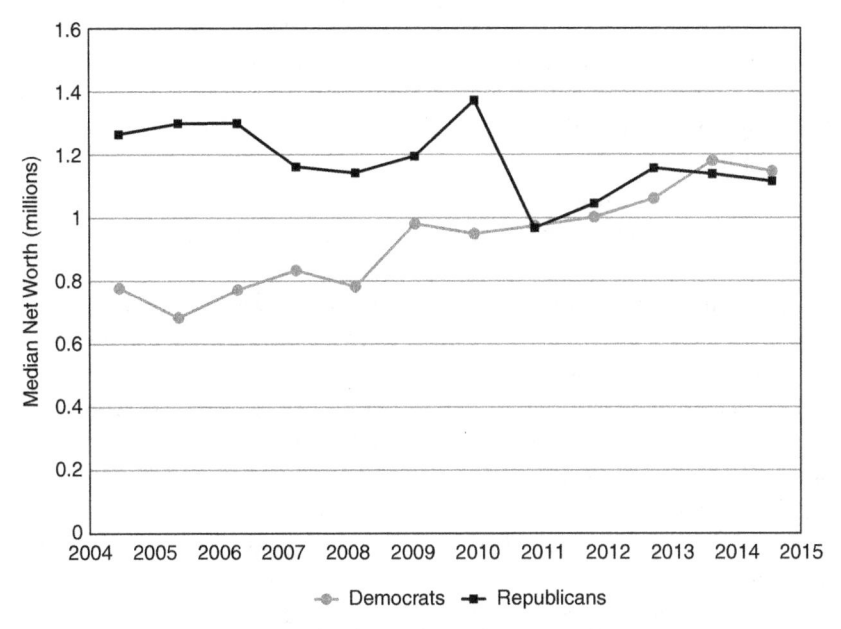

FIGURE 4.5 Median net worth of Members of Congress by party
Source: Center for Responsive Politics; House and Senate combined

between the parties on this measure. The two parties in Congress are thus markedly less sorted in terms of education and income than the parties in the electorate.[31]

Social Sorting Overall

Taken together, the social sorting evident in congressional party composition mirrors or even exaggerates the social sorting that has occurred among the parties in the electorate. The only exception examined here is that social class background matters less for parties in Congress than for parties in the electorate.[32] In short, many of the same sorting processes scholars have documented among partisans in the electorate have also occurred in Congress.

[31] Andrew Gelman, *Red State, Blue State, Rich State, Poor State: Why Americans Vote the Way They Do*, expanded ed. (Princeton: Princeton University Press, 2009); Jeffrey M. Stonecash, *Class and Party in American Politics* (Boulder: Westview Press, 2000).

[32] Notably, recent work on the increased social sorting of parties in the electorate has not focused on social class. See Iyengar et al., "Origins and Consequences"; Mason *Uncivil Agreement*.

It is likely that these cumulating, reinforcing social identities sorted along partisan lines affect members of Congress just as they affect the public at large. We lack survey data on affective polarization among members of Congress that would permit direct comparisons with voters. But it stands to reason that members of congressional parties differing so much in social identity terms would experience growing distrust and animus toward one another. In this respect, the parties' divergence in social identity composition probably engenders feedback effects, deepening partisan antagonisms even beyond the profound issue-based disagreements already at stake in the ideological divide between the parties.

If an absence of cross-pressuring social identities promotes extremism as per Lipset's hypothesis, the Republican Party in Congress would be particularly susceptible to this dynamic. Republican leaders have relatively few identity-based cross-pressures to manage and reconcile in a party that as of 2019–20 is 92 percent male and 96 percent white. By contrast, the Democratic Party is highly diverse in terms of gender (60 percent male) and race (62 percent white); indeed, the congressional Democratic Party has never been more socially diverse than it currently is. Democratic leaders must tread carefully to avoid antagonizing their party's identity-based fault lines. If a group's social homogeneity fosters extremism, the relative lack of diversity within the Republican Party may contribute to the often-noted "asymmetric polarization" in which congressional Republicans have moved more to the right than congressional Democrats to the left.[33]

POLITICAL INSTITUTIONS

American society now exhibits fewer of the crosscutting cleavages that traditionally helped to tamp down party conflict. American politics scholars of the mid-twentieth century often emphasized these crosscutting cleavages as an important source of democratic stability.[34] Indeed, Lipset regarded the presence of crosscutting social cleavages as much more

---

[33] Matt Grossmann and David A. Hopkins, *Asymmetric Politics: Ideological Republicans and Group Interest Democrats* (Oxford: Oxford University Press, 2016); Jacob S. Hacker and Paul Pierson, "Confronting Asymmetric Polarization," in *Solutions to Political Polarization in America*, ed. Nathaniel Persily (Cambridge: Cambridge University Press, 2015), 59–72.

[34] Robert A. Dahl, *A Preface to Democratic Theory* (Chicago: University of Chicago Press, 1956), 104–05; Lipset, "Some Social Requisites"; Seymour Martin Lipset, *Political Man: The Social Bases of Politics* (Garden City, NY: Doubleday, 1963); David B. Truman, *The Governmental Process: Political Interests and Public Opinion* (New York: Alfred A. Knopf, 1960), 157–67.

important for democratic stability than "variations in systems of government."[35] But with crosscutting cleavages in American politics declining, US political institutions need to meet the challenges that identity-based polarization poses for democracy. In such an environment, scholars should consider the virtues of a constitutional system that routinely enforces power-sharing arrangements on the major parties.

Scholars of comparative politics have long wrestled with the challenges of establishing and sustaining democracies in polities divided along lines of social identity.[36] A divided or plural society is one that exhibits "segmental cleavages" in which "political divisions follow very closely ... lines of objective social differentiation," typically of a "religious, ideological, linguistic, regional, cultural, racial, or ethnic nature."[37] In 1977, Lijphart characterized the United States as exhibiting "medium" segmentation,[38] taking note of the "racial cleavage"[39] and the regional divide between North and South.[40] Given the social sorting of American parties in both the electorate and in government, there is no doubt that the United States has become a more divided society since the late 1970s. Although it is not possible to say precisely how much partisan-social sorting is necessary to pose a risk to democracy, it is clear that American democracy has less protection on this dimension than in the past.

Scholars offer various institutional prescriptions to make democracy possible and sustainable in divided societies. *Consociationalists* (e.g., Lijphart) recommend proportional representation, governance by grand coalition, and mutual vetoes to protect key interests. *Centripetalists* (e.g., Horowitz) advocate institutions and procedures that incentivize the formation of broad parties and coalitions, encompassing different societal groups. It would be far beyond the scope of this chapter to adjudicate among these complex and important debates. But what both consociationalists and centripetalists have in common is the desire to foster power sharing across the polity's social divisions.[41] Regardless of what governmental institutions might be best suited for divided societies in general, the

---

[35] Lipset, "Some Social Requisites, 98.
[36] Arend Lijphart *Democracy in Plural Societies: A Comparative Exploration* (New Haven: Yale University Press, 1977); Horowitz, *Ethnic Groups in Conflict*; Horowitz, *A Democratic South Africa?*; Murat Somer and Jennifer McCoy, "Transformations Through Polarizations and Global Threats to Democracy," *ANNALS of the American Academy of Political and Social Science*, January: 1–22, 2019.
[37] Lijphart, *Democracy in Plural Societies*, 3–4.   [38] Ibid., 15.   [39] Ibid., 22.
[40] Ibid., 113.
[41] Matthijs Bogaards, "Consociationalism and Centripetalism: Friends or Foes?" *Swiss Political Science Review* 25, no. 4 (2019): 519–37.

American political system contains several features that have precisely this recommended effect. Despite the evolution in the meso-institutions that Pierson and Schickler (this volume) rightly point out, US political institutions still tend to give each party a share of power and to block one party from running roughshod over the other.

In the following, I will briefly discuss these aspects of American government. Separation of powers, federalism, and bicameralism diffuse power institutionally and geographically, allocating influence to both parties. In addition, constitutional rigidity and central bank independence insulate the structure of governing institutions and monetary policy-making from direct political control. Taken together, these elements of American democracy continue to lower the stakes of elections and necessitate bipartisan negotiation in governance, even under contemporary party-polarized conditions.

Separation of Powers

The balance of power between Congress and the president rests not merely on the enumeration of the branches' separate powers in the Constitution but on electoral realities. Unlike in parliamentary systems, how members vote in Congress does not affect the executive's term of office or force new elections. Members of Congress are thus freer to vote in whatever manner they prefer or will most please their reelection constituency. Party discipline in Congress, as in presidential systems generally, is much lower than in parliamentary systems.[42]

Freed not only from the discipline of sustaining a government in power, members of Congress also gain independence through the decentralized nature of congressional elections. Members win party nominations in open primary competition, mount their own campaigns across geographically dispersed constituencies, and maintain their own bases of political support. Even in today's more nationalized political context,[43] members of Congress still manage to cultivate a personal vote that allows them to outperform the constituency support they would win simply on the basis

---

[42] David J. Samuels, and Matthew S. Shugart, *Presidents, Parties, and Prime Ministers: How the Separation of Powers Affects Party Organization and Behavior* (Cambridge: Cambridge University Press, 2010); Matthew Soberg Shugart and John M. Carey, *Presidents and Assemblies: Constitutional Design and Electoral Dynamics* (Cambridge: Cambridge University Press, 1992).

[43] Daniel J. Hopkins, *The Increasingly United States: How and Why American Political Behavior Nationalized* (Chicago: University of Chicago Press, 2018).

of their party affiliation.[44] In short, members of Congress retain independence as political actors who can only be removed by their constituents, not by presidents or party leaders. Presidents and party leaders must thus engage in continual negotiation and consensus-building to build majorities in Congress.

Nonconcurrent elections for the legislature tend to further fragment power. Consistent with the cross-national pattern, midterm elections in the United States still almost invariably reduce the ranks of the president's party in Congress.[45] In the polarized era, midterm elections have resulted in repeated, severe backlashes against sitting presidents, including a loss of majority control for the president's party in one or both chambers in 1986, 1994, 2006, 2010, 2014, and 2018. In these ways, midterms serve as a potent check on presidential power.

To be sure, presidential elections stand out as the most "winner-take-all" element of American national government. Even after narrow electoral margins of victory, presidents can and often do assemble entire cabinets without a single appointee from the opposing party. But this powerfully majoritarian[46] feature of American government is far less majoritarian than a parliamentary system. As Horowitz writes:

> Systems in which presidents are separately elected make all political assessments more complex. A group that is excluded from power in parliament may still find ways of gaining access to the president. A group that gains the presidency may or may not also form a majority in parliament.[47]

Put simply, compared to parliamentary systems, presidential systems divide power, making it less likely that any single party or coalition in a divided society will have the full reins of power. Indeed, US presidents since World War II have typically lacked majorities of their party in Congress. Separation of powers has meant divided government 75 percent of the time since 1980,

---

[44] Split-ticket voting has markedly declined since the 1980s, but incumbents still maintain a personal vote worth 2–3 percentage points, roughly comparable to that of the 1960s. See Gary C. Jacobson, "It's Nothing Personal: The Decline of the Incumbency Advantage in U.S. House Elections." *Journal of Politics* 77, no. 3 (2015): 861–73; Gary C. Jacobson, "Extreme Referendum: Donald Trump and the 2018 Midterm Elections." *Political Science Quarterly* 134, no. 1 (2019): 9–38. See also Charles R. Hunt, "Beyond Partisanship: Outperforming the Party Label with Local Roots in Congressional Elections," *Congress & the Presidency* (2020), http://doi.org/10.1080/07343469.2020.1811425.

[45] Shugart and Carey, *Presidents and Assemblies*, 242–72.

[46] Of course, presidents are elected by a majority of the electoral college, not a majority of the national electorate.

[47] Horowitz, *A Democratic South Africa?*, 206.

when polarization really began to take off. Divided government obviously forces bipartisan negotiation across all dimensions of policymaking.

Presidential systems are also less able simply to assume a majority in their day-to-day operations than parliamentary systems. A prime minister at the head of a majority in parliament wields far more legislative and budget authority than does the US president. Even in unified government, presidents regularly confront congressional resistance and see their budget requests ignored or heavily modified. During unified government in both 2017 and 2018, for example, congressional Republicans quietly treated the Trump administration's budget proposals as "dead on arrival."[48] The two-year spending deal that Congress agreed to in February 2018 increased domestic discretionary spending by 10 percent rather than cutting it as per the administration's budget request.

Likewise, even with unified government presidents cannot assume that they will be able to muster congressional majorities for their policy agenda.[49] In 2017–18, consistent with the historic norm, Republicans in majority control of Congress not only disregarded President Trump's budget but also rejected central components of his policy agenda. They did not block the president via frontal confrontation or public criticism. Republican resistance to the Trump administration instead largely took the form of what Neustadt called the "enormous power which consists of sitting still."[50] The Republican Congress failed to coalesce to support the repeal and replacement of Obamacare, the southern border wall, any cuts in domestic discretionary spending, or the Trump administration's immigration proposals. For its part, the Republican Senate also declined to support a large number of Trump nominees, who were either rejected or withdrawn. Despite Republican Senate control, the Trump administration faced unusual difficulties staffing the executive branch and confirming nominations.[51]

---

[48] Sylan Lane, "GOP Senator: Trump Budget 'Dead on Arrival,'" *The Hill*, February 28, 2017, http://thehill.com/policy/finance/321576-gop-senator-trump-budget-dead-on-arrival; Andrew Taylor and Martin Crutsinger, "Trump Budget Plan Already Outdated After Budget Deal," *Washington Times*, February 22, 2018, https://m.washingtontimes.com/news/2018/feb/11/trump-budget-plan-already-outdated-after-budget-de/.

[49] David R. Mayhew, *Divided We Govern: Party Control, Lawmaking, and Investigations, 1946–2002*, 2nd ed. (New Haven: Yale University Press, 2005); Mayhew, *Partisan Balance*.

[50] Richard E. Neustadt, *Presidential Power and the Modern Presidents* (New York: Free Press, 1990), 37.

[51] Partnership for Public Service, Center for Presidential Transition, "Senate Confirmation Process Slows to a Crawl," January 20, 2020, https://presidentialtransition.org/wp-content/uploads/sites/6/2020/01/Senate-Confirmations-Issue-Brief.pdf

No doubt, the contemporary Congress conducts less vigorous executive oversight during unified party control than under divided government.[52] Nevertheless, even the Republican-controlled 115th Congress (2017–18) conducted some consequential investigations. Less than three months into the Trump presidency, the House and Senate Intelligence Committees launched formal inquiries into Russian involvement in the 2016 US elections and possible collusion with the Trump presidential campaign. After the president fired FBI Director James Comey, the Senate Judiciary Committee opened a third formal inquiry. These congressional probes were potent drivers of news coverage throughout 2017 and 2018, repeatedly damaging the administration's political standing.[53] The return of divided government after the 2018 elections increased oversight pressure. The power of congressional publicity, for example, forced President Trump to release funds withheld from Ukraine even before the House launched its impeachment inquiry on the matter.

In legislation, budgeting, and oversight, separation of powers remains a meaningful check on majority rule under both unified and divided party control. Although the balance of presidential and congressional power ebbs and flows over time, separation of powers makes American government more complex and less subject to any one party's control. It yields a political system that demands and elicits bipartisan input, negotiation, and accommodation, even under contemporary polarized conditions.

Federalism

Diffusing power geographically gives parties out of power at the national level opportunities for input at other levels. The federal system usually operates so that presidents and majority parties in Congress face a substantial number of states controlled by their party opposition. Federalism is especially likely to require bipartisan power-sharing in an era where there are "blue states" and "red states" and the major parties are polarized on geographic lines.[54] Along with an executive-legislative balance of power, federalism constitutes an element of Lijphart's

---

[52] Mayhew, *Divided We Govern*, 223–26; Kriner and Schickler, *Investigating the President*.
[53] Douglas L. Kriner and Eric Schickler. 2016. "The Resilience of Separation of Powers? Congress and the Russia Investigation," *Presidential Studies Quarterly*, 48, no. 3 (2018): 436–55.
[54] David A. Hopkins, *Red Fighting Blue: How Geography and Electoral Rules Polarize American Politics* (Cambridge: Cambridge University Press, 2017).

"consensus model of democracy"[55] as well as one of Horowitz's "mechanisms of conflict reduction"[56] useful for governing divided societies.

Considering the degree of federal-state cooperation required in most federal policy implementation, opposed state governments have numerous tools to block or dilute national policies.[57] Presidents and parties in power at the federal level routinely struggle to overcome "uncooperative federalism"[58] as they seek to impose national policy. The Trump administration encountered strong opposition from Democratic-leaning states challenging administration policy on immigration, environment, and health policy. The Obama administration's experience was similar in Republican-leaning states. Federalism clearly remains a powerful brake on control of policy from Washington. If anything, polarization may have increased the potency of backlash against federal power from nonaligned states. According to a dataset of state attorney general activity, as of January 2020 there were more than eighty multistate lawsuits against the Trump administration, more than against any other administration since 1982.[59]

Strong Bicameralism

Bicameralism is yet another power-diffusing mechanism recommended for divided societies.[60] Put simply, the bicameral Congress is not a majority-rule institution. The House and Senate are coequal chambers, elected in different constituencies on different timetables. Not even unified government overcomes the consensus-expanding effects of bicameralism. Minority parties in the polarized era are almost always strong enough to wield the Senate filibuster to force compromise.[61] Furthermore, filibusters are not the only obstacle bicameralism erects to majority rule.[62] Majority parties in control of both House and Senate frequently struggle to reach intraparty consensus across the two chambers on even their highest legislative priorities, as is evident in the struggles of Democrats in 2009–10 to

---

[55] Lijphart, *Patterns of Democracy*, 37–38.
[56] Horowitz, *Ethnic Groups in Conflict*, 197–98. [57] Robertson, *Federalism*.
[58] Bulman-Pozen and Gerken, "Uncooperative Federalism," 1256.
[59] State Litigation and AG Activity Database, compiled by Paul Nolette, Associate Professor of Political Science at Marquette University, https://attorneysgeneral.org/multistate-lawsuits-vs-the-federal-government/list-of-lawsuits-1980-present/.
[60] Lijphart, *Pattern of Democracy*, 38; Horowitz, *Ethnic Groups in Conflict*, 598.
[61] Keith Krehbiel, *Pivotal Politics: A Theory of U.S. Lawmaking* (Chicago: University of Chicago Press, 1998).
[62] Binder, *Stalemate*.

enact climate change legislation and Republicans to repeal and replace Obamacare in 2017–18. Bicameral disagreement blocked or diluted much of President Trump's proposed legislation in the 115th Congress, including the efforts to roll back financial regulatory reforms and impose work requirements on food stamp recipients.

Lowering the Stakes

In addition to institutional features that diffuse power – separation of powers, federalism, and bicameralism – the US system also includes important structural features that lower the stakes in elections. Insulating some basic processes from direct political control reduces the capacity of any single party to impose its preferences unilaterally on national government.

Constitutional Rigidity. A constitution that can be easily changed raises the stakes in elections. A constitution subject to alteration by simple majority opens the door to a single party centralizing power over national government.[63] In many countries where democratic backsliding has occurred, the process proceeded via such means – though national elections, referenda, and legitimate lawmaking processes that authorized fundamental systemic change.[64] The procedural barriers to constitutional change in the United States, however, are extraordinarily high.[65] There is little prospect for major institutional reforms to make American government more majoritarian. It is hard to imagine any single party in American politics garnering the breadth of support required to enact constitutional changes. The stability of the system lowers the stakes in politics, tamping down conflict and reducing the threat the parties can pose to one another.

Central Bank Independence. Central bank independence removes key tools of economic management from direct political control. It is therefore also an important mechanism for reducing the political stakes in election. Federal Reserve personnel and policies are, of course, subject to political influence from both Congress and the president.[66] But the Federal Reserve is insulated from politics by long, staggered terms of members of its Board

---

[63] Kurt Weyland, "Populism's Threat to Democracy: Comparative Lessons for the United States," *Perspectives on Politics* 18, no. 2 (2020): 389–406.
[64] Nancy Bermeo, "On Democratic Backsliding," *Journal of Democracy* 27 (2016): 5–18.
[65] Donald S. Lutz, "Toward a Theory of Constitutional Amendment," *American Political Science Review* 88, no. 2 (1994): 355–70.
[66] Sarah A. Binder and Mark Spindel, *The Myth of Independence: How Congress Governs the Federal Reserve* (Princeton: Princeton University Press 2017).

of Governors, nonreliance upon congressional appropriations, and ability to adopt monetary policy decisions without approval from Congress or the president. Via such mechanisms, US monetary policy receives considerable insulation from party politics.

POWER-SHARING VS. EFFECTIVE GOVERNANCE?

Taken together, the US system encompasses an array of institutional mechanisms that diffuse power, force bipartisan negotiation, and set important policies and procedures outside electoral politics. As a consequence, the American political system continually resists any easy answer to the question of "who owns the state?"[67] Such ambiguity is valuable at a time when crosscutting cleavages have declined and Americans are increasingly divided into "us" versus "them" partisan camps along lines of social identity. A political system that resists capture by one party remains more capable of commanding loyalty from both major parties and the societal groups they represent. In these respects, diffusion of power contributes to democratic legitimacy, particularly in a polarized era.

American governing institutions tend to moderate any effect of party polarization on policy outcomes. Despite the rise of party polarization in Congress, there has been no meaningful increase in the tendency of legislation to be adopted on narrow party lines or over the opposition of a majority of the minority party.[68] Even in unified government, most legislation that gets enacted – including landmark laws – still garners broad, bipartisan support. The Affordable Care Act (2010) and the Tax Cuts and Jobs Act (2017) – adopted on straight party line votes – do not represent how American national government works in general, even in the polarized era. Although these are important laws, they are exceptional cases, not indicative of a broader trend. More generally, polarization has not made congressional majority parties any more effective at carrying out their policy agendas.[69] In these ways, the US's complex political institutions still grant both parties a role in national policymaking most of the time.

Polarization also affects the balance of power between Congress and the president, but in contradictory ways. On the one hand, a Congress mired in partisan conflict struggles to assert itself against presidential

---

[67] Horowitz, *A Democratic South Africa*, 206.
[68] Curry and Lee, *Nonparty Government*; Curry and Lee, *Limits of Party*.   [69] Ibid.

action.[70] Congressional deadlock empowers the president in arenas where unilateral action is possible. The authorities available to the executive branch over both domestic regulation and foreign affairs are vast and ambiguous. A president facing congressional stalemate can make more unconstrained use of the presidency's powers and tools, such as executive orders, signing statements, and national security directives. It is also hard to imagine the party-polarized Congress garnering the two-thirds majority necessary to override a presidential veto on any major issue.

On the other hand, party polarization also means that presidents face more tightly cohesive party opposition in Congress. As the parties have polarized, presidents receive dramatically lower levels of cross-party support in Congress.[71] Because major legislation can rarely pass on the strength of one party alone,[72] enhanced support from the president's party cannot offset the downsides of reduced support from the opposition. Polarization also regularly means that even parties in control of unified government find themselves blocked by Senate filibuster. Since the 1990s, the Senate minority party has systematically deployed the filibuster as a veto over much of the majority party's agenda.[73] Congressional polarization grants presidents more freedom of maneuver within the scope of their unilateral powers, but it does not improve their ability to win congressional enactment of their legislative agendas. In this regard, the political system continues to curb partisan ambitions and force bipartisan compromise, even as the decline of crosscutting cleavages renders American political parties less moderate and consensus-oriented.

Given deep social divides between two evenly matched political parties, majority rule would not likely result in broadly acceptable policy outcomes in American politics. If comparative scholars are right that divided societies need institutions that require power-sharing among contending societal groups, the United States may benefit more from these features today than it did in less polarized times. Polarized politics call for institutions that ensure bipartisan negotiation and broader consensus-building.

---

[70] William Howell, *Power Without Persuasion: The Politics of Direct Presidential Action* (Princeton: Princeton University Press, 2003).
[71] Gary C. Jacobson, "Partisan Polarization in Presidential Support: The Electoral Connection" *Congress & the Presidency* 30, no. 3 (2003): 1–36. See also "CQ Vote Studies: Presidential Support – Trump's Last Hurrah," *CQ Magazine*, February 25, 2019, http://library.cqpress.com.ezproxy.princeton.edu/cqweekly/weeklyreport116-000005468046.
[72] Mayhew, *Divided We Govern*.
[73] Barbara Sinclair, *Unorthodox Lawmaking: New Legislative Processes in the U.S. Congress* (Washington, DC: CQ Press, 2012), 153–54.

One implication of this analysis is that today's polarized context argues for increases in congressional capacity. As a political institution, even in these polarized times, Congress is far more oriented toward compromise and consensus-building than the winner-take-all presidency. Presidents do not typically stand at the head of any overwhelming majority. Dating back to 1860, the average winning presidential candidate has received only 52 percent of the national popular vote. Rather than conferring broad legitimacy, presidents are – in Skowronek's words – the "lightning rods" of American politics.[74] By contrast, Congress, now as in the past, is where political conflicts get resolved to both parties' rough satisfaction, at least when those conflicts do get resolved.

The obvious downside of diffused power is that complex governments with many veto players can be hamstrung by their society's internal divides, resulting in immobilism and inability to address major social and political problems. Much work in recent American politics raises precisely these performance concerns. An increasing share of the national policy agenda is mired in political gridlock.[75] Long-standing public policies languish without revision, reform, updating, or repeal.[76] Congress struggles with legislation and mundane tasks of governance, such as budgets, appropriations, and confirmations.[77] With its many checks and balances, the constitutional framework has great difficulty functioning under the pressures of pervasive, intractable conflict between two evenly matched parties.

It is not clear, however, that governmental outcomes would necessarily improve with more majoritarian political institutions. Empowering parties in a deeply divided society has serious downsides for democratic legitimacy and system support. Moreover, even if simple majorities were all that were required, there is no guarantee that the empowered parties would be capable of mustering majorities to deal with the most intractable policy problems facing US national government. The Democratic Party's track record does not inspire confidence that it would be able to coalesce internally around a serious effort to address climate change, for example. For their part, Republicans have shown little capacity to reach internal agreement on how to achieve fiscal balance. In a system in which individual members want to claim credit for popular outcomes and avoid blame

---

[74] Stephen Skowronek, *The Politics Presidents Make: Leadership from John Adams to George Bush* (Cambridge: Harvard University Press, 1993), 20.
[75] Binder, *Stalemate*; Binder, "Polarized We Govern?" [76] Mettler, "Policyscape."
[77] McCarty, "Polarization."

for unpopular outcomes, neither party is inclined to assume or bear responsibility for making hard choices or imposing costs on constituencies. In short, supermajority rule may fall short in governmental decisiveness and effectiveness, but, faced with hard choices, majority rule may not necessarily offer improvements on that dimension. Meanwhile, supermajoritarian outcomes at least rest on broader public support than policies imposed on the basis of simple majorities constructed out of narrow segments of American society.

In short, for those who worry that polarization has undermined traditional checks and balances in the US system, it is important to recognize that many checks and balances still remain. At the same time, for those who rightly fear that the checks and balances of the US system prevent important action, policy inaction in a polarized polity may not be as problematic as the delegitimizing effects of highly controversial action taken on the basis of a bare majority.

5

Unilateralism Unleashed?

Polarization and the Politics of Executive Action

Douglas L. Kriner

Having just fought a war to free themselves from the tyrannical grip of George III, few of the delegates to the constitutional convention shared Alexander Hamilton's enthusiasm for a strong presidency. When James Wilson initially proposed "a single magistrate, as giving most energy dispatch and responsibility to the office," Edmund Randolph denounced the plan as "the foetus of monarchy."[1] Wilson's ideas would eventually win out, but the presidency became one of the most controversial features of the new Constitution during the ratification debates. In his fifth letter, the anti-federalist writer Cato warned that "inexplicitness seems to pervade this whole political fabric," particularly regarding the limits on the powers of the executive magistrate. Without precise limits, Cato warned, "you might as well deposit the important powers of legislation and execution in one or a few and permit them to govern according to their disposition and will."[2]

Cato's warning quickly proved prescient. Washington's unilateral Proclamation of Neutrality prompted howls of executive usurpation from no lesser authorities than Jefferson and Madison.[3] As president, Jefferson would embrace an expanded understanding of the office's unilateral power in securing the Louisiana Purchase. Polk engineered a war with Mexico and presented Congress with a fait accompli, and Lincoln,

---

[1] James Madison, *Notes on the Debates in the Federal Convention*, June 1, 1787, https://avalon.law.yale.edu/18th_century/debates_601.asp/.

[2] Cato, "Letter V," *The New York Journal*, November 22, 1787, www.constitution.org/afp/cato_05.htm.

[3] See Helvidius 1, https://oll.libertyfund.org/titles/hamilton-the-pacificus-helvidius-debates-of-1793-1794.

who had railed against Polk's abuses while in Congress, embraced unilateralism wholeheartedly to preserve, protect, and defend the Union during the Civil War, including by issuing the Emancipation Proclamation. While always a feature of American governance, executive action accelerated under Franklin Roosevelt with the dramatic expansion in the scope of government to combat the twin shocks of the Great Depression and World War II, producing the concomitant rise and consolidation of what King and Milkis in this volume label the executive-centered administrative state.[4]

Today, however, fears that rampant unilateralism threatens the very fabric of our constitutional system of checks and balances have reached a fever pitch. While Watergate and the brief period of congressional resurgence it triggered may have temporarily chastened Schlesinger's "imperial presidency," George W. Bush's aggressive use of the office's unilateral powers in the aftermath of 9/11 precipitated cries of a new imperial presidency.[5] Although Barack Obama pledged to eschew the unilateral impulses of his predecessor, in office he frequently found the siren song of unilateralism irresistible to advance his objectives in both the foreign and domestic spheres. Similarly, candidate Trump routinely denounced Barack Obama's executive actions as constitutionally specious. But as president, Trump advanced assertions of unilateral presidential authority equaling if not even exceeding those of his predecessors in boldness.

Assessing this recent history, many scholars have concluded that the constitutional system of Madisonian checks and balances is on the ropes and unilateralism is the primary culprit. Bruce Ackerman has argued that executive action is the proximate cause underlying the "decline and fall of the American Republic."[6] Analyzing recent American politics from a comparative perspective, Steven Levitsky and Daniel Ziblatt argue that the erosion of norms of institutional forbearance has fueled presidents'

---

[4] This chapter focuses squarely on presidents' unilateral powers – the power to change policy with the stroke of a pen by issuing an executive order, memorandum, proclamation, or other unilateral instrument. For an assessment of how presidents of both parties, since Roosevelt, have aggressively used the administrative reach of the executive branch to pursue their programmatic agendas through other extra-legislative means, including the regulatory process, see the insightful chapter in this volume by King and Milkis.

[5] Andrew Rudalevige, *The New Imperial Presidency: Renewing Presidential Power After Watergate* (Ann Arbor: University of Michigan Press, 2005); Charlie Savage, *Takeover: The Return of the Imperial Presidency* (Boston: Little, Brown, 2008); Arthur Schlesinger Jr., *The Imperial Presidency* (Boston: Houghton Mifflin, 1973).

[6] Bruce Ackerman, *The Decline and Fall of the American Republic* (Cambridge: Harvard University Press, 2010).

increasing willingness to exploit and even abuse their unilateral powers to pursue foreign and domestic policy agendas. This dynamic, in turn, has weakened "the guardrails of democracy" and driven the growing authoritarian tilt in American politics.[7] Rampant presidential unilateralism also threatens to activate two of the pathways of constitutional "retrogression" identified by legal scholars Aziz Huq and Tom Ginsburg: the weakening of institutional checks and the centralization and politicization of executive power. The Constitution's parchment barriers, they warn, provide an imperfect check against democratic retrogression fueled by an authoritarian executive.[8]

A primary force fueling unilateralism in many accounts is the rising tide of partisan polarization in Washington. Since the 1970s, the Democratic and Republican parties have become more internally homogeneous and more ideologically distant from one another.[9] By fueling legislative gridlock on Capitol Hill and frustrating presidential legislative agendas, polarization has strengthened presidents' incentives to go it alone and pursue their policy agendas through non-legislative means while simultaneously weakening the capacity of other institutional actors to check unilateral power grabs.[10] The end result, many warn, is a threat – possibly an existential one – to democratic resilience in the form of presidents increasingly using executive orders, memoranda, proclamations, national emergency declarations, and other unilateral instruments to effect major changes in public policy without congressional consent, let alone action.

But has the rising tide of polarization actually produced a measurable and potentially dangerous increase in significant unilateral action? To examine the threat that unilateralism poses to checks and balances in the contemporary polity, this chapter proceeds in three parts. First, it examines how polarization might weaken the formal institutional checks

---

[7] Steven Levitsky and Daniel Ziblatt, *How Democracies Die* (New York: Crown, 2018).

[8] Ackerman, *Decline and Fall of the American Republic*; Aziz Huq and Tom Ginsburg, "How to Lose a Constitutional Democracy," *UCLA Law Review* 65 (2018): 78–169.

[9] For an exploration of the extent to which this polarization has been asymmetric and driven more by Republicans becoming increasingly conservative, see: Jacob Hacker and Paul Pierson, *Off Center: The Republican Revolution & the Erosion of Democracy* (New Haven: Yale University Press, 2006).

[10] Sarah Binder, *Stalemate: Causes and Consequences of Legislative Gridlock* (Washington: Brookings Institution, 2004); Sarah Binder, "The Dysfunctional Congress," *Annual Review of Political Science* 18, no. 1 (2015): 85–101; George C. III Edwards, *Predicting the Presidency: The Potential for Persuasive Leadership* (Princeton: Princeton University Press, 2016); Keith Krehbiel, *Pivotal Politics: A Theory of U.S. Lawmaking* (Chicago: University of Chicago Press, 1998).

on unilateral action that are the focus of most research on the unilateral presidency. It then discusses the political checks on unilateral action emphasized by recent scholarship and whether they have been weakened by polarization or whether they have remained robust. Second, to explore trends in unilateral action over the last four decades empirically, the chapter introduces a new data set designed to overcome two of the most important limitations of prior scholarship on the unilateral presidency. Most scholarship continues to focus narrowly on executive orders, but presidents increasingly are making recourse to a range of unilateral alternatives to pursue their policy goals. Another challenge is that most unilateral actions – indeed, like most laws – are of limited substantive importance. Thus, any analysis of whether unilateralism is on the rise and threatens checks and balances must focus more narrowly on the subset of significant actions that might plausibly threaten the constitutional order.

Empirically, there is little evidence that presidential unilateralism has increased markedly with rising partisan polarization. Rather, what is perhaps most striking is presidents' relative restraint. To be sure, presidents do occasionally use (abuse?) their unilateral powers to effect significant changes in policy that they would never have secured from Congress. However, the data make clear that presidents also routinely forgo opportunities to act unilaterally and move policies closer to their preferences, even when Congress and the courts are unable to block them. The data suggests that, at least for most of this period, the informal political checks emphasized by recent research have been strong enough to keep unilateralism in check, despite rising polarization.[11]

The chapter concludes by placing President Trump's use of the office's unilateral power in comparative perspective. While some of Trump's claims to unilateral authority have been particularly brazen, even in the Trump era there is evidence that nonlegislative checks remain resilient. However, the Trump presidency has produced a disturbing development with potentially long-lasting implications: the administration's unconditional assault on

---

[11] Dino P. Christenson and Douglas L. Kriner, "Mobilizing the Public Against the President: Congress and the Political Costs of Unilateral Action," *American Journal of Political Science* 69, no. 4 (2017); Dino P. Christenson and Douglas L. Kriner, *The Myth of the Imperial Presidency: How Public Opinion Checks the Unilateral Executive* (Chicago: University of Chicago Press, 2020); Andrew Reeves and Jon C. Rogowski, "Unilateral Powers, Public Opinion, and the Presidency," *Journal of Politics* 78, no. 1 (2016): 137–51; Andrew Reeves and Jon C. Rogowski, "The Public Cost of Unilateral Action," *American Journal of Political Science* 62, no. 2 (April 2018): 424–40.

Congress' oversight powers. In this battle, Trump has been aided and abetted by extreme partisan polarization in Congress, most notably by the almost complete subservience of Senate Republicans during his first impeachment trial in which all but two Republicans rallied behind the president and refused to stand up for Congress' right to have access to the documents and witnesses essential to discharging its constitutional duties. The unparalleled strength of party ties was thrown into even sharper relief when all but ten House Republicans voted against impeachment in the wake of the January 6, 2021, insurrection launched against the Capitol building itself. Trump and his Nixonian efforts to eviscerate Congress' oversight powers may yet prove an aberration. If these efforts instead prove precedential, they could erode the tenuous political checks that have kept the unilateral executive largely in check, and the pendulum of power will swing even more firmly toward the executive branch.

POLARIZATION AND UNILATERALISM

Polarization – and most specifically the widening ideological gap between the parties in Congress – might logically increase unilateral action for two reasons. First, by fueling congressional gridlock polarization both incentivizes presidents to pursue unilaterally policy shifts that they are unable to achieve legislatively and weakens the ability of Congress to reverse unilateral directives. As scholars have long shown, the same institutional gridlock that can doom legislative action on Capitol Hill redounds to the president's advantage when acting unilaterally.[12] Krehbiel's pivotal politics model of lawmaking showed that when a status quo policy lies between the pivotal players in Congress whose votes are essential either to break a filibuster or override a presidential veto, policymaking is hopelessly gridlocked. Any policy change will inevitably make one of these two pivotal players worse off, triggering either a filibuster or a veto. However, when a policy is gridlocked, presidents have the opportunity to move policy unilaterally closer to their preferences. Provided they keep the new status quo within the gridlock interval, Congress will be unable to overturn their action legislatively. By increasing the size of the gridlock interval, polarization should both increase the number of policies

---

[12] William G Howell, *Power Without Persuasion: The Politics of Direct Presidential Action* (Princeton: Princeton University Press, 2003); Terry M Moe and William G Howell, "The Presidential Power of Unilateral Action," *Journal of Law, Economics, and Organization* 15, no. 1 (1999): 132–79.

presidents can move unilaterally and open the door for even larger unilateral policy shifts as presidents can move policy all the way to the preferences of the veto pivot without Congress being able to reverse them legislatively.[13]

Of course, courts can also push back against presidential overreach, and by design the judiciary does not suffer from the same institutional limitations as Congress. However, as Hamilton noted in *Federalist 78*, courts lack independent means of enforcement, and as a result a strategic court has strong incentives to proceed with caution. Empirical analyses of judicial pushback show that judicial challenges to executive orders are exceedingly rare, and that courts are more likely to rule against unilateral directives when they anticipate support from other political actors including Congress.[14] If polarization weakens the legislative check, it may also undermine the prospects for judicial pushback as well.

But it is important not to push the argument too far. The supermajoritarian features of our legislative system create significant opportunities for unilateral action even in periods of relatively low polarization. Indeed, Krehbiel described the core feature of American legislative policymaking as gridlock being "common, but not constant," long before the sharp rise in polarization in recent decades.[15] Similarly, courts have always been highly reticent to strike down unilateral actions. The effects of polarization on unilateralism may therefore be more modest than we might expect. However, the mechanisms through which polarization can further weaken the formal legislative and judicial checks on presidential unilateralism are clear.

An emerging literature argues that other checks, apart from legislation or court orders reversing an executive action, exert the most powerful constraint on unilateralism. One branch of this scholarship hearkening back to Neustadt emphasizes the importance of the bureaucracy as a potential check on the president's unilateral impulses.[16] Recent research

---

[13] A rare instance in which polarization did not expand the size of the gridlock interval was 2009, when Democrats briefly enjoyed a filibuster-proof majority in the Senate. More broadly, scholars differ on whether the combination of polarization and unified government particularly weakens checks and balances. For a discussion of how congressional checks on presidential legislative ambitions may remain resilient even in unified government in a polarized polity, see the Lee chapter in this volume. For a less sanguine view, see the Pierson and Schickler chapter in this volume.

[14] Howell, *Power Without Persuasion*.   [15] Krehbiel, *Pivotal Politics*, 5.

[16] Joshua B. Kennedy, "'"Do This! Do That!" and Nothing Will Happen': Executive Orders and Bureaucratic Responsiveness," *American Politics Research* 43, no. 1 (2015): 59–82; Andrew Rudalevige, "The Letter of the Law: Administrative Discretion and Obama's

by Andrew Rudalevige shows that many draft executive orders are substantially altered over the course of the interagency review process, while hundreds of others, often following significant bureaucratic pushback, are never signed at all.[17] Anticipatory calculations about the need to bargain with bureaucratic actors over program implementation may have even broader effects, constraining presidents' freedom of action.

A second strand of literature argues that informal political costs, rather than institutional resistance, may most influence presidents' unilateral calculus. When contemplating unilateral action, presidents anticipate more than the likelihood of a formal rebuke from Congress or the courts or bureaucratic noncompliance. They also consider the political costs of going it alone. Perhaps most importantly, presidents are concerned with public opinion and whether bold unilateral action risks undermining their reserve of popular support, a valuable resource and index of political capital.[18] Critically, other actors can continue to influence the politics of unilateral action indirectly by shaping how the public responds to unilateralism. For example, even when they cannot check the president legislatively, congressional opponents can hold hearings,[19] shine a light on alleged abuse, and more generally challenge the administration in the public sphere.[20] This public resistance can raise the political costs of executive action and cause presidents to forgo unilateral actions even when they would almost certainly survive any formal legislative or legal challenge.[21] Similarly, even public speculation of a judicial challenge can threaten to erode public support for the president.[22] Thus, if other elites and the media anticipate that judicial challenges are even plausible, reckless unilateral action could threaten a president's base of popular support.

Domestic Unilateralism," *Forum* 12, no. 1 (2014): 29–59; Neustadt, *Presidential Power and the Modern Presidents*.

[17] Andrew Rudalevige, *By Executive Order: Bureaucratic Management and the Limits of Presidential Power* (Princeton: Princeton University Press, 2021).

[18] Dino P. Christenson and Douglas L. Kriner, "Does Public Opinion Constrain Presidential Unilateralism?," *American Political Science Review* 113, no. 4 (2019): 1071–77; Christenson and Kriner, *The Myth of the Imperial Presidency*; Reeves and Rogowski, "Unilateral Powers, Public Opinion, and the Presidency"; Reeves and Rogowski, "The Public Cost of Unilateral Action."

[19] Douglas L. Kriner and Eric Schickler, *Investigating the President: Congressional Checks on Presidential Power* (Princeton: Princeton University Press, 2016).

[20] Josh Chafetz, *Congress' Constitution: Legislative Authority and the Separation of Powers* (New Haven: Yale University Press, 2017); David R Mayhew, *America's Congress: Actions in the Public Sphere* (New Haven: Yale University Press, 2000).

[21] Christenson and Kriner, "Mobilizing the Public Against the President."

[22] Christenson and Kriner, *The Myth of the Imperial Presidency*.

Whether polarization will also weaken these more political checks is less clear. For example, polarization has undoubtedly affected confirmation politics and encouraged presidents to embrace new bureaucratic staffing strategies.[23] However, the consequences of these developments for presidential influence over the bureaucracy have been mixed.[24] The fundamental principal-agent problem remains (witness President Trump's frequent denunciations of a deep state conspiracy against his administration), and so there are strong reasons to believe that bureaucratic checks remain resilient.

It is possible that rising polarization will threaten the indirect check that Congress and other actors wield against presidential overreach through their ability to shape public opinion. Partisan forces have always weakened the institutional incentives for presidential co-partisans to defend Congress' institutional power stakes from presidential encroachments. In an era of intensified partisan loyalties and heightened "teamsmanship," these incentives may be weaker still.[25] Unwavering support from the president's co-partisans in Congress may limit the political fallout from brazenly pushing forward unilaterally. Similarly, previous research shows that courts are highly strategic when choosing to hear cases challenging unilateral action and when ultimately ruling against the White House.[26] If polarization makes these favorable conditions less likely to occur, it may weaken not only the formal judicial check but also the informal one arising from real or anticipated public speculation of a judicial challenge.[27] Finally, if presidents can count on unshakeable support from their fellow partisans in the mass public in an era of base mobilization politics, the electoral risks of going it alone may also be mitigated, even in the face of institutional pushback from Congress or the courts.

However, on each count, recent empirical evidence suggests that the adverse influence of polarization on these informal political checks may be limited. While almost all Republicans stood in lockstep behind Trump on impeachment, many of his most controversial executive actions including

---

[23] Emily H. Moore, "Polarization, Excepted Appointments, and the Administrative Presidency," *Presidential Studies Quarterly* 48, no. 1 (2018): 72–92.

[24] Neal Devins and David E. Lewis, "Not-So Independent Agencies: Party Polarization and the Limits of Institutional Design, *Boston University Law Review* 88 (2008), 459–98.

[25] Frances Lee, *Beyond Ideology: Politics, Principles, and Partisanship in the U.S. Senate* (Chicago: University of Chicago Press, 2009).

[26] Howell, *Power Without Persuasion*.

[27] Contra fears that polarization is weakening the judicial check, there is empirical evidence, particularly within the regulatory realm, that courts are increasingly assertive in checking executive power. Lee Epstein and Eric A. Posner, "The Decline of Supreme Court Deference to the President," *University of Pennsylvania Law Review* 166 (2017): 829–60.

the first travel ban, a draft order to reinstitute torture, the transgender service ban, and the emergency declaration to build the wall did provoke significant congressional criticism even from prominent Republicans. Trump also bowed to congressional pressure and released the Ukraine aid when his actions were discovered, even as he fought tooth and nail to keep the full scope of his machinations secret. In addition, contemporary survey and experimental evidence shows that even in an era of often intense negative partisanship[28] many Americans of all partisan stripes are either innately skeptical of unilateral presidential action[29] or responsive to institutional criticism of the president's actions on constitutional or policy grounds, even when those criticisms are levied only by the opposition.[30] Finally, the Trump administration has suffered an unprecedented string of judicial defeats to its executive actions on multiple fronts, which all but ensures that questions concerning the legality of its unilateral gambits will be omnipresent in the media.

MEASURING THE UNILATERAL PRESIDENCY

Has polarization triggered a dangerous increase in presidential unilateralism? It is a straightforward question. However, problems of measurement complicate the task of providing a compelling answer. For more than two decades, a wealth of presidency scholarship has empirically examined the forces driving the frequency with which presidents use their unilateral powers.[31] However, this literature suffers from two related limitations. While most of the empirical literature has focused exclusively on executive orders, presidents enjoy a range of other tools to accomplish similar policy ends. Presidents are increasingly relying on other unilateral instruments, such as memoranda, to pursue their policy goals, perhaps in part to defend

---

[28] Alan I. Abramowitz and Steven W. Webster, "Negative Partisanship: Why Americans Dislike Parties but Behave Like Rabid Partisans," *Political Psychology* 39, no. 1 (2018): 119–35.

[29] Reeves and Rogowski, "The Public Cost of Unilateral Action"; Andrew Reeves and Jon C. Rogowski, "Public Opinion Toward Presidential Power," *Presidential Studies Quarterly* 4, no 4 (2015): 1–28.

[30] Christenson and Kriner, *The Myth of the Imperial Presidency*.

[31] Michelle Belco and Brandon Rottinghaus, *The Dual Executive: Unilateral Orders in a Separated and Shared Power System* (Stanford: Stanford University Press, 2017); Alexander Bolton and Sharece Thrower, "Legislative Capacity and Executive Unilateralism," *American Journal of Political Science* 60, no. 3 (2016): 649–63; George A. Krause and David B. Cohen, "Presidential Use of Executive Orders, 1953–1994," *American Politics Quarterly* 25, no. 4 (1997): 458–81; Kenneth R. Mayer, "Executive Orders and Presidential Power," *The Journal of Politics* 61, no. 2 (1999): 445–66.

themselves from public criticism by pointing to lower executive order tallies.[32] At the same time, many if not most presidential unilateral actions, be they executive orders, memoranda, proclamations, or other instruments, are of substantively limited importance. Scholars studying executive order issuance have recognized this problem and developed multiple metrics for identifying significant executive orders.[33] However, because these analyses focus exclusively on executive orders, they miss unilateral action implemented through other tools, including many of the most important executive actions of recent administrations, such as President Trump's third travel ban, DACA, DAPA, and expanded NSA surveillance. By contrast, a new wave of scholarship has begun to pay greater systematic attention to presidents' use of other instruments in their unilateral toolkit.[34] However, these studies have largely failed to distinguish between significant and substantively less important actions.

To overcome these limitations, we adapted Howell's method for identifying significant executive orders to develop a new measure of significant executive actions that includes any non-ceremonial unilateral presidential directive mentioned in the *New York Times* within a year of its issuance, regardless of the formal instrument used to put it into effect.[35] Our data spans the entire post-Watergate era from the Carter presidency through the first two years of the Trump administration.[36] Importantly, this measure includes anything the *Times* called an executive order, regardless of whether the unilateral instrument used was actually an executive order. For example, the *Times* routinely called DACA an executive order, even though it was implemented through a memorandum. We also explicitly searched for any mention of executive memoranda, proclamations, executive agreements, or

---

[32] Kenneth S. Lowande, "After the Orders: Presidential Memoranda and Unilateral Action," *Presidential Studies Quarterly* 4, no. 4 (2014): 724–41.

[33] Fang-Yi Chiou and Lawrence S. Rothenberg, *The Enigma of Presidential Power: Parties, Policies, and Strategic Uses of Unilateral Action* (Cambridge: Cambridge University Press, 2017); Howell, *Power Without Persuasion*; Kenneth R. Mayer and Kevin Price, "Unilateral Presidential Powers: Significant Executive Orders, 1949–99," *Presidential Studies Quarterly* 32, no. 2 (2002): 367–86

[34] Lowande, "After the Orders"; Jeffrey S. Peake and Glen S. Krutz, *Treaty Politics and the Rise of Executive Agreements: International Commitments in a System of Shared Powers* (Ann Arbor: University of Michigan Press, 2009); Brandon Rottinghaus and Jason Maier, "The Power of Decree: Presidential Use of Executive Proclamations, 1977–2005," *Political Research Quarterly* 60, no. June (2007): 338–43.

[35] William G Howell, "Unilateral Powers: A Brief Overview," *Presidential Studies Quarterly* 35, no 3 (2005): 417–39.

[36] Ford technically took office after Watergate, however he was forever linked to the scandal and its politics.

anything generally called an "executive action."[37] This measure both casts a much broader net in terms of the types of unilateral actions included than previous research and allows us to focus on the type of publicly salient, substantively important unilateral policy shifts central to arguments that presidential unilateral power has dangerously expanded in contemporary politics and threatens the constitutional system of checks and balances.

HAS POLARIZATION FUELED INCREASING UNILATERALISM?

One of the most commonly used metrics of polarization in Congress is the difference in first dimension NOMINATE scores between the median Democratic and Republican members.[38] As shown in Figure 5.1, while

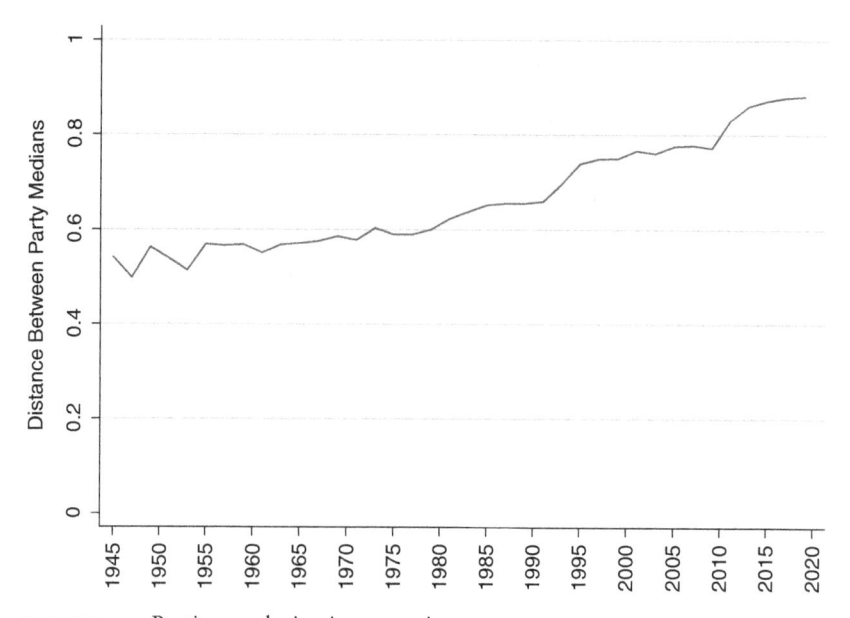

FIGURE 5.1 Partisan polarization over time
Source: First dimension NOMINATE scores from https://voteview.com/

---

[37] Specifically, we searched the *Times* for any article containing at least one of the following words: "executive order"; "executive action"; "proclamation"; "executive agreement"; "memorandum"; or "memoranda."

[38] On the limits of NOMINATE as a measure of ideology, see Lee, *Beyond Ideology*; Frances E. Lee, *Insecure Majorities: Partisanship and the Perpetual Campaign* (Chicago: University of Chicago Press, 2016). While NOMINATE certainly also reflects partisan divisions, the increasing divide between the two parties' median members clearly reflects the growing divide and partisan animosity between the two caucuses.

the two parties' medians grew slowly from the end of World War II through the 1970s, polarization began to accelerate dramatically beginning in the 1980s and continuing through the 1990s. The terrorist attacks of September 11 may have very temporarily served as a unifying force, catapulting George W. Bush to the highest approval ratings in the history of the Gallup Poll. However, it did nothing to slow the rise of polarization, which continued to increase unabated through the present day.

Did this dramatic acceleration in partisan polarization fuel presidential imperialistic tendencies? As an initial and superficial inquiry into this question, Figure 5.2 shows the total number of executive orders, memoranda, and proclamations issued each year from 1977 through 2018. When examining executive action in the aggregate, there is no evidence that presidents have become increasingly unilateral over this period. In raw terms, presidents do indeed seem to rely heavily on their unilateral powers. During this forty-year period, presidents averaged more than 200 executive orders, memoranda, and proclamations per year. However, most of these executive actions are substantively of little import. The tallies in Figure 5.2 include scores of commemorative actions that are purely ceremonial. Even

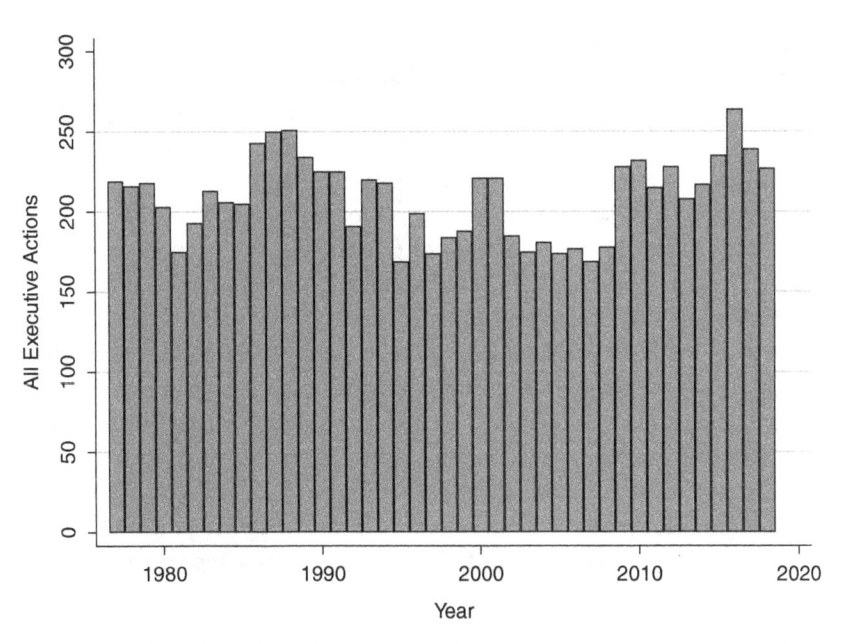

FIGURE 5.2 Total number of executive orders, memoranda, and proclamations, 1977–2018

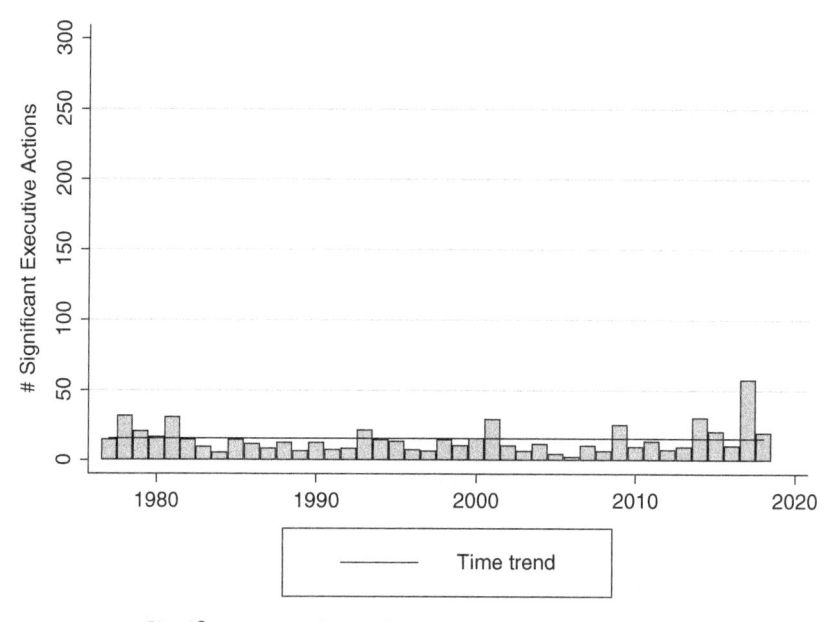

FIGURE 5.3 Significant executive actions, 1977–2018

many actions that are non-ceremonial and of genuine substantive import, such as President Obama's 2014 "Memorandum on Creating a Federal Strategy to Promote the Health of Honey Bees and Other Pollinators," are hardly the unilateral power grabs that concern those worried about rising authoritarianism and an erosion of checks and balances.

To focus more squarely on the types of unilateral action that might represent a threat to the separation of powers, Figure 5.3 plots only those executive orders, memoranda, proclamations, executive agreements, and anything generally labeled an "executive action" that merited even a single mention in the *New York Times*.[39] Of course, it is possible that the *Times* failed to cover at least some executive actions of substantive import, particularly highly classified national security decision directives. Nevertheless, it is highly likely that most executive actions that represent major assertions of unilateral authority and direct threats to checks and balances, particularly in the domestic sphere, will receive at least some coverage in the *Times*, a national newspaper of record. Moreover, it bears repeating that this

---

[39] To emphasize the contrast with tallies of all executive actions, the scale in Figure 5.3 is the same as that in Figure 5.2.

represents a very low threshold for an executive action to be coded as "significant" – indeed, it is a threshold much lower than that routinely used by legislative scholars to identify important or major legislation.[40]

Even using this modest significance threshold, the number of "major" executive actions is relatively modest. On average, presidents issued just fifteen executive actions per year that merited even a single mention in the *New York Times* during this period of steadily rising polarization. While this new data set included the overwhelming majority of the most prominent executive actions of recent years, such as President Bush's creation of military tribunals to try terror suspects and expansion of warrantless surveillance, President Obama's DACA and DAPA memoranda to shield millions of illegal immigrants from deportation, and President Trump's travel bans and transgender military service ban, many other actions that met the significance criteria were of much more limited importance. For example, during the first two years of the Trump presidency alone, our data set includes Trump's order to create his ultimately ineffective Electoral Fraud Commission, his order to take the preliminary steps needed to build the wall in January 2017 (although this had little tangible effect), as well as more technical orders banning American transactions using Venezuela's new crypto-currency and ordering a review of the post office's finances.

Focusing more narrowly on the subset of executive actions that received even a single mention on the front page of the *New York Times* paints an even more restrained portrait of unilateralism even in an era of rising polarization. As shown in Figure 5.4, while there is some considerable variation from year to year, major executive actions that reach this level of media scrutiny and public salience are rare. From 1977 through 2018, presidents averaged only four such actions per year. In eleven of those forty-two years, presidents issued either one or no executive actions of any type that received even a single mention on the front page of the *Times*.

Finally, there is little evidence that presidents are increasingly relying on their unilateral powers as polarization increases. The time trend line shown in Figure 5.3 is essentially flat.[41] There is also no evidence of any

---

[40] William G. Howell et al., "Divided Government and the Legislative Productivity of Congress, 1945–94," *Legislative Studies Quarterly* 25, no. 2 (2000): 285–312; David R Mayhew, *Divided We Govern* (New Haven: Yale University Press, 1991).

[41] And its slope would even be negative if the surge in activity during Trump's first year in 2017 is excluded.

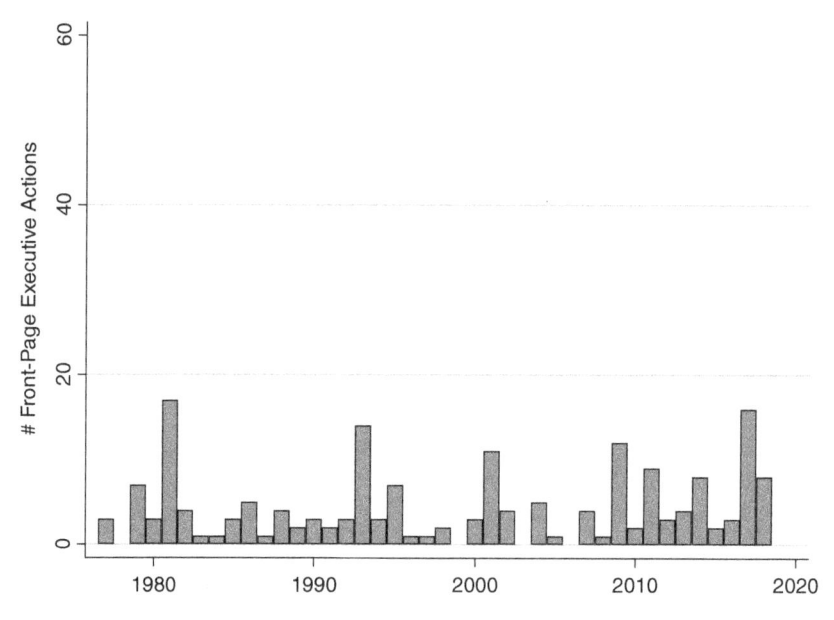

FIGURE 5.4 Executive actions on front page of *New York Times*, 1977–2018

clear temporal increase when looking at the even rarer subset of actions that received front-page coverage in the *Times*.

This is not to say that presidents never achieve significant policy victories when acting unilaterally; presidents of both parties have secured major policy shifts by going it alone that they never would have achieved if forced to secure congressional assent. Moreover, this measure of presidential unilateral activity does not fully capture the extent to which all presidents in the post–World War II years have used their levers of influence over the administrative state – for example, through the regulatory process – to shape the implementation of public policy, in many cases effecting significant shifts in policy outcomes without writing new law (see King and Milkis chapter in this volume).[42] However, the data suggest that

---

[42] If the *Times* refers to a regulatory action as an "executive action" or "executive order," it enters the dataset. However, following the unilateral politics literature we treat regulatory actions as a separate, though inherently important tool of presidential policy influence. As President Trump has learned, regulatory policy cannot be changed with the stroke of a pen, and his administration's failure to follow the Administrative Procedures Act and other procedural requirements has led to many of his de-regulatory initiatives being struck down in Court. See the running tally maintained by the Institute for Policy Integrity, https://policyintegrity.org/trump-court-roundup.

presidents are significantly more constrained in their ability to change policy with the stroke of a pen than both the dominant pivotal politics-based theory of unilateral action and extensions to it assessing the exacerbating role that polarization might play would suggest.[43] Instead, the data is consistent with arguments that bureaucratic and political checks have compensated for the institutional weaknesses of other branches when trying to staunch presidential overreach.[44]

TRUMPIAN EXCEPTIONALISM?

Polarization has not produced an empirically discernible expansion in the exercise of unilateral executive authority. Instead, the political checks on unilateralism have largely remained resilient. However, Donald J. Trump made antipathy for political conventions a defining feature of his campaign for the presidency. Is Trump less sensitive to political checks on his power? Has he exercised the office's unilateral powers differently and more aggressively than his predecessors and, in so doing, created a new precedent opening a Pandora's box for abuse by future presidents in a polarized polity?

With only two years of empirical data, it is perhaps too early to tell, but there are some tantalizing, if conflicting, clues. On the exceptional side of the ledger, Trump's first year in office stands out for producing the most significant actions of any year in our data. Statistical analyses including standard covariates confirm that Trump's rate of issuing executive actions receiving coverage in the *Times* during his first two years in office exceeded the rates of all of his predecessors, save Carter.[45] This result conflicts with a recent empirical assessment of Trump's first year that finds more continuity than change in an assessment of the raw frequency with which presidents have used various directives and regulatory actions across recent administrations.[46] This aggressiveness may reflect Trump's increased willingness to make bold unilateral moves to please his political

---

[43] Howell, *Power Without Persuasion*.
[44] Christenson and Kriner, *The Myth of the Imperial Presidency*; Eric A Posner and Adrian Vermeule, *The Executive Unbound: After the Madisonian Republic* (Oxford: Oxford University Press, 2010); Reeves and Rogowski, "The Public Cost of Unilateral Action"; Rudalevige, *By Executive Order*.
[45] Dino P. Christenson and Douglas L. Kriner, "Beyond the Base: Presidents, Partisan Approval, and the Political Economy of Unilateral Action," *Journal of Political Institutions and Political Economy* 1, no1 (2020): 1–26.
[46] Rachel Augustine Potter et al., "Continuity Trumps Change: The First Year of Trump's Administrative Presidency," *PS – Political Science and Politics* 52, no. 4 (2019): 613–19.

base, even if it risked broader political pushback. However, the larger tallies in Trump's first two years could also be an artifact of measurement error given the media's penchant for (over)covering all things Trump. Indeed, some of the coverage of Trump's actions explicitly discussed how the substantive impact of the directive at hand would be modest.

Perhaps more important is the question of whether Trump has exploited the office's unilateral authority in qualitatively different ways that risk setting dangerous precedents for future administrations. Perhaps Trump's boldest gambit was his 2019 declaration of a national emergency to build the wall along the Mexican border. From a constitutional perspective, this order was particularly troubling as Trump ordered unilaterally a policy course that Congress had explicitly considered and rejected legislatively. Indeed, the government shut down in the winter of 2018/19 precisely because legislators refused to appropriate funds for the wall. Under the framework articulated by Justice Jackson in *Youngstown v. Sawyer*, there is a strong argument that presidential power in this case was therefore "at its lowest ebb." Both chambers quickly passed a resolution revoking the emergency declaration, with twelve Senate Republicans crossing the aisle and voting against the president. However, as predicted by the pivotal politics model, the resistance was futile.[47] Trump vetoed the joint resolution, and his veto was easily sustained by fellow Republicans. The order delighted Trump's base, but was opposed by a strong majority of Americans.[48]

While Trump's emergency declaration was undeniably a bold power grab, it is by far the clearest case of Trump taking a *Youngstown* "lowest ebb" action during his first three years in office.[49] Moreover, Trump's predecessors have also on rare occasions acted unilaterally to effect a shift in policy explicitly refused by Congress. Most recently, President Obama's memorandum establishing the Deferred Action for Childhood Arrivals (DACA) program before his 2012 reelection bid essentially created by executive fiat what Congress refused to enact legislatively through the

---

[47] The 1983 Supreme Court decision *INS v. Chadha* striking down the legislative veto significantly altered the National Emergencies Act, requiring a joint resolution (which can be vetoed) rather than a concurrent resolution to terminate an emergency declaration.

[48] Emily Guskin, "A Clear Majority of Americans Oppose Trump's Emergency Declaration," *Washington Post*, March 15, 2019, www.washingtonpost.com/politics/20 19/03/15/clear-majority-americans-oppose-trumps-emergency-declaration/?arc404=true.

[49] Moreover, in contrast to Truman in *Youngstown*, Trump could point to the delegation of authority in the National Emergencies Act of 1976 to claim that presidential power was actually at its zenith.

DREAM Act.⁵⁰ While President George W. Bush did not ask Congress to create a system of military tribunals to try suspected terrorists as part of the USA Patriot Act, the landmark legislation that he proudly signed on October 26, 2001, explicitly required suspected terrorists to be charged within seven days of being taken into custody and provided access to the civilian court system.⁵¹ Yet less than three weeks later, President Bush signed his Military Order of November 13, 2001, depriving many suspected terrorists of legal rights and protections and creating a parallel system of military tribunals to try terrorism cases under radically different rules of evidence and procedure.⁵² Finally, with Mexico on the verge of default in early 1995, President Clinton sought to strike a deal with congressional leaders for emergency loans to prop up the Mexican economy. While Speaker Gingrich and Majority Leader Dole supported a deal, their members balked, and Congress refused to pass the package. Against the advice of many advisors who warned of great political risk, Clinton unilaterally authorized $20 billion in loan guarantees. From a policy perspective, Clinton's gambit proved a great success. However, from a constitutional one he clearly acted unilaterally contra the express will of Congress.

Presidents do on occasion act unilaterally in direct defiance of Congress' wishes when their power is at its lowest ebb. Trump's border emergency is not unique in this regard. But such cases are empirically quite rare. Speaker Pelosi and other Democrats have openly mused that should a Democrat win in 2020 she or he might declare a national emergency to grapple with climate change or gun violence without congressional action.⁵³ Whether Trump's move has opened the floodgates remains uncertain.

Trump's first years in office provide many more examples of the president taking action opposed by many in Congress, and even by some in his own party, but not explicitly considered and rejected by the legislature. Foremost among these are Trump's trade wars against economic

---

[50] A similar story could be told concerning Obama's post-2014 midterm DAPA memorandum, which was blocked in the courts before going into effect.

[51] Timothy Edgar, "Interested Persons Memo on Military Trials in Terrorism Cases," *ACLU*, November 29, 2001, www.aclu.org/other/interested-persons-memo-military-trials-terrorism-cases.

[52] The Supreme Court ultimately ruled that these tribunals violated the Uniform Code of Military Justice and the Geneva Conventions in *Hamdan v. Rumsfeld*.

[53] Mike Lillis, "Pelosi Warns GOP: Next President Could Declare National Emergency on Guns," *The Hill*, February 14, 2019, https://thehill.com/homenews/house/430098-pelosi-warns-gop-next-president-could-declare-national-emergency-on-guns.

competitors and traditional allies alike. With the Reciprocal Trade Agreements Act of 1934, Congress sought to check its own protectionist impulses by delegating increasing authority over trade to the president.[54] Instead, Trump has used national security exceptions in existing laws to impose tariffs on a range of products, including those from NATO allies, in pursuit of his protectionist agenda. Trump's tariffs are of a different scale; however, he is far from the first to use protectionist policies for electoral purposes.[55] Moreover, the extent to which Trump has backed down in the face of political pressure is illuminating. With great fanfare, Trump followed through on his pledge to withdraw from NAFTA, which he routinely labeled "one of the worst trade deals" in American history. However, the administration quickly replaced it with a revised trade pact that mostly made modest updates to the original treaty.[56] Similarly, facing pressure from fellow Republicans, Trump has repeatedly delayed or canceled new rounds of tariffs against China and, in December 2019, reached a preliminary deal that deferred even more tariffs in exchange for modest concessions from Beijing.[57]

Trump defied congressional critics from both sides of the aisle with his hastily announced ban on transgendered Americans from serving in the military and his almost unprecedented interference with the military justice system through his pardoning of multiple military members accused of war crimes. However, in the case of his family separations policy at the southern border, Trump executed an abrupt about-face and reversed his policy in the face of sharp political pushback and public outcry. In still other cases Trump has openly considered taking unilateral action – including draft executive orders to loosen restrictions on torture and extraordinary renditions; a draft order to crack down on social media companies that "censor" conservatives; and his public threats to end

---

[54] I. M. Destler, *American Trade Politics*, 4th ed. (Washington, DC: Institute for International Economics, 2005).

[55] Douglas L. Kriner and Andrew Reeves, *The Particularistic President: Executive Branch Politics and Political Inequality* (Cambridge: Cambridge University Press, 2015), pp. 52–66; Kenneth S. Lowande, Jeffery A. Jenkins, and Andrew J. Clarke, "Presidential Particularism and US Trade Politics," *Political Science Research and Methods* 6, no2 (2018): 265–81.

[56] Ana Swanson and Jim Tankersley, "Trump Just Signed the U.S.M.C.A. Here's What's in the New NAFTA," *New York Times*, January 29, 2020, www.nytimes.com/2020/01/29/business/economy/usmca-deal.html.

[57] Keith Bradsher, "China's Hard-Liners Win a Round in Trump's Trade Deal," *New York Times*, December 14, 2019, www.nytimes.com/2019/12/14/business/china-trade-hardliners.html.

birthright citizenship through executive action – but backed off in the face of political resistance.[58]

Despite some limited evidence of differences, it is important not to push the argument too far. With a few exceptions, Trump's record of unilateral accomplishment looks neither imperial nor all that exceptional. President Trump has used his unilateral powers to pursue policies that appeal primarily to his political base, perhaps to a greater extent than any of his predecessors. However, in multiple cases, he has shown himself to be sensitive to political pushback, suggesting that political and bureaucratic checks remain resilient. Ultimately, the extent to which Trump's use of the office's unilateral powers represent a precedent-changing break from the past remains highly uncertain.

THE GREATEST THREAT: TRUMP'S WAR ON OVERSIGHT

On balance, perhaps the greatest long-term threat to democratic resilience from the Trump presidency is not its unilateral legacy, but its unconditional war on one of Congress' most important tools when trying to exercise a political check on presidential overreach: its oversight powers. Historically, Congress has used its investigative power to great effect to superintend the executive branch and push back against presidential aggrandizement.[59] Oversight avoids the supermajoritarian requirements that foil most legislative efforts to rein in presidential unilateralism. While the influence of oversight is necessarily indirect, by shining a light on alleged executive misconduct and battling the president in the public sphere, congressional critics have enjoyed considerable success in bringing political pressure to bear on a wayward White House. In some cases, this creates momentum for new legislation that would not have passed without investigative pressure; in others it coerces presidential policy concessions or even outright reversals; and more generally oversight's potential

---

[58] Christenson and Kriner, *The Myth of the Imperial Presidency*, 191–95. See also Brian Fung, "White House Proposal Would Have FCC and FTC Police Alleged Social Media Censorship," *CNN*, August 10, 2019, www.cnn.com/2019/08/09/tech/white-house-social-media-executive-order-fcc-ftc/index.html. Trump did issue an Executive Order alleging to crack down on online censorship in May 2020 after Twitter labeled one the President's tweets alleging widespread voter fraud as false. However, its practical effects were minimal. See: "Executive Order on Preventing Online Censorship," May 28, 2020, www.whitehouse.gov/presidential-actions/executive-order-preventing-online-censorship/.

[59] Mayhew, *Divided We Govern*; Arthur Schlesinger Jr. and Roger Burns, *Congress Investigates: A Documentary History* (New York: Chelsea House Publishers, 1975).

to inflict political damage can influence presidents' anticipatory calculations and moderate their actions.[60]

Yet, for investigative oversight to be effective, Congress must gain access to information and use it to battle the administration in the public sphere. Presidents and Congress have sparred over the scope of the investigative power and Congress' access to information since the very first congressional investigation in 1792. However, Trump's widespread assertions of executive privilege, repeated refusals to comply with congressional subpoenas for testimony, and blanket refusals to turn over documents – even in the context of a formal impeachment inquiry when Congress' constitutional powers are at their highest – threaten to render Congress' investigative power as ineffective as its legislative check.[61] The White House's war on Congress' oversight powers goes far beyond its refusal to cooperate with the impeachment inquiry. Its record of almost total obstruction encompasses a much broader effort to thwart a range of House inquiries into alleged administration improprieties, from the president's personal finances and possible violations of the Emoluments Clause, to evidence of obstruction detailed in the Mueller Report, to allegations that lax security clearance procedures jeopardized national security.[62] Nevertheless, the 2019 impeachment inquiry is particularly instructive.

At its core was President Trump's decision to withhold congressionally appropriated military aid from Ukraine in exchange for investigations of his political rival, Joe Biden, and his son. Notably, President Trump backed down and released the aid in the face of intense political pressure from Congress and after he learned that a whistleblower complaint had been filed that could ultimately end up in the hands of congressional investigators.[63] In this respect, political and bureaucratic checks succeeded in reversing Trump's unilateral gambit. However, Trump

---

[60] Kriner and Schickler, *Investigating the President*.
[61] Exacerbating the long-term threat, Trump's unprecedented and ultimately successfully obstruction comes at a time when changes in meso-level institutions, including state parties and the media, have already weakened congressional incentives, particularly among presidential co-partisans, to engage in oversight that might check presidential power (see the chapter by Pierson and Schickler).
[62] Anita Kumar and Andrew Desiderio, "Trump Showdown with House Democrats Ignites All-Out War," *Politico.com*, April 23, 2019, www.politico.com/story/2019/04/23/trump-investigators-congress-1288795.
[63] Michael Schmidt, Julian Barnes, and Maggie Haberman, "Trump Knew of Whistle-Blower Complaint When He Released Aid to Ukraine," *New York Times*, November 26, 2019, www.nytimes.com/2019/11/26/us/politics/trump-whistle-blower-complaint-ukraine.html.

adamantly refused to cooperate in any respect with the congressional investigation into the Ukraine aid hold and alleged quid pro quo, which the non-partisan General Accountability Office would later determine was illegal. The White House directed current and even former administration officials, including acting chief of staff and head of the Office of Management and Budget Mick Mulvaney and former National Security Adviser John Bolton not to testify before congressional impeachment inquiries. Following White House directives, many officials refused to comply with congressional subpoenas. After releasing a rough transcript of the President's July 25 phone call with Ukrainian President Zelensky that all but confirmed the quid pro quo, the administration refused to turn over virtually every document subpoenaed by investigators.[64] Ultimately, the White House's intransigence led the House to make obstruction of Congress its second article of impeachment.

By crippling Congress' response to this all-out assault on its constitutional prerogatives, polarization has perhaps had the most dangerous and long-lasting consequences for the balance of power between the branches. House Republicans uniformly rallied behind their party leader, even storming the secure location where depositions were taking place to demand greater access to the proceedings and opportunities to defend the president. During the trial phase, Senate Republicans showed no more appetite for bucking a president of their party and standing up for congressional prerogatives than did their compatriots in the House. At the trial's outset, Senate Republicans defeated a series of Democratic motions to subpoena witnesses and documents on party line votes. This party loyalty would be tested when the *New York Times* revealed that in his forthcoming book manuscript, John Bolton undercut a main argument of the president's defense and directly linked Trump to the decision to withhold military aid until Ukraine announced investigations into the Bidens.[65] The startling revelation coupled with Bolton's publicly expressed willingness to testify if subpoenaed led Utah Republican Mitt Romney to judge it "increasingly likely" that the Senate would now vote to hear witnesses. However, Romney was wrong. Retiring swing senator Lamar Alexander (R-TN) announced on January 30 that he would not

---

[64] *Politifact* rated Jim Himes's (D-Conn.) claim that Trump "has not given this Congress a single email, phone record, or document," as "mostly true." www.politifact.com/factchecks/2019/dec/19/jim-himes/himes-says-white-house-snubbed-houses-document-req/.

[65] Maggie Haberman and Michael Schmidt, "Trump Tied Ukraine Aid to Inquiries He Sought, Bolton Book Says," *New York Times*, January 26, 2020, www.nytimes.com/2020/01/26/us/politics/trump-bolton-book-ukraine.html.

support calling witnesses. In his statement, Alexander plainly acknowledged that Trump solicited dirt on the Bidens from Ukraine and that he conditioned military aid, "at least in part," on that assistance.[66] However, Alexander judged that the action, while improper, did not merit removal from office and therefore further investigative action was unnecessary. Alaska Republican Lisa Murkowski echoed Alexander's sentiments. The vote for witnesses failed, and the trial moved toward a speedy acquittal with only a single Republican crossing the aisle.

Ultimately, many Republicans have acknowledged publicly or privately that Trump illegally solicited electoral interference from a foreign government and withheld congressionally appropriated funds in an effort to obtain it. But in an era of intense partisan polarization, almost all judged that the costs of breaking with Trump were so high that they eventually followed Mick Mulvaney's advice: "Get over it!"

Placing partisan imperatives above institutional defense reached its height in the response to the January 6, 2021, insurrection at the Capitol. In the immediate aftermath of the attack, many members from both sides of the aisle denounced the president's role in inciting the mob in a desperate attempt to cling to power more akin to a banana republic than the world's oldest constitutional democracy. However, when confronted with the opportunity to hold Trump accountable for his fundamental assault on the foundations of American democracy, all but ten House Republicans voted against impeachment and forty-three Republican senators ensured his acquittal.

This institutional surrender could have consequences far beyond the Trump presidency; meekly acquiescing to Trump's unprecedented obstruction has set a dangerous precedent that could seriously weaken Congress' investigative oversight powers for the foreseeable future. If presidents can count on iron-clad support from their co-partisans as they all but eviscerate Congress' powers of oversight, then future presidents will have strong incentives to follow in Trump's footsteps. If they do so, it could seriously expand presidential power by weakening one of the most important checks on presidential overreach that has thus far prevented the emergence of a truly imperial presidency.

---

[66] "Alexander Statement on Impeachment," January 30, 2020, www.alexander.senate.gov/public/index.cfm?p=PressReleases&id=AA7E4960-6788-43A9-AF03-5DC456A0D448.

6

Court-Packing and Democratic Erosion

Thomas M. Keck

> [T]he main role of the judge in a democracy is to maintain and protect the constitution and democracy.[1]
> Aharon Barak

> Liberal and democratic constitutionalism is worth defending, but first we need to stop taking for granted that constitutions can defend themselves.[2]
> Kim Lane Scheppele (2018)

The ongoing debate about the ills of American democracy features core disagreements about both diagnosis and cure. The title of this book alludes to what is now a multi-decade lament among scholars and pundits focused on US politics regarding the rise of "polarization." On this account, our problem is that political elites and even ordinary citizens are so divided along partisan lines that they are unable to come together to solve important public problems. Given this diagnosis, the cure would involve institutional changes designed to empower centrists of both parties and to weaken their extremist flanks. Meanwhile, a different group of observers – including students of both democratic procedures in the United States and autocratic governments elsewhere – has diagnosed the

---

I presented earlier drafts of this paper at Cornell University and the University of Utah. I would like to thank members of both audiences for their thoughtful comments and questions. Thanks also to David Bateman, Aaron Belkin, David Driesen, Tom Ginsburg, Aziz Huq, Jane Mansbridge, Seth Tillman, and Mark Tushnet for helpful comments, and to Nathan Carrington for outstanding research assistance.

[1] Aharon Barak, *The Judge in a Democracy* (Princeton: Princeton University Press, 2006).
[2] Kim Lane Scheppele, "Autocratic Legalism," *University of Chicago Law Review* 85 (2018): 583.

problem as partisan degradation rather than polarization. On this account, the key defects facing American democracy are rooted not in a bipartisan refusal to compromise, but in one party's abandonment of the rules of the game. In other words, these observers trace democratic erosion to the transformation of the Republican Party into an anti-system party. Given this alternate diagnosis, the cure would involve institutional changes that weaken the structural pro-GOP biases in our electoral and policymaking systems, thereby frustrating the party's playbook for maintaining its hold on power without offering a platform that appeals to popular majorities.

On both diagnosis and cure, these debates are reflected in contemporary assessments of the US Supreme Court. The current Court is more and differently polarized than the historical norm, but "polarization" is not the best frame for the current Court's democratic defects. Partisan capture is a better frame, and its treatment requires different remedies. If the Court is merely too "polarized," then good-governance reforms like judicial term limits may be an adequate solution, and many good-government reformers have called for them. But if the Court has been captured by an anti-system party, and if it is deploying judicial power to assist that party in maintaining control without appealing to popular majorities, then good-government reforms will be insufficient to meet the threat. In other words, halting and reversing democratic erosion may require bold institutional changes to wrestle the Court away from the anti-system party's control.

Among the boldest such changes is court-packing, which David Kosař and Katarina Šipulová define as "an intentional irregular change in the composition of the existing court, in quantitative as well as qualitative terms, that creates a new majority at the court or restricts the old one."[3] During the 2020 Democratic presidential primary, calls for such court-packing emerged seemingly out of nowhere, with scholars and pundits divided as to whether this development is best understood as a dangerous escalation of partisan polarization or a necessary reckoning with our partisan courts.[4]

Politically motivated alterations in the size of a judicial institution are a quintessential example of the sort of "constitutional hardball" that

---

[3] David Kosař and Katarína Šipulová, "How to Fight Court Packing?" *Constitutional Studies* 6, no. 1 (2020): 135.

[4] Multiple Democratic candidates for both Congress and the presidency expressed openness to expanding the Court's size, with a growing wave of scholars and left-liberal pundits endorsing such reforms as well. Aaron Belkin, "The Case for Court Expansion," Take Back the Court, June 27, 2019, www.takebackthecourt.today/the-case-for-court-expansion; Aaron Belkin, "Court Expansion and the Restoration of Democracy: The Case for

many students of democratic erosion have decried.[5] But the scholar who coined the phrase "constitutional hardball" has himself argued that court-packing and other such tactics are in some circumstances normatively justified.[6] In this chapter, I argue that one such circumstance is when court-packing proves necessary to break a downward spiral of democratic erosion. Even then, however, there are better and worse ways to do it – that is, more and less democratically legitimate ways to engage in Court reform. As such, my account of court-packing and democratic erosion is meant to highlight how pro-democracy elites operating in a context of partial autocratic consolidation might try to escape from that condition in a maximally constitutional fashion.

My argument here is rooted in two central points of reference. First, I review the existing comparative literature on the role of courts in polities where democratic erosion is underway. Second, I turn to the history of court-packing in the United States in an effort to confirm and sharpen the lessons drawn from the comparative literature. The key lesson of the US historical cases is that from almost any normative baseline, court-packing can be used in both positive and negative ways. As such, any assessment of court-reform proposals should distinguish between constitutional hardball in service of

---

Constitutional Hardball," *Pepperdine Law Review* (2019): 19–50; Daniel Epps and Ganesh Sitaraman, "How to Save the Supreme Court," *Yale Law Journal* 129 (2019): 148–206; David Faris, *It's Time to Fight Dirty: How Democrats Can Build a Lasting Majority in American Politics* (Brooklyn: Melville House, 2018), 81–106; Leah Greenberg and Ezra Levin, *We Are Indivisible: A Blueprint for Democracy After Trump* (New York: One Signal, 2019), 273–80; Mondaire Jones, "To Save Our Democracy, We Must Expand the Supreme Court," Salon, April 26, 2020, www.salon.com/2020/04/26/to-save-our-democracy-we-must-expand-the-supreme-court/; Ian Millhiser, "Let's Think About Court-Packing," *Dissent* 51 (Winter 2019), https://democracyjournal.org/magazine/51/lets-think-about-court-packing-2/; Frederick A. O. Schwarz Jr., "Saving the Supreme Court," Brennan Center, September 13, 2019, www.brennancenter.org/our-work/analysis-opinion/saving-supreme-court.

[5] Steven Levitsky and Daniel Ziblatt, *How Democracies Die* (New York: Crown, 2018).
[6] Mark Tushnet coined the term "constitutional hardball" to indicate political tactics that are not unconstitutional under existing law, but that represent unusually aggressive challenges to existing constitutional norms and institutions. More recently, he has spelled out some of the circumstances in which he views such tactics as democratically legitimate. Elsewhere in this volume, David Bateman has likewise argued that hardball tactics undertaken to expand the democratic electorate are more legitimate than those undertaken to constrict it. Mark V. Tushnet, "Constitutional Hardball," *John Marshall Law Review* 37 (2004): 523–53; Mark V. Tushnet, *Taking Back the Constitution: Activist Judges and the Next Age of American Law* (New Haven: Yale University Press, 2020); Bateman, chapter in this volume. See also David E. Pozen, "Hardball and/as Anti-Hardball," *NYU Journal of Legislation and Public Policy* 21 (2019): 949–55.

democratic erosion and constitutional hardball in service of democratic preservation or renewal.

COURTS AND DEMOCRATIC EROSION

Constitutional drafters often establish semi-autonomous executive institutions to serve as guardrails of democracy. In other words, they place important government functions outside the full and direct control of the president or prime minister, particularly those functions that an autocratic leader might abuse in an effort to maintain power. Vote counting should be in the hands of an independent electoral commission, not the governing party, as should regulating the media, enforcing criminal law, collecting census data, and the like. But the literature on democratic erosion teaches us that the very same institutions that operate as guardrails during normal times often become targets of authoritarian leaders, who seek to repurpose those institutions as agents of democratic erosion.[7] For example, once captured by an autocratic leader or an anti-system party, an "independent" electoral commission can change electoral rules in ways that harm the opposition's chances of deposing the party in power.

As such, halting or reversing democratic erosion will often require the recapture and/or reconfiguration of these guardrail institutions. And this recapture or reconfiguration may sometimes require tactics that, at a superficial level, look similar to the tactics used by the autocratic leaders themselves. If an autocratic leader packs an "independent" electoral commission with party loyalists appointed for ten-year terms, then any future democrats seeking to reverse the erosion of democracy will have to figure out a way to disempower or circumvent these loyalists before their terms are up.

A similar dynamic applies to judicial institutions. During normal times, independent courts can provide a valuable check against executive and legislative overreach, and under some conditions they may serve as effective democratic guardrails.[8] Once captured by

---

[7] David M. Driesen, *The Specter of Dictatorship: Judicial Enabling of Presidential Power* (Stanford: Stanford University Press, 2021); Tom Ginsburg and Aziz Z. Huq, *How to Save a Constitutional Democracy* (Chicago: University of Chicago Press, 2018); David Landau and Rosalind Dixon, "Abusive Judicial Review: Courts Against Democracy," *University of California Davis Law Review* 53 (2020): 1380; Levitsky and Ziblatt, *How Democracies Die*, 78–81; Scheppele, "Autocratic Legalism."

[8] Driesen, *Specter of Dictatorship*; Tom Ginsburg, "The Jurisprudence of Anti-Erosion," *Drake Law Review* 66 (2018): 823–53; Tom Ginsburg and Aziz Z. Huq, "Democracy's Near Misses," *Journal of Democracy* 29 (October 2018): 16–30.

authoritarian-minded leaders, however, these same courts can become agents or instruments of democratic erosion.[9] And once courts with strong tenure protections have been packed with party loyalists by an authoritarian leader, the democratic opposition will eventually need to figure out a way to unpack them. This process will necessarily require replacing or circumventing the loyalist judges. In other words, it will require attacks on judicial independence, or at least that is how the governing party loyalists will describe it.

Consider the treatment of judicial institutions by a number of twenty-first-century autocratic leaders. In Hungary, Prime Minister Viktor Orbán expanded the size of the Constitutional Court from eight to fifteen, altered the judicial selection rules to enable his party coalition to approve nominees without consulting the opposition, and declared that Constitutional Court holdings issued prior to 2012 no longer had precedential force.[10] In Poland, the Law and Justice regime refused to seat three recently appointed justices on the Constitutional Tribunal, replacing them with party loyalists. It then required the Tribunal to have a two-thirds majority in order to issue a binding decision, thereby giving a veto to the regime-aligned judges. The government effectively eliminated abstract review (a key jurisdiction-stripping move also pursued in Hungary), then successfully packed the Supreme Court, then reinstated abstract review.[11] In Turkey, President Recep Tayyip Erdoğan won a constitutional referendum in 2010 that increased the Constitutional Court's size from eleven to seventeen.[12] Six years later, he used an unsuccessful coup attempt to justify mass punishment of government critics, including the arrest of two members of the Constitutional Court and hundreds of ordinary

---

[9] Ginsburg and Huq, *How to Save a Constitutional Democracy*, 96–97, 187–91; Robert R. Kaufman and Stephan Haggard, "Democratic Decline in the United States: What Can We Learn from Middle-Income Backsliding," *Perspectives on Politics* 17 (June 2019): 417–32; Landau and Dixon, "Abusive Judicial Review"; Levitsky and Ziblatt, *How Democracies Die*.

[10] Driesen, *Specter of Dictatorship*; Ginsburg and Huq, *How to Save a Constitutional Democracy*, 68–70; Kaufman and Haggard, "Democratic Decline"; Thomas M. Keck, "Is President Trump More Like Victor Orbán or Franklin Pierce?" *Constitutional Studies* 4 (2019): 131–54; Levitsky and Ziblatt, *How Democracies Die*, 80; Kim Lane Scheppele, "Understanding Hungary's Constitutional Revolution," in *Constitutional Crisis in the European Constitutional Area: Theory, Law and Politics in Hungary and Romania*, ed. Armin von Bogdandy and Pál Sonnevend (Portland, OR: Hart Publishing, 2019), 111–24.

[11] Driesen, *Specter of Dictatorship*; Ginsburg and Huq, *How to Save a Constitutional Democracy*, 98–100; Levitsky and Ziblatt, *How Democracies Die*, 80.

[12] Can Yeginsu, "Turkey Packs the Court," *New York Review of Books*, September 22, 2010.

judges.[13] In Venezuela, Hugo Chávez dissolved the Supreme Court in 1999, replacing it with a new Supreme Tribunal of Justice. Five years later, he expanded the Court's size from twenty to thirty-two and filled the new seats with twelve additional loyalist judges.[14] When opposition parties captured Congress in 2015, Chávez's successor, Nicolás Maduro, relied on the loyal Court to invalidate "nearly all" of the opposition-controlled legislature's bills as unconstitutional.[15]

In each case, these court-packing initiatives were an "essential component of the authoritarian playbook."[16] In other words, once they have seized temporary control of state power, authoritarian leaders regularly seek to capture independent courts, including the national apex courts that bear prime responsibility for enforcing the Constitution. By doing so, they remove a potential horizontal check that might limit their own democracy-eroding moves. Even worse, they entrench their own allies in positions of power that extend beyond the normal electoral cycle, such that even if the democratic opposition regains control of the national legislature, the regime-allied Court will be in a position to thwart their democracy-restoring moves.

The post-2016 literature on democratic erosion in the United States has focused mostly on drawing lessons from elsewhere in the world to help understand the Donald Trump presidency, but it has also made some reference to related episodes from American political history. For example, Levitsky and Ziblatt make brief reference to US court-packing controversies following the election of 1800, the assassination of Abraham Lincoln, and FDR's landslide 1936 reelection.[17] In doing so, they endorse the conventional reading of these episodes. On their account, for example, FDR's court-packing plan represented a dangerous presidential assault on a coequal branch, but in the end, our constitutional system of checks and balances prevented its success. This view remains the dominant reading of FDR's effort to alter the Court's size, and it has been advanced with regard to the Jeffersonian Democratic and post–Civil War Republican efforts to do so as well.

---

[13] Kaufman and Haggard, "Democratic Decline," 423; Levitsky and Ziblatt, *How Democracies Die*, 96.

[14] Kaufman and Haggard, "Democratic Decline," 422–24; Levitsky and Ziblatt, *How Democracies Die*, 80–81.

[15] Levitsky and Ziblatt, *How Democracies Die*, 110; see also Landau and Dixon, "Abusive Judicial Review," 1363–70.

[16] Kaufman and Haggard, "Democratic Decline," 426.

[17] Levitsky and Ziblatt, *How Democracies Die*, 118–23, 130–33.

The problem with this conventional view is that it fails to distinguish between constitutional hardball in the service of democratic erosion and constitutional hardball in the service of democratic preservation or renewal. In particular, the conventional story understates the threat posed to core constitutional and democratic values by John Adams, Andrew Johnson, and the early twentieth-century Supreme Court, and hence treats the subsequent court-packing efforts as unfortunate departures from democratic norms, when they might be better understood as constitutional hardball in defense of democratic norms.

By way of analogy, consider Lincoln's famous argument defending his wartime suspension of the writ of habeas corpus. The constitutional text expressly authorized such suspensions, and while it may have implied that the suspension power belonged to Congress, it did not clearly say so. As such, Lincoln did not believe his executive order to have violated the Constitution, and the Attorney General of the United States defended its legality. But even for those who disagreed with this assessment, Lincoln asked them to consider his alternatives. As he took office in March 1861, seven Southern states had already purported to secede, formed a new country, and declared war on the United States. Congress was not in session, and Confederate sympathizers in Maryland were blowing up bridges and cutting rail lines in an effort to prevent Union troops from reaching Washington, DC.[18] Lincoln authorized military detention of such saboteurs because his alternative was to allow "all the laws but one to go unexecuted, and the Government itself go to pieces."[19] In sum, an action that might sometimes (even usually) be a sign of democratic erosion might at other times (perhaps rarely) be a necessary effort to *prevent or reverse* democratic erosion. If this observation is true of executive detentions, it may be true of court-expansion as well.[20]

COURT-PACKING AND AMERICAN POLITICAL DEVELOPMENT

In this light, a closer look at the role of court-packing in American political development is warranted. The history is particularly valuable because the

---

[18] Brian McGinty, *Lincoln and the Court* (Cambridge: Harvard University Press, 2008).
[19] President Abraham Lincoln, "July 4th Message to Congress" (July 4, 1861), https://millercenter.org/the-presidency/presidential-speeches/july-4-1861-july-4th-message-congress.
[20] It may even be true of military coups. Ginsburg and Huq, *How to Save a Constitutional Democracy*, 186.

post-2008 wave of democratic erosion worldwide has not yet provided examples of successful reversals of the erosion process. American political development does provide such examples. The common thread across the historical cases is that court-packing proposals have emerged from fear of democratic collapse or some similarly existential threat. As such, we cannot fairly evaluate the proposals without some assessment of the threat. If the survival of the constitutional order is at stake, norm-breaking may be justified. Or to put the point empirically rather than normatively, norm-breaking may sometimes be necessary to prevent serious threats to the constitutional order.

Court-Packing and the Election of 1800

During periods of extreme polarization, as Suzanne Mettler and Robert Lieberman have shown, political elites sometimes turn to constitutional hardball in an effort to lock rivals out of key institutional sites.[21] Moreover, such deck-stacking sometimes feeds back to reinforce polarization, undermining trust and encouraging rivals to respond in kind.

In the run-up to the election of 1800, President John Adams and his Federalist allies in Congress outlawed public criticism of his administration and jailed roughly a dozen supporters of Adams's opponent, Thomas Jefferson. One of those jailed under the Sedition Act of 1798 was a sitting member of Congress, Representative Mathew Lyon of Vermont.[22] Jefferson and his allies managed to win despite such repression, but following the election, the lame-duck Federalists sought to pack the federal courts before the partisan turnover took place. For example, they persuaded sitting Chief Justice Oliver Ellsworth to resign, replaced him with a Federalist Party loyalist (John Marshall), and then enacted a law reducing the Supreme Court's size from six to five, effective upon the next vacancy. If there were any neutral, nonpartisan reason why a Court of five justices was preferable to one of six, Adams could have elevated a sitting justice to Chief, left the remaining seat vacant, and then signed the bill to eliminate the unneeded seat. Instead, the alteration in the Court's size was clearly intended to deny Jefferson an appointment opportunity. The same law that reduced the Supreme Court's size, the Judiciary Act of

---

[21] Suzanne Mettler and Robert C. Lieberman, *Four Threats: The Recurring Crises of American Democracy* (New York: St. Martin's, 2020).

[22] Michael Kent Curtis, *Free Speech, "The People's Darling Privilege": Struggles for Freedom of Expression in American History* (Durham: Duke University Press, 2000), 80–84.

1801, *increased* the size of the federal judiciary as a whole by more than 70 percent, creating sixteen new Circuit Court judgeships that President Adams and his Senate allies quickly filled with loyal Federalists.[23]

While they were packing the courts, the lame-duck Federalists were also threatening to deny Jefferson the presidency. Jefferson and his running mate, Aaron Burr, had been named on an equal number of electoral ballots. They had a clear majority of the electoral votes (73 of 138), but due to an odd feature of the electoral college's original design, the fact that they were tied with each other meant that the House would choose the winner – the lame-duck House, many of whose Federalist members had recently been unseated. While the House was scheming to give the presidency to Burr or perhaps even Marshall, Virginia's governor laid plans for his state's militia to march on Washington and install Jefferson by force.[24]

This story does not usually appear in the democratic erosion literature, but some of its lessons remain relevant. The Federalists eventually conceded the presidency to Jefferson, but not before they had "retired into the judiciary as a stronghold," in Jefferson's famous words, from which "all the works of Republicanism are to be beaten down and destroyed." As a result, in order to enact the program on which they had been elected – to reverse the country's democratic erosion, as they understood it – Jefferson's Republicans had to attack the courts. They began by impeaching and removing US District Judge John Pickering, whose drunkenness on the bench made him an easy target, and they then impeached Supreme Court Justice Samuel Chase. Levitsky and Ziblatt offer a one-sided characterization of the Chase impeachment as an illegitimate assault on judicial independence, but as Keith Whittington has shown, the lessons of the Chase impeachment were twofold.[25] Chase's acquittal in the Senate helped establish a norm that governing coalitions should not remove federal judges whenever there has been a partisan change in power, but his near-removal also helped establish a norm that sitting federal judges should not use their power for partisan ends. After all, the conduct for which Chase was impeached included his zealous enforcement of the Sedition

---

[23] Bruce Ackerman, *The Failure of the Founding Fathers: Jefferson, Marshall, and the Rise of Presidential Democracy* (Cambridge: Harvard University Press, 2005), 116–41; Thomas M. Keck, *Judicial Politics in Polarized Times* (Chicago: University of Chicago Press, 2014), 131–34.
[24] Ackerman, *Failures of the Founding Fathers*; Mettler and Lieberman, *Four Threats*.
[25] Levitsky and Ziblatt, *How Democracies Die*, 131; Keith Whittington, *Constitutional Construction: Divided Powers and Constitutional Meaning* (Cambridge: Harvard University Press, 1999), 20–71.

Act, preventing Jeffersonian lawyers from questioning its constitutionality in his court and delivering partisan tirades from the bench while doing so.

In addition to targeting particular judges, the Jeffersonians also repealed the Judiciary Act of 1801, returning the Supreme Court's size to six and eliminating the sixteen new circuit judgeships. As a result, those sixteen judges were fired from their life-tenured seats, which no longer existed. Federalists denounced all of these moves as outrageous assaults on judicial independence. Chief Justice Marshall and his Federalist colleagues on the Court thought them clearly unconstitutional, but they acquiesced on the fear that they could not successfully resist, upholding the repeal bill in *Stuart v. Laird* (1803).[26]

Lawyers and judges to this day describe the Jeffersonians as hostile to judicial independence, but those judgments are hard to credit.[27] When a governing regime intentionally packs the courts with partisan loyalists, and those judges then use their power in explicitly partisan ways, the regime's supporters cannot credibly appeal to norms of judicial independence when an opposition regime tries to unpack those courts. It is for this reason that Jefferson's alteration of the Court's size is not best understood as an example of illegitimate court-packing. He and his partisan allies increased the Court's size for political reasons, but they did so in direct response to the Federalists' effort to decrease the Court's size for political reasons. The legitimacy of the later move cannot fairly be evaluated absent the context created by the earlier one.

Court-Packing and the Civil War

A similar episode played out during and after the Civil War. When Lincoln took the oath of office in March 1861, the Court was led by Chief Justice Roger Taney, author of the infamous *Dred Scott* decision, which had held unconstitutional a central policy goal of the Republican platform on which Lincoln had been elected (i.e., banning slavery from federal territories). In addition to Taney himself, the Court inherited by Lincoln included four other justices from Taney's *Dred Scott* majority; one more recent appointee widely derided as a Democratic partisan; and three vacant seats. As early as 1858, the *New York Tribune* was denouncing the Court as "a mere party machine," and by 1861, it was calling for Court expansion.[28]

---

[26] Ackerman, *Failure of the Founding Fathers*.
[27] Keck, *Judicial Politics in Polarized Times*, 131–34.
[28] McGinty, *Lincoln and the Court*, 28, 104.

In addition to the Court's extreme pro-slavery reading of the Constitution, northern Republicans were also concerned with Taney's attempts to use judicial power to undermine the Union war effort. Most well-known is Taney's opinion in *Ex parte Merryman* (C.C.D. Md. 1861), which he was famously unable to enforce.[29] After pro-Confederate mobs fired on Union soldiers seeking to pass through Baltimore en route to Washington, DC, Lincoln had authorized military detention without trial of those engaged in violence against the federal government. Taney held this suspension of habeas corpus to be beyond the scope of presidential power, and the publication of his *Merryman* opinion made it "apparent, if it had not been before, that the chief justice had taken sides in the sectional struggle that threatened to destroy the Union, casting his lot with the South against the North."[30] *Merryman* was not the only such evidence. Taney also ruled against a Treasury Department regulation prohibiting trade of goods from Baltimore to Confederate sympathizers in southern Maryland, and he was one of four judges who argued that Lincoln had unlawfully imposed a naval blockade on Southern ports.[31] He also prepared draft opinions holding unconstitutional the Legal Tender Act (necessary to fund the war), the military conscription act (necessary to wage the war), and indeed the Union war effort itself.[32]

In other words, key members of the Supreme Court were attempting to deploy their power to obstruct a war effort that was necessary to the survival of the Union, and hence of the Constitution. Given this threat, some elected leaders felt compelled to act in norm-violating ways. Abolitionist Sen. John Hale (R-N.H.) called on the Senate Judiciary Committee to explore the possibility of abolishing the Court to get rid of Taney and his obstructionist colleagues. The Congress would then create a new Court fully staffed by Lincoln. On Senator Hale's reading, "the Supreme Court of the United States, as at present established ... is bankrupt in everything that was intended by the creation of such a tribunal." Instead of carefully expounding the law, the justices were more often declaring "what was agreeable to" the party that had put them on the bench. That party was no longer in power, and Hale saw no need "to hold up and maintain what they have built up, as the citadel in our

---

[29] *Ex parte Merryman*, 17 F.Cas. 144 (C.C.D. Md. 1861).
[30] McGinty, *Lincoln and the Court*, 90.
[31] The Prize Cases, 67 U.S. 635, 682–699 (1863). On the Treasury regulation, see McGinty, *Lincoln and the Court*, 199–200.
[32] McGinty, *Lincoln and the Court*, 193–211, 321, n.19.

midst."[33] In other words, Hale had the same objections to the Democratic Court that Jefferson had to the Federalist Court sixty years earlier.

If enacted, Hale's proposal would have been a departure from existing norms, to be sure, but it may well have proven necessary to rein in a Court whose loyalty to the constitutional order was in serious question. Hale's proposal did not prove necessary, as most of Taney's obstructionist efforts proved unsuccessful. But some of them were close calls, and in 1863, Congress created some breathing room by expanding the Court's size from nine to ten, enabling Lincoln to appoint an additional Union supporter to the bench.[34]

Following the Civil War, Lincoln pushed through the Thirteenth Amendment, declared his support for black male suffrage, and then was assassinated by a Confederate sympathizer. His assassination elevated Democrat Andrew Johnson to the presidency, and Johnson set about using all the powers at his disposal to destroy congressional Republicans' attempt to build a multiracial democracy in the US South.[35]

Congress responded to President Johnson's antidemocratic obstructionism with constitutional hardball, most notably by seizing control of the Cabinet and the Army, enacting a law that prohibited the president from removing the Secretary of War without Senate consent. By today's standards, these actions represent congressional violations of the independence of the executive branch, but nineteenth-century executive power jurisprudence tolerated significantly tighter congressional limits on presidential removal powers.[36] And given that President Johnson was systematically trying to make the US South less democratic – firing the US Army generals who were registering African American voters, preventing the Freedmen's Bureau from implementing land redistribution to the former slaves, readmitting States with white supremacist constitutions, and pardoning former Confederates *en masse* to enable them to hold office – congressional Republicans' hardball tactics may have been warranted.[37] These tactics also included the Judiciary Act of 1866,

---

[33] Quoted in Howard Gillman, Mark A. Graber, and Keith E. Whittington, *American Constitutionalism, vol. 1, Structures of Government* (New York: Oxford University Press, 2017), 249. See also Justin Crowe, *Building the Judiciary: Law, Courts, and the Politics of Institutional Development* (Princeton: Princeton University Press, 2012), 138; McGinty, *Lincoln and the Court*, 104.
[34] Crowe, *Building the Judiciary*, 140–46.
[35] Brenda Wineapple, *The Impeachers: The Trial of Andrew Johnson and the Dream of a Just Nation* (New York: Random House, 2019).
[36] Driesen, *Specter of Dictatorship*.   [37] Wineapple, *The Impeachers*.

which reduced the Court's size from ten to seven, thus denying Johnson the opportunity to capture the Court. As Joshua Braver has emphasized, this bill was enacted in direct response to Johnson's nomination of Henry Stanbery to fill a vacancy that had emerged six weeks after Lincoln's assassination.[38] After Republican Ulysses S. Grant was elected in 1868, congressional Republicans increased the Court's size to nine. Again, these congressional actions represented hardball tactics, but they were deployed in response to massive norm-violation on the part of President Johnson. And while Johnson's norm-busting contributed directly to democratic erosion, congressional Republicans were seeking to fulfill Lincoln's vision of a multiracial democracy.

Court-Packing and the New Deal

As noted previously, Levitsky and Ziblatt treat FDR's court-packing plan as a dangerous presidential assault on a coequal branch, but one in which our system of constitutional checks and balances ultimately held firm, with congressional Republicans and Democrats alike pushing back against the president's overreach.[39]

Contrary to this conventional account, FDR's plan is better understood as a necessary and successful effort to rein in a state institution that was threatening the survival of democratic capitalism. When FDR announced the plan in February 1937, prominent left-liberals had for years been advocating the abolition of judicial review or similarly radical alterations to the Court's power.[40] These calls might appear as dangerous assaults on judicial independence, but they were made in a context in which unemployment had reached 25 percent (in 1933), banks had regularly failed (with no federal deposit insurance), thousands of workers died annually in workplace accidents, and bare majorities on the Court repeatedly held that the federal government lacked authority to enact widely popular regulations of the capitalist market. At the time the court-packing plan was announced, Congress had been trying for twenty years to enact a constitutionally acceptable ban on child labor, but the Court had

---

[38] Joshua Braver, "Court-Packing: An American Tradition?" *Boston College Law Review* 61 (2020): 2747–808.

[39] Levitsky and Ziblatt, *How Democracies Die*, 118–19, 130–33.

[40] Kevin J. McMahon, *Reconsidering Roosevelt on Race: How the Presidency Paved the Road to Brown* (Chicago: University of Chicago Press, 2004), 66–67; William G. Ross, *A Muted Fury: Populists, Progressives, and Labor Unions Confront the Courts, 1890–1937* (Princeton: Princeton University Press, 1994).

repeatedly invalidated its attempts.[41] In pending litigation, the Court was widely expected to invalidate the Wagner Act and the Social Security Act as well.[42] In his 1937 State of the Union address, delivered a month before he announced the court-packing plan, FDR reviewed the Court's record of preventing the federal government from effectively responding to the Great Depression, observing that "[t]he process of our democracy must not be imperiled by the denial of essential powers of free government." Indeed, "[t]he judicial branch ... is asked by the people to do its part in making democracy successful."[43] Later that Spring, the Court made its famous "switch in time," upholding first a minimum wage law and then the Wagner and Social Security Acts.[44] The conservative justices then began to step down, allowing FDR to remake the Court without altering its size. By 1941, the Court was unanimously upholding child labor and minimum wage laws in cases like *United States v. Darby Lumber Co.* (1941).

In short, the court-packing plan was motivated at least in part by a desire for preservation and renewal of democracy in the context of industrial capitalism. In this regard, the plan was more successful than not. After all, FDR's goal was not a Court with more people on it. His goal was constitutionalization of the New Deal and a modern reconstruction of the federal balance of power more generally. On that front, he succeeded, largely because the Court backed down in the face of his threat. Had it not backed down, it is likely that some version of the court-packing plan would have been enacted.[45]

Likewise, the bipartisan opposition to the court-packing plan does not easily stand as an example of constitutional guardrails holding against democratic erosion. It is true that FDR's proposal sparked bipartisan opposition, but the opposition from his own party came in significant part from Jim Crow southern Democrats concerned that FDR would use his judicial appointments to undermine segregation. FDR seemed to signal just such an intent by nominating William Hastie as the first African American federal judge in US history – on the same day that he announced

---

[41] *Hammer v. Dagenhart*, 247 U.S. 251 (1918); *Bailey v. Drexel Furniture Co.*, 259 U.S. 20 (1922).
[42] McMahon, *Reconsidering Roosevelt*, 70.
[43] Quoted in McMahon, *Reconsidering Roosevelt*, 76.
[44] *West Coast Hotel v. Parrish*, 300 U.S. 379 (1937); *NLRB v Jones & Laughlin Steel Corp.*, 301 U.S. 1 (1937); *Steward Machine Co. v. Davis*, 301 U.S. 548 (1937); *Helvering v. Davis*, 301 U.S. 619 (1937).
[45] McMahon, *Reconsidering Roosevelt*.

the court-packing plan.[46] Some of FDR's co-partisans did indeed oppose the plan due to fear of excessive concentration of executive power rather than a desire to maintain racial segregation, but it seems clear that there were both democracy-eroding and democracy-enhancing impulses on both sides.[47]

Court-Packing in the Trump Era

Court-packing remains a feature of US politics in the twenty-first century, where heightened polarization has sometimes led partisan elites to bend or break existing norms. Indeed, the second decade of the twenty-first century witnessed efforts by Republican legislators in eight different states to alter the size of their state high courts in order to enhance or cement their party's control over those courts.[48] In Arizona and Georgia, these efforts were successful, with Republican Governors in each state signing bills in 2016 that added two seats to their state Supreme Court, seats which those governors then filled. Arizona Governor Doug Ducey offered nonpolitical explanations for this change, but these explanations do not seem any more credible than were FDR's similar explanations eighty years earlier. While he was increasing the number of justices, Ducey also altered the norms and procedures by which they are selected. Arizona Supreme Court justices have long been nominated by an appellate court commission that is staffed by the governor and state Senate, but with a constitutional mandate to ensure that the commission "reflects the diversity of Arizona's population."[49] After several appointments by Ducey, the fifteen-person commission was left with zero Democratic members.[50] Ducey made several of these appointments after the commission had voted down Maricopa County Attorney Bill Montgomery's candidacy for a Supreme Court seat, and the newly packed commission fell into line by reconsidering and approving Montgomery's nomination in 2019. Montgomery is best known for his longstanding opposition to LGBT rights, and he now sits as one of five Ducey appointees on the seven-member Court. The packed Court has

---

[46] Ibid., 79–86.   [47] Ibid., 77–79.
[48] Marin K. Levy, "Packing and Unpacking State Courts," *William & Mary Law Review* 61 (2020): 1121–58.
[49] Arizona Constitution, Art. 6, Sec. 36.
[50] Mark Joseph Stern, "Arizona's Governor is Leading Republicans' Quiet, Radical Takeover of State Supreme Courts," *Slate*, August 29, 2019, https://slate.com/news-and-politics/2019/08/arizona-supreme-court-rigging-doug-ducey-bill-montgomery.html.

issued a number of conservative rulings, and its members have appeared to skirt conventional norms of judicial behavior – perhaps most notably, with Justice Clint Bolick personally lobbying Governor Ducey on his pick for a vacant US Senate seat.[51]

At the federal level, Republican elites have also built and maintained a judicial majority in part by violating long-established norms regarding judicial selection. During Barack Obama's administration, in particular, Republican Senators effectively shrunk the size of federal courts – twice – in an effort to maintain partisan control. When Democrats held a narrow Senate majority, Minority Leader Mitch McConnell led his caucus in filibustering three consecutive nominations by President Obama to the DC Circuit Court of Appeals, widely regarded as the second most important court in the country. As of November 2013, the DC Circuit was split 4–4 between Democratic and Republican appointees, with three vacant seats, which Senator McConnell pledged to keep vacant no matter whom President Obama nominated.[52] Republican Senator Chuck Grassley, then-ranking member on the Senate Judiciary Committee, proposed legislation formally reducing the court's size from eleven seats to eight.[53] This obstructionism prompted Senate Majority Leader Harry Reid to alter Senate rules to prohibit filibusters of lower-court nominations (the so-called nuclear option).

When the GOP captured the Senate in 2014, now-Majority Leader McConnell slowed judicial confirmations almost to a halt, confirming fewer judges during Obama's last two years than for any administration in recent memory, thereby preserving more than 100 federal judicial vacancies to be inherited by the Trump administration.[54] During the Obama administration, even when Democrats controlled the Senate, the so-called "blue slip" tradition repeatedly allowed a single Republican Senator to block consideration of judicial nominees from their state for years, in some cases for Obama's full two terms in office.[55] During the

---

[51] Joseph Flaherty, "Arizona Supreme Court Justice Urged Governor to Tap Bill Montgomery for Senate," *Phoenix New Times*, November 27, 2018, www.phoenixnewtimes.com/news/arizona-senate-justice-bolick-governor-ducey-appoint-bill-montgomery-11051364.

[52] Jeremy W. Peters, "Obama Pick for Court Is 3rd in a Row Blocked by Republicans," *New York Times*, November 18, 2013.

[53] Millhiser, "Let's Think About Court-Packing."

[54] Aaron Belkin, "Court Expansion and the Restoration of Democracy," 40.

[55] Ian Millhiser, "What Trump Has Done to the Courts, Explained," *Vox*, December 9, 2019, www.vox.com/policy-and-politics/2019/12/19/20962980/trump-supreme-court-federal-judges.

Trump administration, Senate Republicans quickly abandoned this tradition for federal appellate nominees, allowing them to confirm such nominees at a record pace and without regard to objections from Democratic Senators.

The second instance in which Republican Senators effectively shrunk the size of a court to keep it in their party's hands took place following the death of Justice Antonin Scalia in February 2016. On the very day of Scalia's death, McConnell pledged that President Obama would not be allowed to fill the seat. Obama nominated DC Circuit Judge Merrick Garland, a widely respected moderate whom Republican Senators had suggested as a candidate for previous vacancies, but the Republican Senate leadership took the literally unprecedented step of denying Garland a hearing.[56] McConnell argued that the vacancy should be held open until after the 2016 presidential election, giving the people the opportunity to weigh in on who should fill the seat, but several of his Republican colleagues pledged that if Democrat Hillary Clinton were elected, they would hold the seat open for her full four-year term.[57]

When President Trump nominated Neil Gorsuch to fill the Scalia/Garland seat in early 2017, he lacked the votes to overcome a Democratic filibuster. McConnell pushed through a Senate rules change allowing Gorsuch and all future Supreme Court nominees to be confirmed via simple majority. When Trump nominated Brett Kavanaugh to replace Justice Anthony Kennedy the following year, the administration engaged in an unprecedented effort to deny Democratic Senators access to the documentary record of Kavanaugh's long career in government service. And when Christine Blasey Ford and others came forward with credible allegations of sexual assault, Kavanaugh defended himself on live television with angry partisan threats ("what goes around, comes around") and thinly veiled perjury.[58] The administration then conducted a sham, weekend-long FBI investigation that purported to clear Kavanaugh of the charges.[59]

When Justice Ruth Bader Ginsburg passed away in September 2020, less than seven weeks before the presidential election – and indeed with

---

[56] Levitsky and Ziblatt, *How Democracies Die*, 145–46.
[57] Greenberg and Levin, *We Are Indivisible*, 274; Levitsky and Ziblatt, *How Democracies Die*, 166.
[58] Nathan J. Robinson, "How We Know Kavanaugh Is Lying," *Current Affairs*, September 29, 2018, www.currentaffairs.org/2018/09/how-we-know-kavanaugh-is-lying.
[59] Robin Pogrebin and Kate Kelly, "Brett Kavanaugh Fit in with the Privileged Kids. She Did Not," *New York Times*, September 14, 2019, www.nytimes.com/2019/09/14/sunday-review/brett-kavanaugh-deborah-ramirez-yale.html.

early voting already underway in multiple states – Trump nominated Seventh Circuit Judge Amy Coney Barrett to replace her. McConnell immediately announced that he would ignore his "rule" from four years earlier, and the Senate proceeded with accelerated confirmation hearings in advance of the election. When the administration staged a White House ceremony announcing Barrett's nomination without following public health protocols in the midst of the COVID-19 pandemic and multiple Republican Senators then tested positive for the highly contagious virus, McConnell still refused to slow the confirmation process.

As with other recent Republican presidents, Trump's Court appointees have been both younger and more partisan than typical, with no effort to identify nominees who could appeal across the aisle. In several cases, Republicans' ability to successfully seat these nominees has depended on the Senate's built-in overrepresentation of sparsely populated, conservative states. Indeed, the only justices in the Court's history confirmed by Senators who collectively represented fewer people than those who voted against confirmation are Clarence Thomas, Samuel Alito, Gorsuch, Kavanaugh, and Barrett.[60] The three Trump appointees were also nominated by a president who had received fewer popular votes than his opponent.

This combination of norm-breaking by Senate Republicans and structural advantages favoring their position has enabled the GOP to maintain more consistent control of the Supreme Court than their electoral support would predict. Republican presidential candidates won the popular vote in five of six elections from 1968 to 88 (usually by wide margins), but in just one of eight elections from 1992 to 2020 (in 2004, with 50.7 percent). Despite this marked decline in popular support for Republican presidents, Republican-appointed judges have held an unbroken majority on the Supreme Court since 1970, save for one fourteen-month interlude in 2016–17 when the Court's partisan divide was 4–4.

THE ROBERTS COURT AND DEMOCRATIC EROSION

Scholars of democratic erosion have noticed the GOP's partisan capture of the federal courts and flagged it as a potential warning sign, but may well have understated the severity of the danger to democratic norms and institutions. For example, remarking on the Supreme Court twenty

---

[60] Kevin J. McMahon, "Will the Supreme Court Still 'Seldom Stray Very Far'? Regime Politics in a Polarized America," *Chicago-Kent Law Review* 93 (2018): 343–71.

months into Trump's presidency, Kaufman and Haggard diagnosed "a serious threat that a constitutionally-created branch of the government – one that is already deeply divided along partisan lines – will become even more politicized and delegitimated." On their reading, "[t]he most direct threat to American democracy would be judicial acquiescence to restrictions on voting rights."[61] Ginsburg and Huq have likewise noted that partisan judges, like legislators, "may be willing to allow a president to dismantle democratic governance so long as their own policy preferences are furthered."[62] Such judicial acquiescence in the face of legislative restrictions on voting rights is indeed a significant threat, but the bigger danger to American democracy is judicial *evisceration* of legislative *expansions* of voting rights. Consider David Landau and Rosalind Dixon's account of "abusive judicial review," by which they mean the use of judicial power to undermine the "minimum core of electoral democracy." Drawing on comparative evidence from a range of states experiencing democratic erosion, Landau and Dixon identify two variants of the phenomenon. In its weak form, abusive judicial review involves courts "stand[ing] by passively as democracy is dismantled"; in its strong form, it involves courts actively undermining key democratic norms and institutions.[63] The Roberts Court has engaged in both versions of the practice.

In this section, I briefly review two instances in which the contemporary Court has declined to check legislative infringements on fair democratic procedures, and two others in which it has reached out to actively thwart legislative *enhancements* of democratic procedures. In *Crawford v. Marion County Election Board* (2008), the Court upheld Indiana's strict voter ID law, despite clear evidence that the photo identification requirement would "impose nontrivial burdens on the voting rights of tens of thousands of the state's citizens ... [, with] a significant percentage of those individuals ... likely to be deterred from voting."[64] The law had been enacted on a party-line vote in Indiana's Republican-controlled legislature, and Seventh Circuit Judge Terence Evans characterized it as "a not-too-thinly-veiled attempt to discourage election-day turnout by certain folks believed to skew Democratic."[65] In subsequent litigation

---

[61] Kaufman and Haggard, "Democratic Decline," 426.
[62] Ginsburg and Huq, *How to Save and Constitutional Democracy*, 219.
[63] Landau and Dixon, "Abusive Judicial Review," 1316–17.
[64] *Crawford v. Marion County Election Board*, 553 U.S. 181 (2008) (Souter, dissenting).
[65] *Crawford v. Marion County Election Board*, 472 F.3d 949, 954 (7th Cir. 2007) (Evans, dissenting).

regarding an even stricter law from Wisconsin, Circuit Judge Richard Posner noted that roughly 9 percent of registered voters in the state lacked the required state-issued identification. Posner also reviewed sworn testimony from multiple registered voters who had attempted to obtain such identification, but had been unable to do so.[66] Relying on *Crawford*, Posner's colleagues nonetheless upheld the Wisconsin law as well.

A decade after *Crawford*, the Court held in *Rucho v. Common Cause* (2019) that claims of intentional and excessive partisan gerrymandering are not subject to judicial resolution under the US Constitution. The case featured uncontroverted evidence that following the 2010 census, the Republican-controlled North Carolina legislature had "instructed their mapmaker to use political data to draw a map that would produce a congressional delegation of ten Republicans and three Democrats." In all recent election cycles, votes for statewide offices and aggregate votes for House candidates have evinced a state split nearly fifty-fifty, with Democrats winning the aggregate House vote in 2012 and the Governor's race in 2016. But the Republican gerrymander successfully maintained a 10-3 GOP majority in the House delegation across three consecutive election cycles. Despite this context, Chief Justice Roberts declined to impose any constitutional limits on the drawing of district lines to "subordinate adherents of one political party and entrench a rival party in power," even where that desire represents the "predominant purpose" of the line drawing.[67]

The central premise of Roberts's argument for allowing such partisan gerrymandering is that the Constitution grants such authority to state legislatures in the first instance (and to Congress secondarily), and hence that the American people should bring their complaints about existing districting practices to their elected representatives, not to the Court. But relying on self-interested legislators to reform the procedures under which they themselves have been elected has the same shortcomings that it had in *Baker v. Carr* (1962), which authorized courts to weigh in when district maps featured massive departures from the principle of "one person, one vote." With the Court declining to serve as democratic guardrail, *Crawford* and *Rucho* are paradigmatic examples of weak-form abusive judicial review.

Contrast the Court's broad posture of judicial restraint in those cases with its aggressive interference with the 2002 McCain-Feingold Act and

---

[66] *Frank v. Walker*, 773 F.3d 783, 786, 796-8 (7th Cir. 2014) (Posner, dissenting from denial of rehearing).

[67] *Rucho v. Common Cause*, 139 S.Ct. 2484, 2502-3 (2019).

the 1965 Voting Rights Act. In *Citizens United v. FEC* (2010), the Court held that for-profit corporations have a First Amendment right to spend unlimited sums advocating the election or defeat of political candidates, thereby invalidating a central provision of the most significant federal campaign finance law since the Watergate era. *Citizens United* is the most notable in a long string of Roberts Court decisions invalidating campaign finance regulations, with the Court's most conservative justices repeatedly holding that state and federal legislative institutions lack authority to limit election spending.[68] In *Shelby County v. Holder* (2013), the Court gutted a central provision of the Voting Rights Act, holding that Congress had unconstitutionally required certain state and local jurisdictions to get federal approval for all changes to their election laws. Technically, Roberts's opinion for the Court only invalidated the formula that determined which state and local jurisdictions were required to seek such federal "pre-clearance," but both his majority opinion and a concurrence from Justice Thomas suggested that even with a revised coverage formula, the Court's conservative majority would view such a requirement as an unconstitutional intrusion on state sovereignty. The decision unleashed a wave of new state restrictions on voting rights – with Republican legislatures and executives enacting voter ID laws, purging voter rolls, and closing polling sites – that previously would have required federal pre-clearance.[69]

As these examples make clear, the current Court's relevance for democratic erosion is twofold. First, it has significantly scaled back its role as an institutional check against partisan attempts to undermine fair democratic procedures. It is not yet clear that it has abandoned this role altogether, but it is fair to say that its performance is not currently reliable. Indeed, early reports from the Bright Lines Project have shown that "Judiciary can limit executive" and "Judicial independence" are among the democratic norms and institutions on which both expert and mass public confidence dropped most sharply during the Trump era.[70] Consider the Court's response to legal disputes regarding vote counting in the 2020 presidential election. Once it was clear that Joe Biden had won a decisive victory, the

---

[68] *Randall v. Sorrell*, 548 U.S. 230 (2006); *FEC v. Wisconsin Right to Life*, 551 U.S. 449 (2007); *Davis v. FEC*, 554 U.S. 724 (2008); *Arizona Free Enterprise Club v. Bennett*, 564 U.S. 721 (2011); *McCutcheon v. FEC*, 134 S.Ct. 1434 (2014).
[69] Rocco, chapter in this volume.
[70] John M. Carey, Gretchen Helmke, Brendan Nyhan, Mitchell Sanders, and Susan Stokes, "Searching for Bright Lines in the Trump Presidency," *Perspectives on Politics* 17 (September 2019): 699–718.

Court dismissed multiple frivolous lawsuits seeking to reverse the results.[71] But in the weeks leading up to the election, four conservative justices had signaled that they were prepared to give a sympathetic ear to Trump campaign arguments that could have reversed an election defeat if the outcome were close.[72] Justice Barrett was not yet on the Court when those disputes were heard, and there is good reason to worry that she would have provided a fifth vote in such a scenario.[73]

Second, the Court has proven willing on key occasions to thwart *legislative* attempts to *enhance* fair democratic procedures.[74] A variety of signs indicate that this latter effort has not yet run its course. In the campaign finance context, for example, Justices Thomas and Alito have set their sights on disclosure requirements, and Senate Majority Leader McConnell echoed their arguments in a January 2019 op-ed.[75] On the gerrymandering front, reform advocates have used the ballot initiative process in several states to transfer redistricting authority from partisan state legislatures to nonpartisan commissions. The Supreme Court upheld such an initiative from Arizona in 2015, but it did so by a vote of 5-4, with Roberts, Thomas, and Alito (along with Scalia) in

---

[71] *Kelly v. Pennsylvania*, No. 20A98, application for injunctive relief denied, Dec. 8, 2020; *Texas v. Pennsylvania, et al.*, No. 22O155, motion for leave to file a bill of complaint denied, Dec. 11, 2020.

[72] *Andino v. Middleton*, opinion on application for stay, Oct. 5, 2020 (noting votes of Justice Thomas, Alito, and Gorsuch); *Democratic National Committee v. Wisconsin State Legislature*, Kavanaugh, concurring in denial of application to vacate stay, Oct. 26, 2020; *Moore v. Circosta*, Gorsuch, dissenting from denial of application for injunctive relief, Oct. 28, 2020.

[73] President Trump himself repeatedly indicated publicly that he was urging the Senate to confirm Barrett prior to the November 3 election so that she would be available to help decide any election-related disputes. And Barrett's own views on voting rights seem consistent with those of her conservative colleagues. See, for example, *Kanter v. Barr*, 919 F.3d 437, 451-69 (7th Cir. 2019) (Barrett dissent).

[74] Driesen paints a similar picture of the modern Court's doctrine regarding unilateral assertions of executive power. That is, the Court has been insufficiently willing to check presidential abuses of power on its own, and it has also been hostile to some key congressional attempts to rein in presidential abuses of power. Driesen, *Specter of Dictatorship*.

[75] Justice Thomas wrote separately in *Citizens United*, 558 U.S. 310, 480-5, to indicate his view that the McCain-Feingold Act's disclosure requirements were unconstitutional, and Justice Alito echoed these arguments several months later in his concurring opinion in *Doe v. Reed*, 561 U.S. 186 (2010). McConnell objected to congressional Democrats' efforts to expand disclosure requirements in "Behold the Democrat Politician Protection Act," *Washington Post*, January 17, 2019, www.washingtonpost.com/opinions/call-hr-1-what-it-is-the-democrat-politician-protection-act/2019/01/17/dcc957be-19cb-11e9-9ebf-c5fed1b7a081_story.html.

dissent.[76] If any two of Trump's three nominees agree with them, they now have the votes to hold that neither judges nor voters may take districting authority away from partisan legislators. Roberts's dissenting opinion in the Arizona case suggests that this same judicial coalition may invalidate any *congressional* attempt to mandate nonpartisan redistricting as well.[77]

In sum, even before the Trump era, the Roberts Court was sometimes willing to actively deploy judicial power to undermine core features of electoral democracy. President Trump's three appointments have shifted the Court's median justice substantially to the right – both in general and on voting rights in particular. As such, Democratic advocates of democracy reform have reason for concern that, having retaken control of Congress and the White House in 2021, their Republican opponents have retired into the judiciary as a stronghold, from which they will block any new voting rights, gerrymandering reform, or campaign finance policies that Democrats enact. In this context, any comprehensive program of democratic preservation and renewal in the 2020s will need to grapple with the issue of court reform.[78]

CONCLUSION: REESTABLISHING THE COURT'S ROLE AS DEMOCRATIC GUARDRAIL

Calls for Court reform are a recurring feature of US history. They have repeatedly been prompted by controversial actions taken by the justices themselves and by the partisan coalitions with which they are allied. Remarkably, contemporary Republican elites – acting across all three branches of the federal government – have provoked such calls in nearly every way that they have been provoked in the past. When Biden was sworn in as President in January 2021, he found himself facing a Court that had been illegitimately packed by the opposition party on its way out of power; that stands opposed to majoritarian, multiracial democracy; and that is committed to a constitutional vision under which much of the platform on which Biden was elected is constitutionally suspect. If history is any guide,

---

[76] *Arizona State Legislature v. Arizona Independent Redistricting Commission*, 135 S.Ct. 2652 (2015).
[77] Thomas M. Keck, "These Are the Roadblocks to the Democrats' Big Voting Rights Bill," *Washington Post*, March 7, 2019, www.washingtonpost.com/politics/2019/03/07/democrats-introduced-bill-expand-voting-rights-other-democracy-reforms-here-are-roadblocks/.
[78] Jones, "To Save Our Democracy."

Court reform will remain on the table until President Biden's political coalition collapses or Chief Justice Roberts steers a non-obstructionist path. If neither of those paths unfold, serious discussion of Court reform is virtually inevitable, and it was therefore no surprise that Biden appointed a high-profile commission to study the issue in April 2021.[79]

In this concluding section, I highlight some key lessons from our constitutional history regarding how to pursue such reforms in ways that are most beneficial for – and least risky to – democratic health. On my reading of the relevant history, some instances of attempted court-packing contributed to democratic erosion in the United States, while others operated, on balance, to promote democratic preservation and renewal. Indeed, it seems to me incontrovertible that court-packing can be undertaken in ways that both hinder and foster democratic governance. If and when small-d democrats regain control of Hungary, Turkey, or Venezuela, would any decisions on their part to alter the size or structure of their judicial institutions be best understood as undue assaults on democratic norms? Surely we would need to know additional contextual details before reaching that judgment. As Joseph Fishkin and David Pozen have noted, "all acts of constitutional hardball create systemic risks, … [but] specific acts may be justified for a variety of contextual normative reasons; sound political judgment might even require that certain types of hardball be played in certain situations."[80]

In the ongoing debates about how best to respond to processes of democratic erosion once they have been diagnosed, Levitsky and Ziblatt have famously called on opposition party elites to exercise forbearance, resisting the urge to respond to the authoritarian leader's norm-breaking with more norm-breaking of their own. But such forbearance strategies may not be viable when facing incumbents – including judicial incumbents – who are deliberately tilting the playing field. In such circumstances, some sort of hardball opposition may be more effective at protecting and renewing democracy, particularly if small-d democracy advocates deploy such tactics in pursuit not just of their own narrow partisan interests but also

---

[79] Thomas M. Keck, "Biden Is Considering Overhauling the Supreme Court. That's Happened During Every Crisis in U.S. Democracy," *Washington Post*, April 13, 2021, www.washingtonpost.com/politics/2021/04/13/bidens-considering-reforming-supreme-court-thats-happened-during-every-crisis-us-democracy/.

[80] Joseph Fishkin and David E. Pozen, "Asymmetric Constitutional Hardball," *Columbia Law Review* 118 (2018): 925. See also Bateman, chapter in this volume; Tushnet, *Taking Back the Constitution*.

pro-democratic reforms that promise to break the cycle of tit-for-tat escalation.[81]

If systemic threats sometimes justify constitutional hardball, then scholars of democratic erosion and resilience are in a good position to help policymakers reflect on how such tactics can be deployed in maximally legitimate fashion. One issue here is timing – that is, how to know when we have reached the point where hardball tactics are merited. With regard to Court expansion, both its normative legitimacy and its political viability are likely to increase if and when the Roberts Court acts as a partisan roadblock to a Democratic administration. If the conservative justices refrain from doing so, they may be able to forestall Court reform. But the historical pattern suggests that emergence of an obstructionist Court is likely, at which point Democratic Court reformers will be emboldened. I have argued that judicial obstruction of legislative expansions of voting rights (and related democracy reforms) would provide particularly weighty justification for Court reform. In theory, the threat of such judicial contributions to democratic erosion might justify preemptive action – for example, expanding the Court before it eviscerates a new voting rights act – but in practice, such preemptive action would require substantially greater political investment. Convincing the American public that court-packing is called for would be a tall order on any occasion, but it is more likely to succeed once the Court has begun actively obstructing a broadly popular policy agenda.

In addition to the question of *when* to resort to hardball tactics, reformers should reflect on *how* to do so in ways that minimize the threat of tit-for-tat escalation. Here, one's prescription for reform is likely to depend on one's diagnosis of the systemic democratic defects in which the Court plays a role. If the chief threat to US democracy is partisan polarization, then the cure is likely to involve institutional changes designed to empower centrists of both parties and to weaken their extremist flanks. If the diagnosis is partisan degradation rather than polarization – that is, if the key defects facing American democracy are rooted not in a bipartisan refusal to compromise, but in one party's abandonment of the rules of the game – then the prescription would be different. Rather than promoting bipartisanship, the cure would involve institutional changes that weaken the structural pro-GOP biases in our electoral and policymaking systems, thereby disrupting the party's playbook for maintaining its hold on power without offering a platform that appeals to popular majorities.[82]

---

[81] Bateman, this volume; Pozen, "Hardball and/as Anti-Hardball."
[82] Bateman, this volume.

To the extent possible, the goal of Court reform should be reestablishing the Court's role as democratic guardrail, not reestablishing its role as Democratic agent. Given that the reforms would be enacted by partisan legislators, some consideration of partisan payoffs is inevitable, but scholars of democratic erosion and resilience can help call attention to particular reforms that are most beneficial for (or least risky to) democratic health. On this front, Pozen has called for greater consideration of "anti-hardball" reforms, by which he means institutional changes that reduce the likelihood of constitutional hardball being played by either side moving forward.[83] For example, when a new state legislative majority comes to power, they could respond to a prior pattern of partisan gerrymandering by creating a nonpartisan redistricting commission rather than deploying a new partisan gerrymander of their own. The dilemma is that the existing gerrymandered districts may prevent a new state legislative majority from coming to power, or that a captured court might prevent the new majority from altering the redistricting procedures.

With regard to Court reform, anti-hardball measures might include reducing the length of Supreme Court terms and regularizing the occurrence of Supreme Court vacancies, changes that would lower the stakes of any given nomination fight. Scholars were calling for such reforms long before Trump's election, good-government reformers have continued to advocate them, and Biden's Court reform commission is reportedly considering them.[84] The dilemma is that most such reforms would have to survive judicial review by the existing Court.

If the key defect ailing American democracy is partisan degradation rather than polarization, then even anti-hardball reforms that have in the past drawn bipartisan support may require hardball tactics to enact.[85] In other words, successful Court reform may require combining good-government improvements to judicial selection and tenure rules with hardball efforts to wrest judicial institutions away from the anti-system

---

[83] Pozen, "Hardball and/as Anti-Hardball."

[84] Roger C. Cramton, "Reforming the Supreme Court," *California Law Review* 95 (Fall 2007): 1313–34; Roger C. Cramton and Paul D. Carrington, *Reforming the Court: Term Limits for Supreme Court Justices* (Carolina Academic Press, 2005); William A. Galston, Grant Reeher, Nancy Jacobson, and Tom Davis, "Beyond Redistricting and Campaign Finance: Six Bold Ideas to Rebuild Our Democracy," Campbell Public Affairs Institute, Policy Brief No. 1, www.nolabels.org/blog/press/beyond-redistricting-and-campaign-finance/;Charlie Savage, "Supreme Court Commission to Scrutinize Changes Beyond Expanding Justice Seats," *New York Times*, April 15, 2021, www.nytimes.com/2021/04/15/us/politics/supreme-court-commission.html.

[85] Pozen, "Hardball and/as Anti-Hardball."

party's control. The institutional design choices are complex, and I close with one recent proposal that illustrates the challenges.

In September 2020, less than two weeks after Justice Ginsburg's death, Representative Ro Khanna introduced legislation that would authorize the president to nominate a Supreme Court justice every two years, during the first and third years of each four-year presidential term. Once confirmed by the Senate, each justice would serve an eighteen-year, nonrenewable term, after which he or she would rotate off active duty on the Supreme Court. The bill would eventually produce a stable Court membership of nine, but the justices sitting at the time of enactment would be grandfathered, retaining their life terms, thereby producing the possibility of a Court larger than nine until all of those sitting justices have concluded their service.[86] When the basic structure of Rep. Khanna's reform bill was first floated by advocates in 2019, conservatives held a five-to-four majority on the Court.[87] In that context, the combination of temporary Court expansion with permanent improvements to judicial selection and tenure rules may have seemed a workable marriage of hardball and anti-hardball reforms. With Justice Barrett having expanded the conservative majority to six justices, the horns of the dilemma have sharpened. The Khanna bill is one of a variety of anti-hardball reforms that would ameliorate the partisan degradation of the federal courts, but if those reforms cannot survive judicial review by the current Court, then it will take some form of hardball tactics to achieve them.[88] That this dilemma faces Court reform advocates should not be surprising, as it is the same dilemma facing democracy reform more broadly. Solving it will be the central challenge of the post-Trump era in US politics.

---

[86] H.R.8424 (116th Congress), www.congress.gov/bill/116th-congress/house-bill/8424.
[87] Schwarz, "Saving the Supreme Court."
[88] Perhaps for this reason, the leading Court reform bill introduced in the 117th Congress to date would simply add four seats immediately upon enactment. See S.1141: Judiciary Act of 2021, www.congress.gov/bill/117th-congress/senate-bill/1141.

PART III

SOCIAL POLARIZATION AND PARTISANSHIP

7

The Social Roots, Risks, and Rewards of Mass Polarization

Lilliana Mason and Nathan P. Kalmoe

INTRODUCTION

The current moment in American politics feels precipitous. We whipsawed from an era of "hope and change" embodying multiracial democracy into an era with a bigoted president who abused his powers for personal and political advantage, resulting in his impeachment, and who ultimately refused to accept his own reelection loss. It is a wild time in American politics, with democratic norms and institutions tested on a near-daily basis, with many found to be worryingly weak. Political and identity-based violence are also rising,[1] though they remain low by historical standards. Here, we consider polarization in relation to partisan social sorting, including the consequences of those divides for affective polarization and more extreme manifestations. We also consider the potential benefits that this polarization might accrue to American democracy. In particular, as the Republican Party has consolidated the interests of the traditional social hierarchy (with white men at the top of the ladder), the Democratic Party has moved to empower the advocates for social change and bring about a more egalitarian and representative democracy. While polarization is destabilizing, it may also be a necessary step on the path to equality.

Democrats and Republicans are moving apart politically but also culturally, geographically, and socially.[2] Party chasms appear on some of the

---

Note: Some of the ideas and phrasing in this chapter are based on a *Washington Post* article written by Mason on December 2, 2019.

[1] Wesley Lowery, Kimberly Kindy, and Andrew Ba Tran. "In the United States, Right-Wing Violence Is on the Rise." *The Washington Post*, 2018, www.washingtonpost.com/nation al/in-the-united-states-right-wing-violence-is-on-the-rise/2018/11/25/61f7f24a-deb4-11e8 -85df-7a6b4d25cfbb_story.html.

[2] Lilliana Mason, *Uncivil Agreement: How Politics Became Our Identity* (Chicago: University of Chicago Press, 2018).

most historically contentious subjects in American history – race, religion, and sex. Republicans largely believe social equality has been achieved, while Democrats are convinced there is still much work to be done.[3] This partisan disagreement over whether or not American politics and culture has fully empowered all citizens equally is a cause both for concern and for cautious optimism. On the pessimistic side, in other countries the alignment of major social identities with parties has increased the likelihood of violence and civil war.[4] Likewise, the last time American partisan division fell neatly along racial policy lines, the United States itself ended up in a partisan civil war.[5] In that light, we will present new evidence of radical views among contemporary partisans, a significant percentage of whom deny the legitimacy of democratic elections and affirm that of political violence.

However, on the optimistic side, our conception of democratic resilience focuses on that positive case for party polarization defined by hegemonic versus marginalized groups. Despite the conflict it engenders, identity-based polarization means marginalized interests have a major political party as active champion, advancing democracy against its opponents. Oppressed groups have a strong political voice in Democratic Party politics today, to an extent rarely (if ever) seen in the United States. Thus, what we may be witnessing are "the growing pains of a diverse society becoming a full democracy."[6] In this case, we would expect to see a phenomenal backlash from the forces of white supremacy and patriarchy.

In the aftermath of the 2020 election, we saw evidence of this backlash, with Republican leaders and Trump supporters refusing to concede an election they definitively lost. With absolutely no evidence, they spent the months of transition attempting to prevent a peaceful transfer of power to the democratically elected Joe Biden by filing dozens of court cases that

---

[3] Pew Research Center, "Views on Race, Immigration and Discrimination," *Pew Research Center for the People and the Press* (blog). October 5, 2017, www.people-press.org/2017/10/05/4-race-immigration-and-discrimination/.

For evidence that racial *stereotypes* of Blacks have diminished among both Republicans and Democrats since 2016, though a sizeable gap remains between the parties, see Daniel J. Hopkins and Samantha Washington, "The Rise of Trump, the Fall of Prejudice?: Tracking White Americans' Racial Attitudes via a Panel Survey, 2008–2018," *Public Opinion Quarterly* 84, no. 1 (July 9, 2020): 119–40.

[4] Joel Sawat Selway, "Cross-Cuttingness, Cleavage Structures and Civil War Onset," *British Journal of Political Science* 41, no. 1 (2011): 111–38.

[5] Nathan P. Kalmoe, *With Ballots & Bullets* (New York: Cambridge University Press, 2020).

[6] Julia Azari, quoted from the podcast Politics in Question. Julia Azari, Lee Drutman, and James Wallner, "What's the Deal with the Separation of Powers?," Politics In Question, 2019, www.politicsinquestion.com/episodes/whats-the-deal-with-the-separation-of-powers.

sought to throw out legitimately cast votes, a large share of which were cast by voters of color. Trump supporters marched on Washington, demanding a rejection of the election outcome.[7] Most alarmingly, the Attorney General of Texas, joined by 17 other Republican state attorneys general and 126 Republican members of Congress, asked the Supreme Court to throw out the votes cast by four states that Biden had won, in protest of election administration procedures they did not object to in states Trump had won.[8] The Supreme Court summarily rejected the case for lacking standing. This was an assault on democracy itself from the Republican Party, whose only aim was to maintain political (and social) power. This is an example, not of polarization, but of a desperate attempt by Republicans to maintain the traditional social hierarchy at all costs. The problem is not that both parties are too extreme, but that societal changes and the social progress being pushed by the Democratic Party have put the Republican Party in a defensive position so dire that they have become willing to reject democracy itself. In the following, we lay out the roots of these divides, the pessimistic view, and our case for some optimism.

SOCIAL ROOTS OF MASS POLARIZATION

American political behavior research has recently worked to disentangle the traditional study of issue-based polarization from a more identity-based view of partisan conflict. While decades of polarization studies debated the presence or absence of polarization over policy preferences, recent work introduced social and affective partisan divides.[9] In this view, partisans need not be divided on policy to loathe the other side.[10] They must simply hold strong, well-aligned political identities.[11]

---

[7] www.washingtonpost.com/dc-md-va/2020/11/14/million-maga-march-dc-protests/.

[8] www.nytimes.com/2020/12/11/us/politics/supreme-court-election-texas.html.

[9] Alan I. Abramowitz, *The Disappearing Center: Engaged Citizens, Polarization, and American Democracy* (New Haven: Yale University Press, 2011); Morris P. Fiorina, Samuel Abrams, and Jeremy Pope, *Culture War? Great Questions in Politics* (Longman, Paperback, 2004); Mason, *Uncivil Agreement*; Shanto Iyengar, Gaurav Sood, and Yphtach Lelkes, "Affect, Not Ideology: A Social Identity Perspective on Polarization," *Public Opinion Quarterly* 76, no. 3 (September 2012): 405–31.

[10] Shanto Iyengar and Sean J. Westwood, "Fear and Loathing Across Party Lines: New Evidence on Group Polarization," *American Journal of Political Science* 59, no. 3 (July 2015): 690–707.

[11] Lilliana Mason, "'I Disrespectfully Agree': The Differential Effects of Partisan Sorting on Social and Issue Polarization," *American Journal of Political Science* 59, no. 1 (2015): 128–45.

Social Sorting

Crosscutting political cleavages are a key source of the long-standing stability of American democracy.[12] These are social group identifications prevalent across both parties. Republicans and Democrats may disagree about tax policy, but if they attend the same church they may understand each other in a manner outside of politics. This type of crosscutting identity has been gradually disappearing from the American electorate.[13]

Apart from the Reconstruction Era and two decades immediately following, the Republican Party was essentially nonexistent in the American South during the party's first eleven decades, hated by whites for its Civil War associations.[14] The passage of the Civil Rights Act in 1964 occurred amid a long process of partisan-racial realignment as the national Democratic Party became identified with racial liberalism in a way no party had since Republicans were defined by anti-slavery and then full Black citizenship in the mid-nineteenth century. White Southern Democrats grew disaffected with the national party's new support for Civil Rights, and they began to vote for Republican presidential candidates who adopted the white South's views on racial hierarchy.[15] Even then, for a while these long-time Democrats could not bring themselves to identify as Republicans. Instead, they saw themselves as old Democrats whose national party had left them behind.

Nationwide, mid-century Democratic and Republican leaders had a lot in common with partisans on the other side of the aisle. Both groups were predominantly comprised of religiously observant white men, many of them conservative socially and economically. Likewise, each leader's voters shared many social identities with the voters who chose their partisan opponent. These crosscutting partisan, racial, and religious identities created more opportunities for cross-partisan voting, and often facilitated the political compromise that a functioning democracy requires. On the other hand, those compromises often left marginalized groups unrepresented and unprotected, as the common cause in

---

[12] Robert A. Dahl, *Democracy in the United States: Promise and Performance* (Chicago: Rand McNally, 1972).

[13] Lilliana Mason, "A Cross-Cutting Calm: How Social Sorting Drives Affective Polarization," *Public Opinion Quarterly* 80, no. S1 (January 2016): 351–77.

[14] Earl Black and Merle Black, *The Rise of Southern Republicans* (Cambridge: Harvard University Press, 2002).

[15] Nicholas A. Valentino and David O. Sears, "Old Times There Are Not Forgotten: Race and Partisan Realignment in the Contemporary South," *American Journal of Political Science* 49, no. 3 (July 2005): 672–88.

both parties was often rooted in whiteness. Nonetheless, governing was more feasible when Democrats and Republicans shared common identities.

The Southern realignment of white party identification ultimately took several decades as older generations of self-described Democrats died and the new generations that replaced them identified with the Republican Party. Partisanship is "sticky." Like a religious identity, it tends to be a powerful social identification instilled in children by parents and immediate social group contexts.[16] And like religious conversion, partisan change in adulthood is rare and slow. By the 1990s, the younger generations of white Southerners had seen their Democratic parents feel comity with the Republican Party. That younger generation held weaker Democratic ties and found it easier to identify as Republican.

As realignment culminated, the Republican Party grew to represent the white, masculine, and Christian identities sitting atop the American social hierarchy, relative to the rapidly diversifying Democratic Party coalition of varied racial, ethnic, and religious groups. A racial gap between the two parties widened substantially.[17] White Americans who were committed to maintaining their privileged status found that the Republican Party had become most able to represent them. Likewise, whites who strongly identified as Christians coalesced in the Republican Party. At the same time, it became clear to socially marginalized groups that the Republican Party did not have their best interests at heart. Elites in politics and media communicated these racial cues in a changing media landscape that made it easier for average Americans to learn which party looked and thought like them – and to reinforce these group loyalties. As the racial and religious realignment solidified in the 1990s and early 2000s, Americans' views about their partisan opponents soured.[18]

---

[16] Leonie Huddy, Lilliana Mason, and Lene Aarøe, "Expressive Partisanship: Campaign Involvement, Political Emotion, and Partisan Identity," *American Political Science Review* 109, no. 1 (February 2015): 1–17.

[17] Mason, *Uncivil Agreement*; Valentino and Sears, "Old Times There Are Not Forgotten."

[18] Mason, *Uncivil Agreement*. As mentioned previously, the Republican Party defends the traditional social hierarchy, including the patriarchy. As such, battles over feminism were also a potent divide between the parties (see Marjorie J. Spruill, *Divided We Stand: The Battle over Women's Rights and Family Values that Polarized American Politics* (New York: Bloomsbury, 2018). Here, we focus on the racial and religious divides for reasons explained in the following and by Parker and Barreto (this volume). Furthermore, a feminist identity is not equivalent to a female identity, and is thus somewhat harder to measure over time.

Identity Matters

Social identities are not just labels applied to similar groups of people: they have powerful and deeply rooted effects on human interactions. When a person understands themselves to be part of a collection of similar people, they feel an affinity for those people, and think they are better than others.[19] People are willing to sacrifice their own well-being and the greater good of society not only to benefit that group but also to secure the superior status of that group over other groups.[20] This phenomenon emerges even in contexts in which the group identity is itself relatively meaningless (see Minimal Group Paradigm experiments[21]). When a group identity is particularly meaningful – like race, religion, and partisanship – these effects strengthen, producing powerful motives to protect and enhance the group's relative status.

Individual identities are powerful on their own, but they also interact with each other in important ways. Social psychologists Roccas and Brewer (2002) introduced the concept of "identity complexity" to account for the compounding or crosscutting effects of multiple identities.[22] As an example, an Irish Catholic whose national and religious identities are well aligned would know many people who belonged to both groups but perhaps not many people outside of those groups. On the other hand, a person who is Irish and Jewish has crosscutting identities. They would likely know significantly more non-Irish, non-Jewish people, as these identities do not tend to overlap with much frequency. What Roccas and Brewer (2002) discovered is that the person who holds crosscutting identities is likely to be more tolerant of out-group members than the person with well-aligned identities. This is because those with crosscutting identities are aware of their multiple differentiated in-groups that nonetheless represent the individual. Brewer and Pierce (2005)[23] replicated and extended this work, finding that those with crosscutting identities were

---

[19] Henri Tajfel and John Turner, "An Integrative Theory of Intergroup Conflict," in *Intergroup Relations: Essential Readings*, ed. M. A. Hogg and D. Abrams (New York: Psychology Press, 1979), 94–109.

[20] Michael Billig and Henri Tajfel, "Social Categorization and Similarity in Intergroup Behaviour," *European Journal of Social Psychology* 3, no. 1 (1973): 27–52.

[21] Marilynn B. Brewer, "In-Group Bias in the Minimal Intergroup Situation: A Cognitive-Motivational Analysis," *Psychological Bulletin* 86, no. 2 (1979): 307–24.

[22] Sonia Roccas and Marilynn B. Brewer, "Social Identity Complexity," *Personality and Social Psychology Review* 6, no. 2 (2002): 88–106.

[23] Marilynn B. Brewer and Kathleen P. Pierce. "Social Identity Complexity and Outgroup Tolerance," *Personality and Social Psychology Bulletin* 31, no. 3 (March 1, 2005): 428–37.

more accepting of multicultural diversity and affirmative action, even controlling for age, education, and ideology.

These findings are important as American partisans have increasingly come to experience their party attachments as social identities,[24] and have moved into alignment with racial and religious identities. This means that the increasing social divisions between the two parties have lowered tolerance toward partisan opponents and placed racial and ethnic diversity squarely in the center of the political divide.[25]

Political Implications of Social Sorting

Two randomly selected Republicans from the American electorate are likely to share the same race and religion as well as party. For two random Democrats, the likelihood of them sharing a race and religion is far smaller. The Republican Party, by representing the interests of white, mainly rural Christians, has grown to stand against the promotion of the racial and ethnic diversity that has, at least on the surface, been a common refrain of the American reputation.[26] The social homogeneity of the Republican Party also suggests that Republicans on the whole should be inherently less tolerant of racial and ethnic out-groups, in accordance with Brewer and Pierce's (2005) findings.[27] Mason and Wronski (2018)[28] have indeed found that Republicans' partisan identities are more sensitive than Democrats' to the inclusion in the polity of atypical social groups.

Meanwhile, the Democratic Party has come to embody diversity to such an extent that the party cannot ignore the long-standing systemic oppression of the traditionally low-status social groups that make up a significant part of their base. At the same time, Democratic voters have

---

[24] Huddy, Mason, and Aarøe, "Expressive Partisanship"; Steven Greene, "The Social-Psychological Measurement of Partisanship," *Political Behavior* 24, no. 3 (2002): 171–97.

[25] Angie Maxwell and Todd Shields, *The Long Southern Strategy: How Chasing White Voters in the South Changed American Politics* (Oxford: Oxford University Press, 2019); Eric Schickler, *Racial Realignment: The Transformation of American Liberalism, 1932–1965* (Princeton: Princeton University Press, 2016); Michael Tesler, "The Conditions Ripe for Racial Spillover Effects," *Political Psychology* 36 (February 2015): 101–17; Michael Tesler and David O. Sears, *Obama's Race: The 2008 Election and the Dream of a Post-Racial America* (Chicago: University of Chicago Press, 2010).

[26] Jack Citrin, David O. Sears, Christopher Muste, and Cara Wong, "Multiculturalism in American Public Opinion," *British Journal of Political Science* 31, no. 2 (April 2001): 247–75.

[27] Brewer and Pierce. "Social Identity Complexity and Outgroup Tolerance."

[28] Lilliana Mason and Julie Wronski, "One Tribe to Bind Them All: How Our Social Group Attachments Strengthen Partisanship," Political Psychology 39 (February 2018): 257–77.

grown socially and culturally isolated from Republicans, increasing their intolerance for their political opponents.[29] All of this presages an intractable partisan divide that reduces the ability of American partisans to compromise or cooperate.[30]

Unfortunately, a lack of compromise is hardly the worst outcome from a socially sorted, highly partisan electorate. Social identities tend to foster intergroup conflict, especially when the groups are placed into competition (such as an election) on a regular basis.[31] As partisans strengthen their attachment to one party over the other, competitions between the parties begin to feel less like political debate and more like warfare.

SOCIAL RISKS OF MASS POLARIZATION

Our approach to "mass polarization" conveys the partisan intergroup conflict that characterizes social divisions in the mass electorate, rather than issue disagreement-based polarization that does not necessarily implicate those divided social groups. Here, we focus on four negative consequences of that social polarization. First, as crosscutting identities disappear from the American electorate, we should expect to see more emotional reactivity among partisans. Second, partisans will morally disengage by vilifying their political opponents and heralding their own righteousness. Third, the first two consequences should increase risks of violent partisan attitudes and behaviors. Finally, we expect more willingness to reject legitimate elections that threaten the power of one's own party. All four of these outcomes represent escalating forces that threaten the foundations of democratic governance.

Anger

Huddy et al. (2015) have found that threats to the power of one's own party cause the strongest partisans to react with extreme levels of anger. When those same partisans hear about party victory, they feel the

---

[29] Angela Y. He, Amanda Ripley, and Rehka Tenjarla, "The Geography of Partisan Prejudice," *The Atlantic,* March 4, 2019, www.theatlantic.com/politics/archive/2019/03/us-counties-vary-their-degree-partisan-prejudice/583072/.

[30] Diana C. Mutz, *Hearing the Other Side: Deliberative versus Participatory Democracy* (Cambridge: Cambridge University Press, 2006).

[31] Tajfel and Turner, "An Integrative Theory of Intergroup Conflict"; Muzafer Sherif and Carolyn W. Sherif, *Groups in Harmony and Tension: An Integration of Studies of Intergroup Relations,* vol. xiii (New York: Harper & Brothers, 1953).

strongest levels of enthusiasm. Group attachments at the heart of *social identity theory* explain the psychological mechanisms behind these emotional reactions.[32] The framework predicts that strong individual-level social attachments to a partisan identity motivate angry emotional reactions when the party loses.[33] This anger is driven not simply by dissatisfaction with potential policy consequences – it is a much deeper, more primal psychological reaction to group status threat.[34] Party losses are experienced as personal losses. Those who are not closely attached to a party feel less emotional after wins and losses because their sense of self is less closely bound to the status of the group. As partisan identities grow stronger and deeper in the aggregate, we should expect to see a more emotionally reactive electorate.

Mason (2016) found that while socially sorted partisans are not more angry on average, they are more easily provoked to anger, and partisans with crosscutting identities are generally less angry than weakly attached partisans. As a result, average levels of anger may be rising in the electorate because fewer Americans resist the emotional prods of politics given their strengthening partisan ties. As social sorting occurs, fewer people respond to elections and political discussions without becoming emotionally engaged, in a dynamic that places the entire electorate in a more emotionally reactive state.

Given that MacKuen et al. (2010) found that anger can produce "opposition to accommodation," the anger generated by intergroup conflict may be actively harming our ability to reasonably discuss important issues at hand.[35] The angrier the electorate, the less able we are to find common ground on policies or even basic norms. Furthermore, anger can push us toward more aggressive behavior against political opponents.[36]

[32] Tajfel and Turner, "An Integrative Theory of Intergroup Conflict."
[33] Leonie Huddy. "From Group Identity to Political Cohesion and Commitment." *The Oxford Handbook of Political Psychology*, September 4, 2013.
[34] Diane Mackie, Thierry Devos, and Eliot Smith, "Intergroup Emotions: Explaining Offensive Action Tendencies in an Intergroup Context," *Journal of Personality and Social Psychology* 79, no. 4 (2000): 602–16; Eliot R. Smith, Charles R. Seger, and Diane M. Mackie, "Can Emotions Be Truly Group Level? Evidence Regarding Four Conceptual Criteria," *Journal of Personality and Social Psychology* 93, no. 3 (September 2007): 431–46.
[35] Michael MacKuen, Jennifer Wolak, Luke Keele, and George E. Marcus, "Civic Engagements: Resolute Partisanship or Reflective Deliberation," *American Journal of Political Science* 54, no. 2 (2010): 440–58.
[36] Julia Menasce Horowitz, Anna Brown, and Kiana Cox, "Views on Race in America 2019," *Pew Research Center's Social & Demographic Trends Project* (blog), April 9, 2019, www.pewsocialtrends.org/2019/04/09/race-in-america-2019/.

Before addressing physical aggression, however, we need to understand the psychological process by which partisans rationalize such behavior. To harm our opponents, we have to understand them as enemies. If partisans grow morally disengaged from their fellow citizens on the other side of the aisle, this removes the stigma from aggression against them.

Moral Disengagement

Mechanisms of moral disengagement are psychological rationalizations that facilitate harm against others.[37] They give people the moral leeway to harm others in ways they would not otherwise find acceptable without that psychological distancing. They serve to protect one's self-image as a good person even as one harms other people. This constellation of related attitudes is *not* direct support for violence, but it constitutes a key risk factor for developing violent attitudes. Moral disengagement includes vilification and dehumanization of targets, blaming targets and emphasizing their deservingness for punishment, holding morally righteous views of one's own group, displacement of personal and collective responsibility for harm done, and minimizing or misrepresenting the extent of those harms.[38] Moral disengagement reduces pro-social behavior and expectations of self-censure for harmful actions.[39] Vilification of opponents and emphasizing the worthy purposes of one's own side are the strongest predictors of propensity to harm others.

To investigate the prevalence of these attitudes, we developed a battery of items, and first fielded it with a 2017 Cooperative Congressional Election Study (CCES) survey module.[40] All of our radical partisanship

---

[37] Albert Bandura, "Moral Disengagement in the Perpetration of Inhumanities," *Personality & Social Psychology Review (Lawrence Erlbaum Associates)* 3, no. 3 (July 1999): 193, https://doi.org/10.1207/s15327957pspr0303_3.

[38] Political behavior scholars have recently begun to study partisan dehumanization (e.g., Erin C. Cassese, "Partisan Dehumanization in American Politics," *Political Behavior* 43, no. 1 (March 2021): 29–50; James L. Martherus, Andres G. Martinez, Paul K. Piff, and Alexander G. Theodoridis. "Party Animals? Extreme Partisan Polarization and Dehumanization," *Political Behavior* (July 3, 2019). Here, we investigate the broader array of moral disengagement, of which dehumanization is one part.

[39] Albert Bandura, "Mechanisms of Moral Disengagement in the Exercise of Moral Agency," *Journal of Personality and Social Psychology* 71, no. 2 (1996): 364–74.

[40] November and December 2017 as a module in the Cooperative Congressional Election Study (CCES, N = 1,000) an online national stratified sample survey administered by YouGov.

Roots, Risks, and Rewards of Mass Polarization 181

items here and in the following used the respondent's party identification, with "leaners" classified as partisans and pure independents excluded from our results. Figure 7.1 presents the questions and illustrates the percentage of respondents who place themselves on the "morally disengaged" (MD) end of the spectrum for each item, disaggregated by party.

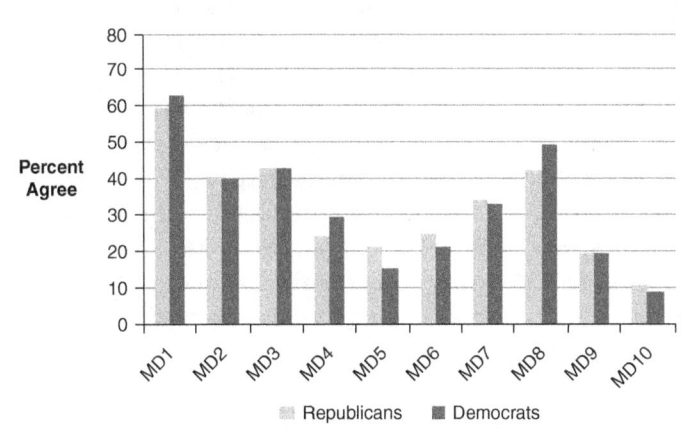

FIGURE 7.1 Partisan moral disengagement (CCES 2017)

	Moral Disengagement
MD1	Would you say [Opposing party] are a serious threat to the United States and its people, or wouldn't you go that far?
MD2	Only [Own party] want to improve our country.
MD3	[Opposing party] are not just worse for politics – they are downright evil.
MD4	If [Own party] break a few rules to oppose [Opposing party], it's because they need to do it for the sake of the country.
MD5	If [Opposing party] are going to behave badly, they should be treated like animals.
MD6	[Opposing party] deserve any mistreatment they get from [Own party].
MD7	[Opposing party] have their heart in the right place but just come to different conclusions about what is best. [reverse-coded]
MD8	[Own party] are not just better for politics – they are morally right.
MD9	Many [Opposing party] lack the traits to be considered fully human – they behave like animals.
MD10	Breaking a few rules to help [Own party] win does no lasting harm.

Partisan moral disengagement is prevalent in both parties, in roughly equal measure.[41] We'll highlight a few parallels. About 60 percent of Republicans and Democrats agree that the opposing party is "a serious threat to the United States and its people" (MD1). This is more moral disengagement than we found in a similar question asked by Pew Research Center in 2014, when over a third of Republicans and a quarter of Democrats viewed their opponents as a threat to national well-being.[42] Half of partisans agree their own party is "not just better for politics – they are morally right" (MD8). Over 40 percent of Republicans and Democrats "strongly" or "somewhat" agree that their opponents are "not just worse for politics – they are downright evil" (MD3). The most disturbing items may be those comparing out-group partisans to animals (MD5 and MD9), with agreement rates around 1 in 6. Taken as a whole, even the lower bounds of partisan moral disengagement provide some cause for concern. Extrapolated to the electorate at large, this figure represents many millions of partisans. These views are far more extreme than the tame "affective polarization" results scholars typically present when calculating differences in "warmth" and "coldness" felt toward the parties. The only solace for people concerned with this level of partisan hostility might be that the most extreme items receive the least support.

Consistent with our theoretical expectations, we find that an additive index of these moral disengagement items is significantly predicted by the strength of partisan social identity, extremity of conventional ideological identity, and levels of political anger and trait aggressiveness. Figure 7.2 illustrates these relationships, along with other traits like college education, age, and sex.

Moral disengagement is of interest here as a sign of extreme partisan hostility in its own right, but also for its role in facilitating violent partisan attitudes and behaviors. The next section identifies levels of violent views that are lower than all but the most extreme moral disengagement items, but the presence of violent attitudes at all is a cause for concern.

---

[41] To be clear, we do not suggest that these attitudes are morally equivalent or equally dangerous coming from both parties. High-status groups dehumanize others frequently – with a long record of harm. Low status groups may dehumanize high-status groups, but with far less ability to generate real harm. The partisan symmetry indicates that both parties believe they are engaged in a dire competition, but not for the same reasons.

[42] Pew Research Center, 2014, "Political Polarization in the American Public." Report, www.people-press.org/2014/06/12/political-polarization-in-the-american-public/.

Moral Disengagement

- Partisan Social Identity
- Ideological Identity Strength
- Anger
- Anxiety
- Trait Aggressiveness
- Education
- Age
- Woman

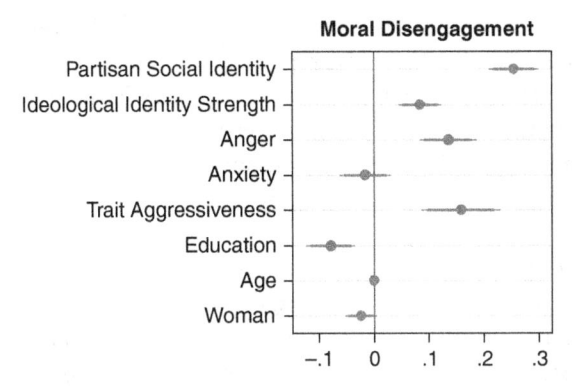

FIGURE 7.2 Correlates of moral disengagement (CCES 2017)
Note: Model presents OLS coefficients. Lines show 90 and 95 percent confidence intervals.

Political Violence

Electioneering from the mid-twentieth century to the present lacked the violence that characterized nineteenth-century partisanship, and we believe that tranquility limited scholarly perspectives on the potential harm that partisanship could do. The nineteenth century saw low-level partisan violence and party militias that accompanied election activity in the antebellum years,[43] partisan conflict over slavery in "Bleeding Kansas" in the 1850s,[44] racialized partisan violence in the Reconstruction and Jim Crow Eras in the South,[45] and the maximal partisan violence of the Civil War following the 1860 presidential election.[46] To be sure, the twentieth century saw plenty of political violence by extremists, including anarchist bombings in the 1920s and radical left bombings in the 1970s, but none of these mapped onto ordinary partisan contestation.

Contemporary US public opinion research has largely ignored the modern potential for partisan violence, and even comparative politics research on partisan violence tends to focus on elite-level mobilization rather than micro-foundations for individual-level partisan violence. Humphreys and

---

[43] David Grimsted, *American Mobbing* (New York: Oxford University Press. 1998).
[44] David Potter, *The Impending Crisis* (New York: Harper Collins, 1976).
[45] Avidit Acharya, Matthew Blackwell, and Maya Sen, *Deep Roots: How Slavery Still Shapes Southern Politics* (Princeton, NJ: Princeton University Press, 2018); Hugh Davis Graham and Ted R. Gurr, *Violence in America* (New York: Sage Publications, 1979).
[46] Kalmoe, *With Ballots & Bullets*; Jennifer L. Weber, *Copperheads* (New York: Oxford University Press, 2006).

Weinstein (2008) diverge from the macro-level scholarly approach in their study of individual-level civil war participation in Sierra Leone, which found some evidence that party affiliation affected willingness to participate as a combatant.[47] Gubler and Selway (2012) and Scarcelli (2014) both point to the effects of ethnic, religious, and ideological (but not explicitly partisan) cleavages in comparative contexts as potential catalysts for civil war.[48]

We present question wording about violent partisanship and the average levels of violent partisan attitudes in Figure 7.3. We were careful to ground these questions in present-day American party contexts, and not some historical or hypothetical case that would elicit broader support (e.g., American Revolution or fighting a totalitarian government). The bars indicate the percentage of respondents who currently believe there are some occasions when threats and violence are appropriate. One in eight Republicans and one in nine Democrats said it is at least occasionally acceptable to send threatening messages to public officials (PV1).[49] The numbers are only slightly lower for online threats against partisans in the public in a way that makes them feel unsafe (PV2). In short, there is a substantial minority of partisans who think violent threats and harassment against partisan opponents are sometimes okay.

The two remaining items justify violence by the in-party to advance political goals: they sanction terrorism, in other words.[50] One asks about violence today (PV3). The other asks for responses if the out-party wins the 2020 presidential election (PV4), a hypothetical but easily imagined scenario. Nine percent of Republicans and Democrats say that, in general, violence is at least occasionally acceptable. However, when imagining an electoral loss in 2020, larger percentages of both parties approve of the use of violence – though this increase is greater for Democrats (18 percent approve) than Republicans (13 percent approve).[51] In sum, most partisans reject violent threats and acts by their side, but a substantial minority does not.

---

[47] Macartan Humphreys and Jeremy M. Weinstein, "Who Fights? The Determinants of Participation in Civil War," *American Journal of Political Science* 52, no. 2 (2008), 436–55.

[48] Joshua R. Gubler and Joel Sawat Selway, "Horizontal Inequality, Crosscutting Cleavages, and Civil War," *Journal of Conflict Resolution* 56, no. 2 (2012): 206–32; Marc Scarcelli, "Social Cleavages and Civil War Onset," *Ethnopolitics* 13, no. 2 (2014): 181–202.

[49] It is possible that some respondents could interpret this item as nonviolent. Perhaps they may consider "threats" to include electoral mobilization, for instance.

[50] Our future work will examine the exact types of violence imagined by respondents when they answered positively to these questions.

[51] It is important to note that these data are from 2017, before the widespread 2020 protests against police brutality and for Black Lives.

Roots, Risks, and Rewards of Mass Polarization

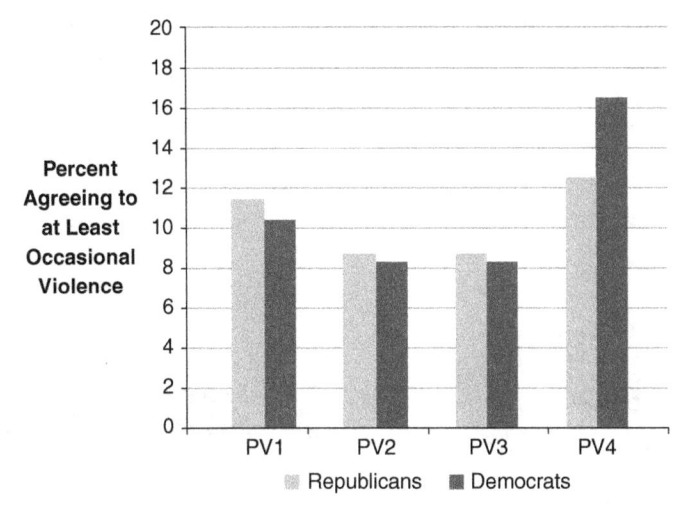

FIGURE 7.3 Partisan violence (CCES 2017)

Political Violence
PV1   When, if ever, is it OK for [Own party] to send threatening and intimidating messages to [Opposing party] leaders?
PV2   When, if ever, is it OK for an ordinary [Own party] in the public to harass an ordinary [Opposing party] on the Internet, in a way that makes the target feel unsafe?
PV3   How much do you feel it is justified for [Own party] to use violence in advancing their political goals these days?
PV4   What if [Opposing party] win the 2020 presidential election? How much do you feel violence would be justified then?

Rejecting Elections

Beyond violence, democracies collapse when leaders and citizens grow unwilling to accept election results and obey legitimately elected leaders. We measured these views in our 2018 CCES pre-election survey. We begin by measuring election confidence: "How much confidence do you have that the 2018 elections for US Congress will be conducted fairly?" Next, we asked whether the country should be split into separate countries along party lines. Election rejection is assessed with: "Should [Own Party] refuse to accept the election result if they do not win majorities in Congress this year?" In the post-election wave, we measured views on whether a respondent's own party's citizens believe they should obey federal laws that go against what they think is right, and we asked the same for what their party's governors should do in that case. We present the basic distribution of these contentious attitudes in Figure 7.4.

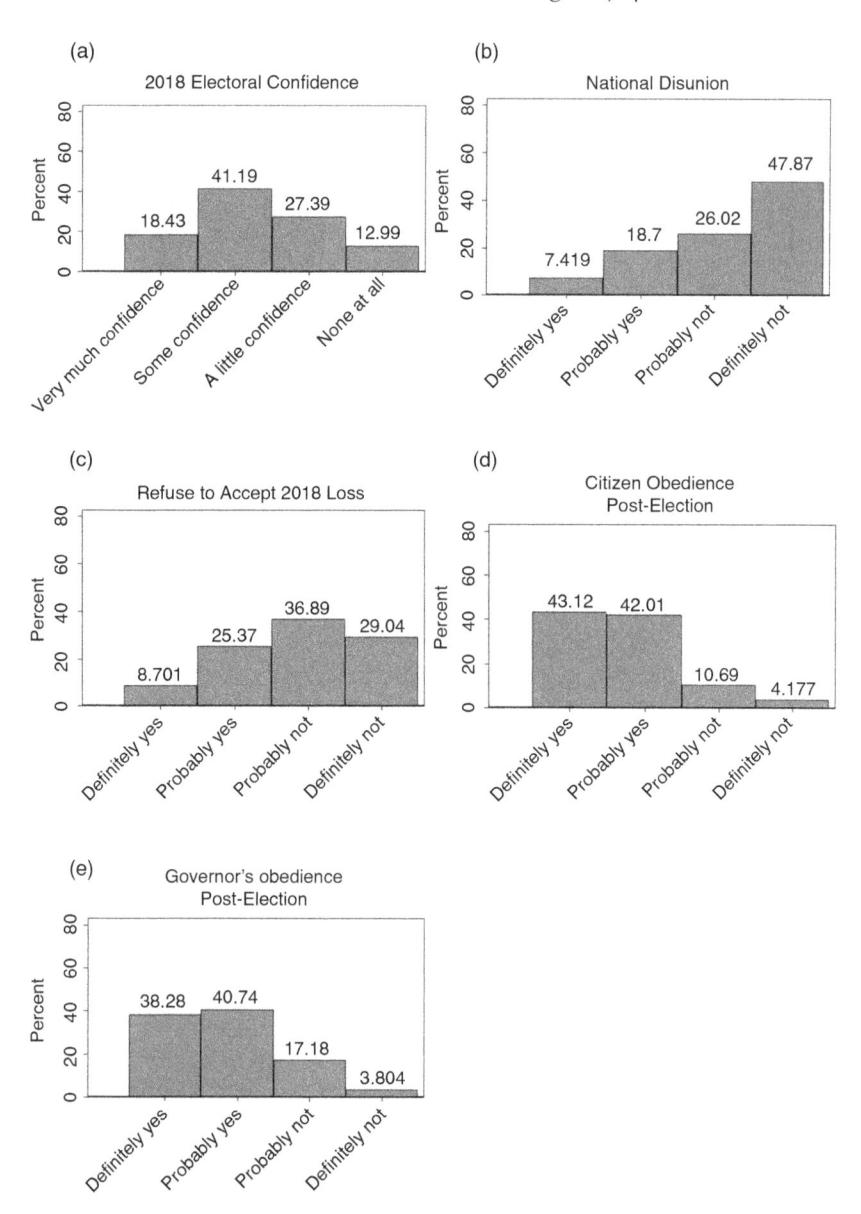

FIGURE 7.4 (a–e): Distributions of election confidence and radical partisanship

Here we see a picture of an American electorate that displays substantial rejections of democratic elections and the obligations of citizens and states to obey the law. Some 13 percent of the electorate had no confidence that the 2018 elections would be conducted fairly. More than one quarter of the electorate endorsed splitting the country apart along party lines, while roughly one third of respondents believed their own party should refuse to accept the outcome of the 2018 election if their party did not win a majority in Congress. About 15 percent of partisans believed that citizens should disobey federal law if it goes against what they think is right, and about 20 percent believed that their state governor should disobey too. These items indicated significant minorities supporting partisan disunion, civil disobedience, and nullification. All of these present disturbing challenges for a functioning democracy. On the other hand, we also take some comfort in the public's democratic resilience, as indicated by majorities opposed to most forms of radical partisanship in our surveys.

Historical Comparisons

We have presented recent survey data indicating some substantial public support for partisan moral disengagement, violence, and rejection of elections. Our evidence comes exclusively from after the 2016 presidential election, which was acrimonious and intense, norm-defying, and extraordinarily hostile. However, partisan acrimony did not begin in 2016.[52] A broader view of American history suggests present conflicts have extreme precedents. Where do we stand now in relation to those troubled times?

The Civil War Era provides the most prominent American examples of partisan authoritarianism and violence, when political parties in the 1850s enfranchised white male voters aligned along racial, religious, and regional lines. That confluence initially spawned "Bleeding Kansas," the site of rampant election fraud, dueling state constitutions and capitols backed by armed militias, and hundreds of deaths in the years before the Civil War.[53] Following Lincoln's 1860 presidential election, Southern partisans – almost all Democrats – refused to accept the legitimate result of a Republican president even before he took office, inaugurating four

---

[52] See, for example, Iyengar, Sood, and Lelkes, "Affect, Not Ideology"; Mason, *Uncivil Agreement*.
[53] Potter, *The Impending Crisis*.

years of warfare that killed three-quarters of a million Americans. War support among leaders in the loyal states polarized by party as the war progressed, and that elite division manifested in disproportionate war service among Republicans and Republican communities.[54] Partisan divides grew so deep that prominent Northern Democrats plotted their own violent insurrections to overthrow the Republican-led federal government.[55] In other words, it was a *partisan* civil war in origin and execution.

During Reconstruction, white Southern Democrats mobilized to attack the white and Black Republicans and the local and federal forces that tried to maintain the tenuous new democracy that recognized Black citizenship and enfranchised Black men. One such attack was the 1874 "Battle of Liberty Place" in New Orleans after a governor's election. Local whites celebrated that racial-partisan violence for a century after with a monument inscribed, "United States troops took over the state government and reinstated the usurpers but the national election November 1876 recognized white supremacy in the South and gave us our state" (DeBerry 2017[56]).

As the monument alluded, the Reconstruction Era ended after 1876, when Northern support for racial equality waned, and the federal government allowed the South's old leaders to reestablish white supremacy in the South. By the late 1890s, the South became a wholly Democratic authoritarian enclave devoted to maintaining white supremacy, including violent coups against multiracial local governments, extra-judicial lynching of thousands, universal segregation, and stringent laws ensuring Black citizens would not participate in elections. Democracy did not return to the Deep South until federal intervention in the 1960s forced reforms that ended de jure segregation and re-enfranchised African Americans after a century of authoritarian suppression.[57]

Lower-level election violence has an even broader precedence, marring free voting in many precincts from the 1830s through the 1850s.[58] Wartime suppression of dissent, as with the Sedition Acts under President Adams, also provide historical examples of partisan authoritarianism, in contrast

---

[54] Kalmoe, *With Ballots & Bullets*.

[55] Weber, *Copperheads*.

[56] Jarvis DeBerry, "Taking down Liberty Place Monument Undoes a Rewrite of History: Opinion." NOLA.com. April 24, 2017, www.nola.com/opinions/article_d42e767e-c6d3-5b9a-8ea9-24f9a0d805d0.html.

[57] Robert Mickey, *Paths out of Dixie: The Democratization of Authoritarian Enclaves in America's Deep South, 1944–1972* (Princeton: Princeton University Press, 2015).

[58] Grimsted, *American Mobbing*.

with the relatively bipartisan authoritarianism and violence of indigenous genocide in the nineteenth century and Japanese internment during World War II, among other travesties.

Recent polling provides some direct benchmarks of public support for political violence from the 1990s to the present, though the available comparison items carry different wordings that inhibit stronger inferences. In 1997, a Pew Research Center survey found that 27 percent of US adults said, "Violence against the government may be justified in some cases."[59] Just over a decade later, Kalmoe (2014) reported on a 2010 Knowledge Networks survey in which 25 percent of American adults declined to agree with the statement, "Citizens upset by government should never use violence to express their feelings."[60] Those levels are stable, assuming the 2010 five-point agree-disagree scale is binned appropriately.

A 2019 YouGov survey with our items shows that, when asked, "How much do you feel it is justified for [Own Party] to use violence in advancing their political goals these days?" 16 percent of partisans responded with something other than "not at all."[61] Interpreting that number in light of the 1997 and 2010 levels is complicated by the contemporary partisan wording that is unspecified in the more general wordings in the older surveys.[62]

Finally, we can examine trends in identically worded violence items with our YouGov surveys in recent years. There, we find the portion of partisans who unequivocally *reject* violence by their party today has declined, from 92 percent in 2017, to 88 percent in 2018 and 84 percent in 2019.[63] Each decline is statistically significant: millions more American partisans express openness to partisan violence than they did just a few short years ago.

Overall, we see today nothing like the levels of partisan authoritarianism and violence that plagued the American past. Nonetheless, the ethno-partisan

---

[59] Andrew Kohut, Kimberly Parker, Gregory Flemming, Molly Sonner, and Beth Donovan, "Deconstructing Distrust: How Americans View Government," March 10, 1998, www.pewresearch.org/wp-content/uploads/sites/4/legacy-pdf/Trust-in-Gov-Report-REV.pdf.
[60] Nathan P. Kalmoe, "Fueling the Fire: Violent Metaphors, Trait Aggression, and Support for Political Violence," *Political Communication* 31, no. 4 (2014), 545–63.
[61] The 2019 YouGov survey with our partisan violence items was designed and funded by Democracy Fund and the Voter Study Group.
[62] We have found no older surveys with which to compare our partisan election rejection items over time.
[63] The 2017 and 2018 YouGov studies were funded by LSU's Manship School of Mass Communication Tom Jarreau Hardin and Howard & Nantelle Mitchiner Gittinger professorships and the University of Maryland's Dept. of Government and Politics.

alignment of political parties suggests more conflict ahead: substantial numbers of Americans already back extreme measures, and those numbers appear to be rising. Those attitudinal trends manifested in the increasingly authoritarian acts of the Trump administration and in increasingly violent actions by partisans, largely Republicans, that have been eroding liberal democracy and public order – including, notably, the violent attack on the United States Capitol by Trump supporters on January 6, 2021. The past is not prologue in any literal sense, but its lessons give cause for grave concern about the current directions of American democracy.

SOCIAL REWARDS OF MASS POLARIZATION

We have painted a worrisome portrait of American public's commitment to democratic norms and practices, motivated by partisan identities that substantially align with major social cleavages. But we find at least one reason for optimism in a contentious time. In prior decades, both parties represented the interests of the white majority. Both housed and welcomed those who wished to legislate on behalf of systems that disproportionately benefitted white America and disadvantaged Black Americans and other communities of color. This racist system of government and society was the compromise position that made other legislation possible, even among racially progressive white legislators. This was the dark side of an unpolarized politics.

Now, we see a new racial and cultural divide *between* the parties, not within them. When asked by Pew whether there is "a lot of discrimination" against Blacks in the United States, Democrats and Republicans answered somewhat similarly as recently as 2013, with 28 percent of Democrats and 11 percent of Republicans agreeing that this was true. However, by 2019, 69 percent of Democrats and 19 percent of Republicans agreed with this statement. As Republican attitudes liberalized by 8 percentage points, Democratic attitudes liberalized by 41 percentage points. A similar trend occurred regarding perceived discrimination against Hispanics. Between 2013 and 2019, Democratic agreement that there was "a lot of discrimination" against Hispanics increased from 32 to 58 percent, while Republican agreement barely changed, moving from 15 to 16 percent. By 2019, when asked "why black people in our country may have a harder time getting ahead than white people," majorities of white Democrats identified systemic barriers and discrimination while majorities of white Republicans blamed the social culture of Black people.[64]

---

[64] Horowitz, Brown, and Cox, "Views on Race in America 2019."

Vast majorities of white Democrats believed in 2019 that Blacks are treated less fairly than whites in dealing with the police (88 percent), by the criminal justice system (86 percent), in hiring, pay, and promotions (72 percent), when applying for a loan or mortgage (64 percent), in stores or restaurants (62 percent), and when voting (60 percent). In comparison, significantly fewer white Republicans agree that Blacks are treated less fairly than whites in dealing with the police (43 percent), by the criminal justice system (39 percent), in hiring, pay, and promotions (21 percent), when applying for a loan or mortgage (17 percent), in stores or restaurants (16 percent), and when voting (7 percent).[65] Beyond acknowledging discrimination against others, 66 percent of white Democrats believed that being white has helped them personally get ahead. Only 29 percent of white Republicans agreed.

Likewise, Pew asked white Republicans and Democrats whether, "when it comes to giving black people equal rights with whites, our country has [not gone far enough/gone too far/ been about right]." Among white Democrats, 64 percent believed the country has not gone far enough. Among white Republicans 84 percent believed the country has either gone *too* far or been about right. In the same study, when asked, "when it comes to racial discrimination" what is "the bigger problem for the country," 77 percent of white Republicans reported that the bigger problem was "seeing discrimination where it does not exist" while 78 percent of white Democrats reported that the bigger problem was "not seeing discrimination where it really does exist." The divide between white Democrats and Republicans in their views of systemic racism is large and rapidly growing.

These changes were exacerbated during the Trump administration, particularly in 2020 after mass national protests against police violence and for racial justice coincided with a global pandemic that disproportionately killed people of color in the United States. In 2016, 40 percent of Hillary Clinton supporters agreed that "White people benefit a great deal from advantages in society that Black people do not have." By August of 2020, 59 percent of Biden supporters agreed with that statement. Over the same period of time, 4 percent of Trump supporters agreed with the statement in 2016, rising only to 5 percent in 2020. When asked whether "It is a lot more difficult to be a Black person in this country than it is to be a White person," 57 percent of Clinton supporters in 2016 agreed, with that number increasing to 74 percent of Biden supporters in 2020. Among

[65] Ibid.

Trump supporters, this number *declined* from 11 percent in 2016 to 9 percent in 2020.[66]

In a two-party system, this level of support for racial justice by half of the political machinery is unprecedented. It does not guarantee progress, but it does offer a stronger possibility than ever before. However, an entrenched system will not disappear quietly. Any time the status of a social group is threatened, individuals identified with that group react with anger, defensiveness, bias, and action. Jardina (2019) described these types of responses among white Americans who hold strong racial identities.[67] A diversifying nation and the accompanying threat of a shrinking status gap between white Americans and everyone else makes strongly identified whites lash out.

But these aggrieved whites are not operating alone. They retain the strong support of a (Republican) political party as well. This means that the racial divide in American politics is now organized around party lines. Americans can base their vote on whether or not they believe that systemic racism exists. Those who do not believe that it does, or those who believe that white Americans are under threat, are able to pursue that case by voting for the Republican Party. The alignment between party and race pushes our electoral institutions into a fight over American identity and the relative humanity of America's citizens.

Kalmoe (2020) describes how nineteenth-century American parties escalated conflict after taking sides on the issue of slavery, resulting in the Civil War.[68] Today's electorate is far more racially liberal than the white population in the nineteenth century, and the partisan divide today is less easily drawn on a map. A massive amount of progress in the battle against systemic racism has already been achieved. The current party divides enable even faster progress, but they also magnify the backlash to that progress. This dynamic entrenches the battle between those who prefer white nationalist politics and those who embrace the democratic future of a diversifying nation. This distinctly racial and ethnic divide between the two parties is a strong echo of violent conflicts in the past, and a harbinger of a white backlash that is sure to resist the emerging forces of change. The fact that 74 million Americans voted for Donald Trump after

---

[66] www.pewresearch.org/politics/2020/09/10/voters-attitudes-about-race-and-gender-are-even-more-divided-than-in-2016/.

[67] Ashley Jardina, *White Identity Politics*, 1st ed. (Cambridge: Cambridge University Press, 2019).

[68] Kalmoe, *With Ballots & Bullets*.

seeing four years of his racial divisiveness suggests that the backlash against social progress is strong and widespread.

CONCLUSIONS

Across our theoretical discussion and original survey evidence, we find reason for both optimism and pessimism regarding political polarization and democratic resilience in American politics. Our pessimistic evidence is powerful. We identify many macro and micro risk factors for democratic unrest in the American electorate. American partisans are not only in disagreement, but they are increasingly intolerant of their opponents and sometimes violently angry about politics. The basic social divide between the parties undermines the common national identity that had been forged through a series of crosscutting social identities within the parties among white Christians in the past. Without a sense of common national identity, the parties are likely to fall victim to the partisanship that George Washington himself warned,

> agitates the community with ill-founded jealousies and false alarms, kindles the animosity of one part against another, foments occasionally riot and insurrection. It opens the door to foreign influence and corruption, which finds a facilitated access to the government itself through the channels of party passions. (1796 Farewell Address)

We have presented survey evidence that Washington's worst worries about riot and insurrection may be worthy concerns in an era of powerful partisanship. Many partisans are perfectly willing to tell survey researchers they reject legitimate electoral outcomes and are also willing to contemplate the circumstances under which they would approve of violence against their partisan opponents. Majorities even see their opponents as threats to the nation. This should be cause for great alarm.

However, there is also cause for optimism. What if the United States seriously addresses its history of racial violence and prejudice, and the present-day manifestations of that history? What if, as a nation, we reckoned with our shameful history in ways akin to the truth and reconciliation processes in Rwanda or Germany? Is it possible for the American electorate to come to terms with the central role of racial oppression and gender inequality in its history?

If we do these things, we will certainly see unrest in response. This type of reckoning would surely deepen social divides and kindle many animosities. It would invite demagogues into political leadership. It may threaten the very institutions on which American democracy rests, because these, after all, were built on a structure of slavery and racial oppression. The disruption inherent in remedying racial inequality has already divided the American citizenry into violent conflict against one another on more than one occasion. It is not difficult to imagine it doing so once again. But, in the optimistic version of events, it is also possible to imagine that this time, American society is ready for this change. In this case, polarization itself is not the problem to be addressed – polarization is simply an inevitable step on a path toward a more representative democracy. The more important problem to address is whether American democracy can survive the journey.

8

The Great White Hope

Threat and Racial Resilience in Trump's America

Christopher Sebastian Parker and Matt A. Barreto

INTRODUCTION

Political polarization, according to the influential text, *How Democracies Die* (HDD), is at the root of the decline of American democracy.[1] In fact, we are more polarized now, as Trump exits the Oval Office, than the country's been in the last seventy-five years.[2] Still, the current round of polarization began in earnest on Obama's watch. Together, Trump and Obama own four of the top five years on record as the most polarizing since 1945. Given the evidence that race has driven partisanship more now than any other time in recent history, it seems to us that racism goes a long way toward explaining the acceleration of polarization in recent years.[3] Even when it comes to the celebrated affective approach to polarization,[4] recent research illustrates that race, more than any other factor, best explains interparty antipathy.[5]

---

[1] Steven Levitsky and Daniel Ziblatt, *How Democracies Die* (New York: Crown, 2018).
[2] https://news.gallup.com/poll/283910/trump-third-year-sets-new-standard-party-polarization.aspx
[3] Marisa Abrajano and Zoltan L. Hajnal, *White Backlash: Immigration, Race, and American Politics* (Princeton: Princeton University Press, 2015); Michael Tesler, *Post Racial or Most Racial: Race and Politics in the Obama Era* (Chicago: University of Chicago Press, 2016).
[4] See, for example, Shanto Iyengar, and Sean J. Westwood, "Fear and Loathing Across Party Lines: New Evidence on Group Polarization," *American Journal of Political Science* 59, no. 3 (2012): 690–707. For a slightly different approach, one that emphasizes social polarization, see Lilliana Mason, *Uncivil Agreement: How Politics Became Our Identity* (Chicago: University of Chicago Press, 2018).
[5] Nicholas A. Valentino and Kirill Zhirkov, "Blue Is Black and Red Is White? Affective Polarization in the Racialized Schemas of US Party Coalitions," Midwest Political Science Association, Chicago, IL, 2018.

Beginning with his candidacy, the most important factor predicting support for Trump is race,[6] a pattern that carried over into the general election of 2016.[7] Missing from these accounts for why Trump won, however, is *why* race is such a key factor. Following others, we argue that underlying the import of race in predicting Trump's success is the anxiety and anger, on the part of many whites, with the increasing diversity taking place in America.[8] This is in keeping with work that shows how whites, when primed with the fact that the United States will be a majority-minority country in 2042, tend to adopt more conservative positions.[9] Trump supporters, in other words, are unsettled at the prospect of losing "their" country. Thus, the ubiquitous refrain, "Make America Great Again," we believe, refers to a time during which WASP cultural dominance remained unchallenged. In short, he won, at least *in part*, because those who supported him believed that the country was changing too fast, a sentiment made popular most recently by the Tea Party movement.[10] (Make no mistake, the Tea Party paved the way for Trump's presidency.[11])

Most accounts of resistance to the Trump presidency identify the #Resistance and the Women's March, both in January 2017, as the beginning of the resistance. We argue, however, that people of color (POC) began to resist before 2017. For POC, Trump represents a reversion to a dated sense of

---

[6] John Sides, Michael Tesler, and Lynn Vavreck, *Identity Crisis: The 2016 Presidential Campaign and the Battle for the Meaning of America* (Princeton: Princeton University Press, 2018).

[7] Jon Green and Sean McElwee, "The Differential Effects of Economic Conditions and Racial Attitudes in the Election of Donald Trump," *Perspectives on Politics* 17, no. 2 (2019): 358–79.

[8] Brenda Major, Alison Blodorn, and Gregory Major Blascovich, "The Threat of Increasing Diversity: Why Many White Americans Support Trump in the 2016 Presidential Election," *Group Processes and Intergroup Relations* 21, no. 6 (2018): 1–10.

[9] Maureen Craig and Jennifer Richeson, "On the Precipice of a 'Majority-Minority' America: Perceived Status Threat from the Racial Demographic Shift Affects White Americans' Political Ideology," *Psychological Science* 25, no. 6 (2014): 1189–97.

[10] Kevin Arceneaux and Stephen P. Nicholson, "Who Wants to Have a Tea Party? The Who, What, and Why of the Tea Party Movement," *PS: Political Science and Politics* 45, no. 4 (2012): 700–10; Matt Barreto, Betsy L. Gonzalez, Benjamin Gonzalez, Christopher S. Parker, and Christopher Towler, "The Tea Party in the Age of Obama: Mainstream Conservatism or Out-Group Anxiety?" *Political Power and Social Theory* 22, no. 1 (2012): 105–37; Christopher S. Parker and Matt A. Barreto, *Change They Can't Believe In: The Tea Party and Reactionary Politics in America* (Princeton: Princeton University Press, 2013).

[11] Bryan T. Gervais and Irwin L. Morris, *Reactionary Republicanism: How the Tea Party in the House Paved the Way for Trump's Victory* (Oxford: Oxford University Press, 2018); see also Rachel M. Blum, *How the Tea Party Captured the GOP: Insurgent Factions in American Politics* (Chicago: University of Chicago Press, 2020).

American national identity, one featuring an ethnocultural understanding of the nation from which they (POC) were excluded. Given what Trump has explicitly said about Mexicans and Muslims, and lecturing "the Blacks," it comes as no great shock that many POC felt threatened by him and by his supporters who displayed xenophobic or racist signs at his campaign rallies. The anxiety and anger associated with the prospect of turning the racial clock back to the 1960s compelled POC to resist, and we can detect resistance to Trump and his supporters in the data during the 2016 election.

In this chapter, we advance theories of threat that are present for whites and POC during Trump's first campaign. We argue that the sentiments expressed by the former are ultimately driven by status threat – the perception that one's way of life is under threat. In other words, the threat is wholly of a symbolic nature; it's not material. In the present context, Trump's supporters are threatened by the loss of "their" country: whites' cultural hegemony. On the flip side, we argue that racial and ethnic minorities saw the emergent Trump movement as a threat to racial progress, mobilizing in response.

We test these propositions by examining the political attitudes and behavior of whites and POC in the 2016 campaign cycle using the American National Election Survey (ANES) and the Collaborative Multiracial Post-Election Survey (CMPS). Ultimately, we find support for our theory of existential threat motivating whites who supported Trump and POC who opposed him. Further, for both groups who responded to the existential threat, we find they were significantly more likely to engage in politics in 2016 than their counterparts who were less convinced of such an existential threat to their group's status.

In the end, this chapter suggests that even as Trump damaged American democracy, his bigotry may, ironically, sow the seeds of its (democracy's) renewal. As it turns out, this is precisely what happened after 2016 when communities of color, led by the Black community, pushed Democrats to victory at the national and subnational level.[12] Findings from this chapter are also indicative of the role race plays in the polarization of American politics. In light of our results, it's beyond shocking that race and racism are almost never included when scholars discuss polarization. This chapter makes plain why such an "oversight" is, at best, unwise, for as the

---

[12] For subnational outcome, see https://thehill.com/opinion/campaign/403977-theres-a-boost-in-black-turnout-especially-among-black-women-voters; for the national level, see https://apnews.com/article/election-2020-joe-biden-race-and-ethnicity-virus-outbreak-georgia-7a843bbce00713cfde6c3fdbc2e31eb7.

outcome 2020 election makes clear, American democracy's resilience was a nonstarter absent the turnout of POC.[13]

This chapter unfolds as follows. First, we furnish the reader with a bit of background on the Trump movement. This is followed by an overview of the origins of resistance on the part of POC. Next, we outline how theories of threat apply to both groups. Briefly, Trump's support is fueled by perceived threats to the WASP way of life, while Trump and supporters are believed to pose a threat to racial progress on the part of POC. The ensuing data analysis first assesses the determinants of Trump support or, in the case of POC, rejection. The second stage of the analysis entails an illustration of how Trump motivates political engagement among his supporters as well as POC. Here, the argument shifts to what Trump represents. For his supporters, he represents a means for them to preserve their way of life. For POC, he represents a threat to racial progress. We end with a brief discussion of how the results fit within a broader framework on the fragility of American democracy in Trump's America.

BACKGROUND AND THEORY: THREAT IN THE AGE OF TRUMP

We argue that the perception of cultural threat, on the part of many whites, drives support for Trump. Similar to the way in which the Tea Party movement represented a reaction to threat stimulated by social change and the election of a Black President, we argue that Trump serves a similar purpose (i.e., as a vessel for reactionary sentiment). In fact, much of what we have to say about Trump supporters references existing work on the Tea Party.[14] After all, the demographic composition of the former and latter are quite similar. According to exit polls, Trump voters were more likely to be male, older, white, strong conservatives, relatively well-off economically, and Christian.[15] This is the same demographic that supported the Tea Party movement. Notwithstanding the time period during which each appeared, we argue that little, if any, daylight separates Trump supporters from its forebears: the Know Nothing Party, the Ku Klux Klan (KKK) of the 1920s, the John Birch Society (JBS), and the Tea Party. Without exception, these groups felt threatened by the social

---

[13] www.brookings.edu/blog/how-we-rise/2020/11/24/how-black-americans-saved-biden-and-american-democracy/

[14] Arceneaux and Nicholson, "Who Wants to Have a Tea Party?"; Parker and Barreto, *Change They Can't Believe In*; Theda Skocpol and Vanessa Williamson, *The Tea Party and the Remaking of Republican Conservatism* (Oxford: Oxford University Press, 2011).

[15] www.cnn.com/election/results/exit-polls.

change happening around them: they were losing "their" country.[16] These effects aren't confined to the American context. Indeed, scholars now point to a consistent finding in America *and* Europe: that cultural, not economic, concerns about immigration are driving these reactionary movements.[17]

Then, as now, a skeptic might offer an alternative hypothesis, such as economic anxiety. Then, as now, we believe it doesn't square with reality: in each of the historic examples we offered, economic anxiety was not a motive for supporting these reactionary movements. Extensive research finds that Tea Party supporters were fueled more by cultural anxiety than concerns over government spending.[18] Likewise, extant research reveals that anti-Obama sentiment among conservatives was mostly explained by racial attitudes, not the price tag of his health care bill.[19] While Trump movement supporters may well have been anxious, it was not about their economic condition, but about their declining status in a changing America.[20] Even when movement supporters explicitly stated economic concerns, a deeper look suggests this was nothing more than a proxy for their cultural anxiety amid changing demographics.[21]

---

[16] Right-wing movements generally emerge to preserve the status, interests, or cultural preferences of dominant groups. Theoretically, this is called the "status politics" model, ultimately made famous by Gusfield, in which an attempt is made to either preserve or restore the power and privilege, or cultural preference of a dominant social group thought to be in decline or completely without influence. Political action, moreover, was seen as an attempt to project their anxiety onto public objects. Bell, Hofstadter and Lipset were the most visible supporters of this approach, which rose to prominence from the late 1950s through the mid-1960s. See Daniel Bell, "The Dispossessed," in *The Radical Right*, ed. Daniel Bell (New York: Doubleday, 1963), 1–46; Joseph R. Gusfield, *Symbolic Crusade: Status Politics and the American Temperance Movement* (Urbana: University of Illinois Press, 1963); Richard Hofstadter, *The Paranoid Style in American Politics* (New York: Alfred A. Knopf, 1965); Seymour Martin Lipset and Earl Raab, *The Politics of Unreason: Right-Wing Extremism in American Politics, 1790–1977* (New York: Harper & Row, 1970).

[17] See for instance, Jens Hainmueller and Daniel Hopkins, "Public Attitudes Toward Immigration," *Annual Review of Political Science* 17 (2014): 225–49; see also Ronald F. Inglehart and Pippa Norris, "Trump, Brexit, and the Rise of Populism: Economic Haves and Have-Nots and Cultural Backlash," Faculty Research Working Paper Series, August 2016.

[18] Parker and Barreto, *Change They Can't Believe In*.

[19] Michael Tesler. 2012. "The Spillover of Racialization into Health Care: How President Obama Polarized Public Opinion by Racial Attitudes and Race," *American Journal of Political Science* 56, no. 3 (July 2012): 690–704.

[20] Diana Mutz, "Status Threat, Not Economic Hardship, Explains the 2016 Presidential Vote," *Proceedings of the National Academy of Science* 115, no. 19 (2018): E4330–39; Green and McElwee, "Differential Effects"; and Sides, Tesler, and Vavreck, *Identity Crisis*.

[21] Others arrive at a similar conclusion, in a different context, in which perceived symbolic threat pushed those in the cultural majority to adopt less tolerant positions far more than

If the economic angst of working-class whites cannot account for emergence of reactionary movements, what can?[22] Historically, partisanship generally informs whether or not one identifies with reactionary movements.[23] But partisanship isn't the only factor: racism is another. Indeed, from the KKK to the Tea Party, both are consistently associated with support for reactionary movements.[24] Building on the Tea Party, Trump ratcheted racial anxiety up another notch. Trump's statements about "Mexicans" and "Muslims," and references to "the Blacks," are clear indicators that racism is part of his appeal. Recent work on support for Trump validates this intuition.[25] Other work indicates that the need for social conformity (authoritarianism) is also associated with support for Trump.[26]

Still, racism and authoritarianism represent marked departures from what we believe is the *principal factor* that explains support for reactionary movements from the past to the present: status threat. We argue that reactionary movements are driven, at least in part, by a desire for the group to regain social prestige by returning to the past. From a substantive perspective, this impulse is associated with all of the reactionary movements we've noted. We cannot say the same for racism. After all, a good portion of the Know Nothing Party in the mid-nineteenth century weren't as concerned about Blacks as they were about Irish immigrants – particularly Catholics.[27] Nor can we say the same for authoritarianism, for it failed to inform the extent to which one identified with the Tea Party.

---

more material concerns, such as one's economic circumstance. See Paul M. Sniderman, Louk Hagendorn, and Markus Prior, "Predisposing Factors and Situational Triggers: Exclusionary Reactions to Immigrant Minorities," *American Political Science Review* 98, no.1 (2014): 35–39.

[22] More recent work arrives at the same conclusion vis-à-vis Trump supporters: www.washingtonpost.com/news/monkey-cage/wp/2017/06/05/its-time-to-bust-the-myth-most-trump-voters-were-not-working-class/?utm_term=.d8545c628400.

[23] Alan Abramowitz and Kyle Saunders, "Ideological Realignment in the U.S. Electorate," *Journal of Politics* 60, no. 3 (1998): 634–52.

[24] Rory McVeigh and Kevin Estep, *The Politics of Losing: Trump, the Klan, and the Mainstreaming of Resentment* (New York: Columbia University Press, 2019); Parker and Barreto, *Change They Can't Believe In*.

[25] Thomas Wood, "Racism Motivated Trump Voters More than Authoritarianism," Monkey Cage, *Washington Post*, April 17, 2017; Jonathan Capehart, "The Real Reason Working-Class Whites Continue to Support Trump," Post Partisan, *Washington Post*, June 6, 2017.

[26] Matthew C. MacWilliams, "Who Decides When the Party Doesn't? Authoritarian Voters and the Rise of Donald Trump," *PS Political Science & Politics* 49, no. 4 (2016): 716–21.

[27] Tyler Anbinder, *Nativism and Slavery: The Northern Know Nothings and the Politics of the 1850s* (Oxford: Oxford University Press, 1992); Bruce Levine, "Conservatism,

Again, like the Tea Party, we picture Trump as a vessel for a certain kind of conservatism, one that fails to mesh well with the more conventional account. As we have outlined elsewhere, perhaps the most dramatic difference between establishment conservatives and what we have called "reactionary conservatives" involves the way in which the rival camps envisage the future, particularly change. Consider the following. Some of the most noted conservative intellectuals of the twentieth century felt that true conservatives must be willing to abide social and economic changes that have proven effective at furthering the American way of life, and in which most Americans are invested. Further, they also held fast to the belief that true conservatives should steadfastly refuse to entertain efforts by some that unravel the bonds of social unity.[28]

Work on the Tea Party confirmed this division between true (or, establishment conservatives) and reactionary conservatives (i.e., Tea Party conservatives, or "true believers"): the former adopted a more measured approach to President Obama and POC, where the latter believed that the president and POC were "destroying the country,"[29] and responsible for the decline of America. Given the bluster of Trump and his campaign, can we really say he and his acolytes can tolerate change, and work to consolidate the bonds that putatively characterize American society?

Another area in which our account of race and politics in the age of Trump improves upon existing scholarship to date, is through the incorporation of POC into the narrative. Indeed, beyond how many white Americans reacted to Trump, there is little doubt that through his rhetoric, campaign promises, and policy prescriptions, Trump was poised to have a significant impact on racial and ethnic minorities in the United States. After decades of fighting for first-class citizenship, it's likely that Trump's presidency threatened to undermine the progress made toward that end. In other words, Trump's presidency represented the latest round of racial retrenchment. By this, we mean a historical pattern by which some racial progress is followed by a backlash of some kind.[30] This pattern is most

---

Nativism, and Slavery: Thomas R. Whitney and the Origins of the Know-Nothing Party," *Journal of American History* 88, no. 2 (2001): 455–88.

[28] Here, among others, we refer to Clinton Rossiter, *Conservatism in America* (Cambridge: Harvard University Press, 1982); and Russell Kirk, *The Conservative Mind: From Burke to Eliot* (Washington: Regnery, 2001).

[29] Parker and Barreto, *Change They Can't Believe In*, chap. 1.

[30] Useful examples of the this can be found in the following: Mario T. Garcia, *Mexican Americans: Leadership, Ideology, and Identity, 1930–1960* (New Haven: Yale University

easily identified when it comes to the Black community if, for no other reason, than that it has happened with more frequency for them than other POC. This dynamic follows a distinct pattern. Progress, for the Black community seems to coincide most frequently with American participation in major wars, but attempts at racial retrenchment are never far behind.[31]

For other POC, those associated with the *voluntary* immigrant experience, the swings between progress and attempts at retrenchment are less frequent, but no less jarring. Perhaps the first contemporary example of the dynamic to which we refer is most readily traceable to mobilization during the Chicano rights movements of the late 1960s, something originating in school-based protest over racist policies.[32]

More recently, California was the epicenter of reactionary politics in the mid-1990s with Republican Governor Pete Wilson and Proposition 187 in 1994. The Wilson/187 campaign was motivated by concern, on the part of many white Californians, that Latinos threatened WASP culture,[33] among other things. The ballot initiative called for withholding education and non-emergency healthcare for the undocumented. What's more, civil servants (school administrators, law enforcement, etc.) were to be charged with reporting suspected "illegal aliens" to the Immigration and Naturalization Service (INS). Needless to say, for many Latinos across California, Wilson's victory and the adoption of Prop 187 represented a threat to their rightful place in California. Latinos reacted to this threat through increased naturalization, voter registration, and voter turnout in subsequent California elections.[34] The Wilson/187 era is perhaps the best documented, but more recent examples are available. These include Latino mobilization against H.R. 4437 and the 2006 immigrant rights

---

Press, 1989); Phillip Klinkner and Rogers M. Smith, *The Unsteady March: The Rise and Decline of Racial Equality in America* (Chicago: University of Chicago Press, 1999); Ronald Takaki, *Strangers from a Different Shore: A History of Asian Americans* (Boston: Little, Brown, 1998).

[31] See for example, Klinkner and Smith, *Unsteady March*; and Christopher S. Parker, *Fighting for Democracy: Black Veterans and the Struggle Against White Supremacy in the Postwar South* (Princeton: Princeton: Princeton University Press, 2009).

[32] Carlos Muñoz Jr., *Youth, Identity, Power: The Chicano Movement* (London: Verso, 2007).

[33] Otto Santa Ana, *Brown Tide Rising: Metaphors of Latinos in Contemporary American Discourse* (Austin: University of Texas Press, 2002).

[34] Matt Barreto, Ricardo Ramirez, Nathan Woods, "Are Naturalized Voters Driving the California Latino Electorate?" *Social Science Quarterly* 86, no. 4 (December 2005): 792–811; Adrian Pantoja, Ricardo Ramirez and Gary Segura, "Citizens by Choice, Voters by Necessity." *Political Research Quarterly* 54, no. 4 (December 2001): 729–50.

marches, and protest movements against Arizona's SB1070 profiling law in 2010.[35]

Notwithstanding the brevity of the Black and Latino examples here, it's easy for one to detect distinct patterns. First, challenges to the racial status quo are always met with resistance of some kind on the part of some whites. To be sure, it's not always the same resistance. During critical phases of the civil rights movement, threats to white supremacy were met with violence; for Latinos, whites reacted at the ballot box. Second, the threats that are perceived, on the part of Blacks and Latinos, are both symbolic and material. For the Black community, the idea that some might think they're not as "American" as they think they are[36] is something with which they take issue. Needless to say, Trump supporters cling to the idea that American identity is a white identity. Likewise, social standing is also important to most members of the Latino community, especially when it comes to citizenship (or, lack thereof) and the threat of deportation.[37] These issues are deeply symbolic for both communities. Further, it hardly bears mentioning that the racism harbored by Trump and his supporters has material implications to the extent that racism, in general, is typically tied to discrimination. It stands to reason, therefore, that POC will resist efforts on the part of whites to reel in whatever advances POC have achieved. In short, the present moment isn't the first time we've observed this pattern of progress followed by retrenchment followed by a reaction on the part of POC.[38]

For many non-whites, Trump merely represents the latest attempt at racial retrenchment. Still, we wish to be clear here: the type of thereat to which we refer represents a marked difference from that which motivates Trump supporters. The existential threat to Trump supporters turns on their belief that their way of life – their *culture* – is under threat, and

[35] Sophia Wallace, Chris Zepeda-Millán, and Michael Jones-Correa, "Spatial and Temporal Proximity: Examining the Effects of Protests on Political Attitudes." *The American Journal of Political Science* 58, no. 2 (2013): 433–48; Chris Zepeda-Millán. 2014. "Weapons of the (Not So) Weak: Immigrant Mass Mobilization in the US South." *Critical Sociology* 42, no. 2 (2014): 269–87.
[36] Efren O. Perez and Entung Kuo, "Racial Order, Racialized Responses: Inter-minority Politics in a Diverse Nation," *Harvard Working Group in Psychology and Political Behavior*, October 9, 2020, Harvard University.
[37] Cecilia Menjivar and Sarah M. Lahkani, "Transformative Effects of Immigration Law: Immigrants' Personal and Social Metamorphoses through Regularization," *American Journal of Sociology* 121, no. 6 (2016): 1818–55.
[38] See for example, Klinkner and Smith, *Unsteady March*; see also Desmond S. King and Rogers M. Smith, *Still a House Divided: Race and Politics in Obama's America* (Princeton: Princeton University Press, 2011).

support for Trump represents their reaction.[39] This is NOT the same as the threat perceived by POC. For them, the election of Trump and his presidency represents *material* and *symbolic* threat, something that suggests that group conflict is the more appropriate model by which to assess the way(s) in which POC ultimately responded to Trump's presidency.

Group conflict involves intergroup competition over scarce resources, ones that confer relative privilege to the advantaged group. The zero-sum nature of competition over such resources is generally responsible for the perception of threat. These resources are typically embedded within the various social, economic, and political institutions of society.[40] Generally material, intergroup competition may also extend beyond, to say, schools, votes, jobs. Winners of this competition (i.e., "dominants") seek to perpetuate their dominance by generating beliefs and values that "justify" the maintenance of their advantage vis-à-vis "subordinate" groups.[41] While this may be the case for those in the cultural majority, subordinate groups are generally more concerned with material ends given the impact of discrimination. As such, consistent with the group competition model in which "outgroups ... desire a greater share of [the] rights, resources and privileges that are 'understood' to 'belong' to the ingroup,"[42] POC seek to resist Trump and what he represents: a threat to their standing as first-class citizens.

On the other hand, it's quite possible that not all POC see Trump as a threat; indeed, some minorities are able to rationalize their position as second-class citizens.[43] However, our theory suggests that many did (view Trump as a threat), and that his occupation of the Oval Office

---

[39] For "Trump-specific" reactions, see Major, Blodorn, and Blascovich, "Threat of Increasing Diversity." For a more general articulation, one that anticipates Trump – especially where it concerns whites' concerns about their shrinking population relative to other racial groups – see Craig and Richeson, "On the Precipice of a 'Majority-Minority' America."

[40] See, for example, Lawrence Bobo, "Whites' Opposition to Busing: Symbolic Racism or Realistic Group Conflict?," *Journal of Personality and Social Psychology* 45, no. 6 (1983): 1196–210; Lawrence Bobo and Vincent L. Hutchings, "Perceptions of Racial Group Competition: Extending Blumer's Theory of Group Competition to a Multiracial Context," *American Sociological Review* 61, no. 6 (December 1996): 951–72.

[41] Jim Sidanius and Felicia Pratto, *Social Dominance Theory: An Intergroup Theory of Social Hierarchy and Oppression* (Cambridge: Cambridge University Press, 1999).

[42] Bobo and Hutchings, "Perceptions of Racial Group Competition," 955.

[43] Sidanius and Pratto, Social Dominance Theory. See also, John T. Jost, Mahzarin R. Banaji, and Brian A. Nosek, "A Decade of System Justification Theory: Accumulated Evidence of Conscious and Unconscious Bolstering of the Status Quo," *Political Psychology* 25, no. 6 (2004): 881–919.

should be especially threatening for minorities who said they strongly oppose Mr. Trump. Of course, this is in comparison to other POC who may not have supported him, or even liked him, but failed to see him as a threat. In the end, we think it likely that *many* Blacks, Latinos, and Asians perceive Trump as a threat, and that beyond their levels of identification with Democrats, or liberal ideology, it was their sense of perceived racism and discrimination that drove POC to oppose Trump. Further, we believe that strong anti-Trump attitudes spur minorities to heightened levels of political engagement, whether that's voting, protesting, or something in-between.

It's beyond question that Trump is a source of racial polarization, where most whites have a much higher regard for Trump relative to POC.[44] Even so, both sides of the racial divide agree on at least one thing: Trump is associated with threat. For Trump supporters it's about symbolic threat: their way of life – their culture – is under siege. In this sense, he represents a *reaction* to this threat. This is the classic status politics model. For POC, and commensurate with group conflict theory, the threat is rooted in material *and* symbolic concerns.[45] In this case, Trump is a proxy for racial retrenchment: HE IS the threat. For this reason, we think the group conflict/group competition model most appropriate. Based on these theoretical expectations we lay out the following four hypotheses:

H1: Whites with a high degree of existential threat are more likely to strongly support Trump

---

[44] www.gallup.com/poll/205832/race-education-gender-key-factors-trump-job-approval.aspx.

[45] Now, a critic may claim that "rights, resources, and privilege" transcend more material interests, that these are more symbolic objectives than material. This is a legitimate concern. Even so, all of the aforementioned are based, at least in part, on the accretion of resources, something that is actual, concrete, and therefore, material. Culture, on the other hand, is virtual, like schema. See William H. Sewell, Jr., "A Theory of Structure: Duality, Agency, and Transformation," *American Journal of Sociology* 98, no. 1 (1992): 1–29. Elsewhere, Parker and Barreto (*Change They Can't Believe In*) address this by estimating the effect of reactionary conservatism (using Tea Party support as the proxy), and controlling for social dominance orientation, authoritarianism, racial resentment, and ethnocentrism. Together, these should roughly cover the four models of group conflict Bobo and Hutchings ("Perceptions of Racial Group Competition") identified: (1) self-interest, (2) prejudice, (3) stratification beliefs, and (4) group position. Still, their proxy predicted various and sundry policy preferences and political choice. Hopefully, this will allay any concerns one may have about a distinction without difference between the status politics and intergroup conflict models we believe appropriate for assessing our claims as they pertain to Trump supporters (who, for reasons mentioned in the text, are like Tea Party supporters), and POC, respectively.

H2: Minorities who perceive racism or discrimination are more likely to strongly oppose Trump

H3: Whites who strongly *support* Trump are more likely to participate in politics than other whites

H4: Minorities who strongly *oppose* Trump are more likely to participate in politics than other racial minorities

DATA AND MEASURES

To fully describe the racial dynamics associated with Trumpism requires the use of more than one source of evidence. As such, our empirical data analysis draws on two large public opinion surveys: the 2016 American National Election Study (ANES), and the 2016 Comparative Multiracial Post-Election Study (CMPS). The ANES includes a total of 4,271 completed interviews from a pre-election/post-election format. In 2016 subjects were interviewed both face-to-face and via the Internet. The overall ANES sample includes 3,022 white, non-Hispanic respondents and 1,249 minority respondents. Throughout our analyses, we rely on the post-election full sample weight (V160102) as provided by the ANES.

Leveraging the impact of Trumpism on POC, however, requires data with sufficient observations, as well as more questions that permit us to explore the range of Trumpism. For this, we turn to the CMPS. The CMPS includes a total of 10,145 interviews, collected online in a respondent self-administered format from December 3, 2016, to February 15, 2017. The survey (and invitation) was available to respondents in English, Spanish, Chinese (simplified), Chinese (traditional), Korean, and Vietnamese. The CMPS includes a total of 1,034 white, non-Hispanic respondents and 3,000 respondents *each* who identified as Black, Latino, or Asian American. The full data are weighted within each racial group to match the adult population in the 2015 Census ACS 1-year data file for age, gender, education, nativity, ancestry, and voter registration status. Data for registered voters comes from the national voter registration database email sample, and respondents were randomly selected to participate in the study, and confirmed they were registered to vote before starting the survey. For the non-registered sample, emails addresses were randomly selected from various online panel vendors.[46]

---

[46] For the CMPS, a total of 298,159 email addresses were selected and sent invitations to participate in the survey and 29,489 people accepted the invitation and started the survey,

We draw on these two datasets because each adds an important dimension to our overall story about the 2016 election and the Trump movement. The ANES contains virtually all of the classic questions on voter attitudes, which may explain why certain subgroups of voters supported Trump. We can account for economic anxiety, authoritarianism, racial resentment, immigrant anxiety, sexism, and much more. By almost any measure, it is the gold-standard public opinion dataset with respect to American elections. We also turn to the CMPS data, which has two principal advantages over the ANES, allowing us to tell a deep and rich story about 2016. First, the CMPS has a much larger sample of racial minorities, with over 3,000 interviews *each* among Blacks, Latinos, and Asians Americans. Second, the CMPS contains many more precise questions about the minority experience in America during the 2016 election that are not found on the ANES. Across these two public opinion surveys, we are quite confident that we can assess and explain the origins and impact of the Trump movement for both white, non-Hispanics as well as for People of Color.

Measuring Existential and Cultural Threat. We begin with the ANES and model support for Trump using the 0–100 feeling thermometer as our dependent variable. This allows us to observe variation in Trump enthusiasm that a simple Trump/Clinton vote measure would miss. To assess threat, we focus on three key independent variables in our models for whites, and three separate variables in our models for POC.

For whites we start with the Tea Party feeling thermometer. Existing work suggests that Tea Party intensity is a good proxy for reactionary sentiment commensurate with status threat.[47] Next, we include a set of questions from the ANES related to what constitutes the cultural meaning of American identity which many see as under attack today.[48] We argue

---

for an effective response rate of 9.9 percent. Among the 29,489 people who started the survey, 11,868 potential respondents were terminated due to quotas being full, which resulted in 17,621 who were eligible to take the survey of which 10,145 completed the full questionnaire for a cooperation rate of 57.6 percent. Respondents were given a $10 or $20 gift card as compensation for their participation. Non-registered voters were randomly selected from one of six online panels of respondents from Federated, Poder, Research Now, Netquest, SSI, and Prodege, and confirmed that they were not registered to vote before starting the survey. Programming and data collection for the full project were overseen by Pacific Market Research in Renton, Washington.

[47] Arceneaux and Nicholson, "Who Wants to Have a Tea Party?"; Corey Robin, *The Reactionary Mind: Conservatism from Edmund Burke to Sarah Palin* (Oxford: Oxford University Press, 2011); Parker and Barreto, *Change They Can't Believe In.*

[48] Items V162271-V162274, POST: To be truly American important to . . .

that central to status threat is the perception of threats to American identity, and a series of four items on the ANES captures this directly. We scale four questions into a single item,[49] ranging from 0 (not important at all) to 12 (very important):

Some people say that the following things are important for being truly American. Others says they are not important. How important do you think the following is for being truly American ...

- To have been born in the United States
- To have American ancestry
- To be able to speak English
- To follow America's customs and traditions

Finally, we include a variable that taps into a preference for tradition, something that suggests resistance to change. This is central to reactionary politics and status threat.[50] The ANES asked respondents if they agreed or disagreed with the statement: "Our country would be great if we honor the ways of our forefathers, do what the authorities tell us to do, and get rid of the 'rotten apples' who are ruining everything."[51] Each of these items, collectively representing symbolic threat, we believe are positively associated with the Trump feeling thermometer, even after controlling for ideology, partisanship, and much more. Specifically, we are also controlling for racial resentment, ethnocentrism, authoritarianism, and other alternative explanations. The question here is whether or not our three unique measures of existential threat will tell their own independent story about Trump support – our theory suggests they will.

For POC, we also identify three key measures on the ANES, as well as on the CMPS. On the ANES, we use two items related to perceived group discrimination against Blacks and Latinos in the United States as a gauge of the threat the Trump movement poses to POC.[52] If we're right, then POC who perceive Blacks and Latinos under attack will be more likely to reject Trump, who represents the likelihood of more discrimination, something that taps into a more material dimension. The third measure we use for minorities is a question about POC needing to "adapt" to

---

[49] Each item has four answer values from (0) not at all important to (3) very important, and together they have an alpha score of 0.79.
[50] Hofstadter, *Paranoid Style*; Lipset and Raab, *Politics of Unreason*; Parker and Barreto, *Change They Can't Believe In*.
[51] Item V162169, POST: Country would be great by getting rid of rotten apples.
[52] Items V162357 (Discrimination against Blacks) and V162358 (Discrimination against Hispanics).

America's culture, an item we use as a means of representing more symbolic concerns. The ANES asked, "Now thinking about minorities in the United States. Do you agree or disagree with the following statement: 'Minorities should adapt to the customs and traditions of the United States.'"[53] Again, we think POC who feel as though minorities should be able to exist as Americans without having to change their culture, would feel threatened by Trump and hence more likely to reject him. Again, we put emphasis on these three items independent of classic controls for ideology, partisanship, and racial attitudes.

In the CMPS data, we are able to pick up many of these same themes, as well as some that are more faithful to our theory in terms of face validity. In addition, the CMPS allows us to estimate composite models for POC, as we did with the ANES, but it also permits us to estimate models by race. We take full advantage of this. Using the CMPS, we include measures for whether respondents mentioned racism as one of the most important problems confronting the nation. We also include a measure for whether respondents have personally experienced discrimination in the past twelve months. Finally, we include a measure that taps into the cultural threat that many POC may have felt as a result of the Trump movement which we term *POC are not valued*. The CMPS also included a question that gets at symbolic threat: "Most Americans value and respect your individual presence in the United States." We expect minorities who think other Americans *do not* value or respect their presence in the United States are likely to reject Trump, relative to those who believe in the desirability of assimilation.

RESULTS

In what follows, we test the aforementioned hypotheses. Foreshadowing our findings, we begin with our first two hypotheses, the ones that assess how symbolic and material threat inform perceptions of Trump. Across both datasets, our regression models predicting support for Trump confirm our theory of threat, for both whites and people of color. In models for whites, proxies for symbolic threat are associated with high levels of Trump support. When examining POC, our measures of material and symbolic threat are statistically associated with opposition to Trump. What's more, our results hold up when including many competing explanations and ruling out alternative theories that have been proposed.

---

[53] Item V162266, POST: Minorities should adapt to the customs/traditions of US.

Likewise, our models confirm our second set of hypotheses vis-à-vis Trump as a proxy for status threat and group conflict for whites and POC, respectively. For whites, status threat pushes them toward political engagement, similar to the way in which group conflict encourages political mobilization on the part of POC.

Feelings Toward Trump

Our first set of models considers both white and POC degree of Trump support using the ANES 2016 dataset. Isolating the impact of the variables we use to highlight threat requires us to account for a number of possible confounds, ones generally associated with support for Trump: moral traditionalism, racial resentment, social dominance order, authoritarianism, ethnocentrism, and sexism. Beyond that, we include the expected controls for partisanship, ideology, size of government, economic anxiety, and demographic controls. Covariates in place, we can now turn to our three proxy variables for existential threat (i.e., threats to their way of life), for whites.

As Figure 8.1 illustrates, all three of the items that tap into symbolic threat are associated with increased support for Trump. The Tea Party thermometer – which prior research suggests reflects a reactionary disposition – is positively associated with Trump support.[54] The "True American" index of four items likewise is a reliable predictor of support for Trump. In other words, whites who feel American nativity, speaking English, having "American" ancestry, and following America's customs are essential to American identity are more likely to rate Trump higher than those who refuse to believe that these traits are essential to American nationhood. Finally, those who felt we need to honor our forefathers and rid the country of any so-called "bad apples" are unreserved in their support for Trump.

Using the same dataset and same set of controls, we next turn to Figure 8.2, where we examine predictors of Trump support among POC. Here, we focus on perceived or experienced racism and discrimination, and the exclusion (or outsider status) that many minorities may have felt in 2016. Our variables that measure perceived discrimination against Blacks and Latinos are both associated with lower levels of Trump support, indicating that increasing levels of perceived discrimination diminishes regard for Trump. Moreover, consistent with our theory, racial

---

[54] See Parker and Barreto, *Change They Can't Believe In*, for more on the relationship between Tea Party support and reactionary politics.

The Great White Hope

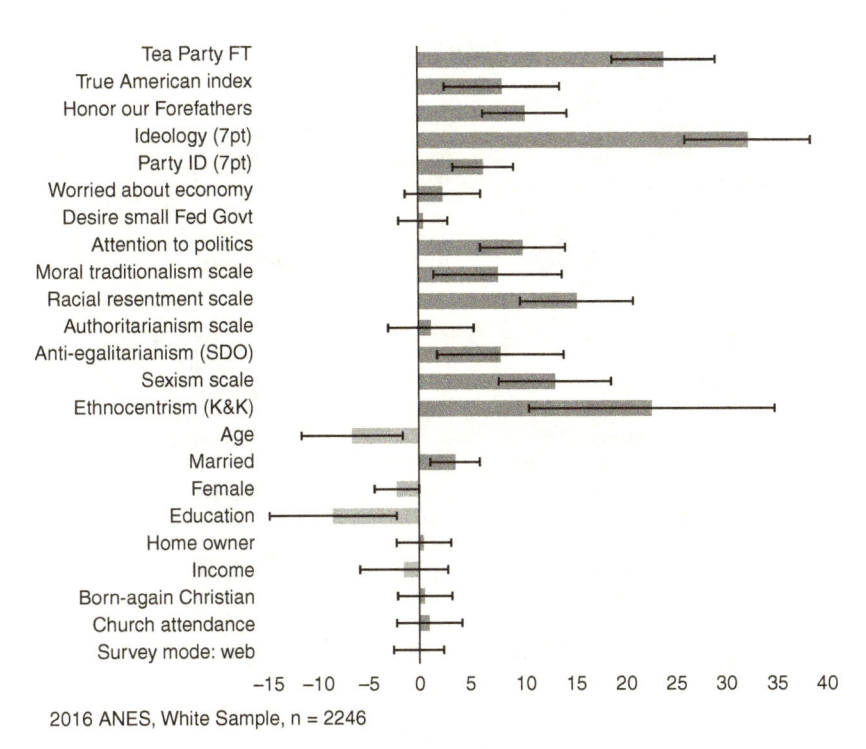

Tea Party FT	
True American index	
Honor our Forefathers	
Ideology (7pt)	
Party ID (7pt)	
Worried about economy	
Desire small Fed Govt	
Attention to politics	
Moral traditionalism scale	
Racial resentment scale	
Authoritarianism scale	
Anti-egalitarianism (SDO)	
Sexism scale	
Ethnocentrism (K&K)	
Age	
Married	
Female	
Education	
Home owner	
Income	
Born-again Christian	
Church attendance	
Survey mode: web	

2016 ANES, White Sample, n = 2246

FIGURE 8.1 Estimated change in Trump thermometer rating among whites, moving each variable from minimum to maximum value

minorities who believe they do not need to adapt their culture to fit in in America are more likely to reject Trump. We think this captures the sense of threat that many POC associated with Trump and his movement, both materially and symbolically. What's more, these results jive with more anecdotal evidence. For instance, Trump campaign rallies were often met with counterprotests by pro-immigrant groups, Black Lives Matter groups, as well as people standing up for American Muslims, women, and other groups who felt threatened by the Make America Great Again (MAGA) movement. Many who protested against Trump attempted to use his language against him by declaring "Immigrants Make America Great" and "Love Trumps Hate" and "No to Racism, No to Trump." These sentiments are supported by our data, showing that POC concerned over cultural threats to make them "adapt" were significantly more likely to oppose Trump, even after we account for factors like racial resentment, ethnocentrism, social dominance, and ideology. One thing we'd like to

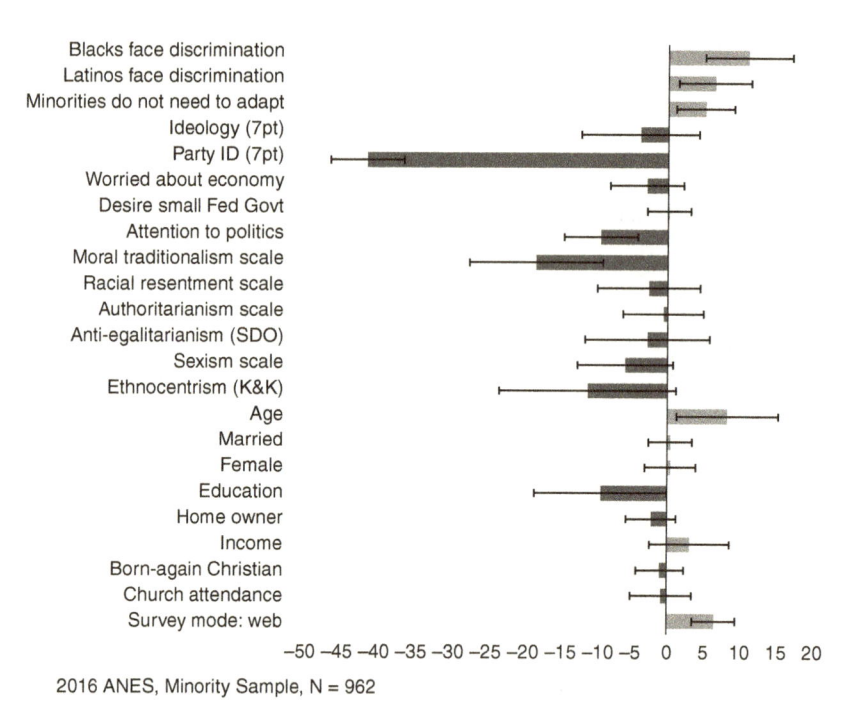

FIGURE 8.2 Estimated point change in oppose Trump (FT) among POC, moving each variable from minimum to maximum value

mention is the role of religion. For whites, it has absolutely no direct effect on support for Trump. The effect is likely mediated by ideology and moral traditionalism.

In Figure 8.3, we continue to examine predictors of Trump opposition among POC, this time with the CMPS dataset, which allows us to explore each minority group to see whether it was just Latinos or Blacks driving the anti-Trump effects. Further, the ANES has only roughly 1,000 total minority respondents, but the CMPS has 3,000 Latino, Black, and Asian-Americans respndents each, which permits us to examine predictors of anti-Trump sentiment among all three groups. Similar to the ANES models, our key independent variables are measures of perceived and experienced racism and the suspicion that the larger society is not inclusive of minorities. As with the ANES models, we find evidence that material and symbolic threat informed all three minority groups' rejection of Trump in 2016.

Minorities who think racism one of the most pressing issues in America are more likely to oppose Trump than those who don't hold this

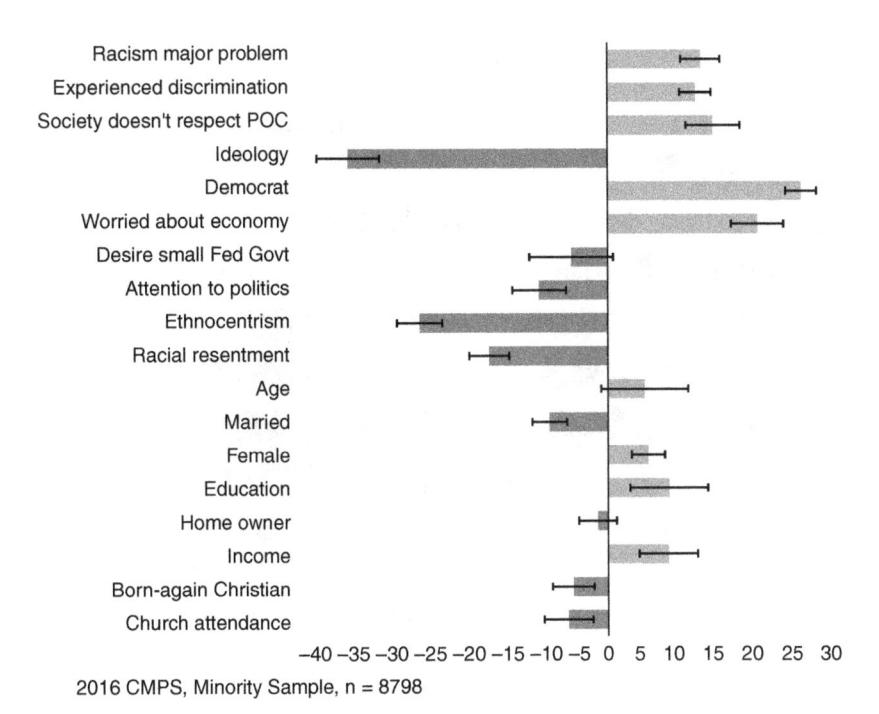

FIGURE 8.3. Estimated point change in strongly oppose Trump among POC, moving each variable from minimum to maximum value

sentiment. Likewise, those who report personally facing discrimination are more likely to oppose Trump. Our final measure, those who believe society as a whole fails to respect or value POC are associated with higher levels of opposition to Trump. On their own, such results are hardly surprising. However, they manage to hold, even after adjusting for important explanatory factors such as party identification, ideology, racial attitudes, and attitudes toward immigrants, as well as socioeconomic status and religiosity.

In Figures 8.4 and 8.5, we disaggregated our models by racial group; for, as we have already suggested, it may well be the case that one group accounts for the lion's share of the variation associated with the rejection of Trump. It just so happens that this isn't the case. Consider Figure 8.4. We find robust support for our hypotheses, across both symbolic (respect) and material domains (racism and discrimination), respectively, for each racial group. Next, in Figure 8.5, we combine the items proxying for symbolic threat (the symbolic item doesn't scale well with the material

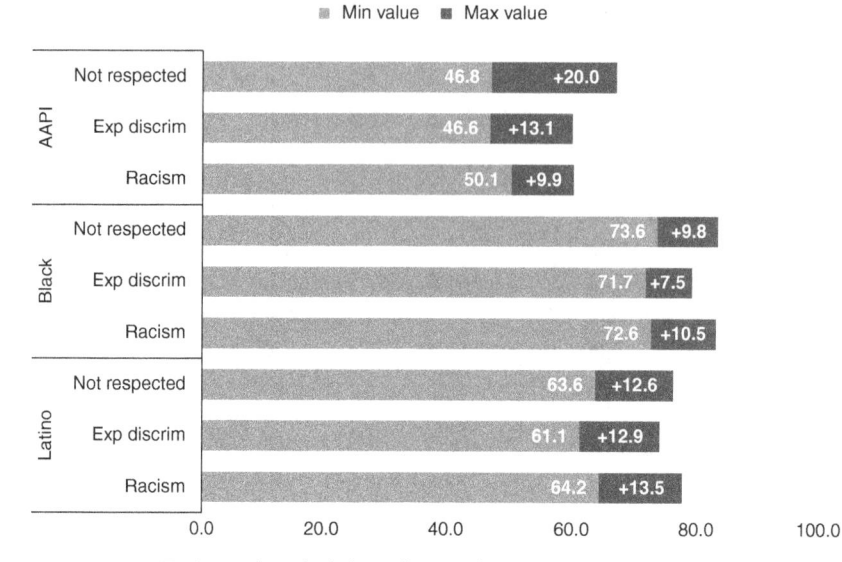

FIGURE 8.4 Estimated probability of strongly opposing Trump by race

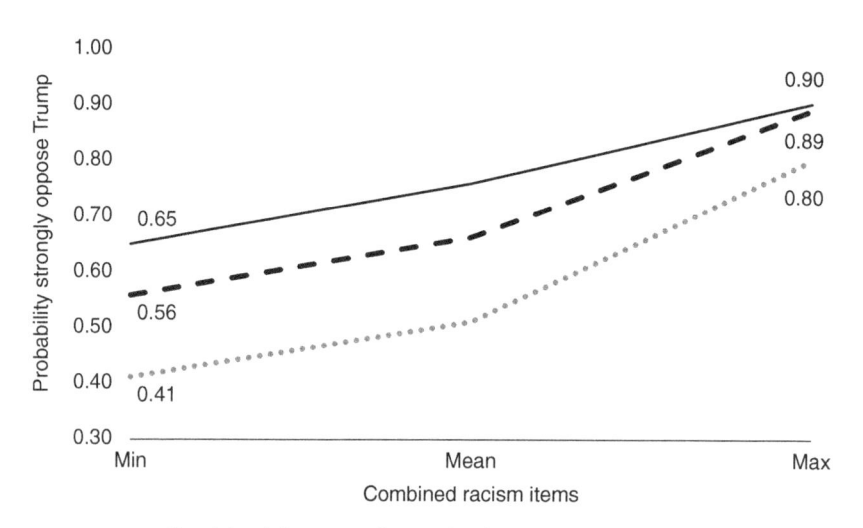

FIGURE 8.5 Combined impact of perceived racism on anti-Trump attitudes among POC

items) for each racial group, estimating their impact on opposition to Trump. While the Black community registered the highest total opposition to Trump once we assess the highest level of anti-Trump sentiment, the substantive effects are roughly comparable across all three groups.

The Great White Hope

Still, the slopes associated with Latinos and Asians are steeper. Of course, this means that material threat is a more meaningful predictor for these groups than it is among Blacks.

Our examination of support for (and opposition to) Trump confirms our priors. Further, it is important to point out that our three variables that tap into class and economic concerns are not associated with support for Trump. For whites, income has no direct bearing on Trump support. Likewise, and most critical, worry about one's financial situation isn't related to support for Trump among whites. This contradicts early widespread (and unfounded) support for the economic anxiety thesis. Yet, among whites, symbolic threat shapes support for Trump. For POC, both symbolic and material threat informs opposition to Trump, something we witnessed in the aggregate (i.e., all racial minorities group together) as well as separately.

Threat and Political Participation

Our theory proposes that the threat Trump represents also had the capacity to mobilize, drawing both his white supporters and POC opponents into political engagement in 2016. Using both the CMPS and the ANES, we assess political participation across a range of dimensions in 2016, from voting and discussing politics online, to volunteering for a campaign and engaging in protest. We examine ten types of non-voting participation in the ANES (Figure 8.6), and thirteen types of participation in the CMPS in addition to validated voting (Figure 8.7).[55] Like the models exploring support and opposition to Trump, we also account for the most important factors that may be associated with political participation. Thus, we are looking for a "Trump bump,"[56] an effect above and beyond standard correlates of political participation.

Using the ANES data, in Figure 8.6, we aggregate across ten political acts, and examine how the "Trump bump" shapes political engagement, across groups, by race: whites and POC. The results conform to our hypotheses. For instance, the probability of becoming politically active – participating in three or more political acts – was highest among whites

---

[55] We exclude voting in the ANES because it was self-reported and validated turnout was not yet available. The CMPS includes validated turnout verified on the voter file.
[56] "Trump bump" as described by Dr. Gabriel Sanchez in an interview with the *Los Angeles Times*, November 3, 2016. www.latimes.com/nation/politics/trailguide/la-na-trailguide-updates-as-many-as-15-million-latinos-may-vote-1478202388-htmlstory.html.

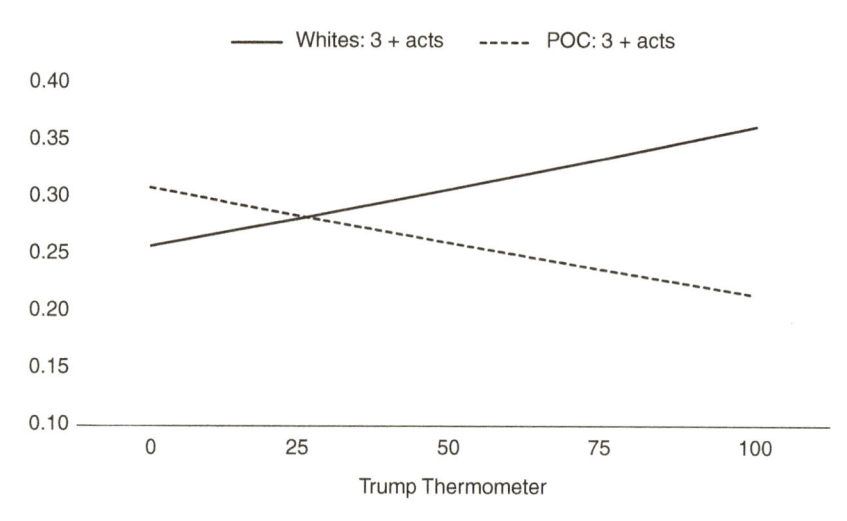

```
          ——— Whites: 3 + acts    ----- POC: 3 + acts
0.40
0.35
0.30
0.25
0.20
0.15
0.10
      0         25         50         75        100
                     Trump Thermometer
```

FIGURE 8.6 Predicted probability of political participation 2016 by race

who supported Trump, and for Minorities it was the opposite: those who rated Trump a "0" on the feeling thermometer were the most engaged among POC.

Now, one might credibly claim that the results in Figure 8.6 are driven by a handful of items, likely led by voting. From discussing politics and attending meetings, to voting and boycotting, the CMPS data in Figure 8.7, affirms our findings in Figure 8.6. Confirming our hypotheses, symbolic threat (for whites) and symbolic *and* material threat (for POC) – both of which are represented by Trump-related sentiment – are associated with multiple modes of political engagement. The main differences between whites and POC appear to be the type of participation encouraged by threat. While symbolic threat among whites spurs more conventional political participation, for POC, the opposite result obtains: the most insistent opponents of Trump were more likely to be pursue political objectives through less conventional participation. Both groups, nonetheless, were active across many domains: whites were active across ten modes of participation, where POC were involved in eight.

Clearly, the patterns are consistent with our argument. For whites it was the (symbolic) threat of a changing America that Trump embodied, and his most loyal supporters were, indeed, politically active in 2016. For minorities, Trump himself (and the MAGA movement) were the (symbolic and material) threat, and Blacks, Latinos, and Asians who rated Trump most negatively, were also the most politically active in 2016. These results

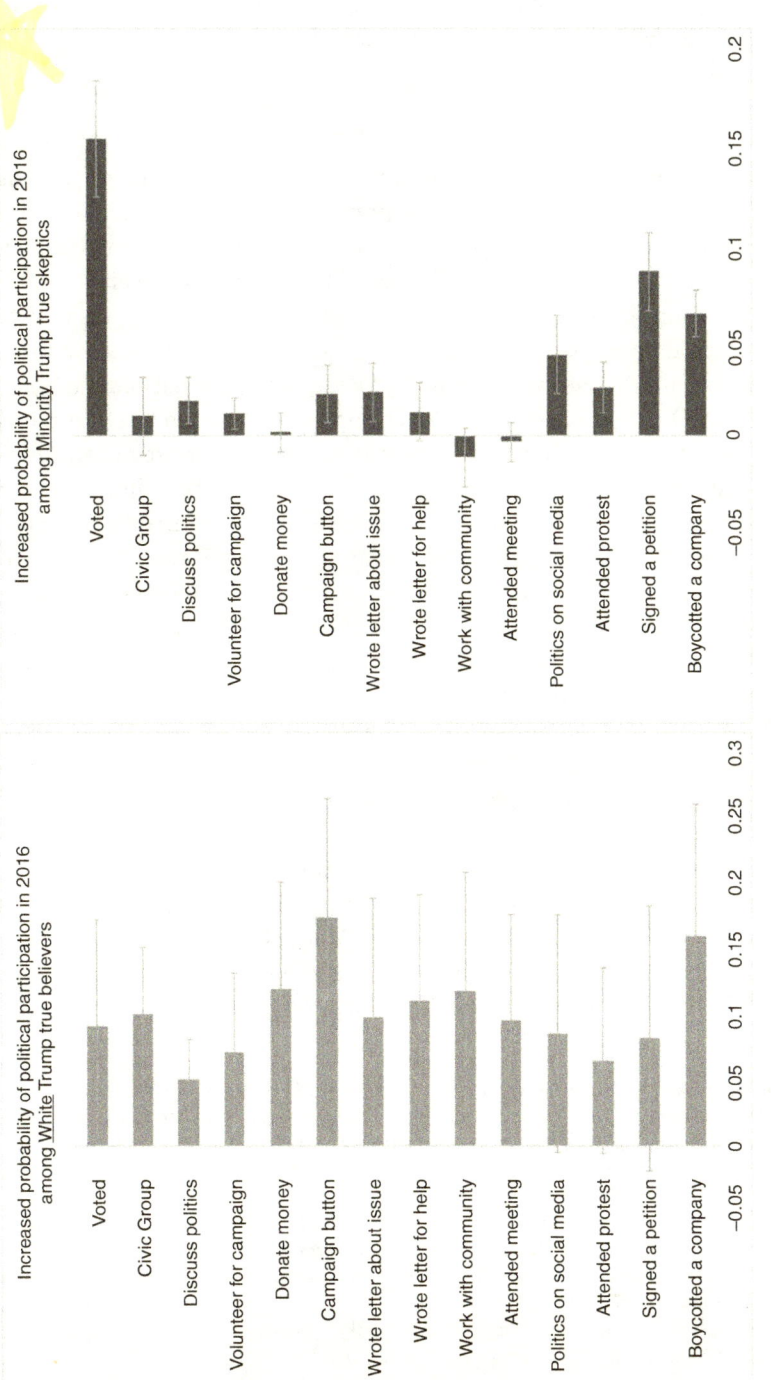

FIGURE 8.7 Threat and political engagement by race

are of a piece with an emerging literature indicating the ways in which threat drives behavior, both on the Right and on the Left.[57]

CONCLUSION

In this chapter, we elaborated an account of the 2016 election, one at odds with existing formulations, the most popular of which is associated with the import of economic anxiety. We argued that the threat over changing demographics, and the perceived loss of status among most whites, would better explain the outcome; it did. In fact, economic anxiety is a complete bust when it comes to explaining support for Trump. At the same time, Trump and his followers represented a threat, both material and symbolic, to POC. POC were concerned that Trump would unleash levels of racial hostility unseen since Jim Crow. (As it turns out, they were right.) Thus, our first two hypotheses are confirmed. We can say the same for our second two hypotheses, on the relationship between threat and mobilization. For whites attracted to the Trump campaign, they participated and engaged politics at higher rates, similar to prior studies documenting elevated participation among Tea Partiers. For minorities, the opposite held. Those most opposed to Trump, who perceived him as a threat, were the most likely to become politically engaged in 2016.

These patterns continue to this day, well after the events of 2016. Since then, POC have proven crucial to coalitions who sought to beat Trump-backed Republicans at the polls. From the special election in Alabama where Democrats won a senate seat over a Trump-backed Republican, to Virginia where another Democrat bested another Trump-affiliated candidate, Black voters have proven key.[58] More recently, Joe Biden owes much to the Black community for winning the White House, one likely attributed to the threat posed by Trump.[59] This is proof positive of the extent to which POC contribute to the resilience of American democracy.

---

[57] On threat and mobilization on the Right, see Blum, *How the Tea Party Captured the GOP*; Gervais and Morris, *Reactionary Republicanism*; Parker and Barreto, *Change They Can't Believe In*; on the Left, see Angela Gutierrez, Angela X. Ocampo, Matt A. Barreto, and Gary Segura, "Somos Más: How Racial Threat and Anger Mobilize Latino Voters in the Trump Era," *Political Research Quarterly* 72, no. 4 (2012): 960–975; Christopher Zepeda-Millán, *Latino Mass Mobilization: Immigration, Racialization, and Activism* (Cambridge: Cambridge University Press, 2017).

[58] https://thehill.com/opinion/campaign/403977-theres-a-boost-in-black-turnout-especially-among-black-women-voters.

[59] Christopher C. Towler and Christopher S. Parker, "Between Anger and Engagement: Donald Trump and Black America," *Journal of Race, Ethnicity, and Politics* 3, no.1

Apparently, Democrats realize the significance of the POC vote, since more racially equitable outcomes take place when Democrats are in charge.[60] Given the import of the Black and Latino vote in the 2020 election cycle, delivering the White House and the Senate, it's apparent that the patterns observed in the present chapter persisted. The only question is whether or not threat is a necessary condition to maintain high levels of turnout among POC, and the maintenance of American democracy. If this is true, we find it deeply ironic that fate of multi-racial American democracy may ultimately rest on threat. A delicate, if dangerous, balance to maintain.

Regression Tables

TABLE 8.1 *Predictors of support for Donald Trump by race in ANES 2016*

	Whites - Trump FT (0-100)		POC - Trump FT (0-100)	
	Coef.	Std.Err	Coef.	Std.Err
Tea Party FT	0.187***	0.025		
True American Index	0.705**	0.226		
Honor our forefathers	2.188***	0.498		
Blacks face discrimination			-2.754***	0.830
Latinos face discrimination			-1.621*	0.820
Minorities do not need to adapt			-1.283*	0.640
Ideology (7pt)	2.053***	0.547	0.623	0.666
Party ID (7pt)	5.647***	0.350	6.780***	0.451
Worried about economy	0.658	0.444	0.702	0.581

(continued)

(2018): 219–253; www.politico.com/news/magazine/2020/03/07/why-bernie-sanders-economic-message-isnt-enough-to-win-over-black-voters-118197.

[60] On racially equitable outcomes, see Zoltan Hajnal, *Dangerously Divided: How Race and Class Shape Winning and Losing in American Politics* (Cambridge: Cambridge University Press, 2019); for more on turnout, race, and support for the Democratic Party, see Bernard L. Fraga, *The Turnout Gap: Race, Ethnicity and Political Inequality in a Diversifying America* (Cambridge: Cambridge University Press, 2018).

TABLE 8.1 *(continued)*

	Whites - Trump FT (0-100)		POC - Trump FT (0-100)	
	Coef.	Std.Err	Coef.	Std.Err
Desire smaller Fed Govt	−2.048+	1.170	−0.020	1.594
Attention to politics	2.730***	0.504	2.266***	0.650
Moral trad.	0.353+	0.189	1.113***	0.283
Racial Resentment Scale	0.751***	0.169	0.157	0.225
Authoritarianism Scale	0.257	0.251	0.065	0.332
SDO	0.285	0.187	0.168	0.271
Sexism Scale	0.803***	0.167	0.358+	0.209
Ethnocentrism	12.873***	2.973	6.557	4.066
Age	−0.040	0.034	−0.115*	0.050
Married	2.614*	1.160	−0.455	1.645
Female	−2.274*	1.054	−0.447	1.489
Education	−0.798**	0.256	0.643+	0.330
Home owner	0.537	1.287	2.154	1.693
Income	−0.111	0.077	−0.116	0.105
Born-again Christian	−0.049	1.278	0.921	1.698
Church attendance	−0.095	0.387	0.194	0.533
Survey mode: web	−0.024	1.167	−6.574***	1.656
Constant	−26.150***	4.417	−6.325	7.385
Adjusted-R2	0.570		0.426	
BIC	20680.005		8791.281	
Log-likelihood	−1.02e+04		−4313.212	
LR-Chi2				
Prob>chi	0.000		0.000	
N	2,246		962	

+ p < 0.10, * p < 0.05, ** p < 0.01, *** p < 0.001
Source: American National Election Study, 2016

TABLE 8.2 *Among POC: Predictors of support for Donald Trump (2016 CMPS)*

	All POC Coef.	Std.Err	Latinos Coef.	Std.Err	Blacks Coef.	Std.Err	AAPI Coef.	Std.Err
Racism major problem in US	-0.604***	0.072	-0.665***	0.144	-0.616***	0.107	-0.400**	0.135
Experienced discrimination	-0.540***	0.051	-0.592***	0.091	-0.407***	0.091	-0.528***	0.087
Society not respect POC	-0.228***	0.033	-0.202***	0.056	-0.196***	0.057	-0.275***	0.058
Ideology (lib->con)	0.404***	0.026	0.502***	0.046	0.280***	0.045	0.431***	0.047
Democrat	-1.176***	0.051	-1.224***	0.093	-1.052***	0.094	-1.092***	0.087
Economy getting worse	-0.227***	0.020	-0.200***	0.036	-0.240***	0.036	-0.242***	0.035
Oppose Fed spending	0.016+	0.010	0.022	0.017	0.020	0.019	0.012	0.015
Interest in politics	0.139***	0.028	0.201***	0.049	0.079	0.051	0.189***	0.049
Deport all undocumented	0.533***	0.033	0.626***	0.062	0.310***	0.063	0.554***	0.052
Racial attitudes	-0.347***	0.030	-0.486***	0.052	-0.187**	0.059	-0.306***	0.050
Actual age 18-98	-0.003+	0.002	-0.002	0.003	-0.004	0.003	-0.002	0.003
Married	0.338***	0.053	0.074	0.094	0.355***	0.103	0.449***	0.088
Male	0.241***	0.050	0.082	0.091	0.493***	0.091	0.142+	0.081
Education level	-0.073**	0.023	-0.114**	0.042	-0.109*	0.047	-0.111**	0.039

(continued)

TABLE 8.2 *(continued)*

	All POC Coef.	Std.Err	Latinos Coef.	Std.Err	Blacks Coef.	Std.Err	AAPI Coef.	Std.Err
Home owner	0.061	0.057	0.146	0.102	0.019	0.110	0.008	0.093
Income level	-0.037***	0.009	-0.026	0.016	-0.060**	0.018	-0.052***	0.014
Evangelical	0.208***	0.062	0.453***	0.111	0.203+	0.105	0.099	0.113
Church attendance	0.046**	0.015	0.002	0.026	0.041	0.027	0.105***	0.024
cut1	0.318	0.241	0.674	0.425	0.037	0.460	0.146	0.410
cut2	1.381***	0.242	1.622***	0.426	1.118*	0.461	1.340**	0.410
cut3	3.045***	0.245	3.216***	0.433	2.442***	0.467	3.342***	0.417
Pseudo–R2	0.157		0.182		0.100		0.163	
BIC	15809.522		5221.496		4751.684		5947.243	
Log-likelihood	-7809.397		-2526.990		-2291.859		-2889.878	
LR-Chi2	2918.223		1124.493		509.195		1127.326	
Prob>chi	0.000		0.000		0.000		0.000	
N	8,798		2,913		2,976		2,909	

+ $p < 0.10$, * $p < 0.05$, ** $p < 0.01$, *** $p < 0.001$
Source: Collaborative Multi-Racial Post-Election Survey, 2016

TABLE 8.3 *Predictors of political participation (0–10) in 2016 by race in ANES*

	Whites - Pol Participation		POC - Pol Participation	
	Coef.	Std.Err	Coef.	Std.Err
Trump FT	0.005***	0.001	−0.005*	0.002
Ideology (7pt)	−0.250***	0.038	−0.162**	0.049
Party ID (7pt)	−0.023	0.027	0.020	0.038
Attention to politics	0.609***	0.038	0.436***	0.052
Age	−0.010***	0.002	−0.006	0.004
Married	−0.018	0.086	−0.184	0.127
Female	0.049	0.075	0.251*	0.114
Education	0.094***	0.018	0.117***	0.025
Home owner	−0.023	0.095	−0.057	0.131
Income	0.016**	0.006	0.010	0.008
Born-again Christian	−0.019	0.091	−0.161	0.129
Church attendance	0.027	0.027	0.132**	0.041
Survey mode: web	0.170*	0.082	0.450***	0.123
cut1	0.270	0.253	0.864*	0.355
cut2	1.507***	0.255	2.161***	0.361
cut3	2.436***	0.257	2.885***	0.366
cut4	3.317***	0.261	3.721***	0.373
cut5	4.093***	0.266	4.437***	0.380
cut6	4.871***	0.275	5.071***	0.390
cut7	5.586***	0.290	5.770***	0.411
cut8	6.595***	0.337	6.580***	0.458
cut9	7.297***	0.401	7.490***	0.564
cut10	9.117***	0.803	7.803***	0.621
Pseudo-R2	0.053		0.045	
BIC	8581.274		843.665	
Log-likelihood	−4200.546		−1842.732	
LR-Chi2	465.621		175.281	
Prob>chi	0.000		0.000	
N	2,525		971	

+ $p < 0.10$, * $p < 0.05$, ** $p < 0.01$, *** $p < 0.001$
Source: American National Election Study, 2016

TABLE 8.4 *Predictors of total participation count (0–13) among whites in CMPS*

	Coef.	SE	p-value
Highly favorable to Trump	1.247***	(0.277)	0.000
Economy getting worse	−0.096	(0.078)	0.219
Democrat	0.223	(0.296)	0.451
Independent	−0.511*	(0.249)	0.040
Ideology (lib->con)	−0.626***	(0.108)	0.000
Political efficacy	−0.119	(0.091)	0.193
Oppose Fed spending	0.041	(0.042)	0.325
Anti-immigrant resentment	−0.144*	(0.059)	0.015
Apologize for slavery	0.136	(0.121)	0.264
Racial linked fate	0.268	(0.163)	0.102
Evangelical	0.663**	(0.247)	0.007
American identity important	−0.180	(0.136)	0.185
Education level	0.762***	(0.091)	0.000
Income level	0.103**	(0.031)	0.001
Actual age 18–98	0.013*	(0.006)	0.025
Male	0.285	(0.197)	0.147
Constant	1.475	(1.241)	0.235
Adjusted-R2	0.231		
BIC	5222.724		
Log-likelihood	−2552.370		
F	20.330		
Prob>F	0.000		
N	1,033		

* p < 00.05, ** p < 00.01, *** p < 00.001
Source: Collaborative Multi-Racial Post-Election Survey, 2016

TABLE 8.5 *Predictors of total participation count (0 – 13) among POC in CMPS*

	Coef.	SE	p-value
Highly unfavorable to Trump	0.269***	(0.063)	0.000
Economy getting worse	−0.144***	(0.024)	0.000
Democrat	−0.161	(0.097)	0.099
Independent	−0.593***	(0.097)	0.000
Ideology (lib->con)	−0.413***	(0.030)	0.000
Political efficacy	−0.174***	(0.028)	0.000
Oppose Fed spending	−0.014	(0.011)	0.217
Deport all undocumented	0.002	(0.043)	0.968
Apologize for slavery	0.180***	(0.037)	0.000
Racial linked fate	0.296***	(0.045)	0.000
Evangelical	0.508***	(0.067)	0.000
American identity important	0.324***	(0.036)	0.000
Education level	0.233***	(0.024)	0.000
Income level	0.058***	(0.010)	0.000
Actual age 18–98	−0.004*	(0.002)	0.018
Male	0.396***	(0.057)	0.000
Constant	1.694***	(0.305)	0.000
Adjusted-R2	0.112		
BIC	42353.647		
Log-likelihood	−2.11e+04		
F	71.139		
Prob>F	0.000		
N	8,883		

* $p < 00.05$, ** $p < 00.01$, *** $p < 00.001$
Source: Collaborative Multi-Racial Post-Election Survey, 2016

9

The Religious Sort

The Causes and Consequences of the Religiosity Gap in America

Michele F. Margolis

The answers to two standard survey questions – "Aside from weddings and funerals, how often to attend religious services?" and "How important is religion in your daily life?" – reveal a great deal about a person's politics, particularly among white Americans. In short, the more religious a person is, the more likely it is that he or she identifies with the Republican Party and supports Republican candidates. This *religiosity* gap brings together religious mainline Protestants, evangelical Protestants, undifferentiated Christians, and Catholics under the Republican umbrella while their less devout co-religionists sit alongside religious non-identifiers – including atheists, agnostics, and those who do not call themselves part of a religion – as Democrats.

The aim of this chapter is to explain how one of the "most important and enduring social cleavages[s]" in American politics came to pass, explore the political and social consequences of the religiosity gap, and consider what all this means for American democracy.[1] The religiosity gap in American politics is powerful not only on account of its size, but because it reflects a reciprocal relationship: not only do religious attachments shape political affiliations, but partisanship and the political landscape also shape religious decisions. I refer to these changes as *religious sorting*, the result of which is that many Americans' religious and political identities are now aligned.[2] This sorting has changed how average

---

[1] Louis Bolce and Gerald DeMaio, "The Evolution of the Religion Gap Metaphor in the Language of American Political Journalists, 1987–2012," *Geolinguistics* 39 (2014): 48.
[2] I do not use the term *polarization* in this chapter, as I interpret polarization to mean Americans separating toward the poles. While there have been a growing number of

Americans view religion, politics, and each other and, in doing so, has the power to bring about democratic erosion. Democratic erosion, by which I mean the intentional undermining of democratic values – including electoral accountability, free exchange of ideas, and recognizing the legitimacy of others' grievances – threatens America's democratic resilience, or the ability to withstand stresses as a nation.

THE RELIGIOSITY GAP EXPLAINED

The religiosity or "God" gap is not just an interesting statistical finding; it represents one of the largest political divides in American society today. In the 2018 General Social Survey (GSS), half of white respondents who report never attending church identify as a Democrat or Democratic leaner while only about a quarter of white respondents who attend church weekly call themselves Democrats. The relationship reverses itself when looking at Republican identification. Only 30 percent of Americans who never attend church identify as Republicans whereas 60 percent of weekly attenders do. This gap – which appears among each of the large Christian traditions – is bigger than political gaps based on gender, education, region of residence, and union status.

While American history is replete with examples of religion's outsized role in politics, particularly during polarized times, the current religious-political landscape is different as it cuts *across* religious groups and not just *between* them. For example, the election of 1800 pitted the established orthodox churches – the Congregationalists and Episcopalians – against the emerging Baptist church. The old-guard churches teamed up with Federalists to attack Jefferson's "heretic," "deist," and "atheist" beliefs, asking voters to impose a *de facto* religion test on the candidates.[3] The Baptists, on the other hand, recognized that Jefferson was not "one of them" when it came to personal theology but that he

---

religious non-identifiers, or "nones," in the United States and many of them identify as Democrats, I think *sorting* more accurately describes the religiosity gap as it currently exists. Matthew Levendusky, *The Partisan Sort: How Liberals Became Democrats and Conservatives Became Republican* (Chicago: University of Chicago Press, 2009).

[3] Matthew Harris and Thomas Kidd, *The Founding Fathers and the Debate over Religion in Revolutionary America: A History in Documents* (Oxford: Oxford University Press, 2011); Frank Lambert, "'God – and a Religious President ... [or] Jefferson and No God': Campaigning for a Voter-Imposed Religious Test," *Journal of Church and State* 39, no. 4 (Autumn 1997): 769–89; Stephen Prothero, *Why Liberals Win (Even When They Lose Elections): How America's Raucous, Nasty, and Mean "Culture Wars" Make for a More Inclusive Nation* (New York: HarperOne, 2017).

would represent their interests in the public sphere, namely, to keep church and state separate.[4] There has also been no shortage of political conflict between Protestants and Catholics, including Prohibition and the presidential campaigns of both Alfred E. Smith and John F. Kennedy.[5] From the country's founding through the mid-twentieth century, differences (sometimes real and sometimes perceived) between religious groups translated into political factions.

What makes today's religious-political environment distinct is that religious groups, in particular Protestants and Catholics, have put aside decades of outward dislike and distrust toward one another in order to work toward a common set of social and political goals.[6] More generally, the political landscape began changing in the 1970s: morality politics took center stage, religious elites of different faiths joined forces with common objectives, and the parties staked out positions such that the Republican Party became associated with culturally conservative policies and traditional values.[7] The new political environment allowed for religiosity – or

---

[4] After the Great Awakening (mid-1700s), it was the Baptists, Methodists, and other evangelicals – religious outsiders at the time – who pushed to disestablish America's state churches, which were Congregationalist or Episcopalian. The evangelicals wanted this separation because they were concerned about how the government would affect their ability practice their faith. Randall Balmer, *The Making of Evangelicism: From Relativism to Politics and Beyond* (Waco, Tex.: Baylor University Press, 2010); Harris and Kidd, *Founding Fathers;* Lambert, "God – and a Religious President."

[5] William G. Carleton, "Kennedy in History: An Early Appraisal," *Antioch Review* 24, no. 3 (Autumn 1964): 277–99; Michael Munger and Thomas Schaller, "The Prohibition-Repeal Amendments: A Natural Experiment in Interest Group Influence," *Public Choice* 90, no. 1 (1997): 139–63; Paul Perl and Mary E. Bendyna, "Perceptions of Anti-Catholic Bias and Political Party Identification Among U.S. Catholics," *Journal for the Scientific Study of Religion* 41, no. 4 (December 2002): 653–68; Ira M. Wasserman, "Prohibition and Ethnocultural Conflict: The Missouri Prohibition Referendum of 1918," *Social Science Quarterly* 70, no. 4 (December 1989): 886–901.

[6] While the shared political goals began with abortion, coalitions of conservative Catholics and evangelicals have worked together to oppose gay marriage, stem-cell research, and euthanasia, and they have worked together in support of school vouchers and religious freedom. Lerond Curry, *Protestant-Catholic Relations in America: World War I Through Vatican II* (Lexington: University of Kentucky Press, 2014); "Evangelicals and Catholics Together," *First Things* (May 1994); Laurie Goodstein, "The 'Hypermodern' Foe: How the Evangelicals and Catholics Joined Forces," *New York Times,* May 30, 2004; Brian T. Kaylor, *Presidential Campaign Rhetoric in an Age of Confessional Politics* (Lanham, Md.: Lexington Books, 2011); Steven Waldman, "How Abortion Unified Catholics and Evangelicals to Become a Power on the Right," *Religion News Services,* May 7, 2019.

[7] For an overview of the changing political-religious landscape beginning in the 1970s onward, see chapter 2 of Michele F. Margolis, *From Politics to the Pews: How Partisanship and the Political Environment Shape Religious Identity* (Chicago: University of Chicago Press, 2018).

how devout a person is or how engaged she is within her religious community – to become a salient dividing line in American politics.

The present-day religiosity sorting is particularly strong because it occurs on two fronts. The common explanation for the present-day religiosity gap is that religious Americans responded to the new political environment by sorting into the Republican Party while less religious and secular Americans responded by joining the Democratic ranks. My own work, however, shows that these same changes in the political environment during the latter part of twentieth century encouraged Americans – particularly white Americans – to become more or less religious on account of their preexisting partisan identities.[8] In other words, partisans took their religious cues from the political environment rather than the other way around: Republicans became further entrenched in their religious communities while Democrats distanced themselves from organized religion. Moreover, the current political-religious landscape continues to shape partisans' decisions about religious identification and church membership.[9]

Importantly, the political-religious environment varies across states and communities, with consequences for religious affiliation. For example, Christian conservatives often wield power in local, and often lower salience, contexts, such as on school boards and at the state level.[10] Religious conservative groups can therefore exert tremendous influence on policy even when the national political environment is not hospitable to their agenda (see Rocco, Chapter 12 in this volume, for a deeper discussion about American federalism and democracy). Moreover, state-level rates of religious non-affiliation increase alongside increases in the state-level presence of the Christian Right movement.[11] More state-level prominence

---

[8] Margolis, *From Politics to the Pews*.
[9] David E. Campbell, Geoffrey C. Layman, John C. Green, and Nathanael G. Sumaktoyo, "Putting Politics First: The Impact of Politics on American Religious and Secular Orientations," *American Journal of Political Science* 62, no. 3 (July 2018): 551–65; Paul A. Djupe, Jacob R. Neiheisel, and Anand E. Sokhey, "Reconsidering the Role of Politics in Leaving Religion: The Importance of Affiliation," *American Journal of Political Science* 62, no. 1 (January 2018): 161–75; Margolis, *From Politics to the Pews*.
[10] Ruth Murray Brown, *For Christian America: A History of the Religious Right*, 1st ed. (Amherst, NY: Prometheus, 2002); Kimberly H. Conger, *The Christian Right in Republican State Politics* (New York: Palgrave Macmillan, 2009); Kimberly H. Conger, "Same Battle, Different War: Religious Movements in American State Politics," *Politics and Religion* 7, no. 2 (June 2014): 395–417; Melissa Deckman, *School Board Battles: The Christian Right in Local Politics* (Washington: Georgetown University Press, 2004).
[11] Paul A. Djupe, Jacob R. Neiheisel, and Kimberly H. Conger, "Are the Politics of the Christian Right Linked to State Rates of the Nonreligious? The Importance of Salient Controversy," *Political Research Quarterly* 62, no. 1 (December 2018): 910–22.

is associated with greater increases in non-identification during the first decade of the twenty-first century. In shaping individuals' religious decisions, politics has transformed the religious makeup of America.

On the surface, demonstrating the reverse relationship between religion and politics seems like an academic exercise. What matters is that a correlation exists, not how it forms. But the ability of politics to affect whether a person identifies with a faith, what church a person goes to, and how involved a person should be in a religious community poses threats to our democracy, two of which I will highlight here.

One consequence of politics affecting religious identities and involvement, or really any social group attachment, is that voters may be less able to hold elected officials accountable. Americans have low levels of political knowledge, making it difficult for them to form political attitudes, choose candidates, and evaluate policy options. Social group membership, however, can offer a workaround to this problem by offering shortcuts to group members. A person does not need to know the details of a policy or specifics of a candidate's platform. Instead, she can follow the lead of others in her group and can make decisions that we might reasonably think are in her best interest. Social group membership can therefore assuage concerns about citizen competence in the United States. But, if a person's religious identity is, in part, a function of her political identity, group cues can no longer effectively compensate for low levels of political knowledge, making it more difficult for voters to identify policies that, and candidates who, support their interests. Adopting or modifying a social identity to align with a political identity threatens one of democracy's main virtues: its ability to represent the will of the people.

Politics shaping religious decisions has also stymied political discourse, shutting out views that at one time were in the political sphere. We often think of religious leaders as, well, leaders – holding sway over their flock and operating as a moral compass. Religion has a great deal to say about the political questions of the day and religious leaders have traditionally represented an important voice in our pluralist society. Politics, however, now constrains these dissident voices.

One notable example is of this is Russell Moore. Moore, the president of the Ethics & Religious Liberty Commission of the Southern Baptist Convention, received public pushback for his pointed criticisms of Donald Trump throughout the 2016 election.[12] Many Baptists called for his job

---

[12] Ana Marie Cox, "Russell Moore Can't Support Either Candidate," *New York Times Magazine*, October 12, 2016.

and Moore even went on what some dubbed an "apology tour" after the election, trying to make clear that his criticisms of President-elect Trump did not extend to Trump supporters.[13] The blowback Moore faced highlights that evangelical Republicans will not tolerate criticism of their political leaders and views. This constraint also extends to religious leaders with less visible public profiles. Over the course of six weeks in Alabama in the Summer of 2018, I interviewed dozens of religious leaders who expressed some degree of frustration or weariness about President Trump but who also said they would not air any such grievance from the pulpit in fear of alienating members. Indeed, virtually every pastor had at least one recent story of congregants becoming upset after hearing messages that church members believed conflicted with their political outlooks.[14] Rather than lead, local pastors take their cues from their followers in order to maintain their position of power, and doing so has changed – and I would argue, undermined – democratic discourse in the United States.

Having discussed what the religiosity gap is, how it formed, and some of the democratic implications of politics affecting religion, I now turn to discuss more general consequences stemming from today's religiously sorted political environment. Both religiously induced political sorting and politically induced religious sorting have created an inextricable link in the minds (and behaviors) of average Americans. This relationship, in turn, has important consequences that extend beyond Americans' decisions about who to vote for and how often to go to church. The next sections discuss a few consequences stemming from sorting as well as what these mean for our democracy.

ASYMMETRIC SORTING

Today's religiously sorted political environment can best be categorized as an asymmetric sorting. While the religious makeup of the parties differs,

---

[13] Chris Moody, "The Survival of a Southern Baptist Who Dared to Oppose Trump," *CNN State Magazine*, July 2017, www.cnn.com/interactive/2017/politics/state/russell-moore-donald-trump-southern-baptists/.

[14] My favorite example of this comes from a pastor of a Baptist church in the eastern part of the state who, after giving a sermon about Jesus emphasizing compassion, received the criticism that: "I don't come to church to hear liberal propaganda." At the time of the interview, the pastor was seeking to leave the congregation since "it is not a good match, particularly since the election." The pastor did, in fact, leave the congregation (and the state of Alabama) in summer, 2020.

Democrats and Republicans are not equally (non)religious. Indeed, while it would be accurate to categorize the Republican Party as the party of religion (among white Americans), the Democratic Party is not the party of non-religion or secularism. Instead, the Democratic Party is a religiously pluralistic party.

Religiously induced political sorting and politically induced religious sorting has given way to a relatively homogenous Republican Party. Some 35 percent of the Republican Party is made up of white evangelical Christians, making white evangelicals the single largest religious constituency within the Republican ranks. After including mainline Protestants and Catholics, just under three-quarters of Republican identifiers are white Christians.[15] Moreover, only 11 percent of Republicans do not identify with a religion, 44 percent report attending church at least once a week, 84 percent believe that religion is very or somewhat important in their lives, and 73 percent believe in God with absolute certainty.[16]

The Democratic Party, on the other hand, includes both believers and non-believers. Here 26 percent of Democrats do not identify with a religion, and this group has received a great deal of attention in the media, rightfully so, as it now represents the single largest religious bloc within the Democratic Party.[17] But this means that the overwhelming majority of Democrats identify with a faith. And while 35 percent of Democrats report that they never or seldom attend church, about 30 percent report attending church on a weekly basis, just under 75 percent report that religion is very or somewhat important in their lives, and 55 percent believe in God with absolute certainty.[18] While Democrats are less religious than the Republicans on virtually every dimension, the party is best thought of as a religious coalition.

Moreover, members of the most devout religious group in America are also the strongest Democrats. Black Protestants – many of whom self-identify as born again and adhere to an evangelical theology – are not only

---

[15] Public Religion Research Institute, "America's Changing Religious Identity," PRRI (blog), 2017, www.prri.org/research/american-religious-landscape-christian-religiously-unaffiliated/.

[16] Pew Research Center, "Party Affiliation – Religion in America: U.S. Religious Data, Demographics and Statistics," Religion and Public Life Project, 2018, www.pewforum.org/religious-landscape-study/.

[17] The second largest religious constituency – making up 17 percent of the Democratic Party – are Black Protestants. Public Religion Research Institute, "America's Changing Religious Identity."

[18] Importantly, even some Democrats who do not identify with a religion report that religion is very or somewhat important in their lives. Pew Research Center, "Party Affiliation."

one of the most religious racial groups in the United States, they also represent the most politically cohesive racial or ethnic group, overwhelmingly identifying as Democrats and supporting Democratic candidates.[19] There are numerous reasons why Black Americans are both highly religious and strongly Democratic, including the origins of Black Protestantism stemming from racial segregation and oppression, Black Protestant theology's emphasis on social justice and equality rather than personal morality, and the continued tradition of political mobilization and activism within Black churches on the political left.[20] Black Protestants therefore do not see their religious and political identities as being in conflict and do not feel internal pressure to update one identity to be consistent with the other. Because the religiosity gap does not extend to African Americans, secular white Americans and highly devout Black Americans are now on the same political team.

To further underscore the religious asymmetry across the parties, religious non-identifiers in the Democratic Party are not the counterpoint to highly devout Republicans. Non-religion in America is not synonymous with hostility toward religion or strong secular identities. Over 60 percent of religious "nones" believe in God or a universal spirit, just under 40 percent report praying at least monthly, and 34 percent report that religion is somewhat or very important in their lives.[21] Despite not identifying with a religious tradition, many non-identifiers retain basic religious beliefs.

Moreover, while Christianity is a group that people identify with and feel connected to, secularism is not a strongly held social identity. In 2018, I asked Christians and religious non-identifiers a series of questions

---

[19] For example, in the 2018 GSS, 30 percent of Black Protestants attended church at least weekly, over 80 percent reported praying at least daily, and over 80 percent identify as a Democrat with about 7 percent identifying as a Republican. Additionally, 15 percent of Black Democrats do not identify with a religion. By way of comparison, 33 percent of white Democrats are religious non-identifiers.

[20] Khari R. Brown and Ronald E. Brown, "Faith and Works: Church-Based Social Capital Resources and African American Political Activism," *Social Forces* 82, no. 2 (2003): 617–41; Allison Calhoun-Brown, "African American Churches and Political Mobilization," *Journal of Politics* 58, no. 4 (1996): 935–53; Eric L. McDaniel and Christopher G. Ellison, "God's Party? Race, Religion and Partisanship Over Time," *Political Research Quarterly* 61 no. 2 (2008): 180–91; Brian D. McKenzie, "Religious Social Networks, Indirect Mobilization, and African-American Political Participation" *Political Research Quarterly* 57 no. 4 (2004): 621–32; Robert D. Putnam and David E. Campbell, *American Grace: How Religion Divides and Unites Us* (New York: Simon and Schuster, 2010).

[21] Pew Research Center, "Party Affiliation."

tapping into their attachment to their respective groups.[22] For example, respondents offered their level of agreement to statements like "When someone criticizes [group], it feels like a personal insult" and "When talking about [group], I usually say "we" rather than "they."[23] I scaled these six measures together to range between 0 and 1, with higher numbers indicating stronger group attachment. Figure 9.1 shows the distributions of group attachments for Christians (gray boxes) and religious non-identifiers (white boxes with black outlines).

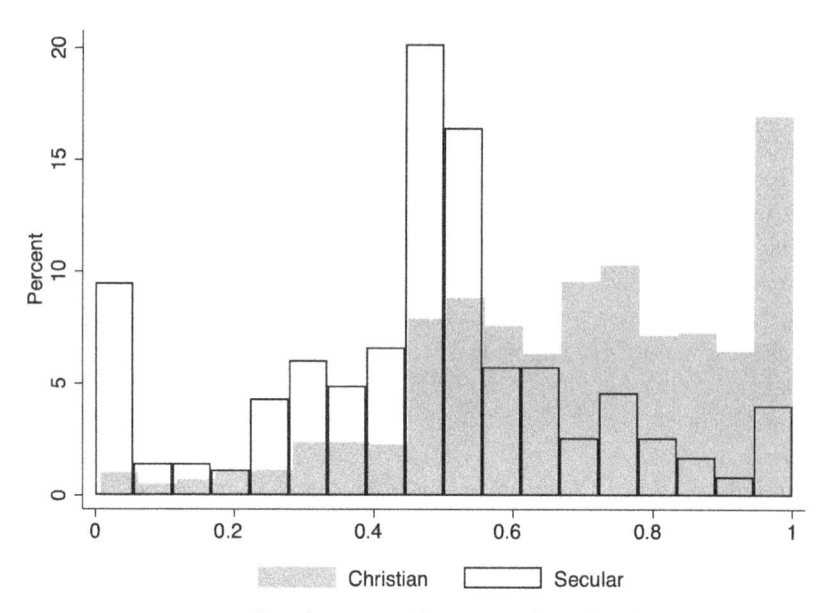

FIGURE 9.1 Attachment to Christian and secular identities

[22] The data come from a nationally diverse sample collected in the fall of 2018. The data has been weighted back to the Current Population Survey (CPS).
[23] Question wordings for self-identified Protestants and other Christians. 1. How well does the term Christian describe you. Agree-disagree statements: 2. When someone criticizes Christians, it feels like a personal insult. 3. I do not act like a typical Christian. 4. If a story in the media criticized Christians, I would feel upset. 5. When someone praises Christians, it feels like a personal compliment. 6. When talking about Christians, I usually say "we" rather than "they." [Leonie Huddy, Lilliana Mason, and Lene Aarøe, "Expressive Partisanship: Campaign Involvement, Political Emotion, and Partisan Identity," *American Political Science Review* 109, no. 1 (February 2015): 1–17; Lilliana Mason, "A Cross-Cutting Calm: How Social Sorting Drives Affective Polarization," *Public Opinion Quarterly* 80, no. S1 (2016): 351–77.] For religious non-identifiers, I ran studies that both used the group "non-religious person/people" and "secular person/people." The two sets of results are substantively similar to one another.

Among Christians, there is a notable skew in the data toward strongly identifying as a Christian and with other Christians. Indeed, the mean is 0.62, over 15 percent of the data have scores between 0.9 and 1, and less than 2 percent have scores between 0 and 0.1. In contrast, non-identifiers do not embrace the secular or non-religious labels to the same extent. There is a peak in the middle of the distribution – indicating that a large number of religious non-identifiers feel neither particularly close to nor distant from other group members.[24] Here, the mean is 0.40, only 3 percent of religious non-identifiers have scores in the 0.9 to 1 range, and 15 percent have scores between 0 and 0.1.

This asymmetry found among voters extends to asymmetric representation in Congress. Frances Lee (Chapter 4 of this volume) illustrates religious sorting among evangelical members of Congress. While the share of white evangelicals elected to Congress from the Democratic and Republicans parties was the same in the late 1960s and 1970s, a 35-point gap existed by 2016. Evangelicals make up 40 percent of Republicans elected to Congress compared to just 5 percent of Democrats elected to Congress. Consequently, white evangelicals – who make up approximately one-third of the Republican Party – are somewhat overrepresented by Republicans in Congress. A corresponding trend does not exist within the Democratic Party. Despite religious non-identifiers making up the largest Democratic constituency, only a single member of the 116th Congress reports having no religion (Senator Krysten Sinema, D-Arizona) and 18 members (representing 3 percent of Congress) decline to specify.[25] Non-identifiers, therefore, do not have descriptive representation in Congress.

All told, Republicans are more unified in their religion than the Democrats are in their secularism, which means that the parties' abilities to mobilize and energize their bases is now different, which can ultimately threaten democratic values. Republicans take part in similar activities – such as attending religious services and being involved in their religious communities – hold similar views about God and identify strongly with

---

[24] Another interpretation of the middle peak is that respondents offered neutral positions because they had not given much thought to their secular identities. I would argue that the interpretation that a large number of people have not given this identity much thought is still evidence of a weakly held identity.

[25] One of the members who would not disclose his faith – Rep. Jared Huffman, D-California – identifies as a humanist and has said that he is not sure whether God exists. Pew Research Center, "Faith on the Hill: The Religious Composition of the 116th Congress," Religion and Public Life Project, January 2, 2019, https://pewforum.org/2019/01/03/faith-on-the-hill-116/.

the Christian label and feel attached to other Christians. Religious-political sorting therefore allows Republicans to engage in what Lacombe calls *identity-based mobilization* (Chapter 10 of this volume), a strategy emphasizing that group members' values and status are under attack. Donald Trump campaigning against the left's "War on Christmas" and Vice President Mike Pence lamenting the difficulties religious people face in America are examples of Republicans using threats to religious identity as a political tactic.[26] And as Lacombe argues, identity-based mobilization can transform policy debates into highly charged and personal struggles where one's survival (or in this case, soul) is at stake, thereby making compromise a less unacceptable option. While identity-based mobilization represents a politically expedient strategy for Republicans, this strategy can decrease the perceived legitimacy of political outsiders and willingness to compromise – two core values underpinning a healthy democracy.

SOCIAL SORTING AND SUPPORT FOR TRUMP

A socially sorted society, in which social and political identities are aligned, unites people on multiple dimensions, thereby increasing the possibility of generating an "us" versus "them" mentality.[27] For example, Republicans no longer simply share a political identity, but they also share a religious identity. Sharing multiple identities make it easier to develop an us-versus-them mentality; after all, "they" differ not only in their politics but in their faith as well. Mason goes on to show that this social sorting has observable implications, including higher levels of political bias and out-party anger. The consequences of religious sorting, therefore, goes beyond religious people supporting one party and secular people supporting another. This sorting has laid the groundwork for increasing hostility and animosity in American society.

---

[26] Democrats, on the other hand, can be anywhere on a Sunday morning – church, the grocery store, or yoga. Moreover, even the party's non-religious constituency is not avowedly secular with respect to members' beliefs or identity, making it difficult to design a strategy meant to appeal to these voters. Saba Hamedy, "Did Trump Stop the 'War on Christmas'? Some Say Yes," CNN Politics, December 22, 2017, https://cnn.com/2017/12/22/politics/donald-trump-war-on-christmas/index.html; Eugene Scott, "Mike Pence's Speech to Christian College Graduates Furthers 'Evangelical Persecution Complex,'" *Washington Post*, May 13, 2019.

[27] Lilliana Mason, *Uncivil Agreement: How Politics Became Our Identity* (Chicago: University of Chicago Press, 2018).

Indeed, the consequences of sorting help explain Trump's electoral support among religious Americans, particularly white evangelical Christians. There was a great deal of discussion surrounding whether white evangelicals – who are not only more religious on average than other religious traditions but have also tried to bring religion and morality into politics – would support Donald Trump. Donald Trump, it may go without saying, does not resemble the type of candidate religious Americans, like white evangelicals, would theoretically support.[28] As it turns out, they did. An extension of the social sorting argument can help us understand why.

We can think of devout, theologically defined evangelical Republicans – those who believe many or all of the core tenets associated with evangelicalism and are deeply ensconced in their religious communities – as being more effectively sorted than *nominal* evangelical Republicans – those who, despite identifying as an evangelical and a Republican, hold their religious identities less tightly. And since the consequences of social sorting include a bias in favor of one's own party and negative emotions toward the political out-party, we might expect theologically defined or highly devout evangelical Republicans to be less likely to abandon their party's standard bearer and more likely to hold negative feelings toward the out-party's candidate compared to their *nominal* or *cultural* evangelical counterparts. This is precisely what I find when looking at white evangelicals in the 2016 election. Not only did more devout evangelical Republicans support Trump at higher rates than their less devout co-partisans, but they also held much more negative affect toward Hillary Clinton and Barack Obama.[29]

Helping make sense of the 2016 election is only one example of the consequences stemming from religious-political sorting. On the one hand, religion is an important social identity – it is a group that members can feel a part of and connected to, it is a set of people with whom members can have regular interactions, and it is a set of core beliefs that can guide all aspects of members' lives. Partisanship, on the other hand, is also an important social identity – it is not only a driver of how people vote, but also serves as a lens through which to see the world, interpret events, and evaluate others. Each identity is individually strong enough to motivate group members to take action to protect the group's status, and their

---

[28] If the reader does need it to be said – Donald Trump is currently married to his third wife, has committed adultery, owns casinos, was caught on tape denigrating women, frequently uses foul language, and committed a series of religious gaffes during the campaign.

[29] Michele F. Margolis, "Who Wants to Make America Great Again? Understanding Evangelical Support for Donald Trump," *Politics and Religion* 13, no. 1 (March 2020): 89–118.

combined power is even stronger.³⁰ Religious-political sorting can therefore enhance emotional responses in politics and discourage deviations from expected behaviors, sometimes to deleterious ends. Mason and Kalmoe (Chapter 7 in this volume) show that partisans feel pleasure when members of the partisan opposition suffer and some even support political violence toward them. Social sorting, including religious-political sorting, has undoubtedly contributed to partisans' intolerance and anger toward their political opponents.

SORTING AND PERCEPTIONS OF VICTIMIZATION

Not only is religious-political sorting the first step in changing how Americans view the political arena, but this sorting has also created fundamental differences in how people view the non-political world, including which groups experience discrimination and bias in society.

Pew and PRRI have been asking whether various groups face discrimination in the United States over the past decade. I pooled together five surveys between 2009 and 2015 – the survey responses are remarkably stable across time – and look at the two largest religious constituencies in the parties, white evangelicals and religious non-identifiers.³¹ Generally speaking, members of a given social group are more likely to report that their group faces discrimination compared to non-group members. This might occur because group members are more sensitive toward slights aimed at their own group or more likely to hear more about discrimination aimed at their group.³² Indeed, while just over half of white

---

[30] Importantly, social sorting does not have to produce overarching combined identities. For example, while many Democrats are not particularly religious, a non-religious or secular identity is not nearly as strong as a religious identity.

[31] Americans recognize the political attachments of evangelicals and non-religious people. When asked about the partisanship of evangelicals, just under three-quarters reported that they are "mainly Republicans," less than 20 percent reported "a pretty even mix of both" and less than 5 percent reported that they are "mainly Democrats." For non-religious people, 48 percent said the group are mainly Democrats, 45 percent said they are a mix of both parties, and only 3 percent said they are mainly Republicans. David E. Campbell, John C. Green, and Geoffrey C. Layman. "The Party Faithful: Partisan Images, Candidate Religion, and the Electoral Impact of Party Identification," *American Journal of Political Science* 55, no. 1 (January 2011): 42–58.

[32] I also look at other social group identities in the survey and similarly find that Jews are more likely to report that Jews face "a lot" of discrimination compared to non-Jews; Catholics (not asked in all five survey waves) report that Catholics face more discrimination than non-Catholics do; Blacks report that Blacks face more discrimination than non-Blacks do; Hispanics report that Hispanics face more discrimination than non-Hispanics

evangelicals report that evangelicals face "a lot" of discrimination in the United States, only about one-quarter of non-evangelicals do so.[33] Similarly, while 38 percent of religious non-identifiers report that atheists face "a lot" of discrimination in the United States today, that number is less than 25 percent among those who identify with a faith.[34] These results, while consistent with existing literature, mask important similarities and differences when we simultaneously consider partisan identity.

Whereas 56 percent of white evangelical Republicans believe that evangelicals face "a lot" of discrimination, non-evangelical Republicans and white evangelical Democrats perceive roughly similar rates of discrimination against evangelicals (35 percent versus 32 percent).[35] Members of social groups usually perceive more discrimination against their own group than others do; however, non-evangelical Republicans seem as attuned to the plight of their political compatriots, despite not being members of the religious group, as white evangelical Democrats who are, themselves, members of the group in question. Non-evangelical Democrats report that evangelicals face discrimination at the lowest rate: 22 percent.[36]

I find a similar, but reversed, relationship when looking at perceptions of discrimination against atheists. As noted, 38 percent of religious non-identifiers report that atheists face "a lot" of discrimination in the United States today.[37] That number rises to 43 percent when looking at religiously unaffiliated Democrats. Once again, partisan identities seem to matter in perceptions of discrimination. Roughly one-in-three Democrats who identify with a faith report that atheists experience "a lot" of discrimination in the United States today while only one-in-four Republican

---

do; and women report that women face more discrimination than men do. Katie Wang and John F. Dovidio, "Perceiving and Confronting Sexism: The Causal Role of Gender Identity Salience," *Psychology of Women Quarterly* 41, no. 1 (March 2017): 65–76.

[33] Evangelicalism is measured using a self-identification question: "Do you consider yourself to be an evangelical or born-again Christian?"

[34] Importantly, the overwhelming majority of religious non-identifiers are not atheists. Unfortunately, due to limitations of sample size and what survey questions are available, I look at religious non-identifiers' perceptions of discrimination against atheists, which generally represent a subsample of religious non-identifiers.

[35] N of white evangelical Democrats = 404.

[36] The Democratic results do not appear on account of religious non-identifiers. Looking only at non-evangelical Democrats who *do* identify with a religious faith, the percent only increases to 25.

[37] Importantly, the overwhelming majority of religious non-identifiers are not atheists. Unfortunately, due to limitations of sample size and what survey questions are available, I look at religious non-identifiers' perceptions of discrimination against atheists, which represent a subsample of religious non-identifiers.

non-identifiers do so.[38] Put another way, Democrats who are *not* part of the non-religious group perceive *higher* levels of discrimination against atheists compared to Republicans who are group members. And finally, religiously affiliated Republicans are the least likely to report that atheists face a lot of discrimination (18 percent).

Three patterns emerge when considering the two identities together. First, perceptions of discrimination are highest when answering about a religious in-group and when religious group membership and partisanship match. In other words, evangelical Republicans and Democratic non-identifiers perceive the highest rates of discrimination against evangelicals and atheists, respectively. Second, when partisanship and religious group membership do not match, political identity matters a great deal. Non-evangelical Republicans (Religiously affiliated Democrats) perceive the same levels of (more) discrimination against evangelicals (atheists) as white evangelical Democrats (Republican non-identifiers). And third, perceptions of discrimination are the lowest when answering about a religious out-group and when group membership and partisanship match. White evangelical Republicans (Democratic non-identifiers) perceive the lowest rates of discrimination against atheists (evangelicals).

Importantly, the causal direction underpinning these trends likely runs both ways. For example, respondents who think that evangelicals face a lot of discrimination are 17 percent more likely to identify as a Republican compared to respondents who do not believe evangelicals face a lot of discrimination (p-value < 0.01).[39] Conversely, perceiving that atheists are on the receiving end of discrimination is associated with a 10 percent decrease in the likelihood of identifying as a Republican (p-value < 0.01).[40] It is quite possible that individuals' perceptions of the world around them – who is discriminated against and which party will better help the aggrieved group – shape their political attachments.

The reverse is also quite likely occurring. Democrats – by virtue of being on the Democratic team – identify with and feel affinity toward

---

[38] N of Republican non-identifiers = 432.

[39] This coefficient comes from a regression model that includes perceptions of discrimination against other groups, religious identification, church attendance, and socioeconomic indicators. When also controlling for political ideology, perceiving a lot of discrimination increases the likelihood of identifying as a Republican by 11 percent (p-value < 0.01).

[40] This number comes from a regression model that includes perceptions of discrimination against other groups, church attendance, and socioeconomic indicators. When also controlling for political ideology, respondents who perceive a lot of discrimination against atheists are 6 percent less likely to identify as a Republican (p-value < 0.01).

other groups in their political tent. In this case, even religiously affiliated Democrats may be sensitive toward slights aimed at their co-partisans or be more likely to hear about discrimination aimed at this group. And when the political and social identities match (evangelical Republicans and non-identifying Democrats), I find maximum sensitivity toward in-group slights and the least sensitivity toward the discrimination that out-groups may face. These findings illustrate how religious-political sorting corresponds with systematic differences in how Americans' view the plight of others. Recognizing that others have legitimate grievances is an essential component of creating equitable policies in a diverse society.

IDENTITY VERSUS ISSUES

While this chapter has focused on the importance of Americans' religious and political identities, issues also matter a great deal. "It's about abortion" and "It's about the Supreme Court" are two common refrains explaining religious Americans' support for Trump. Indeed, there are legitimate policy reasons for religious Americans to identify with the Republican Party and support Republican candidates for elected office. As I describe at the beginning of the chapter, the origins of the religiosity gap began when social and moral issues became salient in American politics, religious elites across multiple faiths joined forces to be a loud conservative political voice, and the Republican Party became aligned with culturally conservative positions not only on abortion, but also on policies related to the LGBTQ+ community, contraceptives, prayer in school, vouchers, and religious liberty. To this end, abortion attitudes lead to changing party affiliations in the 1980s and 1990s and more devout white mainline Protestants, evangelical Protestants, and Catholics take more conservative policy positions on a host of issues compared to their less devout co-religionists.[41] But policy preferences alone cannot explain the social consequences associated with religious-political sorting, including feelings of anger, out-party hostility, and victimization (discussed in this chapter), as these consequences appear after

---

[41] Christopher H. Achen and Larry M. Bartels, *Democracy For Realists: Why Elections Do Not Produce Responsive Government* (Princeton: Princeton University Press, 2017); Michael Tesler, "Priming Predispositions and Changing Policy Positions: An Account of When Mass Opinion Is Primed or Changed," *American Journal of Political Science* 59, no. 4 (October 2015): 806–24.

accounting for policy positions.[42] Rather, identities and feelings toward groups now play an important role in the religious-political sorting story, even if issues helped precipitate the sorting.

WHAT DOES THE FUTURE HAVE IN STORE?

The religious-political sorting described in this chapter has implications that extend far beyond who votes for whom. Indeed, these consequences affect core components of how our democracy functions. Moreover, these ties are unlikely to weaken – indeed, I would argue they will continue to grow stronger – in the future.

First, America now has a generation of Democratic (Republican) parents raising their children with little (a great deal of) religion. In other words, parents who have either sorted into the parties on account of their religion or sorted into religion on account of their politics are raising an entire generation with political and religious beliefs that cohere at the national level. And while neither partisanship nor religion are inherited identities, a person's upbringing is a strong predictor of these identities in adulthood. And, by virtue of the parent generation being sorted along religious and political lines, many members of the next generation will come of age with already-sorted identities. Inertia is strong and therefore many of these people will likely remain sorted unless given a reason to revisit one or another identity.

Second, the religious environment is unlikely to separate itself from conservative politics any time soon. There have been multiple political moments recently in which conservative religion had the opportunity to distance itself from the political right and the Trump administration. One example of this was President Trump's family separation policy at the border coupled with stories about the horrific treatment recent arrivals to the country received. Even in this extreme case in which the Bible takes a pretty unequivocal position, there was no unified religious voice speaking out against these actions and policies. On the one hand, many religious leaders may not feel comfortable criticizing Trump's policies due to concerns about potential blowback. For example, Russell Moore's more

---

[42] Margolis, "Who Wants to Make America Great Again?"; Lilliana Mason, "'I Disrespectfully Agree': The Differential Effects of Partisan Sorting on Social and Issue Polarization," *American Journal of Political Science* 59, no. 1 (January 2015): 128–45; Mason, *Uncivil Agreement*.

recent attempts to wade into politics indicate what he has learned since the 2016 election. Moore expressed his frustration and disappointment about how children are being treated at detention centers along the border on Twitter; however, he was careful not to mention President Trump by name: "The reports of the conditions for migrant children at the border should shock all of our consciences. Those created in the image of God should be treated with dignity and compassion, especially those seeking refuge from violence back home. We can do better than this."[43] On the other hand, there are also many vocal supporters of Trump's immigration policies among evangelical elite. James Dobson – founder of Focus on the Family – wrote in the response to his visit to a detention center that, "without an overhaul of the law and the allocation of resources, millions of illegal immigrants will continue flooding to this great land from around the world. Many of them have no marketable skills. They are illiterate and unhealthy. Some are violent criminals. Their numbers will soon overwhelm the culture as we have known it, and it could bankrupt the nation." The presence of continued support at the elite level for President Trump and his policies coupled with dissenters being silenced or antagonized creates an environment that promotes further religious-political sorting.

Third, Christianity continues to become a smaller share of the American religious landscape, which might further fuel anxiety among religious and political conservatives. Recent Pew data show that 65 percent of Americans described themselves as Christian (down from 77 percent in 2009), while non-identification rates have increased from 17 to 26 percent in the same ten-year period.[44] This trend is expected to continue, with Christianity – specifically white Christianity – making up a smaller share of the country in the future. Building on social psychology findings showing that threats to whites' numerical dominance gives rise to conservative racial and political attitudes, including support for Trump, we might expect a similar response to the declining dominance of Christianity in America.[45] As Christianity's numeric size and relative

---

[43] Jerry Falwell Jr. – the president of Liberty University and a vocal Trump supporter – still lashed out in response to Moore's statement.
[44] Pew Research Center, "In U.S., Decline of Christianity Continues at Rapid Pace," Religion and Public Life Project, October 17, 2019, www.pewforum.org/2019/10/17/in-u-s-decline-of-christianity-continues-at-rapid-pace/.
[45] Maureen A. Craig and Jennifer A. Richeson, "On the Precipice of a 'Majority-Minority' America: Perceived Status Threat from the Racial Demographic Shift Affects White Americans' Political Ideology," *Psychological Science* 25, no. 6 (June 2014): 1189–97;

influence wanes, those remaining in the faith may turn to politics as a way to maintain power.

While there has been some discussion about what could disrupt these trends, none seem particularly promising. For example, some have pinned their hopes on young evangelicals and generational replacement to loosen the tight grip between evangelical Christianity and Republican politics. The data, however, do not warrant a great deal of optimism. Young evangelicals look quite similar to their older counterparts on key dimensions, including partisanship, ideology, abortion, and 2016 Trump support.[46] While there are admittedly some differences in which young evangelicals are more progressive than older generations of evangelicals, for example, gay marriage and the environment, younger evangelicals remain significantly more conservative on these issues compared to their younger non-evangelical counterparts and these issues do not rank among young evangelicals' top priorities.[47] Others have raised the possibility that a particular issue – like immigration or climate change – can serve as a wedge between white evangelicals and the Republican Party. There are, after all, clear theological reasons to support progressive immigration reform and pro-environmental policies. But once again, the data do not show evidence of a wedge. White evangelicals hold the most conservative views on immigration and are starkly out of step with the general American population on immigration.[48] While I do not have a crystal ball and cannot say with certainty that the status quo will continue, the evidence does not support some of the commonly cited potential disruptors of this trend.

Despite the official separation of church and state, religion has never been separate from politics in the United States. This chapter sought to

---

Brenda Major, Alison Blodorn, and Gregory Major Blascovich, "The Threat of Increasing Diversity: Why Many White Americans Support Trump in the 2016 Presidential Election," *Group Processes & Intergroup Relations* 21, no. 6 (September 2018): 931–40.

[46] Ryan P. Burge, "Just How Far Are White Evangelicals Out of the Mainstream? A Case Study of Immigration and Abortion," Religion in Public, 2019, https://religioninpublic.blog/2019/12/26/just-how-far-are-white-evangelicals-out-of-the-mainstream-a-case-study-of-immigration-and-abortion/; Jeremiah J. Castle, *Rock of Ages: Subcultural Religious Identity and Public Opinion Among Young Evangelicals* (Philadelphia: Temple University Press, 2019).

[47] Ryan P. Burge, "Young Evangelicals Are as Republican as Their Grandparents," Religion in Public, 2018, https://religioninpublic.blog/2018/07/18/young-evangelicals-are-as-republican-as-their-grandparents/; Ryan P. Burge, "Let's Talk About Young Evangelicals and the Environment," Religion in Public, 2018, https://religioninpublic.blog/2018/11/27/lets-talk-about-young-evangelicals-and-the-environment/.

[48] Burge, "Let's Talk"; Burge, "Just How Far."

explain the ways in which religion and politics are linked today and discuss how these linkages have changed our society. The religiosity gap in the United States could simply represent differences in party attachment and vote choice; however, the divisions have had downstream consequences. Religious sorting has helped create a global us-versus-them mentality that supersedes differences between Democrats and Republicans, religious and secular. This sorting has changed the way partisans view each other, political elites, and their surroundings. Democracy functions best when its citizens hold elected officials accountable; are exposed to public discourse representing a wide variety of views, including dissenting ones; and consider alternative viewpoints as legitimate and compromise as an option. Religious sorting, both directly and indirectly, has undermined these key components of a healthy democracy.

10

Weaponized Group Identities and the Health of Democracy

Why the National Rifle Association Is Good at Democracy but Bad for It

Matthew J. Lacombe

The National Rifle Association (NRA) is good at using democracy to advance its agenda. Over the course of many decades, the United States' foremost advocate of gun rights has built substantial political power by cultivating a politically unified and engaged base of grassroots supporters. The political intensity of US gun owners – and the NRA's ability to mobilize them into action – has enabled the organization to consistently defeat proposed gun regulations and is a key reason that it has become a central pillar of the contemporary Republican Party.

The NRA, as I discuss in the following pages, is a prime example of how organized groups can cultivate social identities among their members and then appeal to those identities in order to mobilize support on behalf of their policy agendas. This sort of approach to politics is, in certain ways, quite democratic; in a political system that is often responsive to the interests of a relatively small number of wealthy elites, groups that build power by encouraging political participation among their mass-level supporters might be viewed as democratic success stories.

In practice, however, the NRA's use of identity to mobilize its members – a usage that relies on fear – has had deleterious consequences for democracy, creating a paradox in which, despite being good *at* democracy, it is nonetheless bad *for* it. More specifically, I argue that the NRA's tactics make compromise less achievable, contribute to polarization and the delegitimization of its opponents, encourage politicians to engage in constitutional "hardball," and ultimately reduce democratic accountability and responsiveness. I also discuss how the negative consequences of the NRA's use of a group identity have been magnified by its rise within the

Republican Party and argue that the dynamics present in the NRA case are likely becoming more common. Finally, I note that, despite being mass-based, the type of political mobilization used by the NRA ultimately provides cover for the often hidden, inequality-enhancing political efforts of ultra-wealthy Americans.

THE NRA'S WEAPONIZATION OF GUN OWNERS AND THE HEALTH OF AMERICAN DEMOCRACY

The NRA is frequently credited with (or, depending on one's view, blamed for) keeping US firearms regulations comparatively weak, even in the face of strong public support for stricter laws, high rates of gun-related deaths, and heart-wrenching mass shootings. Popular discourse often asserts that the NRA's power is a product of its financial resources. The NRA, the theory goes, pours huge sums of money into electoral campaigns and lavish lobbying efforts, which enable it to effectively purchase the support of policymakers. In a related argument, some politicians, activists, and commentators suggest that the NRA is a front organization for the gun industry and that its primary mission is to boost gun sales. These perspectives portray gun policy as another issue area in which majority will has been subverted by the corrosive influence of money and view the NRA as fitting neatly into scholarship showing that groups representing businesses and wealthy Americans have disproportionate policy influence.[1]

Upon closer inspection, however, it is apparent that this popular emphasis on the NRA's use of financial resources offers, at best, an incomplete explanation of the group's notable political sway. Indeed, the magnitude of the NRA's spending during most election cycles does not stand out relative to that of numerous other mass-based groups, its annual lobbying expenditures pale in comparison to those of powerful business organizations, and – although the organization does in certain ways have a symbiotic relationship with the gun industry – its history with gun manufacturers suggests that it has more power over them than they

---

[1] Larry M. Bartels, *Unequal Democracy: The Political Economy of the New Gilded Age* (Princeton: Princeton University Press, 2008); Martin Gilens, *Affluence and Influence: Economic Inequality and Political Power in America* (Princeton: Princeton University Press, 2012); Martin Gilens and Benjamin I. Page, "Testing Theories of American Politics: Elites, Interest Groups, and Average Citizens," *Perspectives on Politics* 12, no. 3 (2014): 564–81; Benjamin I. Page and Martin Gilens, *Democracy in America: What Has Gone Wrong and What We Can Do About It* (Chicago: University of Chicago Press, 2018).

have over it.[2] Moreover, accounts of important gun policy battles – occurring as early as the 1930s and as recently as the 2010s – demonstrate that the NRA's influence over gun control legislation has often been related to the organization's ability to mobilize its mass-level supporters into action on behalf of its agenda.[3]

The NRA is one of the largest mass-based interest groups in the United States, with a reported membership of about 5 million people – a total that actually understates the size of its constituency. Over 30 percent of Americans report personally owning a gun and over 40 percent indicate that they live in a household with one.[4] Moreover, 19 percent of gun owners *say* that they are NRA members, which indicates that around 14 million people believe (or at the very least feel like) they are part of the NRA.[5] Beyond its size, the NRA's base is unusually politically active and committed to their cause; gun owners and NRA members, for instance, heavily emphasize candidates' gun-rights stances when deciding whom to support and tend to contact public officials with unusual frequency.[6] These high levels of political engagement enable the NRA to punch above its weight – consistently defeating gun control proposals

---

[2] Richard Feldman, *Ricochet: Confessions of a Gun Lobbyist* (Hoboken: Wiley, 2008); Jarrett Murphy, "How the Gun Industry Got Rich Stoking Fear About Obama," *The Nation*, August 22, 2012; "National Rifle Assn," Center for Responsive Politics. www.opensecrets.org/orgs/summary.php?id=d000000082.

[3] Kristin A. Goss, *Disarmed: The Missing Movement for Gun Control in America* (Princeton: Princeton University Press, 2006); Matthew J. Lacombe, "The Political Weaponization of Gun Owners: The National Rifle Association's Cultivation Dissemination, and Use of a Group Social Identity," *Journal of Politics* 81, no. 4 (2019): 1342–56; Matthew J. Lacombe, *Firepower: How the NRA Turned Gun Owners into a Political Force* (Princeton: Princeton University Press, 2021).

[4] Lydia Saad, "What Percentage of Americans Own Guns?" Gallup's The Short Answer, August 14, 2019, https://news.gallup.com/poll/264932/percentage-americans-own-guns.aspx.

[5] Kim Parker, "Among Gun Owners, NRA Members Have a Unique Set of Views and Experiences," Pew Research Center report, July 5, 2017. Accessed January 20, 2019. www.pewresearch.org/fact-tank/2017/07/05/among-gun-owners-nra-members-have-a-unique-set-of-views-and-experiences/; Megan R. Wilson, "The NRA's Power: By the Numbers," *The Hill*, October 8, 2017, https://thehill.com/business-a-lobbying/business-a-lobbying/354317-the-nras-power-by-the-numbers.

[6] Peter M. Aronow and Benjamin T. Miller, "Policy Misperceptions and Support for Gun Control Regulations," *The Lancet* 387, 10015 (2016): 23; Matt Grossmann, *The Not-So-Special Interests: Interest Groups, Public Representation, and American Governance* (Palo Alto: Stanford University Press, 2012); Parker, "Among Gun Owners, NRA Members Have a Unique Set of Views and Experiences"; Howard Schuman and Stanley Presser, "The Attitude-Action Connection and the Issue of Gun Control," *The ANNALS of the American Academy of Political and Social Science* 455, no.1 (1981): 40–47.

even when they are broadly popular – and are a key reason for its prominence within the GOP coalition.[7]

The deep political engagement of NRA supporters is not an accident, but is instead a product of a shared collective identity that exists among gun owners. In a 2017 survey, about half of American gun owners said that owning guns is important to their personal identity, a figure that rose to 69 percent when looking only at NRA members.[8] Moreover, nearly three-quarters of gun owners – and 92 percent of NRA members – said that the right to own guns is essential to their personal sense of freedom.[9] Personal identification with gun ownership – that is, one's feeling that owning a gun is an important part of who they are – is a strong predictor of gun-related activism; in addition to being more likely to oppose gun control, those who more strongly identify as gun owners are also more likely to contact public officials, join gun-related organizations, and vote based on candidates' gun stances.[10]

The NRA has played a central role in cultivating this gun-owner identity, working hard over the course of many decades to inculcate a sense among many of its supporters that their status *as gun owners* is central to who they are, what they value, and how they view their place in the world. It has disseminated this identity through its widely circulated media outlets – via magazines like the *American Rifleman* – and its very popular firearms-related programs,[11] which draw more than a million annual participants.[12] These communications outlets and programs associate gun ownership with a number of desirable characteristics and collective values – depicting gun owners as self-sufficient, deeply patriotic, law-abiding citizens who are protectors of the American tradition – and

---

[7] Benjamin G. Bishin, *Tyranny of the Minority: The Subconstituency Politics Theory of Representation* (Philadelphia: Temple University Press, 2009); Lacombe, *Firepower*.
[8] Sixty-nine percent figure calculated using Pew data that can be accessed here: www.pewsocialtrends.org/2017/06/22/americas-complex-relationship-with-guns/
[9] Parker, "Among Gun Owners, NRA Members Have a Unique Set of Views and Experiences"; Kim Parker et al., "America's Complex Relationship with Guns," Pew Research Center report, June 22, 2017, www.pewsocialtrends.org/2017/06/22/americas-complex-relationship-with-guns/.
[10] Matthew J. Lacombe, Adam J. Howat, and Jacob E. Rothschild, "Gun Ownership as a Social Identity: Estimating Behavioral and Attitudinal Relationships," *Social Science Quarterly* 100, no.6 (2019): 2408–24.
[11] These programs, which are often administered by state and local NRA-affiliated clubs, also establish sites for building relationships and developing leaders – factors that, according to Hahrie Han, are crucial for grassroots organization. See Hahrie Han, *How Organizations Develop Activists: Civic Associations and Leadership in the 21st Century* (Oxford: Oxford University Press, 2014).
[12] See https://firearmtraining.nra.org/.

juxtapose gun owners with a number of perceived out-groups, each of which is associated with negative traits.[13]

This gun-owner identity is central to the NRA's ability to politically mobilize its supporters on its behalf. More specifically, the NRA's effectiveness at rallying its members into action is a product of *fear-based mobilization*; rather than relying mostly on evidence-based appeals that critique gun control policies on their merits, the NRA has instead frequently framed gun control proposals as deeply harmful to the group's collective values and paired such frames with calls to action on behalf of gun rights. Its supporters – under the belief that gun control threatens their identities – tend to respond in large numbers to its fear-based messaging, which then – via numerous distinct mechanisms – sharply reduces the prospects of gun reform. The collective identity that exists around gun ownership has, in other words, been "politically weaponized" by the NRA and is a key factor for understanding the organization's power.[14]

On the one hand, the NRA tactics described here actually amount to a rather democratic approach to politics, at least along certain dimensions: The organization advances its agenda by driving political participation among its members and supporters, most of whom are not financial, social, or political elites. As such, rather than being another example of the negative effects of money in politics, the NRA is in fact an example of how groups can achieve substantial success by mobilizing average citizens. Indeed, even the NRA's opponents might acknowledge that it provides a template for how other groups can use identity to advance their interests.

On the other hand, despite the NRA's success *at* democracy, the following sections present a much grimmer view of the consequences of its fear-based mobilization *for* democracy. To be clear, the NRA's opposition to gun control is not inherently harmful to democracy simply because most Americans favor additional regulations on guns. Rather, the NRA's harm to democracy is a product of *how* and *with what effects* it pursues its agenda. I argue that the identity-based politics practiced by the NRA weakens American democracy in a number of distinct ways, including by reducing the viability of compromise, increasing polarization, encouraging politicians to violate long-standing constitutional norms, and more generally diminishing the government's ability to implement popular solutions that address important social problems (such as the misuse of guns).[15]

---

[13] Lacombe, *Firepower*; Lacombe, "Political Weaponization of Gun Owners." [14] Ibid.
[15] Although certainly not the only (or even the most crucial) dimension along which democratic health might be assessed, the responsiveness of public policy to mass opinion is

PERCEIVED THREAT AND POLITICAL COMPROMISE

Perceived threat is a key characteristic of fear-based mobilization. When individuals believe that salient identities are under attack, they are highly motivated to defend them.[16] As such, groups can mobilize their members into politics by portraying candidates and legislative proposals as deeply threatening to the group's values and interests. These sorts of fear-based appeals may be made in lieu of evidence-based arguments that attempt to persuade individuals based on policy merits or candidate qualifications. Of course, in some (relatively rare) cases, particular candidates or pieces of legislation *do* pose genuinely dire threats to groups; using fear to mobilize group members when they have good reason to be fearful is certainly appropriate and perhaps even desirable. In most political contests, however, unfavorable outcomes do not spell doom for interested parties on any side of the conflict. In instances of the latter, organized groups that rely on fear-based appeals have an incentive to vastly overstate the extent to which their members are threatened in order to increase their likelihood of taking action. Such groups might even portray *all* instances of political conflict – regardless of their actual stakes – as existential battles in which group members are under attack.

Fear-based mobilization's emphasis on threat – especially if the extent to which the group is threatened is exaggerated – can have harmful effects on democracy. When elections and policy debates are viewed as highly personal, high-stakes battles – the outcomes of which might even determine the group's survival – policy content is heavily deemphasized and compromise is seemingly impossible.[17] Notably, this can even be the case

---

nonetheless important, especially when (a) public opinion overwhelmingly and durably falls on one side of a policy debate (as is the case in regards to gun control), and (b) the policies in question would address a clear and important social problem (like US gun violence). In other words, while some forms of democratic erosion (e.g., violations of voting rights) may be more alarming, it is still appropriate to assess the health of a democracy in part based on its ability to enact popular policies that address major problems.

[16] Leonie Huddy, Lilliana Mason, and Lene Aarøe, "Expressive Partisanship: Campaign Involvement, Political Emotion, and Partisan Identity," *American Political Science Review* 109, no. 1 (2015): 1–17; Diane M. Mackie, Thierry Devos, and Eliot R. Smith, "Intergroup Emotions: Explaining Offensive Action Tendencies in an Intergroup Context," *Journal of Personality and Social Psychology* 79, no. 4 (2000): 602–16.

[17] James N. Druckman, Erik Peterson, and Rune Slothuus, "How Elite Partisan Polarization Affects Public Opinion Formation," *American Political Science Review* 107, no. 1 (2013): 57–79; David K. Sherman and Geoffrey L. Cohen, "The Psychology of Self-Defense: Self-Affirmation Theory," *Advances in Experimental Social Psychology* 38 (2006): 183–242; Michael R. Wolf, J. Cherie Strachan, and Daniel M. Shea, "Forget the Good

when substantial policy agreement exists between members of competing groups, as Lilliana Mason makes clear in her compelling book, *Uncivil Agreement*; among many other things, Mason finds that political participation driven by identity threat is much more related to group competition than to issue preferences.[18]

These dynamics are clearly present in the realm of pro-gun politics. A majority of gun owners and NRA members say that they favor expanded background checks, which suggests that they would hypothetically be willing to accept certain legislative compromises that result in new gun control laws.[19] But when any and all gun control proposals are viewed as attacks on who gun owners are as a social group, the stakes change in ways that make compromise seem like surrender. Take, for example, the description NRA chief Wayne LaPierre gave of a relatively benign early 2000s bill that would have expanded background checks to cover sales at gun shows – the exact type of policy most gun owners support in the abstract. LaPierre wrote that the bill would "put private sales of firearms between peaceable Americans – you, me, our families and friends – under the total control of the Federal government" and told NRA members that "[o]ur very culture is the target." He then made a slippery slope argument, telling NRA members that gun control advocates would not stop after closing the so-called gun show loophole because "[w]hat our enemies are really after is the 'freedom loophole.'" LaPierre then closed by imploring NRA members to contact their representatives in opposition to the bill.[20] This example is useful for explaining why gun owners often mobilize against proposals containing policies that they claim to support; the NRA's fear-based tactics mislead its members about the severity of such proposals and encourage them to view efforts to pass gun laws as personal attacks.

Over time, in order to maintain the level of alarm among its members, the NRA – especially given its track record of success – has had to continually up the ante rhetorically; it has done so by, among other things, portraying an increasingly wide range of factors as potentially threatening and going even further when exaggerating the threat posed by particular candidates or bills. For example, during a period of unified Republican

---

of the Game: Political Incivility and Lack of Compromise as a Second Layer of Party Polarization," *American Behavioral Scientist* 56, no. 12 (2012): 1677–95.

[18] Lilliana Mason, *Uncivil Agreement: How Politics Became Our Identity* (Chicago: University of Chicago Press, 2018), chapter 7.

[19] Parker, "Among Gun Owners, NRA Members Have a Unique Set of Views and Experiences."

[20] Wayne LaPierre, "Standing Guard," *American Rifleman*, July 2002.

government in the early 2000s – when gun control proposals stood little chance of even being considered – the NRA turned to international organizations as sources of threat; in one instance, LaPierre warned members of a "mounting effort by more than 100 members of the United Nations to impose a worldwide ban on civilian ownership of firearms" aimed at "outlawing your guns, extinguishing your hunting, prohibiting your shooting sports, ending your right to self-defense and destroying your Second Amendment rights forever."[21]

Although the NRA's use of these tactics may be effective for rallying support on behalf of its agenda, they make the stakes of elections and policy battles seem misleadingly high to many gun owners. These misleadingly high stakes help explain why compromise on gun control is exceedingly difficult to achieve despite the magnitude of the United States' gun violence problem and the relatively widespread agreement that exists about a number of policy options. And although gun policy is only one issue area, the NRA's impact on politics – as the following sections demonstrate – is much wider as a result of its important place in the conservative movement and the wide range of topics with which it now engages.

VIRTUOUS IN-GROUPS, VILLAINOUS OUT-GROUPS, AND AFFECTIVE POLARIZATION

Beyond creating a state of constant alarm, the NRA's fear-based mobilization also involves the vilification of its political opponents. In order to develop and use a weaponized social identity, organizations like the NRA must juxtapose a "good" in-group with one or more "bad" out-groups.[22] This involves associating the in-group with positive characteristics and values; the NRA's previously mentioned portrayal of gun owners as the patriotic defenders of (its version of) the American tradition is an example of this. In addition to building up the in-group, the creation of politically weaponized identities also involves depicting out-groups – like gun control supporters – as not merely having differing opinions, but as being enemies of the in-group and its core beliefs.

This approach to politics can produce effects that are harmful to democracy. Viewing political opponents as enemies who are attacking one's very identity can increase affective polarization by producing

---

[21] Wayne LaPierre, "Standing Guard," *American Rifleman*, September 2005.
[22] Lacombe, "Political Weaponization of Gun Owners."

feelings of prejudice and anger toward those opponents.[23] Moreover, this sort of politics can eliminate any space that might otherwise exist for a broader sense of national unity; when one's political opponents are seen as not just misguided but as intentionally working against the national interest, it is difficult share a broader sense of American identity with them in any context. Taken to an extreme, this type of politics encourages the delegitimization of the group's opponents, including elected officials, whose actions might be explained using conspiratorial thinking.

The NRA frequently vilifies a number of distinct out-groups – portraying them as out-of-touch urban elitists who want to impose tyranny via big-government socialism – and at times even associates its opponents with broader far-right conspiracy theories. Moreover, the out-groups it vilifies are not limited to outspoken advocates of gun control, but instead include a much wider range of figures, including Democratic Party leaders. Speaking at the 2018 Conservative Political Action Conference, for instance, LaPierre said that the Democratic Party "is now infested with saboteurs who don't believe in capitalism, don't believe in the Constitution, don't believe in our freedom, and don't believe in America as we know it. Obama may be gone, but their utopian dream, it marches on." He then connected all of this to a range of movements on the left, commenting,

> socialism is a movement that loves a smear. Racist, misogynist, sexist, xenophobe and more ... They keep their movement growing by finding someone to be offended by something every minute of every day. From the Occupy movement, to Black Lives Matter, to Antifa, they agitate the offended, promote uncivil discourse and ignore any sense of due process and fairness to destroy their enemies.[24]

LaPierre also propagated a right-wing conspiracy theory, suggesting that, following Donald Trump's 2016 victory, a deep state embedded in the government continued to push a left-wing agenda behind the scenes.[25] This sort of appeal is perhaps unsurprising given that the NRA was an early and powerful promoter of anti-Semitic conspiracy theories targeting George Soros; it ran a feature on Soros's "Anti-Gun Vision For America"

---

[23] Mason, *Uncivil Agreement*.
[24] "NRA CEO Speaks at Conservative Forum After School Massacre; NRA Chief: Schools are 'Wide-Open' Target," CNN Newsroom transcript, February 22, 2018. Accessed February 9, 2019. www.cnn.com/TRANSCRIPTS/1802/22/cnr.03.html.
[25] Ibid.

in 2004 – years before Soros-related theories gained broader traction – and has continued to frequently link its opponents to Soros since then.[26]

The NRA's efforts to vilify its opponents have had important mass-level effects that go well beyond the advancement of gun rights. The NRA's longstanding criticisms of the media, for example – in which it accuses mainstream news outlets of pushing an elitist, anti-gun agenda and suggests that they serve as propaganda arms for liberal politicians – clearly show up in the views of NRA members. Compared to other gun owners, NRA members are significantly more likely to say that the media "keeps political leaders from doing their job" as opposed to serving as an important watchdog that "keeps political leaders from doing things that should not be done."[27] These anti-media sentiments are very similar to – and work in conjunction with – President Trump's attacks on the media. When speaking at the NRA's annual meeting in 2019, for instance, Trump drew loud applause when he gestured to the media area in the back of the room and said, "We call them the 'fake news' ... They're fake. They're fake," before going on to say, "The level of dishonesty and corruption in the media is unbelievable."[28]

Although it is not necessarily alone in using these tactics, it is worth emphasizing that the NRA's fear-based mobilization is especially alarming for democracy because it is often built upon an implied threat of armed force – a threat which is sometimes even directed against the state. In portraying its members as patriots ready to protect the "real" American tradition from the intrusion of an abusive state, the NRA implies that its members are willing to violently resist political outcomes that they oppose. It describes the Second Amendment as "America's first freedom" – which is also the title of a magazine it offers – in order to advance a belief that gun rights are necessary to defend all of the other rights guaranteed by the Constitution. LaPierre has connected gun rights and resistance against the state even more explicitly, telling an audience that "Our Founding Fathers knew that without Second Amendment freedom, all of our freedoms could be in jeopardy ... If you aren't free to protect yourself – when government puts its thumb on that freedom – then you aren't free at all."[29]

---

[26] James O. E. Norell, "George Soros' Anti-Gun Vision for America," *American Rifleman*, April 2004.
[27] Lacombe, *Firepower*.
[28] Dwight Adams, "Read Donald Trump's Speech from the NRA Convention in Indianapolis," *Indianapolis Star*, April 26, 2019.
[29] "Wayne LaPierre Remarks at Conservative Political Action Conference," C-Span, March 15, 2013. Accessed February 8, 2019. www.c-span.org/video/?311543-6/wayne-lapierre-remarks-conservative-political-action-conference&start=83.

These developments are even more troubling in light of the NRA's increasing prominence in the Republican coalition, as well as its need, mentioned earlier, to consistently expand the severity of the threats it describes to its members in order to maintain a sense of alarm. Especially during the Trump era and then following Trump's 2020 defeat, the sorts of NRA appeals discussed throughout this essay were echoed by conservative and GOP leaders. Prominent pro-gun politicians, including Trump himself, have used rhetoric that is notably similar to the NRA's rhetoric; during the 2016 campaign, for example, Trump told a crowd that Hillary Clinton wants to "abolish the Second Amendment" and that "if she gets to pick her judges, nothing you can do," before noting, "although, the Second Amendment people, maybe there is."[30]

The NRA's intense vilification of its political opponents and its exaggerated portrayals of the threats faced by its members are very concerning. They make cleavages that exist between gun owners and other groups in society deeper and more emotional. Moreover, they encourage NRA members to view their political opponents as illegitimate in ways that make the existence of a broader sense of national unity incredibly difficult to imagine. And these negative impacts on democracy are magnified by the NRA's increased influence in the Republican Party.

IDENTITY ALIGNMENT AND CONSTITUTIONAL DEMOCRACY

The negative effects of the NRA's use of identity threat to mobilize gun owners have been further exacerbated by the relatively recent alignment of the gun owner identity with a number of other politically relevant social identities, as well as the related rise of the NRA within the Republican Party. Identity alignment – in which the range of identities held by individuals tend to fit together politically – contributes to affective polarization by causing individuals to be exposed to fewer cross-pressures (i.e., competing influences that pull them in different political directions) and reinforcing each of the aligned identities.[31] As Lilliana Mason and Nathan Kalmoe's chapter in this volume demonstrates, this identity sorting –

---

[30] "Trump on Clinton and the Second Amendment," TimesVideo, August 9, 2016. Accessed October 3, 2019. www.nytimes.com/video/us/politics/100000004579354/trump-on-clinton-and-the-second-amendment.html.

[31] Lilliana Mason and Julie Wronski, "One Tribe to Bind Them All: How Our Social Group Attachments Strengthen Partisanship," *Political Psychology* 39, S1 (2018): 257–77; Sonia Roccas and Marilynn B. Brewer, "Social Identity Complexity," *Personality and Social Psychology Review* 6, no.2 (2002): 88–106.

especially when individuals' racial views align with partisan divides – is also associated with increased support for political violence and feelings of pleasure in response to the suffering of one's political opponents. Less directly – but no less importantly – identity alignment also has the potential to reduce democratic accountability and encourage parties to play constitutional hardball; it decreases the likelihood of voters punishing extremism and enforcing their policy views, which in turn provides party leaders with more leeway to pursue unpopular policies using aggressive tactics that violate preexisting norms of governance.

The NRA's gun owner social identity has gradually come into alignment with a number of other identities associated with the Republican Party, especially in the Trump era.[32] This includes both Republican partisan identification itself and electoral support for Republican candidates, which are strongly and statistically significantly predicted by gun ownership, even when controlling for numerous other factors.[33] Beyond their association with Republican partisan identity, gun ownership and opposition to gun control are also enmeshed with numerous other group memberships and identities related to the Trump-era Republican Party. These include white racial identity, traditional masculine identity, conservative Christian identity, and rural identity. Each of these identities is closely related – statistically and rhetorically – to both Trumpism and one's experience with and attitudes about guns.[34]

---

[32] Indeed, in the Trump era, the NRA likely represents what Sidney Milkis and Daniel Tichenor would describe as an institutionalized movement; it has significant conventional political leverage as a result of its mobilizational capabilities and works within the existing political order to achieve its goal. Sidney M. Milkis and Daniel J. Tichenor, *Rivalry and Reform: Presidents, Social Movements, and the Transformation of American Politics* (Chicago: University of Chicago Press, 2019).

[33] Mark R. Joslyn, Donald P. Haider-Markel, Michael Baggs, and Andrew Bilbo, "Emerging Political Identities? Gun Ownership and Voting in Presidential Elections," *Social Science Quarterly* 98, no. 2 (2017): 382–96; Lacombe, *Firepower*.

[34] Alexandra Filindra and Noah J. Kaplan, "Racial Resentment and Whites' Gun Policy Preferences," *Political Behavior* 38, no. 2 (2015): 255–75; Kristin A. Goss, "The Socialization of Conflict and Its Limits: Gender and Gun Politics in America," *Social Science Quarterly* 98, no. 2 (2017): 455–70; Lacombe et al., "Gun Ownership as a Social Identity"; Stephen M. Merino, "God and Guns: Examining Religious Influences on Gun Control Attitudes in the United States," *Religions* 9, no. 6 (2018), 189; Diana C. Mutz, "Status threat, not economic hardship, explains the 2016 presidential vote," *PNAS* 115, no. 9 (2018), E4330–E4339; Kerry O'Brien, Walter Forrest, Dermot Lynott, and Michael Daly, "Racism, Gun Ownership and Gun Control: Biased Attitudes in US Whites May Influence Policy Decisions," *PLoS ONE* 8, no. 10 (2013): e77552–e77552; Parker, "Among gun owners, NRA members have a unique set of views and experiences"; Brian F. Schaffner, Matthew Macwilliams, and Tatishe Nteta, "Understanding White

The alignment of the gun owner identity with numerous other GOP-aligned identities suggests that the social psychological *meaning* of guns is now wrapped up with Republican partisan identification. That is, rather than simply being a plank in the GOP platform and a component of conservative ideology, support for gun rights – and the symbolic meaning attached to guns – is an element of what it means for many people to identify as Republicans and/or conservatives.[35] This is visible, for example, in the clear overlap that exists between the sorts of right-wing, populist NRA appeals described throughout this essay and the feelings of resentment toward urban elites that Katherine Cramer has documented among conservative rural Wisconsinites. Indeed, although the gun owner identity is not the same as rural consciousness per se, they are similar enough to likely reinforce one another and, together, help explain the political success of candidates like Donald Trump in rural areas of the Upper Midwest.[36]

Polarization in the 2016 Vote for President: The Sobering Role of Racism and Sexism," *Political Science Quarterly* 133, no. 1 (2018): 9–34; John Sides, Michael Tesler, and Lynn Vavreck, "The 2016 U.S. Election: How Trump Lost and Won," *Journal of Democracy* 28, no. 2 (2017): 34–44; Angela Stroud, *Good Guys with Guns: The Appeal and Consequences of Concealed Carry* (Chapel Hill: University of North Carolina Press, 2016); Andrew L. Whitehead, Samuel L. Perry, and Joseph O. Baker, "Make America Christian Again: Christian Nationalism and Voting for Donald Trump in the 2016 Presidential Election," *Sociology of Religion* 79, no. 2 (2018): 147–71; Andrew L. Whitehead, Landon Schnabel, and Samuel L. Perry, "Gun Control in the Crosshairs: Christian Nationalism and Opposition to Stricter Gun Laws," *Socius: Sociological Research for a Dynamic World* 4 (2018): 1–13; David Yamane, "Awash in a Sea of Faith and Firearms: Rediscovering the Connection Between Religion and Gun Ownership in America," *Journal for the Scientific Study of Religion* 55, no. 3 (2016): 622–36.

[35] This observation generally aligns with the conclusions drawn by Michele Margolis in her study of how political factors (e.g., party identification) can shape individuals' religious identities. Margolis argues that political identities are not only a product of other social identities but are themselves also a cause of those identities and the strength with which they are held. What I describe here is similar in that it involves a political factor – the group composition of party coalitions – shaping the broader set of identities held by individuals who are part of groups that are themselves part of a party coalition. Similarly, in the conclusion of his study of racial realignment, Eric Schickler gets at the notion that distinct partisan policy positions sometimes are not just a product of "separate cases of new policy demanders being incorporated into one party or the other" but can instead be mutually reinforcing when they bring together what he describes as an "interlocking set" of identities. See Michele F. Margolis, *From Politics to the Pews: How Partisanship and the Political Environment Shape Religious Identity* (Chicago: University of Chicago Press, 2018); Eric Schickler, *Racial Realignment: The Transformation of American Liberalism, 1932–1965* (Princeton: Princeton University Press, 2016), 283.

[36] Katherine J. Cramer, *The Politics of Resentment: Rural Consciousness in Wisconsin and the Rise of Scott Walker* (Chicago: University of Chicago Press, 2016).

The alignment of the gun-owner identity with other right-leaning identities has altered the nature of the NRA's fear-based mobilization in important ways. Rather than relying exclusively on portrayals of gun rights as under threat in order to mobilize its supporters, the NRA now portrays conservatism and the Republican Party as under attack in order to maintain a sense of alarm. Not only is this useful to the NRA during periods in which gun control is off the agenda, it also enables the organization to describe the threats faced by its supporters as even larger and more existential.

This development has been associated with both increasing extremism from the NRA and a deepening of its relationship with the GOP. Along these lines, the organization's rhetoric in recent years has pushed a right-wing brand of nationalistic populism. It has focused on what it describes as a dire threat posed by socialism – which it associates with "Antifa" and a desire for mob rule – while also linking opposition to President Trump to conspiracy theories about billionaires like George Soros and Michael Bloomberg.[37] The NRA has also essentially stopped providing support to Democratic candidates, ending a previous pattern of endorsing and contributing to a small, but non-negligible number of pro-gun Democrats.[38] Although these trends have surely alienated some potential gun rights supporters who are put off by the NRA's non-gun stances, they have also likely intensified the views of core members, many of whom are motivated by a neatly aligned set of political identities which they believe must be protected from a set a common threats.

Although the NRA is only a single organization, increasing issue-based, partisan polarization – which definitionally involves a reduction to the number of bipartisan issue areas – likely generates broader incentives for organized groups to align with one party or the other. One factor that is likely both a cause and a consequence of this broader trend is the increasing commonality and institutionalization of close relationships between political parties and organized groups. Deeper and more frequent

---

[37] See, for example, the cover stories of the NRA's *America's 1st Freedom* magazine from March 2018 (which warned of a "[c]oming socialist wave that will drown your guns"), November 2017 (which focused on Antifa), January 2017 (which contained images of Soros and Bloomberg and suggested that they would undermine the Trump administration from behind the scenes), and December 2018 (which depicted a raised arm holding Molotov cocktail and accused Trump's opponents of favoring mob rule "that threatens the foundations of our democracy").

[38] Center for Responsive Politics, "National Rifle Association Contributions," www.opensecrets.org/orgs/totals.php?id=d000000082&cycle=2018.

alignments between groups and parties have contributed to polarization by decreasing the extent to which the parties compete for the support of groups; as the number of bipartisan groups declines, so do incentives and opportunities for compromise.[39] Moreover, the general trend toward closer bonds between organized groups and parties can then become self-reinforcing, as increased polarization – and the diminished willingness of the parties to work together – encourages remaining groups to choose a side. This – along with the tribalism, vitriol, and gridlock of recent politics – suggests that the dynamics present in the NRA case may be more broadly applicable.

Greater interrelation of politically salient identities is problematic for democracy because it contributes to a political environment in which voters view politics as a competition between one good team and one bad team, pay minimal attention to policy, and are almost exclusively concerned with whether their side is winning.[40] This sort of environment is one in which voters may frequently fail to enforce their issue preferences; this, in turn, gives policymakers greater latitude to pursue highly unpopular policies – for instance, as discussed in the next section, tax cuts for billionaires – and ultimately decreases democratic accountability.[41]

Indeed, insofar as fear-based politics generally take voters away from a focus on candidates' issue stances, they may create – borrowing from Kathleen Bawn and her co-authors – something of an "electoral blind spot." The formulation of the electoral blind spot developed by Bawn and colleagues applies to relatively ignorant voters and describes a range of policy positions over which such voters do not detect real differences between the parties. As a result, these voters then fail to enforce their issue preferences (i.e., they fail to hold political parties accountable for a lack of long-term policy representation).[42] Identity-based politics may produce a somewhat similar effect, except it instead applies to rather

---

[39] Katherine Krimmel, "The Efficiencies and Pathologies of Special Interest Partisanship," *Studies in American Political Development* 31, no.2 (2017): 149–69; Katherine Krimmel, "Special Interest Partisanship: The Transformation of American Political Parties" (PhD Dissertation, Columbia University, 2013).

[40] Mason, *Uncivil Agreement*.

[41] Christopher H. Achen and Larry M. Bartels, *Democracy for Realists: Why Elections Do Not Produce Responsive Government* (Princeton: Princeton University Press, 2016); Jacob S. Hacker and Paul Pierson, *Let Them Eat Tweets: How the Right Rules in an Age of Extreme Inequality* (New York: Liveright, 2020).

[42] Kathleen Bawn, Martin Cohen, David Karol, Seth Masket, Hans Noel, and John Zaller, "A Theory of Political Parties: Groups, Policy Demands and Nominations in American Politics," *Perspectives on Politics* 10, no. 3 (2012): 571–97.

attentive voters who have strong feelings about politics and see political contests as zero-sum competitions between a virtuous in-group and an evil out-group. These voters – despite their attentiveness to politics – may also fail to enforce their policy preferences as a result of their intensely negative feelings toward the opposing side. For the same reasons, they may also be willing to tolerate constitutional hardball – actions that advance partisan causes by pushing the boundaries of the Constitution in ways that may be technically legal but that violate preexisting norms – so long as it helps their side win.[43]

Such developments can be devastating to the health of democracy. Indeed, Philip Rocco's chapter in this volume highlights the effects that hardball tactics have already had on state-level democracy. When hardball is not punished, crucial democratic norms and the rule of law are imperiled: Actions that make elections less free and fair, that make political participation less inclusive, that harm the protection of civil rights and liberties, and that undermine – or ignore – the rule of law are all accepted by some voters to a greater extent than they would be otherwise.[44]

WEAPONIZED IDENTITIES AND THE HIDDEN INFLUENCE OF THE ULTRA-WEALTHY

Finally, in decreasing the likelihood that even attentive voters will enforce their policy preferences, fear-based politics may paradoxically complement the efforts of ultra-rich individuals to advance narrowly self-interested economic policies that are opposed by most Americans. In this sense, the NRA's tactics help us further understand how politicians can promote unpopular economic policies without facing substantial electoral consequences – a topic that is more closely explored in chapters written by Alexander Hertel-Fernandez and Philip Rocco that appear elsewhere in this volume.[45]

Many American billionaires engage in what I – along with co-authors Benjamin Page and Jason Seawright – describe as stealth politics. In

---

[43] Joseph Fishkin and David E. Pozen, "Asymmetric Constitutional Hardball," *Columbia Law Review* 118 (2018) 915–82; Jacob S. Hacker and Paul Pierson, "The Republican Devolution," *Foreign Affairs* 98, no. 4 (July/August 2019): 42–50; Mark Tushnet, "Constitutional Hardball," *John Marshall Law Review* 37 (2004): 523–53.

[44] Robert C. Lieberman, Suzanne Mettler, Thomas B. Pepinsky, Kenneth M. Roberts, and Richard Valelly, "The Trump Presidency and American Democracy: A Historical and Comparative Analysis," *Perspectives on Politics* 17, no. 2 (2019): 470–79.

[45] See also, Rocco, "Laboratories of What?"

a systematic study of the 100 wealthiest Americans, we found that many billionaires are exceptionally politically active and work hard to move public policy – especially on issues related to redistribution – in a conservative direction that is opposed by average Americans. However, despite this activity and their abundant opportunities to speak out, billionaires – especially those who favor conservative policies – tend to be totally silent about policy specifics in public. As a result, the (likely substantial) political influence billionaires have often comes without the potential for public accountability or countermobilization from ordinary citizens.[46]

As a political strategy, stealth politics differs from fear-based politics in important ways; in the former, a relatively tiny number of individuals very quietly use financial resources to advance their agendas, whereas in the latter organizations build mass-based, ideational power that enables them to mobilize relatively large numbers of individuals on behalf of their agendas.

However, despite these differences, the two strategies are similar in that they contribute to the advancement of policies favored by wealthy political actors that are unpopular with most Americans. Moreover, fear-based politics can actually provide cover for stealth politics; when voters are driven more by group allegiances than policy and are unwilling or unable to enforce their issue preferences, it is easier for politicians to pass unpopular policies without being punished. Billionaires' use of stealth politics to pursue unpopular economic policies is by design already difficult to detect – and fear-based politics may make it even harder for voters to identify the political actions of the ultra-rich.

Not only could this further reduce democratic accountability, but it might also contribute to broader trends that have harmed American democracy. Most notably, it fits neatly with what Jacob Hacker and Paul Pierson have termed "plutocratic populism," in which politicians win elections using populistic rhetoric but then enact policies favored by plutocrats (which then seems to increase subsequent demand for populism).[47] In line with this theme, Trumpian populism – which closely resembles the NRA's worldview – has been used to advance policies favored by the ultra-rich. Indeed, despite clashes between Trump and some prominent billionaires (most notably the Koch brothers), many

---

[46] Benjamin I. Page, Jason Seawright, and Matthew J. Lacombe, *Billionaires and Stealth Politics* (Chicago: University of Chicago Press, 2019).
[47] Hacker and Pierson, *Let Them Eat Tweets*.

wealthy Americans ultimately supported Trump – and he delivered them some major policy wins, including a massive and highly unequal tax cut in 2017.[48] In sum, although the identity-based efforts of organized groups like the NRA are distinct from the efforts of ultra-wealthy Americans who engage in stealth politics, they may threaten democratic resilience in interrelated ways.

CONCLUSION

The NRA has achieved substantial political success by working the levers of mass democracy in ways that advance its agenda. Despite its success at using democracy to its advantage, however, this chapter makes the case that the NRA has contributed to the sorts of troubling trends discussed throughout this volume. Its approach to politics enhances polarization, encourages the use of hardball tactics that erode democratic norms, and reduces democratic accountability.

In light of the argument made here, the NRA's prominent position within the Republican Party should be troubling not just to proponents of gun control, but to anyone who is concerned about the problems currently facing American democracy. The NRA's prominence in the GOP does indeed help it advance gun rights; more broadly, however, it also provides wider traction to the NRA's fear-based, right-wing populist political worldview. This worldview predates the rise of Donald Trump and – given its alignment with so many other conservative-leaning identities – will outlast his presidency.

This chapter also raises questions about what other groups – including those that favor gun control – can learn from the NRA, as well as the extent to which it is *desirable* for other groups to adopt its approach to politics. The NRA's successful use of democracy should in some ways be inspiring to other groups. Insofar as the NRA's political success is related more to mass-mobilization than to its use of financial resources, it suggests that groups can build and use power by cultivating mass-based resources – such as group identities – rather than relying solely on the help of moneyed interests. But the case of the NRA also shows that an identity-based approach to group mobilization can have some negative consequences

---

[48] Ibid.; Alexander Hertel-Fernandez, Theda Skocpol, and Jason Sclar, "When Political Mega-Donors Join Forces: How the Koch Network and the Democracy Alliance Influence Organized U.S. Politics on the Right and Left," *Studies in American Political Development* 32, no. 2 (2018): 127–65.

for democracy, which suggests that it may not be desirable for groups to wholesale adopt the NRA's use of fear-based tactics.

The challenge, then, is for groups to build identity-based, mobilizational power in a way that does not rely on fear and vilification. And this is indeed a substantial challenge; in an era characterized by intense polarization, many groups may be tempted to use their political opponents as foils in order to mobilize their members. In fact, ascendant groups working *on behalf* of gun control have recently started vilifying the NRA as part of their mobilization efforts. In a fundraising message sent in early 2019, for example, Everytown for Gun Safety described the NRA as being "fueled by profit-hungry gun manufacturers and right-wing zealots." The appeal then said that "[t]oday's NRA is unaccountable, unhinged, and must be stopped" before asking for contributions.[49] Although gun control advocacy groups may believe that the use of such appeals is warranted by the severity of the gun violence problem in the United States and the pro-gun dogmatism of the NRA, their adoption of fear-based tactics may nonetheless produce democratically harmful externalities, enhancing affective polarization among Americans who feel strongly about the gun debate and further inflaming gun owners who believe their political opponents are out to get them.

Building mobilizational power while also resisting the temptation to rely on fear and vilification likely involves hard work, but it has the potential to help groups advance their causes in ways that produce positive – rather than negative – externalities for democracy. As Hahrie Han, Elizabeth McKenna, and Michelle Oyakawa's work on activism demonstrates, by bringing people together in person and providing them with skills to collectively act on behalf of their shared interests – not just their shared resentments – groups can build shared identities around communities that transcend (rather than reinforce) "the differences that normally divide Americans."[50] The source of the NRA's power, in other words, can – at least under the right conditions – be replicated without the use of its tactics.

---

[49] Rob Wilcox, "Celebration of Extremism," email message sent to Everytown for Gun Safety members, April 16, 2019.
[50] Hahrie Han, Elizabeth McKenna, and Michelle Oyakawa, *Prisms of the People: Power and Organizing in Twenty-First-Century Century America* (Chicago: University of Chicago Press, 2021).

PART IV

VICIOUS CIRCLES? THE RELATIONSHIP BETWEEN POLARIZED BEHAVIOR AND INSTITUTIONS

11

Polarization, the Administrative State, and Executive-Centered Partisanship[*]

Desmond King and Sidney M. Milkis

Fierce partisan conflict in the United States is not new. Throughout American history, there have been polarizing struggles over fundamental questions relating to the meaning of the Declaration, the Constitution, and the relationship between the two. These struggles over ideals have become all encompassing when joined to battles over what it means to be an "American" – conflicts that have become more regular and dangerous with the rise of the administrative state. The idea of a "State" cuts more deeply than suggested by Max Weber's definition of "a human community that (successfully) claims the monopoly of the legitimate use of physical force within a given territory."[1] Beyond the powers of government, the State represents a centralizing ambition (at least for progressive reformers) to cultivate, or impose, a vision of citizenship. In Randolph Bourne's words, the State is a "concept of power" that comes alive in defense of or in conflict with an ideal of how such foundational values of Americanism as "free and enlightened" are to be interpreted and enforced. The ideal is symbolized not by the Declaration and the Constitution but rather in rallying emblems such as the flag and Uncle Sam. A key mobilizing force is patriotism, a concept at once centralizing and conflictual.[2]

---

[*] The authors thank Sidney Tarrow of Cornell University and the editors of this volume for their incisive and helpful comments on earlier drafts of this chapter. We also express our gratitude to Jacob Asch and Katharine Huiskes, University of Virginia students, for their dedicated research in support of this project.
[1] From *Max Weber: Essays in Sociology*, ed. Hans H. Gerth and C. Wright Mills (London: Routledge & Kegan Paul, 1948), p51.
[2] Randolph Bourne, "The State," 1918 Accessed January 3, 2018. http://fair-use.org/randolph-bourne/the-state/.

For a time, a fragile consensus that obscured partisan conflict over national administrative power sustained the executive-centered administrative state, consolidated during the protracted presidency of Franklin Roosevelt. The subordination of partisanship to administration was abetted by the development of independent regulatory commissions and a civil service that endowed the New Deal State with a commitment to expertise – "neutral competence" – that privileged pragmatic policymaking in the service of economic and national security,[3] and sought impeccable standards of public service. Partisan politics reached a low ebb as citizens held high trust in government, and majorities of both parties largely agreed about the direction of domestic and foreign policy, so long as national programs did not disturb a racialized political order with partial civil rights.

The public support for the national state that prevailed from the 1940s through the late 1960s and early 1970s fractured in the wake of the cultural, civil rights, and political upheavals of the Sixties. The attempt to realize the Great Society exposed the liberal State's central fault lines (notably racial inequalities), and with violent upheaval in Vietnam and in the nation's urban core, the pragmatic center that buttressed the New Deal disintegrated. Once contested by conservative Democrats and Republicans as an existential threat to constitutional government, national administrative power gained acceptance on the right as both parties came to see the advantages of claiming credit for administrative accomplishment.

As a consequence, partisanship in the United States is no longer a struggle over the size of the State. It is an executive-centered struggle for the services of national administrative power. Despite rhetorical appeals to "limited government," since the late 1960s, conservatives have sought to deploy state power as ardently as liberals.

This is not to suggest that the conservative attack on government is unimportant. Republicans' rhetorical assault on the Liberal State is consistent with their persistent efforts to weaken social welfare programs and, more generally, to remake the administrative state through "privatization" and outsourcing. By the same token, less hostile to government than conservatives, liberals display a lingering commitment to the pragmatism and expertise that are the cachet of the administrative state forged during the New Deal. However, since the late Sixties, conservatives have pursued

---

[3] Herbert Kaufman identifies the "quest for neutral competence" as a core commitment in the development of the administrative state. "Emerging Conflicts in the Doctrines of Public Administration, *The American Political Science Review* 50, no. 4 (December 1956): 1057–73.

programs and policies that would restore traditional values and commitments that they alleged liberalism had weakened. Consequently, while Liberals seek to build administrative capacity to design and implement social welfare policies, conservatives have sought to redeploy and extend that power in pursuit of their own partisan goals (while often espousing anti-state sentiments): enhancing national defense, homeland security, border-protection, and local policing; and establishing more market-oriented policies in education, climate change, and government service.

The election and presidency of Donald Trump confirms that executive power is the vanguard of an enervating contest between liberal and conservative policy demands, which weakens the system of checks and balances, diminishes the integrity of decentralizing constitutional institutions like Congress and the states, and erodes citizens' trust in the competence and fairness of the national government. Because his administration has used executive power so aggressively, most scholars and pundits place Trump outside the tradition of American conservative thought, and many regard him as a disruptive force inside conservatism's institutional vessel, the Republican Party. We deny this presumption.

Our core argument is that the association of conservative Republicanism and retrenchment elides a critical change in the relationship between party politics and executive power, which Donald Trump determinedly nurtured – the rise of executive-centered partisanship characterized by presidential unilateralism, social activism, and polarizing struggles over questions of national identity that sharply divide the nation by race, ethnicity, and religion.[4]

As the first impeachment inquiry in Congress highlighted, however, the Trump presidency represents a challenge to American constitutional government, in the sense that long-standing rules and norms are belittled and circumnavigated. Although both Democrat and Republican presidents have centralized power in the White House since the Nixon years, attenuating protocols and institutions that maintain departments and agencies as neutral sites of public policy, the Trump administration represents the strongest expression to date of this denigration of "bureaucratic autonomy,"[5] a disdain confirmed in the dramatic Executive Order on

---

[4] Nicholas F. Jacobs, Desmond King, and Sidney M. Milkis, "Building a Conservative State: Partisan Polarization and the Redeployment of Administrative Power, *Perspectives on Politics* 17, no. 2, June 2019: 453–69.

[5] Daniel P. Carpenter, *The Forging of Bureaucratic Autonomy: Reputations, Networks, and Policy Innovation in Executive Agencies, 1862–1928* (Princeton: Princeton University Press, 2001).

October 22, 2020, re-politicizing the civil service by reversing the foundational Pendleton Act of 1883.[6]

BATTLING FOR THE SERVICES OF THE ADMINISTRATIVE STATE

Executive-centered partisanship in the United States sits at the crosscurrents of two related phenomena in American political development. First, the form of party contestation that allowed Trump to capture the Republican nomination is a consequence of organizational and electoral reforms that weakened the decentralized, patronage-based parties that dominated most of the nineteenth century. Throughout the twentieth century, both parties were pressured by insurgent movements to alter the rules governing the presidential selection process – ostensibly to give more power to "the people" in selecting candidates for office and in determining party priorities. However, the pursuit of "participatory democracy" did not empower the Downsian median-voter; rather, the weakening of traditional party organizations enhanced the influence of donors, interest groups and social activists who scorned the pragmatic politics and compromises hitherto credited with forging majority coalitions.[7] Median-voter theory becomes redundant as radical Republicans shift further to the right and Democrats gradually follow suit.

The effect of those reforms is enhanced by a second development: the creation of a presidential institution formed in pursuance of the 1939 Executive Reorganization Act. With the creation of the Executive Office of the President, comprised of the White House Office (the West Wing) and important staff agencies like the Office of Management and Budget, the president could form alliances with activists and outside groups who disdained the party "establishment," thus subordinating decentralized and pluralistic party coalitions to the more national and programmatic networks that shape contemporary partisan politics.

The support for an executive-centered administrative state was consolidated by the programmatic commitments of New Deal liberalism. As FDR argued in his State of the Union message of 1941, traditional freedoms like speech and religion needed to be supplemented by two new

---

[6] www.washingtonpost.com/politics/trump-order-federal-civil-service/2020/10/22/c73783 f0-1481-11eb-bc10-40b25382f1be_story.html. President Joseph Biden quickly rescinded this executive action on taking office.
[7] Morton Keller, *America's Three Regimes: A New Political History* (Oxford: Oxford University Press, 2007).

rights: "freedom from want" and "freedom from fear." These new freedoms, representing for all intents and purposes the charter of the modern American state, were given institutional form by the welfare and national security states. The "Four Freedoms" speech ushered in a new understanding of rights, sanctified by the "Constitutional Revolution of 1937," under which domestic programs like Social Security and international causes like the Cold War called not for partisanship, but for "enlightened administration" (as Roosevelt had described his New Deal aspiration in his 1932 speech at the Commonwealth Club). Politics was now a search for pragmatic solutions to the challenging responsibilities that America had to assume, at home and abroad, in the wake of the Great Depression and World War II.[8] From the end of the Second World War to the late 1960s, party politics was largely subordinated to a policy-making state, where partisan conflict and resolution were displaced by a new understanding of rights and the delivery of services associated with those rights.[9]

However, recent institutional developments and changes in the dynamics of partisanship in the wake of the Sixties upheaval, encouraged the White House to deploy executive power in the service of partisan objectives. Beginning with the presidency of Richard Nixon, party conflict has roiled the administrative state forged during the Progressive and New Deal eras. Most accounts of our present discontents emphasize polarization in Congress, but the modern executive has embraced and advanced partisan polarization itself as White House incumbents become more single-party identified and less national unifiers. The fractious politics in Congress, which have not only sharply divided Democrats and Republicans but also created internal disputes within the legislative caucuses, have made parties even more dependent on presidents to advance their objectives. Republican presidents, especially Ronald Reagan and George W. Bush, pioneered the art of mobilizing partisan opinion and exploiting administrative power for their partisan objectives.[10] During the

---

[8] Sidney M. Milkis, "Ideas, Institutions, and the New Deal Constitutional Order," *American Political Thought* 3, no. 1 (Spring 2014): 167–76.

[9] Sidney M. Milkis, *The President and the Parties: The Transformation of the American Party System Since the New Deal* (Oxford: Oxford University Press, 1993), 143; Karen Orren and Stephen Skowronek, *The Policy State: An American Predicament* (Cambridge: Harvard University Press, 2017).

[10] Daniel J. Galvin, *Presidential Party Building: Dwight D. Eisenhower to George W. Bush.* (Princeton: Princeton University Press, 2010); Daniel J. Galvin, "Presidents as Agents of Change," *Presidential Studies Quarterly* 44, no. 1 (March 2014): 95–119.

2008 campaign, Barack Obama presented himself as a transcendent leader who could imbue the policy state with new causes and moral fervor. Yet, by the time he reached office, it no longer seemed possible for presidents to stand apart from partisan combat; more to the point, partisan polarization had come to so divide Congress and advocacy groups in Washington that the Obama administration had strong incentives to take refuge and pursue progressive policies in the administrative presidency.

Obama's partisanship was a critical prelude to Trump's tactics and policies. Indeed, it is impossible to understand the momentum and force of Trump's presidency without taking account of Obama's sustained reliance on partisan administration. Scholars and pundits have usually depicted Obama as a prisoner of partisan rancor in Congress, which was especially fierce and obstructive on the Republican side of the aisle during his two terms in office. To the contrary, he actively – if sometimes reluctantly – embraced the role of party leader, even in the management of the bureaucracy, the arena in which the modern presidency's claim to transcend partisanship was nurtured.[11]

During the final six years of this presidency, when Obama faced a Congress with at least one chamber controlled by Republicans, he surpassed the institutional strategies of the Bush administration in combining programmatic achievement and partisan calculation.[12] Most of his executive actions were directed to strengthening a widely scattered but potentially powerful coalition that had been forming since the Great Society: minorities, youth, the LGBTQ community, and educated white voters, especially single women. Many of Obama's administrative actions in the service of environmental protection, women's rights, and criminal justice reform appealed to those constituencies. Similarly, the administration's direction to the Justice Department in February 2011 to stop defending the Defense of Marriage Act (DOMA), which barred federal recognition of same-sex marriage, against constitutional challenges sealed the White House's partnership with the LGBTQ movement. Perhaps the most significant and polarizing action the Obama administration took to strengthen support of this coalition was in the controversial matter of immigration. Failing to reach an agreement with the Republican Congress on comprehensive immigration reform, Obama took strong administrative action that provided deportation relief and work authorizations to

---

[11] Kenneth Lowande and Sidney M. Milkis, "'We Can't Wait': Barack Obama, Partisan Polarization, and the Administrative Presidency," *The Forum* 12, no. 1 (2014): 3–27.
[12] Ibid.

more than 5 million undocumented immigrants. These administrative initiatives in support of the "Dreamers" (DACA) and parents of permanent residents and citizens (DAPA) greatly strengthened Obama's often-fraught relationship with the immigration rights movement. As Marielena Hincapié of the National Immigration Law Center announced, this meeting of the minds between the Obama administration and social movement organizations was "one of the rare times in history when the White House and activists are completely in agreement."[13] It is not coincidental, therefore, that Obama's immigration initiatives defined the lines of rancorous partisan conflict in Congress, the courts, and the 2016 election campaign.

Although the political philosophies and policy objectives of Obama and Trump could not be more antithetical, the style of politics they practice reflects two key areas of common ground: a detachment from party organization and a vision of the White House as the vanguard of a movement. Obama planned his administration as a progressive crusade that marked a new stage in the fusion of executive power and partisan politics. He coupled his ambitious administrative strategy with an innovative political organization dedicated to linking him directly with potential supporters. Born during the 2008 campaign as "Obama for America," this mass mobilization effort was incorporated into the Democratic National Committee as "Organizing for America" during Obama's first term in the White House; after 2012, the group was spun off as a non-profit social welfare agency called "Organizing for Action" (OFA). Obama's information-age, grassroots tool was critical not only to his two presidential campaigns, but also to the enactment of major legislative reform including the 2010 Affordable Care Act. When Obama removed his organization from the Democratic National Committee with the promise that it would strengthen its potential as a grassroots movement, he further solidified an executive-centered Democratic Party. Candidate-centered organizations had been a staple of American politics since the Kennedy administration, but Obama was the first president to keep his electoral machine intact as the vanguard of a movement that would free

---

[13] News Conference of Immigration Advocacy Leaders, White House, February 25, 2015, SM, https://docs.google.com/presentation/d/11CrmZFoMLxxLH-EUrG7aOWTFggDF KI62WxD5U4w3xQ/edit#slide=id. The DAPA initiative was blocked by the courts until the Trump administration repealed it. Muzaffar Chishti and Faye Hipsman, "Supreme Court DAPA Ruling a Blow to Obama Administration: Moves Immigration Back to the Political Realm," *Immigration Information Service,* June 29, 2016, www.migrationpo licy.org/article/supreme-court-dapa-ruling-blow-obama-administration-moves-immigra tion-back-political-realm.

him from the constraints of the Democratic "establishment" and connect him directly to a new progressive coalition. Significantly, just as Obama's attention shifted to executive action in 2011, OFA redeployed his staff and volunteers to defend the president's administrative initiatives, touting with special urgency the unilateralism which would advance climate change policy, LGBTQ rights, and immigration reform.[14]

Trump's odds-defying ascendance to the presidency in 2016 appeared to complete the fusion of centralized administration and partisanship. Trump lacked an independent grassroots machine as organized or as institutionally sophisticated as Obama's. However, his reliance on variegated media platforms (social and traditional) galvanized his supporters with the same fervor and passion as liberal advocates under OFA. Trump did not disband his movement at the end of the campaign; rather, the president-elect took off on a "thank you tour" during the transition period, revealing his determination to continue to holding mass rallies after he entered the White House.[15] In campaign-style rallies since then – averaging two a month – he has energized his supporters and renewed their faith that the president speaks for them, and them alone. With the approach of the 2020 election, Trump rallies became more meticulously produced than the spontaneous and thinly staffed events of his first presidential campaign. Although no longer covered by cable networks, the campaign turned them into "giant, roving field offices that vacuum up personal data from rallygoers, register new voters and sign up his most enthusiastic supporters as volunteers."[16] Despite a raging and deadly pandemic in the closing months of the 2020 presidential contest, Trump appeared personally without a face mask at a rolling sequence of rallies.

Obama saw himself as the leader of a new "coalition of the ascendant"; Trump and his strategists positioned him as the steward of a "coalition of restoration" comprised of blue-collar, religiously devout, and nonurban

---

[14] Sidney M. Milkis and John W. York, "Barack Obama, Organizing for America, and Executive-Centered Partisanship," *Studies in American Political Development* 31, no. 1 (2017): 1–23.

[15] For Donald Trump's full remarks, see: "Read: Full Transcript of Trump's Rally Speech in Florida," *Palm Beach Post*, February 28, 2017, www.palmbeachpost.com/news/national/read-full-transcript-trump-rally-speech-florida/DeDCpoNEKLQmWcIKndWBoM/.

[16] Michael C. Bender, "Trump Rallies Are No Longer Side Shows: They Are the Campaign." October 22, 2019, *Wall Street Journal*, www.wsj.com/articles/trumps-rallies-arent-just-part-of-his-campaign-they-are-the-campaign-11571753199?emailToken=4e4ef9f43181f d56dbccf3obe4144e2eCy3Snv74/29dkuJoflIGiRljcDyayQDuansy8YT+aFdHmnOA5Bt PbcNaXt2QDHoguAsltZJXgf3vm/UpXA+vZKgqGM4ec2okJogoKVBcho1KSllp3w4jiv SOytga9xdp5+IycUXbjoloYmuCS7qVdQ%3D%3D&reflink=article_email_share.

whites who feel that traditional Republican politicians had forsaken their needs and demands.[17] As president, Trump surpassed Obama in attending to his base. As much as Obama paid tribute to the civil rights activists of a previous generation who made his political ascendance possible, and as much as he hoped to channel the popular energies of his 2008 campaign into a formidable movement of his own, the imperatives of his administration and of social movements remained at odds. Emblematic of the Democratic Party's regnant allegiance to nonpartisan administration, Obama accommodated his message of change to persistent efforts to reprise the policy state. "Obama himself was an activist and a community organizer ... – but he is not, by temperament, a protester," noted Ta-Nehisi Coates after a series of interviews with the president.

> He is a consensus builder; consensus, he believes, ultimately drives what gets done. He understands the emotional power of protest, the need to vent before authority – but that kind of approach does not come naturally to him ... The notion that a president would attempt to achieve change within the boundaries of the accepted consensus is appropriate. But Obama is almost constitutionally skeptical of those who seek to achieve change outside the consensus.[18]

In contrast to Obama's persistent, albeit frustrated, efforts to transcend partisanship, Trump's efforts to mobilize support for his controversial plans to "Make America Great Again" entailed unrelenting appeals to core supporters. Despite pleas among fellow Republicans to act "more presidential," Trump relished his administration's unapologetic support for, as one White House aide put it, the former businessman's most "loyal customers."[19] The diminishing but still spirited band of Never-Trump conservatives have bewailed Trump's war cry that America is no longer a great nation, but the stooge of its international trading partners and the victim of predatory immigrants. (Accruing an additional 5 million votes in 2020 over his 2016 win, seemed to vindicate Trump's strategy.) Such a dire message, they lamented, abandoned the more uplifting conservatism that Ronald Reagan expressed – a conservatism that insisted, in opposition to the post-Sixties Liberals anti-imperialism, that America still was a "city on a hill." This message of resilience and religious tolerance inspired the position that Reagan heir-apparent George W. Bush projected in the wake of the attacks of September 11, 2001. The first

---

[17] Ronald Brownstein, "The Clinton Conundrum," *The Atlantic* April 17 2015, at www.theatlantic.com/politics/archive/2015/04/the-clinton-conundrum/431949/.
[18] Ta-Nehisi Coates, "My President Was Black," *Atlantic*, January/February 2017.
[19] Interview with White House Aide, not for attribution, May 28, 2019.

sentence of the 2016 Republican platform read: "We believe in American exceptionalism," an uplifting sentiment that Trump virtually ignored during the long and bitter 2016 contest.

Nevertheless, this nostalgia for the Reagan "Revolution" overlooks how, under these kinder and gentler partisans, the Republican Party built a conservative base whose foot soldiers, most notably the Christian Right (which Reagan enlisted in his administration's conservative crusade) and the Obama-era Tea Party, which Republican presidential candidates had been courting since its inception, rallied around the belief that liberalism had so corrupted the country that the national government had the responsibility to support "family values" (a view that permeates proposals to restrict abortion and same-sex marriage; to require work for welfare; and to impose standards on secondary and elementary schools). The unyielding opposition of the Christian Right and the Tea Party to Obama's efforts to change the arc of the Reagan Revolution decisively turned the Republican Party against the liberal administrative state, and its ferocious opposition to the nation's first African American president, although first aroused by Obama's pursuit of comprehensive health insurance reform, was rooted in deep cultural issues that reopened the festering wounds of the civil rights revolution and the opposition it spawned.

Significantly, Trump, a thrice-married and one-time New York liberal, received strong support not only from Tea Party activists but also from conservative evangelical leaders. One of his strongest champions was Ralph Reed, chairman of the Faith and Reform Coalition. Recounting the Christian Right's long march toward a leading place in the conservative coalition, Reed expressed appreciation for Trump's strong pledge to make appointments to the administration and the Supreme Court who would oppose abortion, stand up to for the traditional family, and protect Christian Schools from the Department of Education.[20] Other crucial defenders included Liberty University President Jerry Falwell, Jr., Focus on the Family's James Dobson, and Family Research Council's Tony Perkins. "We're not electing a pastor-in-chief," Falwell, echoing the pragmatism his father expressed in championing the candidacy of Ronald Reagan, explained to Fox News during the campaign. "Sometimes you have to be pragmatic. You have to choose the one with the best chance of winning and who is closest to your views."[21]

---

[20] Katie Glueck, "Christian Leaders See Influence Growing on Trump," *Politico*, November 25, 2016.
[21] Jerry Falwell, Jr. interview on Fox Business News, September 27, 2016.

Appealing to a restive Republican base agitated by movement conservatives, the 2012 Republican candidate Mitt Romney embraced a punitive immigration policy – endorsing Arizona's ultimately unconstitutional "show-me-your-papers" law and calling on undocumented immigrants to "self-deport" by denying them public benefits and fostering a subclass status that would drive most to leave. GOP state officials and congressional members soon embraced harsh crackdowns on unauthorized immigration and demonized undocumented immigrants.

Consequently, as Douglas McAdams and Karina Kloos argue, conservative activists were ensconced in the Republican Party before the 2016 election.[22] Against this backdrop, Trump's ascendance was not only due to demagogic anti-immigrant appeals. His political success is also attributable to his giving unfiltered expression to the marriage of Republican presidents and right-wing social movements that was more than four decades in the making. Foreign-born individuals now make up about 14 percent of the US population, historically the same levels as in the late nineteenth and early twentieth century, which, as Nolan McCarty has pointed out, is the other period in American history roiled by ritualized partisan combat.[23] This era ended in a draconian immigration law, enacted in 1924, which "settled" this issue for a generation. To a point, Trump's appeal to the Republican base has been fueled by the economic despair of a declining working class. Yet the major factor in his elevation to the White House was an appeal to fear, often racialized, and to the feeling of a large number of Americans that immigrants are responsible not only for the country's economic problems, but also for the terrible threat that "radical Islamic terrorism" and undocumented immigrants pose to the security of the homeland.

DONALD TRUMP AND THE REDEPLOYMENT OF THE AMERICAN STATE

As a candidate, Trump denounced the Obama administration's "major power grabs of authority." But as president, he not only rescinded Obama-era actions, but also redeployed administrative power to serve conservative objectives. Moreover, Trump has appointed three Supreme

---

[22] Douglas McAdams and Karina Kloos, *Deeply Divided: Racial Policies and Social Movements in Postwar America* (Oxford: Oxford University Press, 2014).

[23] Nolan McCarty, "Polarization and American Political Development," in *Oxford Handbook of American Political Development*, ed. Richard M. Valelly, Suzanne Mettler, and Robert C. Lieberman (Oxford: Oxford University Press, 2016), pp. 492–515.

Court justices – Neil Gorsuch, Brett Kavanaugh, and Amy Coney Barret – and a large number of District and Appellate judges – who will likely shift the balance on the court toward greater acceptance of public action that advances conservative policies in national security, protection of the homeland, policing, and civil rights. Trump's imprint on the judiciary loomed large in the sharply divided Supreme Court's approval of a Muslim ban, albeit a modified version of the original order that was blocked by the lower courts, and the emergency decree to build the Wall.

Trump's partisanship did not abrogate the administrative state, as many critics alleged. Rather, by shifting resources between departments and agencies, inserting policy activists in key administrative positions, and repurposing policies, he redeployed administrative power to serve a racialized politics of fear. Ignoring the burden of Senate confirmation for senior appointments, Trump relied excessively on making 'acting' appointees to key offices. As Figures 11.1 and 11.2 show, Trump's substantial cuts to the Departments of State, Labor, and Education were more than offset by his administration's expansion of personnel in the Departments of Veteran Affairs, Defense, and Homeland Security. However, the Trump White House's partisan strategy also included concerted efforts to protect favored constituencies by recasting social welfare policies as conservative programs and redistributing resources in the Departments of Health and Human Services, Education, and Justice (see Table 11.1).

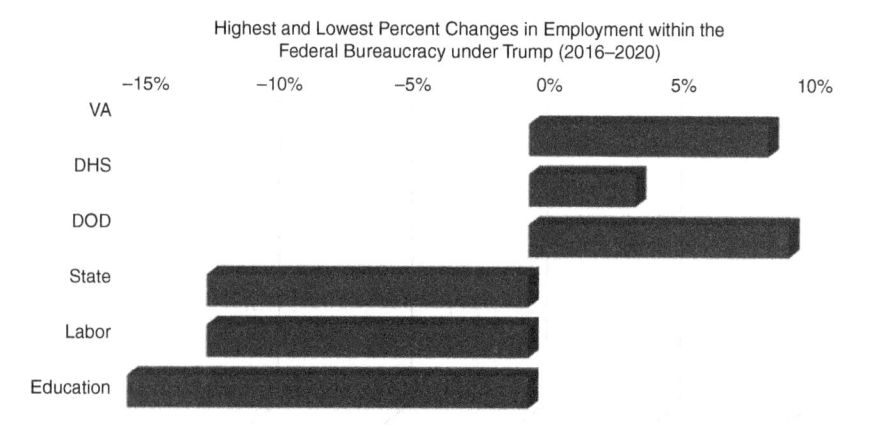

FIGURE 11.1 Highest and lowest percent changes in employment within the federal bureaucracy under Trump (2016–2020)
Source: www.govexec.com/pay-benefits/2019/04/all-three-cabinet-level-departments-have-shed-jobs-under-trump/156500/

On-Board Personnel (Federal Civilian Employees) 2016–2019

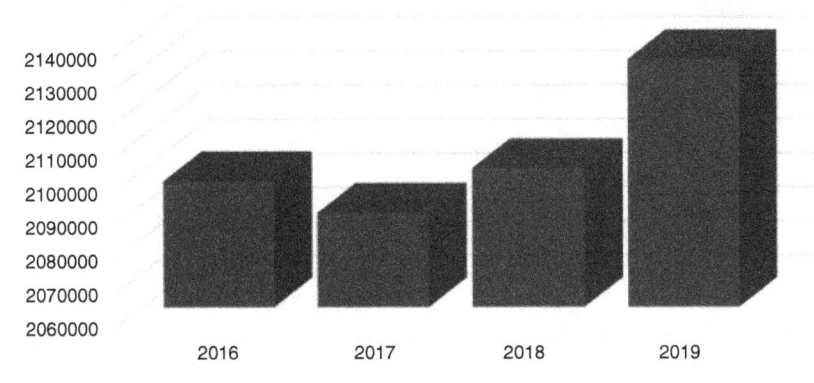

FIGURE 11.2 On-board personnel (federal civilian employees), 2016–2019
Note from the original report: Each total is an "on-board" count for September of the year noted. Current coverage does not include the Board of Governors of the Federal Reserve, Central Intelligence Agency, Defense Intelligence Agency, foreign service personnel at the State Department, National Geospatial-Intelligence Agency, National Security Agency, Office of the Director of National Intelligence, Office of the Vice President, Postal Regulatory Commission, Tennessee Valley Authority, US Postal Service, White House Office, foreign nationals overseas, Public Health Service's Commissioned Officer Corps, non-appropriated fund employees, selected legislative branch agencies, the judicial branch, or the military.
Source: https://fas.org/sgp/crs/misc/R43590.pdf

Protecting the Homeland

Trump's partisan administration on immigration has been especially polarizing. For decades, no Republican candidate had been able to unite the party behind a comprehensive immigration plan. However, by constantly stoking his base, the president rallied partisan support for his immigration policies. Again, Trump galvanized rather than created party differences. Republican voters had been trending toward nativist positions before Trump's candidacy. But Trump made undocumented immigration his signature issue and a core commitment of Republican partisanship: just 10 percent of Americans in February 2016 believed immigration to be the primary problem facing the country; by July 2019, immigration had risen to the top of the list of the most important issues in the country,

TABLE 11.1 *Trump Administration Executive Actions: 2017–2019*

Social welfare policies	National and Homeland Security
– Medicaid work requirement waivers for states, which reportedly were never studied thoroughly and may cost the federal government millions of dollars	– Increase in the budget of DHS to handle the border
– Rules allowing the importation of prescription drugs from other countries	– The Trump administration was prepared to add a citizenship question to the census (Blocked by the Supreme Court)
– CMS rule requiring that drug makers list prices on consumer advertising	– Drastic cuts to refugee admittance during the Trump administration
– Reduced outreach substantially for the Affordable Care Act.	– Public Charge regulations **to prevent less fortunate migrants from coming to America and** to make it difficult for undocumented immigrants to access safety-net resources
– Secretary of Education Betsy Devos worked with private collection agencies to crack down on student loan borrowers	– Plans to build 450 miles of border wall in addition to the hundreds of miles of repaired fencing with DOD funds, which increased drastically during Trump's tenure
– Proposed Tax Credits to encourage school choice	– Threatened to sue California over homelessness crisis
– Made it far more difficult for students to get their loans discharged or reduced through various avenues	– Deployed national guard and military to southern border
– Used federal funds to buy out employees of the Education Dept.	– Increased worksite enforcement of immigration law
– HUD disparate impact rule, which would raise the burden of proof for those seeking to prove discrimination in housing	– Presided over a large increase in ICE budget requests in order to handle the new, stricter immigration enforcement regime
– Rescinded Title IX guidelines in Department of Education	– Rapidly increased, or threatened tariffs on various countries creating trade tensions with adversaries and allies alike.
– The DOJ supported state laws that could remove thousands of people from voter rolls; pulled back on robust oversight of police	– Rescinded DAPA and DACA

(continued)

TABLE 11.1 *(continued)*

Social welfare policies	National and Homeland Security
departments found to have violated the rights of citizens in their jurisdictions; supported religious conservatives in business and local government who have resisted the advance of LBGTQ rights; and sided with plaintiffs challenging affirmative action plans in higher education	
– Created Conscience and Religious Freedom Division in HHS to "more vigorously and effectively enforce existing laws protecting the rights of conscience and religious freedom"	– Attempted to use the power of the federal government to crack down on sanctuary cities
Issued a rule that would require "able-bodied" adults without dependents to work at least 20 hours a week to keep their Supplemental Nutrition Assistance Program benefits (formerly known as food stamps)	Established a new form of information sharing between the Office of Refugee Resettlement, which sits within Health and Human Services, and Immigration and Customs Enforcement (ICE), housed in the Department of Homeland Security, that puts those who seek to take custody of migrant children at risk of deportation

Source: Authors' Compilation

with 22 percent of Americans – and 35 percent of Republicans – citing it as the major problem facing the nation.[24]

Given the way he centered Republican partisanship on immigration, Trump's decision to declare a national emergency and redirect nearly $3.6 billion in military construction appropriations for a border wall was neither a show of force nor a sign of institutional weakness.[25] It was a rational strategy for an institution that derives its power from

---

[24] The percentage of Americans indicating immigration as the most important problem was so small in 2016 that Gallup did not record a partisan differential. Information on 2016 and 2019 numbers were documented in the Internet Archive, www.gallup.com. See also, Frank Newport, "Immigration Surges to Top of Most Important Problem List," *Gallup*, July 18, 2018.

[25] "Declaring a National Emergency Concerning the Southern Border of the United States," Proclamation 9844. February 15, 2019. Federal Registrar, vol. 84, no. 34, pp. 4949–50.

exacerbating partisan divisions, energizing its most ardent supporters, and flouting constitutional restraints in the name of "the people." By the time Congress exercised its statutory obligation, according to the terms established by the National Emergency Act of 1976, to approve or disavow the president's emergency declaration, esoteric constitutional deliberation gave way completely to visceral presidential partisanship. As Trump threatened in an interview with Fox News several weeks before the vote, "I really think that Republicans that vote against border security and the wall ... put themselves at great jeopardy."[26] Not surprisingly, few Republicans challenged the president, and those who did risked the ire of his fiercely loyal supporters. Senator Thom Tillis (R-NC) witnessed the specter of a potential primary challenge after he disavowed the president's emergency declaration; so credible was the threat that even after Tillis authored a widely publicized op-ed against Trump, he switched his position and voted for the president's declaration.[27] In the House of Representatives, just 13 Republicans voted to overturn the president's declaration. In the Senate, a significantly higher proportion of the caucus – twelve members – broke party ranks. Noticeably, just one of those Senators – Susan Collins of Maine – was up for reelection in 2020.

Trump's eager deployment of executive power also reflects a strategy to obviate divisions within his party over America First conservatism. Indeed, Trump's estrangement from the GOP establishment over the tenets and policies of conservative nationalism has resulted in some striking evidence of how presidents now dominate their party's "brand" – how they can denigrate parties as collective organizations with a past and a future. Although Trump's harsh positions on immigration and trade might not have won over Washington, he forged strong ties with the GOP's base through tweets, mass rallies, and administrative action – dramatically transforming GOP loyalists' views on issues such as the "Wall" and tariffs.[28] These defining issues of Trump conservatism were joined in the

---

[26] Erica Werner and John Wagner, "GOP Opposition to Emergency Declaration Grows as Trump Warns Lawmakers," *Washington Post*, February 28, 2019, www.washingtonpost.com/politics/trump-republicans-who-cross-him-on-national-emergency-are-at-great-jeopardy/2019/02/28/07d3d334-3b6a-11e9-a2cd-307b06d0257b_story.html.

[27] Scott Wong and Alexander Bolton, "GOP'S Tillis Comes Under Pressure for Taking on Trump." *The Hill*, March 13, 2019, https://thehill.com/homenews/senate/433929-gops-tillis-comes-under-pressure-for-taking-on-trump.

[28] For example, during the 2016 presidential campaign, Pew tracked a massive drop in the share of Republicans and Republican-leaning independents claiming that free trade agreements had been a "good thing" for the United States from 56 percent in early 2015 to 29 percent in October 2016; see Ashley Parker, "A Sturdy Plank in the GOP Platform:

president's threat in June 2019 to deploy tariffs as a surrogate barrier to the surge of Central American migrants coming to the United States through Mexico. Threatening to slap tariffs as high as 25 percent on all goods from Mexico unless it thwarted the transit of undocumented immigrants and refugees to the United States, Trump adumbrated America First policies that mobilize his base. The threat to deploy tariffs to stem the flow of immigrants to the United States, which risked harming the economy and undermining a trade deal to replace NAFTA as a potential legislative achievement under divided government, testified dramatically to how struggles over national identity have become all-consuming, sharply dividing the country and weakening the national resolve.[29]

The Trump White House's all-out fight to add a citizenship question to census forms is another example of how policy battles became red meat for the president's base. The White House lost this fight in the Supreme Court, when Chief Justice Roberts, who sided with the Trump admiration in the cases pertaining to the Muslim ban and declaration of an emergency to build the Wall, ruled against its effort to weaponize the census. Nonetheless, the contretemps over the citizenship question allowed the president to cast himself as a strong leader, willing to shake things up in defense of the "silent majority."[30]

Although battles over controversial measures to control the border and the rescission of the Obama administration's policy for the Deferred Action for Childhood Arrivals (DACA) were divisive measures that garnered extraordinary media coverage, the contours of the modern administrative state also created multiple, subtler avenues for the exercise of presidential power.[31]

Trumpism," *Washington Post*, March 25, 2018, A1, A21. Trump also managed during his first two years in office to make the Wall the core of Republican immigration policy, a partisan symbol of their support for border security. Colby Itkowitz, "Republicans Spent Two Years Resisting Trump's Border Wall: What Happened?" *Washington Post*, January 15, 2019, www.washingtonpost.com/politics/2019/01/15/republicans-spent-two-years-resisting-trumps-border-wall-what-changed/?utm_term=.2a2eed8bcf78.

[29] Toluse Olorunnipa, "Trump's Frenetic Immigration Approach Becomes a Central Part of the 2020 Bid," *Washington Post*, June 3, 2019, A2.

[30] Toluse Olorunnipa, "'A Willingness to Fight': Win or Lose, Trump's Push for Citizenship Question in the Census Is Red Meat for the Base," *Washington Post*, July 6, 2019, www.washingtonpost.com/politics/a-willingness-to-fight-win-or-lose-trumps-push-for-a-citizenship-question-in-the-census-is-red-meat-for-his-base/2019/07/06/4950889c-9f5c-11e9-b27f-ed2942f73d70_story.html.

[31] After DACA was gutted by the Trump Administration on December 4, 2020, a federal US District Court justice, Judge Nicholas G. Garaufis, ordered the administration to resume the program by admitting new applications and reversed the Homeland Security's

Seemingly benign changes add up and seep through departments and agencies that hold secondary, and even tertiary responsibility for policy change. Collaborating with anti-immigration activists who staffed positions throughout the federal bureaucracy, Trump deployed the full force of the executive branch to implement his desired immigration policy, from revising the rules that the Department of Housing and Urban Development uses in order to curtail rental assistance to unauthorized migrants; to delaying and often suspending the enlistment of foreign-national military recruits; to Homeland Security's expansion of the "Public Charge" rule to prevent less-fortunate migrants from coming to America and to deter legal and undocumented immigrants from accessing health, housing, and food assistance benefits; to establishing a new form of information sharing between the Office of Refugee Resettlement, which sits within Health and Human Services (HHS), and Immigration and Customs Enforcement (ICE), housed in the Department of Homeland Security, that puts those who seek to take custody of migrant children at risk of deportation.[32] The White House also instructed ICE officials to arrest unauthorized immigrants deep in the US interior, even targeting sensitive sites long viewed as off limits to immigration enforcement, such as courthouses and churches.[33]

Remaking the Welfare State

In addition to redeploying national state power to serve conservative causes in homeland security, the Trump administration sought to recast

---

memorandum made by its then-acting secretary Chad Wolfe to restrict the program to those already enrolled.

[32] Sarah Holder, "How Rule Changes about Public Benefits Could Affect Immigrants," *City Lab*, August 13, 2019, www.citylab.com/equity/2019/08/public-charge-rule-legal-immigration-welfare-services-dhs/595987/; A. M. Kurta, "Memorandum: Military Service Suitability Determinations for Foreign Nationals Who Are Lawful Permanent Residents," *Office of the Secretary of Defense*, October 13, 2017; Nick Miroff, "Under Secret Stephen Miller Plan, ICE to Use Data on Migrant Children to Expand Deportation Efforts," *Washington Post*, December 20, 2019, www.washingtonpost.com/immigration/under-secret-stephen-miller-plan-ice-to-use-data-on-migrant-children-to-expand-deportation-efforts/2019/12/20/36975b34-22a8-11ea-bed5-880264cc91a9_story.html?utm_campaign=news_alert_revere&utm_medium=email&utm_source=alert&wpisrc=al_news__alert-politics–alert-national&wpmk=1.

[33] Immigrant Defense Project, "Safeguarding the Integrity of Our Courts: The Impact of ICE Courthouse Operations in New York State," 2019, www.immigrantdefenseproject.org/wp-content/uploads/Safeguarding-the-Integrity-of-Our-Courts-Final-Report.pdf.

social welfare policies to serve national conservative objectives. Trump's Department of Education (DOEd) Secretary Betsy DeVos had long championed local control of public schools, but once in power, she did not hesitate to take administrative measures that encouraged market-driven education reforms such as charter schools and vouchers.[34] DeVos thus weakened the authority of some department divisions, while retooling and empowering others. Not surprisingly, DOEd's Office of Civil Rights has lost much of the independent regulatory authority it built for itself over the last decade. Trump issued an executive order in April 2017 that called for a review of the department's regulations and guidance documents[35]; four months later, DeVos rescinded the Obama-era "dear colleague letter" that universities and colleges used to adjudicate Title IX complaints.[36] While DeVos curbed the Office of Civil Rights' authority, she creatively used the department's student loan division to support for-profit colleges and universities, and to protect student loan providers. By rewriting the gainful employment regulations and contracting with private collection agencies to more aggressively recoup student loan debt, the Department was not weakened; rather, it was retooled to provide State support for market-driven education providers.[37]

Similarly, the Trump Justice Department sought to redefine decades of civil rights enforcement, and to reshape the notion of whose rights the federal government should protect. Since its founding six decades ago, the

---

[34] Erica L. Green, "DeVos's Hard Line on Education Law Surprises States," *New York Times*, July 7, 2017, www.nytimes.com/2017/07/07/us/politics/devos-federal-education-law-states.html?mcubz=0.

[35] "Enforcing Statutory Prohibitions on Federal Control of Education," Executive Order 13791. April 26, 2017. Federal Registrar, vol. 82, no. 82, p. 20427–20428.

[36] US Department of Education, "Department of Education Issues New Interim Guidance on Campus Sexual Misconduct," September 22, 2017, www.ed.gov/news/press-releases/department-education-issues-new-interim-guidance-campus-sexual-misconduct. The following May, the DOE issued a rule that gave a stricter definition of sexual harassment, and required more due process protections for the accused. Some critics of the Obama guidelines praised the new rule as providing a fairer adjudication of sexual harassment charges; however, the due process requirements imposed more burdensome regulations on higher and secondary education. www.ed.gov/news/press-releases/secretary-devos-takes-historic-action-strengthen-title-ix-protections-all-students.

[37] Danielle Douglas-Gabriel, "Trump Administration Welcomes Back Student Debt Collectors Fired by Obama," *Washington Post*, May 3, 2017, wwwwashingtonpost.com/news/grade-point/wp/2017/05/03/trump-administration-welcomes-back-student-debt-collectors-fired-by-obama/?utm_term=.7bc1472cd35d; Michael Stratford, "Education Department Forges Ahead with Loan Servicing Overhaul." *Politico*, May 9, 2017, www.politico.com/tipsheets/morning-education/2017/05/education-department-forges-ahead-with-loan-servicing-overhaul-220209.

Justice Department's civil rights division (CRD) has used the Constitution and federal law to expand protections of African Americans, gays, lesbians and transgender people, immigrants, and other minorities – efforts that have extended the government's reach from polling stations to police stations. During Republican administrations, the division has been restrained, particularly during the Reagan and George W. Bush presidencies.

But civil rights enforcement was not curbed under Trump's Attorneys General Jeff Sessions and William Barr; instead, it shifted to people of faith, police officers, and local government officials who maintain they have been treated with contempt by the federal government. The department supported state laws that could wind up removing thousands of people from voter rolls, pulled back on robust oversight of police departments found to have violated the rights of citizens in their jurisdictions, supported religious conservatives in business and local government who have resisted the advance of LBGTQ rights, and sided with plaintiffs challenging affirmative action plans in higher education.[38]

In redefining the mission of civil rights enforcement, the Trump administration did not gutthe CRD; rather, it was repurposed. In one telling example, the Trump White House started a new project to spearhead the redeployment of federal civil rights enforcement in higher education, which enlisted lawyers who were interested in working on "investigations and possible litigation related to intentional race-based discrimination in college and university admissions." The project has not operated out of the civil rights division's Educational Opportunities Section, where career Justice attorneys oversee cases on universities, but instead in the front office of the division.[39]

Perhaps the most telling example of the Trump administration's commitment to repurpose social welfare policies was its plan to reconstitute the Affordable Care Act (ACA). After the Republican Congress failed to repeal and replace Obamacare, Trump resorted to an administrative approach to recast a centerpiece of the ACA: the extension of Medicaid

---

[38] Katie Benner, "Trump's Justice Department Redefines Whose Civil Rights to Protect," *New York Times*, September 3, 2018, www.nytimes.com/2018/09/03/us/politics/civil-rights-justice-department.html.

[39] Sara Horwitz and Emma Brown, "Justice Department Plans New Project to Sue Universities Over Affirmative Action Policies, *Washington Post*, August 1, 2017, www.washingtonpost.com/world/national-security/justice-department-plans-new-project-to-sue-universities-over-affirmative-action-policies/2017/08/01/6295eba4-772b-11e7-8f39-eeb7d3a2d304_story.htmn.

benefits to those with annual incomes below 138 percent of the federal poverty level. Almost one year after taking office, the Trump administration informed each state's Medicaid office of a new demonstration project, encouraged by Republican Governors' demands. With the permission of the Centers for Medicare and Medicaid (CMS), housed in HHS, states may rescind the Medicaid benefits of able-bodied adults if they are not seeking work or demonstrating active "community engagement." To this point, amid legal battles that have set aside work requirements in four states, eight states have received approval and seven more states have waiver applications pending.[40] These administrative changes to the Affordable Care Act encouraged Republicans in the seventeen States that had previously opposed Medicaid expansion to do so. But, signaling the Trump administration to remake health benefits for the working poor, CMS director, Seema Verma, who worked with then-Governor Mike Pence to impose premiums on Medicaid recipients in Indiana, wanted to alert state leaders across the nation that a new era was dawning: some people would be required to work in exchange for Medicaid benefits.

The press and pundits viewed the Republicans' inability to repeal and replace Obamacare as a great failure. But with a waiver from CMS, state officials siezed the opportunity to remake health care for the poor into a more conservative program – to redeploy the most redistributive features of "Obamacare" through administrative fiat. In fact, because of the incentives these waivers provided for red states, Medicaid was projected to expand as a result of this policy – but only for individuals who live up to the conservative credo of the "deserving poor."[41]

Given the Trump administration's close ties with the Christian Right, it is not surprising that political appointees in HHS also sought to reduce

---

[40] www.kff.org/medicaid/issue-brief/medicaid-waiver-tracker-approved-and-pending-section-1115-waivers-by-state/.

[41] The Trump administration's attempt to remake the Medicaid program is modeled on the playbook for welfare reform that the Clinton White House and a Republican-controlled Congress enacted in 1996, replacing cash payments for low income households with temporary, strict work requirement-based assistance. The Trump presidency envisioned using a similar strategy in remaking the federal government's principal nutrition program. Toward the end of 2019, the administration issued a rule that would require "able-bodied" adults without dependents to work at least twenty hours a week to keep their Supplemental Nutrition Assistance Program benefits (formerly known as food stamps). Margarette Purvis, "The SNAP Rule Will Cause More Hunger than We Can Handle," *New York Times*, December 20, 2019, www.nytimes.com/2019/12/12/opinion/trump-snap-food-stamps.html.

health benefits for the LGBTQ community and women seeking reproductive-health services. In January 2018, HHS established a new division in its Office for Civil Rights (OCR), which was headed by Roger Severino: the Conscience and Religious Freedom Division (CRFD). According to HHS, CRFD was established to "more vigorously and effectively enforce existing laws protecting the rights of conscience and religious freedom." Prior to joining the Trump administration, Severino used his platform at the conservative think tank, the Heritage Foundation, to oppose the rule implementing the nondiscrimination provision of the Affordable Care Act – Section 1557 – since it agreed with a growing number of federal courts that interpreted gender identity discrimination as prohibited sex discrimination. As director of the OCR, he was tasked with enforcing this rule. In a request for information titled "Removing Barriers for Religious and Faith-Based Organizations to Participate in HHS Programs and Receive Public Funding," Severino sought public comments from health care providers on potential changes to regulations or guidance. Some of the comments submitted – expressing the opposition of conservative health care providers to LGBTQ rights – foreshadowed how his office's prioritization of, and funding for, the promotion of expansive religious exemptions would permit discrimination against transgender patients to go unchecked. More broadly, Severino issued a rule that radically redefines federal laws to expand religious, moral, and conscience exemptions that threatened to reverse decades of case law expanding what constitutes discrimination on the basis of sex.[42]

Given the fractious state of American politics, and the vast network of progressive social movements and advocacy groups that had formed during the Obama presidency, Trump's executive actions in the service of conservative causes aroused ferocious opposition from the Democratic Party's base. Mounting a "Trump Resistance Movement," progressive activists employed grassroots protest, social media and legal action to protect the hard-won programmatic achievements in health care, immigration, climate change, and civil rights. Moreover, one of the most vibrant movements in existence when Trump was elected – Black Lives Matter – formed an aspirational coalition that championed

---

[42] *Center for American Progress*, April 25, 2019, www.americanprogress.org/issues/lgbt/news/2019/04/25/468377/hhs-budget-fund-discrimination-expense-civil-rights-enforcement/. The religious conscience rule was blocked by a New York district court ruling, which the Trump administration appealed, news.bloomberglaw.com/health-law-and-business/trump-administration-appeals-religious-health-care-rule-decision.

comprehensive criminal justice reform, the rights of the LGBTQ community, and the protection of immigrants laboring under the heightened scrutiny of INS and economic equality.[43] From the first day of his presidency, therefore, the Trump presidency found itself governing in a political war zone, which grew all the more combative after Democrats took control of the House in the 2018 elections. Given the president' truculent temperament, it is hardly surprising that he responded in kind, using Twitter and mass rallies in small towns and nonurban areas to attack, indeed declare illegitimate, the insurgent opposition to his program.

Although the relationship between presidents and social movement organizations had become commonplace since the 1960s, Trump appeared to become especially dependent on conservative activists. As the president's poll numbers dropped to historically low numbers during the first year of his presidency and the administration became embroiled in a scandal that risked exposing collusion between his campaign and the Russian government and obstructive tactics to hinder the Special Prosecutor Robert Mueller's investigation of potential high crimes and misdemeanors, Trump maintained the close ties to the leaders of the conservative movement that he had cultivated during the general election. Trump's efforts to take credit for a robust economy were overshadowed by his championing of the issues that had become the template of movement conservatives over the past four decades: "traditional" family values, law and order, enhanced border security, opposition to affirmative civil rights policy, and the war against "radical Islamic terrorism." Relentlessly emphasizing these issues in the 2018 elections and the early days of his 2020 reelection effort, Trump doubled down on the politics of fear – conservative statism – gambling that the mobilization of a passionate base can substitute for the cultivation of a majority coalition.[44] The decision of Nancy Pelosi and the Democratic Caucus to launch an impeachment inquiry into the president's machinations in Ukraine – leading to the House's enactment of two articles of impeachment – only served to expand the theater of harsh partisan combat.

---

[43] For an excellent analysis of the anti-Trump resistance, see Sidney Tarrow, "Rhythms of Resistance: The Anti-Trumpian Movement in a Cycle of Contention," in *The Resistance: The Dawn of the Anti-Trump Movement*, ed. David S. Meyer and Sidney Tarrow (Oxford: Oxford University Press, 2018): 187–206.

[44] Jonathan Martin and Alexander Burns, "Abortion Fight or Strong Economy: Cultural Issues Undercut 2020 Message," May 19, 2019, www.nytimes.com/2019/05/19/us/politics/republicans-abortion-economy-issues.html.

THE HAZARDS OF EXECUTIVE PARTISANSHIP

The American party system was formed during the first four decades of the nineteenth century to restrain presidential power. But over the course of the twentieth and twenty-first centuries, especially since the late Sixties, parties have been made integral to the personalized political wars President Trump relished. Former Speaker of the House John Boehner gave colloquial expression to our thesis in 2018: "There is no Republican Party. There's a Trump party. The Republican Party is kind of taking a nap somewhere."[45] Boehner failed to appreciate the fact that this is an ingrained feature of modern presidential politics, and that the Trump administration fits a pattern of partisan and administrative centralization – a pattern to which Boehner, in his courting of Tea-Party voters, contributed. Faced with a divided party, Trump delivered on promises to enact important programmatic changes long sought by Republican leaders in Congress. And despite Boehner's concern, Republicans relished the president's use of unilateral action to sidestep the arduous process of legislative deal making.

As the outcome of the 2018 midterms showed, Trump's partisan administration put moderate Republicans at risk. In effect, Trump's rancorous politics and the prerogatives of the modern presidency combined to forge a leaner and more united Republican Party. The Republican Party's support was increasingly confined to those places – rural and outer-ring suburban areas – where Trump performed well in 2016. Of the 170 contested races that a Republican won in the 2018 midterms, the president's 2016 numbers outperformed the Republican candidate in 94 districts, or 55.3 percent. Trump won those districts with an average 58.8 percent of the vote, while Republican congressional candidates averaged 59.1 percent of the vote. Trump thus tied the fate of Republican candidates to his political fortunes.[46]

The results of the 2020 campaign suggested that Trump's influence on his party would endure. Predictably, Trump's response to the twin crises that dominated his final year in the White House – the outbreak of a global

---

[45] Jennifer Rubin, "John Boehner: 'There Is No Republican Party,'" *Washington Post*, May 31, 2018.
[46] Nicholas Jacobs and Sidney M. Milkis, "Our 'Undivided Support': Donald Trump, the Republican Party, and Executive-Centered Partisanship," in *Partisanship in the Age of Trump*, ed. Eric Patashnik and Wendy Schiller (Lawrence: University Press of Kansas, forthcoming); Sabrina Tavernese and Robert Gebeloff, "Are the Suburbs Turning Democratic? It Depends on Which Ones," *Washington Post*, October 26, 2019, A1, A12.

pandemic and the racial reckoning that erupted after the horrifying police brutality that led to George Floyd's death – further polarized rather than unified the country. After a campaign during which each side accused the other as posing an existential threat to the nation, Trump lost a close contest to former Vice President Joe Biden; however, his party picked up eleven seats in the House diminishing the majority the Democrats had achieved in the 2018 elections. The Democrats did pick up three seats in the Senate, winning two remarkable special elections in Georgia, leaving the upper chamber evenly divided, with Vice President Kamala Harris the deciding vote in the event of a tie. Thus, for the first time since 2010, the Democrats controlled the White House and both chambers of Congress – albeit by the narrowest of margins in a country that remained sharply divided. Even in defeat, moreover, Trump reigned over his party and reveled in the adulation of its base supporters, most of whom supported his groundless claims that the election was fraudulent.

Like those many instances where Trump had not achieved policy successes, such as adding a citizenship question to the census form, the president blamed his failure to win reelection on the "deep state" and "radical" Democrats, arousing resentment among his most loyal supporters. Trump has thus been an instrumental figure in buttressing a highly personalized constituency, and through aggressive administrative action and a determined political strategy to remake the Republican Party, he has further embittered partisan conflict. Joining executive prerogative, grassroots mobilization and high-stakes battles over domestic and foreign policy, executive-centered partisanship provided the Trump White House with a range of administrative and political powers to promote his agenda and to forge a visceral connection with his base of supporters who disdain the virtues of deliberation, compromise, and pragmatic governance.

Although Trump tapped into long-standing developments in the Republican Party, his aberrant behavior, such as interference with independent counsel investigations, refusal to comply with congressional subpoenas, and condemnation of the press as "the enemy of the people," poses unprecedented dangers to the norms and institutions of liberal democracy. The House impeachment conviction over Trump's effort to pressure Ukraine to investigate the "corruption" of the leading Democratic candidate for the 2020 Democratic nomination, former Vice President Joe Biden, and his son Hunter starkly revealed just how novel and dangerous executive partisanship has become. Trump fought the impeachment battle by stoking support from his base. The Trump reelection campaign quickly raised funds for a $10 million advertising blitz against the Bidens. The Trump White House also was intent on deploying the powers of the modern executive to escalate his attack on the "deep state" – especially career diplomats and civil servants in the Justice and State Departments as well as the intelligence agencies who testified in the impeachment investigations or waivered in their support of the president.[47] The dénouement shook the foundations of American democracy. Denying that he lost a close but decisive election, Trump pursued all legal and political avenues he and his campaign strategists could devise to impede a peaceful transfer of power – a protracted and in the end futile effort that nevertheless denigrated the vital principle of a republic, popular sovereignty.

Nor should any attempt to identify the political developments that help explain the emergence of Trumpism elide his calculated appeal to racial prejudice and virulent nativism.[48] Nevertheless, focusing solely on the exceptional aspects of Trump's presidency, as disruptive and dangerous as they are, risks overlooking the more routinized dynamics of party politics, which will continue to disrupt the constitutional system long after President Trump leaves office. It is true that many actions taken during Trump's term in office were not deliberate and seemed to exist outside the normal working arrangement of executive politics and party leadership. Nevertheless, despite all the travails and self-inflicted controversies, the president's support among loyal and independent-leaning Republicans did not waver.

Donald Trump's raw and disruptive partisanship seemed so hazardous not only because of the divisions it fomented, but also because it exposed the lack of political will on the part of Congress and the Supreme Court to restrain it. The authority for many of the president's actions were based on questionable, and reckless, constitutional interpretation; and on other fronts, statutory changes might significantly curb the president's authority to act unilaterally. Nixon's pioneering and corrupt advance of executive-centered partisanship resulted in efforts to restore the "guardrails" of

---

[47] Greg Miller and Greg Jaffe, "In the Aftermath of the Ukraine Crisis, a Climate of Mistrust and Threats," *Washington Post*, December 25, 2019, www.washingtonpost.com/national-security/in-aftermath-of-ukraine-crisis-a-climate-of-mistrust-and-threats/2019/12/24/03831e3e-2359-11ea-a153-dce4b94e4249_story.html; Philip Rucker and Robert Costa, "A Presidency of One: Key Federal Agencies Increasingly Compelled to Benefit Trump," *Washington Post*, October 2, 2019, www.washingtonpost.com/politics/a-presidency-of-one-key-federal-agencies-increasingly-compelled-to-benefit-trump/2019/10/01/f80740ec-e453-11e9-a331-2df12d56a80b_story.html.

[48] Desmond King and Rogers M. Smith, "White Reconstruction in America," *Perspectives on Politics*, https://doi.org/10.1017/S1537592720001152.

liberal democracy. One might hope that the Trump administration's highly disruptive leadership might result in a renewed effort to restore constitutional norms and institutional constraints.

Yet Trump's bellicose partisanship might have influenced the Democratic Party almost as much as his own. During the campaign, President Biden, promising to restore civility to American politics and celebrating his ability to broker legislative compromises with Congress, managed to win the Democratic nomination by rallying the diverse coalition that Obama summoned, which was united by the pragmatic imperative of beating Donald Trump. However, even before public health and racial crises engulfed the nation – and pushed the Democratic Party further to the left – Biden found himself on the defensive as ardent progressives Bernie Sanders and Elizabeth Warren promised to take aggressive executive action to jump-start the transformation of American politics on day one. The bitterly contested election, which Trump and many of his followers claim was fraudulent, and the prospect of resistance to his policy priorities by a narrowly divided Congress made it more likely that the Biden administration, as progressive Democrats urged in a memo, would be forced to "use the full power of the executive branch to deliver immediate and tangible results."[49] Acknowledging his precarious political position, and the crises he would inherit from the Trump administration, Biden promised to sign a series of executive orders to forecast immediately that his presidency would be guided by radically different priorities in matters of climate change, immigration, civil rights, and the pandemic. Progressives were determined to press the new administration further, arguing that Trump had left a loaded administrative weapon on the desk of the Oval office. As Adam Green, co-founder of the Progressive Change Campaign Committee, referring to Trump's emergency declaration to build a wall along the border with Mexico that was upheld in court, asked "Why wouldn't that same exact concept apply to relief for homeowners and relief for student debt?"[50]

The displacement of party politics by executive administration has not made formal party organizations inconsequential. Rather, as Democrats

---

[49] Memo, "The Path Forward for Democrats," November 29, 2020, www.washingtonpost.com/context/memo-on-the-path-forward-for-democrats/ba38467b-05fa-4334-a268-fc6c3e2b172d/?itid=lk_interstitial_manual_37.

[50] Sean Sullivan and Rachel Blade, "Criticized by Moderates and Pressured by Their Base, Liberals Fight for a Voice in the Democratic Party," November 29, 2020, www.washingtonpost.com/politics/democratic-party-future-liberals/2020/11/29/3da05bfe-2ba5-11eb-92b7-6ef17b3fe3b4_story.html.

and Republicans have come to rely on partisan administration to fulfil their collective goals, they have ceded greater authority to the White House. This commitment to executive prerogative has gone hand-in-hand with the denigration of the bureaucracy as a site of neutral competence. The increasing consolidation of policy responsibility in the White House Office as well as the partisan and politicized shape of the federal government's senior appointments since the Nixon years are a visible corollary of the State in perpetual redeployment. It is an ineluctable implication of the "unitary executive" since presidents want to appoint civil servants who will deploy State resources in their preferred way.[51]

Time will tell whether the critical role whistleblowers and career diplomats played in the first Trump impeachment marks a renaissance of the civil service. But as David Lewis points out, the civil service has been under assault at least since the Reagan presidency.[52] Moreover, the Trump administration, through savvy conservative populists like the West Wing's immigration czar Stephen Miller, installed handpicked political appointees across key departments and agencies, many recruited from conservative social movement networks and organizations, who exploited the listlessness of the federal bureaucracy.[53] Although his network was not as extensive as Miller's, Peter Navarro, who headed the White House Office of Trade and Manufacturing, outflanked more moderate voices in the West Wing and regular Departments and Agencies in the formulation of the Trump administration's controversial trade policies.[54] Given the outsize influence of Miller and Navarro, the politics and policies pertaining to the pillars of Trump's America First agenda – immigration and trade – were insulated from regular bureaucratic procedures.

Fear abounds that the Trump presidency went so far in hollowing out and intimidating valued political servants in many Departments and agencies that restoring a measure of bureaucratic autonomy that moderates rancorous partisanship and constrains executive aggrandizement

---

[51] Joel Aberbach and Bert A Rockman, "The Appointments Process and the Administrative Presidency," *Presidential Studies Quarterly* 39 no.1 (2009): 38–59; Milkis, *The President and the Parties*, 132–34.

[52] David Lewis, "Deconstructing the Administrative State," *Journal of Politics* 81, no. 3 (July 2019): 767–89.

[53] Nick Miroff and Josh Dawsey, "The Advisor Who Scripts Trump's Border Policy," *Washington Post,* August 18, 2019, A1, A20-21.

[54] Josh Dawsey and Damien Paletta, "'My Peter': Rising Influence of Controversial Trade Advisor Worries Critics," *Washington Post,* June 12, 2019, www.washingtonpost.com/p olitics/my-peter-rising-influence-of-controversial-trump-trade-adviser-navarro-concerns-his-critics/2019/06/12/e4fcb81c-8b96-11e9-b162-8f6f41ec3c04_story.html.

might prove impossible. Conservative Republicans have demonized civil servants since the Reagan administration. But in the past, civil servants could lay low and bide their time until a more supportive administration occupied the executive branch. The Trump administration sent a message that all career staff are suspect, indeed enemies of the people, who should be forced out of the government or made completely subservient to political appointees.[55] Characteristic of executive-centered partisanship, the Trump administration's "deconstruction of the administrative state" was selective – but conservative state building in Homeland Security, the Defense Department, and Veteran Affairs emphasized empowering Trump loyalists and tasking career employees and civil servants with the unenviable task of maintaining their professional integrity amid disruptive and polarizing tactics that fractured the nation.

The maintenance of professionalism even became a problem for the military establishment – the most respected government institution – which fretted over the possibility of losing its prized credibility while assuming the challenging task of explaining the President's bellicose tweets and controversial actions, such as his use of the drone strike on Iranian general Qassem Soleimani, which risked a dangerous escalation of bellicosity between the United States and Iran.[56] Trump's threat to invoke the Insurrection Act to deploy active military troops to squelch the protests aroused by George Floyd's death in Washington, DC, and other "Democrat-run" cities caused a public break between the White House and Secretary of Defense Mark Esper. Risking Trump's wrath, Esper insisted, "The option to use active-duty forces in a law enforcement role should only be used as a matter of last resort, and only in the most urgent and dire of situations. We are not in one of those situations now. I do not support invoking the Insurrection Act."[57] When Trump fired Esper soon after the election it was an all-too-predictable episode in a series of actions designed to domesticate the executive branch. Deconstructing the administrative state does not mean a smaller state, just a state less encumbered

---

[55] Brad Plummer and Coral Davenport, "Science Under Attack: How Trump Is Sidelining Researchers and Their Work," *New York Times*, December 28, 2019, www.washingtonpost.com/national-security/in-aftermath-of-ukraine-crisis-a-climate-of-mistrust-and-threats/2019/12/24/03831e3e-2359-11ea-a153-dce4b94e4249_story.html.

[56] Brian Bender and Jaqueline Feldsher, "'It's Terrible: Fear Grows that Trump Is Kneecapping the Pentagon," *Politico*, January 8, 2020, www.politico.com/news/2020/01/08/donald-trump-created-pentagon-credibility-problem-096146.

[57] Meghan Myers, "Esper, on His Way Out, Says He Was No Yes Man," *Military Times*, November 9, 2020, www.militarytimes.com/news/your-military/2020/11/09/exclusive-esper-on-his-way-out-says-he-was-no-yes-man/.

by oversight or regulation and politically integrated into an executive-centered partisan White House.

In an era marked by vigorous party competition, divided government, and tribal struggles to control the judiciary, these dangerous trends are likely to continue after Trump's tenure.[58] Trump's disruptive presidency is testament to political developments that have fused executive prerogative and fierce partisanship – and instilled in the country an obsession with the modern presidency's pseudo grandeur and the false hope that a single individual could ever truly serve as the sole steward of the public welfare. Until this misplaced faith in a presidency-centered democracy is decisively disabused, the hope of restoring the constitutional norms and institutions of the American republic will be a chimera.

In sum, democracy necessarily involves conflict, most notably in struggles over national identity. But the joining of social activism, executive prerogative and party conflict since the cultural crack-up of the Sixties has eroded many of the norms and institutions that have constrained the most dangerous tendencies of fundamental democratic combat. Intense polarization originated in a struggle over inclusiveness centered on the 1960s. The enactment of civil rights legislation in that decade and the reaction to it was so polarizing because it finally forced the United States to confront, after a century of false promises, the shameful limits of its grand experiment in self-rule. Only then did America truly become a democracy as voting rights were at last enforced. But that very democratization exposed the deep fault lines fundamentally unresolved and now testing the very essence of American democracy. Whether that test tranquilizes or perverts democracy is the nation's pressing question.

*The authors thank Sidney Tarrow of Cornell University and the editors of this volume for their incisive and helpful comments on earlier drafts of this chapter. We also express our gratitude to Jacob Asch and Katharine Huiskes, University of Virginia students, for their dedicated research in support of this project.

---

[58] Frances E. Lee, *Insecure Majorities: Congress and the Perpetual Campaign* (Chicago: University of Chicago Press, 2018).
  Desmond King, "Forceful Federalism Against Racial Inequality." *Government and Opposition*, 52 (April 2017): 356–82.

12

Laboratories of What?

American Federalism and the Politics of Democratic Subversion

Philip Rocco

> From time to time public attention is focused on scandalous situations in state government... These moments pass; state affairs recover their wonted obscurity and it is assumed that the wrongdoers have been exposed and punished.
> Grant McConnell (1966)[1]

The 2016 presidential election brought on a blizzard of foreboding announcements about American democracy. Yet as political scientists and pundits alike turned their gaze toward the spectacle of Trump's Washington, fewer seemed as concerned about what was happening in places like Raleigh or Jefferson City. In fact, scholars and commentators troubled by abuses of power in the executive branch pointed to federalism as "the most effective tool" for protecting democracy, "especially if other constitutional checks fail."[2] States, it was argued, provided crucial venues for dissent and the formation of alternative governing coalitions.[3] And while new analyses of democratic backsliding mentioned gerrymandering in state legislatures and state-level episodes of "constitutional hardball," they tended to focus their attention on the national level.[4]

Acknowledgments: I am grateful to Rob Lieberman, Sid Tarrow, and Rick Valelly, as well as to the anonymous reviewers, for comments on earlier drafts of this chapter.

[1] Grant McConnell, *Private Power and American Democracy* (New York: Alfred A. Knopf, 1966), 193.

[2] Corey Brettschneider, "Local and State Government Can Protect the Constitution from Trump," *Time*, November 30, 2016.

[3] Heather Gerken, "Progressive Federalism: A User's Guide," *Democracy: A Journal of Ideas* 44 (2017).

[4] Tom Ginsburg and Aziz Huq, *How to Save a Constitutional Democracy* (Chicago: University of Chicago Press, 2018); Steven Levitsky and Daniel Ziblatt, *How Democracies Die* (New York: Crown, 2018).

Four years later, in the midst of a pandemic and a presidential election, appraisals of federalism's virtues carried some weight. Around the country, states governed by both Republicans and Democrats approved an unprecedented number of changes in election law designed to facilitate absentee voting and to slow the spread of COVID-19.[5] Similarly, governors, state election administrators, and judges from both parties refused to support President Trump's feckless effort to use false allegations of voter fraud as a means of overturning election results.[6] If crises of democracy are like diseases, these observations might lead one to conclude that the states are – with a small number of exceptions – immune.

Such benign images of the states – what V. O. Key called the "pleasant fictions of American political mythology" – are nothing new.[7] That the most commonly applied sobriquet for the states is "the laboratories of democracy" is evidence enough. Tellingly, mass-level trust in state and local governments has remained remarkably resilient, even as trust in national institutions has cratered.[8] To some extent, empirical research confirms the states' role as democratic laboratories. Structurally speaking, state constitutions contain numerous positive rights that are not to be found at the national level.[9] Nearly half allow for some form of direct democracy, enhancing opportunities for mass influence.[10] A variety of scholars have also argued that state governments are, on balance, responsive to mass opinion.[11]

---

[5] "Absentee and Mail Voting Policies in Effect for the 2020 Election," National Conference of State Legislatures, November 3, 2020, accessed December 10, 2020, www.ncsl.org/research/elections-and-campaigns/absentee-and-mail-voting-policies-in-effect-for-the-2020-election.aspx.

[6] Miles Parks, "As Trump's Election Pressure Campaign Hits Republican Officials, Some Hit Back," National Public Radio, December 4, 2020, accessed December 10, 2020, www.npr.org/2020/12/04/941284401/as-trumps-election-pressure-campaign-hits-republican-officials-some-hit-back.

[7] V. O. Key, *American State Politics: An Introduction* (New York: Alfred A. Knopf, 1956).

[8] Justin McCarthy, "Americans Still More Trusting of Local than State Government," Gallup.com, October 8, 2018.

[9] Emily Zackin, *Looking for Rights in All the Wrong Places* (Princeton: Princeton University Press, 2013).

[10] Patrick Flavin, "Direct Democracy and Political Equality in the American States," *Social Science Quarterly* 96, no. 1 (2015): 119–32.

[11] Devin Caughey and Christopher Warshaw, "Policy Preferences and Policy Change: Dynamic Responsiveness in the American States, 1936–2014," *American Political Science Review* 112, no. 2 (2018): 249–66; James Stimson, Michael MacKuen, and Robert S. Erikson, "Dynamic Representation," *American Political Science Review* 89, no. 3 (1995): 543–65.

Laboratories of What? 299

Yet the notion that state governments are a cause of democratic resilience neglects the complex dynamics of American federalism.[12] Some of the same governors who resisted Trump's calls to overturn the results of the 2020 elections were responsible for instituting restrictions on voter participation.[13] State legislators perpetuated the myth of voter fraud to justify new restrictions on voting.[14] Led by Ken Paxton of Texas, a group of Republican attorneys general filed lawsuits to enjoin the certification of elections in other states which Trump had lost.[15] Simultaneously, ten states had filed briefs in federal court supporting the Trump administration's unprecedented effort to remove undocumented immigrants from congressional apportionment counts.[16] Thus while states may not have fully leapt into the darkness of a constitutional crisis, they had already helped to delimit democratic participation and delegitimate elections.

Indeed, the empirical pattern of subnational democracy in the United States is not one of recent *erosion*, but the endurance of unevenness, even after the democratic transition of the 1960s. Consider the following contrast. In cross-national indices of democracy, the United States has improved markedly over the last sixty years. Figure 12.1 compares the United States to seven older democracies with federal systems on the Varieties of Democracy (V-Dem) Institute's Electoral Democracy Index. Between 1958 and 2018, the United States shifts from being a low-outlier on the index to achieving near parity with older federal democracies. Yet the same cannot be said for *subnational* democracy. Figure 12.2 plots a measure of the evenness of free and fair elections at the subnational level for the same set of countries at the same two points in time. Indeed, while democracy in the states has no doubt improved over the last sixty years, it remains substantially more uneven than in peer countries. Not only do cross-sectional analyses reveal significant differences among states in opinion-policy congruence, the character of state

---

[12] David Brian Robertson, *Federalism and the Making of America* (New York: Routledge, 2018).

[13] Lisa Marshall Manheim and Elizabeth G. Porter, "The Elephant in the Room: Intentional Voter Suppression," *The Supreme Court Review 2018*, no. 1 (2019): 213–55.

[14] Jane C. Timm, "Trump's False Fraud Claims Are Laying Groundwork for New Voting Restrictions, Experts Warn," NBC News, December 6, 2020, accessed December 10, 2020, www.nbcnews.com/politics/elections/trump-s-false-fraud-claims-are-laying-groundwork-new-voting-n1250059.

[15] Jeremy Peters and Maggie Haberman, "17 Republican Attorneys General Back Trump in Far-Fetched Election Lawsuit," *New York Times*, December 9, 2020, accessed December 10, 2020, www.nytimes.com/2020/12/09/us/politics/trump-texas-supreme-court-lawsuit.html.

[16] These states included Alabama, Arkansas, Kentucky, Louisiana, Mississippi, Missouri, Nebraska, South Carolina, South Dakota, and West Virginia.

■ 1958   □ 2018

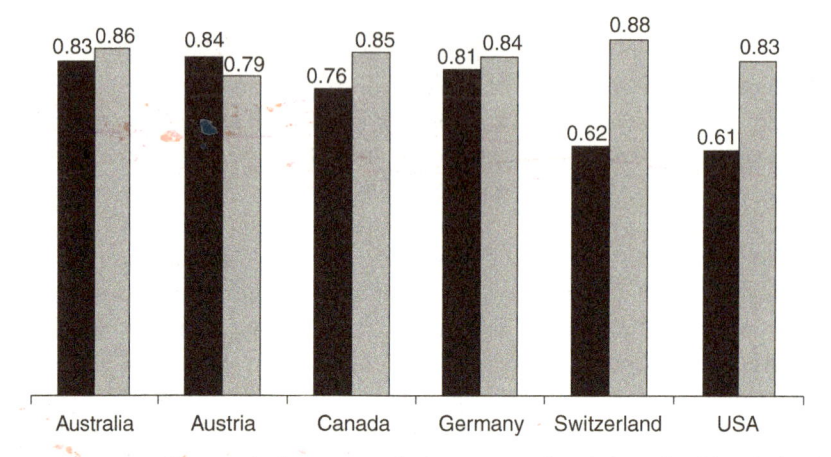

	Australia	Austria	Canada	Germany	Switzerland	USA
1958	0.83	0.84	0.76	0.81	0.62	0.61
2018	0.86	0.79	0.85	0.84	0.88	0.83

FIGURE 12.1 Electoral democracy index scores for US and older federal democracies, 1958 and 2018
Note: Scores are based on a weighted average of five component indices measuring freedom of association, clean elections, freedom of expression, elected officials, and suffrage and the five-way multiplicative interaction between those indices.
Source: Author's analysis based on data from Michael Coppedge, John Gerring, Carl Henrik Knutsen, et al., V-Dem Country-Year Dataset v9, Varieties of Democracy (V-Dem) Project, https://doi.org/10.23696/vdemcy1

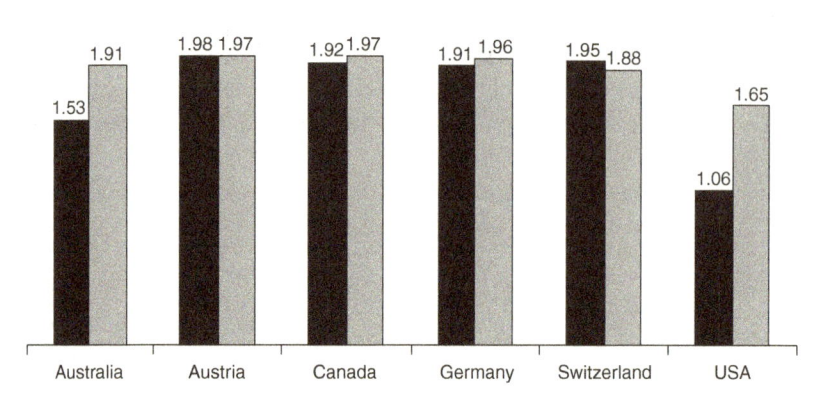

■ 1958   □ 2018

	Australia	Austria	Canada	Germany	Switzerland	USA
1958	1.53	1.98	1.92	1.91	1.95	1.06
2018	1.91	1.97	1.97	1.96	1.88	1.65

FIGURE 12.2 Subnational election evenness in US and older federal democracies, 1958 and 2018
Note: Scores are based on expert ratings of countries using an ordinal measure ranging from 0 to 2.
Source: Author's analysis based on data from Michael Coppedge, John Gerring, Carl Henrik Knutsen, et al., V-Dem Country-Year Dataset v9, Varieties of Democracy (V-Dem) Project, https://doi.org/10.23696/vdemcy1

electoral and representative institutions diverges in meaningful ways.[17] States that make it easier for voters to participate in direct democracy tend to produce a greater amount of collective goods and tend to feature greater levels of political equality.[18] In other states, however, the manipulation of electoral and legislative rules curtails basic democratic rights.[19]

While uneven subnational democracy is preferable to a situation in which territorial governments are evenly undemocratic, the existence of undemocratic outliers nevertheless helps to undermine democracy as a whole. Inequality in democratic rights and liberties was itself baked into the Constitution. These inequalities have been dismissed, however, because scholars tend to conceptualize states as relatively isolated laboratories of democracy. Yet the Constitution makes the states into the *infrastructure* of democracy: state laws shape the exercise of rights and liberties, structure national elections and legislative districts, and affect the development of civil-society institutions in ways that have national reach. Indeed, episodes of democratic collapse at the state level have had profound reverberations for national politics.

To understand the endurance of uneven subnational democracy, it is worth remembering that subnational authoritarianism persisted in the US South until the 1960s, yielding only after the nationalization of political conflict and protracted interventions by central state authorities. Yet, territorial democratization was not self-enforcing. Racial apartheid and localized economic oligarchies have had enduring effects on state politics. More important, soon after the democratic transition, conservative political elites countermobilized, and began to chip away at the new rights regime. State parties motivated by counter-majoritarian ideological agendas have, among other things, violated informal governing norms, actively limited ballot-box access through enacting new administrative burdens, and employed increasingly sophisticated approaches to gerrymandering to lock in seat shares.

The erosion of subnational democracy after the consolidation of the 1960s has depended upon efforts to localize and privatize conflict – what

---

[17] Patrick Flavin, "Political Equality in the American States: What We Know and What We Still Need to Learn," *State and Local Government Review* 49, no. 1 (2017): 60–69; Jeffrey Lax and Justin Phillips, "The Democratic Deficit in the States," *American Journal of Political Science* 56, no. 1 (2012): 148–66.
[18] Patrick Flavin and William Franko, "Government's Unequal Attentiveness to Citizens' Political Priorities," *Policy Studies Journal* 45, no. 4 (2017): 659–87.
[19] Heather Gerken, *The Democracy Index* (Princeton: Princeton University Press, 2009); Quan Li, Michael J. Pomante II, and Scott Schraufnagel, "Cost of Voting in the American States," *Election Law Journal: Rules, Politics, and Policy* 17, no. 3 (2018): 234–47.

Adam Przeworski calls "subversion by stealth."[20] Research on subnational democratization suggests that reversing these dynamics requires the renationalization of contests over the boundaries of political incorporation. Yet given the highly polarized state of national parties, nationalizing conflict may, paradoxically, entail a more highly coordinated *local* strategy. While this strategy has drawbacks, I argue, it may help to depolarize issues of democratic participation by focusing national attention on the material realities of democratic erosion.

INFRASTRUCTURE, NOT LABORATORIES

The language scholars use to describe American state governments may contribute to the shock we experience when democratic norm violations occur at the ballot box or on the legislative floor. One source of confusion here is the phrase "laboratories of democracy," famously coined by Louis Brandeis in 1937, but which did not gain wide traction until the 1980s.[21] This metaphor refers to states' capacity to learn from one another's policy successes (and, less frequently, their mistakes). It thereby emphasizes experimentation itself as a democratic good. The tacit assumption here is that subnational governments have the capacity to resist undemocratic maneuvers and to adopt and promote democratizing reforms when Congress is resistant to them. Further, it is assumed that reforms which undermine democracy in a single state can be costlessly observed by others, rejected, and thereby contained – at worst contained to a delimited region. Those subject to these reforms can also hypothetically exit the regime by "voting with their feet."[22]

The laboratory metaphor, as numerous scholars have noted, fails to account for structural limitations on states' capacity as innovators and sites of representation.[23] Yet the problem goes deeper: conceptualizing the states as relatively isolated laboratories fundamentally ignores the multiple roles they play in co-constituting the national polity.[24] First, and

---

[20] Adam Przeworski, *Crises of Democracy* (Cambridge: Cambridge University Press, 2019).
[21] Google Ngram data are illustrative: https://tinyurl.com/y56hz3r9.
[22] Ilya Somin, "Foot Voting, Decentralization, and Development," *Minnesota Law Review* 102 (2017): 1649–70.
[23] Susan Rose-Ackerman, "Risk Taking and Reelection: Does Federalism Promote Innovation?" *Journal of Legal Studies* 9, no. 3 (1980): 593–616; David Super, "Laboratories of Destitution: Democratic Experimentalism and the Failure of Antipoverty Law," *University of Pennsylvania Law Review* 157, no. 2 (2008): 541–616.
[24] Jessica Bulman-Pozen, "From Sovereignty and Process to Administration and Politics: The Afterlife of American Federalism," *Yale Law Journal* 123 (2014): 1920–57.

perhaps most important, states construct the national electorate through their administration of federal elections. Notwithstanding the nationalization of voting rights in the 1960s and increasing judicial scrutiny of state election practices, state election practices have continued to vary; following the Supreme Court's elimination of the Voting Rights Act preclearance formula in *Shelby County v. Holder*, states' discretion over election laws expanded yet further. The effects of election laws do not stop at the state line, however. Racial apartheid in the South constructed a "Jim Crow Congress"; insulated from electoral competition, Southern committee chairs became the fulcrum of national policymaking – foreclosing the New Deal's social democratic aspirations.[25] Even after the dismantling of Jim Crow laws, Southern states continue to exhibit lower levels of voter turnout in national elections, and lower levels of responsiveness to reforms intended to reduce the cost of voting.[26] Regardless of geography, enduring unevenness in electoral democracy continues to shape national politics. The disfranchisement of felons significantly shaped the outcome of the 2000 presidential election as well as several Senate elections in the latter half of the twentieth century.[27] While the effect of photo ID laws on turnout is much disputed, they clearly depress voter registration in presidential election years by as much as 7.6 percentage points.[28] Setting aside any concerns about voter suppression, state voter registration requirements, when implemented in municipalities with weak administrative capacity, can lower turnout in national elections by as much as two percentage points.[29] In short, an assessment of US electoral democracy would be incomplete without attending to unevenness in state election laws and practices.

Just as state election laws reconstitute the national electorate, states decennially reconstitute Congress through redistricting. States' discretion over this process has diminished since the so-called judicial "reapportionment revolution." Even so, state legislative redistricting continues to vary

---

[25] Ira Katznelson, *Fear Itself: The New Deal and the Origins of Our Time* (New York: Liveright, 2013).
[26] Melanie J. Springer, "State Electoral Institutions and Voter Turnout in Presidential Elections, 1920–2000," *State Politics & Policy Quarterly* 12, no. 3 (2012): 252–83.
[27] Jeffrey Manza and Christopher Uggen, *Locked Out: Felon Disenfranchisement and American Democracy* (Oxford: Oxford University Press, 2008).
[28] Francesco Maria Esposito, Diego Focanti, and Justine S. Hastings, "Effects of Photo ID Laws on Registration and Turnout: Evidence from Rhode Island," No. w25503. National Bureau of Economic Research, 2019.
[29] Barry C Burden, and Jacob R. Neiheisel, "Election Administration and the Pure Effect of Voter Registration on Turnout," *Political Research Quarterly* 66, no. 1 (2013): 77–90.

in ways that are consequential for national governance. Partisan gerrymandering skews the ideological distribution of state legislatures and the policy outputs of state government. Republican gerrymanders advantage conservative politicians and yield higher levels of conservative policy output.[30] As such, gerrymandering invariably affects federal policy, especially given the substantial role states play in administering federal grants (which make up over 30 percent of states' annual budgets) and implementing federal regulations. While it was not the only factor impeding states' expansion of Medicaid, aggressive gerrymanders in states like North Carolina and Wisconsin helped to undermine state legislators' incentives to do so, even though expansion is supported by majorities of voters in both states.[31] To be sure, partisan control of redistricting has a smaller effect on seat shares in Congress than it did before the Supreme Court's decision in *Wesberry v. Sanders* (1964).[32] Nevertheless, partisan gerrymandering has significant downstream effects on the integrity of political parties. In districts where gerrymandering disadvantages their party, prospective congressional candidates are far less likely to challenge incumbents. Candidates who do run in congressional districts biased against their party also have significantly weaker resumes and receive significantly fewer campaign contributions than their peers in unbiased districts.[33]

Finally, governance in the fifty states plays a formative role in structuring both the public and private spheres. Prior to the judicial construction of what William Leuchtenburg calls the "Second Bill of Rights" in the 1960s, states used their police powers in ways that limited the exercise of individual rights.[34] Perhaps most infamously, states exerted the power – with the

---

[30] Devin Caughey, Christopher Tausanovitch, and Christopher Warshaw, "Partisan Gerrymandering and the Political Process: Effects on Roll-Call Voting and State Policies," *Election Law Journal: Rules, Politics, and Policy* 16, no. 4 (2017): 453–69.

[31] Marquette University Law School Poll, April 3–7, 2019, accessed December 10, 2020, https://law.marquette.edu/poll/wp-content/uploads/2019/04/MLSP52Toplines.pdf; Meredith College Poll, Policy Issues and the 2019 Legislative Session, February, 2019, accessed December 10, 2020, www.meredith.edu/assets/images/content/Meredith_College_Poll_Report_February_2019.pdf.

[32] Michael Peress and Yangzi Zhao, "How Many Seats in Congress Is Control of Redistricting Worth?," *Legislative Studies Quarterly* 45, no. 3 (2020): 433–68.

[33] Nicholas Stephanopoulos and Christopher Warshaw, "The Impact of Partisan Gerrymandering on Political Parties," *Legislative Studies Quarterly* 45, no. 4 (2020): 609–43.

[34] Gary Gerstle, *Liberty and Coercion: The Paradox of American Government from the Founding to the Present* (Princeton: Princeton University Press, 2017); William Leuchtenburg, *The Supreme Court Reborn: The Constitutional Revolution in the Age of Roosevelt* (Oxford: Oxford University Press, 2015).

Supreme Court's blessing – to sterilize tens of thousands of "undesirable" people, including people of color, immigrants, unwed mothers, the poor, the disabled, and the mentally ill.[35] On the other hand, positive rights contained in state constitutions played a pivotal role in creating civil society through the guarantee of free primary and secondary education. Even as the federal government gained greater control over other areas of public provision, states have retained substantial leverage in the sphere of education. State choices on education policy, in turn, construct citizens' participatory behaviors and views of government.[36] Education is not the only such "formative" institution shaped by the states. As Jamila Michener's research shows, citizens' experience with state Medicaid programs has a sizable impact on their propensity to participate in politics. Medicaid beneficiaries in states making the largest reductions in benefits were between "four and nine percentage points less likely to vote, register, or participate" when compared to those in states that did not reduce their benefits.[37]

To sum up, we cannot treat democratic deficits in the states as mere variation in a dataset where N equals 50. Instead, the states *compose* the national polity through the administration of national elections, the construction of Congress, the implementation of federal policies, and the structuring of public and private spheres. By drawing attention to the states, I do not intend to diminish the important role of the federal government in structuring the boundaries of democratic participation. Nor do I mean to imply that nationalizing the administration of rights and liberties has a necessarily democratizing effect. Especially where the emergence of the national security state is concerned, there is no shortage of evidence to the contrary.[38] Rather, assessing democracy in the states adds much-needed depth to the analysis of democratic resilience in the United States as a single case.

---

[35] Randall Hansen and Desmond King, *Sterilized by the State: Eugenics, Race, and the Population Scare in Twentieth-Century North America* (Cambridge: Cambridge University Press, 2013).

[36] Sarah K. Bruch and Joe Soss, "Schooling as a Formative Political Experience: Authority Relations and the Education of Citizens," *Perspectives on Politics* 16, no. 1 (2018): 36–57; David Campbell and Richard Niemi, "Testing Civics: State-Level Civic Education Requirements and Political Knowledge," *American Political Science Review* 110, no. 3 (2016): 495–511.

[37] Jamila Michener, *Fragmented Democracy: Medicaid, Federalism, and Unequal Politics* (Cambridge: Cambridge University Press, 2018), 82.

[38] Katznelson, *Fear Itself*.

ENDURING UNEVENNESS

While the quality of subnational democracy has ramifications for the national polity, few studies treat democracy in the states as a subject of study in its own right.[39] Rather than comparative assessments of regime type in, say, Wisconsin and Minnesota, political scientists have produced a great mass of empirical studies comparing party competitiveness,[40] election administration,[41] the effects of state policy on civic participation,[42] and opinion-policy congruence.[43] While voluminous, the fragmentation of this literature impedes our understanding of subnational democracy in the United States. This is especially important if we want to assess the endurance of the democratic transition ushered in by the Second Reconstruction.[44]

We can begin to evaluate the unevenness in subnational democracy by considering how states vary on three basic criteria. First, do states extend equal voting rights to all adult citizens and do their votes have roughly equal weight? Second, do the vast majority of citizens in a state participate in elections? Third, is there effective competition among organized political parties? According to Kim Quaile Hill, when analyzed with these criteria, only fifteen states qualified as at least modestly "polyarchic" in the middle of the twentieth century.[45] By contrast, eleven states – exclusively in the South – constitute closed or relatively closed party oligarchies. While state-level democracy persisted in the South even after the end of Reconstruction,

---

[39] Carol Weissert, "Beyond Marble Cakes and Picket Fences: What US Federalism Scholars Can Learn from Comparative Work," *Journal of Politics* 73, no.4 (2011): 965–79.

[40] Austin Ranney, "Parties in State Politics," in *Politics in the American States*, ed. Herbert Jacob and Kenneth Vines (Boston: Little, Brown, 1956), 52–92; Thomas Holbrook and Elizabeth Van Dunk, "Electoral Competition in the American States," *American Political Science Review* 87, no. 4 (1993): 955–62.

[41] Li et al., "The Cost of Voting in the American States."

[42] Michener, *Fragmented Democracy*; Amy Lerman and Vesla Weaver, *Arresting Citizenship: The Democratic Consequences of American Crime Control* (Chicago: University of Chicago Press, 2014); Chris Zepeda-Millán, *Latino Mass Mobilization: Immigration, Racialization, and Activism* (Cambridge: Cambridge University Press, 2017).

[43] See Caughey and Warshaw, "Policy Preferences and Policy Change"; Lax and Phillips, "The Democratic Deficit in the States"; Stimson et al., "Dynamic Representation."

[44] Edward Gibson, *Boundary Control: Subnational Authoritarianism in Federal Democracies* (Cambridge: Cambridge University Press, 2013); Robert Mickey, *Paths out of Dixie: The Democratization of Authoritarian Enclaves in America's Deep South, 1944–1972* (Princeton: Princeton University Press, 2015).

[45] Kim Quaile Hill, *Democracy in the Fifty States* (Lincoln: University of Nebraska Press, 1994).

it eroded as the result of racial violence, election fraud, and ostensibly race-neutral laws that disenfranchised the Black population.[46] In the years that followed, state governments in the South existed as one-party authoritarian enclaves – denying the right to vote to African Americans and poor whites, brutally repressing dissent, and monopolizing control over the political arena. Even when we look outside the South, the quality of democracy is mixed. Prior to the reapportionment revolution, incumbent parties in many state legislatures also strategically leveraged malapportionment to constrain their political opponents, making the state legislature "ill equipped" to serve the "basic function of dissent."[47]

By the 1980s, the passage and reauthorization of the Voting Rights Act had virtually eliminated the *de jure* forms of vote suppression that had existed under Jim Crow (see Table 12.1). Yet pockets of resistance remained, and systematic efforts to erect "second generation" barriers to voting rights emerged in a number of states.[48] Registration systems in all but one state continued to pose barriers to voting.[49] State scores on an index measuring the cost of voting increased on average by 20 percent between 1996 and 2012.[50] Malapportionment disappeared, yet new technologies permitted more sophisticated forms of partisan gerrymandering. Following the 2010 Census, fourteen states severely gerrymandered their congressional districts and six did the same to their state assemblies.

Second, while the Voting Rights Act helped to correct major racial disparities in voter registration and turnout, substantial variation remained. Between 1980 and 1986, the range in state turnout rates compressed, but it did not improve across the fifty states. Moreover, four states (Georgia, South Carolina, Texas, and Virginia) had average voter-turnout rates below one third of the voting-age population. By 2018, the floor for turnout had risen from 28 to 36 percent, yet the ceiling fell slightly from 65 to 63 percent. In other words, the greatest improvement in turnout rates came from those that had historically performed poorly. Turnout did not markedly improve, however, among "middle-of-

---

[46] Richard M. Valelly, *The Two Reconstructions: The Struggle for Black Enfranchisement* (Chicago: University of Chicago Press, 1994).
[47] Key, *American State Politics*, 279.
[48] Jesse Rhodes, *Ballot Blocked: The Political Erosion of the Voting Rights Act* (Stanford: Stanford University Press, 2017).
[49] Burden and Neiheisel, "Election Administration."
[50] Li et al., "The Cost of Voting in the American States."

TABLE 12.1 *Significant features of subnational democracy*

	1946–52	1980–86	2012–18
Voting Rights Restrictions	De jure restrictions based on race / ethnicity: 11 states Malapportionment: 50 states Other major restrictions: 3 states	Systematic efforts to infringe rights: 7 states Systematic efforts to dilute minority vote: 7 states Registration-system barriers: 49 states	New voting rights restrictions: 28 states Extreme partisan gerrymanders (congressional): 14 states Extreme partisan gerrymanders (state assembly): 6 states
Turnout: (Average % Voting Age Population for Highest Office)	Median: 55 St. Dev: 15 Range: 17–73	Median: 45 St. Dev: 9 Range: 28–65	Median: 39 St. Dev: 6 Range: 36–63
Party Competitiveness: (Ranney Index)	One-Party Dem.: 11 Modified Dem.: 6 Two-Party: 13 Modified Rep.: 15 One-Party Rep.: 3	One-Party Dem.: 3 Modified Dem.: 22 Two-Party: 16 Modified Rep.: 9 One-Party Rep.: 0	One-Party Dem.: 1 Modified Dem.: 3 Two-Party: 17 Modified Rep.: 28 One-Party Rep: 1

Notes: Extreme partisan gerrymanders are all plans with an Efficiency Gap of +/− 8%; party competitiveness is measured using the Ranney Index.
Sources: Data for 1946–52 and 1980–86 tabulated by author from Hill (1994); Data for 2012–18 tabulated by author from: US Commission on Civil Rights, An Assessment of Minority Voting Rights Access in the United States (Washington, DC: USCCR, 2018); Michael Li and Laura Royden, *Extreme Maps* (New York: Brennan Center, 2017); United States Elections Project, Voter Turnout Data, www.electproject.org/home/voter-turnout/v oterturnout-data; National Conference of State Legislatures, State Partisan Composition Maps, www.ncsl.org/research/about-state-legislatures/partisan-composition.aspx.

the-pack" states, many of which began implementing tighter voter restrictions during this period.[51]

Third, the democratization of the South brought with it the end of closed party oligarchies in the states. Even so, party competitiveness – as

---

[51] David A. Bateman, "Race, Party, and American Voting Rights," *The Forum* 14, no. 1 (2016): 39–65.

measured by the Ranney Index – remained limited in the latter two periods of analysis. Whereas Democrats dominated the largest share of states in the 1980s, between 2012 and 2018, nearly two-thirds of the states were dominated by Republicans. By contrast, only seventeen states could be classified as competitive two-party systems. Indeed, while the end of party oligarchies opened up the possibility of two-party competition in the South, one-party Republican dominance soon emerged there due to several factors, including the increasing ideological alignment between the Republican Party and conservative Southern voters, the fact that loyal Southern Democratic voters have gradually aged out of the electorate, and incumbency advantages enjoyed by Republicans in majority-white jurisdictions.

Broadening our conceptualization of democracy beyond these political characteristics reveals additional evidence of unevenness.[52] Three examples will suffice. First, the organizational capacity of non-elite actors to make demands on government is highly inconsistent across states. In 2018, wage and salary workers with union representation varied from 3.6 percent in South Carolina to 24 percent in Hawaii.[53] The rise of right-to-work legislation in the states over the latter half of the twentieth century has significantly weakened the working class's capacity to effectively represent the interests of non-elite Americans.[54]

Second, states vary considerably in their protection of basic civil rights. North Dakota, which has seen a rash of recent hate crimes, provides only limited recourse for victims.[55] In recent years, the Kansas legislature has violated the state constitution by failing to provide "reasonably equal access to substantially similar equal educational opportunity."[56] Perhaps most importantly, state policies across the country have injured democratic citizenship by constructing an uneven, but ever-widening system of mass incarceration.[57] In 2017, the state-prison incarceration rate (per 100,000 people) ranged from 134 in Massachusetts to 720 in

---

[52] Michael Coppedge, John Gerring, David Altman, et al. "Conceptualizing and Measuring Democracy: A New Approach," *Perspectives on Politics* 9, no. 2 (2011): 247–67.
[53] Bureau of Labor Statistics, Union Affiliation of Employed Wage and Salary Workers by State, accessed December 10, 2020, www.bls.gov/news.release/union2.t05.htm.
[54] Laura C. Bucci, "Organized Labor's Check on Rising Economic Inequality in the US States," *State Politics & Policy Quarterly* 18, no. 2 (2018): 148–73.
[55] US Commission on Civil Rights, Advisory Memorandum on Hate Crime in North Dakota, accessed December 10, 2020, www.usccr.gov/pubs/2019/09-30-North-Dakota-Advisory-Memo-Hate-Crimes.pdf.
[56] *Gannon v. State*, 306 Kan. 1170 (Kan. 2017).
[57] Lerman and Weaver, *Arresting Citizenship*.

Louisiana.[58] This maps onto broader variation in the punitiveness of state-level policies on sentencing, parole, and juvenile justice.[59]

Third, state policies affecting social rights have also been historically uneven.[60] Variation among states in per-person Medicaid spending, for example, reflects stark differences in states' philosophies about income-transfer programs.[61] Thin Medicaid benefit packages, in turn, have a negative effect on low-income citizens' political participation.[62] Because states cannot engage in countercyclical spending, economic downturns can also yield retrenchment in state commitments to social rights. Since the Great Recession, spending on higher education has fallen in nearly every state. In eight states, for example, including Alabama, Arizona, Pennsylvania, and South Carolina, funding for higher education fell by more than 30 percent between 2008 and 2017. Over the same period, tuition at public colleges increased by 35 percent.

The evidence here points to persistent inequalities in state-level democracy, even in the wake of a significant democratic transition. To be sure, the closed party oligarchies of the past have disappeared. Yet the foundations of democratic rule – free and fair elections, competitive parties, and institutional support for civil and social rights – are not even across the fifty states. Such territorial variation is perhaps to be expected in a large, diverse polity.[63] If anything, however, this suggests that the quality of state-level democracy is understudied. This is especially troublesome, given both the historical roots of the variation as well as present trends that may undermine subnational democracy.

INSTITUTIONAL EROSION AND POLARIZED DEMOCRACY

How should we understand the endurance of unevenness in democratic rule following the belated consolidation of American democracy? Several factors seem important. First, the legal instruments of that consolidation

---

[58] Prison Policy Project, Data toolbox. prisonpolicy.org/data.
[59] Katharine A. Neill, Juita-Elena Yusuf, and John C. Morris, "Explaining Dimensions of State-Level Punitiveness in the United States: The Roles of Social, Economic, and Cultural Factors," *Criminal Justice Policy Review* 26, no. 8 (2015): 751–72.
[60] Suzanne Mettler, *Dividing Citizens: Gender and Federalism in New Deal Public Policy* (Ithaca: Cornell University Press, 1998).
[61] John Holahan, "State Variation in Medicaid Spending: Hard to Justify," *Health Affairs* 26, Suppl2 (2007): w667–w669.
[62] Michener, *Fragmented Democracy*.
[63] Kelly M. McMann, "Measuring Subnational Democracy: Toward Improved Regime Typologies and Theories of Regime Change," *Democratization* 25, no. 1 (2018): 19–37.

Laboratories of What? 311

have been subject to gradual institutional erosion. Consider the Voting Rights Act (VRA), arguably the keystone of what Edward Gibson calls the "territorial regime" supporting subnational democracy.[64] Its powerful preclearance provisions, routinely reauthorized and expanded by wide bipartisan majorities, gave it the reputation for being the most effective civil rights law ever enacted. Yet the VRA's solid majorities in Congress concealed a sustained antipathy to the law on the political right, and enduring partisan polarization on the question of racial justice.[65] Between 1982 and 2006, the Department of Justice blocked over 700 attempts by VRA-covered jurisdictions to enact discriminatory election rules. Core coalition partners within the Republican Party – including representatives of organized business who feared the potential redistributive implications of minority political incorporation – turned to administrative and legal venues to contest the law soon after the VRA's enactment. By the 1980s, the Reagan administration helped to slow action on preclearance enforcement at the Department of Justice. Conservative judicial nominees advocated for strong limitations on majority-minority redistricting and application of preclearance provisions. By the early 2000s, these efforts had grown more aggressive. At the same time, after a decade of movement toward less restrictive voter-registration procedures, states began to experiment with new forms of voter restriction, including limits on early voting, tightening registration requirements, voter-identification rules, and greater barriers to felon re-enfranchisement.[66] The Supreme Court's 5–4 decision to strike the VRA's preclearance formula in *Shelby County v. Holder* thus represented a culmination of a decades-long series of maneuvers to dismantle the territorial regime that emerged following the Second Reconstruction. After it came a deluge. Twenty-eight states adopted new restrictions on voter registration, including identification requirements, purges of voter rolls, cuts to early voting, and the elimination of polling locations.

De-consolidating democracy required the displacement of debates over voting rights from high-salience venues like Congress to arenas where public attention would be minimal: the bureaucracy and the courts. It also demanded a legal means to weaken federal agencies' leverage over the conduct of local elections – further parochializing conflict. Indeed, the recipe for what Przeworski calls "subversion by stealth" need not be unlawful. Rather, subversive maneuvers can include legal (or legally

---

[64] Gibson, *Boundary Control.*   [65] Rhodes, *Ballot Blocked.*
[66] Bateman, "Race, Party, and American Voting Rights."

ambiguous) manipulations of rules and norms that diminish access to elections, rights, or accountability.[67]

Yet if subversion by stealth is the means of deconstructing subnational democracy, where is the motive? To find the answer, we have to consider the shifting incentives of state-level politicians. Not all elected officials pursue strategies of boundary control.[68] Rather, what matters is whether politicians can achieve their desired ends through electoral politics. After they are elected, officials intensely committed to an unpopular ideological goal face a stark choice. They must decide whether or not to use the power of the state to entrench themselves in office and weaken their opponents' opportunities for electoral and policy success.

It bears mentioning, then, that the period following the democratic transition witnessed a major shift in the ideological landscape of American politics. With the decline of the one-party South, the centralization of government, and the decline of local media landscapes, state governments became increasingly ideologically aligned with national, polarized parties.[69] The recent rise of undemocratic maneuvers at the state level is at least in part attributable to asymmetric polarization in the states. Consider restrictions on voting. Whereas many states expanded access to the ballot in the 1990s and early 2000s via voting by mail and early voting, a growing number of states have passed laws increasing the cost of voting through tightening voter registration deadlines, rolling back early voting, limiting the number of polling stations, and reducing polling hours.[70] Voter restrictions are the subject of intensely polarized battles.[71] Between 2006 and 2011, states with an unencumbered Republican majority in the state legislature were significantly more likely to enact voter restrictions than states where Democrats had control. Yet when it comes to voting rights, partisanship intersects with race: legislatures were significantly more likely to restrict voting in states with larger Black populations or where minority turnout had increased sharply in the 2008 presidential

---

[67] Ellen Lust and David Waldner, "Unwelcome Change: Understanding, Evaluating, and Extending Theories of Democratic Backsliding" (Washington, DC: US Agency for International Development, 2015), 7.

[68] Gibson, *Boundary Control*.

[69] Daniel J. Hopkins, *The Increasingly United States: How and Why American Political Behavior Nationalized* (Chicago: University of Chicago Press, 2018).

[70] Li et al., "The Cost of Voting in the American States."

[71] William D. Hicks, Seth C. McKee, and Daniel A. Smith, "The Determinants of State Legislator Support for Restrictive Voter ID Laws," *State Politics & Policy Quarterly* 16, no. 4 (2016): 411–31.

election.[72] In general, new restrictions on voting have a depressing effect on voter turnout.[73] When North Carolina enacted a strong photo ID requirement for voting, it resulted in a 2.6 percent decrease in turnout for voters without an ID in the general election.[74] Notably, this deterrent effect persisted *even after the law was suspended*, likely because the law created confusion and because voters lacked information about changing requirements for voting. Countermobilization may help to minimize the impact of these laws on turnout.[75] Even so, administrative barriers to voting are undeniably "real, nontrivial, and unequal in impact."[76]

Next, consider the rise of partisan gerrymandering in the 1990s and 2000s. Here, it is not merely the asymmetric polarization of the parties that matters, but also Republicans' increasingly sophisticated efforts to coordinate redistricting plans across state legislatures. In 2010, the Republican State Leadership Committee launched REDMAP (short for Redistricting Majority Project) to invest in swing-state races with the explicit aim of controlling redistricting in swing states like Wisconsin and North Carolina. The availability of sophisticated mapping software like Maptitude enabled Republicans to redraw districts to lock in their electoral gains in the 2010 midterms. By 2012, Wisconsin's gerrymander had ensured that, while Democrats won 53 percent of the votes for State Assembly, they won only 39 percent of assembly seats. This case is emblematic of a broader asymmetric pattern in gerrymandering. Since 1972, unified Democratic control of state government has had a consistent effect on one prominent measure of gerrymandering, the efficiency gap.[77] By contrast, the treatment effect of unified Republican control on the efficiency gap in state legislatures nearly doubled between the 1972–90 period and the years between 1992 and 2014. In other words, both parties gerrymander, but in recent years Republicans have engaged in a far more intense form of gerrymandering than Democrats.

---

[72] Keith G. Bentele and Erin E. O'Brien, "Jim Crow 2.0? Why States Consider and Adopt Restrictive Voter Access Policies," *Perspectives on Politics* 11, no. 4 (2013): 1088–116.

[73] Li et al., "The Cost of Voting in the American States."

[74] Justin Grimmer and Jesse Yoder, "The Durable Deterrent Effects of Strict Photo Identification Laws," Working Paper, University of Pennsylvania, 2019.

[75] Nicholas Valentino and Fabian Neuner, "Why the Sky Didn't Fall: Mobilizing Anger in Reaction to Voter ID Laws," *Political Psychology* 38, no. 2 (2017): 331–50.

[76] Ben Highton, "Voter Identification Laws and Turnout in the United States," *Annual Review of Political Science* 20 (2017): 164.

[77] Nicholas Stephanopoulos, "The Causes and Consequences of Gerrymandering," *William and Mary Law Review* 59, no. 5 (2018): 2115–58.

Party polarization has also intersected with another trend that threatens democracy in the states: the infiltration of ideological networks into party organizations. Over the latter half of the twentieth century, successive waves of reform and organizational change gradually hollowed out local party organizations, disconnecting party actors from the work of candidate selection and policy development.[78] Taking their place has been a looser assemblage of intense policy demanders, who leverage party apparatuses to pursue their interests. Within the Republican Party, conservative network organizations such as the American Legislative Exchange Council (ALEC) and the State Policy Network (SPN) organized to advance an agenda of upwardly redistributive policies that lack a mass base of support.[79] Understandably, then, these organizations have also promoted policies that weaken mass participation and civil-society infrastructure. Among other model legislation promoted by ALEC are bills that restrict ballot-box access through imposing administrative burdens and limit the use of ballot initiatives on issues like the minimum wage. ALEC has also promoted right-to-work laws, which weaken the organizational capacity of labor unions, as well as preemption laws which bar local governments from crafting worker protections.[80] Other model bills have the capacity to undermine civic engagement through privatizing public education systems.[81]

When ideologically extreme parties experience costly electoral threats, "constitutional hardball" is never far behind. Forty-eight hours after Democrat Roy Cooper's victory in the 2016 North Carolina gubernatorial election, Republicans introduced a package of legislation that, among other things, restricted Cooper's ability to make cabinet appointments, cut the size of the executive branch by 275 percent, and gave Republicans control over the state Board of Elections during election years. The legislation was soon signed by outgoing governor Pat McCrory (R). Two years later,

---

[78] Advisory Commission on Intergovernmental Relations, *The Transformation in American Politics: Implications for Federalism* (Washington, DC: ACIR, 1986); Julia Azari, "Weak Parties and Strong Partisanship Are a Bad Combination," *Vox.com*, November 3, 2016; Daniel Schlozman and Sam Rosenfeld, "The Hollow Parties," in *Can America Govern Itself*, ed. Frances E. Lee and Nolan McCarty (Cambridge: Cambridge University Press, 2019), 120–54.

[79] Alexander Hertel-Fernandez, *State Capture: How Conservative Activists, Big Businesses, and Wealthy Donors Reshaped American Politics – and the Nation* (Oxford: Oxford University Press, 2019).

[80] Ibid.

[81] Julie Underwood and Julie Mead, "A Smart ALEC Threatens Public Education," *Phi Delta Kappan* 93, no. 6 (2012): 51–55.

Laboratories of What? 315

Republicans in Wisconsin introduced a similar package of legislation, which cabined the authority of governor-elect Tony Evers (D) over key state commissions, the state's Medicaid and nutritional assistance programs. Signed into law by outgoing governor Scott Walker (R), the package also restricted the number of days allotted for early voting. Both McCrory and Walker's ideological commitments mattered here. In Michigan, outgoing governor Rick Snyder (R) – who had frequently disagreed with hard-right members of his own party – vetoed similar legislation, introduced after the election of Gretchen Whitmer (D) to the office in 2018.

As the Michigan example shows, institutional veto points are a conditional bulwark against democratic erosion. The courts provide another illustration. Despite numerous district court rulings overturning partisan gerrymanders, the Supreme Court's 5–4 decision in *Rucho v. Common Cause* (2019) effectively deemed the subject nonjusticiable, closing the window of opportunity offered by Anthony Kennedy's concurrence in *Vieth v. Jubelirer* (2006). A similar pattern has played out on the issue of partisan power grabs. In an ideologically divided 4–3 decision, Wisconsin's Supreme Court upheld lame-duck legislation passed in 2018, ruling that the state's Constitution "affords the Legislature absolute discretion to determine the rules of its own proceedings."[82] Less than a year later, a federal district-court ruling effectively punted the Wisconsin legislation, suggesting that it lacked jurisdiction to "police the boundaries" between the branches "in the absence of a concrete and particularized harm and the violation of a federal constitutional right."[83]

Judicial deference on issues of subnational democracy highlights a broader epistemic challenge in strengthening subnational democracy. If "subversion by stealth" is the most common form of democratic erosion, policing it requires a great deal of societal consensus on when so-called "bright line" rules have been violated. Yet public opinion studies suggest that, despite a surprising level of consensus on what the "bright lines" are, assessments of their violation diverge, in predictable ways, along party lines.[84] In other words, polarization may not only drive

---

[82] *League of Women Voters v. Evers*, 75 Wisc. 2019.
[83] *Democratic Party of Wisconsin v. Vos*. W.D. Wis. Sep. 30, 2019.
[84] John M. Carey, Gretchen Helmke, Brendan Nyhan, Mitchell Sanders, and Susan Stokes, "Searching for Bright Lines in the Trump Presidency," *Perspectives on Politics* 17, no. 3 (2019): 699–718.

democratic erosion – it may preclude efforts to reverse it. What is to be done?

STRENGTHENING SUBNATIONAL DEMOCRACY

Subnational democratization is best described as a slow-moving institutional process – slow moving, in part, because the US Constitution imposes rigid barriers to changing the territorial regime.[85] These structural impediments also enable local elites who wish to preserve countermajoritarian arrangements to engage more easily in strategies of boundary control. This includes designing electoral and legislative structures to preempt competition and monopolizing links to the national polity to limit outside influence in territorial affairs. In a nationally democratic polity, efforts at boundary control are often designed to fly under the radar, making their identification and eradication all the more difficult.

Given the challenges of parochialized politics, strengthening subnational democracy typically requires the nationalization of conflict.[86] This can occur through either party-led transitions, in which national leaders invest in state-level resources to defeat incumbents, or center-led transitions, in which national authorities intervene to transform the rules of the game. Indeed, the central reason *why* urban voters brought the issue of state legislative malapportionment before the federal courts is because malapportionment itself had deprived them of leverage in the subnational political process. Absent mass mobilization for the passage of a national Voting Rights Act in Congress, widespread disenfranchisement of Black voters would have no doubt continued.

Yet in an intensely polarized polity, nationalizing conflict presents problems of its own. If the federal judiciary is unwilling to wade into the "political thicket," legislative or executive action will be necessary. The *Shelby* majority, for example, framed its decision as an invitation for Congress to rewrite Section 4(b) of the Voting Rights Act (VRA). Yet in part because political conflict over the rights of citizenship is *already* so nationalized, efforts to restore the Voting Rights Act – let alone enhance it – have faced stiff political opposition.

Members of every Congress since *Shelby* have introduced stand-alone legislation to restore the preclearance formula, updating it to reflect new forms of voter suppression, including photo ID laws. Yet, with only

---

[85] Arend Lijphart, *Patterns of Democracy* (New Haven: Yale University Press, 1999).
[86] Gibson, *Boundary Control*.

a modicum of Republican support – gathered by its sponsor, Rep. James Sensenbrenner (R–WI) – the legislation has never received a vote in either chamber. Rather than reintroducing this legislation when they retook the House in 2019, Democrats broadened the scope of democracy reform legislation to include, among other things, measures to require automatic voter registration, nationwide early voting, a ban on partisan gerrymandering, and voter restoration for citizens with past criminal convictions. The legislation passed on a strict party-line vote in the House and was dead on arrival in the Republican-controlled Senate.[87]

In addition to elite polarization on the expansion of voting rights, attitudes at the mass level are mixed. In advance of the 2016 election, a third of the country expected voter fraud to be a "major problem." Such fears have not abated, especially given President Trump's circulation of the myth that there was widespread voter fraud in 2016. Self-identified Democrats overwhelmingly support doing "everything possible" to make it easier to vote. Yet self-identified Republicans appear evenly divided on the question.[88] By contrast, 85 percent of self-identified Republicans and 93 percent of Democrats – at least in the abstract – support measures to limit partisan gerrymandering.[89]

Do the present challenges of nationalizing conflict suggest that democracy activists ought to concentrate their attention locally? There is some evidence that the localization of issues can have a depolarizing effect.[90] And in the last several years, social movements have advanced measures across a number of American states to restrict partisan gerrymandering and to expand voting rights.[91] Yet the replicability of these strategies across the country is an open question. Suppose there is a broad-based social movement whose main goal is to enhance access to the ballot box. Assuming its resources are limited, it can choose to concentrate its attention in one of two ways. First, it can seek to expand voter participation

---

[87] Max Feldman, "Voting Rights in America, Six Years After *Shelby v. Holder*," Brennan Center for Justice, June 25, 2019.
[88] John Laloggia, "Conservative Republicans Are Least Supportive of Making It Easy for Everyone to Vote," Pewresearch.org, October 31, 2018.
[89] Kathy Frankovic, "Few Support Partisan Gerrymandering," YouGov, October 4, 2017, accessed December 10, 2020, https://today.yougov.com/topics/politics/articles-reports/2017/10/04/few-support-partisan-gerrymandering
[90] Amalie Jensen, William Marble, Kenneth Scheve, and Matthew Slaughter, "City Limits to Partisan Polarization in the American Public." Unpublished ms (Princeton University), 2019.
[91] David Daley, *Unrigged: How Americans Are Battling Back to Save Democracy* (New York: Liveright, 2020).

through Automatic Voter Registration (AVR) in ten states where the "cost of voting" is already the lowest in the country.[92] Because incumbent office-holders – and judges drawn from the governing party – are difficult to persuade directly on AVR, the movement chooses to pursue the issue at the ballot box, which is permitted in seven of the ten states.[93] Alternatively, the movement could concentrate its resources on the ten states where the cost of voting is the highest.[94] In these states, it would not pursue AVR, but a package of four basic reforms (same-day registration, expanded early voting, no-excuse absentee voting, and felon enfranchisement). In this case, the movement would, as before, prefer to pursue these reforms at the ballot box. Yet only *three* of these ten states allow for initiatives and referenda.[95] Under these circumstances, it seems at least plausible that a movement with limited resources would have an incentive to pursue the first of the two strategies, resulting in the under-provision of resources to states with higher barriers to ballot-box access.

The downside of this state-by-state strategy is thus the persistence, for a time, of uneven subnational democracy. Even so, these localized campaigns may help to enhance the visibility of democratic deficits and their material consequences for the lives of ordinary voters. As such, they may not be an alternative to the nationalization of conflict, but a *precursor* to effective conflict expansion. It is worth remembering that the legislative record supporting the 2006 reauthorization of the VRA came to roughly 15,000 pages, which were littered with examples of localized contestation of attempts to undermine voting rights. Despite Congress's failure to revise the preclearance formula, field hearings on voting rights have continued. But legislative action on reauthorization is stalled, and is unlikely to resume in the absence of unified control of government by the Democratic Party.

Yet a nationally coordinated, but localized, mass movement may well be far more effective than hearings at creating a greater social consciousness about democratic deficits in the states. Such a movement would help

---

[92] Li et al., "The Cost of Voting in the American States." These states are: California, Colorado, Iowa, Maine, Maryland, Massachusetts, New Jersey, North Dakota, Oregon, and Utah.
[93] California, Colorado, Maine, Massachusetts, North Dakota, Oregon, Utah. Maryland allows only veto referenda.
[94] Indiana, Kansas, Kentucky, Michigan, Mississippi, Ohio, South Carolina, Tennessee, Texas, Virginia.
[95] Michigan, Mississippi, Ohio.

to generate a spatially distributed "observatory" of democracy.[96] It could, for example, produce information about local compliance with democratic norms, state-level institutional obstacles to democratization, opportunities for coalition building, and a better sense of the means necessary to enforce compliance with democracy-enhancing reforms.

In any case, if partisan polarization on the question of subnational governance persists at its current level, and if the courts are not willing partners in Gibson's model of a "center-led intervention," popular mobilization by non-elites – in the form of protests, boycotts, and strikes – may ultimately be necessary to defend democratic values in the states.[97] Democratization depends in no small part on the ability of non-elites to engage in disruptive action.[98] If this is so, strengthening democracy in the states requires restoring – and indeed deepening – the capacity of ordinary Americans to engage in organized struggle. The raw materials of this capacity are evident in recent social movements, including the protests against police brutality that followed the murder of George Floyd in the summer of 2020, which offer "broad and decentralized challenges to institutionalized inequality."[99] In the midst of tremendous political setbacks for organized labor, more American workers went on strike in 2018 than at any time since 1986.[100] Whether these movements can be stitched together, expanded, and targeted at institutional change, remains to be seen. This uncertainty should remind us that the American states are not so much "laboratories of democracy" as sites of an ongoing democratization project.

---

[96] Michael Schudson, "Political Observatories, Databases & News in the Emerging Ecology of Public Information," *Daedalus* 139, no. 2 (2010): 100–09.
[97] Maria J. Stephan and Erica Chenoweth, "Why Civil Resistance Works: The Strategic Logic of Nonviolent Conflict," *International Security* 33, no. 1 (2008): 7–44.
[98] Adaner Usmani, "Democracy and the Class Struggle," *American Journal of Sociology* 124, no. 3 (2018): 664–704.
[99] David S. Meyer and Sidney Tarrow, "Introduction," in *The Resistance: The Dawn of the Anti-Trump Movement*, ed. David S. Meyer and Sidney Tarrow (Oxford: Oxford University Press, 2018), 15.
[100] Bureau of Labor Statistics, "Major Work Stoppages in 2018," accessed December 10, 2020, www.bls.gov/news.release/wkstp.nr0.htm.

13

Conservative Extra-Party Coalitions and Statehouse Democracy

Alexander Hertel-Fernandez

Over a month after 2020 election night had ended, the results of the presidential contest between former Vice President Joe Biden and Donald J. Trump seemed obvious to all except President Trump and his supporters in the Republican Party. Even as Biden's victory over Trump became clear in the days following the election, a campaign unfolded to overturn the vote totals and deny Biden his victory. The most worrisome elements involved armed supporters of President Trump threatening election officials with violence or death.[1] No less extreme was unprecedented litigation supported by seventeen Republican state attorneys general and more than half of House Republicans asking the US Supreme Court to reverse the election.[2] That case lost. But in the process, broad swaths of the Republican Party leadership indicated they are willing to use every institutional lever at their disposal to overturn public opinion as expressed in the voting booth.

In explaining why Republican leaders were so quick to try to overturn the votes cast by millions of Americans, many observers pointed to Trump. As the *New York Times* argued, the ongoing campaign to reverse the election showed "how singular a figure Mr. Trump remains in the G.O.P."[3] Reaching further back in political history and looking at the states, rather than federal politics, this chapter challenges the view that the

---

[1] Nick Corasaniti, Jim Rutenberg, and Kathleen Gray, "As Trump Rails Against Loss, His Supporters Become More Threatening," *New York Times*, December 8, 2020.
[2] Jeremy W. Peters and Maggie Haberman, "17 Republican Attorneys General Back Trump in Far-Fetched Election Lawsuit," *New York Times*, December 9 2020.
[3] Peters and Haberman, "17 Republican Attorneys General Back Trump in Far-Fetched Election Lawsuit."

GOP's anti-majoritarianism is an exclusive outgrowth of the Trump presidency in 2020. Instead, it shows a much longer trajectory of efforts by conservative leaders, prodded on by networks of organized interests, to overturn or bypass public opinion, with the states as key battlegrounds.

For one clue, consider developments from two years prior, in the 2018 elections. Most of the attention on that election night focused on whether Democrats, buoyed by the national resistance movement against President Donald J. Trump, could retake control of the US House. But further down ballot, voters had the opportunity to enact sweeping changes to state policy that had previously languished in Republican-controlled state legislatures. In Utah, Idaho, and Nebraska, for instance, voters were deciding whether their states ought to expand Medicaid to cover previously uninsured poor adults as part of the Affordable Care Act.[4]

With all the votes tallied, it became clear that voters backed the new policies, sometimes by wide margins, in each of the states. Yet despite these public mandates, conservative legislators in these states moved quickly to either ignore or undermine the results of the election. In Utah, for instance, legislators replaced the full expansion approved by voters with a partial expansion and a cap on federal funding, as well as onerous new work requirements on beneficiaries that will likely reduce access to medical care and financial security among low-income households.[5] GOP legislators in Idaho, for their part, similarly sought a more limited expansion than authorized by voters as well as work requirements. In addition, responding directly to the Medicaid vote, Idahoan legislators tried to make it harder for citizens to pass ballot initiatives at all.[6]

These state episodes, set against the GOP's campaign against the 2020 election results, pose a puzzle for standard political science accounts that emphasize the centrality of voter preferences. They also challenge our shared norms of democratic participation. Over 60 percent of Idahoans, for instance, had voted in favor of full expansion of Medicaid, including

---

[4] Sarah Kliff, "4 States Could Expand Medicaid This Year. That's a Big Deal," *Vox*, June 4, 2018.

[5] Akeiisa Coleman and Rachel Nuzum, "Medicaid Expansion across the Country: An Update on the Ballot States," *To the Point (The Commonwealth Fund)*, June 20, 2019; Hannah Katch, Jennifer Wagner, and Aviva Aron-Dine, *Taking Medicaid Coverage Away from People Not Meeting Work Requirements Will Reduce Low-Income Families' Access to Care and Worsen Health Outcomes*, Center on Budget and Policy Priorities (Washington, 2018).

[6] Audrey Dutton, McKenna King, and Mike Sharp, "GOP Bill to Toughen Voter Initiative Standards Would Have Killed Medicaid Expansion," *Idaho Statesman*, March 15, 2019.

many Republicans.[7] (The measure passed in all but nine of the forty-two Idaho counties that voted for Trump in 2016.) Shouldn't politicians feel pressure to respond to the preferences of their constituents, especially when public opinion was so supportive of a particular policy and expressed through the ballot box?

To answer this question, this chapter tracks how a collision of new institutional and organizational developments over the past four decades – well before Trump's entry to Republican Party politics – have undermined democratic responsiveness and representation in the states. More specifically, I highlight the role of coalitions of wealthy donors, ideological activists, and private-sector businesses in redefining the stands held by Republican state legislators. The result of these conservative activists' efforts has been to polarize the Republican party – that is, to pull the GOP toward far-right policy positions often opposed by majorities of the public, including Republicans, on a range of policy issues.[8] These coalitions have also encouraged GOP politicians to pursue policies that tilt the political playing field toward further conservative electoral and legislative victories by weakening their political opponents and raising obstacles to broader political participation. Both outcomes suggest concerning ways that polarization on the right, prodded on by political organizations, may be challenging – and even eroding – important aspects of American democracy, including the political representation of ordinary Americans and the balance of political competition and participation. My account thus complements Phil Rocco and David Bateman's chapters in this volume by documenting the organizational roots of state-level efforts to restrict democratic participation in recent years. It also sheds important light on the Republicans anti-majoritarian campaign to overturn election results after the 2020 presidential election.

I develop this argument as follows. I first consider the evidence for whether states are bolstering democratic representation and participation in recent decades, arguing that the outlook is gloomier than research in

---

[7] See www.cnn.com/election/2018/results/idaho/ballot-measures/1/.
[8] See also Jacob S. Hacker and Paul Pierson, *Let them Eat Tweets: How the Right Rules in an Age of Extreme Inequality* (New York: Liveright 2020); Jacob S. Hacker and Paul Pierson, *Off Center: The Republican Revolution and the Erosion of American Democracy* (New Haven: Yale University Press, 2005); Thomas E. Mann and Norman J. Ornstein, *It's Even Worse Than It Looks: How the American Constitutional System Collided with the New Politics of Extremism* (New York: Basic Books, 2012); Theda Skocpol and Alexander Hertel-Fernandez, "The Koch Network and Republican Party Extremism," *Perspectives on Politics* 14, no. 3 (2016).

political science would suggest. States are not only ignoring large majorities to pursue unpopular agendas, but also taking aggressive steps to limit democratic participation. My brief tour of recent state policy underscores that anti-majoritarian tendencies in the states are increasingly concentrated in one wing of one party – the conservative end of the GOP – and therefore in the roughly half of states that are under partial or full Republican control. In the following two sections, I describe the organizational and institutional forces that have enabled conservative activists to successfully press policy positions on the Republican party that run against public opinion and that often serve to weaken or even incapacitate the right's political opposition. The final section concludes by reflecting on the implications of these findings for understanding broader trends in contemporary American politics.

STATEHOUSE DEMOCRACY: (STILL) ALIVE AND WELL?

How well are the states living up to their promise as laboratories of democracy, responding to the evolving preferences and needs of their citizens, or bulwarks of democracy, protecting and deepening the political representation of Americans and their ability to participate in the political process?

Considering state developments in response to the Trump administration, the answer might seem promising. In the face of efforts by the Trump White House to erode democratic norms, procedures, and institutions, many states have responded by using their legislative and constitutional authority to challenge the president.[9] States have, for instance, sued the administration to prevent partisan meddling with the 2020 census and efforts to limit immigration from majority-Muslim countries. Indeed, in the early days of the Trump administration, one leading legal scholar urged fellow liberals to consider how federalism could be a source of "progressive resistance"[10] against the president's worst policies and another saw federalism as the safeguard against moves toward autocracy under the Trump administration.[11] The idea that federalism checks

---

[9] Greg Goelzhauser and David M. Konisky, "The State of American Federalism 2018–2019: Litigation, Partisan Polarization, and the Administrative Presidency," *Publius* 49, no. 3 (2019).

[10] Heather Gerken, "We're About to See States' Rights Used Defensively Against Trump," *Vox*, January 20, 2017.

[11] Ian Millhiser, "Federalism in a Time of Autocracy," *Yale Law & Policy Review* 35, no. 2 (2017).

authoritarian impulses has a long lineage: James Madison, writing in the *Federalist Papers*, argued that with their independent bases of power and support, state governments would surely join together in "plans of resistance" against any "ambitious encroachments of the federal government."[12]

Looking more systematically at the responsiveness of state policy to public opinion, some political scientists have argued that statehouse democracy is alive and well[13], supporting generations of scholars who argued that federalism and decentralization enhance political representation by accommodating ethnic, racial, and political diversity and permitting citizens to vote with their feet.[14]

That picture of responsiveness, however, looks dimmer when we consider very recent legislative battles and look at specific policies instead of aggregations of policies.[15] Doing so reveals that many state governments are failing to act on policies preferred by majorities of their public, while also frequently pursuing large-scale policy shifts intended to bypass voters altogether. Medicaid expansion is clearly one example of the former. But there are a number of other policy areas where states, especially under full Republican control, are failing to respond to their citizens – with significant social and economic consequences.

Consider a highly salient and substantively important economic policy – the minimum wage – where we might expect to see responsiveness.[16] GOP states have failed to increase the minimum wage beyond the level set by the federal government ($7.25/hour) over a decade ago. While some states have responded by increasing their minimum wages to reflect this inaction, twenty-one mostly Republican-controlled states have not.

---

[12] The Federalist Papers No. 46.

[13] Devin Caughey, Yiqing Xu, and Chris Warshaw, "Incremental Democracy: The Policy Effects of Partisan Control of State Government," *Journal of Politics* 79, no. 4 (2016); Devin Caughey and Christopher Warshaw, "Policy Preferences and Policy Change: Dynamic Responsiveness in the American States, 1936–2014," *American Political Science Review* 112, no. 2 (2018); Matt Grossmann, *Red State Blues: How the Republican Revolution Stalled in the States* (Cambridge: Cambridge University Press, 2019). See also Robert S. Erikson, Gerald C. Wright, and John P. McIver, *Statehouse Democracy* (Cambridge: Cambridge University Press, 1993).

[14] See, e.g., Ugo M. Amoretti and Nancy Bermeo, *Federalism and Territorial Cleavages* (Baltimore: Johns Hopkins University Press, 2004); Charles M. Tiebout, "A Pure Theory of Local Expenditures," *Journal of Political Economy* 64, no. 5 (1956). See also the intellectual history documented in the Rocco chapter.

[15] See also Jeffrey R. Lax and Justin H. Phillips, "The Democratic Deficit in the States," *American Journal of Political Science* 56, no. 1 (2012).

[16] See, e.g., Lax and Phillips, "The Democratic Deficit in the States."

But states are not just failing to update their minimum wages. In reaction to the pressure from the "Fight for Fifteen" mass movement pushing for a higher minimum wage, especially for retail and service workers,[17] GOP states have passed new laws blocking the ability of cities within their borders from passing their *own* local increases in the minimum wage, even when such measures pass by wide margins in ballot measures and are supported by majorities of a city's residents. Twenty-six states, disproportionately those under full or partial Republican control, have passed preemption laws. In a similar vein, many GOP controlled states have also banned city-level efforts to pass paid sick or family leave programs (with twenty-three states preempting such programs). In all, well over half of Americans now live in a state that has barred cities from raising local wages and nearly four in ten are in a state that restricts city-level efforts on paid leave.[18] States' inaction on, and preemption of, minimum wages and paid leave thus often runs against the preferences of broad swaths of their citizens. It also has significant economic consequences: over 21 million workers in minimum wage–preempted states would be affected by an increase in the state minimum wage to $15 an hour by 2024 and about 16 million minimum wage workers would gain access to leave in states barring local-level paid leave programs.[19]

Conservative legislatures are not just bypassing public opinion on crucial economic policies. These states are also increasingly passing policies that curb political participation more generally, aimed squarely at their opponents on the political left. Such power-tilting policies are perhaps most obvious in election administration, where conservative lawmakers have, in recent years, embarked on widespread efforts to restrict access to the ballot box.[20]

These efforts include voter ID laws, which have received outsized media attention for the ways in which they often target Democratic constituencies, like college students or minority communities, while

---

[17] Steven Greenhouse, *Beaten Down, Worked Up: The Past, Present, and Future of American Labor* (New York: Alfred A. Knopf, 2019), chapter 16.
[18] Alexander Hertel-Fernandez, *State Capture: How Conservative Activists, Big Businesses, and Wealthy Donors Reshaped the American States – and the Nation* (New York: Oxford University Press, 2019), 241.
[19] David Cooper, *Raising the Federal Minimum Wage to $15 by 2024 Would Lift Pay for Nearly 40 Million Workers*, Economic Policy Institute (Washington, 2019).
[20] Keith G. Bentele and Erin E. O'Brien, "Jim Crow 2.0? Why States Consider and Adopt Restrictive Voter Access Policies," *Perspectives on Politics* 11, no. 4 (2013); Ari Berman, *Give Us the Ballot: The Modern Struggle for Voting Rights in America* (New York: Farrar, Straus and Giroux, 2015).

shielding Republican-leaning groups (like gun owners) from their provisions.[21] But these election meddling efforts go well beyond ID laws to include reforms curtailing early voting, closing polling locations, instituting "purges" of voter rolls to force infrequent voters to re-register to vote, and raising barriers to registering new voters.[22] Political scientists are still debating the net effect of these measures on turnout,[23] but it is clear that they raise the costs of voting – and force campaigns and canvassing groups to expend additional resources to mobilize the same voters. In private – and sometimes even in public, too – Republican lawmakers make clear that the intention of these laws is to make it harder for their political opponents to win elections.[24]

A similar tendency is on full display with conservative efforts to aggressively redistrict state legislative and Congressional districts to undermine Democratic electoral prospects – made substantially easier by the natural geographic concentration of Democratic voters in urban areas[25] – as well as the move by right-wing electoral consultants to push for redistricting on the basis of citizens, rather than all adults.[26] Counting only citizens for the purpose of drawing legislative districts would reduce the electoral clout of areas with large immigrant populations (documented or not).

Attempts to weaken or suppress conservatives' political opposition altogether extend beyond the ballot box into civil society. In the wake of progressive mass mobilizations in recent years related to climate change, police shootings, immigrant detention, and labor standards, GOP legislatures have pursued laws restricting the rights of protesters.[27] These include efforts to criminalize demonstrations on private property, increase penalties on protests deemed riots, punish activists who wear masks

---

[21] Rebecca Leber, "In Texas, You Can Vote with a Concealed Handgun License – but Not a Student ID," *The New Republic*, October 20, 2014.
[22] Matt Vasilogambros, "Voter Access Matters in 2020, and These Lawmakers Know It," *Pew Stateline*, August 1, 2019.
[23] Benjamin Highton, "Voter Identification Laws and Turnout in the United States," *Annual Review of Political Science* 20 (2017).
[24] Jamelle Bouie, "Republicans Admit Voter ID Laws Are Aimed at Democratic Voters," *The Daily Beast*, August 28, 2013; Michael Wines, "Some Republicans Acknowledge Leveraging Voter ID Laws for Political Gain," *New York Times*, September 16, 2016.
[25] Jonathan Rodden, *Why Cities Lose* (New York: Basic Book, 2019).
[26] Nick Brown, "Republicans Want Census Data on Citizenship for Redistricting," *Reuters*, April 8, 2019; Tierney Sneed, "Key Voter Fraud Alarmist Pushing States to Adopt Anti-Immigrant Redistricting Change," *Talking Points Memo*, August 19, 2019.
[27] Chan S. Suh and Sidney Tarrow, "'Wholesale' Legal Repression: Threat and Political Advantage in State Legislative Repression of Protest," Unpublished working paper (2020).

during protests to avoid identification by the police, and make protestors liable for any property damages. Some restrictions are laser-targeted to specific kinds of activism, as in Oklahoma, where legislators sought to make it a crime for environmental activists to set foot on land intended for oil pipelines. In all, since 2016, thirty-one states have considered anti-protest bills or measures and fifteen states – including Iowa, Louisiana, North Dakota, South Dakota, Oklahoma, and Tennessee – have enacted such restrictions.[28] Campus protests by college students have been a particular target of conservative legislative attention, and Republican legislatures in at least three states – Arizona, Georgia and North Carolina – have passed laws restricting or punishing student protestors who are seen to have infringed on the free expression and speech of others.[29]

Perhaps the clearest example of conservative attacks on their political opponents involve the surge of state laws curtailing the rights of labor unions, especially those representing public sector employees.[30] New measures that cut public employee collective bargaining rights, impose onerous requirements for enrolling and retaining members, and that make it harder for unions to collect dues do not just weaken unions as economic organizations. These laws also have significant political consequences as well, diminishing the strength and capacity of one of the few remaining mass-membership organizations mobilizing working class Americans into politics and representing their interests in elections and in the policy-making process at all levels of government.[31] With a weaker labor movement, working-class Americans are less likely to participate in elections and to have their preferences reflected in state and federal decisions.[32]

---

[28] ACLU, *Anti-Protest Bills Around the Country*, American Civil Liberties Union (Washington, DC, June 23, 2017 2017); Nicolas Kusnetz, "Harsh New Anti-Protest Laws Restrict Freedom of Speech, Advocates Say," *The Washington Post*, August 22, 2018.

[29] Jeremy W. Peters, "In Name of Free Speech, States Crack Down on Campus Protests," *New York Times*, June 14, 2018.

[30] Hertel-Fernandez, *State Capture*, chapters 1 and 6.

[31] Ibid., chapter 6.

[32] Michael Becher and Daniel Stegmueller, "Reducing Unequal Representation: The Impact of Labor Unions on Legislative Responsiveness in the U.S. Congress," *Perspectives on Politics* 19, no. 1 (2021): 92–109; Michael Becher, Daniel Stegmueller, and Konstantin Kappner, "Local Union Organization and Law-making in the U.S. Congress," *Journal of Politics* 80, no. 2 (2018): 539–54; James Feigenbaum, Alexander Hertel-Fernandez, and Vanessa Williamson, "From the Bargaining Table to the Ballot Box: Political Effects of Right to Work Laws," 2019, National Bureau of Economic Research Working Paper No. 24259; Patrick Flavin, "Labor Union Strength and the Equality of Political Representation," *British Journal of Political Science* 48, no. 4 (2018): 1075–91.

Taken together, these developments give us good reason to doubt that the states are living up to their full potential as either laboratories or bulwarks of democracy. Not only are state legislators regularly ignoring majority opinions on policies with significant bearing on the living standards of many Americans, but they are also increasingly passing laws to curb expressions of individual and organized political voice.

Of course, these are not new concerns. State efforts to restrict political participation and curb democratic representation date back to the Founding and stretch through the ugly history of Redemption and Jim Crow.[33] Indeed, the repression of democratic participation in the American South reflects the more general capacity of federal or decentralized political systems to foster authoritarian enclaves that fragment citizenship[34] – or at least to facilitate parochial governments more responsive to concentrated interests than to the mass public.[35] And traditionally left-leaning constituencies have engaged in their share of power-tilting reforms to restrict political participation, for instance, how teachers unions have historically sought to dampen turnout in municipal elections by holding elections off-cycle.[36] But what is relatively new is just how much these antidemocratic impulses are concentrated along the rightward edge of the GOP.[37] To grasp this transformation of the Republican Party in the states, we need to understand the emergence of new activists and donors on the right – best exemplified by a trio of cross-state networks I dub the "right-wing troika" – and how the troika has exploited both long-standing and recent developments in the states.

---

[33] For example, Alexander Keyssar, *The Right to Vote: The Contested History of Democracy in the United States* (New York: Basic Books, 2001).

[34] Edward L. Gibson, *Boundary Control: Subnational Authoritarianism in Federal Democracies* (Cambridge: Cambridge University Press, 2013); V. O. Key Jr, *Southern Politics in State and Nation* (Knoxville: University of Tennessee Press, 1984[1949]); Suzanne Mettler, *Dividing Citizens: Gender and Federalism in New Deal Public Policy* (Ithaca: Cornell University Press, 1998); Jamila Michener, *Fragmented Democracy: Medicaid, Federalism, and Unequal Politics* (Cambridge: Cambridge University Press, 2018); Robet Mickey, *Paths out of Dixie: The Democratization of Authoritarian Enclaves in America's Deep South, 1944–1972* (Princeton: Princeton University Press, 2015).

[35] Grant McConnell, *Private Power and American Democracy* (New York: Alfred Knopf, 1966).

[36] Sarah F. Anzia, *Timing and Turnout: How Off-Cycle Elections Favor Organized Groups* (Chicago: University of Chicago Press, 2013).

[37] Berman, *Give Us the Ballot*.

THE RESURGENT RIGHT SEIZES THE STATES

By the early 1970s, conservative activists and organized business felt lost in the political wilderness, having faced decades of Democratic dominance in Congress and state governments, as well as the recent victories scored by the civil rights, consumer rights, and environmental rights movements in Great Society and then Nixon-era reforms.[38] But perhaps most worrisome for right-leaning political operatives was the rise of a new powerful liberal interest group: the government employee unions. Over the span of just a few decades, public employees joined forces with the civil rights movement to push for greater legal rights and better working conditions for federal, state, and local employees. The result – an explosion of state laws recognizing the right of public employee unions to organize and collectively bargain with government – helped to fuel the expansion of union membership rolls and political influence. One telling trend: the number of states where a National Education Association teachers union affiliate had established a PAC increased from just one in 1965 to twenty-two four years later, and these committees quickly became heavyweights in their respective states.

In response, a group of concerned philanthropists, activists, state legislators, and members of Congress helped to launch the American Legislative Exchange Council (ALEC) to provide policy ideas (including model bill proposals), research assistance, and political advice to conservative state lawmakers. Although the organization got off to a shaky start and nearly went under, by the early 1990s ALEC had grown into a powerful force shaping state policy and politics for the Republican Party. Combining state legislators (around a third to a fourth of all legislators at its peak in the mid-2000s), around 200 of the largest Fortune 500 companies, and various heavyweight conservative philanthropies, advocacy groups, and think tanks, ALEC helped to shepherd a business-friendly and socially conservative agenda across state legislatures. At the height of its strength, I have estimated that ALEC was responsible for around 1 percent of all introduced and enacted legislation across the states, amounting to hundreds of new bills drafted in whole or part from its suggested legislative text each session.

As we will see, ALEC was especially appealing for junior lawmakers and legislators in states who lacked the experience and staff help to draft

---

[38] This section draws from Hertel-Fernandez, *State Capture*, chapters 1 and 5.

legislation on their own. But ALEC had an even more important function beyond the immediate bills it ghost-wrote for harried legislators: defining the positions that conservative, pro-business lawmakers felt they needed to hold to be successful in state politics. Most state legislative candidates do not enter the legislature with a well-defined platform of issues that they want to pursue. ALEC and the two other members of the "right-wing troika" I will soon introduce helped to signal to ambitious state legislators what kind of policies were important for conservatives to take on.

As ALEC grew in the mid-1980s, its head realized that the group could be even more successful if it had support from outside state legislatures. To that end, ALEC's head opened his donor list to a fledging network of state-level conservative think tanks struggling to get off the ground. ALEC's head during this period also helped to get that network of think tanks participating in ALEC conferences and providing technical support to ALEC's legislators interested in various policy issues. Over time, ALEC's decision to support the network of conservative state-level think tanks would reap considerable dividends. That loose coalition of think tanks eventually expanded into the State Policy Network, which by now counts over sixty affiliated think tanks as members in all fifty states. SPN affiliates support ALEC efforts directly, by providing technical support to friendly legislators, offering testimony on ALEC-backed bills, and publishing op/eds in support of that legislation. These affiliates also help ALEC indirectly, by launching strategic lawsuits in support of broader ALEC priorities (including several landmark cases that have weakened the labor movement, like the recent *Janus* Supreme Court decision) and by trying to shape the public discourse in their respective states.

The third member of the right-wing troika, Americans for Prosperity (AFP), is the most recent but in some ways also the most significant. AFP formed in 2004 out of the remains of an older organization, Citizens for a Sound Economy (CSE), which was created by Charles and David Koch to offer lobbying support (especially "astro-turf" campaigns) to companies seeking policy change in Washington, DC. AFP retained some features of CSE, including a role for grassroots citizen activists, but in other ways represented a big departure from both CSE and many other interest groups in US politics. AFP is a federated advocacy organization, with local, state, regional, and national offices and paid staff and usually additional volunteers and activists at each level. As we will see, this federated structure – as with past organizations throughout American politics – affords it leverage over politics and especially the GOP.[39] Yet although AFP operates with a federated model and a broad volunteer base, decision-making is highly centralized, with little to no role for its volunteer membership. Further unlike many organizations, AFP is simultaneously active in both policymaking debates and elections ranging from local school boards and city-level governments to state legislatures and Congress.

Where does AFP direct that clout? As the central part of the Koch political network, AFP lobbies governments for lower taxes, especially on wealthy individuals and businesses, cuts to government social programs, above all the Affordable Care Act in recent years, reductions in business regulations related to the environment and labor standards, and, with laser-like focus, curbs to the power of labor unions, especially in the public sector. As I have documented in joint work with Theda Skocpol, AFP has worked hand-in-glove with the two other members of the troika to pursue those objectives.[40] With ALEC providing model bills and SPN offering technical and policy support, AFP takes a more bare-knuckled approach, organizing grassroots rallies, lobby days at state capitols, radio, television, and print ad blitzes, and door-to-door canvassing in support of ALEC and SPN's policy priorities.

AFP can count on continued financial support as the centerpiece of the Koch political network, directed by Charles Koch (David Koch passed away in 2019). By now, the Koch network has matured from a collection of various libertarian think tanks and foundations into a fully integrated political operation that combines grassroots mobilization and lobbying functions (in the form of AFP) with voter data analytics (Themis/i360) and fundraising (in the form of the Koch seminars). Those seminars, which have grown from attracting just a dozen or so participants into formalized, twice-annual convenings, now regularly count over 500 guests in attendance who each pledge at least $100,000 a year to groups identified by Koch operatives. Most guests pledge much, much more, since the seminars raise hundreds of millions of dollars each election cycle. In 2007–8, the seminars raised about $90 million, but that jumped to $412 million by the 2012 election, and a stratospheric $700 to $800 million by 2016. The network reportedly gathered around $300 to $400 million in the 2018 election

---

[39] Theda Skocpol, Marshall Ganz, and Ziad Munson, "A Nation of Organizers: The Institutional Origins of Civic Voluntarism in the United States," *American Political Science Review* 94, no. 3 (2000): 527–546.

[40] e.g., Alexander Hertel-Fernandez, Theda Skocpol, and Daniel Lynch, "Business Associations, Conservative Networks, and the Ongoing Republican War over Medicaid Expansion," *Journal of Health Politics, Policy and Law* 41, no. 2 (2016): 239–286.

cycle. Those are fundraising totals that approach, and in some cases even rival, the sums controlled by official Republican Party committees.

Together, AFP, ALEC, and SPN have had an outsized role in defining the positions and priorities held by Republican state legislators – especially the cases where Republican politicians were pushing policies unpopular with their voters or that were seeking to hobble their opposition. The organization and pressure exerted by the troika, for instance, helps to explain why some Republicans were willing to accept Medicaid expansion as part of the Affordable Care Act while others were not.[41] The troika's advocacy also helps to account for which states decided to pursue aggressive new limits on union collective bargaining rights and dues collections in recent years[42] and why state Republicans arrived at preemption as a strategy for rolling back city-level efforts to raise the minimum wage and enact new paid sick leave provisions.[43] The troika has helped develop the legislative push to curtail protest rights, especially on college campuses.[44] And the troika, and ALEC in particular, played an important role in making an early case for changes to election administration and gerrymandering that would hobble Democratic constituencies.[45]

Importantly, while operating across the states, the troika's development has had implications for *both* state *and* national politics. Many of the state policies pursued by the troika – like curbs on union rights or preempting minimum wage increases – are also changes to national policy. When states fail to update their minimum wages, it makes the federal government's decision not to raise the federal floor all the more significant by changing the context for the overall "policyscape."[46] Equally relevant,

---

[41] Hertel-Fernandez, Skocpol, and Lynch, "Business Associations, Conservative Networks, and the Ongoing Republican War over Medicaid Expansion."

[42] Hertel-Fernandez, *State Capture*, chapter 6.

[43] Ibid., chapter 7; see also NELP, *Wage Suppression: Inside ALEC's Legislative Campaign Against Low-Paid Workers*, National Employment Law Project (New York, 2013).

[44] Teri Lyn Hinds, *Untangling the Threads: 2018 State Legislation Addressing Campus Speech Concerns*, NASPA – Student Affairs Administrators in Higher Education (2018); but see Suh and Tarrow, "'Wholesale' Legal Repression."

[45] Berman, *Give Us the Ballot*; David Daley, "How to Get Away with Gerrymandering," *Slate*, October 2, 2019; Ethan Magoc, "Flurry of Photo ID Laws Tied to Conservative Washington Group," *News21*, August 14, 2012, http://votingrights.news21.com/article/movement/index.html; see also Hertel-Fernandez, *State Capture*, chapter 1.

[46] Jacob S. Hacker, "Privatizing Risk without Privatizing the Welfare State: The Hidden Politics of Social Policy Retrenchment in the United States," *American Political Science Review* 98, no. 2 (2004): 243–60; Suzanne Mettler, "The Policyscape and the Challenges of Contemporary Politics to Policy Maintenance," *Perspectives on Politics* 14, no. 2 (2016): 369–90.

legislation that the troika enacts often has spillover effects across state borders. When states weaken labor unions or suppress civil protests, it diminishes the national reach of these efforts.[47] And perhaps most directly, any changes to state-level policy that shape national elections – whether by weakening civic organizations or making it harder for certain groups to vote – have immediate consequences for who is elected to Congress and the White House.

WEAK INSTITUTIONS AND NATIONALIZED POLITICS UNDERMINE STATEHOUSE DEMOCRACY

The success of the troika at reshaping the stands of GOP politicians, especially at the state level, rests in part on the structure of the organizations themselves: in the case of ALEC, for instance, creating broad, nation-spanning networks of legislators where there were none before. At the same time, these organizations also exploited several features of American federalism. Some of these are longstanding characteristics of the states, while others are more recent developments. But together, they form a toxic brew that has been increasingly exploited by the conservative troika in the pursuit of policies often opposed by majorities of Americans and that seek to demobilize and defang their left-leaning opponents. These four developments include the following:

Diminished visibility of state politics for many voters: The Framers of the Constitution assumed that state governments would loom larger in the minds of Americans than the more distant federal government, making it easier for citizens to hold their state politicians to account than officials in Congress or the White House.[48] In practice, the reverse has tended to be true in recent years: Americans know much more about the federal government than their own states. About four out of ten Americans say that they cannot name the party in control of their state senate or house, twice as many as for the party in control of the US Senate or House.[49] Indeed, voters are less likely to be able to name their governor now than in decades past.[50]

---

[47] See also Leslie Finger and Michael Hartney, "Financial Solidarity: The Future of Unions in the Post-Janus Era," *Perspectives on Politics* 19, no. 1 (2021): 19–35.
[48] See, e.g., *The Federalist Papers* 45 and 46.
[49] Hertel-Fernandez, *State Capture*, Introduction.
[50] Daniel J. Hopkins, *The Increasingly United States: How and Why American Political Behavior Nationalized* (Chicago: University of Chicago Press, 2018), 68.

Media coverage of state politics and legislation plays a role in explaining the diminished visibility of statehouse events for voters.[51] While scholars have bemoaned the lack of media coverage of state politics compared to national politics for decades, the problem has worsened in recent years with the demise of statehouse reporting and a drop in consumption of news sources focused on local and state issues.[52] The Pew Research Center, for instance, has found that the number of full-time reporters covering state capitols fell by 35 percent from 2003 to 2014.[53] This low and diminishing visibility of state politics means that state officials can more easily pursue policies that may not be popular among their constituents with less risk of electoral punishment. If less than one in five voters can correctly identify their state legislator,[54] how many are likely to know whether or not their legislator voted against otherwise popular bills, like increasing the minimum wage or expanding Medicaid? Indeed, studying the accountability that state legislators face for the votes that they take, Steven Rogers has found that state officials face little risk of backlash from backing bills out of step with their constituents' preferences – and in fact face *less* accountability than do members of Congress.[55]

Nationalized and polarized state politics: One reason why politicians can pass otherwise unpopular or anti-majoritarian troika policies is that voters may not have a good picture of what is happening in state politics. But another reason is that voters may not care since they are casting their ballots for state governors and legislators based on national issues, rather than state or local ones. Since the 1980s, Americans' choices about whom to support in state elections increasingly mirror voting patterns for national office.[56]

As the parties have moved toward two very distinct bundles of beliefs, policy positions, and identities, state politicians have less room to develop their own stands independent of the national party – and that polarization is reflected in voter behavior. With voters casting ballots for state offices

---

[51] Daniel J. Moskowitz, "Local News, Information, and the Nationalization of U.S. Elections," *American Political Science Review* 115, no. 1 (2021): 114–29.
[52] Hopkins, *The Increasingly United States*.
[53] Katerina Eva Matsa and Jan Lauren Boyles, *America's Shifting Statehouse Press* (Pew Research Center, 2014).
[54] Steven Rogers, "National Forces in State Legislative Elections," *Annals of the American Academy of Political and Social Sciences* 667, no.1 (2016), 210.
[55] Steven Rogers, "Electoral Accountability for State Legislative Roll Calls and Ideological Representation," *American Political Science Review* 111, no. 3 (2017): 555–71.
[56] Hopkins, *The Increasingly United States*, 55–58.

on the basis of their national partisan identities, state politicians face far less accountability from voters, especially their co-partisans – forming an electoral "blindspot" similar to the concept described in the UCLA school's reconceptualization of political parties.[57] The troika has both *contributed* to the nationalization and polarization of state politics, by helping to define the common positions held by conservative lawmakers (especially in the case of ALEC) all across the country, and has *benefited* from nationalization and polarization as state politicians pursue otherwise unpopular measures insulated against backlash from voters who may dislike some of their positions – but fear the election of Democrats even more.[58]

There is a direct connection here with the behavioral research presented in the chapters in this volume by Nathan Kalmoe and Liliana Mason, Michele Margolis, Matthew Lacombe, and Matthew Barreto and Christopher Parker. Together, these four sets of authors identify how particular identities, and especially social identities tied to whiteness, Christianity, gun ownership, and racial conservatism, have fueled conservative voters' attachment to the Republican Party. The strong appeal of these identities suggests that conservative state politicians can campaign on nonmaterial, "second-dimension" issues[59] even while prioritizing legislation, especially economic policy, that runs against the preferences of majorities of voters.[60]

Understaffed and under-resourced legislatures: A third and more enduring feature of the states that the troika has exploited is the fact that most states do not provide many resources for legislators to make and implement policy on their own. Legislatures meet for only a few months a year (with some states only meeting every other year), legislators are paid a part-time salary, and there is generally minimal staff help throughout the legislative process. As of 2019, for instance, twenty states either did not pay an annual legislative salary (instead opting for per-diem rates) or offered legislators salaries of $20,000 or less per year. Strikingly,

---

[57] Kathleen Bawn et al., "A Theory of Political Parties: Groups, Policy Demands and Nominations in American Politics," *Perspectives on Politics* 10, no. 3 (2012): 571-97.
[58] Lilliana Mason, *Uncivil Agreement: How Politics Became Our Identity* (Chicago: University of Chicago Press, 2018).
[59] Moses Shayo, "A Model of Social Identity with an Application to Political Economy: Nation, Class, and Redistribution," *American Political Science Review* 103, no. 2 (2009): 147-74.
[60] See also Jacob S. Hacker and Paul Pierson, "Plutocrats with Pitchforks: The Distinctive Politics of Right-Wing Populism in the United States," Unpublished working paper (2019).

sixteen states decline to provide lower chamber members with personal staff and twelve states do not provide personal staff to upper chamber members. And even resources in the most professionalized legislatures – like New York, California, and Illinois – are constrained. In a recent interview, a New York state senator bemoaned to me that his office did not have access to either Westlaw or Lexis – two major (and expensive) databases necessary for legal research – and so often needed to rely on the goodwill of advocacy groups or experts with access to those subscriptions.

This story underscores a key weakness of state legislatures: faced with these constraints and the need to weigh in on important policies in a range of areas, many state legislators must rely heavily on outside interest groups for bill ideas, research, and political advice. Recognizing this dependency, the troika (and especially ALEC and SPN) have provided exactly the sort of legislative support that lawmakers need. As I have documented in other work, it is members of the least-resourced legislatures – even net of party and ideology – who have tended to rely most heavily on ALEC's services and model bills.[61] In turn, this leaves legislators reliant on the priorities set by the troika, not necessarily their constituents.

Hollow state and local political parties: Lastly, the troika has taken advantage of, and contributed to, what Sam Rosenfeld and Daniel Schlozman have described as the "hollowness" of the contemporary political parties – that is, that the parties are "neither organizationally robust beyond their roles raising money nor meaningfully felt as a real, tangible presence in the lives of voters or in the work of engaged activists."[62] Though Schlozman and Rosenfeld describe this hollowness in all levels of government, it is especially apparent across counties and states, where party organizations remain underdeveloped. According to one GOP consultant, "state parties have become really a shadow of what they used to be," failing to either independently set agendas among elected officials or mobilize long-term support in the mass public.[63] That has left state and local parties open to takeover – sometimes hostile, sometimes cordial – by outside groups that leverage existing party structures to set their own agendas for politicians. In the case of the troika, these are

---

[61] Hertel-Fernandez, *State Capture*, chapter 4.
[62] Daniel Schlozman and Sam Rosenfeld, "The Hollow Parties," in *Can America Govern Itself?*, ed. Frances E. Lee and Nolan McCarty (Cambridge: Cambridge University Press, 2019), 121.
[63] See, e.g., Alan Greenblatt, "The Waning Power of State Political Parties," *Governing the States and Localities*, December, 2015.

agendas set not with an eye to maximizing the party's long-run legitimacy or appeal to the mass public, but rather to appeasing their activist, donor, and business base and minimizing electoral backlash.

Americans for Prosperity offers a clear example of how outside groups can take advantage of hollow party structures at the state and local level. By providing well-compensated opportunities for bright, talented, and motivated state and local Republican operatives in a successful conservative advocacy group, AFP has become an important way station in conservative activists' careers. This means that current staffers bring with them contacts and relationships that they can use to pull state and local GOP agendas toward Koch priorities. (In fact, in some cases, after helping to elect state legislators and governors, campaign staff will head to AFP, meaning that they are lobbying the very politicians they put in office.) State and local Republican staffers outside of the Koch network, for their part, may be angling for a future job in AFP and may thus become more receptive to the Koch agenda to secure future employment within the network.

THE COSTS OF CONSERVATIVE STATE CAPTURE

To be sure, the troika has not succeeded in pushing its agenda across every policy area and in each state. The close intertwining of the troika with the Republican Party has meant that ALEC, SPN, and AFP are most likely to secure changes in state policy when Republicans enjoy full control of both state legislatures and governorships. That limits the troika's immediate reach now to just under half of all states – and that reach could slip further as GOP electoral fortunes ebb and flow with campaign cycles. Kansas provides one instructive example: after the election of a Democratic governor broke the GOP trifecta in 2018, the Republican-controlled state legislature finally acquiesced to expanding Medicaid.[64] Still, as I noted previously, troika changes in some state-level policies can have significant spillovers, even to blue states with little or no troika presence, as when states weaken federated civic organizations or change voting rules.

In addition, ALEC, SPN, and AFP have tended to be most successful in preventing new expansions of government (as with Medicaid) or rolling back existing regulations or standards (as with environmental protections or labor rights) as compared to enacting new initiatives or making very

---

[64] Mitch Smith and Abby Goodnough, "Expanding Medicaid Was a Pipe Dream in Kansas. Now It May Become Reality," *New York Times*, January 9, 2020.

large cuts to taxes or public spending. As Matt Grossmann has argued persuasively, the overall size of state governments tends to steadily increase under both Democratic and Republican control alike.[65] Relatedly, the troika tends to be relatively more effective when it pushes policies well-aligned with *both* its business and more ideological activist members and less so on other issues that create more coalitional tensions. And in some cases troika-backed politicians have reached too far and have faced backlash from Democrats and Republicans alike. That was the case in Kansas, where massive cuts in taxes – and thus public spending and programs – led to an abrupt reversal after widespread bipartisan anger.[66] The statewide teacher strikes that have spread across a number of conservative states in response to low teacher pay and cutbacks in school spending similarly indicate the limits of troika policies, especially when such policies threaten highly valued public services.[67]

Notwithstanding these limits, the troika has enjoyed growing influence over GOP agendas in state politics and policy in recent years, and as this chapter has documented, this influence has meant that Republican legislatures push policies that often undermine statehouse democracy. When ALEC, AFP, and SPN succeed, they tend to be doing so *against*, not *in line with* what majorities of American citizens say they want from government. The troika may thus be pulling government policy away from the preferences held by most Americans and toward those of a smaller group of businesses, activists, and donors.

The policies that the troika is pulling away from public preferences do not simply represent a handful of proposals on trivial issues. Instead, the troika's economic stands – especially those related to taxation, regulation, labor organizing, and social policy – are systematically opposed to public preferences and represent substantial changes in government authority. As we have seen, policies like the minimum wage, labor organizing rights, Medicaid expansion, and education spending affect the economic livelihood of millions of Americans – above all, already vulnerable Americans like low-income households and racial and ethnic minorities. The troika's political mobilization carry significant material costs to these Americans and contribute to the striking mismatches in political representation by

---

[65] Grossmann, *Red State Blues*.
[66] Russell Berman, "Kansas Republicans Sour on Their Tax-Cut Experiment," *The Atlantic*, February 24, 2017.
[67] Eric Blanc, *Red State Revolt: The Teachers' Strike Wave and Working-Class Politics* (Brooklyn: Verso Books, 2019).

income documented by Larry Bartels, Martin Gilens, and Benjamin Page, among others, at the federal level.[68] That disjuncture directly undermines the promise of democratic representation for many Americans. But it may also erode democratic institutions indirectly as well, as the lack of political responsiveness to the middle class fuels further resentment and distrust in the traditional political parties and in government more generally.[69]

The activism of the troika lastly clarifies the willingness of Republican politicians to push for anti-majoritarian reforms that attempt to hobble their political opposition – like restricting access to the voting booth, aggressive partisan gerrymanders, and limits on civic mobilization and organization. Pursuing policies that are relatively unpopular, even with their own voters, the troika recognizes that it is most likely to win when it can "play for the rules" and diminish the odds of opposition. One concern with these policies is that they directly reduce the sort of political participation that underpins a healthy democracy, undermining norms of mutual toleration and forbearance to one's opposition.[70] But coupled with the overrepresentation that Republicans can count on because of the rural bias in American political institutions[71] and the advantage Republicans enjoy because of the relatively more homogenous social identities they can deploy (as identified in the chapters by Frances Lee and Nathan Kalmoe and Liliana Mason in this volume[72]), these power-shifting policies threaten a fair balance of competition between the parties and entrench the possibility of minority rule. Over the longer run, these power-shifting plays may thus represent an even more significant threat to democracy than the troika's counter-majoritarian stands. They may also help to explain why the GOP was so receptive to President Trump's appeals to overturn the 2020 election results: that campaign represented a set of

---

[68] Larry M. Bartels, *Unequal Democracy: The Political Economy of the New Gilded Age* (Princeton: Princeton University Press, 2008); Martin Gilens and Benjamin I. Page, "Testing Theories of American Politics: Elites, Interest Groups, and Average Citizens," *Perspectives on Politics* 12, no. 3 (2014).

[69] Katherine J. Cramer, *The Politics of Resentment: Rural Consciousness in Wisconsin and the Rise of Scott Walker* (Chicago: University of Chicago Press, 2016); Jacob S. Hacker and Paul Pierson, *American Amnesia: How the War on Government Led Us to Forget What Made America Prosper* (New York: Simon and Schuster, 2016); Stephanie L. Mudge, *Leftism Reinvented: Western Parties from Socialism to Neoliberalism* (Cambridge: Harvard University Press, 2018).

[70] Steven Levitsky and Daniel Ziblatt, *How Democracies Die* (New York: Crown, 2018).

[71] Rodden, *Why Cities Lose*.

[72] See also Matt Grossmann and David A. Hopkins, *Asymmetric Politics: Ideological Republicans and Group Interest Democrats* (Oxford: Oxford University Press, 2016).

tactics that conservative leaders had already developed and deployed over several decades across the states.

Ultimately, conservative Republicans are unlikely to abandon the strategies or stands pushed by the troika so long as the institutional conditions that enabled the troika's rise persist and so long as these strategies and stands continue to yield victories at the ballot box. Changing the former means figuring out how to revive accountability and bolster legislative capacity across state governments. Changing the latter will require large-scale GOP electoral losses, combined with a subsequent – and broadly shared – interpretation that the party must pursue policies more aligned with majorities of voters and with democratic norms. Absent those shifts, it seems doubtful that we can realize the promise of the states as laboratories or bulwarks of democracy – if that promise ever held.

PART V

CAN POLITICAL ACTION SAVE DEMOCRACY IN POLARIZED TIMES?

14

Elections, Polarization, and Democratic Resilience

David A. Bateman

> To watch an elected official – who claims to represent the people of this state, baldly pin his hopes for election on the suppression of the people's democratic right to vote – has been truly appalling. So, to be clear, this is not a speech of concession. Concession means to acknowledge an action is right, true or proper. As a woman of conscience and faith, I cannot concede.
> Stacey Abrams[1]

> One perennial problem of opposition is that there is either too much or too little.
> Robert Dahl[2]

THE PROBLEM OF ELECTIONS IN DEMOCRATIC POLITICS

Elections are at the core of democratic politics. We rely on them to perform the vital tasks of organizing and aggregating preferences, of determining leadership, of instituting accountability, of regulating conflict, and – more amorphous but no less important – of regenerating a broadly shared sense that the institutions and persons who govern us do so legitimately. As "moments of heightened citizenship" they focus the collective attention of the public on questions of who should be delegated

---

[1] Heather Timmons, "Stacey Abrams' Concession Speech Is a Powerful Critique of US Civil Rights," *Quartz*, November 19, 2018, https://qz.com/1468560/read-stacey-abrams-full-concession-speech/.
[2] Robert A. Dahl, *Political Oppositions in Western Democracies* (New Haven: Yale University Press, 1966), 397.

governing authority and to what end it should be dedicated.³ They are among the only moments in which "the people" is allowed to speak authoritatively in its collective capacity, and the rituals surrounding them positively affirm community ties while also marking out its boundaries of exclusion.

It is unsurprising, then, that the integrity of the electoral process is regularly treated as one of the most important metrics of democratic development and consolidation. If elections are not inclusive, free, fair, and transparent, then we cannot trust that the individuals and institutions that govern us have been democratically authorized.⁴ Elections in which the process has been or is widely suspected to have been rigged have failed in one of their core democratic functions, not because they did not produce a winner but because they will have failed to generate a shared sense that the winner's claim to governing authority is legitimate. A coin toss could select a leader – we generally ask more than that of elections.⁵

By this metric, American elections are faltering. After November 2016 there was a chorus of complaints that the Electoral College impeded the will of the majority by installing the loser of the popular vote in office, the endpoint of its more generally distorting effect on the supposed equality of voters. November 2020 was met with far-more destabilizing insistences that the election was illegitimate, as the sitting president, his immediate political allies, as well as many members of his broader political coalition claimed against all evidence that fraud or illegal manipulations of voting rules had resulted in his opponent claiming a majority of the College votes. The most spectacular consequence was the invasion of the US Capitol on January 6. More troubling results were taking place inside the Capitol, as 147 Republicans voted to object to the certified Electoral College votes of at least one state, and in the country at large, as more than half of Republican voters indicated a belief that the Democratic victory was

---

[3] Jaimie Bleck and Nicolas van de Walle, *Electoral Politics in Africa Since 1990: Continuity in Change* (Cambridge: Cambridge University Press, 2018), 21.

[4] Pippa Norris, "Do Perceptions of Electoral Malpractice Undermine Democratic Satisfaction? The US in Comparative Perspective," *International Political Science Review* 40, no. 1 (2019): 5–22.

[5] An essential feature of democratic regimes is their reliance on an openly competitive process for public support, in which the winner is entitled to govern for some limited period before the competition recurs. This so-called minimal definition is obviously insufficient to qualify a regime as democratic. "The people" who chose must also be defined in a broadly inclusive manner, embracing all citizens (with only a limited set of ideally temporary exceptions) and with citizenship covering all persons subject to the direct authority of the state (again, with only temporary or voluntary exceptions).

illegitimate. This victory likely dampened, for the moment, Democratic voters' concerns about the legitimacy of the process.[6] But the institutions that validate such concerns endure. The US Senate remains the most egregiously malapportioned legislative body in the world, and the same demographic and political transformations that have made the Electoral College an unreliable translator of popular majorities into political power operate with even greater distortions here. The aggregate effects of gerrymandering in the House of Representatives and state assemblies can be difficult to establish, and yet here too there is a growing recognition that deliberate manipulation of the line-drawing process has resulted in an unfair advantage to one party over the other. Recent voter suppression policies are even harder to study empirically.[7] And yet the partisan pattern and rhetoric accompanying their proliferation has fuelled a belief that they were deliberate efforts to disadvantage Democratic candidates.

One way to think about these trends is that the relatively young democracy established in the United States between the 1960s and 1970s is in the process of deconsolidating.[8] While a reasonable concern, the language of consolidation is inadequate for understanding the nature of the problem, insofar as it posits some end-state in which democratic rituals and rules are so embedded that they have become the "only game in town."[9] Thinking of democracy in this way, I suggest, ultimately obscures the source of the danger to democratic institutions and draws our attention away from the types of practices needed to sustain them.

Rather than something that will no longer be a worry once the country's democracy has "consolidated," today's cycle of voter suppression and district manipulation is part of a familiar pattern in American history.

---

[6] Candace Jaimungal, "Three-quarters of voters think fraud occurred during the election," *YouGov.com*, November 12, 2020, https://today.yougov.com/topics/politics/articles-reports/2020/11/12/voters-think-fraud-occurred-during-elec; Chris Kahn, "Half of Republicans say Biden won because of a 'rigged' election," *Reuters.com*, November 18, 2020, www.reuters.com/article/us-usa-election-poll/half-of-republicans-say-biden-won-because-of-a-rigged-election-reuters-ipsos-poll-idUSKBN27Y1AJ. For evidence that winning can help reduce concerns with illegitimacy, see Betsy Sinclair, Steven S. Smith, and Patrick D. Tucker, "'It's Largely a Rigged System': Voter Confidence and the Winner Effect in 2016," *Political Research Quarterly* 71, no. 4 (2018): 854–68.
[7] Barry C. Burden, "Disagreement over ID Requirements and Minority Voter Turnout," *Journal of Politics* 80, no. 3 (2018): 1060–63.
[8] Roberto Stefan Foa and Yascha Mounk, "The Danger of Deconsolidation: The Democratic Disconnect," *Journal of Democracy* 27, no. 3 (2016): 5–17.
[9] Juan J. Linz and Alfred C. Stepan, *Problems of Democratic Transition and Consolidation: Southern Europe, South America, and Post-Communist Europe* (Baltimore: Johns Hopkins University Press, 1996), 5.

It is also an inherent danger of democratic politics. In any democratic regime, the electoral rules and procedures will be structured at some point by those who will be contending for office under their terms. There will inevitably be an opportunity to instrumentally manipulate the process to advantage or entrench in power certain persons or interests. And, paradoxically, if elections are producing the close competition that we hope they will, then there will be an *incentive* to do so as well. The more heatedly parties and other interests vie for power, the more fragile their incumbency, and the more they perceive to be at stake in their defeat, the greater the incentive to win by altering the conditions of play.

The basic problem – that political institutions are endogenous to politics, and thus can be manipulated by the persons they are supposed to constrain – has repeatedly attracted the attention of social scientists.[10] But while efforts to rig the machinery of elections are common around the world, they are not universal. Scholars have identified a variety of factors that might insulate democratic institutions from self-entrenchment and manipulation, including explicit constitutional constraints, independent electoral agencies, ideological commitments, norms of mutual toleration and institutional forbearance, or an underlying public or elite consensus on either democratic values or public policy.

The United States is lacking many of these, and strengthening them should be part of any democracy-preserving agenda. Doing so, however, is unlikely to result in a consolidated democracy. Elections where there is real competition between meaningful alternatives (i.e., elections that work), inevitably encourage its players to think about how they might gain an advantage. And while additional constraints such as insulated administrative agencies might be vital to electoral integrity, they likewise are endogenous to politics, potentially inheriting the problem rather than solving it.[11] Institutions or norms intended to constrain electoral manipulation are just as vulnerable to politics as elections themselves.

This does not make democracy "impossible" in any practical sense. A recognition of the theoretical dynamic, however, might encourage us to think of democracy less as an end-point awaiting consolidation, and more as a varyingly brittle regime that will always be wrought by internal

---

[10] Andreas Schedler, "The Nested Game of Democratization by Elections," *International Political Science Review / Revue Internationale de Science Politique* 23, no. 1 (2002): 103–22; Alberto Simpser, *Why Governments and Parties Manipulate Elections: Theory, Practice, and Implications* (Cambridge: Cambridge University Press, 2013).

[11] William H. Riker, "Implications from the Disequilibrium of Majority Rule for the Study of Institutions," *The American Political Science Review* 74, no. 2 (1980): 432–46.

contradictions and recurring patterns of self-erosion. In this case, *resilience* is the more appropriate frame, insofar as it draws our attention to the need for an ongoing, indeed Sisyphean, recalibration and updating of democracy's buttresses.

In what follows, I lay out the tension between elections' *polarizing* and *integrative* functions, each of which is necessary if elections are to perform the tasks assigned them by democratic theory. I describe how elections' polarizing logic has repeatedly led to electoral manipulation in American history, and then consider the types of institutional or normative constraints that have been devised to protect against this. This view from history isn't comforting. Much of what earlier generations did to insulate elections effectively threw the democratic baby out with the political bathwater. Efforts to construct a national supervisory structure were repeatedly defeated, or, when established, were often used for partisan purposes; state-level efforts to end fraud through administrative innovations were advocated in part because they were expected to provide a partisan advantage, and were passed because they facilitated the self-entrenchment of local politicians. One form of manipulation replaced another, or the institutions intended to prevent against manipulation were subverted for partisan purposes.

In fact, the most reliable way that way that Americans have muted electoral manipulations has been by reducing and localizing political competition. These efforts crystallized in the successive "political regimes" that characterize American political development – the "era of good feelings," the Age of Jackson, the Republican Ascendancy, or the New Deal order – each of which rested in part on new institutions and practices explicitly designed to secure a partisan advantage, whether through stacking the Senate or manipulating electoral rules to provide one party with a persistent advantage. The result was less intense national competition and a less polarized national politics existing alongside regional patterns that could include outright authoritarianism, manipulative party machines, and sometimes even highly functioning electoral institutions backed up by broadly shared normative commitments. Preserving America's electoral integrity at the national level has been accomplished in no small part through manipulations that diffused the potentially corrosive effects of competition away from the center, empowering local elites and dissolving any pretext of equal citizenship.

A central theme of this chapter, however, is that not all forms of electoral manipulations are equally suspect. Expanding the electorate, reforming voter registration procedures, admitting new states, or establishing non-partisan districting agencies can all be pursued with an eye toward partisan advantage even as they also promote a more inclusive politics and dampen the intensity of polarization. The paradox of American elections might simply be that certain forms of electoral "hardball" (i.e., otherwise legitimate and legal changes that bias outcomes in favor of one party over the other), have been one of the most important forces advancing both democratic inclusion and democratic resilience.[12]

WHAT WE ASK OF ELECTIONS

Democratic regimes integrate competition for power directly into their foundational rituals and decision-making procedures, and do so in order to forestall some of competition's more destructive consequences. What democratic theory asks of elections is that they be both *polarizing*, providing citizens with genuine choices over governing officials and public policy; and *integrative*, serving as mechanisms by which claims to govern can be founded on a form of consensual authority that rests not on outcomes but on the legitimacy of the process.

These tasks are in fundamental tension with each other. Some level of polarization is endogenous to electoral institutions that allow competition and reasonably free entry and campaigning. But free and fair elections in turn need to be protected from the efforts of ambitious politicians to gain a competitive edge, and the institutions and commitments that we rely on to provide this protection are vulnerable to the same threat of self-interested manipulation. Elections, then, should be thought of as potentially self-undermining institutions, whose ability to effectively regulate conflict rests in part on the degree to which the polarization they encourage can be contained by other institutions that are themselves liable to be eroded by the dynamics elections unleash.

ELECTIONS AS INTEGRATIVE INSTITUTIONS

Democratic regimes formalize the competition latent in all regimes, swearing off the suppression of political opposition so long as it goes through the appropriate channels, while expanding the number of persons who may compete for office and whose votes will determine the winner. Predicting who will be invested with political authority can consequently

---

[12] Mark Tushnet, "Constitutional Hardball," *John Marshall Law Review* 37, no. 2 (2003): 523–53.

become more difficult. On its face, this would seem to increase the always-dangerous possibility of disputed outcomes. The promise of elections, however, is that regularizing competition before an extensive body of voters will not only move contests over succession out of the domain of palace or barracks intrigue and into the public spotlight, but will generate greater clarity among potential contenders about their prospects of winning as well as a decent assurance, at least among those that care, that losing isn't forever.

These dynamics are crucial to elections' ability to reconcile losers to the outcomes and regulate potentially deadly conflict. Ambitious people have an endless capacity to delude themselves about their popularity, cleverness, and capacity to manage a complex political situation. Elections promise to channel such ambitions and beliefs, however unfounded, in socially useful directions (while also testing them against reality). Elections create a predictable and recurring process on which the energies of both would-be leaders and allied intriguers can be concentrated. Better hustling for cash in Martha's Vineyard, or demagoguing in Boca Raton, than plotting in the Army and Navy Club. The process of campaigning can provide aspiring rulers with important information about the distribution and level of their support, while the process of presenting oneself and one's policies for critique can suggest pathways for future success. So long as contestants believe that next time they can win, or that their political inheritors or defenders of their interests can win, they can graciously concede. And if they come to believe that they cannot win, it is often because their own supporters have gone as far as they're willing to go, and have begun to throw their lot in with one of the hundreds of other ambitious persons that elections in mass democracies force to work together in extensive coalitions. They are left with reduced prospects for successfully gaining or seizing power by any other means, and if they decide to intrigue at that point it will be with a smaller base and with everyone having full knowledge that there are other, more popular combinations of political forces in the country.

In more optimistic accounts, this concentration of focus among would-be leaders can have useful consequences.[13] The fact that a difficult-to-manage electorate determines the outcome might discipline political elites into believing the most reliable way of winning is through providing or promising to provide policies that will improve the lives of most voters.

---

[13] Staffan Lindberg, *Democracy and Elections in Africa* (Baltimore: Johns Hopkins University Press, 2006); Schedler, "The Nested Game."

Even when this is not true, however, coordinated engagement in elections can lead political elites to act *as though* they believe elections are the right way to select leaders; elections "may force, trick, lure, or cajole nondemocrats into democratic behavior."[14] The consequence over time can be a widening sense among the electorate (and a more calculated acceptance among elites) that elections are the only legitimate way to allocate power, and that manipulations which change the rules of the game are an illegitimate form of cheating.

When this happens, elections can be *integrative,* providing not just for the selection of leaders but the more difficult task of getting the losers to accept the results.

ELECTIONS AS POLARIZING INSTITUTIONS

Most of the desirable qualities of elections stem from their ability to produce choice, to organize an electorate's attention around this choice, and to "cajole" leaders into accepting this choice. Any realistic hope for inducing a collective-orientation among political elites, whether in the form of substantive representation or bare accountability, requires that voters have the capacity to punish those who fail to provide for the common good or engage in self-dealing. Fortunately, so long as entry is relatively open, there is almost always someone who thinks they can win and who is willing to critique the existing leadership's performance. And so long as candidates are relatively free in their campaign strategies, a sufficient number of choices ought to be available for the electorate to make a meaningful decision.

But elections do more than just provide choice: they also encourage polarization, the drawing of contrasts between choices so that they either are or appear to be crisply distinct. This might be because the parties are coalitions of interests or are unable to perfectly screen out candidates, resulting in parties that appeal more to their respective poles than to a median voter.[15] Political parties operating in competitive environments also draw symbolic contrasts between themselves and their opponents in

---

[14] Dankwart Rustow, "Transitions to Democracy," *Comparative Politics* 2, no. 3 (1970): 344–45.

[15] Kathleen Bawn, Martin Cohen, David Karol, Seth Masket, Hans Noel, and John Zaller, "A Theory of Political Parties: Groups, Policy Demands and Nominations in American Politics," *Perspectives on Politics* 10, no. 3 (2012): 571–97; Nolan McCarty, "Reducing Polarization by Making Parties Stronger," in *Solutions to Political Polarization in America*, ed. Nathaniel Persily (Cambridge: Cambridge University Press, 2015), 136–45.

the hopes of creating the impression that a party's rivals are extreme relative to public opinion. As one political operative put it, "you're seeking to draw a contrast .... And of course, it goes without saying, you want to put the other party on the wrong side of that contrast."[16] Since much electoral choice is mediated through perceptions of commonality and difference, one effective strategy is to cultivate a sense among potential constituencies that their opponents' policies or persons pose a fundamental threat to their interests, values, and standing. The consequence can be to heighten affective polarization, a form of out-group antagonism in which the opposition is imagined in highly negative terms.[17]

Competition and polarization likely encourage electoral manipulation: when the stakes are high, whether for politicians' reelection or the policy or symbolic interests of their supporting constituencies, then the incentive to bend the rules is likely to be higher as well. The flip side of this basic calculus has long been central to theories of democratization, where leaders are expected to be willing to accept elections or the expansion of voting rights only when the costs of doing so are lower than the costs of repression.[18] The logic applies equally to leaders' propensity to engage in electoral manipulation, which should be more likely when the anticipated cost of losing under free and fair elections is higher than the political, social, or economic costs of cheating. Put differently, it is when aspirants for office, or their social backers, cannot tolerate the prospect of losing that the incentive to rig the game becomes most acute. In these cases, it becomes – as *The Nation* lamented in 1879 – "of more importance to elect your own man than to satisfy your opponents that he has been fairly elected."[19] The polarizing logic of elections will have then capsized their integrative logic.

---

[16] Frances E. Lee, *Insecure Majorities: Congress and the Perpetual Campaign* (Chicago: University of Chicago Press, 2016), 47.
[17] Shanto Iyengar, Yphtach Lelkes, Matthew Levendusky, Neil Malhotra, and Sean J. Westwood, "The Origins and Consequences of Affective Polarization in the United States," *Annual Review of Political Science* 22, no. 1 (2019): 129–46; Mason and Kalmoe, this volume.
[18] Robert A. Dahl, *Polyarchy: Participation and Opposition* (New Haven: Yale University Press, 1971).
[19] Mark Wahlgren Summers, "Party Games: The Art of Stealing Elections in the Late-Nineteenth-Century United States," *The Journal of American History* 88, no. 2 (2001): 431.

ELECTORAL MANIPULATION IN AMERICAN HISTORY

All this is bad news for the United States. Affective polarization among politically attentive Americans is on the rise. When combined with ideological polarization among the most politically active Americans, it seems that a not-insignificant proportion sees the stakes of each election as existentially large. Contributing to both is partisan competition, which is experiencing one of its relatively rare moments of national high-intensity and which leaves political elites – the most significant class of actors in the drama – with uncertain prospects for holding office and exercising power.

Today's combination of polarization and competition is not entirely unique in American history.[20] While the usual pattern is for intense political competition to be localized in a few states or districts, where it can do little national harm, there have been at least three other eras when competition for national offices was so close that partisan control could not be reliably anticipated: the late 1790s, the decade or so leading up to the organization of the Republican Party in 1856 and the immediate pre-Civil War years that followed, as well as the two decades from the end of Reconstruction to the crushing defeats of the Democratic party between 1894 and 1900. Each of these earlier moments saw a thoroughgoing disparagement of the opposition in terms suggestive of heightened ideological and affective polarization. Not coincidentally, each also saw substantial electoral manipulation.[21]

In the early Republic, the competition between Federalists and Jeffersonian Republicans contributed to gerrymandering and to open disregard of electoral laws and qualifications. The parties mobilized men to the polls regardless of eligibility, while partisan election judges interpreted the rules to enfranchise legally unqualified voters advanced by their

---

[20] There are distinctive characteristics to contemporary polarization, including the degree to which social movements have penetrated both parties and to which politics is nationalized and conducted by many non-politicians. Still, American elections were highly nationalized in the nineteenth century, all major parties since 1856 have had at least some ideological and social movement connections, and while the balance between transactional politicians and moralistic amateurs has shifted, we should not overstate the demise of the former or the ascendancy of the latter. Erik J. Engstrom and Samuel Kernell, *Party Ballots, Reform, and the Transformation of America's Electoral System* (Cambridge: Cambridge University Press, 2014); Byron E. Shafer and Regina L. Wagner, *The Long War over Party Structure: Democratic Representation and Policy Responsiveness in American Politics* (Cambridge: Cambridge University Press, 2019).

[21] Tova Andrea Wang, *The Politics of Voter Suppression: Defending and Expanding Americans' Right to Vote* (Ithaca: Cornell University Press, 2012), xiii.

party and disfranchise legally qualified voters advanced by their opponents. Ultimately, the most important form of electoral manipulation was not fraud but otherwise legitimate reforms of voting procedures that had the express purpose of reducing the share of the vote won by the opposing party or the sensitivity with which this vote share was translated into political office. Faced with a threat to their party's electoral hegemony in Connecticut, for example, Federalists passed laws abolishing the written ballot and requiring voters to stand up and be counted by elites associated with the dominant party. Subsequent amendments denied African Americans access to the vote, required partisan state officials to approve the addition of new voters, lengthened the time required to have owned property, raised the personal property requirement, and mandated that real property be free of mortgage. These were added to the state's two-stage election system, the design of which intentionally facilitated incumbent manipulation, and its gerrymandered at-large elections.

Partisan efforts to gain an advantage have also been one of the principal motivations for *expanding* the electorate.[22] While more attractive from the perspective of democratic theory, extensions of voting rights were identical in objective to voter suppression or gerrymandering. Legislation tilting the playing field toward one party or the other was passed in most of the original states of the Union, while decisions about voting eligibility, electoral proceedings, and district (or even statehood) lines were fraught with partisan calculations in new states.[23] The aggregate effect likely weakened the Federalist party and laid the foundations for the "era of good feelings," a period of hegemonic Republican rule with correspondingly low levels of polarization.

Regular electoral manipulation returned with the re-emergence of national parties again competing for control of national institutions. Whigs and their successor parties set out to suppress voting through cumbersome registration procedures, longer residency periods – including twenty-one years for naturalized citizens – and passage of the country's first literacy tests. Democrats supported some disenfranchisements, against free Black citizens in particular, but more generally sought to

---

[22] Richard M. Valelly, "How Suffrage Politics Made – and Makes – America," in *The Oxford Handbook of American Political Development*, eds. Richard M. Valelly, Suzanne Mettler, and Robert C. Lieberman (Oxford: Oxford University Press, 2016), 445–72.
[23] Alexander Keyssar, *The Right to Vote: The Contested History of Democracy in the United States* (New York: Basic Books, 2001).

mobilize ineligible voters to the polls and to turn naturalization proceedings into an arm of a partisan election campaign.

When this party system collapsed, the country went with it. During the Civil War, the new Republican Party stationed officials at polling booths to threaten Democratic voters with being placed on the army draft roll; Republican state-legislatures passed absentee ballot laws to enfranchise men in military service, and the combination of open voting, military hierarchy, and intimidation ensured that votes returned from military encampments were counted overwhelmingly for the Republican party.[24] With their grip on power slipping after the War, Republicans enfranchised nearly all adult African American men, first in the South and then in the North. What ultimately persuaded the party to take these boldly democratizing steps, which in the case of the 15th Amendment required flagrant violations of state legislative norms and procedures, was the threat of electoral defeat.[25] Republicans were willing to shatter norms to stay in power, and the fact that it amounted to a substantial democratization was for many white Republicans merely incidental. For us, by contrast, this should be instructive: Both democratization and de-democratization in America have been in large part the result of political efforts at self-entrenchment, and the norms of democracy should not always be raised above the substance of democracy.[26]

Voting rights for African American men briefly suppressed national competition, and for a time led portions of the Democratic Party to moderate their stance on white supremacy and to depolarize their campaigns. The promise of this moment should not be overlooked, even if it was short-lived. The Democratic party ultimately re-embraced a combination of fraud and violence that eroded Black southerners' rights and allowed the party to again become a contender for national office. For the remainder of the nineteenth century, elections would be intensely competitive and polarizing. The close margins between the major parties, and the need for each to generate a sufficient level of moral outrage to "mobilize their rank and file," gave license to real fraud but also fake news, in the form of exaggerated accounts of fraud and its prevalence.

---

[24] Richard Franklin Bensel, *The American Ballot Box in the Mid-Nineteenth Century* (Cambridge: Cambridge University Press, 2004), chapter 6.
[25] Richard M. Valelly, *The Two Reconstructions: The Struggle for Black Enfranchisement* (Chicago: University of Chicago Press, 2004).
[26] Julia R. Azari, "Forget Norms: Our Democracy Depends on Values," *FiveThirtyEight.com*, May 24, 2018, https://fivethirtyeight.com/features/forget-norms-our-democracy-depends-on-values/.

"Satan must be fought with his own weapons at times," equivocated one New Hampshire paper. A Louisiana newspaper was franker: "It is the religious duty of Democrats to rob Populists and Republicans of their votes whenever and wherever the opportunity presents itself."[27]

Overtly illegal behavior waned over the course of the twentieth century, and we will come back to one possible reason for that in a moment.[28] By contrast, today's efforts at legal voter suppression easily meet standard criteria of electoral manipulation around the world.[29] These include restrictive voter identification laws, purges of the registration rolls using what are known to be discriminatory processes, the curtailing of early voting reforms, reducing the number of polling booths, requiring proof of citizenship for new voters, and efforts to roll back or block the implementation of reforms intended to re-enfranchise citizens caught up in the expansion of the carceral state.[30] The vast majority of these have been partisan proposals, and are best understood as a consequence of the last few decades' brew of heightened political competition and its intensification of polarization.[31]

CONSTRAINING ELECTIONS

There is nothing uniquely American about this dynamic. "Electoral competition," writes Paul Collier, "creates a Darwinian struggle for political survival in which the winner is the one who adopts the most cost-effective means of attracting votes. In the *absence of restraints* the most cost-effective

---

[27] Summers, "Party Games, 424, 433, 435. As a group of conservative activists was told in 2020, "be not afraid of the accusations that you're a voter suppressor." Robert O'Harrow Jr., "Videos show closed-door sessions of leading conservative activists: 'Be not afraid of the accusations that you're a voter suppressor,'" *Washington Post*, October 14, 2020, www.washingtonpost.com/investigations/council-national-policy-video/2020/10/14/367f24c2-f793-11ea-a510-f57d8ce76e11_story.html.

[28] On the decline, see Didi Kuo and Jan Teorell, "Illicit Tactics as Substitutes: Election Fraud, Ballot Reform, and Contested Congressional Elections in the United States, 1860–1930," *Comparative Political Studies* 50, no. 5 (2017): 665–96, 666.

[29] Andreas Schedler, "Elections Without Democracy: The Menu of Manipulation," *Journal of Democracy* 13, no. 2 (2002): 36–50; Simpser, *Why Governments and Parties Manipulate Elections*.

[30] David A. Bateman, "Race, Party, and American Voting Rights," *The Forum* 14, no. 1 (2016): 39–65; Wang, *Politics of Voter Suppression*.

[31] Keith G. Bentele and Erin E. O'Brien, "Jim Crow 2.0? Why States Consider and Adopt Restrictive Voter Access Policies." *Perspectives on Politics* 11, no. 4 (2013): 1088–116; Lorraine C. Minnite, *The Myth of Voter Fraud* (Ithaca: Cornell University Press, 2011).

means" will be bribery, intimidation, and – most important – electoral manipulation.[32]

As Collier suggests, it is precisely because the polarizing logic of elections can undermine their integrative function that democracy needs to rely on additional constraints to either limit the intensity of polarization or to check politicians' ability to manipulate the process. Even in the United States, there are many places – probably most – where electoral manipulation has been the exception across their history; there have also been sustained periods, including the last few decades of the twentieth century, in which such activities were less common across the country, though still occurring. Perhaps such places or times just happened to enjoy a Goldilocks level of electoral competition, just hot enough to produce choice and accountability, but not so hot as to incentivize politicians to run polarizing campaigns or engage in fraud or otherwise legal "hardball." Such a nice balance, I suggest, is unlikely to be sustainable over time given the centrifugal force of electoral competition.

Perhaps politicians' behavior in these times and places has been effectively restrained, as Collier suggests, by other institutions or normative commitments? If we could identify such restraints and build our electoral machinery around them, then perhaps there would be a way out of the self-undermining logic of polarizing elections. Democratic theorists, attuned to the dangers of polarization, have devised numerous solutions to this problem, most of which aim to either constrain elites or limit the scope and intensity of competition. Perhaps the first and most important line of defense against electoral manipulation is to insulate the institutions that set the rules from self-interested actors.[33] A growing body of research into electoral integrity finds that insulating electoral qualifications, processes, and administration from executive or direct legislative control, and ensuring that the organizations responsible for conducting elections have a high level of functional capacity and a professional administrative ethos

---

[32] Emphasis added. Paul Collier, *Wars, Guns, and Votes: Democracy in Dangerous Places* (New York: Harper Collins, 2009), 40.

[33] Constitutions might perform such a function, insofar as they outline explicit rules whose violation might provide a focal point for collective action against malfeasant leaders. If these distribute authority in such a way as to make coordinated alterations or violations of electoral rules more difficult, then their effective adherence can help prevent manipulation. But assuming constitutions' effectiveness is never a safe bet. Barry R. Weingast, "The Political Foundations of Democracy and the Rule of Law," *The American Political Science Review* 91, no. 2 (1997): 245–63.

helps prevent manipulation and improve the overall operation of the system.[34]

Insulated institutions have an important to role to play in protecting democracy from self-entrenching behavior. But they are unlikely to be effective in the face of coordinated and sustained efforts to rig the game. The reason is that they too are endogenous to politics. Administrative agencies can be captured and repurposed by party actors, or cowed into submission by threats of funding withdrawal; laws can be changed to give control over electoral processes to politicians; constitutions can be amended, or courts packed with supporters willing to interpret the text in light of political expediency.[35] None of this is easy, and it might be more difficult in countries where democratic practices are well established and where there is a vibrant and organized public life that can identify and resist such incursions. It might also be more difficult in countries where the conduct of elections is administratively fragmented, multiplying the number of officials a party looking to subvert an election needs to persuade and coordinate.[36] But the incentive to do so is inherent in the quest for power.

---

[34] Michael R. Alvarez and Bernard Grofman, eds., *Election Administration in the United States: The State of Reform After Bush v. Gore* (Cambridge: Cambridge University Press, 2014); Sarah Birch, *Electoral Malpractice* (Oxford: Oxford University Press, 2011); Svitlana Chernykh and Milan W. Svolik, "Third-Party Actors and the Success of Democracy: How Electoral Commissions, Courts, and Observers Shape Incentives for Electoral Manipulation and Post-Election Protests," *Journal of Politics* 77, no. 2 (2015): 407–20; Toby S. James, Holly Ann Garnett, Leontine Loeber, and Carolien van Ham, "Electoral Management and the Organisational Determinants of Electoral Integrity: Introduction," *International Political Science Review* 40, no. 3 (2019): 295–312; Pippa Norris, *Strengthening Electoral Integrity* (Cambridge: Cambridge University Press, 2017); Charles Stewart III, "The 2016 U.S. Election: Fears and Facts About Electoral Integrity," *Journal of Democracy* 28, no. 2 (2017): 50–62; .

[35] Michael Blauberger and R. Daniel Kelemen, "Can Courts Rescue National Democracy? Judicial Safeguards Against Democratic Backsliding in the EU," *Journal of European Public Policy* 24, no. 3 (2017): 321–36; Nuno Garoupa and Tom Ginsburg, "Guarding the Guardians: Judicial Councils and Judicial Independence," *The American Journal of Comparative Law* 57, no. 1 (2009): 103–34; Thomas M. Keck, "Court Packing and Democratic Erosion," in *Democratic Resilience: Can the United States Withstand Rising Polarization*, eds. Robert C. Lieberman, Suzanne Mettler, and Kenneth M. Roberts (Cambridge: Cambridge University Press, 2021).

[36] In the end, this seems to have been among the more important factors in defeating Republican efforts to subvert the presidential elections of 2020. Had the results of only one or two states been needed to overturn the process, the pressure the president and his allies could have brought on the relevant officials and judges – as well as the promise implicit in pleasing both the president and his fervent supporters among influential politicos and backers – would have been immense. The difficulties of coordinating such a steal across many more states, then under intense public scrutiny, were considerable.

For this reason, democratic theorists have also stressed the importance of a variety of non-institutional constraints. Much mid-century American social science hypothesized that democracies "required some degree of consensus on required and permissible forms and purposes of political action," as well as the removal of certain topics from the issue agenda.[37] The purpose of value consensus – or some thinner source of basic agreement, such as a common nationality – was to "ensure that there was the right amount" of contestation, neither so much as would overwhelm the system nor so little that there was no real choice.[38] Crosscutting cleavages were invoked for the same reason.[39]

What good, though, is societal consensus if elites set the agenda, or if the political system makes it difficult for voters to differentiate and punish them? It is not usually the public that needs to be constrained, after all, but those who have the ability and incentive to subvert democratic institutions. The outsized importance of elites to questions of regime type led some to argue that what democracy required was for these elites to adhere to a shared public philosophy, to have "agreement on fundamentals" or to at least share "a mutual attachment to the requirements of the [constitutional] system."[40] Recent insistence on the centrality of norms fit this same mold: norms such as mutual toleration or institutional forbearance, featured prominently in Levitsky and Ziblatt's *How Democracies Die*, are elite-centered, intended to stop them from engaging in the types of behaviors that might subvert the democratic system.[41]

Each of these shares the same weakness of the institutions they are invoked to protect in the first place, in that they are endogenous to politics and so are potentially undermined by elections' polarizing dynamic. Consider elite-constraining norms: the often-explicit argument is that those interested in preserving democratic institutions need to prioritize the maintenance of these norms at all costs, even in the face of their repeated violation by partisan rivals. But norms depend on a continued

---

[37] David B. Truman, "The American System in Crisis," *Political Science Quarterly* 74, no. 4 (1959): 485, 488; Weingast, "Political Foundations."
[38] Rustow, "Transitions to Democracy," 355
[39] Lewis A. Coser, *The Functions of Social Conflict* (Glencoe, IL: Free Press, 1956), 70.
[40] Walter Lippmann, *Essays in the Public Philosophy* (New Brunswick, NJ: Transaction Publishers, 2009); Truman, "The American System," 485, 488; Fred H. Willhoite Jr., "Political Order and Consensus: A Continuing Problem," *The Western Political Quarterly* 16, no. 2 (1963): 294–304
[41] Steven Levitsky and Daniel Ziblatt, *How Democracies Die* (New York: Crown, 2018).

Elections, Polarization, Democratic Resilience 359

expectation of sanction, usually by other elites.[42] They have no mystical effect outside of this expectation, and politicians bent on gaining an advantage can do as Newt Gingrich urged his colleagues to do: ignore the norms, and don't sanction co-partisans for ignoring them.[43]

Norms, like insulated institutions, are perhaps especially vulnerable to subversion, given how much their effectiveness rests on the calculations of those they are intended to constrain. Societal-level mechanisms have the advantage of being distant from the immediate back-and-forth of politics, though this might also make them more weakly constraining. But they too can be eroded by the intense competition of elections. Parties are adept at finding the fault lines in public opinion, even in the face of broad consensus over values, and can be adroit manipulators of the perceived importance or immediate relevance of divisive issues. That is precisely their value in a democratic society. But there is little way to limit them to a juxtaposition of policy positions and to not take the often-more-effective step of attacking the social groups associated with their partisan rivals. The affective polarization this can unleash is powerful not because of its ideological content, but because it speaks to existing senses of social belonging and reorients these toward politics and conflictual visions of political interests, many of which will be well-founded no matter whether there are other values or nationality that are shared.

For this reason, neither societal values nor national unity – any more than norms or insulated institutions – can be reliable protections against political manipulation. We share nothing with them, they are unbound in their audacity, and, at the extreme, *they* are not *us*.[44] The degree to which we come to such evaluations is not a straightforward function of any objective condition of society; rather, these evaluations are constructed through the very antagonistic political processes that democratic life depends upon. When democracies reach this level of polarization, giving symbolic and ideological justification for politicians' existing professional incentive to rig the game, then norms, insulated institution, national unity,

---

[42] Julia R. Azari and Jennifer K. Smith, "Unwritten Rules: Informal Institutions in Established Democracies," *Perspectives on Politics* 10, no. 1 (2012): 40, 46
[43] Sean M. Theriault, *The Gingrich Senators: The Roots of Partisan Warfare in Congress* (Oxford: Oxford University Press, 2013).
[44] Or as Bill Walton, the executive committee president of the far-right Council for National Policy told his highly influential network of conservative activists, "this is a spiritual battle we are in. This is good versus evil .... And we have to do everything we can to win." O'Harrow, "Videos Show."

and values consensus – all the bulwarks keeping democratic competition in check – can be quickly eroded away.[45]

ELECTIONS UNBOUND

This has happened on several occasions in American history, when polarized competition (usually at the state level) crashed over the levees, resulting in widespread electoral manipulation and even the outright dismantling of democratic institutions in large portions of the country. And yet national politics has generally retained some essential features of a democracy, with rotations in office only rarely rejected and long stretches where threats to electoral integrity seemed to be local or regional exceptions, of not much consequence for the national result.[46]

On balance, I suggest, America's institutional solutions have been more effective than its normative ones. But their history also points to their deep inadequacy and ambivalence from a democratic perspective. Among the most significant institutional factors have been the fragmented structure of America's elections. The Constitution leaves it to the states to organize national elections, draw district boundaries, and establish voting qualifications and procedures. The actual administration has been left in many cases to counties or other subunits. This fragmented structure has persisted despite the punctuated layering of national standards and institutions over top of it, and likely makes it difficult to coordinate fraud or other illegal malfeasance in such a way as would secure a national victory. Legal forms of manipulation are not eliminated, but are rather multiplied so that they have no consistent national direction and are generally localized in their consequences. Illegal forms of manipulation, difficult to

---

[45] Arguments that democratic elections are "self-enforcing" rest on parties' anticipation that they will rotate in and out of office, which leads them to act with restraint. Electoral manipulations unsettle this expectation, and since it is better to gain office and not rotate out, elections themselves should be understood as "constantly at some risk of generating from within the forces of [their] own demise." Tom Ginsburg and Aziz Z. Huq, *How to Save a Constitutional Democracy* (Chicago: University of Chicago Press, 2018), 78, 84–85.

[46] Only in 1861 did the losers of an election clearly reject not only the result but the system which produced it. The danger of this happening was also pronounced in 1801, 1825, 1877, and to a lesser extent in 2000 and 2016. The losers of the 2020 presidential elections not only rejected the result but attempted to use various legal means, some potentially illegal ones, as well as the influence of the office to subvert the result. The country's fragmented electoral system – namely its administration by thousands of local officials with no subordinate or institutional relationship to the president – seems to have been critical to preventing the election's full subversion.

coordinate at the national or even the state level, especially with the organizational decline of political parties over the last century, have become relatively rare and are often highly idiosyncratic when they do occur.[47] Fragmentation, however, is responsible for the high levels of inequality Americans face in casting a ballot, having it counted as intended, and having it equally weighed. This inequality intersects with correlates of partisanship – such as race, income, age – and means that the direction of bias does not exactly average out across the country. One party often enjoys a biased advantage, with the constituencies associated with the other experiencing a diminished citizenship, their voices persistently counting for less.

This fragmentation not only generates persistent biases, but has frustrated efforts to secure electoral integrity and equal electoral rights for the nation as a whole. More immediately relevant, from the perspective of this chapter's argument, is that many of the historical efforts to erect institutions capable of preventing manipulation were themselves subverted toward the goal of advancing one party's political fortunes. The Civil War and Reconstruction saw the first federal attempts to regulate national elections, with Republicans creating a limited supervisory layer for elections and empowering federal marshals to preserve the peace at the polls. This machinery protected Republican voting in the South, especially by African American men. It was also simultaneously put to work in the North to make voting by Democratic constituencies more difficult. Unsurprisingly, there was no cross-party consistency in its application: the protection of Black southerners' voting rights largely ceased under Democratic president Grover Cleveland, while enforcement against Democratic activists and constituencies in the North slowed considerably. Congressional efforts at protecting electoral integrity showed a similar partisan bias. The House of Representatives and Senate became much more active in policing congressional elections during this period – with

---

[47] Consider the election fraud uncovered in the 9th congressional district of North Carolina in 2018, which seems to have hinged on a small number of Republican operatives seeking to subvert the integrity of both the Republican primary and the general election. Molly E. Reynolds, "Understanding the election scandal in North Carolina's 9th District," *Brookings*, December 7, 2018, www.brookings.edu/blog/fixgov/2018/12/07/understanding-the-election-scandal-in-north-carolinas-9th-district/. Some forms of illegal manipulation are easier to coordinate at the state or national level than others, such as voter intimidation through otherwise protected forms of electoral observation. The recent ending of the 1982 consent decree prohibiting the Republican National Committee from mobilizing "task force" observers will possibly lead to more coordinated efforts than we have seen in recent decades.

contested elections in some years exceeding 10 percent of the total – but the chambers generally used this power as a tool for buttressing partisan majorities.[48] Good-government reformers saw little advantage in sustaining either the Reconstruction-era institutions, tainted in an increasingly racist environment for their association with equal citizenship, or congressional control over its membership; this disassociation was so thorough that a final effort to pass a limited but important supervisory act in the 1890s is even today usually understood as the last gasp of the Civil War, and not as a potentially important component of the vibrant efforts at electoral reform sweeping the states. Once national competition had ceased to be white-hot, Congress created new norms and institutions for dealing with contested elections in a less partisan manner: these considerably diminished congressional interest in using this power to highlight or redress abuses. By the turn of the century, almost all of the electoral machinery built up to insulate national elections from partisan manipulation had been subverted, fallen into abeyance, or outright dismantled.

It was only with the civil rights legislation of the 1960s – and a corresponding judicial activism – that federal-level mechanisms for limiting or undoing entrenched manipulations came to be of any significance. Decisions requiring the equal apportionment of legislative districts and striking down the poll tax and lengthy residency requirements narrowed the scope of actions that state legislators could undertake to manipulate the electorate to their advantage. This "jurisprudence-building" was one of the key factors securing America's "second reconstruction" from erosion.[49] The upholding of federal voting rights protections helped fortify a new check on electoral manipulations and empowered an increasingly important and relatively insulated administrative agency – the Civil Rights Division in the Department of Justice – in protecting the right to vote. Operating in part in coalition with civil rights organizations, the federal government and judiciary used their new authority to dismantle the electoral manipulations that had maintained America's subnational authoritarianism for generations.[50]

---

[48] Jeffrey A. Jenkins, "Partisanship and Contested Election Cases in the House of Representatives, 1789–2002," *Studies in American Political Development* 18, no. 2 (2004): 112–35; Kuo and Teorell, "Illicit Tactics," 678.

[49] Valelly, *The Two Reconstructions*.

[50] Robert Mickey, *Paths out of Dixie: The Democratization of Authoritarian Enclaves in America's Deep South, 1944–1972* (Princeton: Princeton University Press, 2015).

This coalition frayed somewhat during the Reagan and Bush presidencies, but federal and state judges continued to enforce voting rights and federal lawyers continued to work with civil rights organizations in protecting and even expanding access to the ballot. National legislation to further expand access and improve election administration even passed in the 1990s and 2000s with bipartisan support. The result is that today's electoral administration is more integrated, professional, and effective, and elections' jurisprudence more thickly developed and consequential, than at any point in American history.

Still, this infrastructure has important limitations, and is already showing signs of erosion. For one, it remains relatively thin at the national level. The Federal Elections Commission is tasked primarily with enforcing federal campaign finance laws, themselves considerably undermined by the Supreme Court. The 1993 National Voting Registration Act and the 2002 Help America Vote Act have seen widely varying rates of state compliance, and federal legislation has only modestly, if at all, limited states' prerogatives to determine voter identification standards, the location of polling booths, the maintenance of registration lists, and the drawing of districts, some of the more important mechanisms for producing partisan bias.[51]

The courts have over the last fifty years served as a bulwark, using the now-considerable jurisprudence it has built up around federal statutes and the 14th Amendment to limit states' discretion in setting qualifications or in drawing district lines. But it seems likely that the Supreme Court is no longer willing to play this role, at least as aggressively as it has in the past. Its decision in *Shelby County*, moreover, suggests that it does not want other branches of the federal government to play it either. This case, which struck down a vital section of the 1965 Voting Rights Act, was the culmination of a decades-long partisan effort: Republican administrations since the 1970s have sought to politicize the Justice Department and its Civil Rights Division with the deliberate goal of undercutting voting rights protections.[52] These remain powerful tools for protecting elections, and have not been fully dismantled; but that they have become targets is no

---

[51] Valentina A. Bali and Brian D. Silver, "Politics, Race, and American State Electoral Reforms after Election 2000," *State Politics & Policy Quarterly* 6, no. 1 (2006): 21–48; Jamila Michener, "Race, Poverty, and the Redistribution of Voting Rights: Race, Poverty, and Voting Rights," *Poverty & Public Policy* 8, no. 2 (2016): 106–28.
[52] Jesse H. Rhodes, *Ballot Blocked: The Political Erosion of the Voting Rights Act* (Stanford: Stanford University Press, 2017), 131–41.

surprise, for neither the courts nor the bureaucracy are immune to the logic of partisan subversion.

SUPPRESSION OVER INSULATION

Perhaps the most reliable way that Americans have dealt with the threat of polarization has not been through fragmenting or insulating the electoral machinery, nor by artificially restraining elite behavior through norms, but by suppressing or localizing the competition that encouraged electoral malfeasance in the first place. Consider the three eras discussed previously: each of these ended with the crystallization of what scholars of American political development have termed a political regime, in which one party dominated national politics with the other confined to regional strongholds and a relatively small number of truly competitive districts.[53]

The political and ideological dominance of these "regimes," as well as their periodicity, can be overstated. But once installed they have tended to have a similar effect on political discourse as mid-century theorists hoped would be produced by values consensus, namely a modest restriction in the types of appeals that aspiring rulers believed could gain traction among elites and voters. By leaving one party reasonably secure in the expectation of holding power, they have encouraged minority partisans to act more as supplicants for policy and patronage than as serious contenders for national influence, and they have lessened the incentive for both sides to draw sharp contrasts. They have, for a period, limited the scope and intensity of political conflict.[54]

Many of the constraints that theorists have pointed to as buttressing the democratic aspects of America's polity have been neither intrinsic to American culture nor durable features of its politics, but entirely contingent features of the balance of political strength in the country. American history has regularly seen sharp disagreements among politically attentive and active publics on issues of values and culture, but political regimes have often suppressed the salience of these divergences and thereby provided the institutional and electoral conditions for the *appearance* of values consensus among the actually politically relevant classes. They have at times altered the incentives of political elites,

---

[53] Andrew J. Polsky, "Partisan Regimes in American Politics," *Polity* 44, no. 1 (2012): 51–80.
[54] Lee, *Insecure Majorities*.

reducing the value of maximalist hardball and facilitating a contingent recognition of norms. And on more than one occasion, they have occasioned the emergence of a seeming form of national unity, either by installing a cross-sectional coalition as the politically dominant force in the country or by localizing the importance of cultural and political minorities under the national hegemony of a particular party and its associated constituencies.

A number of commentators have been relatively sanguine about the dangers of contemporary polarization for precisely this reason, maintaining that high levels of polarization reflect a transition period in which an old and fracturing regime is locked in intense competition with an emerging one.[55] The hope, for them at least, is that the next few years will see a new political coalition dominate national politics, leading to de-polarization as the now-minority coalition finds itself expecting to lose for the foreseeable future and unable to advance its interests or ideals without making substantial compromises. This recommendation has been repeated in different forms by a variety of political and academic commentators: to protect American democracy requires the repeated defeat of the GOP – the major threat to democratic institutions at the moment – until it has been sufficiently chastened to once again adhere to the democratic rules of the game.[56]

Insofar as one-party dominance has been among the most effective tools for preserving America's electoral integrity this advice seems sound, albeit a little dispiriting to anyone who might champion the supposed virtues of the American constitutional order. But this historical pattern sits uneasily with calls to protect norms and to refrain from responding to manipulations with tit-for-tat hardball, lest this provoke a spiraling escalation. America's political regimes have never been secured solely by their strength in public opinion. Each of them has rested, at least in part, on new manipulations that have biased the electoral playing field at the national level in their favor, while relying on America's fragmented electoral system to allow the nationally subordinate party to similarly entrench themselves in various regions or localities. The "era of good feelings," for example, came after an expansion of the electorate and the admission of new states whose number, borders, and electoral qualifications were intentionally designed to benefit the Republicans. The Civil War–era Republican Party almost achieved

[55] Jack M. Balkin, "The Recent Unpleasantness: Understanding the Cycles of Constitutional Time," *Indiana Law Journal* 94, no. 1 (2019): 253–96.
[56] Levitsky and Ziblatt, *How Democracies Die.*

a similar entrenchment through the Reconstruction Acts and the 15th Amendment, which briefly saw the Democratic Party reduced to a shell of its former self. The eventual collapse of national competition at the beginning of the twentieth century was sustained in part by a new state-level electoral machinery in the North, which had the dual purpose of reducing fraud and making party management of elections less costly, as well as a new machinery in the South, which had a similar dual purpose of reducing fraud and suppressing Black voting.[57] The advance of electoral "integrity" that these new institutions achieved was real, but they also embedded a more fundamental manipulation of partisan bias into America's governing institutions. The Republican Party was installed as the dominant party in the North and the Democrats in the South. Competition declined, polarization declined, fraud declined, norms emerged, national unity was secured, and democracy disappeared in nearly a third of the country.

CONCLUSION

This is the conundrum that confronts anyone interested in preserving American democracy. The institutions and norms used to safeguard electoral integrity have either sustained deep inequalities and authoritarian enclaves, or they have been subverted under conditions of intense competition. This reflects the fundamental tension between the integrative and polarizing tasks assigned to elections: choice encourages polarization, which can in turn erode the external constraints needed for elections to be reliable regulators of conflict over succession.

Elections can fail in either direction, and democratic *resilience* requires us to assess at any given moment whether the polarizing logic is overly constrained or running rampant, whether the integrative logic is operating well-enough or is in danger of eroding, and whether the institutions that preserve elections against this self-undermining dynamic need updating, fortification, or redesign altogether.

So which choice should we make today? The contemporary era is the longest sustained period in American history in which the electoral process has been reasonably well insulated against political self-entrenchment,

---

[57] J. Morgan Kousser, *The Shaping of Southern Politics: Suffrage Restriction and the Establishment of the One-Party South, 1880–1910* (New Haven: Yale University Press, 1974); Alan Ware, "Anti-Partism and Party Control of Political Reform in the United States: The Case of the Australian Ballot," *British Journal of Political Science* 30, no. 1 (2000): 1–29.

a consequence of the institutions established during the mid-twentieth century, most prominently the VRA. These institutions remain in place, but seem increasingly brittle in the face of intense national competition. Shoring them up should be first on the list of democratic reforms, though doing so will – like passage of the 15th Amendment or the Civil Rights Act – inevitably require shattering some norms. We should not shirk from the task. Institutional and normative conservatism can have some merit, but should not be prioritized above the goals and values that these institutions and norms are supposed to secure.[58] The insistence on norms' centrality to democracy, despite their obvious fragility in the face of a coordinated ambition to power, is less a prescription for democratic preservation than a testament to democracy's inherent instability. To insist on abiding by no-longer-operational norms is to disregard their purpose and the context of their significance in favor of their superficial form.

Encouraging political actors' re-commitment to norms of mutual restraint and forbearance might be valuable over the long run, but this first requires a political context in which it would make sense for them to do so. America's history with democratization and political regimes points to ways in which such a context can be established. In particular, we ought to recognize the potential virtues of electoral innovations that are both deliberately designed to extend democracy and, for a period, to limit the intensity of competition by giving one party a durable advantage over the other. This is the history of the expansion of voting rights, and there is no shortage of contemporary possibilities that might serve the same function: Automatic voter registration, a statutory requirement that congressional districts be drawn by non-partisan electoral boards, the admission of at least one and possibly several states out of the District of Columbia and – if its residents were to choose so – at least one formed out of Puerto Rico, and the application of the 14th Amendment's equal protection clause to Senate malapportionment.[59] Despite being "hardball," each of these would enrich democracy along standard metrics while shifting the playing field, advantaging what is at the moment the only pro-democracy national party, in the short- to medium-term. Crucially, these

---

[58] Julia R. Azari, "Forget Norms: Our Democracy Depends on Values," *FiveThirtyEight.com*, May 24, 2018, https://fivethirtyeight.com/features/forget-norms-our-democracy-depends-on-values/.

[59] Subjugating the interests and preferences of already subjugated territories, such as Puerto Rico or other American colonies, to the interests of metropolitan factions only continues a history of imperialism. An expansion of the electorate is not inherently democratic, especially if it reproduces inherently undemocratic patterns of rule.

partisan consequences are not locked in, which indeed would be undemocratic. Instead, such reforms provide a structure around which the initially disadvantaged party can reorganize. They reorient the direction of bias in America's electoral system, securing the temporary national dominance of what is for the moment the party more committed to democracy and electoral integrity even as they make America's electoral institutions more equal and inclusive.

Establishing a new political regime in turn might generate a context of lowered polarization akin to that in which the norms of toleration and forbearance emerged in the first place at the end of the nineteenth century. This time, however, it would be achieved by expanding rather than restricting democracy. The United States is perhaps fortunate in that, like in the immediate aftermath of the Civil War, it confronts a political landscape in which competition can be reduced, the active threat to democracy pushed back, and democratic rights advanced all at the same time. Still, nothing is permanent, and, as the Reconstruction example reminds us, there are no sure things in politics. Even if democratizing and representation-equalizing reforms were to succeed in dampening national competition, the United States would again have to recalibrate its institutions, whether to preserve it from the eventual renewal of polarization or from an anemic *de*polarization. But doing so is an intrinsic responsibility of a democratic order, and it is time to face up to this and its implications.

15

Citizen Organizing and Partisan Polarization from the Tea Party to the Anti-Trump Resistance

Theda Skocpol, Caroline Tervo, and Kirsten Walters

The November 2020 elections delivered a big victory for Democratic presidential challenger Joseph R. Biden along with gains or holds for many Republicans running in congressional and state contests. Reinforced partisan divisions were not, however, the most remarkable aspect of this election. Amid a raging deadly pandemic and sharp economic retraction, about two-thirds of eligible Americans registered their votes by mail or in-person, marking the highest eligible voter turnout in more than a hundred years. Some 74 million voted for Donald Trump, while more than 81 million supported the winner, Joe Biden. This remarkably high voter turnout continued through the early January 2021 Georgia runoffs, where upset victories for Democrats Jon Ossoff and Raphael Warnock delivered control of the US Senate to their party through 2022. A modern US electoral system that has, for decades, exhibited extraordinary slack in voter participation suddenly experienced engaged citizens on both ends of the partisan spectrum, as many more Americans than the usual ideologically attuned elites, interest groups, and party-oriented activists jumped into a high-stakes, emotionally and morally infused referendum on the meaning and future of US democracy.

In this chapter, we argue that the stage was set for the high stakes and massive turnouts of 2020 by two precursor upsurges of citizen activism, the Tea Party launched in early 2009 and the anti-Trump resistance that took to the field in late 2016. As readers of this volume have learned,

---

The authors would like to thank Michael A. Bailey, Rachel Blum, and Michael Zoorob for their assistance with some of the data employed here. For feedback on early versions of this work, we thank Lara Putnam and Michael Tomasky.

America's Republicans and Democrats have been pulling apart for decades and the separation has become increasingly right-tilted since the 1990s. By the early twenty-first century, elites, activists, and many voters embraced opposite hopes and fears about government's role in managing the market economy and dealing with the nation's increasing ethnic, racial, and cultural diversity. Then came two closely spaced 2008 and 2016 electoral shocks of the kind that had previously been relatively rare in the divided-powers US system. Just eight years apart, two highly usual presidential contenders won the White House – first Democrat Barack Hussein Obama (a Black former community organizer and college professor) and then Republican Donald Trump (a New York real estate operator and bombastic reality TV impresario). Their messages about the meaning and promise of America were diametrically opposite, yet both won the presidency backed by House and Senate majorities from their respective parties, positioning each to advance sweeping policy changes. After such startling results in November 2008 and November 2016, pushback was instant. Alarmed partisans on the losing side mounted massive protests and launched waves of political organizing aimed at blocking threatened policy shifts and winning the next rounds of US elections.

Early analyses of the anti-Obama Tea Party and the anti-Trump resistance focused on public protests and national advocacy initiatives. Indeed, both movements were propelled by the Tea Party Tax Day rallies of mid-April 2009 and the Women's Marches of January 21, 2017, and both included all-out mobilizations by national advocacy and donor organizations. Much more remarkably, however, ordinary Americans living everywhere upped their ongoing civic and political engagement under the Tea Party and resistance banners. Starting in the spring of 2009, conservative citizens voluntarily organized what grew to around two thousand regularly meeting local Tea Party groups across all fifty states. Similarly, after the November 2016 election, liberal-leaning citizens created what became about three thousand volunteer-led grassroots resistance groups to sustain pushback against President Trump and the GOP-led Congress across states and communities of all stripes.

When widespread popular activism occurs, many observers presume it will feed polarizing policy agendas and uncompromising styles of political engagement. Activists do tend to lean more toward ideological purity than non-activists and voters in general. From this perspective, the resistance that gathered force after 2016 should function like "a Tea Party of the left" to push the Democrats toward extremes, as happened earlier on the right. Challenging this conventional wisdom, we show that the elite and grassroots components of the Tea Party and the anti-Trump resistance have influenced the major political parties in different ways. After 2009, grassroots Tea Party activism went beyond bolstering elite advocacy for ultra-free-market policies to supercharge new forms of ethnonationalist extremism and prod GOP officeholders toward uncompromising, even extra-Constitutional practices.

Nothing analogous has happened on the other side. Although some self-styled progressive advocates in the post-2016 resistance have challenged moderate Democrats in primaries and urged congressional Democrats to take maximal policy stands, most grassroots resistance groups have worked for moderate-liberal as well as left-progressive candidates and remain open to step-by-step reforms and governing compromises within established institutional rules.

DISSECTING TWO CIVIC EXPLOSIONS

Most previous scholarly work on the Tea Party and the anti-Trump resistance has documented early waves of public protests and the demographics and attitudinal outlooks of initial participants and sympathizers, setting the stage for the more organizationally focused approach we develop here.

Nationwide Protest Waves

The kick-off of the Tea Party is usually pegged to a February 19, 2009, "rant" by MSNBC financial commentator Rick Santelli in which he called for protestors to dress up in Colonial costumes to oppose Obama administration mortgage relief policies. Nationally networked conservatives encouraged rallies in dozens of cities on February 27, 2009; and Fox News and other right-wing media outlets publicized grander plans for Tax Day rallies, which ended up drawing between 250,000 and a million participants to events in 642 counties across the country.[1] Recurrent

---

[1] Patrik Jonsson, "Arguing the Size of the 'Tea Party' Protest," *Christian Science Monitor*, April 18, 2009; A. Madestam, D. Shoag, S. Veuger, and D. Yanagizawa-Drott, "Do Political Protests Matter? Evidence from the Tea Party Movement," *Quarterly Journal of Economics* 128, no. 4 (August 2013): 1633–85; and Nate Silver, "Tea Party Nonpartisan Attendance Estimates: Now 300,000+," *FiveThirtyEight* blog, April 16, 2009. Fox News and other media coverage is analyzed in Theda Skocpol and Vanessa Williamson, *The Tea Party and the Remaking of Republican Conservatism* (New York: Oxford University Press, 2012), chapter 4.

protest waves followed – including coordinated July 4th rallies; protests at Democratic Town Hall meetings; and a large September 12, 2009, March on Washington, DC.[2] Through 2010 and beyond, raucous Tea Party demonstrations continued. Eight years later mass public protests marked the national debut of the anti-Trump resistance.

Within days of the November 8, 2016, election, national and local networks started preparing for a "Women's March" the day after Donald Trump's inauguration.[3] On January 21, 2017, between 500,00 and a million marchers massed in the streets of Washington, DC, and millions more joined "sister" events held in more than 650 US cities and towns across all fifty states. The estimated 3.3 to 5.3 million marchers, more than 1 percent of the population, mounted the "the largest single-day demonstration in recorded U.S. history" to date.[4] These women's marches were a prelude to recurrent protests.[5] At regular intervals during 2017 and into 2018, multi-city waves of issue-focused rallies proliferated, including a March for Science, People's Climate March, and Families Belong Together protests against the separation of immigrant children from their parents at the border.[6] Judged by standard protest metrics of size and speed, the early resistance was more potent, because Trump's 2016 victory created a bigger shock and resistance protestors could take inspiration from the earlier Tea Party and use faster internet modalities to coordinate.

---

[2] Matthew Bigg and Nick Carey, "Protests Disrupt Town-Hall Healthcare Talks," *Reuters*, August 8, 2009; Chris Good, "Lawmakers Will Face Tea Parties, and More, in August," *The Atlantic*, July 30, 2009; Rachel Streitfeld, "Tea Party Activists Rally at Capital," *CNN Politics*, July 4, 2009; Jeff Zeleny, "Thousands Rally in Capital to Protest Big Government," *New York Times*, September 12, 2009.

[3] Marie Berry and Erica Chenoweth, "Who Made the Women's March?," in *The Resistance*, ed. David S. Meyer and Sidney Tarrow (New York: Oxford University Press, 2018), 75–89; Kraig Beyerlein, Peter Ryan, Aliyah Abu-Hazeem, and Amity Pauley, "The 2017 Women's March: A National Study of Solidarity Events," *Mobilization: An International Quarterly* 23, no. 4 (December 2018): 425–49; and Rachel G. McKane and Holly J. McCammon, "Why We March: The Role of Grievances, Threats, and Movement Organizational Resources in the 2017 Women's Marches," *Mobilization: An International Quarterly* 23, no. 4 (December 2018): 401–24.

[4] Erica Chenoweth and Jeremy Pressman, "This Is What We Learned by Counting the Women's Marches," Monkey Cage blog post, *Washington Post*, February 7, 2017.

[5] Kenneth T. Andrews, Noel Caren and Alyssa Browne, "Protesting Trump," *Mobilization: An International Quarterly* 23, no. 4 (December 2018): 393–400.

[6] The succession of major protests is covered by Dana R. Fisher in *American Resistance* (New York: Columbia University Press, 2019), 23–24 and chapter 2, plus references. Further details on many early protests appear in David S. Meyer and Sidney Tarrow, eds., *The Resistance* (New York: Oxford University Press, 2018).

Who Are the Tea Partiers and Resisters?

Investigators have used various kinds of surveys to decipher the social characteristics and political outlooks of Americans active in these upsurges. By 2010, well-designed surveys made it clear that both Tea Party activists and sympathizers were middle-class whites, about 60 percent men, with higher incomes and levels of educational attainment than Americans in general.[7] People with some college or bachelors' degrees predominated. As for political views, the vast majority of Tea Party participants were very conservative-minded Republicans or independents located to the right of the GOP, with some variations in outlooks. Most Tea Party-aligned elites claim that the movement is solely focused on fiscally conservative "small government" goals, but many grassroots Tea Partiers want government to enforce traditional cultural norms and national identity.[8] Various polls and studies, including a major contribution by political scientists Christopher Parker and Matt Barreto, show that Tea Party supporters are more inclined than other conservatives and Republicans to view President Obama as threatening, express strong support for Donald Trump, and espouse negative stereotypes about immigrants, racial-ethnic minorities, and Muslims.[9]

Turning to post-2016 resistance, we know of no national surveys that asked specifically about demographics and detailed policy views of activists and sympathizers. Instead, scholars have used field surveys, internet questionnaires, and interviews to understand those most actively engaged, especially in major city protests. Sociologist Dana Fisher and her collaborators administered surveys to samples of participants in six large-scale Washington, DC, protests during 2017 or 2018, and also did follow-up

---

[7] Findings from many contemporaneous polls are discussed in Skocpol and Williamson, *Tea Party and Republican Conservatism*, chapters 1 and 2, especially pages 21–34. See especially Kate Zernike and Megan Thee-Brenan, "Poll Finds Tea Party Backers Wealthier and More Educated," *New York Times*, April 14, 2010.

[8] Michelle Boorstein, "Tea Party, Religious Right Often Overlap, Poll Shows," *Washington Post*, October 5, 2010.

[9] Christopher S. Parker and Matt A. Barreto, *Change They Can't Believe In: The Tea Party and Reactionary Politics in America* (Princeton: Princeton University Press, 2014). See also Jonathan Allen, "The Tea Party Finally Has Its Very Own Presidential Candidate: Donald Trump," *Vox*, August 7, 2015; Michael Dimock, Carroll Doherty, and Jocelyn Kiley, "'Borders First' a Dividing Line in Immigration Debate," *Pew Research Center/USA Today Survey*, June 23, 2013; Bruce Drake, "Tea Party Republicans Believe Legal Status Would Reward Undocumented Immigrants," *Pew Research Center*, July 11, 2013; "Warmer Feelings About Trump Among Republicans Critical of Immigration, Growing Diversity, Islam," *Pew Research Center* survey conducted April 5–May 2, 2016.

surveys with some respondents in May and November 2018.[10] Across the DC protests they studied, the Fisher group found that between 70 and 80 percent of the participants were women and whites, and three quarters or more had earned bachelors' or advanced college degrees.[11] Resisters include some young adults, but, as in the Tea Party, many of these activists were middle-aged to retirees. The vast majority of resisters (80 to 90 percent) had voted for Hillary Clinton in 2016, and most also described their political orientations as "left" (rather than "moderate/middle of the road" or "right"). Research on organizers of local Women's Marches outside Washington, DC, and studies of local resistance group members find much the same profile, but also suggest that along with the liberals and progressives some centrist-independents and dissident Republicans have been active in the resistance nationwide.[12]

All told, researchers have documented that, prior to the Black Lives Matter street protests in US cities during the summer of 2020, middle-class, middle-aged whites dominated America's recent waves of civic activism on both sides of a fierce political war about the nation's identity and immediate governmental future. Tea Partiers want to restrict immigration, cut back on government regulation of the economy and the environment, and spend much less public money to help less privileged groups.

Resisters, by contrast, want to welcome immigrants and refugees, advance racial equality, and use government to fight climate change and build a more equitable economy and society.[13] Yet important as it has been to pin down that these civic explosions have involved mostly middle-class whites promoting clashing visions, such previous studies cannot tell us very much about whether – and how – these movements have changed US political parties, elections, and governance. For that, we must probe their evolving organizational networks.

AN ORGANIZATIONAL PERSPECTIVE

Organizations are vital players in social movements, not only because they help to orchestrate protest events but because they influence elections and

---

[10] For methods, see Fisher, *American Resistance*, 31–33 and Methodological Appendix.
[11] Ibid., chapter 2.
[12] Beyerlein et al., "The 2017 Women's March," 436–37; Gose and Skocpol, "Resist, Persist, and Transform," especially p. 299; Skocpol and Tervo, *Upending American Politics*, chapters 8, 9, 11, 12, and 13.
[13] The goals and issue priorities of resisters are measured in Fisher, *American Resistance*; Gose and Skocpol, "Resist, Persist, and Transform"; Meyer and Tarrow, *The Resistance*.

governing agendas by deploying paid staffers or committed volunteers to raise money, shape and disseminate messages, coordinate activities, recruit participants, manage media relations, and build alliances.

What kind of organizations matter? Through much of US history, civic life centered in volunteer-led federated membership associations grounded in vast networks of local chapters and dues-paying mass memberships.[14] Major mid-twentieth-century social movements usually included such membership federations able to influence US government and political parties at local, state, and national levels. After the 1960s, however, the civic center of gravity shifted toward nationally centralized, professionally led organizations, including issue advocacy groups, think tanks, lobbying operations, and fundraising organizations, mostly headquartered in Washington, DC, New York City, or other major US metropolises.[15] Lacking wide networks of chapters, these entities rely on wealthy donors and foundations for funding and recruit citizen adherents, if at all, initially through mass mailings and later via email or social media. They exert political influence through media outreach, lobbying, policy research, and legal filings. Now, many important American civic operations do not even have physical headquarters; like the well-known MoveOn organization, they may operate entirely through virtual staff connections and internet communications with mass adherents.[16]

Oriented to this new civic world, scholarship on the Tea Party and resistance has focused on national, professionally run organizations and said little, apart from anecdotes, about thousands of volunteer-run local groups. Data about local groups is hard to find, of course, but there are also conceptual blinders. Most researchers presume that professionals operating from (virtual or brick and mortar) national headquarters can use mass communications and occasional training sessions to inspire ground-level individual activists, regardless of where they live. "Distributed organizing" is the moniker for this approach, seen as

---

[14] Theda Skocpol, Marshall Ganz, and Ziad Munson, "A Nation of Organizers: The Institutional Origins of Civic Voluntarism in the United States," *American Political Science Review* 94 (2000): 527–46; Theda Skocpol, *Diminished Democracy: From Membership to Management in American Civic Life* (Norman: University of Oklahoma Press, 2003), chapters 1–3.

[15] Jeffrey M. Berry, *The New Liberalism: The Rising Power of Citizen Groups* (Washington: Brookings Institution Press, 1999); Robert Putnam, *Bowling Alone* (New York: Simon and Schuster, 2001); Skocpol, *Diminished Democracy*, chapters 4–6.

[16] David Karpf, *The MoveOn Effect: The Unexpected Transformation of American Political Advocacy* (Oxford: Oxford University Press, 2012).

dominant in the social media era.[17] But this model is a misleading guide to the Tea Party and the anti-Trump resistance, because both have included ongoing, voluntarily organized *collective* activities in most communities and congressional districts, not always responsive to the behest of national professionals.

Overall, the Tea Party and the anti-Trump resistance are best conceptualized, as we do here, as evolving, loosely coupled organizational fields – including dozens of professionally managed funding and advocacy organizations pushing from the top, along with thousands of local groups run by volunteers pushing from below. We describe these fields before explaining how their dynamic interplay has buffeted and changed Republican and Democratic politics – furthering extremism on the right but, so far, not on the left.

NATIONAL CONVENERS AND PROFESSIONAL ADVOCATES

From the start, national organizations have been key players in both the Tea Party and the anti-Trump resistance – some newly formed (usually as nonprofit 501cs or c4s), others previously functioning advocacy organizations, electoral operations, or think tanks that revamped some of their activities to ride the new waves of civic energy. Relying on organizational self-identifications and previous studies, we have identified the most important players.

To start with the top-down Tea Party, following Rick Santelli's February 2009 call for protests, an initial "steering committee" of conservative orchestrators "launched a coordinated test marketing" of the concept through April.[18] Thereafter, the original steering coalition gave way to formal organizations, of which the most important has always been FreedomWorks, an already established DC-based free-market advocacy and lobbying operation.[19]

---

[17] Fisher, *American Resistance*, 14–18; and David Karpf, *The MoveOn Effect* (Oxford: Oxford University Press, 2012).

[18] Quote is from Clarence Y. H. Lo "Astroturf versus Grass Roots," in *Steep: The Precipitous Rise of the Tea Party*, ed. Lawrence Rosenthal and Christine Trost (Berkeley: University of California Press, 2012), 100–01.

[19] Ibid., 100; see also Devin Burghart, "View from the Top: Report on Six National Tea Party Organizations," in *Steep*, ed. Rosenthal and Trost, 69–73. This chapter draws from a much longer report prepared in the fall of 2020. See Devin Burghart and Leonard Zeskind, *Tea Party Nationalism: A Critical Examination of the Tea Party Movement and the Size, Scope, and Focus of Its National Factions* (Kansas City, MO: Institute for Research & Education on Human Rights, 2010). The Institute (IREHR) has

After FreedomWorks CEO Matt Kibbe and director of campaigns Brandon Steinhauser helped inspire early protests, the organization went on to cosponsor national Tea Party campaigns and marches, convene strategy meetings and activist training sessions, and plot ways to channel Tea Party energies into key GOP election races for November 2010 and beyond.[20] Some observers regard the Tea Party movement as no more than an "Astroturf" creation because FreedomWorks, along with another free-market organization called Americans for Prosperity (AFP), were offshoots of a progenitor organization called Citizens for a Sound Economy that was part of the political network created by multibillionaire industrialists Charles and David Koch.[21] However, by 2009, FreedomWorks was no longer a Koch-run operation and was much smaller than AFP, which focuses strictly on advancing free-market candidates and policies through paid state directors who orchestrate electoral and policy campaigns.[22] Rather than posit that the Koch network created the Tea Party, it makes more sense that association with this upsurge buoyed the previously waning fortunes of FreedomWorks – and also created new ad hoc opportunities for AFP operatives to counter Democrats.

During the late winter and spring of 2009, various other new and repurposed national organizations jumped onto the Tea Party bandwagon. Prior to 2009, an operation called ResistNet had offered social networking services and run conservative internet petition drives. In 2009, it turned to building lists of movement supporters, sending "blasts" against President Obama and congressional Democrats, and promoting "Tea Parties at every state capitol."[23] By late 2010, ResistNet claimed 142 local chapter followers in 34 states and relabeled itself the Political Action Network. Another preexisting California-based Republican political action committee called "Our Country Deserves Better" similarly relabeled itself Tea Party Express

---

done periodic follow ups to update narratives and statistics on Tea Party national organizations.

[20] Kate Zernike, "Shaping Tea Party Passion into Campaign Force," *New York Times*, August 25, 2010.

[21] See, for example, Amanda Fallin, Rachel Grana, and Stanton A. Glantz, "'To Quarterback Behind the Scenes, Third-Party Efforts': The Tobacco Industry and the Tea Party," Tobaccocontrol.bmj.com, August 3, 2020.

[22] Using detailed state-level data harvested from internal reports, AFP websites, and the Wayback machine, we have found no significant associations between prior AFP presence and the growth of Tea Party groups and activists after 2008.

[23] Burghart, "View from the Top," 76.

and proceeded to run Tea Party bus tours and make donations to GOP candidates running against Democratic incumbents.[24]

Several newly launched Tea Party organizations proclaimed cultural conservative priorities. Radio and TV host Glenn Beck's 9/12 Project was launched on March 13, 2009, to tout a blend of nationalist, religious, and family-centered "principles and values shared by the Founding Fathers of the United States."[25] Two other new creations, the 1776 Tea Party and Tea Party Nation, similarly pushed openly ethno-nationalist and Christian conservative priorities that appealed to many individual activists and some local groups that signed up on their websites.[26] In early April 2009, a Nashville attorney set up Tea Party Nation (TPN) to organize a Tax Day rally and orchestrate an ongoing national network that eventually attracted some 318 local Tea Parties in dozens of states, especially in the South and West.

TPN convened a February 2010 convention, got involved in some Senate and House elections, and lobbied congressional and other Republicans on behalf of "culture-war staples, such as opposition to gay marriage, anti-immigration policies and opposition to abortion."[27]

By far the most important newly created national organization was (and remains) Tea Party Patriots (TPP), launched on March 10, 2009, as a self-styled umbrella coordinating body to push Constitutional, limited government and "faith in the Founding Fathers" with encouragement from FreedomWorks. At first, TPP was a relatively low-budget and lightly staffed operation that raised small donations to pay for travel by the directors and commission consultants to do further rounds of fundraising from followers.[28] Later it became a major cosponsor and convener of high-profile Tea Party protests. By 2012, TPP had one of the largest web-enrolled lists of individual Tea Party activists all over the country, and by 2015 it also boasted very large Facebook and Twitter followings. Although TPP's national leaders originally seemed content to spark public protests and enroll individual supporters, from the late spring of 2009 the Atlanta headquarters encouraged emerging local groups to register on its website, and by fall, TPP was regularly updating its expanding online list of local Tea Parties classified by home states.[29]

---

[24] For the 2010 midterms, the Tea Party Express endorsed Republicans in 15 Senate races and 102 House contests, three-fifths of whom prevailed in their races. See Burghart, "View from the Top," 82–87.
[25] Quotes from Wikipedia 2020 write up of "9-12-Project."
[26] Burghart, "View from the Top," 73–75.
[27] Ibid., 77–80.
[28] Direct evidence appears in the group's IRS 990s.
[29] Heath Brown, *The Tea Party Divided* (Santa Barbara, CA: Praeger, 2015), 26–30.

Top-down players in the anti-Trump resistance also included both preexisting and start-up organizations. But a wider array leaped into the post-2016 fray – in part because the preexisting universe of left-leaning national advocacy organizations was already densely populated and also because US liberals suddenly faced a constricted opportunity structure. Back in 2009, conservative elites could count on the Senate filibuster to obstruct the full Obama agenda for six months, until after the contested Minnesota Senate election was settled; but after the Trump-GOP sweep of November 2016 there were no Democratic powerholders in Washington, DC, to whom opponents could turn. Outside action was the whole ball game, so literally hundreds of groups could therefore be considered "resistance aligned." We focus here on a smaller core of key players.

Soon after Hillary Clinton's defeat, women who had earlier signed up on the Facebook site Pantsuit Nation grieved and contacted one another via tools added to the site.[30] Meanwhile, a formal national Women's March organization was established, misleadingly portrayed by some analysts as the primary orchestrator of the overall resistance movement because it assembled a sponsoring coalition of dozens of long-standing progressive and liberal groups, including a few cosponsors with significant organizational heft like Planned Parenthood.[31] With or without prior organizational ties, millions of liberal-minded Americans were eager to join protests.

Other resistance-aligned organizations dedicated their efforts to electoral resource mobilization for Democrats. Start-ups such as Swing Left, Flippable, Sister District, and Run for Something deployed internet-facilitated means to recruit new candidates, especially women, and channel money and volunteers into Democratic campaigns.[32] Swing Left evolved by 2018 into a uniquely impactful endeavor, with a few dozen staffers providing election analysis and tactical suggestions to a nationwide network of affiliated groups run by volunteers prepared to help defeat Republicans in targeted districts.

---

[30] *Hollywood Reporter*, "In the Wake of Clinton Defeat, Pantsuit Nation Mobilizes for More Action," Yahoo.com, November 11, 2016.

[31] Anna North, "How the Women's March Made Itself Indispensable," *Vox*, January 19, 2018. For broader overviews, see Marie Berry and Erica Chenoweth, "Who Made the Women's March?," 75–89 in *The Resistance*, ed. Meyer and Tarrow; and McKane and McCammon, "Why We March."

[32] Tim Murphy, "The Secret Slack Group Plotting to Turn Your State Government Blue," *Mother Jones*, February 13, 2017; Lisa Rab, "Star Search: The Race to Rebuild the Democratic Party," *Harper's Magazine*, November 2017; Jia Tolentino, "Swing Left and the Post-Election Surge of Progressive Activism," *The New Yorker*, January 26, 2017.

Flush with eager new volunteers and millions of dollars in new contributions, long-standing leftist advocacy, lobbying, community-organizing, and legal organizations simultaneously also stepped up their agitations.[33] MoveOn became a regular convener of anti-Trump protests and lobbying campaigns, working with diverse advocacy group partners depending on the issues at hand. In orchestrating outside activist pressures, MoveOn was often joined by the Working Families Party, and by perhaps the most important new resistance organization to take to the field after November 2016, an outfit called Indivisible that sought to inspire, coordinate, and support local resistance efforts, much as Tea Party Patriots had done in the earlier right-wing movement.[34]

Eventually formalized in a twinned 501c4 and 501c3 formation, Indivisible got going in mid-December 2016, when two former Democratic congressional staffers who had experienced 2009 Tea Party protests gathered a group of peers to write an online *Indivisible Guide* to help alarmed liberals organize locally in opposition to congressional and Trump administrative initiatives.[35] At first, the *Guide* was just a Google document that went viral, but the authors soon created a website and a map where activists could list local resistance projects. Soon the Indivisible founders quit their previous jobs and set about fundraising to build their own nonprofit organization staffed by DC-area professionals.[36]

By the fall of 2017, the national office employed more than 40 professionals in communications, development, policy, politics, digital and regional organizing, and (with considerable exaggeration) the organization claimed close to 6,000 affiliated "chapters" and a presence in every US congressional district. The DC office sent regular alerts about congressional twists and turns and issued calls for local resisters to protest and lobby against the Trump-GOP regime's efforts. Local groups did not always heed DC urgings, and many either never formally affiliated with Indivisible or dropped out after a time.

---

[33] Many details about organizational contributions are covered in Meyer and Tarrow, *The Resistance*, parts two and three; and in Fisher, *American Resistance*, chapters 3 and 4.

[34] Useful overviews of Indivisible appear in Megan E. Brooker, "Indivisible: Investigating and Redirecting the Grassroots," 162–84 in *The Resistance*, ed. Meyer and Tarrow; Fisher, *American Resistance;* Casey Tolan, "Meet the Husband-Wife Duo Who Are Sparking a Liberal Tea Party Movement," *Mercury.News.com*, May 13, 2017, updated May 17.

[35] Ezra Levin, Leah Greenberg, and Angel Padilla, *Indivisible: A Practical Guide for Resisting the Trump Agenda*. Originally posted December 14, 2016.

[36] For the founders' narration, see Leah Greenberg and Ezra Levin, *We Are Indivisible: A Blueprint for Democracy After Trump* (New York: Once Signal Publishers, Atria Books, 2019). We also draw on our own research about Indivisible's structure and development.

Nevertheless, Indivisible became the most important newly formed national resistance organization because, like Tea Party Patriots back in 2009, it served as an umbrella in touch with local voluntary groups across the country. This model appealed to many wealthy liberal donors and foundations who, in 2017, 2018, and 2019, poured at least 35 million dollars into Indivisible's coffers. Most of the new resources were spent to hire and support 75 to 100 professional staffers.[37] As had happened earlier with Tea Party Patriots, only small dribbles of the tens of millions raised by DC Indivisible flowed to subnational groups or networks, which continued to rely on their own volunteers and small dollar donations.

THE SPREAD OF LOCAL TEA PARTIES AND RESISTANCE GROUPS

Repeatedly in post-1960s US civic life, protest waves have proved ephemeral or have transmogrified into new donor-funded rounds of professionally managed advocacy politics. Such tendencies have also happened in Tea Party and resistance, yet to a remarkable degree committed citizen volunteers in both turned to organizing regularly meeting local groups that sustained participation over months and years. The vignettes offered here – two each for the Tea Party and the anti-Trump resistance – indicate how that happened, drawing examples from our research network's interviews and field visits.

> **How Local Tea Parties Emerged**
>
> "We do Tea Party stuff to take the country back to where we think it should be," said *Stella Fisher* of Surprise, Arizona, as she explained how she and her sixty-nine-year-old husband *Larry* got involved as retirees. In April 2009, they attended a Tax Day rally at the state capitol and visited several Tea Party groups before helping set up a local Tea Party in their neighborhood. "We think the federal government is overstepping their authority. Take health care, take education. All those things.... The EPA, they've shut down I forget how many timber plants in Arizona because of the spotted owl."

---

[37] Information drawn from Indivisible's online annual financial summaries, IRS 990s, a summer 2019 staff roster document, and internet postings of staff openings.

When *John Patterson* of Lynchburg, Virginia, heard the February 19, 2009, Rick Santelli rant replayed on his truck radio, he explains that "I related to him ... saying what a lot of people think." After Obama's election, John, a longtime Republican, wondered what could be done. His son served in Iraq and it filled him with "seething rage" to hear Obama say the war could not be won. John is "not calling Obama a Muslim," but he was glad when people who "love the same things" about this country started organizing. Several "local ladies" got a local Tea Party group going in spring 2009 with email and leaflets stuffed under windshield wipers in the Walmart parking lot. Lynchburg Tea Partiers participated in several city and regional protests and about fifty carpooled to the huge 9/12 rally in Washington, DC.

How Local Resistance Groups Emerged

On November 12, 2016, in Luzerne County, Pennsylvania, a grassroots anti-Trump resistance group got going when two women met for the first time at a "bitch session" to lament Hillary Clinton's election loss. Pulled together via local campaign volunteers and contacts on the Pantsuit Nation website, participants met then and again in December at a restaurant in Wilkes-Barre. After three busloads of seventy-five people traveled to Washington, DC, for the January 21 Women's March, the group was formalized as the Luzerne chapter of a network called Action Together. It went on to form task forces, lobby representatives, engage in community and voter registration projects, and support Democratic candidates for local, state, and national office while pressing for party reforms. By the spring of 2017, the Luzerne group became a core driver in Action Together Northeast Pennsylvania, a multi-county 501c4 federation that is the powerhouse of grassroots resistance activity in the region.

> In Tomah, Wisconsin, on February 26, 2017, a female physician convened sixteen people concerned about the Trump presidency to found "Indivisible WI-03," a resistance group named for the US House district that encompasses conservative-leaning Monroe County and the town of Sparta as well as Tomah. Inspired by the Women's March and the *Indivisible Guide*, members have mounted occasional street demonstrations, participated in parades and community fairs, and supported Democrats running for state and national offices. At times, the group worked with Indivisible LaCrosse, based in the nearest small city.

Despite clashing values and goals, there were only subtle differences in the starts and operations of Tea Parties and resistance groups. Unpaid organizers often did not know one another until they met electronically or while traveling to early protests. Local groups took inspiration but never detailed direction from national organizations. Both kinds of groups have convened in similar kinds of places – public libraries, back rooms of restaurants, church basements – but Tea Party meetings start with participants standing for the Pledge of Allegiance and perhaps a prayer before hearing from a visiting lecturer or planning attendance at lobbying days or regional protests. Resistance meetings usually move directly from informal socializing to reports from leaders and subgroups engaged in ongoing activities like voter outreach, lobbying elected officials, or special community projects. Both sets of groups give participants many chances to learn about the nitty-gritty of US politics, the doings of local government, the mechanics of running for office, the timing of state legislative decisions, and tactics for pressuring Congress. Tea Party meetings attract more married couples, higher shares of men, and tend to include many active or retired small businesspeople and military veterans, while resistance meetings feature mostly women, particularly teachers, health-care professionals, public-sector employees, and owners of creative businesses, with the occasional male partner or friend in tow.

Elsewhere we have written more about the internal organization and ongoing activities of local Tea Party and resistance groups.[38] Here we address more challenging macroscopic issues: How and when did these

---

[38] Leah E. Gose and Theda Skocpol, "Resist, Persist, and Transform: The Emergence and Impact of Grassroots Resistance Groups Opposing the Trump Presidency," *Mobilization: An International Journal* 24, no. 3 (2019): 293–317; Skocpol and Tervo, *Upending*

local voluntary groups take shape and accumulate; and where did Tea Parties and grassroots resistance groups spread across the vast US social and political landscape?

To track trends in numbers of local Tea Parties and anti-Trump resistance groups, we have worked, in the first instance, from date-specific lists of affiliated local groups compiled by two umbrella organizations, Tea Party Patriots and Indivisible. Their website lists are not entirely parallel, because Indivisible used an internet map that recorded all sorts of local projects, only about half of which were groups, whereas the early Tea Party Patriots website included state-level associations and some allied organizations as well as local Tea Party groups. Both lists contain errors and duplications we have tried to clean up. With appropriate cleaning and adjustments to approximate trends in the overall numbers of actual local groups, we find that both local Tea Parties and resistance groups accumulated quickly, but the upward trajectory was much sharper and faster for the resistance locals. By February 2017, we estimate that there were already between 1,500 and 2,000 resistance groups operating over all fifty states.

Eight years earlier, local Tea Parties emerged more slowly after the April 2009 Tax Day rallies: by August that year there were some 175 groups in two-thirds of states, and six months in, during the late fall of 2009, the numbers grew to more than 750 in all fifty states.[39] Beyond the initial periods, we believe that the overall number of resistance groups grew to between 2,000 and 3,000 within one year and persisted at that level into year two, while the ranks of local Tea Party groups grew to more than 1,600 during the first year and seem to have peaked between 2,000 and 3,000 in the second year.

Sheer numbers aside, we wondered from the start whether grassroots resistance organizing after November 2016 occurred as widely across the country as Tea Party organizing did after April 2009. In this era of sharp US partisan polarization, voters have sorted by places of residence, with Republicans spread across counties in rural, small town, and exurban areas, and Democrats clustered tightly into a relatively small share of counties, homes to big cities, some metropolitan suburbs, and scattered university or college towns. It did not surprise us that Tea Parties emerged in most counties and congressional districts, because all major movements establish at least some presence in state capitals and big cities and Republicans are also prevalent everywhere else. By contrast, it seemed

---

American Politics, chapters 8 and 9; Skocpol and Williamson, *Tea Party and Remaking Republicanism*.
[39] See also Brown, *Tea Party Divided*, 29, figure 2.1.

plausible that grassroots resistance groups might end up heavily clustered in the same enclaves as Democratic voters.

Although we imagined ex ante that resistance groups might have a stronger left partisan tilt across the US political geography than any rightward tilt for Tea Parties, that is not what our data show.[40] By late 2010, we document local Tea Parties in all fifty states and in all but three-dozen congressional districts; and by late 2017 we see actual local resistance groups in all fifty states and in all but eight congressional districts. Both the Tea Party and the resistance arrays of local groups clearly spread very widely across the country. Yet their partisan tilt is counterintuitively different. Across the states, the late 2010 distribution of Tea Parties normalized per 100,000 voting-age population has a moderate correlation of 0.36 with the two-party presidential vote shares won by GOP contender John McCain in 2008. And the distribution of Tea Parties across congressional districts shows an even more pronounced correlation (0.46) with McCain's 2008 vote shares. A scholar of the Tea Party, Rachel Blum, used 2013 data to show that even though most Tea Parties clustered in swing districts with two-party splits in the 2012 presidential election between 40 percent and 60 percent, they were nevertheless at that point most numerous in very conservative districts where Republican Mitt Romney won overwhelmingly.[41] We have arrived at a similar finding about the earlier rightward tilt of Tea Parties, using 2008 presidential data and our own late 2010 group counts by congressional districts.

Importantly, however, we do NOT find a comparable leftward tilt in the local distribution of grassroots resistance groups at a correspondingly early stage in movement development. Using our carefully cleaned late 2017 list of local groups, we find a moderate (0.33) liberal partisan tilt across the fifty states in the relative densities of resistance groups (controlling for voting-age populations). But at the more fine-grained congressional district level, we do not find a liberal partisan tilt (close to zero

[40] For this analysis, we use our most carefully cleaned nationwide lists for fifty states excluding the District of Columbia, consisting of 1,991 named and geocoded local Tea Parties listed with Tea Party Patriots in late 2010 provided by Michael A. Bailey from a 2010 study conducted by Devin Burghart and Leonard Zeskind, and of 2,302 named and geocoded actual local groups on an internal Indivisible Project roster assembled in late 2017. Uncleaned national lists have higher totals but include nonlocal and duplicate listings that distort variations across states and districts, especially on the resistance side. We attempted two methods of assigning groups to congressional districts and arrived at substantively similar results.
[41] Rachel M. Blum, *How the Tea Party Captured the GOP* (Chicago: University of Chicago Press, 2020), 57, figure 4.9.

correlation of group densities with Clinton 2016 vote shares). In short, our two-level analysis yields the *surprising and important finding that local resistance groups have not been as tilted toward liberal Democratic voting strongholds as local Tea Parties tilted toward conservative GOP strongholds.* Both types of groups achieved a widespread presence spanning all US states and virtually all congressional districts, but across both states and congressional districts Tea Parties tend to reinforce the very conservative GOP presence across the US political geography, whereas resistance groups extend the Democratic presence across more local districts.

TOP-DOWN VERSUS BOTTOM-UP

The widespread and varied densities of local voluntarily organized Tea Partiers and resistance groups matter because these citizen-organized initiatives have propelled their movements from below, creating clout on behalf of grassroots values and priorities that are, at times, quite different from the policy priorities and styles of politics favored by aligned top-down, professionally managed national organizations.

In the Tea Party, the most resourceful big-donor-funded and professionally staffed operations – such as FreedomWorks, Americans for Prosperity, Tea Party Express, and Tea Party Patriots – have from the start pushed ultra-free-market priorities, including the defunding of social programs, weakening of business and environmental regulations, curbing of labor unions and regulatory protections for workers, and – above all – slashing of tax rates for the wealthy and big businesses. More often than not, grassroots Tea Party groups and activists back these goals, yet they often place equal or greater emphasis on restricting immigration and deploying government authority to enforce conservative Christian "family" values. There are stylistic differences, too. National, elite Tea Party organizations are willing to advance policy goals via legislative bargaining and inside lobbying bolstered by occasional televised protests or activist contacts with legislators. In contrast, grassroots Tea Partiers are more likely to mount angry protests and press legislators and professional advocates to refuse governing compromises. As grassroots Tea Partiers see it, they alone are the true patriots working to "save America" from the evils of liberalism and a squishy GOP "establishment." They want advocates and Republicans who claim to be on their side to go all out for their own ethnocultural as well as free-market priorities – and because more

Tea Parties emerged in the most conservative GOP districts, those pressures have hit already right-leaning Republicans the hardest.

In the post-2016 resistance, tensions between advocacy professionals and grassroots groups have less to do with policy differences – which are not as great as the gap between free-market and ethno-nationalist priorities in the Tea Party – but have more to do with differences of generation and place.

Most national resistance organizations are headquartered in big cities and liberal states, and function through paid professional employees who tend to be racially and ethnically diverse college graduates in their late twenties to early forties. Grassroots groups are spread across communities of all sizes and partisan compositions, and their leaders and most devoted participants are mostly older white women who might be (and sometimes actually are) the mothers or grandmothers of the youthful metropolitan advocates. Virtually all resistance professionals think of themselves as leftist "progressives," while many grassroots group leaders and participants are mainstream, long-standing Democratic liberals who want to cooperate with neighbors ranging from disgruntled Republicans to left progressives. Resistance groups often adopt quite different tactics depending on the overall partisan lean of their districts.

Within the overall resistance, variations in political style can be quite striking; but in this case, unlike in the Tea Party, the elites are the ones less prone to compromise. Youthful resistance professionals tend to be intensely moralistic in outlook, and they spend lots of time networking with each other in Washington, DC, New York City, Boston, or San Francisco, collecting signatures on public letters and negotiating among themselves about ways to pressure elected Democrats to the left. Their advocacy efforts bash congressional Democrats for making governing compromises on morally charged issues like immigrant rights or police reform; and these advocates also hope to move the Democratic Party to the left with endorsements of leftist challengers to party officeholders they deem overly moderate or responsive to for-profit business concerns. Grassroots groups, in contrast, focus as much on local and state issues and elections as on national controversies. They are often willing to back moderate candidates and officeholders if those are the only kinds of Democrats likely to prevail over Republicans in their areas. With the exception of some groups often located in the most liberal districts and states, grassroots resistance groups do not function like Tea Partiers of the left.

PARALLEL AND DIVERGENT POLITICAL IMPACTS

The intra-movement tensions just described in broad brushstrokes have waxed and waned. During the first two years, all participants in both the Tea Party and the resistance pushed in the same directions against the respective presidents and Congresses they reviled. After the first pivotal midterms in 2010 and 2018, though, internal tensions grew between national and local players, creating new cross-pressures for aligned party politicians.

Elites and Grassroots Push Together in Year One

From early 2009, Tea Party advocates and grassroots activists denounced and fought against everything the Obama administration and congressional Democrats did – pushing Republicans to oppose economic recovery measures, labor protections, and efforts to fight global warming. Yet front and center for all Tea Party participants was the fight against comprehensive health reform, dubbed "Obamacare." National and local Tea Party groups had distinct reasons for fighting this reform. Free-market advocates like FreedomWorks and Americans for Prosperity opposed new taxes and business regulations and feared that new social insurance measures would redound to the political benefit of Democrats, whereas many grassroots Tea Partiers worried that this measure, backed by a Black president, would tax "real Americans" like themselves to give health care to "freeloading" low-income people, including undocumented immigrants.[42] Through March 2010, when the Affordable Care Act was signed into law, protracted fights against health reform made it easy for all Tea Party players to work together to lobby the congressional GOP, mount public demonstrations, and harry Democratic representatives at their town hall meetings with constituents.

In an eerie way, a similar interplay between congressional and movement politics played out in reverse during 2017. This time, professional advocates and grassroots groups in the burgeoning resistance waged nine months of protests, media efforts, and lobbying campaigns to keep congressional Republicans from repealing the Affordable Care Act. Again, resistance players had various reasons for engagement. Most national

---

[42] Many of the Tea Partiers interviewed by Skocpol and Williamson in 2011 insisted, without factual basis, that undocumented immigrants were major beneficiaries of the Affordable Care Act.

advocates and some grassroots participants would have preferred to push for Medicare for All rather than wage a rear-guard effort to save Obamacare, but a shared fight against the first big move to reverse the Obama legacy by a hated president and GOP Congress overrode disagreements about how to expand health care coverage. In the end, Congress came one vote short of repealing Obamacare, and resistance forces could claim that coordinated advocacy and grassroots pressures on Senators in Arizona, Maine, and Alaska contributed to this victory.[43]

Electioneering for the 2010 and 2018 Midterms

As congressionally centered battles played out, professional advocates, big-money donors, and grassroots activists focused on special elections, primaries, and the 2010 and 2018 midterm elections that offered the best chance to deal ballot-box rebukes to the president and party each movement opposed. In this phase, we see parallels and differences.

On both sides, national movement-aligned organizations endorsed and channeled some funding to primary and general-election candidates. Leading into 2010, Tea Party Express endorsed 138 Republicans (85 of whom eventually won) and also ran bus tours and paid for advertising to go after targeted congressional Democrats; and FreedomWorks supported conservative challengers in GOP primaries and endorsed 113 Republicans running to defeat Democrats in the 2010 general election (72 of whom won).[44] In the 2018 cycle on the resistance side, many national organizations endorsed or supported Democratic candidates, and some got behind left-progressive challengers in primaries.

National Indivisible leaders joined other left advocates in such primary interventions, but other national resistance groups such as Swing Left as well as most grassroots groups focused on helping Democrats beat Republicans in November.

---

[43] Ezra Levin, Leah Greenberg, and Angel Padilla, "Who Saved Obamacare from the GOP? The American People," *Washington Post*, July 31, 2017. The Tea Party and resistance waged other congressional legislative campaigns in year one, but not as successfully, arguably because local groups were not as involved – for example, free market advocates' efforts to block the 2009 House cap-and-trade bill and liberal advocates' efforts to defeat the 2017 upward-tilted Trump-GOP tax cuts.

[44] Jonathan Mummolo, "Nimble Giants: How National Interest Groups Harnessed Tea Party Enthusiasm," 193–212 in *Interest Groups Unleashed*, ed. Paul Herrnson, Christopher Deering, and Clyde Wilcox (Thousand Oaks, CA: Sage Publishers, 2013), 203–05.

In 2010 and 2018, the opposition movements and parties generated record numbers of new candidates at all levels of government. In the crucial fights to flip control of the House of Representatives, the 2010 cycle saw a surge of conservative Republican contenders, many touting Tea Party ties, and the 2018 cycle brought an even higher surge of "resistance" aligned Democratic contenders, disproportionately female and more racially and ethnically diverse than earlier candidate cohorts.[45] Of course not all new contenders won, but many did. In November 2010, Republicans netted six governorships and a remarkable 675 state legislative seats.[46] Republicans and their allies also flipped 63 House seats from Democrats to deliver the GOP a 242 to 193 majority, while also cutting the Democratic majority in the Senate from 59/41 to 53/47. Eight years later, Democrats challenging the Trump-GOP made major advances of their own, despite needing to win more votes for every seat in many highly gerrymandered state legislative and congressional districts: Democrats netted seven new governorships and 309 state legislative seats. Democrats lost Senate seats as they faced contests in mostly conservative states, but in House elections their "blue wave" netted a considerable 41 seats, enough to take control.[47]

Grassroots Tea Parties and resistance groups may have played somewhat different roles in these midterms. Although local Tea Party groups held candidate forums and sometimes endorsed conservative 2010 candidates, as far as we can tell their members did not usually engage in voter registration or get-out-the-vote efforts. Because older whites reliably vote in midterm as well as presidential elections, local Tea Partiers could just spread messages and take it for granted that most of their neighbors and age-peers would turn out in November. In fact, although Republicans increased their 2010 performance over the previous midterm election in 2006, overall voter participation in 2010 was relatively low as it usually is in midterms.[48] Just 45.5 percent of eligible US adults went to the polls, many Democratic-leaners stayed home, and turnout ended up heavily

---

[45] Figures tracking both candidate surges appear in Jonathan Martin and Denise Lu, "Democrats' Best Recruitment Tool? President Trump," *New York Times*, April 6, 2018.

[46] Aaron Blake, "Which Election Was Worse for Democrats: 2010 or 2014? It's a Surprisingly Close Call," *Washington Post*, November 5, 2014; Karen Hansen, "A GOP Wave Washed over State Legislatures on Election Day," *National Conference of State Legislatures*, December 2010.

[47] Dylan Scott, "Democratic Wins in These 9 States Will Have Seismic Policy Consequences," *Vox*, November 10, 2020.

[48] Daniel Q. Gillion, *The Loud Minority: Why Protests Matter in American Democracy* (Princeton: Princeton University Press, 2020), 136.

skewed toward the older whites most receptive to conservative, anti-Obama messages.[49]

After 2016, by contrast, resistance groups, like all others on the left, focused doggedly on boosting voter turnout for special elections and the 2018 midterms. Local and national organizations alike scrambled to register voters and persuade neighbors and coworkers to support Democrats, even if just to express opposition to President Trump. In these efforts, resistance groups often cooperated with labor unions, local party committees, candidate campaigns, and groups representing African Americans and Latinos. In early 2019, our research group used an online questionnaire to collect information from the leaders of grassroots resistance groups operating in forty-nine of sixty-seven Pennsylvania counties. Remarkably, we learned that members of all but four of the eighty-two responding groups engaged in election activities, usually four to six types of activities out of nine types we listed, and the most frequent undertaking was local canvassing, "knocked on doors."[50] Similar reports from many states suggest that resistance volunteers similarly went door to door for many weeks leading into 2017 special elections and the November 2018 midterms. Their efforts contributed to an unusually elevated 2018 turnout of 53.4 percent of eligible adults, including increased participation of women, minorities, and young people.[51]

If there had been no Tea Party or resistance upsurges at all, would the two parties have done just as well in 2010 and 2018? Although causal impacts are very hard to pin down, two studies with sophisticated statistical controls show that districts with larger mass participation in the Tea Party's 2009 Tax Day rallies and the resistance's January 2017 Women's Marches subsequently registered higher vote shares to 2010 GOP candidates and 2018 Democratic candidates, respectively.[52] In the 2010 GOP primaries, endorsements from national Tea Party organizations and sponsors may have given favored conservatives and the "Tea Party" label a boost, but most organizational endorsements do not seem to have mattered in November, when other conditions favorable to GOP

---

[49] Midterm turnouts tracked over time in Jordan Misra, "Voter Turnout Rates Among All Voting Age and Major Racial and Ethnic Groups Were Higher Than in 2014," US Census Bureau, *Current Population Survey*, April 23, 2019.
[50] Gose and Skocpol, "Resist, Persist, and Transform," 311, figure 3.
[51] Misra, "Voter Turnout Rates."
[52] Andreas Madestam, Daniel Shoag, Stan Veuger, and David Yanagizawa-Drott, "Do Protests Matter? Evidence from the Tea Party Movement," *Quarterly Journal of Economics* 128, no. 4 (October 2013): 1633–85; Jonathan Pinckney, "Did the Women's March Work? Re-evaluating the Political Efficacy of Protest," Working Paper for the 2019 Mobilization Conference.

candidates are taken into account.[53] FreedomWorks' general election endorsements are an exception; some researchers find they had a statistically significant positive effect on GOP House fortunes. Furthermore, one key study found that GOP candidates also did better in districts with greater numbers of individual grassroots activists who had signed up on national Tea Party organizational websites, including the FreedomWorks site.[54] Analogous studies have not been done to parse any similar impact from activists who signed up with, say MoveOn or other national resistance organizations engaged in the 2018 election.

Aside from individuals enrolled on national lists, actual local Tea Party and resistance groups may have impacted congressional elections. Preliminary evidence from our documentation of district densities for local Tea Parties and resistance groups indicates that both types were associated with boosting turnout on their side and flipping control of the House of Representatives to the GOP in 2010 and to the Democrats in 2018. Figure 15.1 displays average numbers of local groups in congressional districts that did, and did not, change party hands in these midterms.[55] In 2010, local Tea Parties were most numerous in the 176 House districts where Republicans continued in House seats, but by the fall of 2010 had also become very dense on the ground in the 66 "flipped" districts where Republicans defeated or replaced Democrats. Similarly, in 2017–18, grassroots anti-Trump resistance groups were numerous both in districts where Democrats were reelected or replaced by other Democrats and also in the 41 flipped districts where Democrats displaced Republicans. Although these are correlations not causal findings, the numbers are consistent with the idea that organized local citizens can make a difference – by influencing local public opinion, boosting like-minded voter participation, or both. Especially for resistance groups in the 2018

---

[53] Christopher F. Karpowitz, J. Quin Monson, Kelly D. Patterson, and Jeremy C. Pope, "Tea Time in America? The Impact of the Tea Party Movement on the 2010 Midterm Elections," *PS: Political Science & Politics* 44 (2011): 303–09; Jonathan Mummolo, "Nimble Giants: How National Interest Groups Harnessed Tea Party Enthusiasm," in *Interest Groups Unleashed*, ed. Paul Herrnson, Christopher Deering, and Clyde Wilcox (Thousand Oaks, Cal.: Sage Publishers, 2013), 193–212.

[54] Michael A. Bailey, Jonathan Mummolo, and Hans Noel, "Tea Party Influence: A Story of Activists and Elites," *American Politics Research* 40, no. 5 (2012): 769–804.

[55] The figure omits small sets of congressional districts in each midterm. There were only three districts that flipped from the GOP to Democrats in 2010 and only three that flipped from the Democrats to the GOP in 2018 – in both cases too few to make calculation of averages meaningful.

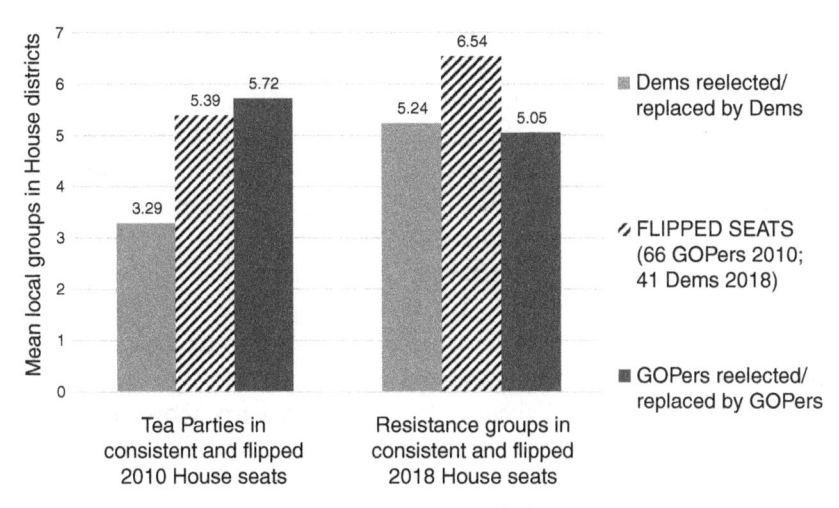

FIGURE 15.1 Local Tea Parties/resistance groups and partisan turnover in the 2010 and 2018 congressional midterm elections

midterms, ethnographically rich field studies suggest that both of these processes probably helped Democrats capture dozens of previously GOP-held suburban House seats.[56]

Tea Party Elites and Grassroots Fuel GOP Extremism

After triumphs in the 2010 midterms, the markedly more conservative GOP House majority that took control included dozens of returning and new Republicans who touted Tea Party loyalties or support.[57] Thereafter, researchers tried to discern whether "Tea Party Republicans" voted differently than other GOP representatives. Such exercises often find no statistically significant relationships, in part because there is no straightforward way to measure Tea Party membership, and also because most Republicans have stampeded together toward hard-right fiscal and cultural positions. The most convincing findings come from a uniquely nuanced study, *Reactionary Republicanism* by Bryan T. Gervais and Irwin L. Morris, that classifies GOP House members into subsets, including some with no Tea Party ties and others who are actively supported by national Tea Party organizations and/or who take active, public steps to court the movement (by joining

---

[56] See Skocpol and Tervo, *Upending American Politics*, chapters 11–13.
[57] Skocpol and Williamson, *Tea Party and Republican Conservatism*, 169, figure 5.1; and "How the Tea Party Fared," *New York Times*, November 4, 2010.

a relevant House Caucus, attending public Tea Party rallies or events, or issuing press releases or Tweets that express Tea Party loyalties).[58] This scheme usefully recognizes that both GOP officeholders and Tea Party organizations make their own strategic choices (e.g., officeholders may hope to avoid primary challenges and organizations may want to align with surefire winners or cultivate up-and-coming conservatives).

With the aid of such distinctions, the *Reactionary Republicanism* researchers analyze congressional votes from 2011 through 2014 and find that "Republicans are quite fiscally conservative whether or not they align themselves with the Tea Party" and national Tea Party organizations do not allocate support based on policy stances. At the same time, "legislators who make an effort to attach themselves to the Tea Party movement have significantly more conservative roll call voting records than fellow Republicans who are not attached to the Tea Party." Those courting the Tea Party often hail from districts where constituents are relatively more resentful of racial and ethnic minorities and more worried about immigrants than Republicans in general. Accordingly, their ultra-conservative voting records "stand out on issues related to fair housing, consumer protection, immigration policy, voter ID laws, healthcare, and programs providing support for the poor and working class," policy areas that have a "disproportionate effect on minority communities... where the brand of conservatism espoused by Tea Party adherents in the general population is most clearly apparent."[59]

These findings make sense if we recognize the different priorities of the top-down and bottom-up Tea Party forces. From 2009 on, national free-market advocacy organizations like FreedomWorks proclaimed that they spoke for the entire Tea Party, which was devoted to federal budget and tax cuts and other fiscal priorities. But actual grassroots activists and many local Tea Party groups were always equally or more passionate about blocking new social benefits for low-income people and pushing Christian conservative, anti-civil rights, and anti-immigrant causes. Not surprisingly, GOP congressional representatives who took the most active steps to reach out to Tea Party supporters also voted in increasingly right-wing ways on ethnocultural issues.

Fatefully, when the Obama administration and a bipartisan Senate coalition tried to advance comprehensive immigration reform in 2013,

---

[58] Bryan T. Gervais and Irwin L. Morris, *Reactionary Republicanism: How the Tea Party in the House Paved the Way for Trump's Victory* (Oxford: Oxford University Press, 2018).
[59] Ibid., 106–07.

Tea Partiers adamantly opposed to any path to citizenship for undocumented immigrants successfully pressured the GOP House Republicans to kill the legislation.[60] Florida GOP Senator Marco Rubio, originally a Tea Party favorite, faced intense grassroots criticism for his cosponsorship of immigration reform, and thereafter shifted toward hardline stands.[61] A year later, shock waves again rocked Republican officeholders when Virginia Representative Eric Cantor, a free-market-minded member of the House leadership, was defeated in a GOP primary by a grassroots Tea Party-backed upstart who stressed anti-immigrant stands.[62]

Even as public approval declined, Tea Party influences persisted and grew in Congress.[63] Soon those congressional Republicans most boastful of Tea Party ties became prolific issuers of bombastic hyper-partisan Tweets, starting down a polarizing communication path that Donald Trump would later turn into an expressway. Both elite and grassroots Tea Party forces thus ended up pushing elected Republicans not just toward far right policy positions, but also toward bombastic politics and uncompromising governance. High-stakes budget and debt ceiling standoffs ensued, and the 112th and 113th Congresses were among the least legislatively productive to date.[64] After the 2012 elections, GOP House Speaker John Boehner was pressured against compromises and congressional Republicans fiercely opposed regulatory efforts by the second Obama administration to deal with climate change or protect undocumented immigrants from deportation. Free market elites worried more about Obama's economic measures, while grassroots Tea Party groups and activists passionately opposed his immigrant protections, but both pushed the GOP away from governing compromises. Writing in March 2014 in *The Texas Tribune*, Ross Ramsey reached a conclusion that describes national as well as state dynamics. "The Tea Party," he said, "got its start five years ago, and has become the favorite label for a no-compromises variety of

---

[60] Fox News, "Tea Party Groups Ramp Up Fight Against Immigration Bill, as August Recess Looms," *Fox News*, July 5, 2013.

[61] Ed Kilgore, "Marco Rubio's Endless Drift to the Right on Immigration Policy Continues," *New York Magazine*, January 25, 2018; and Dana Milbank, "Tea Party Scalds Marco Rubio," *Washington Post*, June 19, 2013.

[62] Jonathan Martin, "Eric Cantor Defeated by David Brat, Tea Party Challenger, in G.O.P. Primary Upset," *New York Times*, June 10, 2014. This was a very low-turnout election, but the results were nevertheless interpreted by GOP leaders as a rebuke to a supporter of immigration reform.

[63] Gervais and Morris, *Reactionary Republicanism*, 107.

[64] Holly Fechner, "Managing Political Polarization in Congress: A Case Study on the Use of the Hastert Rule," *Utah Law Review* 4 (2014), article 3.

conservatism ... standing not as a separate entity or movement so much as the label for the most energetic faction within the Republican Party."[65]

Resistance Tensions and Democratic Party Politics

If the Tea Party after 2010 essentially goaded the GOP toward ever more extremism and obstruction, the post-2018 effects of the resistance have invigorated a "broad tent" Democratic Party while modestly intensifying tensions between mainstream liberals and left progressives. The full complexity of post-2018 resistance dynamics cannot be captured briefly, but we can gain crucial insights from growing disconnects between local resistance groups and the campaigns pursued by the DC headquarters of Indivisible.

At an accelerating pace after the November 2018 midterms, Indivisible's DC staffers turned to advocacy lobbying in alliance with other left-leaning progressive "partner organizations." In early 2019, for example, Indivisible and other advocacy staffers formed coalitions to push the Democratic congressional leaders Nancy Pelosi, House Speaker, and Chuck Schumer, Senate minority leader, to threaten government shutdowns if Trump and the GOP Senate did not act to protect Dreamers, undocumented youth brought to the country as children.[66] Even before the 2018 midterms, national Indivisible leaders decided to follow the lead of immigrant and minority advocates to press congressional Democrats toward bold or uncompromising stands on racial and immigrant issues. More such efforts would ensue, including participation in an alliance to promote a "Medicare for All" bill introduced in March 2019 by Representative Pramila Jayapal, cochair of the House Progressive Caucus. Speaker Pelosi did accede to progressive demands to hold hearings on this and other health-care reform bills, but little came from Indivisible leaders' participation in progressive advocacy campaigns beyond briefly publicized letters, occasional appearances on MSNBC, and a constant stream of emails from DC headquarters urging local groups and activists to "contact your congressional representative" and also send a contribution to help fund the campaign du jour. The political opportunity structure for left progressives simply was not analogous to that facing the Tea Partiers – in part because most of

---

[65] Ross Ramsey, "Five Years Later, Tea Party Is a Faction Republicans Must Court," *The Texas Tribune*, March 6, 2014.
[66] Greenberg and Levin, *We Are Indivisible*, 158–78.

the grassroots-backed Democrats who won new House seats in 2018 hailed from moderate or swing districts, not leftist strongholds.[67]

Another disconnect grew from Indivisible's determination to join with other national groups in endorsing progressives running in Democratic primaries. Leading into 2018, Indivisible encouraged local groups to do such endorsements for congressional and state races, and made similar efforts for 2020 – but to little avail, because many local leaders worried that primary fights would divide their memberships unnecessarily.[68] According to reports on the Indivisible website, DC-orchestrated endorsement campaigns never attracted more than dozens of participating local groups (out of the thousands the network claims). When the presidential cycle started in 2019, Indivisible's DC leaders redoubled their endorsement push, this time trying to cajole local groups and activists to get behind one Democratic contender (their obvious preference was Elizabeth Warren). Again, most local groups resisted, and in fact Indivisible's own internal canvasses always showed scattered preferences, with small pluralities of respondents from the national email list at various points favoring Bernie Sanders, Elizabeth Warren, or Kamala Harris, but others lining up for other contenders, including the moderates.[69] As late as March 2020, when Joe Biden began to rack up primary victories, Indivisible argued strongly against his nomination, denouncing him as anathema to "grassroots democratic values."[70] Yet as soon as Democratic primary voters, especially African Americans, propelled Biden to victory, most local resistance groups moved quickly to get behind his candidacy. As in 2018, when "progressive energy helped moderate Democrats win," local resisters everywhere were prepared to go all out for whichever Democrat could defeat Donald Trump in November 2020.[71]

More disconnects happened in the wake of the massive summer 2020 Black Lives Matter protests against the police killing of George Floyd and

---

[67] Nate Cohn, "Moderate Democrats Fared Best in 2018," *New York Times*, September 11, 2019; and Ella Nilsen, "Progressive Democrats Running in Competitive House Districts Had a Bad Night on Tuesday," *Vox*, November 7, 2018.
[68] For an overview and thoughtful discussion, see Joan Walsh, "Indivisible Is Working Hard to Live Up to Its Name," *The Nation*, September 9–16, 2019.
[69] For example, see "Indivisible February 2020 Survey Results," *Indivisible Guide*, Medium Blog, February 27, 2020.
[70] *Indivisible Guide*, "The Grassroots Knows How to Beat Trump – Biden and Bloomberg Aren't Listening," March 2, 2020. The DC leaders eventually endorsed Biden, but not until after many local groups got behind him.
[71] The quote comes from Nilsen, "Progressive Democrats Had a Bad Night."

other Blacks. Virtually all Democrats and resistance activists joined these protests calling for fundamental revamping of police practices.

Nevertheless, unity in June gave way over time to disagreement about the slogan "Defund the Police" amid waning white support for ongoing protests. Even as Democratic candidates ran away from this provocative slogan, left advocates including Indivisible leaders continued to tout it, urging activists to call local officials and "tell them to defund your local police department."[72] Meanwhile at the grassroots, many local resistance groups worked for specific police reforms. For example, when their city council was about to vote on police funding, a group of college-educated white women in one North Carolina resistance group responded to calls for action from young Black organizers in the area by contacting relevant officials about specific demands – including establishing a citizen review board, requiring body cameras and cultural competency training, and placing less priority on misdemeanor drug offenses. These resisters also assisted organizers with registering voters at recurrent Black Lives Matter demonstrations, furthering difficult pandemic-era election work.

Within the overall wave of renewed activism in and around the Democratic Party, divergences in policy goals and political styles are likely to persist. To be sure, disagreements were held in abeyance as summer 2020 turned to fall with all elements of the resistance and the Democratic Party pushing together to achieve, in the end, their shared goal of defeating Donald Trump's reelection. Nevertheless, splits are likely to recurrently flare between, on the one hand, progressive advocates who want maximal policy changes and practice a moralistically uncompromising style of politics and, on the other hand, many of the party candidates and on-the-ground volunteer citizens who have to fight uphill for election victories and incremental changes in districts of many stripes.[73] That some of those splits – on racially charged issues – were highly visible in 2020 may help to explain why the November results in congressional and state races were much less pleasing to Americans liberals, progressives, and anti-Trump independents than the 2020 presidential result and the 2018 congressional results. Unlike the Tea Party in relation to the GOP,

---

[72] Email from Indivisible Team, "This week and every week: Black Lives Matter. Without qualifications. Without asterisks. Without add-ons," to the authors, June 1, 2020.

[73] As of early 2021, for example, DC Indivisible has called along with other progressive advocates for a House progressive voting bloc that would imitate the GOP Freedom Caucus to enforce ideological preferences on Democratic leaders operating with a narrow majority. This may worsen intraparty tensions leading into future elections where Democratic candidates will have to appeal to a broad center-left swath of voters.

the anti-Trump resistance has not, overall, pulled the Democratic Party toward extreme styles and stands. But neither has this burst of intense national and local liberal activism overcome the internal tensions that inevitably challenge a party that must be geographically and ideologically inclusive to have any real chance at achieving and retaining national power.

AN INTERIM BOTTOM LINE

Any conclusion for our comparison of these two movements to "save America" in very different ways cannot truly be definitive – because the effects of these upsurges will continue to play out for years to come. Our analysis has focused on the lead into and aftermath of the 2010 and 2018 midterm elections and associated developments in Congress. Widespread grassroots volunteer groups made both the Tea Party and the anti-Trump resistance more potent and different from many other kinds of political undertakings limited to urban street protests or professionally run advocacy operations. By virtue of including thousands of volunteer groups, both movements have clearly invigorated American small-d democracy. Ordinary middle-class people have upped their citizen participation beyond voting and drawn others around them into the high-stakes, high-turnout elections of 2018 and 2020.

Beyond this shared contribution to small-d democracy, however, the Tea Party and the resistance have had contradictory impacts. On the right, the Republican Party has been transformed, first by the Tea Party and then by the candidacy and presidency of Donald Trump, who expanded and centralized the ethnocultural and authoritarian tendencies fueled by that movement. As one of America's two major parties, the GOP is willing to ride this surging energy and is, by now, also committed to manipulating every institutional lever – to the edge of legality and perhaps beyond – to ensconce right-wing rule even if without majority voter support. The Tea Party has thus turned out to be both a democratizing and an authoritarian force – and certainly has furthered both economic and sociocultural extremism on the right. As of 2021, surviving Tea Party groups and individuals originally involved with the Tea Party are among the most fervent believers of the false notion that the 2020 presidential election was "stolen" from Donald Trump. Along with many other grassroots Republican activists, some Tea Party identifiers celebrate the January 6, 2021, assault on the US Capitol and are willing to accept violence or threats of violence as ways to assert their goals in future US elections and policy struggles.

Although still being told, the story seems different on the left. The anti-Trump resistance has engaged more citizens in continuous collective action, boosted candidacies and voter participation in all types of elections, and – perhaps most important of all – extended the grassroots reach of the Democratic Party by creating nodes of activism outside of blue strongholds and adding organized college-credentialed people, mostly women, to ongoing party alliances. Nationally organized progressive advocates have been part of this, too, but not as big a part as they believe – and they are the ones on the left who sometimes push polarization beyond the limits of majority understanding and consent, an undemocratic tendency.

Considered as intersecting fields of top-down and bottom-up organized efforts, the Tea Party and the resistance have – together – furthered the increasing and asymmetric partisan polarization that helped give rise to both movements in the first place. Ironically, each movement's internal tensions have contributed in opposite ways. In the Tea Party, organized grassroots activism has supercharged no-compromise extremism by adding ethnonationalist fears into the free-market anti-government mix. In the resistance, national elites have been more likely to toy with no-compromise, highly ideological styles of politics, while the grassroots groups by virtue of their widespread presence and outreach activities have reinforced pluralistic coalitions and muscular reformism. By expanding as well as invigorating liberal citizenship, the grassroots anti-Trump resistance has given the Democratic Party its best chance to come through this era of mobilized extreme polarization as a healthy center-left majority party prepared to govern a diversifying nation.

Index

Abrams, Stacey, 343
Adams, John, 147, 148–49, 188
Administrative Procedures Act, The, 132
Administrative state, 119, 132, 268, 270–77
 and Trump, 277–81, 295
 Definition of, 267
Affordable Care Act, The, 79, 110, 113, 114, 273, 280, 286, 321, 332, 388
 Weakening of, 286–88
Alabama, 218, 231, 310
Alaska, 389
Alexander, Lamar, 139–40
Alito, Samuel, 158
American carnage, 87
American Legislative Exchange Council (ALEC), 79, 314, 329–33
 Exploitation of federalism, 333–37
 State capture, 337–40
Americans For Prosperity (AFP), 18, 330–32, 377, 386, 388 *See also* Koch, Charles and David
 Exploitation of federalism, 333–37
 State capture, 337–40
Antifa, 254, 259
Anti-Federalist Papers, The, 118
Arizona, 155, 162, 163, 203, 235, 277, 310, 327, 381, 389
Australia, 80

Baker v. Carr, 160
Bandwagoning, 58
Bangladesh, 65
Barr, William, 286

Bicameralism. *See* Constitutional system: Bicameralism
Biden, Joseph R., 11, 77, 89, 140, 161, 163, 172, 218, 291, 293, 320, 369, 397
 and the election of 2020, . *See* Election of 2020
Black Lives Matter, 85, 184, 211, 254, 288, 374
Bleeding Kansas, 187
Boehner, John, 290, 395
Bolton, John, 139
Brandeis, Louis, 302
Brazil, 80
Budget and Impoundment Control Act of 1974, The, 53
Burr, Aaron, 149
Bush, George W., 21, 119, 129, 131, 135, 271, 272, 275, 286

California, 45, 280
Cantor, Eric, 395
Carter, James E., 83, 133
Chase, Samuel, 149
Chávez, Hugo, 69, 85–86, 146
China, 136
Citizens United v. FEC, 160–61
Civic organizations. *See* Mobilization
Civil Rights Act of 1964, The, 13, 84, 174, 367
Civil War, The, 12, 83, 119, 147, 150–53, 187–90, 352, 354, 361, 368
Cleavages, 4, 13, 59, 63, 64, 66, 72, 75, 190, 226, 256

401

Cleavages (cont.)
  Crosscutting cleavages, 26, 40, 43, 78, 95–99, 106–8, 358
Cleveland, Grover, 361
Clinton, Hillary, 157, 237, 256, 374, 379, 382
Clinton, William J., 17, 135, 287
Coates, Ta-Nehisi, 275
Collier, Paul, 355–56
Collins, Susan, 9, 282
Comey, James, 111
Competitive authoritarianism, 6
Compromise of 1876, 188
Coney Barrett, Amy, 162, 167, 278
  Supreme Court confirmation of, 157–58
Constitutional hardball, 9, 29, 33, 77, 86, 87, 88, 91, 142, 143, 164, 166, 187–90, 246, 257, 261, 297
  at the state level, 314–15
Constitutional system, 4, 8, 25–27, 113, 114
  and polarization, 37–41, 114–17
  Bicameralism, 8, 26, 76, 97, 112–13
  Checks and balances, 47–56, 59–60
  Counter-majoritarian institutions, 79–82
  Federalism, 4, 8, 25, 26, 31, 38, 39–40, 43–45, 76, 97, 111–12
  Separation of powers, 4, 8, 25, 26, 38, 40, 52, 57, 70, 76, 97, 108–11, 130
Contract with America, 92
Cooper, Roy, 314
Court-packing, 27
  and the Election of 1800, 148–50
  under Andrew Johnson, 152–53
  under Franklin Roosevelt, 146, 153–55
  under Lincoln, 150–53
  under Trump, 155–58
Crawford v. Marion County Election Board, 159

Dahl, Robert A., 27, 38, 343
Deep state, The, 125, 254, 291, 292
Defense of Marriage Act (DOMA), The, 272
Deferred Action for Childhood Arrivals (DACA), 127, 131, 134, 273, 280, 283
Democracy, 310
  and elections, 343–51
  at the state level, 31, 306–10, 316–19, 323–28
  definition of, 6
Democratic backsliding, 4–5, 7, 119–20
  and polarization, 68–71
  and the courts, 144–47, 163–67
  at the state level, 31, 298–302, 310–16
Democratic resilience
  Definition of, 7–12
DeVos, Betsy, 280, 285
Disengagement, Moral, 180–82
Dole, Robert J., 135
Downs, Anthony, 12, 47, 59, 82, 270
Dred Scott v. Sanford, 150
Ducey, Douglas, 155–56

Economic anxiety, 28, 84, 199, 207, 210, 215, 218
Egypt, 74
Eisenhower, Dwight D., 39
Election of 1800, 148–50, 227
Election of 1860, 187
Election of 2008, 86, 313, 370
Election of 2010, 85, 109, 313, 377, 389–93, 399
Election of 2012, 44, 56, 84, 160, 277, 313, 331, 385, 395
Election of 2016, 11, 28, 84, 87, 91, 101, 111, 157, 160, 187, 196–98, 206–25, 237, 243, 256, 269, 274, 276, 297, 314, 317, 370
Election of 2018, 11, 88, 90, 109, 111, 185–87, 289, 315, 321, 332, 337, 389–93, 396, 399
Election of 2020, 11, 89–90, 157, 161, 171, 274, 282, 289, 291, 293, 369, 398, 399
  Attempts to overturn, 58, 77–78, 172–73, 291, 292, 298, 320–21, 322, 339, 357
Elections, 4, 6, 10, 21, 28, 31, 32–33, 38, 43, 66, 67, 76, 81, 108–10, 113, 158, 160–61, 172, 178, 185–87, 261, 299, 302–3, 306, 310, 311, 325, 327, 333, 343–51, 352–60, 361, 366–68
Electoral College, 80, 81, 344, 345
Equal Rights Amendment, 13
Era of Good Feelings, 347, 353, 365
Erdoğan, Recep Tayyip, 70, 145
Evers, Tony, 315
Ex parte Merryman, 151
Executive Reorganization Act of 1939, The, 270

Fake news, 255, 354
Federal Election Commission (FEC), 363
Federal Reserve, The, 113–14

Index

Federalism. *See* Constitutional system: Federalism
Federalist Papers, The, 8, 38, 123, 324
Federalist Party, The, 148–50, 352–53
Fifteenth Amendment, The, 354, 366, 367
Fight for Fifteen. *See* Minimum wage policy
Filibuster, 52, 76, 77, 86–87, 112, 115, 122, 156, 157, 379
Fisher, Dana, 373, 374
Floyd, George, 85, 91, 291, 295, 319, 397
Four Freedoms, The, 271
Fourteenth Amendment, The, 363
Fox News, 51, 55, 276, 371
FreedomWorks, 18, 376, 377, 386, 388, 392, 394

Garland, Merrick, 157
Gender, 10, 19, 26, 84, 89, 90, 96, 98, 99, 106, 193, 206, 227
  and polarization, 99–101
  Gender gap, The, 100–1
Georgia, 155, 307, 327
Germany, 193
Gerrymandering, 10, 69, 80, 81, 82, 90, 92, 160, 162–63, 166, 297, 301, 303–4, 307, 313, 315, 317, 326, 332, 339, 345, 352, 390
Gibson, Edward, 311
Gingrich, Newt, 14, 92, 135, 359
Ginsburg, Ruth Bader, 157, 167
God gap. *See* Religion, Religiosity gap
Gorsuch, Neil, 157, 158, 278
Grant, Ulysses S., 153
Grassley, Charles, 156
Great Society, 268

Hale, John, 151, 152
Hamilton, Alexander, 118, 123
Harris, Kamala, 397
Hawaii, 309
Help America Vote Act of 2002, The, 363
Hershey, Marjorie Randon, 40
Hofstadter, Richard, 199
Horowitz, Donald I., 107, 109, 112
How Democracies Die. *See* Levitsky, Steven; Ziblatt, Daniel
Howell, William G., 127
Hungary, 23, 69, 71, 145, 164

Idaho, 321
Indiana, 159

Indivisible. *See* Resistance to Trump, The
INS v. Chadha, 134
Insurrection Act, The, 295
Investigations. *See* Oversight
Iowa, 327

Jayapal, Pramila, 396
Jefferson, Thomas, 83, 118, 148, 227
  and court-packing. *See* Court packing, and the Election of 1800
John Birch Society, 29, 198
Johnson, Andrew, 147, 152–53
  and court-packing. *See* Court packing, Under Andrew Johnson
Johnson, Lyndon B., 83
Judiciary Act of 1801, The, 149, 150
Judiciary Act of 1866, The, 153

Kansas, 309, 337, 338
Kavanaugh, Brett, 158, 278
  Supreme Court confirmation of, 88, 157
Kennedy, Anthony, 157, 315
Kennedy, John F., 228, 273
Key, V.O., 39, 298
Khanna, Ro
  Supreme Court reform proposal, 167
Klein, Ezra, 82
Kloos, Karina, 86, 277
Know Nothing Party, The, 198, 200
Koch, Charles and David, 56, 79, 262, 377
Krehbiel, Keith, 123
  Pivotal politics model, 122–23
Ku Klux Klan, 29, 198, 200

Labor unions, 18, 55, 314, 328, 331, 332–33, 338, 386, 391
  Attacks on, 327
Laboratories of democracy, 298, 301, 302, 319, 323
Lepore, Jill, 83
Levitsky, Steven, 6, 77, 119, 146, 149, 153, 164, 195, 358
Lijphart, Arend, 75–76, 95, 107, 111
Lincoln, Abraham, 118, 146, 150–53
  and court-packing. *See* Court packing, Under Lincoln
  and suspension of *habeas corpus*, 147, 151
  Election of. *See* Election of 1860
Linz, Juan J., 41, 52, 57

Lipset, Seymour Martin, 95, 98, 106, 199
Louisiana, 310, 327
Louisiana Purchase, The, 118

Madison, James, 8, 37, 38, 40, 118, 324
Maduro, Nicolás, 146
Maine, 389
Marshall, John, 148, 149, 150
Massachusetts, 309
Mayhew, David R., 51, 54
McAdam, Douglas, 86, 277
McCain, John, 385
McCain-Feingold Act of 2002, The, 160, 162
McCarty, Nolan, 16, 277
McConnell, Mitch, 162
  and federal court confirmations, 156–58
McCrory, Patrick, 314
Media, 36, 41, 47, 49, 51, 54, 55, 59, 312, 334, 371, 375
  as a meso-institution, 45–46
Median voter theorem, The, 12, 47, 81, 82, 270
Medicaid, 280, 286–87, 304, 305, 310, 315, 321, 324, 332, 334, 337, 338
Medicare, 86, 389, 396
Meso-institutions, 25, 46–47, 57–60
  Definition of, 46
  Interest Groups, 42–43
  Media, 45–46
  States, 43–45
Mexico, 80
Michener, Jamila, 305
Mickey, Robert, 31
Midterm election of 2018, . See Election of 2018
Minimum wage policy, 154, 314, 324–25, 332–33, 334, 338
Minnesota, 306, 379
Mobilization, 28, 236, 264, 326–27, 370–72, 374–76
MoveOn, 375, 380
Mueller investigation, The, 138
Mulvaney, Mick, 139, 140
Murkowski, Lisa, 140

National Rifle Association (NRA), 29
  and affective polarization, 253–56
  and fear-based mobilization, 248–53
  and identity alignment, 256–61
  and stealth politics, 261–63
  Financial resources of, 247–48
National Voter Registration Act of 1993, The, 363
Nebraska, 321
Neustadt, Richard, 47, 110, 123
New Deal, The, 13, 40, 48, 50, 153–55, 268, 271, 303, 347
Nixon, Richard M., 9, 30, 53, 54, 58, 271, 292
North American Free Trade Agreement (NAFTA), The, 17, 136
North Carolina, 160, 304, 313, 327, 361
North Dakota, 309, 327

Obama for America. See Organizing for Action
Obama, Barack, 31, 79, 84, 86–87, 89, 119, 130, 134, 135, 156–57, 195, 199, 201, 237, 254, 276, 293, 370, 373, 377, 382, 391, 395
  and executive-centered partisanship, 271–75
  and immigration policy, 272–73
  and nomination of Merrick Garland, 87, 157
Obamacare. See Affordable Care Act, The
Oklahoma, 327
Orbán, Victor, 69, 70, 145
Organizing for Action, 273
(Organizing for America). see Organizing for Action
Orren, Karen, 8
Oversight, 26, 47–49, 111

Partisanship
  and polarization. See Polarization
  Executive-centered partisanship, 30–31, 268–77, 290–96
  Negative partisanship, 20, 126
  Partisan competition, 20–21, 352–55, 359–66
PATRIOT Act, The, 135
Pelosi, Nancy, 55, 88, 135, 289, 396
Pence, Michael, 236, 287
Pendleton Act of 1883, 270
Pennsylvania, 310
Philippines, The, 23, 70
Poland, 23, 145
Polarization, 3–4, 12–18, 24–25, 95–96, 120, 350–51
  Affective polarization, 182

and gender. *See* Gender, and polarization
and meso-institutions, 41–47, 57–60
and political violence, 183–85, 187–90
and presidential power, 114–15, 122–26, 128–33
Counter-polarization, 73–74, 85–90
Definition of, 16
Pernicious polarization, 25, 61–65, 66–68, 71–73, 82–85, 90–92
Social polarization, 19–20, 173–82, 190–93
Policyscape, The, 332
Polk, James K., 118
Polsby, Nelson, 39
Poole, Keith, 16
Populism, 15, 68, 69, 74, 89, 258, 259, 294
Plutocratic populism, 262
Protest. *See* Mobilization
Przeworski, Adam, 302, 311

Quaile Hill, Kim, 306

Race, 4, 10, 14, 20, 23, 24, 26, 28, 30, 75, 83–84, 86, 89, 90, 91, 96, 98, 99, 106, 107, 155, 172, 177, 183, 188, 193, 195–98, 233, 243, 254, 268, 269, 286, 291, 301, 303, 307, 312, 335, 338, 361, 370, 390, 394, 396, 398 *See also* Sorting: Racial sorting
and Trump, 28–29, 84–85, 195–225, 277, 292, 373 *See also* Status threat: and support for Trump
Randolph, Edmund, 118
Reagan, Ronald, 83, 271, 275, 276, 286, 363
Reid, Harry, 156
Religion, 30, 83, 84, 90, 96, 98, 99, 172, 177, 281
and support for Trump, 211, 236, 276
Perceptions of victimization, 238–41
Religiosity gap, 226, 227–31
Religious representation in Congress, 102, 235
Religious sorting, 29, 101–2, 175, 226, 241
Resistance to Trump, The, 18, 33–34, 196–97, 288–89, 321, 379–81
and the Democratic Party, 396–99
Emergence of, 379–81, 382–83
Strength compared with the Tea Party, 381–86
Roberts, John, 164

Roberts Court, The, 158–63, 165
Roberts, Kenneth M., 58
Roe v. Wade, 13, 83
Romney, Mitt, 9, 56, 87, 139, 277, 385
Roosevelt, Franklin Delano, 49, 146, 270
and court-packing. *See* Court packing, Under Franklin Roosevelt
Rosenthal, Howard, 16
Rubio, Marco, 395
Rucho v. Common Cause, 81, 160, 315
Russia, 77, 111
Rwanda, 193

Sanders, Bernie, 17, 37, 74, 89, 293, 397
Scalia, Antonin, 157, 162
Schlesinger, Arthur, 119
Schmitt, Carl, 67
Schumer, Charles E., 396
Schumpeter, Joseph, 6
Sedition Act of 1798, The, 148, 150, 188
Sensenbrenner, James, 317
Separation of powers. *See* Constitutional system: Separation of powers
September 11, 2001 attacks, 119, 129
Sessions, Jeff, 286
Shelby County v. Holder. *See* Voting Rights Act of 1965: Weakening of
Skowronek, Stephen, 8, 116
Smith, Alfred E., 228
Snyder, Rick, 315
Social identity theory, 179
Social Security Act, The, 154
Soros, George, 69, 254, 259
Sorting, 14
and religion. *See* Religion: Religious sorting
and social class, 103–5
Racial sorting, 41, 84–85, 102–3, 174–75, 190–93, 257, 311
Social sorting, 19–20, 27–30, 95–96, 98–99, 105–6, 174–78
South Carolina, 307, 309, 310
South Dakota, 327
Southern realignment. *See* Polarization; Sorting
State Policy Network, 314, 330
Exploitation of federalism, 333–37
State capture, 337–40
State, The. *See* Administrative state

Status threat, 179, 197, 200
    and support for Trump, 28–29, 205–6, 209–18
Stuart v. Laird, 150
Subnational democracy. *See* Democracy: at the state level

Taney, Roger, 150–52
Tax Cuts and Jobs Act of 2017, The, 79, 114, 389
Tea Party, The, 18, 29, 33, 86, 196, 198, 199–201, 205, 207, 276, 290
    and opposition to President Obama, 201
    Emergence of, 371–72, 376–78
    Strength compared with the Resistance, 381–86
Teapot Dome scandal, The, 50
Tennessee, 327
Texas, 45, 173, 307
Thailand, 70, 73
Thirteenth Amendment, The, 152
Thomas, Clarence, 158, 161, 162
Tillis, Thom, 282
Truman, David, 39
Trump, Donald J., 5–6, 11, 21, 51, 57, 110, 113, 125, 187–90, 298, 317, 320, 339, 369, 370, 373, 395
    and attacks on the Affordable Care Act (ACA). *See* Affordable Care Act (ACA), Weakening of
    and court-packing. *See* Court packing, Under Trump
    and economic protectionism, 135–36, 280
    and immigration policy, 52–53, 134, 136–37, 279–84, 293
    and presidential power, 121–22, 133–40
    and race. *See* Race, and Trump
    and status threat, *See* Status threat, and support for Trump
    and the 2016 election. *See* Election of 2016
    and the 2020 election. *See* Election of 2020
    and the administrative state. *See* Administrative state, and Trump
    and the welfare state, 284–89
    Impeachment of, 9, 55, 57–58, 77, 87, 88, 111, 122, 125–26, 138–39, 269, 289, 291
    Religious criticism of, 230–31
    Support from religious leaders, 276
Turkey, 23, 70, 71, 73, 145, 164

Ukraine, 88, 111, 126, 138–40, 289, 291
Unions. *See* Labor Unions
United States v. Darby Lumber Co., 154
Utah, 321

Venezuela, 23, 70, 71, 85, 131, 146, 164
Vieth v. Jubelirer, 315
Vietnam, 268
Violence, political, 11, 183–85, 187–90, 307
Virginia, 149, 218, 307
Voter identification laws, 80, 159–60, 161, 303, 325–26, 355, 363, 394
Voter registration, 202, 317, 318, 347
Voting Rights Act of 1965, The, 7, 161, 307
    Weakening of, 80, 161, 310–11, 316, 363–64

Wagner Act, The, 154
Walker, Scott, 315
Warren, Elizabeth, 74, 89, 293, 397
Washington, George, 26, 118, 193
Way, Lucan, 6
Whitmer, Gretchen, 315
Whittington, Keith E., 149
Wilson, James, 118
Wilson, Pete, and the Proposition 187 campaign, 202–3
Wisconsin, 160, 258, 304, 306, 313, 315
Women's March, 196, 370, 372, 374, 379, 382, 383, 391
Working Families Party, 380

Ziblatt, Daniel, 77, 119, 146, 149, 153, 164, 195, 358
Zimbabwe, 65